What follows is the full text of the
Trump-Ukraine Impeachment Inquiry Report issued
by the House Permanent Select Committee on
Intelligence. Turn the book over to read the response to
this report by Republican Representatives
Devin Nunes, Jim Jordan, and Michael McCaul.

THE TRUMP-UKRAINE
IMPEACHMENT INQUIRY REPORT

TRUMP-UKRAINE IMPEACHMENT INQUIRY REPORT

House Permanent Select Committee on Intelligence

THE
TRUMP-UKRAINE IMPEACHMENT INQUIRY REPORT

House Permanent
Select Committee on
Intelligence

MELVILLE HOUSE
BROOKLYN · LONDON

The Trump-Ukraine Impeachment Inquiry Report
House Permanent Select Committee on Intelligence
First Melville House printing December 2019

Melville House Publishing
46 John Street
Brooklyn NY 11201

mhpbooks.com

ISBN: 978-1-61219-870-5

Cover design by Marina Drukman
Prepress production by Beste M. Doğan

Printed in the United States of America
10 9 8 7 6 5 4 3 2 1

THE TRUMP-UKRAINE
IMPEACHMENT INQUIRY REPORT

Report of the House Permanent Select Committee on Intelligence,
Pursuant to H. Res. 660 in Consultation with the
House Committee on Oversight and Reform and the
House Committee on Foreign Affairs

December 2019

House Permanent Select Committee on Intelligence

Rep. Adam B. Schiff (CA), Chairman

Rep. Jim Himes (CT)
Rep. Terri Sewell (AL)
Rep. André Carson (IN)
Rep. Jackie Speier (CA)
Rep. Mike Quigley (IL)
Rep. Eric Swalwell (CA)
Rep. Joaquin Castro (TX)
Rep. Denny Heck (WA)
Rep. Peter Welch (VT)
Rep. Sean Patrick Maloney (NY)
Rep. Val Demings (FL)
Rep. Raja Krishnamoorthi (IL)

Rep. Devin Nunes (CA), Ranking Member
Rep. Mike Conaway (TX)
Rep. Michael Turner (OH)
Rep. Brad Wenstrup (OH)
Rep. Chris Stewart (UT)
Rep. Elise Stefanik (NY)
Rep. Will Hurd (TX)
Rep. John Ratcliffe (TX)
Rep. Jim Jordan (OH)

Majority Staff
Timothy S. Bergreen, Staff Director
Daniel S. Goldman, Director of Investigations
Maher Bitar, General Counsel
Rheanne Wirkkala, Deputy Director of Investigations
Patrick M. Boland, Communications Director

Impeachment Inquiry Investigative Staff

William M. Evans
Patrick Fallon
Sean A. Misko
Nicolas A. Mitchell

Daniel S. Noble
Diana Y. Pilipenko
Ariana N. Rowberry

Carly A. Blake, Deputy Staff Director
William Wu, Budget and Policy Director
Wells C. Bennett, Deputy General Counsel

Oversight Staff

Linda D. Cohen
Thomas Eager
Abigail C. Grace
Kelsey M. Lax
Amanda A. Rogers Thorpe

Lucian D. Sikorskyj
Conrad Stosz
Kathy L. Suber
Aaron A. Thurman
Raffaela L. Wakeman

Non-Partisan Security and Information Technology Staff

Kristin Jepson

Kimberlee Kerr

Claudio Grajeda

House Committee on Oversight and Reform

Rep. Carolyn B. Maloney (NY), Chairwoman
Rep. Elijah E. Cummings (MD), Chairman

Operations and Press Team

Zachary Barger, Intern

Jamitress Bowden

Kristen Charley, Intern

Kenyatta Collins

James Darlson, Intern

Emma Dulaney

Evan Elizabeth Freeman, Intern

Christophe Godshall, Intern

Brandon Jacobs

Elisa LaNier

Kellie Larkin

Olivia Letts, Intern

Anna Rose Marx, Intern

Courtney Miller

Noah Steimel, Intern

Travis Stoller, Intern

Amy Stratton

Laura Trevisani, Intern

Joshua Zucker

House Committee on Foreign Affairs

Rep. Eliot L. Engel (NY), Chairman

Rep. Brad Sherman (CA)
Rep. Gregory Meeks (NY)
Rep. Albio Sires (NJ)
Rep. Gerald Connolly (VA)
Rep. Theodore Deutch (FL)
Rep. Karen Bass (CA)
Rep. William Keating (MA)
Rep. David Cicilline (RI)
Rep. Ami Bera (CA)
Rep. Joaquin Castro (TX)
Rep. Dina Titus (NV)
Rep. Adriano Espaillat (NY)
Rep. Ted Lieu (CA)
Rep. Susan Wild (PA)
Rep. Dean Phillips (MN)
Rep. Ilhan Omar (MN)
Rep. Colin Allred (TX)
Rep. Andy Levin (MI)
Rep. Abigail Spanberger (VA)
Rep. Chrissy Houlahan (PA)
Rep. Tom Malinowski (NJ)
Rep. David Trone (MD)
Rep. Jim Costa (CA)
Rep. Juan Vargas (CA)
Rep. Vicente Gonzalez (CA)

Rep. Michael McCaul (TX) *Ranking Member*
Rep. Christopher Smith (NJ)
Rep. Steve Chabot (OH)
Rep. Joe Wilson (SC)
Rep. Scott Perry (PA)
Rep. Ted Yoho (FL)
Rep. Adam Kinzinger (IL)
Rep. Lee Zeldin (NY)
Rep. James Sensenbrenner (WI)
Rep. Ann Wagner (MO)
Rep. Brian Mast (FL)
Rep. Francis Rooney (FL)
Rep. Brian Fitzpatrick (PA)
Rep. John Curtis (UT)
Rep. Ken Buck (CO)
Rep. Ron Wright (TX)
Rep. Guy Reschenthaler (PA)
Rep. Tim Burchett (TN)
Rep. Greg Pence (IN)
Rep. Steve Watkins (KS)
Rep. Michael Guest (MS)

Majority Staff
Jason Steinbaum, Staff Director
Doug Campbell, Deputy Staff Director
Laura Carey, Senior Professional Staff Member, State Department Oversight
Tim Mulvey, Communications Director
Jacqueline Ramos, Senior Professional Staff Member, Europe and Russia

Operations and Press Staff

Evan Bursey
Jacqueline Colvett

Rachel Levitan

5

TABLE OF CONTENTS

PREFACE

This report reflects the evidence gathered thus far by the House Permanent Select Committee on Intelligence, in coordination with the Committee on Oversight and Reform and the Committee on Foreign Affairs, as part of the House of Representatives' impeachment inquiry into Donald J. Trump, the 45th President of the United States.

The report is the culmination of an investigation that began in September 2019 and intensified over the past three months as new revelations and evidence of the President's misconduct towards Ukraine emerged. The Committees pursued the truth vigorously, but fairly, ensuring the full participation of both parties throughout the probe.

Sustained by the tireless work of more than three dozen dedicated staff across the three Committees, we issued dozens of subpoenas for documents and testimony and took more than 100 hours of deposition testimony from 17 witnesses. To provide the American people the opportunity to learn and evaluate the facts themselves, the Intelligence Committee held seven public hearings with 12 witnesses—including three requested by the Republican Minority—that totaled more than 30 hours.

At the outset, I want to recognize my late friend and colleague Elijah E. Cummings, whose grace and commitment to justice served as our North Star throughout this investigation. I would also like to thank my colleagues Eliot L. Engel and Carolyn B. Maloney, chairs respectively of the Foreign Affairs and Oversight and Reform Committees, as well as the Members of those Committees, many of whom provided invaluable contributions. Members of the Intelligence Committee, as well, worked selflessly and collaboratively throughout this investigation. Finally, I am grateful to Speaker Nancy Pelosi for the trust she placed in our Committees to conduct this work and for her wise counsel throughout.

I also want to thank the dedicated professional staff of the Intelligence Committee, who worked ceaselessly and with remarkable poise and ability. My deepest gratitude goes to Daniel Goldman, Rheanne Wirkkala, Maher Bitar, Timothy Bergreen, Patrick Boland, Daniel Noble, Nicolas Mitchell, Sean Misko, Patrick Fallon, Diana Pilipenko, William Evans, Ariana Rowberry, Wells Bennett, and William Wu. Additional Intelligence Committee staff members also assured that the important oversight work of the Committee continued, even as we were required to take on the additional responsibility of conducting a key part of the House impeachment inquiry. Finally, I would like to thank the devoted and outstanding staff of the Committee on Oversight and Reform, including but not limited to Dave Rapallo, Susanne Sachsman Grooms, Peter Kenny, Krista Boyd, and Janet Kim, as well as Laura Carey from the Committee on Foreign Affairs.

* * *

In his farewell address, President George Washington warned of a moment when "cunning, ambitious, and unprincipled men will be enabled to subvert the power of the people and to usurp for themselves the reins of government, destroying afterwards the very engines which have lifted them to unjust dominion."

The Framers of the Constitution well understood that an individual could one day occupy the Office of the President who would place his personal or political interests above those of the nation. Having just won hard-fought independence from a King with unbridled authority, they were attuned to the dangers of an executive who lacked fealty to the law and the Constitution.

In response, the Framers adopted a tool used by the British Parliament for several hundred years to constrain the Crown—the power of impeachment. Unlike in Britain, where impeachment was typically reserved for inferior officers but not the King himself, impeachment in our untested democracy was specifically intended to serve as the ultimate form of accountability for a duly-elected President. Rather than a mechanism to overturn an election, impeachment was explicitly contemplated as a remedy of last resort for a president who fails to faithfully execute his oath of office "to preserve, protect and defend the Constitution of the United States."

Accordingly, the Constitution confers the power to impeach the president on Congress, stating that the president shall be removed from office upon conviction for "Treason, Bribery, or other high Crimes and Misdemeanors." While the Constitutional standard for removal from office is justly a high one, it is nonetheless an essential check and balance on the authority of the occupant of the Office of the President, particularly when that occupant represents a continuing threat to our fundamental democratic norms, values, and laws.

Alexander Hamilton explained that impeachment was not designed to cover only criminal violations, but also crimes against the American people. "The subjects of its jurisdiction," Hamilton wrote, "are those offenses which proceed from the misconduct of public men, or, in other words, from the abuse or violation of some public trust. They are of a nature which may with peculiar propriety be denominated political, as they relate chiefly to injuries done immediately to the society itself."

Similarly, future Associate Justice of the United States Supreme Court James Wilson, a delegate from Pennsylvania at the Constitutional Convention, distinguished impeachable offenses from those that reside "within the sphere of ordinary jurisprudence." As he noted, "impeachments are confined to political characters, to political crimes and misdemeanors, and to political punishments."

* * *

As this report details, the impeachment inquiry has found that President Trump, personally and acting through agents within and outside of the U.S. government, solicited the interference of a foreign government, Ukraine, to benefit his reelection. In furtherance of this scheme, President Trump conditioned official acts on a public announcement by the new Ukrainian President, Volodymyr Zelensky, of politically-motivated investigations, including one into President Trump's domestic political opponent. In pressuring President Zelensky to carry out his demand, President Trump withheld a White House meeting desperately sought by the Ukrainian President, and critical U.S. military assistance to fight Russian aggression in eastern Ukraine.

The President engaged in this course of conduct for the benefit of his own presidential reelection, to harm the election prospects of a political rival, and to influence our nation's upcoming presidential election to his advantage. In doing so, the President placed his own personal and political interests above the national interests of the United States, sought to undermine the integrity of the U.S. presidential election process, and endangered U.S. national security.

At the center of this investigation is the memorandum prepared following President Trump's July 25, 2019, phone call with Ukraine's President, which the White House declassified and released under significant public pressure. The call record alone is stark evidence of misconduct; a demonstration of the President's prioritization of his personal political benefit over the national interest. In response to President Zelensky's appreciation for vital U.S. military assistance, which President Trump froze without explanation, President Trump asked for "a favor though": two specific investigations designed to assist his reelection efforts.

Our investigation determined that this telephone call was neither the start nor the end of President Trump's efforts to bend U.S. foreign policy for his personal gain. Rather, it was a dramatic crescendo within a months-long campaign driven by President Trump in which senior U.S. officials, including the Vice President, the Secretary of State, the Acting Chief of Staff, the Secretary of Energy, and others were either knowledgeable of or active participants in an effort to extract from a foreign nation the personal political benefits sought by the President.

The investigation revealed the nature and extent of the President's misconduct, notwithstanding an unprecedented campaign of obstruction by the President and his Administration to prevent the Committees from obtaining documentary evidence and testimony. A dozen witnesses followed President Trump's orders, defying voluntary requests and lawful subpoenas, and refusing to testify. The White House, Department of State, Department of Defense, Office of Management and Budget, and Department of Energy refused to produce a single document in response to our subpoenas.

Ultimately, this sweeping effort to stonewall the House of Representatives' "sole Power of Impeachment" under the Constitution failed because witnesses courageously came forward and testified in response to lawful process. The report that follows was only possible because of their sense of duty and devotion to their country and its Constitution.

Nevertheless, there remain unanswered questions, and our investigation must continue, even as we transmit our report to the Judiciary Committee. Given the proximate threat of further presidential attempts to solicit foreign interference in our next election, we cannot wait to make a referral until our efforts to obtain additional testimony and documents wind their way through the courts. The evidence of the President's misconduct is overwhelming, and so too is the evidence of his obstruction of Congress. Indeed, it would be hard to imagine a stronger or more complete case of obstruction than that demonstrated by the President since the inquiry began.

The damage the President has done to our relationship with a key strategic partner will be remedied over time, and Ukraine continues to enjoy strong bipartisan support in Congress. But the damage to our system of checks and balances, and to the balance of power within our three branches of government, will be long-lasting and potentially irrevocable if the President's ability to stonewall Congress goes unchecked. Any future President will feel empowered to resist an investigation into their own wrongdoing, malfeasance, or corruption, and the result will be a nation at far greater risk of all three.

* * *

The decision to move forward with an impeachment inquiry is not one we took lightly. Under the best of circumstances, impeachment is a wrenching process for the nation. I resisted calls to undertake an impeachment investigation for many months on that basis, notwithstanding the existence of presidential misconduct that I believed to be deeply unethical and damaging to our democracy. The alarming events and actions detailed in this report, however, left us with no choice but to proceed.

In making the decision to move forward, we were struck by the fact that the President's misconduct was not an isolated occurrence, nor was it the product of a naïve president. Instead, the efforts to involve Ukraine in our 2020 presidential election were undertaken by a President who himself was elected in 2016 with the benefit of an unprecedented and sweeping campaign of election interference undertaken by Russia in his favor, and which the President welcomed and utilized.

Having witnessed the degree to which interference by a foreign power in 2016 harmed our democracy, President Trump cannot credibly claim ignorance to its pernicious effects. Even more pointedly, the President's July call with Ukrainian President Zelensky, in which he solicited an investigation to damage his most feared 2020 opponent, came the day after Special Counsel Robert Mueller testified to Congress about Russia's efforts to damage his 2016 opponent and his urgent warning of the dangers of further foreign interference in the next election. With this backdrop, the solicitation of new foreign intervention was the act of a president unbound, not one chastened by experience. It was the act of a president who viewed himself as unaccountable and determined to use his vast official powers to secure his reelection.

This repeated and pervasive threat to our democratic electoral process added urgency to our work. On October 3, 2019, even as our Committee was engaged in this inquiry, President Trump publicly declared anew that other countries should open investigations into his chief political rival, saying, "China should start an investigation into the Bidens," and that "President Zelensky, if it were me, I would recommend that they start an investigation into the Bidens." When a reporter asked the President what he hoped Ukraine's President would do following the July 25 call, President Trump, seeking to dispel any doubt as to his continuing intention, responded: "Well, I would think that, if they were honest about it, they'd start a major investigation into the Bidens. It's a very simple answer."

By doubling down on his misconduct and declaring that his July 25 call with President Zelensky was "perfect," President Trump has shown a continued willingness to use the power of his office to seek foreign intervention in our next election. His Acting Chief of Staff, Mick Mulvaney, in the course of admitting that the President had linked security assistance to Ukraine to the announcement of one of his desired investigations, told the American people to "get over

10

it." In these statements and actions, the President became the author of his own impeachment inquiry. The question presented by the set of facts enumerated in this report may be as simple as that posed by the President and his chief of staff's brazenness: is the remedy of impeachment warranted for a president who would use the power of his office to coerce foreign interference in a U.S. election, or is that now a mere perk of the office that Americans must simply "get over"?

* * *

Those watching the impeachment hearings might have been struck by how little discrepancy there was between the witnesses called by the Majority and Minority. Indeed, most of the facts presented in the pages that follow are uncontested. The broad outlines as well as many of the details of the President's scheme have been presented by the witnesses with remarkable consistency. There will always be some variation in the testimony of multiple people witnessing the same events, but few of the differences here go to the heart of the matter. And so, it may have been all the more surprising to the public to see very disparate reactions to the testimony by the Members of Congress from each party.

If there was one ill the Founding Founders feared as much as that of an unfit president, it may have been that of excessive factionalism. Although the Framers viewed parties as necessary, they also endeavored to structure the new government in such a way as to minimize the "violence of faction." As George Washington warned in his farewell address, "the common and continual mischiefs of the spirit of party are sufficient to make it the interest and duty of a wise people to discourage and restrain it."

Today, we may be witnessing a collision between the power of a remedy meant to curb presidential misconduct and the power of faction determined to defend against the use of that remedy on a president of the same party. But perhaps even more corrosive to our democratic system of governance, the President and his allies are making a comprehensive attack on the very idea of fact and truth. How can a democracy survive without acceptance of a common set of experiences?

America remains the beacon of democracy and opportunity for freedom-loving people around the world. From their homes and their jail cells, from their public squares and their refugee camps, from their waking hours until their last breath, individuals fighting human rights abuses, journalists uncovering and exposing corruption, persecuted minorities struggling to survive and preserve their faith, and countless others around the globe just hoping for a better life look to America. What we do will determine what they see, and whether America remains a nation committed to the rule of law.

As Benjamin Franklin departed the Constitutional Convention, he was asked, "what have we got? A Republic or a Monarchy?" He responded simply: "A Republic, if you can keep it."

Adam B. Schiff
Chairman, House Permanent Select Committee on Intelligence

EXECUTIVE SUMMARY

The impeachment inquiry into Donald J. Trump, the 45th President of the United States, uncovered a months-long effort by President Trump to use the powers of his office to solicit foreign interference on his behalf in the 2020 election. As described in this executive summary and the report that follows, President Trump's scheme subverted U.S. foreign policy toward Ukraine and undermined our national security in favor of two politically motivated investigations that would help his presidential reelection campaign. The President demanded that the newly-elected Ukrainian president, Volodymyr Zelensky, publicly announce investigations into a political rival that he apparently feared the most, former Vice President Joe Biden, and into a discredited theory that it was Ukraine, not Russia, that interfered in the 2016 presidential election. To compel the Ukrainian President to do his political bidding, President Trump conditioned two official acts on the public announcement of the investigations: a coveted White House visit and critical U.S. military assistance Ukraine needed to fight its Russian adversary.

During a July 25, 2019, call between President Trump and President Zelensky, President Zelensky expressed gratitude for U.S. military assistance. President Trump immediately responded by asking President Zelensky to "do us a favor though" and openly pressed for Ukraine to investigate former Vice President Biden and the 2016 conspiracy theory. In turn, President Zelensky assured President Trump that he would pursue the investigation and reiterated his interest in the White House meeting. Although President Trump's scheme intentionally bypassed many career personnel, it was undertaken with the knowledge and approval of senior Administration officials, including the President's Acting Chief of Staff Mick Mulvaney, Secretary of State Mike Pompeo, and Secretary of Energy Rick Perry. In fact, at a press conference weeks after public revelations about the scheme, Mr. Mulvaney publicly acknowledged that the President directly tied the hold on military aid to his desire to get Ukraine to conduct a political investigation, telling Americans to "get over it."

President Trump and his senior officials may see nothing wrong with using the power of the Office of the President to pressure a foreign country to help the President's reelection campaign. Indeed, President Trump continues to encourage Ukraine and other foreign countries to engage in the same kind of election interference today. However, the Founding Fathers prescribed a remedy for a chief executive who places his personal interests above those of the country: impeachment. Accordingly, as part of the House of Representatives' impeachment inquiry, the Permanent Select Committee on Intelligence, in coordination with the Committees on Oversight and Reform and Foreign Affairs, were compelled to undertake a serious, sober, and expeditious investigation into whether the President's misconduct warrants that remedy.

In response, President Trump engaged in an unprecedented campaign of obstruction of this impeachment inquiry. Nevertheless, due in large measure to patriotic and courageous public servants who provided the Committees with direct evidence of the President's actions, the Committees uncovered significant misconduct on the part of the President of the United States. As required under House Resolution 660, the Intelligence Committee, in consultation with the Committees on Oversight and Reform and Foreign Affairs, has prepared this report to detail the evidence uncovered to date, which will now be transmitted to the Judiciary Committee for its consideration.

12

SECTION I—THE PRESIDENT'S MISCONDUCT

The President Conditioned a White House Meeting and Military Aid to Ukraine on a Public Announcement of Investigations Beneficial to his Reelection Campaign

The President's Request for a Political Favor

On the morning of July 25, 2019, President Donald Trump settled in to the White House Executive Residence to join a telephone call with President Volodymyr Zelensky of Ukraine. It had been more than three months since President Zelensky, a political neophyte, had been swept into office in a landslide victory on a platform of rooting out corruption and ending the war between his country and Russia. The day of his election, April 21, President Zelensky spoke briefly with President Trump, who had called to congratulate him and invite him to a visit at the White House. As of July 25, no White House meeting had materialized.

As is typical for telephone calls with other heads of state, staff members from the National Security Council (NSC) convened in the White House Situation Room to listen to the call and take notes, which would later be compiled into a memorandum that would constitute the U.S. government's official record of the call. NSC staff had prepared a standard package of talking points for the President based on official U.S. policy. The talking points included recommendations to encourage President Zelensky to continue to promote anti-corruption reforms in Ukraine, a pillar of American foreign policy in the country as far back as its independence in the 1990s when Ukraine first rid itself of Kremlin control.

This call would deviate significantly from that script. Shortly before he was patched through to President Zelensky, President Trump spoke with Gordon Sondland, who had donated $1 million to President Trump's 2016 presidential inauguration and whom the President had appointed as the United States Ambassador to the European Union. Ambassador Sondland had helped lay the groundwork for a very different kind of call between the two Presidents.

Ambassador Sondland had relayed a message to President Zelensky six days earlier that "assurances to run a fully transparent investigation" and "turn over every stone" were necessary in his call with President Trump. Ambassador Sondland understood these phrases to refer to two investigations politically beneficial to the President's reelection campaign: one into former Vice President Joe Biden and a Ukrainian gas company called Burisma, on which his son sat on the board, and the other into a discredited conspiracy theory alleging that Ukraine, not Russia, interfered in the 2016 U.S. election. The allegations about Vice President Biden were without evidence, and the U.S. Intelligence Community had unanimously determined that Russia, not Ukraine, interfered in the 2016 election to help the candidacy of Donald Trump. Despite the falsehoods, Ambassador Sondland would make it clear to Ukrainian officials that the public announcement of these investigations was a prerequisite for the coveted White House meeting with President Trump, an effort that would help the President's reelection campaign.

The White House meeting was not the only official act that President Trump conditioned on the announcement of these investigations. Several weeks before his phone call with President Zelensky, President Trump ordered a hold on nearly $400 million of congressionally-appropriated security assistance to Ukraine that provided Kyiv essential support as it sought to repel Russian forces that were occupying Crimea and inflicting casualties in the eastern region of the country. The President's decision to freeze the aid, made without explanation, sent shock waves through the Department of Defense (DOD), the Department of State, and the NSC, which uniformly supported providing this assistance to our strategic partner. Although the suspension of aid had not been made public by the day of the call between the two Presidents, officials at the Ukrainian embassy in Washington had already asked American officials about the status of the vital military assistance.

At the outset of the conversation on July 25, President Zelensky thanked President Trump for the "great support in the area of defense" provided by the United States to date. He then indicated that Ukraine would soon be prepared to purchase additional Javelin anti-tank missiles from the United States as part of this defense cooperation. President Trump immediately responded with his own request: "I would like you to do us a favor though," which was "to find out what happened" with alleged Ukrainian interference in the 2016 election.

President Trump then asked President Zelensky "to look into" former Vice President Biden's role in encouraging Ukraine to remove a prosecutor widely viewed by the United States and numerous European partners to be corrupt. In so doing, President Trump gave currency to a baseless allegation that Vice President Biden wanted to remove the corrupt prosecutor because he was investigating Burisma, a company on whose board the Vice President's son sat at the time.

Over the course of the roughly thirty-minute call, President Trump repeated these false allegations and pressed the Ukrainian President to consult with his personal attorney, Rudy Giuliani, who had been publicly advocating for months for Ukraine to initiate these specific investigations. President Zelensky promised that he would "work on the investigation of the case." Later in the call, he thanked President Trump for his invitation to join him at the White House, following up immediately with a comment that, "[o]n the other hand," he would "ensure" that Ukraine pursued "the investigation" that President Trump had requested.

During the call, President Trump also disparaged Marie Yovanovitch, the former U.S. ambassador to Ukraine, who championed anti-corruption reforms in the country, and whom President Trump had unceremoniously removed months earlier following a smear campaign waged against her by Mr. Giuliani and others. President Trump claimed that she was "bad news" and was "going to go through some things." He praised the current prosecutor at the time, who was widely viewed as corrupt and who helped initiate the smear campaign against her, calling him "very good" and "very fair."

Hearing the call as it transpired, several White House staff members became alarmed. Far from giving the "full-throated endorsement of the Ukraine reform agenda" that had been hoped for, the President instead demanded a political investigation into an American—the presidential candidate he evidently feared most, Joe Biden.

Lieutenant Colonel Alexander Vindman, an NSC staff member responsible for Ukraine policy who listened to the call, immediately reported his concerns to NSC lawyers. His supervisor, NSC Senior Director for Europe and Russia Timothy Morrison, also reported the call to the lawyers, worrying that the call would be "damaging" if leaked publicly. In response, the lawyers placed the memorandum summarizing the call onto a highly classified server, significantly limiting access to the materials.

The call record would not remain hidden forever. On September 25, 2019, facing immense public pressure to reveal the contents of the call and following the announcement the previous day of a formal impeachment inquiry in the House of Representatives into President Trump's actions toward Ukraine, the White House publicly released the memorandum of the July 25 call.

The record of the call would help explain for those involved in Ukraine policy in the U.S. government, the Congress, and the public why President Trump, his personal attorney, Mr. Giuliani, his hand-picked appointees in charge of Ukraine issues, and various senior Administration officials would go to great lengths to withhold a coveted White House meeting and critical military aid from Ukraine at a time when it served as a bulwark against Russian aggression in Europe.

The answer was as simple as it was inimical to our national security and election integrity: the President was withholding officials acts while soliciting something of value to his reelection campaign—an investigation into his political rival.

The story of that scheme follows.

* * *

The President Removed Anti-Corruption Champion Ambassador Yovanovitch

On April 24, 2019, President Donald Trump abruptly called back to Washington the United States Ambassador to Ukraine, Marie "Masha" Yovanovitch, after a ruthless smear campaign was waged against her. She was known throughout Ukraine and among her peers for aggressively advocating for anti-corruption reforms consistent with U.S. foreign policy and only recently had been asked to extend her stay in Ukraine. Her effectiveness in anti-corruption efforts earned her enemies in Kyiv and in Washington. As Deputy Assistant Secretary of State George Kent testified in praising Ambassador Yovanovitch: "You can't promote principled anticorruption action without pissing off corrupt people."

Beginning on March 20, *The Hill* newspaper published several op-eds attacking Ambassador Yovanovitch and former Vice President Joe Biden, relying on information from a Ukrainian prosecutor, Yuriy Lutsenko, who was widely viewed to be corrupt. Mr. Lutsenko had served as the chief prosecutor in Ukraine under the then-incumbent president who lost to Volodymyr Zelensky in April 2019. Although he would later recant many of his allegations, Mr. Lutsenko falsely accused Ambassador Yovanovitch of speaking negatively about President Trump and giving Mr. Lutsenko a "do-not-prosecute list."

The attacks against Ambassador Yovanovitch were amplified by prominent, close allies of President Trump, including Mr. Giuliani and his associates, Sean Hannity, and Donald Trump Jr. President Trump tweeted the smears himself just a month before he recalled the Ambassador from Ukraine. In the face of attacks driven by Mr. Lutsenko and the President's allies, Ambassador Yovanovitch and other senior State Department officials asked Secretary of State Mike Pompeo to issue a statement of support for her and for the U.S. Embassy in Ukraine. The Secretary declined, fearing that President Trump might publicly undermine those efforts, possibly through a tweet.

Following a ceremony in which she presented an award of courage to the family of a young female anti-corruption activist killed in Ukraine for her work, Ambassador Yovanovitch received an urgent call from the State Department regarding her "security," and imploring her to take the first plane back to Washington. When she arrived, she was informed that she had done nothing wrong, but that the President had lost confidence in her. She was told to leave her post as soon as possible.

In her place, the President would designate three new agents to spearhead Ukraine policy, political appointees far more willing to engage in an improper "domestic political errand" than an ambassador known for her efforts to fight corruption.

The President's Hand-Picked Agents Began the Scheme

Just three days before Ambassador Yovanovitch's abrupt recall to Washington, President Trump had his first telephone call with President-elect Zelensky. During that conversation, President Trump congratulated the Ukrainian leader on his victory, complimented him on his country's Miss Universe Pageant contestants, and invited him to visit the White House. A White House meeting would help demonstrate the United States' strong support for Ukraine as it fought a hot war with Russia and attempted to negotiate an end to the conflict with Russian President Vladimir Putin, as well as to bolster President-elect Zelensky's standing with his own people as he sought to deliver on his promised anti-corruption agenda. Although the White House's public summary of the call included some discussion of a commitment to "root out corruption," President Trump did not mention corruption at all.

Shortly after the conversation, President Trump asked Vice President Mike Pence to attend President Zelensky's inauguration. Vice President Pence confirmed directly to President Zelensky his intention to attend during a phone conversation on April 23, and Vice President Pence's staff and the U.S. Embassy in Kyiv began preparations for the trip.

At the same time, President Trump's personal attorney, Mr. Giuliani, intensified his campaign to pressure Ukraine's newly-elected President to initiate investigations into Joe Biden, who had officially entered the race for the Democratic nomination on April 25, and the baseless conspiracy theory about Ukrainian interference in the 2016 election. On May 9, the *New York Times* published an article in which Mr. Giuliani declared that he intended to travel to Ukraine on behalf of his client, President Trump, in order to meddle in an investigation. After public backlash, Mr. Giuliani canceled the trip, blaming "some bad people" around President Zelensky. Days later, President Trump rescinded the plans for Vice President Pence to attend President

Zelensky's inauguration, which had not yet been scheduled. The staff member planning the trip was not provided an explanation for the about-face, but staff in the U.S. Embassy in Kyiv were disappointed that President Zelensky would not receive a "high level" show of support from the United States.

In Vice President Pence's stead, Secretary of Energy Rick Perry led the American delegation to the Ukrainian President's inauguration. Ambassador Sondland, Special Representative for Ukraine Negotiations Ambassador Kurt Volker, and Lt. Col. Vindman also attended. In comments that would foreshadow troubling events to come, Lt. Col. Vindman warned President Zelensky to stay out of U.S. domestic politics to avoid jeopardizing the bipartisan support Ukraine enjoyed in Congress.

The delegation returned to the United States impressed with President Zelensky, especially his focus on anti-corruption reforms. Ambassador Sondland quickly organized a meeting with President Trump in the Oval Office on May 23, attended by most of the other members of the delegation. The three political appointees, who would describe themselves as the "Three Amigos," relayed their positive impression of President Zelensky to President Trump and encouraged him to schedule the Oval Office meeting he promised in his April 21 phone call with the new leader.

President Trump reacted poorly to the suggestion, claiming that Ukraine "tried to take me down" in 2016. In order to schedule a White House visit for President Zelensky, President Trump told the delegation that they would have to "talk to Rudy." Ambassador Sondland testified that he understood the President's instruction to be a directive to work with Mr. Giuliani if they hoped to advance relations with Ukraine. President Trump directed the three senior U.S. government officials to assist Mr. Giuliani's efforts, which, it would soon become clear, were exclusively for the benefit of the President's reelection campaign.

As the Three Amigos were given responsibility over the U.S. government's Ukraine portfolio, Bill Taylor, a former Ambassador to Ukraine, was considering whether to come out of retirement to accept a request to succeed Ambassador Yovanovitch in Kyiv. As of May 26, Ambassador Taylor was "still struggling with the decision," and, in particular, whether anyone can "hope to succeed with the Giuliani-Biden issue swirling." After receiving assurances from Secretary Pompeo that U.S. policy toward Ukraine would not change, Ambassador Taylor accepted the position and arrived in Kyiv on June 17. Ambassador Taylor would quickly come to observe an "irregular channel" led by Mr. Giuliani that, over time, began to undermine the official channel of diplomatic relations with Ukraine. Mr. Giuliani would prove to be, as the President's National Security Advisor Ambassador John Bolton would tell a colleague, a "hand grenade that was going to blow everyone up."

The President Froze Vital Military Assistance

For fiscal year 2019, Congress appropriated and authorized $391 million in security assistance to Ukraine: $250 million in funds administered by DOD and $141 million in funds administered by the State Department. On June 18, DOD issued a press release announcing its intention to provide $250 million in taxpayer-funded security assistance to Ukraine following the certification that all legitimate conditions on the aid, including anti-corruption reforms, had been met. Shortly after this announcement, however, both the Office of Management and Budget (OMB) and DOD received inquiries from the President related to the funds. At that time, and throughout the next few months, support for Ukraine security assistance was overwhelming and unanimous among all of the relevant agencies and within Congress.

By July 3, OMB blocked a Congressional notification which would have cleared the way for the release of $141 million in State Department security assistance funds. By July 12, President Trump had placed a hold on all military support funding for Ukraine. On July 18, OMB announced the hold to all of the relevant agencies and indicated that it was directed by the President. No other reason was provided.

During a series of policy meetings involving increasingly senior officials, the uniform and consistent position of all policymaking agencies supported the release of funding. Ukraine experts at DOD, the State Department, and the NSC argued that it was in the national security interest of the United States to continue to support Ukraine. As Mr. Morrison testified, "The United States aids Ukraine and her people so that they can fight Russia over there, and we don't have to fight Russia here."

Agency officials also expressed concerns about the legality of President Trump's direction to withhold assistance to Ukraine that Congress had already appropriated for this express purpose. Two OMB career officials, including one of its legal counsels, would resign, in part, over concerns regarding the hold.

By July 25, the date of President Trump's call with President Zelensky, DOD was also receiving inquiries from Ukrainian officials about the status of the security assistance. Nevertheless, President Trump continued to withhold the funding to Ukraine without explanation, against the interests of U.S. national security, and over the objections of these career experts.

The President Conditioned a White House Meeting on Investigations

By the time Ukrainian officials were first learning about an issue with the anticipated military assistance, the President's hand-picked representatives to Ukraine had already informed their Ukrainian counterparts that President Zelensky's coveted White House meeting would only happen after Ukraine committed to pursuing the two political investigations that President Trump and Mr. Giuliani demanded.

Ambassador Sondland was unequivocal in describing this conditionality, testifying, "I know that members of this committee frequently frame these complicated issues in the form of a simple question: Was there a quid pro quo? As I testified previously with regard to the requested White House call and the White House meeting, the answer is yes." Ambassadors Sondland and Volker worked to obtain the necessary assurance from President Zelensky that he would personally commit to initiate the investigations in order to secure both.

On July 2, in Toronto, Canada, Ambassador Volker conveyed the message directly to President Zelensky, specifically referencing the "Giuliani factor" in President Zelensky's engagement with the United States. For his part, Mr. Giuliani made clear to Ambassadors Sondland and Volker, who were directly communicating with the Ukrainians, that a White House meeting would not occur until Ukraine announced its pursuit of the two political investigations. After observing Mr. Giuliani's role in the ouster of a U.S. Ambassador and learning of his influence with the President, Ukrainian officials soon understood that "the key for many things is Rudi [sic]."

On July 10, Ambassador Bolton hosted a meeting in the White House with two senior Ukrainian officials, several American officials, including Ambassadors Sondland and Volker, Secretary Perry, Dr. Fiona Hill, Senior Director for Europe and Russia at the NSC, and Lt. Col. Vindman. As had become customary each time Ukrainian officials met with their American counterparts, the Ukrainians asked about the long-delayed White House meeting. Ambassador Bolton demurred, but Ambassador Sondland spoke up, revealing that he had worked out an arrangement with Acting Chief of Staff Mick Mulvaney to schedule the White House visit after Ukraine initiated the "investigations." Ambassador Bolton "stiffened" and quickly ended the meeting.

Undaunted, Ambassador Sondland ushered many of the attendees to the Ward Room downstairs to continue their discussion. In the second meeting, Ambassador Sondland explained that he had an agreement with Mr. Mulvaney that the White House visit would come only after Ukraine announced the Burisma/Biden and 2016 Ukraine election interference investigations. At this second meeting, both Lt. Col. Vindman and Dr. Hill objected to intertwining a "domestic political errand" with official foreign policy, and they indicated that a White House meeting would have to go through proper channels.

Following these discussions, Dr. Hill reported back to Ambassador Bolton, who told her to "go and tell [the NSC Legal Advisor] that I am not part of whatever drug deal Sondland and Mulvaney are cooking up on this." Both Dr. Hill and Lt. Col. Vindman separately reported the incident to the NSC Legal Advisor.

The President's Agents Pursued a "Drug Deal"

Over the next two weeks, Ambassadors Sondland and Volker worked closely with Mr. Giuliani and senior Ukrainian and American officials to arrange a telephone call between President Trump and President Zelensky and to ensure that the Ukrainian President explicitly promised to undertake the political investigations required by President Trump to schedule the White House meeting. As Ambassador Sondland would later testify: "Mr. Giuliani was expressing the desires of the President of the United States, and we knew these investigations were important to the President."

On July 19, Ambassador Volker had breakfast with Mr. Giuliani and his associate, Lev Parnas, at the Trump Hotel in Washington, D.C. Mr. Parnas would subsequently be indicted for campaign finance violations as part of an investigation that remains ongoing. During the conversation, Ambassador Volker stressed his belief that the attacks being leveled publicly against Vice President Biden related to Ukraine were false and that the former Vice President was "a person of integrity." He counseled Mr. Giuliani that the Ukrainian prosecutor pushing the false narrative, Mr. Lutsenko, was promoting "a self-serving narrative to preserve himself in power." Mr. Giuliani agreed, but his promotion of Mr. Lutsenko's false accusations for the benefit of President Trump did not cease. Ambassador Volker also offered to help arrange an in-person meeting between Mr. Giuliani and Andriy Yermak, one of President Zelensky's most trusted advisors, which would later take place in Madrid, Spain in early August.

After the breakfast meeting at the Trump Hotel, Ambassador Volker reported back to Ambassadors Sondland and Taylor about his conversation with Mr. Giuliani, writing in a text message that, "Most impt [sic] is for Zelensky to say that he will help investigation—and address any specific personnel issues—if there are any," likely referencing President Zelensky's decision to remove Mr. Lutsenko as prosecutor general, a decision with which Mr. Giuliani disagreed. The same day, Ambassador Sondland spoke with President Zelensky and recommended that the Ukrainian leader tell President Trump that he "will leave no stone unturned" regarding the political investigations during the upcoming presidential phone call.

Ambassador Sondland emailed several top Administration officials, including Secretary of State Pompeo, Acting Chief of Staff Mulvaney, and Secretary Perry, stating that President Zelensky confirmed that he would "assure" President Trump that "he intends to run a fully transparent investigation and will 'turn over every stone.'" According to Ambassador Sondland, he was referring in the email to the Burisma/Biden and 2016 election interference investigations. Secretary Perry and Mr. Mulvaney responded affirmatively that the call would soon take place, and Ambassador Sondland testified later that "everyone was in the loop" on plans to condition the White House meeting on the announcement of political investigations beneficial to President Trump. The arrangement troubled the Ukrainian President, who "did not want to be used as a pawn in a U.S. reelection campaign."

The President Pressed President Zelensky to Do a Political Favor

On the morning of July 25, Ambassador Volker sent a text message to President Zelensky's top aide, Mr. Yermak, less than 30 minutes before the presidential call. He stated: "Heard from White House—assuming President Z convinces trump he will investigate / 'get to the bottom of what happened' in 2016, we will nail down date for visit to Washington. Good luck!" Shortly before the call, Ambassador Sondland spoke directly with President Trump.

President Zelensky followed this advice during his conversation with President Trump. President Zelensky assured that he would pursue the investigations that President Trump had discussed—into the Bidens and 2016 election interference—and, in turn, pressed for the White House meeting that remained outstanding.

The following day, Ambassadors Volker, Sondland, and Taylor met with President Zelensky in Kyiv. The Ukrainian President told them that President Trump had mentioned "sensitive issues" three times during the previous day's phone call. Following the meeting with the Ukrainian leader, Ambassador Sondland had a private, one-on-one conversation with Mr. Yermak in which they discussed "the issue of investigations." He then retired to lunch at an outdoor restaurant terrace with State Department aides where he called President Trump directly from his cellphone. The White House confirmed that the conversation lasted five minutes.

At the outset of the call, President Trump asked Ambassador Sondland whether President Zelensky "was going to do the investigation" that President Trump had raised with President Zelensky the day before. Ambassador Sondland stated that President Zelensky was "going to do it" and "would do anything you ask him to." According to David Holmes, the State Department aide sitting closest to Ambassador Sondland and who overheard the President's voice on the phone, Ambassador Sondland and President Trump spoke only about the investigation in their discussion about Ukraine. The President made no mention of other major issues of importance in Ukraine, including President Zelensky's aggressive anti-corruption reforms and the ongoing war it was fighting against Russian-led forces in eastern Ukraine.

After hanging up the phone, Ambassador Sondland explained to Mr. Holmes that President Trump "did not give a shit about Ukraine." Rather, the President cared only about "big stuff" that benefitted him personally, like "the Biden investigation that Mr. Giuliani was pitching," and that President Trump had pushed for in his July 25 call with the Ukrainian leader. Ambassador Sondland did not recall referencing Biden specifically, but he did not dispute Mr. Holmes' recollection of the call with the President or Ambassador Sondland's subsequent discussion with Mr. Holmes.

The President's Representatives Ratcheted up Pressure on the Ukrainian President

In the weeks following the July 25 call, the President's hand-picked representatives increased the President's pressure campaign on Ukrainian government officials—in person, over the phone, and by text message—to secure a public announcement of the investigations beneficial to President Trump's reelection campaign.

In discussions with Ukrainian officials, Ambassador Sondland understood that President Trump did not require that Ukraine *conduct* investigations as a prerequisite for the White House meeting so much as publicly *announce* the investigations—making clear that the goal was not the investigations, but the political benefit Trump would derive from their announcement and the cloud they might put over a political opponent.

On August 2, President Zelensky's advisor, Mr. Yermak, traveled to Madrid to meet Mr. Giuliani in person. There, they agreed that Ukraine would issue a public statement, and they discussed potential dates for a White House meeting. A few days later, Ambassador Volker told Mr. Giuliani that it "would be good" if Mr. Giuliani would report to "the boss," President Trump, about "the results" of his Madrid discussion so that President Trump would finally agree to a White House visit by President Zelensky.

On August 9, Ambassador Volker and Mr. Giuliani spoke twice by phone, and Ambassador Sondland spoke twice to the White House for a total of about 20 minutes. In a text message to Ambassador Volker later that day, Ambassador Sondland wrote, "I think potus [sic] really wants the deliverable," which Ambassador Sondland acknowledged was the public statement announcing the two political investigations sought by President Trump and Mr. Giuliani.

The following day, Ambassador Sondland briefed State Department Counselor Ulrich Brechbuhl, a top advisor to Secretary Pompeo, on these discussions about President Zelensky issuing a statement that would include an announcement of the two political investigations. Ambassador Sondland also emailed Secretary Pompeo directly, copying the State Department's executive secretary and Mr. Brechbuhl, to inform them about the agreement for President Zelensky to give the press conference. He expected to see a draft of the statement, which would be "delivered for our review in a day or two." Ambassador Sondland noted his hope that the draft statement would "make the boss happy enough to authorize an invitation."

On August 12, Mr. Yermak sent the proposed statement to Ambassador Volker, but it lacked specific references to the two investigations politically beneficial to President Trump's reelection campaign. The following morning, Ambassadors Sondland and Volker spoke with Mr. Giuliani, who made clear that if the statement "doesn't say Burisma and 2016, it's not credible." Ambassador Volker revised the statement following this direction to include those references and returned it to the Ukrainian President's aide.

Mr. Yermak balked at getting drawn into U.S. politics and asked Ambassador Volker whether the United States had inquired about investigations through any appropriate Department of Justice channels. The answer was no, and several witnesses testified that a request to a foreign country to investigate a U.S. citizen "for political reasons" goes "against everything" the United States sought to promote in eastern Europe, specifically the rule of law. Ambassador Volker eventually agreed with Mr. Yermak that the announcement of the Biden/Burisma and 2016 elections investigations would "look like it would play into our domestic politics," so the statement was temporarily "shelved."

Nevertheless, Ambassador Sondland, in accordance with President Trump's wishes, continued to pursue the statement into early September 2019.

Ukrainians Inquired about the President's Hold on Security Assistance

Once President Trump placed security assistance on hold in July, "it was inevitable that it was eventually going to come out." On July 25, DOD officials learned that diplomats at the Ukrainian Embassy in Washington had made multiple overtures to DOD and the State Department "asking about security assistance." Separately, two different contacts at the Ukrainian Embassy approached Ambassador Volker's special advisor, Catherine Croft, to ask her in confidence about the hold. Ms. Croft was surprised at the effectiveness of their "diplomatic tradecraft," noting that they "found out very early on" that the United States was withholding critical military aid to Ukraine. By mid-August, before the freeze on aid became public, Lt. Col. Vindman had also received inquiries from an official at the Ukrainian Embassy.

The hold remained in place throughout August against the unanimous judgment of American officials focused on Ukraine policy. Without an explanation for the hold, which ran contrary to the recommendation of all relevant agencies, and with President Trump already conditioning a White House visit on the announcement of the political investigations, it became increasingly apparent to multiple witnesses that the military aid was also being withheld in exchange for the announcement of those. As both Ambassador Sondland and Mr. Holmes would later testify, it became as clear as "two plus two equals four."

On August 22, Ambassador Sondland emailed Secretary Pompeo again, recommending a plan for a potential meeting between President Trump and President Zelensky in Warsaw, Poland on September 1. Ambassador Sondland noted that President Zelensky should "look him in the eye" and tell President Trump that once new prosecutorial officials were in place in Ukraine, "Zelensky should be able to move forward publicly and with confidence on those issues of importance to Potus and the U.S." Ambassador Sondland testified that this was a reference to the political investigations that President Trump discussed on the July 25 call, that Secretary Pompeo had listened to. Ambassador Sondland hoped this would "break the logjam"—the hold on critical security assistance to Ukraine. Secretary Pompeo replied three minutes later: "Yes."

The President's Security Assistance Hold Became Public

On August 28, *Politico* published a story revealing President Trump's weeks-long hold on U.S. military assistance to Ukraine. Senior Ukrainian officials expressed grave concern, deeply worried about the practical impact on their efforts to fight Russian aggression, but also about the public message it sent to the Russian government, which would almost certainly seek to exploit any real or perceived crack in U.S. resolve toward Ukraine.

On August 29, at the urging of National Security Advisor Bolton, Ambassador Taylor wrote a first-person cable to Secretary Pompeo. This was the only first-person cable the Ambassador had ever sent in his decades of government service. He explained the "folly" of withholding security assistance to Ukraine as it fought a hot war against Russia on its borders. He wrote that he "could not and would not defend such a policy." Ambassador Taylor stated that Secretary Pompeo may have carried the cable with him to a meeting at the White House.

The same day that Ambassador Taylor sent his cable, President Trump cancelled his planned trip to Warsaw for a World War II commemoration event, where he was scheduled to meet with President Zelensky. Vice President Pence traveled in his place. Ambassador Sondland also traveled to Warsaw and, at a pre-briefing discussion with the Vice President before he met President Zelensky, Ambassador Sondland raised the issue of the hold on security assistance. He told Vice President Pence that he was concerned that the security assistance "had become tied to the issue of investigations" and that "everything is being held up until these statements get made." Vice President Pence nodded in response, apparently expressing neither surprise nor dismay at the linkage between the two.

At the meeting, President Zelensky expressed concern that even an appearance of wavering support from the United States for Ukraine could embolden Russia. Vice President Pence reiterated U.S. support for Ukraine, but could not promise that the hold would be lifted. Vice President Pence said he would relay his support for lifting the hold to President Trump so a decision could be made on security assistance as soon as possible. Vice President Pence spoke with President Trump that evening, but the hold was not lifted.

Following this meeting, Ambassador Sondland pulled aside President Zelensky's advisor, Mr. Yermak, to explain that the hold on security assistance was conditioned on the public announcement of the Burisma/Biden and the 2016 election interference investigations. After learning of the conversation, Ambassador Taylor texted Ambassador Sondland: "Are we now saying that security assistance and WH meeting are conditioned on investigations?"

The two then spoke by phone. Ambassador Sondland explained that he had previously made a "mistake" in telling Ukrainian officials that only the White House meeting was conditioned on a public announcement of the political investigations beneficial to President Trump. He clarified that "everything"—the White House meeting and hundreds of millions of dollars of security assistance to Ukraine—was now conditioned on the announcement. President Trump wanted President Zelensky in a "public box," which Ambassador Taylor understood to mean that President Trump required that President Zelensky make a public announcement about the investigations and that a private commitment would not do.

On September 7, President Trump and Ambassador Sondland spoke. Ambassador Sondland stated to his colleagues that the President said, "there was no quid pro quo," but that President Zelensky would be required to announce the investigations in order for the hold on security assistance to be lifted, "and he should want to do it." Ambassador Sondland passed on a similar message directly to President Zelensky and Mr. Yermak that, "although this was not a quid pro quo, if President Zelensky did not clear things up in public, we would be at a stalemate," referring to the hold on security assistance. Arrangements were made for the Ukrainian President to make a public statement during an interview on CNN.

After speaking with Ambassador Sondland, Ambassador Taylor texted Ambassadors Sondland and Volker: "As I said on the phone, I think it's crazy to withhold security assistance for help with a political campaign." Notwithstanding his long-held understanding that the White House meeting was conditioned on the public announcement of two political investigations desired by President Trump—and not broader anti-corruption concerns—Ambassador Sondland responded hours later:

> Bill, I believe you are incorrect about President Trump's intentions. The President has been crystal clear: no quid pro quo's of any kind. The President is trying to evaluate whether Ukraine is truly going to adopt the transparency and reforms that President Zelensky promised during his campaign. I suggest we stop the back and forth by text. If you still have concerns, I recommend you give Lisa Kenna or [Secretary Pompeo] a call to discuss with them directly. Thanks.

Ambassador Sondland's subsequent testimony revealed this text to be a false exculpatory—an untruthful statement that can later be used to conceal incriminating information. In his public testimony, Ambassador Sondland testified that the President's direction to withhold a presidential telephone call and a White House meeting for President Zelensky were both quid pro quos designed to pressure Ukraine to announce the investigations. He also testified that he developed a clear understanding that the military aid was also conditioned on the investigations, that it was as simple as 2+2=4. Sondland confirmed that his clear understanding was unchanged after speaking with President Trump, which he then communicated to the Ukrainians—President Zelensky had to publicly announce the two investigations if he wanted to get the meeting or the military aid.

In Ambassador Sondland's testimony, he was not clear on whether he had one conversation with the President in which the subject of a quid pro quo came up, or two, or on precisely which date the conversation took place during the period of September 6 through 9. In one version of the conversation which Ambassador Sondland suggested may have taken place on September 9, he claimed that the President answered an open question about what he wanted from Ukraine with an immediate denial—"no quid pro quo." In another, he admitted that the President told him that President Zelensky should go to a microphone and announce the investigations, and that he should want to do so—effectively confirming a quid pro quo.

Both Ambassador Taylor and Mr. Morrison, relying on their contemporaneous notes, testified that the call between Ambassador Sondland and President Trump occurred on September 7, which is further confirmed by Ambassador Sondland's own text message on September 8 in which he wrote that he had "multiple convos" with President Zelensky and President Trump. A call on September 9, which would have occurred in the middle of the night, is at odds with the weight of the evidence and not backed up by any records the White House was willing to provide Ambassador Sondland. Regardless of the date, Ambassador Sondland did not contest telling both Mr. Morrison and Ambassador Taylor of a conversation he had with the President in which the President reaffirmed Ambassador Sondland's understanding of the quid pro quo for the military aid.

As Ambassador Sondland acknowledged bluntly in his conversation with Mr. Holmes, President Trump's sole interest with respect to Ukraine was the "big stuff" that benefited him personally, such as the investigations into former Vice President Biden, and not President Zelensky's promises of transparency and reform.

The President's Scheme Unraveled

By early September, President Zelensky was ready to make a public announcement of the two investigations to secure a White House meeting and the military assistance his country desperately needed. He proceeded to book an interview on CNN during which he could make such an announcement, but other events soon intervened.

On September 9, the House Permanent Select Committee on Intelligence, the Committees on Oversight and Reform, and the Committee on Foreign Affairs announced an investigation into the scheme by President Trump and his personal attorney, Mr. Giuliani "to improperly pressure the Ukrainian government to assist the President's bid for reelection." The Committees sent document production and preservation requests to the White House and the State Department related to the investigation. NSC staff members believed this investigation might have had "the effect of releasing the hold" on Ukraine military assistance because it would have been "potentially politically challenging" to "justify that hold."

Later that day, the Inspector General of the Intelligence Community (ICIG) sent a letter to Chairman Schiff and Ranking Member Nunes notifying the Committee that a whistleblower had filed a complaint on August 12 that the ICIG had determined to be both an "urgent concern" and "credible." Nevertheless, the Acting Director of National Intelligence (DNI) took the unprecedented step of withholding the complaint from the Congressional Intelligence Committees, in coordination with the White House and the Department of Justice.

The White House had been aware of the whistleblower complaint for several weeks, and press reports indicate that the President was briefed on it in late August. The ICIG's notification to Congress of the complaint's existence, and the announcement of a separate investigation into the same subject matter, telegraphed to the White House that attempts to condition the security assistance on the announcement of the political investigations beneficial to President Trump— and efforts to cover up that misconduct—would not last.

On September 11, in the face of growing public and Congressional scrutiny, President Trump lifted the hold on security assistance to Ukraine. As with the implementation of the hold, no clear reason was given. By the time the President ordered the release of security assistance to Ukraine, DOD was unable to spend approximately 14 percent of the funds appropriated by Congress for Fiscal Year 2019. Congress had to pass a new law to extend the funding in order to ensure the full amount could be used by Ukraine to defend itself.

Even after the hold was lifted, President Zelensky still intended to sit for an interview with CNN in order to announce the investigations—indeed, he still wanted the White House meeting. At the urging of Ambassador Taylor, President Zelensky cancelled the CNN interview on September 18 or 19. The White House meeting, however, still has not occurred.

The President's Chief of Staff Confirmed Aid was Conditioned on Investigations

The conditioning of military aid to Ukraine on the investigations sought by the President was as clear to Ambassador Sondland as "two plus two equals four." In fact, the President's own Acting Chief of Staff, someone who meets with him daily, admitted that he had discussed security assistance with the President and that his decision to withhold it was directly tied to his desire to get Ukraine to conduct a political investigation.

On October 17, at a press briefing in the White House, Acting Chief of Staff Mick Mulvaney confirmed that President Trump withheld the essential military aid for Ukraine as leverage to pressure Ukraine to investigate the conspiracy theory that Ukraine had interfered in the 2016 U.S. election. As Dr. Hill made clear in her testimony, this false narrative has been promoted by President Putin to deflect away from Russia's systemic interference in our election and to drive a wedge between the United States and a key partner.

According to Mr. Mulvaney, President Trump "[a]bsolutely" mentioned "corruption related to the DNC server" in connection with the security assistance during his July 25 call. Mr. Mulvaney also stated that the server was part of "why we held up the money." After a reporter attempted to clarify this explicit acknowledgement of a quid pro quo, Mr. Mulvaney replied:

"We do that all the time with foreign policy." He added, "I have news for everybody: get over it. There is going to be political influence in foreign policy."

Ambassador Taylor testified that in his decades of military and diplomatic service, he had never seen another example of foreign aid conditioned on the personal or political interests of the President. Rather, "we condition assistance on issues that will improve our foreign policy, serve our foreign policy, ensure that taxpayers' money is well-spent," not specific investigations designed to benefit the political interests of the President of the United States.

In contrast, President Trump does not appear to believe there is any such limitation on his power to use White House meetings, military aid or other official acts to procure foreign help in his reelection. When asked by a reporter on October 3 what he had hoped President Zelensky would do following their July 25 call, President Trump responded: "Well, I would think that, if they were honest about it, they'd start a major investigation into the Bidens. It's a very simple answer."

SECTION II—THE PRESIDENT'S OBSTRUCTION OF THE HOUSE OF REPRESENTATIVES' IMPEACHMENT INQUIRY

The President Obstructed the Impeachment Inquiry by Instructing Witnesses and Agencies to Ignore Subpoenas for Documents and Testimony

An Unprecedented Effort to Obstruct an Impeachment Inquiry

Donald Trump is the first President in the history of the United States to seek to completely obstruct an impeachment inquiry undertaken by the House of Representatives under Article I of the Constitution, which vests the House with the "sole Power of Impeachment." He has publicly and repeatedly rejected the authority of Congress to conduct oversight of his actions and has directly challenged the authority of the House to conduct an impeachment inquiry into his actions regarding Ukraine.

President Trump ordered federal agencies and officials to disregard all voluntary requests for documents and defy all duly authorized subpoenas for records. He also directed all federal officials in the Executive Branch not to testify—even when compelled.

No other President has flouted the Constitution and power of Congress to conduct oversight to this extent. No President has claimed for himself the right to deny the House's authority to conduct an impeachment proceeding, control the scope of a power exclusively vested in the House, and forbid any and all cooperation from the Executive Branch. Even President Richard Nixon—who obstructed Congress by refusing to turn over key evidence— accepted the authority of Congress to conduct an impeachment inquiry and permitted his aides and advisors to produce documents and testify to Congressional committees.

Despite President Trump's unprecedented and categorical commands, the House gathered overwhelming evidence of his misconduct from courageous individuals who were willing to follow the law, comply with duly authorized subpoenas, and tell the truth. In response, the President engaged in a brazen effort to publicly attack and intimidate these witnesses.

If left unanswered, President Trump's ongoing effort to thwart Congress' impeachment power risks doing grave harm to the institution of Congress, the balance of power between our branches of government, and the Constitutional order that the President and every Member of Congress have sworn to protect and defend.

Constitutional Authority for Congressional Oversight and Impeachment

The House's Constitutional and legal authority to conduct an impeachment inquiry is clear, as is the duty of the President to cooperate with the House's exercise of this authority.

Article I of the U.S. Constitution gives the House of Representatives the "sole Power of Impeachment." The Framers intended the impeachment power to be an essential check on a President who might engage in corruption or abuse of power. Congress is empowered to conduct oversight and investigations to carry out its authorities under Article I. Because the impeachment power is a core component of the nation's Constitutional system of checks and balances, Congress' investigative authority is at its zenith during an impeachment inquiry.

The Supreme Court has made clear that Congress' authority to investigate includes the authority to compel the production of information by issuing subpoenas, a power the House has delegated to its committees pursuant to its Constitutional authority to "determine the Rules of its Proceedings."

Congress has also enacted statutes to support its power to investigate and oversee the Executive Branch. These laws impose criminal and other penalties on those who fail to comply with inquiries from Congress or block others from doing so, and they reflect the broader Constitutional requirement to cooperate with Congressional investigations.

Unlike President Trump, past Presidents who were the subject of impeachment inquiries—including Presidents Andrew Johnson, Richard Nixon, and Bill Clinton—recognized and, to varying degrees, complied with information requests and subpoenas.

President Nixon, for example, agreed to let his staff testify voluntarily in the Senate Watergate investigation, stating: "All members of the White House Staff will appear voluntarily when requested by the committee. They will testify under oath, and they will answer fully all proper questions." President Nixon also produced documents in response to the House's subpoenas as part of its impeachment inquiry, including more than 30 transcripts of White House recordings and notes from meetings with the President. When President Nixon withheld tape recordings and produced heavily edited and inaccurate records, the House Judiciary Committee approved an article of impeachment for obstruction.

The President's Categorical Refusal to Comply

Even before the House of Representatives launched its investigation regarding Ukraine, President Trump rejected the authority of Congress to investigate his actions, proclaiming, "We're fighting all the subpoenas," and "I have an Article II, where I have the right to do whatever I want as president."

When the Intelligence, Oversight and Reform, and Foreign Affairs Committees began reviewing the President's actions as part of the House's impeachment inquiry, the President repeatedly challenged the legitimacy of the investigation in word and deed. His rhetorical attacks appeared intended not only to dispute reports of his misconduct, but to persuade the American people that the House lacks authority to investigate the President.

On September 26, President Trump argued that Congress should not be "allowed" to impeach him under the Constitution and that there "should be a way of stopping it—maybe legally, through the courts." A common theme of his defiance has been his claims that Congress is acting in an unprecedented way and using unprecedented rules. However, the House has been following the same investigative rules that Republicans championed when they were in control.

On October 8, White House Counsel Pat Cipollone sent a letter to House Speaker Nancy Pelosi and the Chairmen of the investigating Committees confirming that President Trump directed his entire Administration not to cooperate with the House's impeachment inquiry. Mr. Cipollone wrote: "President Trump cannot permit his Administration to participate in this partisan inquiry under these circumstances."

Mr. Cipollone's letter advanced remarkably politicized arguments and legal theories unsupported by the Constitution, judicial precedent, and more than 200 years of history. If allowed to stand, the President's defiance, as justified by Mr. Cipollone, would represent an existential threat to the nation's Constitutional system of checks and balances, separation of powers, and rule of law.

The President's Refusal to Produce Any and All Subpoenaed Documents

Following President Trump's categorical order, not a single document has been produced by the White House, the Office of the Vice President, the Office of Management and Budget, the Department of State, the Department of Defense, or the Department of Energy in response to 71 specific, individualized requests or demands for records in their possession, custody, or control. These subpoenas remain in full force and effect. These agencies and offices also blocked many current and former officials from producing records directly to the Committees.

Certain witnesses defied the President's sweeping, categorical, and baseless order and identified the substance of key documents. For example, Ambassador Gordon Sondland attached ten exhibits to his written hearing testimony reflecting reproductions of certain communications with high-level Administration officials, including Acting White House Chief of Staff Mick Mulvaney, former National Security Advisor John Bolton, Secretary of State Mike Pompeo, and Secretary of Energy Rick Perry. Other witnesses identified numerous additional documents that the President and various agencies are withholding that are directly relevant to the impeachment inquiry.

Like the White House, the Department of State refused to produce a single document in response to its subpoena, even though there is no legal basis for the Department's actions. In fact, on November 22, the Department was forced to produce 99 pages of emails, letters, notes, timelines, and news articles to a non-partisan, nonprofit ethics watchdog organization pursuant to a court order in a lawsuit filed under the Freedom of Information Act (FOIA). Although limited in scope, this production affirms that the Department is withholding responsive documents from Congress without any valid legal basis.

The President's Refusal to Allow Top Aides to Testify

No other President in history has issued an order categorically directing the entire Executive Branch not to testify before Congress, including in the context of an impeachment inquiry. President Trump issued just such an order.

As reflected in Mr. Cipollone's letter, President Trump directed government witnesses to violate their legal obligations and defy House subpoenas—regardless of their offices or positions. President Trump even extended his order to former officials no longer employed by the federal government. This Administration-wide effort to prevent all witnesses from providing testimony was coordinated and comprehensive.

At President Trump's direction, twelve current or former Administration officials refused to testify as part of the House's impeachment inquiry, ten of whom did so in defiance of duly authorized subpoenas:

- Mick Mulvaney, Acting White House Chief of Staff
- Robert B. Blair, Assistant to the President and Senior Advisor to the Chief of Staff
- Ambassador John Bolton, Former National Security Advisor
- John A. Eisenberg, Deputy Counsel to the President for National Security Affairs and Legal Advisor, National Security Council
- Michael Ellis, Senior Associate Counsel to the President and Deputy Legal Advisor, National Security Council
- Preston Wells Griffith, Senior Director for International Energy and Environment, National Security Council
- Dr. Charles M. Kupperman, Former Deputy Assistant to the President for National Security Affairs, National Security Council
- Russell T. Vought, Acting Director, Office of Management and Budget
- Michael Duffey, Associate Director for National Security Programs, Office of Management and Budget
- Brian McCormack, Associate Director for Natural Resources, Energy, and Science, Office of Management and Budget
- T. Ulrich Brechbuhl, Counselor, Department of State
- Secretary Rick Perry, Department of Energy

These witnesses were warned that their refusal to testify "shall constitute evidence that may be used against you in a contempt proceeding" and "may be used as an adverse inference against you and the President."

The President's Unsuccessful Attempts to Block Other Key Witnesses

Despite President Trump's orders that no Executive Branch employees should cooperate with the House's impeachment inquiry, multiple key officials complied with duly authorized subpoenas and provided critical testimony at depositions and public hearings. These officials not only served their nation honorably, but they fulfilled their oath to support and defend the Constitution of the United States.

In addition to the President's broad orders seeking to prohibit all Executive Branch employees from testifying, many of these witnesses were personally directed by senior political appointees not to cooperate with the House's impeachment inquiry. These directives frequently cited or enclosed copies of Mr. Cipollone's October 8 letter conveying the President's order not to comply.

For example, the State Department, relying on President Trump's order, attempted to block Ambassador Marie Yovanovitch from testifying, but she fulfilled her legal obligations by appearing at a deposition on October 11 and a hearing on November 15. More than a dozen current and former officials followed her courageous example by testifying at depositions and public hearings over the course of the last two months. The testimony from these witnesses produced overwhelming and clear evidence of President Trump's misconduct, which is described in detail in the first section of this report.

The President's Intimidation of Witnesses

President Trump publicly attacked and intimidated witnesses who came forward to comply with duly authorized subpoenas and testify about his misconduct, raising grave concerns about potential violations of criminal laws intended to protect witnesses appearing before Congressional proceedings. For example, the President attacked:

- Ambassador Marie Yovanovitch, who served the United States honorably for decades as a U.S. diplomat and anti-corruption advocate in posts around the world under six different Presidents;

- Ambassador Bill Taylor, who graduated at the top of his class at West Point, served as an infantry commander in Vietnam, and earned a Bronze Star and an Air Medal with a V device for valor;

- Lieutenant Colonel Alexander Vindman, an active-duty Army officer for more than 20 years who earned a Purple Heart for wounds he sustained in an improvised explosive device attack in Iraq, as well as the Combat Infantryman Badge; and

- Jennifer Williams, who is Vice President Mike Pence's top advisor on Europe and Russia and has a distinguished record of public service under the Bush, Obama, and Trump Administrations.

The President engaged in this effort to intimidate these public servants to prevent them from cooperating with Congress' impeachment inquiry. He issued threats, openly discussed possible retaliation, made insinuations about their character and patriotism, and subjected them to mockery and derision—when they deserved the opposite. The President's attacks were broadcast to millions of Americans—including witnesses' families, friends, and coworkers.

It is a federal crime to intimidate or seek to intimidate any witness appearing before Congress. This prohibition applies to anyone who knowingly "uses intimidation, threatens, or corruptly persuades" another person in order to "influence, delay, or prevent the testimony of any person in an official proceeding." Violations of this law can carry a criminal sentence of up to 20 years in prison.

In addition to his relentless attacks on witnesses who testified in connection with the House's impeachment inquiry, the President also repeatedly threatened and attacked a member of the Intelligence Community who filed an anonymous whistleblower complaint raising an "urgent concern" that "appeared credible" regarding the President's conduct. The whistleblower filed the complaint confidentially with the Inspector General of the Intelligence Community, as authorized by the relevant whistleblower law. Federal law prohibits the Inspector General from revealing the whistleblower's identity. Federal law also protects the whistleblower from retaliation.

In more than 100 public statements about the whistleblower over a period of just two months, the President publicly questioned the whistleblower's motives, disputed the accuracy of the whistleblower's account, and encouraged others to reveal the whistleblower's identity. Most chillingly, the President issued a threat against the whistleblower and those who provided information to the whistleblower regarding the President's misconduct, suggesting that they could face the death penalty for treason.

The President's campaign of intimidation risks discouraging witnesses from coming forward voluntarily, complying with mandatory subpoenas for documents and testimony, and disclosing potentially incriminating evidence in this inquiry and future Congressional investigations.

KEY FINDINGS OF FACT

Based on witness testimony and evidence collected during the impeachment inquiry, the Intelligence Committee has found that:

I.   Donald J. Trump, the 45th President of the United States—acting personally and through his agents within and outside of the U.S. government—solicited the interference of a foreign government, Ukraine, in the 2020 U.S. presidential election. The President engaged in this course of conduct for the benefit of his reelection, to harm the election prospects of a political opponent, and to influence our nation's upcoming presidential election to his advantage. In so doing, the President placed his personal political interests above the national interests of the United States, sought to undermine the integrity of the U.S. presidential election process, and endangered U.S. national security.

II.   In furtherance of this scheme, President Trump—directly and acting through his agents within and outside the U.S. government—sought to pressure and induce Ukraine's newly-elected president, Volodymyr Zelensky, to publicly announce unfounded investigations that would benefit President Trump's personal political interests and reelection effort. To advance his personal political objectives, President Trump encouraged the President of Ukraine to work with his personal attorney, Rudy Giuliani.

III.   As part of this scheme, President Trump, acting in his official capacity and using his position of public trust, personally and directly requested from the President of Ukraine that the government of Ukraine publicly announce investigations into (1) the President's political opponent, former Vice President Joseph R. Biden, Jr. and his son, Hunter Biden, and (2) a baseless theory promoted by Russia alleging that Ukraine—rather than Russia—interfered in the 2016 U.S. election. These investigations were intended to harm a potential political opponent of President Trump and benefit the President's domestic political standing.

IV.   President Trump ordered the suspension of $391 million in vital military assistance urgently needed by Ukraine, a strategic partner, to resist Russian aggression. Because the aid was appropriated by Congress, on a bipartisan basis, and signed into law by the President, its expenditure was required by law. Acting directly and through his subordinates within the U.S. government, the President withheld from Ukraine this military assistance without any legitimate foreign policy, national security, or anti-corruption justification. The President did so despite the longstanding bipartisan support of Congress, uniform support across federal departments and agencies for the provision to Ukraine of the military assistance, and his obligations under the Impoundment Control Act.

V.   President Trump used the power of the Office of the President and exercised his authority over the Executive Branch, including his control of the instruments of the federal government, to apply increasing pressure on the President of Ukraine and the Ukrainian government to announce the politically-motivated investigations desired by President Trump. Specifically, to advance and promote his scheme, the President withheld official acts of value to Ukraine and conditioned their fulfillment on actions by Ukraine that would benefit his personal political interests:

A. President Trump—acting through agents within and outside the U.S. government—conditioned a head of state meeting at the White House, which the President of Ukraine desperately sought to demonstrate continued United States support for Ukraine in the face of Russian aggression, on Ukraine publicly announcing the investigations that President Trump believed would aid his reelection campaign.

B. To increase leverage over the President of Ukraine, President Trump, acting through his agents and subordinates, conditioned release of the vital military assistance he had suspended to Ukraine on the President of Ukraine's public announcement of the investigations that President Trump sought.

C. President Trump's closest subordinates and advisors within the Executive Branch, including Acting Chief of Staff Mick Mulvaney, Secretary of State Mike Pompeo, Secretary of Energy J. Richard Perry, and other senior White House and Executive Branch officials had knowledge of, in some cases facilitated and furthered the President's scheme, and withheld information about the scheme from the Congress and the American public.

VI. In directing and orchestrating this scheme to advance his personal political interests, President Trump did not implement, promote, or advance U.S. anti-corruption policies. In fact, the President sought to pressure and induce the government of Ukraine to announce politically-motivated investigations lacking legitimate predication that the U.S. government otherwise discourages and opposes as a matter of policy in that country and around the world. In so doing, the President undermined U.S. policy supporting anti-corruption reform and the rule of law in Ukraine, and undermined U.S. national security.

VII. By withholding vital military assistance and diplomatic support from a strategic foreign partner government engaged in an ongoing military conflict illegally instigated by Russia, President Trump compromised national security to advance his personal political interests.

VIII. Faced with the revelation of his actions, President Trump publicly and repeatedly persisted in urging foreign governments, including Ukraine and China, to investigate his political opponent. This continued solicitation of foreign interference in a U.S. election presents a clear and present danger that the President will continue to use the power of his office for his personal political gain.

IX. Using the power of the Office of the President, and exercising his authority over the Executive Branch, President Trump ordered and implemented a campaign to conceal his conduct from the public and frustrate and obstruct the House of Representatives' impeachment inquiry by:

A.   refusing to produce to the impeachment inquiry's investigating Committees information and records in the possession of the White House, in defiance of a lawful subpoena;

B.   directing Executive Branch agencies to defy lawful subpoenas and withhold the production of all documents and records from the investigating Committees;

C.   directing current and former Executive Branch officials not to cooperate with the Committees, including in defiance of lawful subpoenas for testimony; and

D.   intimidating, threatening, and tampering with prospective and actual witnesses in the impeachment inquiry in an effort to prevent, delay, or influence the testimony of those witnesses.

In so doing, and despite the fact that the Constitution vests in the House of Representatives the "sole Power of Impeachment," the President sought to arrogate to himself the right to determine the propriety, scope, and nature of an impeachment inquiry into his own misconduct, and the right to deny any and all information to the Congress in the conduct of its constitutional responsibilities.

SECTION I.

THE PRESIDENT'S MISCONDUCT

1. The President Forced Out the U.S. Ambassador to Ukraine

> *The President forced out the United States Ambassador to Ukraine, Marie Yovanovitch, following a baseless smear campaign promoted by President Trump's personal attorney, Rudy Giuliani, and others. The campaign publicized conspiracy theories that benefited the President's personal political interests and undermined official U.S. policy, some of which the President raised during his July 25 call with the President of Ukraine.*

Overview

On April 24, 2019, President Donald J. Trump abruptly recalled the U.S. Ambassador to Ukraine, Marie Yovanovitch. Ambassador Yovanovitch, an award-winning 33-year veteran Foreign Service officer, aggressively advocated for anti-corruption reforms in Ukraine consistent with U.S. foreign policy. President Trump forced her out following a baseless smear campaign promoted by his personal attorney, Rudy Giuliani, associates of Mr. Giuliani, and corrupt Ukrainians.

Ambassador Yovanovitch was told by the State Department that President Trump had lost confidence in her, but she was never provided a substantive justification for her removal. Her ouster set the stage for other U.S. officials appointed by President Trump to work in cooperation with Mr. Giuliani to advance a scheme in support of the President's reelection.

Mr. Giuliani and his associates promoted false conspiracy theories about Ukraine colluding with Democrats to interfere in the 2016 U.S. election. This false claim was promoted by Russian President Vladimir Putin in February 2017—less than a month after the unanimous U.S. Intelligence Community assessment that Russia alone was responsible for a covert influence campaign aimed at helping President Trump during the 2016 election. Mr. Giuliani also made discredited public allegations about former Vice President Joe Biden and his son, Hunter, in an apparent effort to hurt President Trump's political rival in the 2020 presidential election. Mr. Giuliani's associates, with their own ties to President Trump, also worked to enter into arrangements with current and former corrupt Ukrainian officials to promote these false allegations—the same unfounded allegations President Trump requested that Ukraine investigate on his July 25 call with Ukrainian President Volodymyr Zelensky.

President Trump amplified these baseless allegations by tweeting them just a month before he recalled Ambassador Yovanovitch. Despite requests from Ambassador Yovanovitch and other senior State Department officials, Secretary of State Mike Pompeo refused to issue a statement of support for the Ambassador or the U.S. Embassy in Ukraine for fear of being undermined by a tweet by President Trump.

The removal of Ambassador Yovanovitch left a vacuum in the leadership of the U.S. Embassy in Ukraine at an important time. A new president had just been elected on an anti-corruption platform, and the country was in a period of transition as it continued to defend itself against Russia-led military aggression in the east.

Anti-Corruption Ceremony Interrupted to Recall Anti-Corruption Ambassador

Ambassador Yovanovitch represented the United States of America as the U.S. Ambassador to Ukraine from 2016 to 2019. She is a non-partisan career public servant, first selected for the American Foreign Service in 1986. President George W. Bush named her as his Ambassador twice, to the Kyrgyz Republic and Armenia, and President Barack Obama nominated her for the posting in Kyiv.[1]

On the evening of April 24, Ambassador Yovanovitch approached a podium in front of gold drapes at the U.S. Ambassador's residence in Ukraine's capital city. She was hosting an event to present an award of courage to the father of Kateryna Handziuk, who was brutally murdered by people who opposed her efforts to expose and root out public corruption in Ukraine. In 2018, attackers threw sulfuric acid at Ms. Handziuk, burning more than 30 percent of her body. After months of suffering and nearly a dozen surgeries, she died at the age of 33.[2] Her attackers have still not been held to account.[3]

Ambassador Yovanovitch began her speech by noting that Ms. Handziuk "was a woman of courage who committed herself to speaking out against wrongdoing." She lamented how Ms. Handziuk had "paid the ultimate price for her fearlessness in fighting against corruption and for her determined efforts to build a democratic Ukraine." She pledged that the United States would "continue to stand with those engaged in the fight for a democratic Ukraine free of corruption, where people are held accountable" and commended Ukrainians who "have demonstrated to the world that they are willing to fight for a better system."[4]

Ambassador Yovanovitch concluded her remarks by holding Ms. Handziuk's story up as an inspiration to the many Ukrainians striving to chart a new course for their country in the face of Russian interference and aggression:

> I think we can all see what a remarkable woman Kateryna Handziuk was, but she continues to inspire all of us to fight for justice. She was a courageous woman, who wanted to make Ukraine a better place. And she is continuing to do so. And I'll just leave you with one thought that was expressed in Washington at the ceremony—that courage is contagious. I think we saw that on the Maidan in 2014, we see that on the front lines every day in the Donbas, we see it in the work that Kateryna Handziuk did here in Ukraine. And we see it in the work of all of you—day in, day out—fighting for Ukraine and the future of Ukraine.[5]

Ambassador Yovanovitch's evening was interrupted around 10:00 p.m. by a telephone call from the State Department's headquarters in Washington, D.C.

Director General of the Foreign Service and Director of Human Resources Ambassador Carol Perez warned that the Department's leaders had "great concern" and "were worried" about her. Ambassador Yovanovitch testified that it is "hard to know how to react to something like that." Ambassador Perez said she did not know what the concerns were but pledged she would "try to find out more" and would try to call back "by midnight."[6]

Finally, at 1:00 a.m. in Kyiv, Ambassador Perez called again: The "concerns" were from "up the street" at the White House. Ambassador Perez said that Ambassador Yovanovitch needed to "come home immediately, get on the next plane to the U.S." She warned that there were concerns about Ambassador Yovanovitch's "security." When Ambassador Yovanovitch asked if Ambassador Perez was referring to her physical safety, Ambassador Perez relayed that she "hadn't gotten that impression that it was a physical security issue," but that Ambassador Yovanovitch "needed to come home right away."[7]

Ambassador Yovanovitch asked Ambassador Perez specifically whether this order had anything to do with President Trump's personal attorney, Rudy Giuliani, who had been making unfounded allegations against her in the media. Ambassador Perez said she "didn't know."[8] Ambassador Yovanovitch argued that this order to return to Washington, D.C. was "extremely irregular" and that no one had provided her a reason.[9] In the end, however, Ambassador Yovanovitch swiftly returned to Washington.[10]

Rudy Giuliani, on Behalf of President Trump, Led a Smear Campaign to Oust Ambassador Yovanovitch

Ambassador Yovanovitch's recall followed a concerted smear campaign by Mr. Giuliani and his associates, promoted by President Trump. The campaign was largely directed by Rudy Giuliani, President Trump's personal attorney since early 2018.[11] A cast of supporting characters, which included corrupt Ukrainian prosecutors, now-indicted middlemen, conservative media pundits, and attorneys close to President Trump, assisted Mr. Giuliani. Among those associates were two U.S. citizens, Lev Parnas and Igor Fruman. Mr. Parnas and Mr. Fruman were Florida-based businessmen who were represented by Mr. Giuliani "in connection with their personal and business affairs" and who also "assisted Mr. Giuliani in connection with his representation of President Trump."[12] Both Mr. Parnas and Mr. Fruman were criminally indicted in the Southern District of New York in October and face charges of conspiring to violate the federal ban on foreign donations and contributions in connection with federal and state elections.[13] Dr. Fiona Hill, former Deputy Assistant to the President and Senior Director for Europe and Russian Affairs, National Security Council (NSC), learned from her colleagues that "these guys were notorious in Florida and that they were bad news."[14]

The campaign was also propelled by individuals in Ukraine, including two prosecutors general. Yuriy Lutsenko served as the Prosecutor General of Ukraine under former Ukrainian President Petro Poroshenko—the incumbent who lost to President Zelensky in April 2019—and previously was the head of President Poroshenko's faction in the Ukrainian parliament.[15] Viktor Shokin was Mr. Lutsenko's predecessor and was removed from office in 2016.[16] Mr. Shokin has been described as "a typical Ukraine prosecutor who lived a lifestyle far in excess of his government salary, who never prosecuted anybody known for having committed a crime," and "covered up crimes that were known to have been committed."[17]

In late 2018, Ukrainian officials informed Ambassador Yovanovitch about Mr. Giuliani's and Mr. Lutsenko's plans to target her. They told her that Mr. Lutsenko "was in communication with Mayor Giuliani" and that "they were going to, you know, do things, including to me."[18]

Soon thereafter, Ambassador Yovanovitch learned that "there had been a number of meetings" between Mr. Giuliani and Mr. Lutsenko, who was looking to "hurt" her "in the U.S."[19]

The allegations against Ambassador Yovanovitch, which later surfaced publicly, concerned false claims that she had provided a "do-not-prosecute list" to Mr. Lutsenko and made disparaging comments about President Trump.[20]

Ambassador Yovanovitch inferred that Mr. Lutsenko was spreading "falsehoods" about her because she was "effective at helping Ukrainians who wanted reform, Ukrainians who wanted to fight against corruption, and … that was not in his interest."[21] Anti-corruption reform was not in Mr. Lutsenko's interest because he himself was known to be corrupt.[22] David Holmes, Counselor for Political Affairs at the U.S. Embassy in Kyiv, Ukraine, explained that:

> In mid-March 2019, an Embassy colleague learned from a Ukrainian contact that Mr. Lutsenko had complained that Ambassador Yovanovitch had, quote, unquote, destroyed him, with her refusal to support him until he followed through with his reform commitments and ceased using his position for personal gain.[23]

Deputy Assistant Secretary of State George Kent similarly summarized Mr. Lutsenko's smear campaign against Ambassador Yovanovitch, which was facilitated by Mr. Giuliani and his associates, as motivated by revenge:

> Over the course of 2018 and 2019, I became increasingly aware of an effort by Rudy Giuliani and others, including his associates Lev Parnas and Igor Fruman, to run a campaign to smear Ambassador Yovanovitch and other officials at the U.S. Embassy in Kyiv. The chief agitators on the Ukrainian side of this effort were some of those same corrupt former prosecutors I had encountered, particularly Yuriy Lutsenko and Viktor Shokin. They were now peddling false information in order to extract revenge against those who had exposed their misconduct, including U.S. diplomats, Ukrainian anticorruption officials, and reform-minded civil society groups in Ukraine.[24]

Mr. Kent succinctly summarized, "[y]ou can't promote principled anti-corruption efforts without pissing off corrupt people."[25] By doing her job, Ambassador Yovanovitch drew Mr. Lutsenko's ire.

In late 2018 and early 2019, Mr. Lutsenko also risked losing his job as Prosecutor General and possible criminal investigation, if then-candidate Volodymyr Zelensky won the presidency. Special Representative for Ukraine Negotiations, Ambassador Kurt Volker, explained:

> As is often the case in Ukraine, a change in power would mean change in prosecutorial powers as well, and there have been efforts in the past at prosecuting the previous government. I think Mr. Lutsenko, in my estimation, and I said this to Mayor Giuliani when I met with him, was interested in preserving his own position. He wanted to avoid being fired by a new government in order to prevent prosecution of himself, possible prosecution of himself.[26]

Officials in Ukraine have also speculated that Mr. Lutsenko cultivated his relationship with Mr. Giuliani in an effort to hold on to his position.[27] Ambassador Yovanovitch described Mr. Lutsenko as an "opportunist" who "will ally himself, sometimes simultaneously ... with whatever political or economic forces he believes will suit his interests best at the time."[28]

Mr. Lutsenko promoted debunked conspiracy theories that had gained traction with President Trump and Mr. Giuliani. Those debunked conspiracy theories alleged that the Ukrainian government—not Russia—was behind the hack of the Democratic National Committee (DNC) server in 2016, and that former Vice President Biden had petitioned for the removal of Mr. Shokin to prevent an investigation into Burisma Holdings, a Ukrainian energy company for which Vice President Biden's son, Hunter, served as a board member.

Both conspiracy theories served the personal political interests of President Trump because they would help him in his campaign for reelection in 2020. The first would serve to undercut Special Counsel Robert Mueller's investigation, which was still underway when Mr. Giuliani began his activities in Ukraine and was denounced as a "witch hunt" by the President and his supporters.[29] The second would serve to damage Democratic presidential candidate Vice President Biden.

These conspiracies lacked any basis in fact. The Intelligence Community, the Senate Select Committee on Intelligence, both the Majority and Minority of the House Permanent Select Committee on Intelligence, and the investigation undertaken by Special Counsel Robert Mueller concluded that Russia was responsible for interfering in the 2016 election.[30] President Trump's former Homeland Security Advisor, Tom Bossert, said that the idea of Ukraine hacking the DNC server was "not only a conspiracy theory, it is completely debunked."[31]

Russia has pushed the false theory that Ukraine was involved in the 2016 election to distract from its own involvement.[32] Mr. Holmes testified that it was to President Putin's advantage to promote the theory of Ukrainian interference in the 2016 U.S. elections for several reasons:

> First of all, to deflect from the allegations of Russian interference. Second of all, to drive a wedge between the United States and Ukraine which Russia wants to essentially get back into its sphere of influence. Thirdly, to besmirch Ukraine and its political leadership, [and] to degrade and erode support for Ukraine from other key partners in Europe and elsewhere.[33]

The allegations that Vice President Biden inappropriately pressured the Ukrainians to remove Mr. Shokin also are without merit. Mr. Shokin was widely considered to be ineffective and corrupt.[34] When he urged the Ukrainian government to remove Mr. Shokin, Vice President Biden was advocating for anti-corruption reform and pursuing official U.S. policy.[35] Moreover, Mr. Shokin's removal was supported by other countries, the International Monetary Fund, and the World Bank, and was "widely understood internationally to be the right policy."[36] In May 2019, even Mr. Lutsenko himself admitted that there was no credible evidence of wrongdoing by Hunter Biden or Vice President Biden.[37]

Nevertheless, Mr. Giuliani engaged with both Mr. Lutsenko and Mr. Shokin regarding these baseless allegations. According to documents provided to the State Department Office of Inspector General, in January 23, 2019, Mr. Giuliani, Mr. Parnas, and Mr. Fruman participated in a conference call with Mr. Shokin. According to notes of the call, Mr. Shokin made allegations about Vice President Biden and Burisma. Mr. Shokin also claimed that Ambassador Yovanovitch had improperly denied him a U.S. visa and that she was close to Vice President Biden.[38]

Mr. Giuliani separately met with Mr. Lutsenko in New York.[39] Over the course of two days, on January 25 and 26, Mr. Giuliani, Mr. Lutsenko, Mr. Parnas, and Mr. Fruman, reportedly discussed whether Ambassador Yovanovitch was "loyal to President Trump," as well as investigations into Burisma and the Bidens.[40] For his part, Mr. Lutsenko later said he "understood very well" that Mr. Giuliani wanted Mr. Lutsenko to investigate former Vice President Biden and his son, Hunter. "I have 23 years in politics," Lutsenko said. "I knew. … I'm a political animal."[41]

Mr. Giuliani later publicly acknowledged that he was seeking information from Ukrainians on behalf of his client, President Trump. On October 23, Mr. Giuliani tweeted "everything I did was to discover evidence to defend my client against false charges."[42] Then, in a series of tweets on October 30, Mr. Giuliani stated:

> All of the information I obtained came from interviews conducted as … private defense counsel to POTUS, to defend him against false allegations. I began obtaining this information while Mueller was still investigating his witch hunt and a full 5 months before Biden even announced his run for Pres.[43]

President Trump and Mr. Giuliani's efforts to investigate alleged Ukrainian interference in the 2016 U.S. election and Vice President Biden negatively impacted the U.S. Embassy in Kyiv. Mr. Holmes testified:

> Beginning in March 2019, the situation at the Embassy and in Ukraine changed dramatically. Specifically, the three priorities of security, economy, and justice and our support for Ukrainian democratic resistance to Russian aggression became overshadowed by a political agenda promoted by former New York City Mayor Rudy Giuliani and a cadre of officials operating with a direct channel to the White House.[44]

U.S. national interests in Ukraine were undermined and subordinated to the personal, political interests of President Trump.

The Smear Campaign Accelerated in Late March 2019

The smear campaign entered a more public phase in the United States in late March 2019 with the publication of a series of opinion pieces in *The Hill*.

On March 20, 2019, John Solomon penned an opinion piece quoting a false claim by Mr. Lutsenko that Ambassador Yovanovitch had given him a do-not-prosecute list.[45] Mr. Lutsenko later retracted the claim.[46] Mr. Solomon's work also included false allegations that Ambassador Yovanovitch had "made disparaging statements about President Trump."[47] Ambassador Yovanovitch called this allegation "fictitious," and the State Department issued a statement describing the allegations as a "fabrication."[48]

The Committees uncovered evidence of close ties and frequent contacts between Mr. Solomon and Mr. Parnas, who was assisting Mr. Giuliani in connection with his representation of the President. Phone records show that in the 48 hours before publication of *The Hill* opinion piece, Mr. Parnas spoke with Mr. Solomon at least six times.[49] In addition, *The Hill* piece cited a letter dated May 9, 2018, from Representative Pete Sessions (R-Texas) to Secretary Pompeo, in which Rep. Sessions accused Ambassador Yovanovitch of speaking "privately and repeatedly about her disdain for the current administration."[50] A federal criminal indictment alleges that in or about May 2018, Mr. Parnas sought a congressman's assistance to remove Ambassador Yovanovitch, at the request of one or more Ukrainian government officials.[51]

On March 20, 2019, the day *The Hill* opinion piece was published, Mr. Parnas again spoke with Mr. Solomon for 11 minutes.[52] Shortly after that phone call, President Trump promoted Mr. Solomon's article in a tweet.[53]

Following President Trump's tweet, the public attacks against Ambassador Yovanovitch were further amplified on social media and were merged with the conspiracy theories regarding both Ukrainian interference in the 2016 U.S. election and the Bidens. On March 22, 2019, Mr. Giuliani tweeted: "Hillary, Kerry, and Biden people colluding with Ukrainian operatives to make money and affect 2016 election." He also gave an interview to *Fox News* in which he raised Hunter Biden and called for an investigation.[54] Then, on March 24, Donald Trump Jr. called Ambassador Yovanovitch a "joker" on Twitter and called for her removal.[55]

This campaign reverberated in Ukraine. Mr. Kent testified that "starting in mid-March" Mr. Giuliani was "almost unmissable" during this "campaign of slander" against Ambassador Yovanovitch.[56] According to Mr. Kent, Mr. Lutsenko's press spokeswoman retweeted Donald Trump, Jr.'s tweet attacking the Ambassador.[57]

Concerns About President Trump Kept State Department from Issuing Statement of Support

At the end of March, as this smear campaign intensified, Ambassador Yovanovitch sent Under Secretary of State for Political Affairs David Hale an email identifying her concerns with the false allegations about her and asking for a strong statement of support from the State Department. She explained that, otherwise, "it makes it hard to be a credible ambassador in a country."[58] Ambassador Hale had been briefed on the smears in a series of emails from Mr. Kent.[59] Ambassador Hale agreed that the allegations were without merit.[60]

Ambassador Yovanovitch was told that State Department officials were concerned that if they issued a public statement supporting her, "it could be undermined" by "[t]he President."[61] Ambassador Hale explained that a statement of support "would only fuel further negative reaction" and that "it might even provoke a public reaction from the President himself about the

Ambassador."[62] In short, State Department officials were concerned "that the rug would be pulled out from underneath the State Department."[63]

Ambassador Yovanovitch turned to the U.S. Ambassador to the European Union, Gordon Sondland, for advice. According to Ambassador Yovanovitch, Ambassador Sondland suggested that, in response to the smear campaign, she make a public statement in support of President Trump. She said Ambassador Sondland told her, "you need to go big or go home" and "tweet out there that you support the President, and that all these are lies and everything else."[64] Ambassador Yovanovitch said she felt that this "was advice that I did not see how I could implement in my role as an Ambassador, and as a Foreign Service officer."[65]

Ultimately, Secretary Pompeo refused to issue a public statement of support for Ambassador Yovanovitch. At the same time Secretary Pompeo was refusing to issue a statement, he was communicating with one of the individuals involved in the smear campaign against her. State Department records show that Secretary Pompeo spoke to Mr. Giuliani on March 26 and 28, not long after Mr. Solomon's first article in *The Hill*.[66]

The Smear Campaign was a Coordinated Effort by Mr. Giuliani, His Associates, and One or More Individuals at the White House

In April, Mr. Solomon continued to publish opinion pieces about Ambassador Yovanovitch and other conspiracy theories being pursued by Mr. Giuliani on behalf of President Trump. Mr. Solomon was not working alone. As further described below, there was a coordinated effort by associates of President Trump to push these false narratives publicly, as evidenced by public statements, phone records, and contractual agreements.

On April 1, Mr. Solomon published an opinion piece in *The Hill* alleging that Vice President Biden had inappropriately petitioned for the removal of Mr. Shokin to protect his son, Hunter.[67] The opinion piece was entitled, "Joe Biden's 2020 Ukrainian Nightmare: A Closed Probe is Revived." Many of the allegations in the piece were based on information provided by Mr. Lutsenko. The following day, Donald Trump, Jr. retweeted the article.[68]

Phone records obtained by the Committees show frequent communication between key players during this phase of the scheme. Between April 1 and April 7, Mr. Parnas exchanged approximately 16 calls with Mr. Giuliani (longest duration approximately seven minutes) and approximately 10 calls with Mr. Solomon (longest duration approximately nine minutes).[69]

On April 7, Mr. Solomon followed up with another opinion piece. The piece accused Ambassador Yovanovitch of preventing the issuance of U.S. visas for Ukrainian officials who wished to travel to the United States to provide purported evidence of wrongdoing by "American Democrats and their allies in Kiev."[70] One of those Ukrainian officials allegedly denied a visa was Konstiantyn Kulyk, a deputy to Mr. Lutesenko. Mr. Kulyk participated in a "wide-ranging interview" with Mr. Solomon and was extensively quoted.[71]

These Ukrainian officials claimed to have evidence of wrongdoing about Vice President Biden's efforts in 2015 to remove Mr. Shokin, Hunter Biden's role as a Burisma board member,

Ukrainian interference in the 2016 U.S. election in favor of Hillary Clinton, and the misappropriation and transfer of Ukrainian funds abroad.[72] The opinion piece also made clear that Mr. Giuliani was pursuing these very same theories on behalf of the President:

> More recently, President Trump's private attorney Rudy Giuliani—former mayor and former U.S. attorney in New York City—learned about some of the allegations while, on behalf of the Trump legal team, he looked into Ukrainian involvement in the 2016 election.

According to Mr. Solomon's piece, Mr. Lutsenko was reported to have sufficient evidence, "particularly involving Biden, his family and money spirited out of Ukraine—to warrant a meeting with U.S. Attorney General William Barr."[73]

On the same day that Mr. Solomon published these allegations, Mr. Giuliani appeared on *Fox News*. Mr. Giuliani discussed how he learned about alleged Ukrainian interference in the 2016 U.S. elections and the Bidens' purported misconduct in Ukraine:

> Let me tell you my interest in that. I got information about three or four months ago that a lot of the explanations for how this whole phony investigation started will be in the Ukraine, that there were a group of people in the Ukraine that were working to help Hillary Clinton and were colluding really—[LAUGHTER]—with the Clinton campaign. And it stems around the ambassador and the embassy, being used for political purposes. So I began getting some people that were coming forward and telling me about that. And then all of a sudden, they revealed the story about Burisma and Biden's son ... [Vice President Biden] bragged about pressuring Ukraine's president to firing [sic] a top prosecutor who was being criticized on a whole bunch of areas but was conducting investigation of this gas company which Hunter Biden served as a director.[74]

The next day, April 8, Mr. Giuliani tweeted about Mr. Solomon's opinion piece.[75]

Over the course of the four days following the April 7 article, phone records show contacts between Mr. Giuliani, Mr. Parnas, Representative Devin Nunes, and Mr. Solomon. Specifically, Mr. Giuliani and Mr. Parnas were in contact with one another, as well as with Mr. Solomon.[76] Phone records also show contacts on April 10 between Mr. Giuliani and Rep. Nunes, consisting of three short calls in rapid succession, followed by a text message, and ending with a nearly three minute call.[77] Later that same day, Mr. Parnas and Mr. Solomon had a four minute, 39 second call.[78]

Victoria Toensing, a lawyer who, along with her partner Joseph diGenova, once briefly represented President Trump in connection with Special Counsel Robert Mueller's investigation,[79] also was in phone contact with Mr. Giuliani and Mr. Parnas at the beginning of April.[80]

Beginning in mid-April, Ms. Toensing signed retainer agreements between diGenova & Toensing LLP and Mr. Lutsenko, Mr. Kulyk, and Mr. Shokin—all of whom feature in Mr. Solomon's opinion pieces.[81] In these retainer agreements, the firm agreed to represent Mr.

46

Lutsenko and Mr. Kulyk in meetings with U.S. officials regarding alleged "evidence" of Ukrainian interference in the 2016 U.S. elections, and to represent Mr. Shokin "for the purpose of collecting evidence regarding his March 2016 firing as Prosecutor General of Ukraine and the role of Vice President Biden in such firing, and presenting such evidence to U.S. and foreign authorities."[82] On July 25, President Trump would personally press President Zelensky to investigate these very same matters.

On April 23, Mr. Parnas had a call with Mr. Solomon, and multiple phone contacts with Mr. Giuliani.[83] On that same day, Mr. Giuliani had a series of short phone calls (ranging from 11 to 18 seconds) with a phone number associated with the White House, followed shortly thereafter by an eight minute, 28 second call with an unidentified number that called him.[84] Approximately half an hour later, Mr. Giuliani had a 48 second call with a phone number associated with Ambassador John Bolton, National Security Advisor to the President.[85]

That same day, Mr. Giuliani tweeted:

Hillary is correct the report is the end of the beginning for the second time...NO COLLUSION. Now Ukraine is investigating Hillary campaign and DNC conspiracy with foreign operatives including Ukrainian and others to affect 2016 election. And there's no Comey to fix the result.[86]

The next day, on the morning of April 24, Mr. Giuliani appeared on *Fox and Friends*, lambasting the Mueller investigation. Mr. Giuliani also promoted the false conspiracy theories about Ukraine and Vice President Biden:

And I ask you to keep your eye on Ukraine, because in Ukraine, a lot of the dirty work was done in digging up the information. American officials were used, Ukrainian officials were used. That's like collusion with the Ukrainians. And, or actually in this case, conspiracy with the Ukrainians. I think you'd get some interesting information about Joe Biden from Ukraine. About his son, Hunter Biden. About a company he was on the board of for years, which may be one of the most crooked companies in Ukraine. … And Biden bragged about the fact that he got the prosecutor general fired. The prosecutor general was investigating his son and then the investigation went south.[87]

Later that day, Mr. Giuliani had three phone calls with a number associated with OMB, and eight calls with a White House number.[88] One of the calls with the White House was four minutes, 53 seconds, and another was three minutes, 15 seconds.

Later that evening, the State Department phoned Ambassador Yovanovitch and abruptly called her home because of "concerns" from "up the street" at the White House.[89]

Ambassador Yovanovitch Was Informed That the President "Lost Confidence" in Her

When Ambassador Yovanovitch returned to the United States at the end of April, Deputy Secretary of State John Sullivan informed her that she had "done nothing wrong," but "there had been a concerted campaign" against her and that President Trump had "lost confidence" in her leadership.[90] He also told her that "the President no longer wished me to serve as Ambassador to Ukraine, and that, in fact, the President had been pushing for my removal since the prior summer."[91] Ambassador Philip T. Reeker, Acting Assistant Secretary of State for the Bureau of European and Eurasian Affairs, offered a similar assessment. He explained to Ambassador Yovanovitch that Secretary Pompeo had tried to "protect" her, but "was no longer able to do that."[92]

Counselor of the Department of State T. Ulrich Brechbuhl, who had been handling Ambassador Yovanovitch's recall, refused to meet with her.[93]

Ambassador Yovanovitch's final day as U.S. Ambassador to Ukraine was May 20, 2019. This was the same day as President Zelensky's inauguration, which was attended by Secretary of Energy Rick Perry, Ambassador Sondland, and Ambassador Volker.[94] Rather than joining the official delegation at the inaugural festivities, she finished packing her personal belongings and boarded an airplane for her final flight home. Three days later, President Trump met in the Oval Office with his hand-picked delegation and gave them the "directive" to "talk with Rudy [Giuliani]" about Ukraine.[95]

The President Provided No Rationale for the Recall of Ambassador Yovanovitch

Ambassador Yovanovitch testified that she was never provided a justification for why President Trump recalled her.[96] Only two months earlier, in early March 2019, Ambassador Yovanovitch had been asked by Ambassador Hale to extend her assignment as Ambassador to Ukraine until 2020.[97]

Ambassador Hale testified that Ambassador Yovanovitch was "an exceptional officer doing exceptional work at a very critical embassy in Kyiv."[98] He added, "I believe that she should've been able to stay at post and continue to do the outstanding work that she was doing."[99]

During her more than three-decade career, Ambassador Yovanovitch received a number of awards, including: the Presidential Distinguished Service Award, the Secretary's Diplomacy in Human Rights Award, the Senior Foreign Service Performance Award six times, and the State Department's Superior Honor Award five times.[100]

Career foreign service officer Ambassador P. Michael McKinley, former Senior Advisor to Secretary Pompeo, testified that Ambassador Yovanovitch's reputation was "excellent, serious, committed."[101] Ambassador Reeker described her as an "[o]utstanding diplomat," "very precise, very—very professional," "an excellent mentor," and "a good leader."[102]

Ambassador Yovanovitch Strongly Advocated for the U.S. Policy to Combat Corruption

Throughout the course of her career, and while posted to Kyiv, Ambassador Yovanovitch was a champion of the United States' longstanding priority of combatting corruption.

Mr. Kent described U.S. foreign policy in Ukraine as encompassing the priorities of "promoting the rule of law, energy independence, defense sector reform, and the ability to stand up to Russia."[103] Ambassador Yovanovitch testified that it "was—and remains—a top U.S. priority to help Ukraine fight corruption" because corruption makes Ukraine more "vulnerable to Russia."[104] Additionally, she testified that an honest and accountable Ukrainian leadership makes a U.S.-Ukrainian partnership more reliable and more valuable to the United States.[105]

Mr. Holmes testified that Ambassador Yovanovitch was successful in implementing anti-corruption reforms in Ukraine by achieving, for example, "the hard-fought passage of a law establishing an independent court to try corruption cases."[106] Mr. Holmes said Ambassador Yovanovitch was "[a]s good as anyone known for" combatting corruption.[107] The reforms achieved by Ambassador Yovanovitch helped reduce the problem faced by many post-Soviet countries of selective corruption prosecutions to target political opponents.[108]

There was a broad consensus that Ambassador Yovanovitch was successful in helping Ukraine combat pervasive and endemic corruption.

President's Authority Does Not Explain Removal of Yovanovitch

While ambassadors serve at the pleasure of the president, the manner and circumstances of Ambassador Yovanovitch's removal were unusual and raise questions of motive.[109]

Ambassador Yovanovitch queried "why it was necessary to smear my reputation falsely."[110] She found it difficult to comprehend how individuals "who apparently felt stymied by our efforts to promote stated U.S. policy against corruption" were "able to successfully conduct a campaign of disinformation against a sitting ambassador using unofficial back channels."[111]

Dr. Hill similarly testified that while the President has the authority to remove an ambassador, she was concerned "about the circumstances in which [Ambassador Yovanovitch's] reputation had been maligned, repeatedly, on television and in all kinds of exchanges." Dr. Hill "felt that that was completely unnecessary."[112]

Recall of Yovanovitch Threatened U.S.-Ukraine Policy

The smear campaign questioning Ambassador Yovanovitch's loyalty undermined U.S. diplomatic efforts in Ukraine, a key U.S. partner and a bulwark against Russia's expansion into Europe. As Ambassador Yovanovitch explained:

Ukrainians were wondering whether I was going to be leaving, whether we really represented the President, U.S. policy, et cetera. And so I think it was—you know, it really kind of cut the ground out from underneath us.[113]

Summarizing the cumulative impact of the attacks, she emphasized: "If our chief representative is kneecapped it limits our effectiveness to safeguard the vital national security interests of the United States."[114]

President Trump's recall of Ambassador Yovanovitch left the U.S. Embassy in Ukraine without an ambassador at a time of electoral change in Ukraine and when the Embassy was also without a deputy chief of mission. Mr. Kent explained:

> During the late spring and summer of 2019, I became alarmed as those efforts bore fruit. They led to the outer [ouster] of Ambassador Yovanovitch and hampered U.S. efforts to establish rapport with the new Zelensky administration in Ukraine.[115]
>
> ...
>
> One of the unfortunate elements of the timing was that we were also undergoing a transition in my old job as deputy chief of mission. The person who replaced me had already been moved early to be our DCM and Charge in Sweden, and so we had a temporary acting deputy chief of mission. So that left the embassy not only without—the early withdrawal of Ambassador Yovanovitch left us not only without an Ambassador but without somebody who had been selected to be deputy chief of mission.[116]

It was not until late May that Secretary Pompeo asked Ambassador Bill Taylor, who had previously served as Ambassador to Ukraine, to return to Kyiv as Chargé d'Affaires to lead the embassy while it awaited a confirmed Ambassador. Ambassador Taylor did not arrive in Kyiv until June 17, more than a month after Ambassador Yovanovitch officially left Kyiv.[117] His mission to carry out U.S. objectives there would prove challenging in the face of ongoing efforts by Mr. Giuliani and others—at the direction of the President—to secure investigations demanded by the President to help his reelection.

2.   The President Put Giuliani and the Three Amigos in Charge of Ukraine Issues

After President Trump recalled Ambassador Yovanovitch, his personal agent, Rudy Giuliani, intensified the President's campaign to pressure Ukraine's newly-elected president to interfere in the 2020 U.S. election. President Trump directed his own political appointees to coordinate with Mr. Giuliani on Ukraine, while National Security Council officials expressed alarm over the efforts to pursue a "domestic political errand" for the political benefit of the President. Officials at the highest levels of the White House and Trump Administration were aware of the President's scheme.

Overview

On April 21, 2019, the day that Ukrainian President Volodymyr Zelensky was elected as president of Ukraine, President Trump called to congratulate him. After a positive call—in which Mr. Zelensky complimented President Trump and requested that President Trump attend his inauguration—President Trump instructed Vice President Mike Pence to lead the U.S. delegation to the inauguration. However, on May 13—before the inauguration date was even set—President Trump instructed Vice President Pence not to attend.

Rudy Giuliani also announced a plan to visit Ukraine in mid-May 2019—not on official U.S. government business, but instead to pursue on behalf of his client, President Trump, the debunked conspiracy theories about alleged Ukrainian interference in the 2016 election and discredited claims about the Bidens. After public scrutiny in response to his announced visit, Mr. Giuliani cancelled his trip and alleged that President-elect Zelensky was surrounded by "enemies of the President."

Secretary of Energy Rick Perry, Ambassador to the European Union Gordon Sondland, and Ambassador Kurt Volker, Special Representative for Ukraine Negotiations, ultimately led the U.S. delegation to President Zelensky's inauguration. Upon returning to Washington, D.C., the three U.S. officials—who dubbed themselves the "Three Amigos"—debriefed the President in the Oval Office and encouraged him to engage with President Zelensky. Instead of accepting their advice, President Trump complained that Ukraine is "a terrible place, all corrupt, terrible people," and asserted that Ukraine "tried to take me down in 2016." The President instructed the "Three Amigos" to "talk to Rudy" and coordinate with him on Ukraine matters. They followed the President's orders.

Dr. Fiona Hill, Deputy Assistant to the President and Senior Director for Europe and Russian Affairs at the National Security Council, would later observe that Ambassador Sondland "was being involved in a domestic political errand, and we [the NSC staff] were being involved in national security foreign policy, and those two things had just diverged."

On April 21, popular comedian and television actor, Volodymyr Zelensky, won a landslide victory in Ukraine's presidential election, earning the support of 73 percent of voters and unseating the incumbent Petro Poroshenko. Mr. Zelensky, who had no prior political experience, told voters a week before his victory: "I'm not a politician. I'm just a simple person who came to break the system."[118] Five years earlier, in late 2013, Ukrainians had gathered in Kyiv and rallied against the corrupt government of former President Viktor Yanukovych, eventually forcing him to flee to the safety of Vladimir Putin's Russia. Mr. Zelensky's victory in April 2019 reaffirmed the Ukrainian people's strong desire to overcome an entrenched system of corruption and pursue closer partnership with the West.[119]

Following the election results, at 4:29 p.m. Eastern Time, President Trump was connected by telephone to President-elect Zelensky and congratulated him "on a job well done … a fantastic election." He declared, "I have no doubt you will be a fantastic president."[120]

According to a call record released publicly by the White House, President Trump did not openly express doubts about the newly-elected leader.[121] And contrary to a public readout of the call originally issued by the White House, President Trump did not mention corruption in Ukraine, despite the NSC staff preparing talking points on that topic.[122] Indeed, "corruption" was not mentioned once during the April 21 conversation, according to the official call record.[123]

In the call, President-elect Zelensky lauded President Trump as "a great example" and invited him to visit Ukraine for his upcoming inauguration—a gesture that President Trump called "very nice."[124] President Trump told Mr. Zelensky:

> I'll look into that, and well—give us the date and, at a very minimum, we'll have a great representative. Or more than one from the United States will be with you on that great day. So, we will have somebody, at a minimum, at a very, very high level, and they will be with you.[125]

Mr. Zelensky persisted. "Words cannot describe our country," he went on, "so it would be best for you to see it yourself. So, if you can come, that would be great. So again, I invite you to come."[126] President Trump responded, "Well, I agree with you about your country and I look forward to it."[127] In a nod to his past experience working with Ukraine as a businessman, President Trump added, "When I owned Miss Universe … Ukraine was always very well represented."[128]

President Trump then invited Mr. Zelensky to the White House to meet, saying: "When you're settled in and ready, I'd like to invite you to the White House. We'll have a lot of things to talk about, but we're with you all the way." Mr. Zelensky promptly accepted the President's invitation, adding that the "whole team and I are looking forward to that visit."[129]

Mr. Zelensky then reiterated his interest in President Trump attending his inauguration, saying, "it will be absolutely fantastic if you could come and be with us." President Trump promised to let the Ukrainian leader know "very soon" and added that he would see Mr. Zelensky "very soon, regardless."[130]

Shortly after the April 21 call, Jennifer Williams, Special Advisor to the Vice President for Europe and Russia, learned that President Trump asked Vice President Pence to attend Mr. Zelensky's inauguration.[131] Ms. Williams testified that in a separate phone call between Vice President Pence and President-elect Zelensky two days later, "the Vice President accepted that invitation from President Zelensky, and looked forward to being able to attend … if the dates worked out."[132] Ms. Williams and her colleagues began planning for the Vice President's trip to Kyiv.[133]

Rudy Giuliani and his Associates Coordinated Efforts to Secure and Promote the Investigations with Ukrainian President Zelensky

As previously explained in Chapter 1, Mr. Giuliani, acting on behalf of President Trump, had for months engaged corrupt current and former Ukrainian officials, including Ukrainian Prosecutor General Yuriy Lutsenko. The April election of Mr. Zelensky, however, raised the possibility that Mr. Lutsenko might lose his job as Prosecutor General once Mr. Zelensky took power.

In the immediate aftermath of President-elect Zelensky's election, Mr. Giuliani continued publicly to project confidence that Ukraine would deliver on investigations related to the Bidens. On April 24—before Ambassador Yovanovitch received calls abruptly summoning her back to Washington—Mr. Giuliani stated in an interview on *Fox and Friends* that viewers should,

> [K]eep your eye on Ukraine… I think you'd get some interesting information about Joe Biden from Ukraine. About his son, Hunter Biden. About a company he was on the board of for years, which may be one of the most crooked companies in Ukraine.[134]

Behind the scenes, however, Mr. Giuliani was taking steps to engage the new Ukrainian leader and his aides.

The day before, on April 23, the same day that Vice President Pence confirmed his plans to attend President-elect Zelensky's inauguration, Mr. Giuliani dispatched his own delegation—consisting of Lev Parnas and Igor Fruman—to meet with Ihor Kolomoisky, a wealthy Ukrainian with ties to President-elect Zelensky. Instead of going to Kyiv, they booked tickets to Israel, where they met with Mr. Kolomoisky.[135] Mr. Kolomoisky owned Ukraine's largest bank until 2016, when Ukrainian authorities nationalized the failing financial institution. Although he denied allegations of committing any crimes, Mr. Kolomoisky subsequently left Ukraine for Israel, where he remained until President Zelensky assumed power.[136]

Mr. Kolomoisky confirmed to *The New York Times* that he met with Mr. Parnas and Mr. Fruman in late April 2019. He claimed they sought his assistance in facilitating a meeting between Mr. Giuliani and President-elect Zelensky, and he told them, "you've ended up in the wrong place," and declined to arrange the requested meeting.[137]

Mr. Giuliani was not deterred.

During the time surrounding Ambassador Yovanovitch's recall, Mr. Giuliani and Mr. Parnas connected over a flurry of calls around a planned trip to Ukraine by Mr. Giuliani, which he would eventually cancel after growing public scrutiny. As previously described in Chapter 1, call records obtained by the Committees show a series of contacts on April 23 and 24 between Mr. Giuliani, the White House, Mr. Parnas, and John Solomon, among others.[138]

On April 25, 2019, former Vice President Biden publicly announced his campaign for the Democratic nomination for President of the United States and launched his effort to unseat President Trump in the 2020 election.[139]

That evening, Mr. Solomon published a new opinion piece in *The Hill* entitled, "How the Obama White House Engaged Ukraine to Give Russia Collusion Narrative an Early Boost." Like Mr. Solomon's previous work, this April 25 piece repeated unsubstantiated conspiracy theories about alleged Ukrainian interference in the 2016 U.S. presidential election.[140]

Meanwhile, in Kyiv, David Holmes, Counselor for Political Affairs at U.S. Embassy Kyiv, learned on April 25 that Mr. Giuliani had reached out to Mr. Zelensky's campaign chair, Ivan Bakanov, seeking a channel to the newly-elected leader. Mr. Bakanov told Mr. Holmes "that he had been contacted by, quote, someone named Giuliani, who said he was an advisor to the Vice President, unquote."[141] Mr. Holmes clarified that Mr. Bakanov was "speaking in Russian" and that he did not "know what he [Bakanov] meant" by his reference to the Vice President, "but that's what he [Bakanov] said."[142] Regardless of Mr. Bakanov's apparent confusion as to who Mr. Giuliani represented, Mr. Holmes explained that by this point in time, Ukrainian officials seemed to think that Mr. Giuliani "was a significant person in terms of managing their relationship with the United States."[143]

At 7:14 p.m. Eastern Time on April 25, Mr. Giuliani once again received a call from an unknown "-1" number, which lasted four minutes and 40 seconds.[144] Minutes later, Mr. Giuliani held a brief 36 second call with Sean Hannity, a *Fox News* opinion host.[145]

On the night of April 25, President Trump called into Mr. Hannity's prime time *Fox News* show. In response to a question about Mr. Solomon's recent publication, President Trump said:

> It sounds like big stuff. It sounds very interesting with Ukraine. I just spoke to the new president a little while ago, two days ago, and congratulated him on an incredible race. Incredible run. A big surprise victory. That's 75 percent of the vote. But that sounds like big, big stuff. I'm not surprised.[146]

As Mr. Holmes later learned on July 26 from Ambassador Sondland, President Trump did not care about Ukraine, he cared about this "big stuff"—such as the investigation into Vice President Biden.[147]

In the same *Fox News* interview, Mr. Hannity asked President Trump whether America needed to see the purported evidence possessed by the unnamed Ukrainians noted in Mr. Solomon's piece. The President replied, invoking Attorney General William P. Barr:

> Well, I think we do. And, frankly, we have a great new attorney general who has done an unbelievable job in a very short period of time. And he is very smart and tough and I would certainly defer to him. I would imagine he would want to see this. People have been saying this whole—the concept of Ukraine, they have been talking about it actually for a long time. You know that, and I would certainly defer to the attorney general. And we'll see what he says about it. He calls them straight. That's one thing I can tell you.[148]

Ukraine's current Prosecutor General Ruslan Ryaboshapka, who assumed his new position in late August 2019, told *The Financial Times* in late November 2019 that Attorney General Barr had made no contact regarding a potential investigation into allegations of wrongdoing by former Vice President Biden.[149] In an apparent reference to President Trump's demand for Ukrainian interference in U.S. elections, Mr. Ryaboshapka stated: "It's critically important for the west not to pull us into some conflicts between their ruling elites, but to continue to support so that we can cross the point of no return."[150]

President Trump Promoted False Information About Former Vice President Joe Biden

In early May, Mr. Giuliani continued his outreach to President-elect Zelensky and promoted the need for Ukrainian investigations into former Vice President Biden that served President Trump's political needs.

On May 2, at 6:21 a.m. Eastern Time, President Trump retweeted a link to an article in *The New York Times,* which assessed that Mr. Giuliani's efforts underscored "the Trump campaign's concern about the electoral threat from the former vice president's presidential campaign" and noted that "Mr. Giuliani's involvement raises questions about whether Mr. Trump is endorsing an effort to push a foreign government to proceed with a case that could hurt a political opponent at home."[151]

Later that evening, in an interview with *Fox News* at the White House, President Trump referenced the false allegations about the firing of a corrupt former Ukrainian prosecutor, Viktor Shokin, that Mr. Giuliani had been promoting. He was asked, "Should the former vice president explain himself on his feeling in Ukraine and whether there was a conflict … with his son's business interests?"[152] President Trump replied:

> I'm hearing it's a major scandal, major problem. Very bad things happened, and we'll see what that is. They even have him on tape, talking about it. They have Joe Biden on tape talking about the prosecutor. And I've seen that tape. A lot of people are talking about that tape, but that's up to them. They have to solve that problem.[153]

"The tape" President Trump referenced in his interview was a publicly available video of former Vice President Biden speaking in January 2018 at an event hosted by the Council on Foreign Relations (CFR), a nonpartisan think-tank focused on foreign policy matters. During an interview with the CFR president, Vice President Biden detailed how the United States—consistent with the policy of its European allies and the International Monetary Fund (IMF)—withheld $1 billion in loan guarantees until the Ukrainian government acceded to uniform American and international demands to fire the corrupt prosecutor.[154]

By late 2015, Ukrainians were agitating for Mr. Shokin's removal, and in March 2016, Ukraine's parliament voted to dismiss the prosecutor general.[155] Multiple witnesses testified that Mr. Shokin's dismissal in 2016 made it *more*—not less—likely that Ukrainian authorities might investigate any allegations or wrongdoing at Burisma or other allegedly corrupt companies.[156] Nonetheless, President Trump and his supporters sought to perpetuate the false narrative that Mr. Shokin should not have been removed from office and that Vice President Biden had acted corruptly in carrying out U.S. policy.

Rudy Giuliani Was "Meddling in an Investigation" on Behalf of President Trump

On May 7, 2019, Christopher Wray, the Director of the Federal Bureau of Investigation, testified before the U.S. Senate Appropriations Subcommittee on Commerce, Justice, Science, and Related Agencies regarding foreign interference in U.S. elections:

> My view is that, if any public official or member of any campaign is contacted by any nation-state or anybody acting on behalf of a nation-state about influencing or interfering with our election, then that is something that the FBI would want to know about. [157]

Mr. Giuliani nonetheless pressed forward with his plan to personally convey to President-elect Zelensky, on behalf of his client President Trump, the importance of opening investigations that would assist President Trump's reelection campaign.

On the morning of May 8, Mr. Giuliani called the White House Switchboard and connected for six minutes and 26 seconds with someone at the White House.[158] That same day, Mr. Giuliani also connected with Mr. Solomon for almost six minutes, with Mr. Parnas, and with Derek Harvey, a member of Representative Nunes' staff on the Intelligence Committee.[159]

During a meeting that same day, Ukraine Minister of Interior Arsen Avakov disclosed to Deputy Assistant Secretary of State George Kent that Mr. Parnas and Mr. Fruman would soon visit Kyiv "and that they were coming with their associate, the Mayor Giuliani."[160] Minister Avakov confided to Mr. Kent that "Mayor Giuliani had reached out to him and invited him to come and meet the group of them in Florida" in February 2019.[161] Although he declined that offer, Minister Avakov indicated that he intended to accept their new invitation to meet in Kyiv.[162]

The next day, on May 9, *The New York Times* publicized Mr. Giuliani's plan to visit Ukraine.[163] Mr. Giuliani confirmed that he planned to meet with President Zelensky and press the Ukrainians to pursue investigations that President Trump promoted only days earlier on *Fox News*.[164] *The New York Times* described Mr. Giuliani's planned trip as:

[P]art of a monthslong effort by the former New York mayor and a small group of Trump allies working to build interest in the Ukrainian inquiries. Their motivation is to…undermine the case against Paul Manafort, Mr. Trump's imprisoned former campaign chairman; and potentially to damage Mr. Biden, the early front-runner for the 2020 Democratic presidential nomination.[165]

Mr. Giuliani claimed, "We're not meddling in an election, we're meddling in an investigation, which we have a right to do."[166]

Only a few days after Director Wray's public comments about foreign interference in U.S. elections, Mr. Giuliani acknowledged that "[s]omebody could say it's improper" to pressure Ukraine to open investigations that would benefit President Trump. But, Mr. Giuliani argued:

[T]his isn't foreign policy—I'm asking them to do an investigation that they're doing already, and that other people are telling them to stop. And I'm going to give them reasons why they shouldn't stop it because that information will be very, very helpful to my client, and may turn out to be helpful to my government.[167]

Mr. Giuliani's "client" was President Trump, as Mr. Giuliani repeatedly stated publicly. According to Mr. Giuliani, the President fully supported putting pressure on Ukraine to open investigations that would benefit his 2020 reelection campaign.[168] Mr. Giuliani emphasized that President Trump "basically knows what I'm doing, sure, as his lawyer."[169] Underscoring his commitment to pressuring Ukraine until it opened the investigations President Trump promoted on *Fox News*, Mr. Giuliani told *The Washington Post* that he would "make sure that nothing scuttles the investigation that I want."[170]

On May 9, following public revelation of his trip by the *New York Times*, Mr. Giuliani connected in quick succession with Mr. Solomon and then Mr. Parnas for several minutes at a time.[171] Mr. Giuliani then made brief connections with the White House Switchboard and Situation Room several times, before connecting at 1:43 p.m. Eastern Time with someone at the White House for over four minutes.[172] He connected, separately, thereafter with Mr. Parnas several times in the afternoon and into the evening.[173]

That evening, Mr. Giuliani tweeted:

If you doubt there is media bias and corruption then when Democrats conspiring with Ukrainian officials comes out remember much of the press, except for Fox, the Hill, and NYT, has suppressed it. If it involved @realDonaldTrump or his son it would have been front page news for weeks.[174]

Shortly thereafter, on the night of May 9, he made an appearance on *Fox News* and reiterated that his trip to Ukraine was intended to further the President's personal and political interests by pressuring the Ukrainian government to investigate the Bidens:

It's a big story. It's a dramatic story. And I guarantee you, Joe Biden will not get to election day without this being investigated, not because I want to see him investigated. This is collateral to what I was doing.[175]

The next morning, on May 10, amidst the press coverage of his trip, Mr. Giuliani tweeted:

Explain to me why Biden shouldn't be investigated if his son got millions from a Russian loving crooked Ukrainian oligarch while He was VP and point man for Ukraine. Ukrainians are investigating and your fellow Dems are interfering. Election is 17 months away. Let's answer it now[176]

He then had another flurry of calls with Mr. Parnas. Shortly after 2:00 p.m., Eastern Time, Mr. Giuliani also spoke with Ambassador Volker on the phone. [177] Ambassador Volker had learned that Mr. Giuliani intended to travel to Ukraine "to pursue these allegations that Lutsenko had made, and he was going to investigate these things"—specifically, the debunked story that Vice President Biden had improperly pressured Ukraine to fire a corrupt prosecutor general, as well as the Russian-backed conspiracy that the Ukrainians interfered in the 2016 U.S. election.[178] Ambassador Volker testified that he had a simple warning for Mr. Giuliani: Prosecutor General Lutsenko "is not credible. Don't listen to what he is saying."[179] Call records obtained by the Committees reveal that their call lasted more than 30 minutes.[180]

Call records also show that around midday on May 10, Mr. Giuliani began trading aborted calls with Kashyap "Kash" Patel, an official at the National Security Council who previously served on Ranking Member Devin Nunes' staff on the Intelligence Committee. Mr. Patel successfully connected with Mr. Giuliani less than an hour after Mr. Giuliani's call with Ambassador Volker. Beginning at 3:23 p.m., Eastern Time, Mr. Patel and Mr. Giuliani spoke for over 25 minutes.[181] Five minutes after Mr. Patel and Mr. Giuliani disconnected, an unidentified "-1" number connected with Mr. Giuliani for over 17 minutes.[182] Shortly thereafter, Mr. Giuliani spoke with Mr. Parnas for approximately 12 minutes.[183]

That same afternoon, President Trump conducted a 15-minute long phone interview with *Politico*. In response to a question about Mr. Giuliani's upcoming visit to Kyiv, the President replied, "I have not spoken to him at any great length, but I will … I will speak to him about it before he leaves."[184]

Recently, when asked what Mr. Giuliani was doing in Ukraine on his behalf, the President responded: "Well, you have to ask that to Rudy, but Rudy, I don't, I don't even know. I know he was going to go to Ukraine, and I think he canceled a trip."[185] Prior to that, on October 2, the President publicly stated; "And just so you know, we've been investigating, on a personal basis—through Rudy and others, lawyers—corruption in the 2016 election."[186] On October 4, the President publicly stated: "If we feel there's corruption, like I feel there was in the 2016 campaign—there was tremendous corruption against me—if we feel there's corruption, we have a right to go to a foreign country."[187]

By the evening of May 10, Mr. Giuliani appeared to have concerns about the incoming Ukrainian president. He appeared on *Fox News* and announced, "I'm not going to go" to Ukraine "because I think I'm walking into a group of people that are enemies of the President."[188] In a text message to *Politico*, Mr. Giuliani alleged the original offer for a meeting with Mr. Zelensky was a "set up" orchestrated by "several vocal critics" of President Trump who were advising President-elect Zelensky.[189] Mr. Giuliani declared that President-elect Zelensky "is in [the] hands of avowed enemies of Pres[ident] Trump."[190]

Like Mr. Giuliani, President Trump would express hostility toward Ukraine in the days and weeks to come.

Russian President Putin and Hungarian Prime Minister Orban Counseled President Trump on Ukraine

In early May, Mr. Giuliani was not the only person who conveyed his skepticism of Ukraine to President Trump. The President reportedly discussed Ukraine with Russian President Vladimir Putin when they spoke by phone on May 3. President Trump posted on Twitter that he "[h]ad a long and very good conversation with President Putin of Russia" and discussed "even the 'Russian Hoax'"—an apparent reference to the unanimous finding by the U.S. Intelligence Community that Russia interfered in the 2016 election with the aim of assisting President Trump's candidacy.[191] Mr. Kent subsequently heard from Dr. Hill, the NSC's Senior Director for Europe and Russia, that President Putin also expressed negative views about Ukraine to President Trump. He testified that President Putin's motivation in undercutting President-elect Zelensky was "very clear":

> He denies the existence of Ukraine as a nation and a country, as he told President Bush in Bucharest in 2008. He invaded and occupied 7 percent of Ukraine's territory and he's led to the death of 13,000 Ukrainians on Ukrainian territory since 2014 as a result of aggression. So that's his agenda, the agenda of creating a greater Russia and ensuring that Ukraine does not survive independently.[192]

On May 13, President Trump met one-on-one for an hour with Hungarian Prime Minister Viktor Orban. President Trump offered the leader a warm reception in the Oval Office and claimed Prime Minister Orban had "done a tremendous job in so many different ways. Highly respected. Respected all over Europe."[193] The European Union and many European leaders, however, have widely condemned Mr. Orban for undermining Hungary's democratic institutions and promoting anti-Semitism and xenophobia.[194]

Mr. Kent explained to the Committees that Prime Minister Orban's "animus towards Ukraine is well-known, documented, and has lasted now two years." Due to a dispute over the rights of 130,000 ethnic Hungarians who live in Ukraine, Kent noted that Prime Minister Orban "blocked all meetings in NATO with Ukraine at the ministerial level or above," undercutting U.S. and European efforts to support Ukraine in its war against Russia.[195] Nonetheless, President Trump told reporters prior to his meeting with Prime Minister Orban to not "forget they're a member of NATO, and a very good member of NATO."[196]

Commenting on what Dr. Hill shared with him following the May 3 call and May 13 meeting, Mr. Kent said he understood President Trump's discussions about Ukraine with President Putin and Prime Minister Orban "as being similar in tone and approach." He explained that "both leaders" had "extensively talked Ukraine down, said it was corrupt, said Zelensky was in the thrall of oligarchs" the effect of which was "negatively shaping a picture of Ukraine, and even President Zelensky personally."[197] The veteran State Department diplomat concluded, "[T]hose two world leaders [Putin and Orban], along with former Mayor Giuliani, their communications with President Trump shaped the President's view of Ukraine and Zelensky, and would account for the change from a very positive first call on April 21 to his negative assessment of Ukraine."[198]

President Trump Instructs Vice President Pence Not to Attend President Zelensky's Inauguration

On Monday, May 13, at approximately 11:00 a.m. Eastern Time, Ms. Williams received a call from an assistant to the Vice President's chief of staff.[199] President Trump, the assistant relayed, had "decided that the Vice President would not attend the inauguration in Ukraine," despite the fact that Vice President Pence previously had accepted the invitation.[200] Ms. Williams was never given a reason for the change in President Trump's decision.[201]

Mr. Holmes later testified that:

[The U.S. Embassy in Kyiv had] gone back and forth with NSC staff about proposing a list of potential members of the delegation. It was initially quite a long list. We had asked who would be the senior [U.S.] member of that delegation. We were told that Vice President Pence was likely to be that senior member, it was not yet fully agreed to. And so we were anticipating that to be the case. And then the Giuliani event happened, and then we heard that he was not going to play that role.[202]

Asked to clarify what he meant by "the Giuliani event," Mr. Holmes replied, "the interview basically saying that he had planned to travel to Ukraine, but he canceled his trip because there were, quote, unquote, enemies of the U.S. President in Zelensky's orbit."[203]

One of the individuals around President-elect Zelensky whom Mr. Giuliani publicly criticized was the oligarch Mr. Kolomoisky, who had refused to set up a meeting between Mr. Giuliani and President Zelensky. On May 18, Mr. Giuliani complained on Twitter that the oligarch "returned from a long exile and immediately threatened and defamed two Americans, Lev Parnas and Igor Fruman. They are my clients and I have advised them to press charges."[204]

Mr. Kolomoisky responded to Mr. Giuliani in a televised interview and declared, "Look, there is Giuliani, and two clowns, Lev Parnas and Igor Fruman, who were engaging in nonsense. They are Giuliani's clients." He added: "They came here and told us that they would organize a meeting with Zelensky. They allegedly struck a deal with [Prosecutor-General Yuriy] Lutsenko about the fate of this criminal case—Burisma, [former Vice President] Biden, meddling in the U.S. election and so on."[205] He warned that a "big scandal may break out, and not only in

Ukraine, but in the United States. That is, it may turn out to be a clear conspiracy against Biden."[206]

Despite Ukraine's significance to U.S. national security as a bulwark against Russian aggression and the renewed opportunity that President Zelensky's administration offered for bringing Ukraine closer to the United States and Europe, President Trump did not ask Secretary of State Michael Pompeo, Acting Secretary of Defense Patrick Shanahan, or National Security Advisor John Bolton to lead the delegation to President Zelensky's inauguration. Instead, according to Mr. Holmes, the White House "ultimately whittled back an initial proposed list for the official delegation to the inauguration from over a dozen individuals to just five."[207]

Topping that list was Secretary Perry. Accompanying him were Ambassador Sondland, U.S. Special Representative for Ukraine Negotiations Ambassador Volker, and NSC Director for Ukraine Lt. Col. Alexander Vindman.[208] Acting Deputy Chief of Mission (Chargé d'Affaires) of U.S. Embassy Kyiv Joseph Pennington joined the delegation, in place of outgoing U.S. Ambassador to Ukraine Marie Yovanovitch. U.S. Senator Ron Johnson also attended the inauguration and joined several meetings with the presidential delegation. When asked if this delegation was "a good group," Mr. Holmes replied that it "was not as senior a delegation as we [the U.S. embassy] might have expected."[209]

Secretary Perry, Ambassador Volker, and Ambassador Sondland subsequently began to refer to themselves as the "Three Amigos." During the delegation's meeting with President Zelensky, Mr. Holmes recounted that "Secretary Perry passed President Zelensky a list of, quote, 'people he trusts' from whom Zelensky could seek advice on energy sector reform, which was the topic of subsequent meetings between Secretary Perry and key Ukrainian energy sector contacts, from which Embassy personnel were excluded by Secretary Perry's staff."[210]

Mr. Holmes assessed that the delegation's visit proceeded smoothly, although "at one point during a preliminary meeting of the inaugural delegation, someone in the group wondered aloud about why Mr. Giuliani was so active in the media with respect to Ukraine."[211] Ambassador Sondland responded: "Dammit, Rudy. Every time Rudy gets involved he goes and effs everything up."[212] Mr. Holmes added: "He used the 'F' word."[213]

By the time of the inauguration, Mr. Holmes assessed that President Zelensky and the Ukrainians were already starting to feel pressure to conduct political investigations related to former Vice President Biden.[214] Lt. Col. Vindman also was concerned about the potentially negative consequences of Mr. Giuliani's political efforts on behalf of President Trump—both for U.S. national security and also Ukraine's longstanding history of bipartisan support in the U.S. Congress.[215]

During the U.S. delegation's meeting with President Zelensky on the margins of the inauguration, Lt. Col. Vindman was the last person to speak.[216] He "offered two pieces of advice" to President Zelensky. First, he advised the new leader, "be particularly cautious with regards to Russia, and its desire to provoke Ukraine."[217] And second, Lt. Col. Vindman warned, "stay out of U.S. domestic ... politics."[218] Referencing the activities of Mr. Giuliani, Lt. Col Vindman explained:

[I]n the March and April timeframe, it became clear that there were—there were actors in the U.S., public actors, nongovernmental actors that were promoting the idea of investigations and 2016 Ukrainian interference. And it was consistent with U.S. policy to advise any country, all the countries in my portfolio, any country in the world, to not participate in U.S. domestic politics. So I was passing the same advice consistent with U.S. policy.[219]

U.S. Officials Briefed President Trump About their Positive Impressions of Ukraine

Ambassadors Volker and Sondland left Kyiv with "a very favorable impression" of the new Ukrainian leader.[220] They believed it was important that President Trump "personally engage with the President of Ukraine in order to demonstrate full U.S. support for him," including by inviting him to Washington for a meeting in the Oval Office.[221] It was agreed that the delegation would request a meeting with President Trump and personally convey their advice. They were granted time with President Trump on May 23.

According to Mr. Kent, the delegation was able to secure the Oval Office meeting shortly after the return from Kyiv because of Ambassador Sondland's "connections" to Acting White House Chief of Staff Mick Mulvaney and President Trump.[222] Christopher Anderson, Special Advisor to Ambassador Kurt Volker, also attributed the delegation's ability to quickly confirm a meeting with President Trump to Ambassador Sondland's "connections to the White House."[223]

At the May 23 meeting, Ambassadors Sondland and Volker were joined by Secretary Perry, Senator Johnson, and Dr. Charles M. Kupperman, the Deputy National Security Advisor. Mr. Mulvaney may have also participated.[224]

Lt. Col. Vindman, who had represented the White House at President Zelensky's inauguration, did not participate in the meeting. Dr. Hill directed him not to join, because she had learned that "there was some confusion" from the President "over who the director for Ukraine is."[225] Specifically, Dr. Hill testified that around the time of the May 23 debriefing in the Oval Office, she "became aware by chance and accident" that President Trump had requested to speak with the NSC's Ukraine director about unspecified "materials."[226] A member of the NSC executive secretary's staff stated that in response to the President's request, "we might be reaching out to Kash."[227]

Dr. Hill testified that she understood the staff to be referring to Mr. Patel, who then served as a director in the NSC's directorate of International Organizations and Alliances, not the directorate of Europe and Russia.[228] She subsequently consulted with Dr. Kupperman and sought to clarify if Mr. Patel "had some special ... Ambassador Sondland-like representational role on Ukraine" that she had not been informed about, but "couldn't elicit any information about that."[229] All Dr. Kupperman said was that he would look into the matter.[230] Dr. Hill also testified that she never saw or learned more about the Ukraine-related "materials" that the President believed he had received from Mr. Patel, who maintained a close relationship with Ranking Member Nunes after leaving his staff to join the NSC.[231]

President Trump Put the Three Amigos in Charge of the United States' Ukraine Relationship and Directed Them to "Talk to Rudy" About Ukraine

According to witness testimony, the May 23 debriefing with the President in the Oval Office proved consequential for two reasons. President Trump authorized Ambassador Sondland, Secretary Perry, and Ambassador Volker to lead engagement with the President Zelensky's new administration in Ukraine. He instructed them, however, to talk to and coordinate with his personal attorney, Mr. Giuliani.

Ambassador Sondland, Ambassador Volker, Secretary Perry, and Senator Johnson "took turns" making their case "that this is a new crowd, it's a new President" in Ukraine who was "committed to doing the right things," including fighting corruption.[232] According to Ambassador Sondland, the group "emphasized the strategic importance of Ukraine" and the value to the United States of strengthening the relationship with President Zelensky.[233] They recommended that President Trump once again call President Zelensky and follow through on his April 21 invitation for President Zelensky to meet with him in the Oval Office.[234]

President Trump reacted negatively to the positive assessment of Ukraine. Ambassador Volker recalled that President Trump said Ukraine is "a terrible place, all corrupt, terrible people" and was "just dumping on Ukraine."[235] This echoed Mr. Giuliani's public statements about Ukraine during early May.

According to both Ambassadors Volker and Sondland, President Trump also alleged, without offering any evidence, that Ukraine "tried to take me down" in the 2016 election.[236] The President emphasized that he "didn't believe" the delegation's positive assessment of the new Ukrainian president, and added "that's not what I hear" from Mr. Giuliani.[237] President Trump said that Mr. Giuliani "knows all of these things" and knows that President Zelensky has "some bad people around him."[238] Rather than committing to an Oval Office meeting with the Ukrainian leader, President Trump directed the delegation to "[t]alk to Rudy, talk to Rudy."[239]

Ambassador Sondland testified that the "Three Amigos" saw the writing on the wall and concluded "that if we did not talk to Rudy, nothing would move forward on Ukraine."[240] He continued:

> [B]ased on the President's direction we were faced with a choice. We could abandon the goal of a White House meeting for President Zelensky, which we all believed was crucial to strengthening U.S.-Ukrainian ties … or we could do as President Trump directed and talk to Mr. Giuliani to address the President's concerns. We chose the latter path.[241]

Ambassador Volker reached a similar conclusion. He believed "that the messages being conveyed by Mr. Giuliani were a problem, because they were at variance with what our official message to the President was, and not conveying that positive assessment that we all had. And so, I thought it was important to try to step in and fix the problem."[242] Ultimately, however, the "problem" posed by the President's instruction to coordinate regarding Ukraine with his personal attorney persisted and would become more acute.

After the May 23 meeting, Ambassador Sondland stayed behind with President Trump and personally confirmed that the Three Amigos "would be working on the Ukraine file."[243]

Multiple witnesses testified about this shift in personnel in charge of the Ukraine relationship.[244] Mr. Kent recalled that, after the Oval Office meeting, Secretary Perry, Ambassador Sondland, and Ambassador Volker began "asserting that, going forward, they would be the drivers of the relationship with Ukraine."[245] Catherine Croft, Special Advisor to Ambassador Kurt Volker, recalled that "Sondland, Volker, and sort of Perry, as a troika, or as the Three Amigos, had been sort of tasked with Ukraine policy" by President Trump.[246] Under Secretary of State for Political Affairs David Hale testified about his understanding of the meeting, "[I]t was clear that the President, from the readout I had received, the President had tasked that group, members of that delegation to pursue these objectives: the meeting, and the policy goals that I outlined earlier. So I was, you know, knowing I was aware that Ambassador Volker and Ambassador Sondland would be doing that."[247]

On a June 10 conference call with the Three Amigos, "Secretary Perry laid out for Ambassador Bolton the notion that" they "would assist Ambassador Taylor on Ukraine and be there to support" him as the U.S.-Ukraine relationship "move[ed] forward."[248]

This *de facto* change in authority was never officially communicated to other officials, including Dr. Hill, who had responsibility for Ukraine at the National Security Council.[249]

U.S. Officials Collaborated with Rudy Giuliani to Advance the President's Political Agenda

Ambassador Sondland testified that in the weeks and months after the May 23 Oval Office meeting, "everyone was in the loop" regarding Mr. Giuliani's role in advancing the President's scheme regarding Ukraine.[250] The "Three Amigos" did as the President ordered and began communicating with Mr. Giuliani. E-mail messages described to the Committees by Ambassador Sondland showed that he informed Mr. Mulvaney, Ambassador Bolton, and Secretaries Pompeo and Perry, as well as their immediate staffs, of his Ukraine-related efforts on behalf of the President.[251]

According to Ambassador Sondland, Secretary Perry agreed to reach out to Mr. Giuliani first "given their prior relationship."[252] Secretary Perry discussed with Mr. Giuliani the political concerns that President Trump articulated in the May 23 meeting.[253]

Dr. Hill testified that Ambassador Volker, Ambassador Sondland, and Secretary Perry "gave us every impression that they were meeting with Rudy Giuliani at this point, and Rudy Giuliani was also saying on the television, and indeed has said subsequently, that he was closely coordinating with the State Department."[254] These meetings ran counter to Ambassador Bolton's repeated declarations that "nobody should be meeting with Giuliani"[255]

Like Dr. Hill, Ambassador Bolton also closely tracked Mr. Giuliani's activities on behalf of the President. According to Dr. Hill, Ambassador Bolton closely monitored Mr. Giuliani's public statements and repeatedly referred to Mr. Giuliani as a "hand grenade that was going to blow everyone up."[256] During a meeting on June 13, Ambassador Bolton made clear that he supported more engagement with Ukraine by senior White House officials but warned that "Mr. Giuliani was a key voice with the President on Ukraine."[257] According to Ambassador Bolton, Mr. Giuliani's influence "could be an obstacle to increased White House engagement."[258] Ambassador Bolton joked that "every time Ukraine is mentioned, Giuliani pops up."[259]

Ambassador Bolton also reportedly joined Dr. Hill in warning Ambassador Volker against contacting Mr. Giuliani.[260] Dr. Hill was particularly concerned about engagement with Mr. Giuliani because "the more you engage with someone who is spreading untruths, the more validity you give to those untruths."[261] She further testified that she also discussed Mr. Giuliani's activities with Dr. Kupperman, specifically her concern that "Ukraine was going to be played by Giuliani in some way as part of the campaign."[262]

On June 18, Ambassador Volker, Acting Assistant Secretary of State Ambassador Philip T. Reeker, Secretary Perry, Ambassador Sondland, and State Department Counselor T. Ulrich Brechbuhl participated in a meeting at the Department of Energy to follow up to the May 23 Oval Office meeting.[263] Ambassador Bill Taylor, Chargé d'Affaires for U.S. Embassy in Kyiv, who had arrived in Ukraine just the day before, participated by phone from Kyiv.[264] The group agreed that a meeting between President Trump and President Zelensky would be valuable.[265] However, Ambassadors Volker and Sondland subsequently relayed to Ambassador Taylor that President Trump "wanted to hear from Zelensky before scheduling the meeting in the Oval Office."[266] Ambassador Taylor testified that he did not understand, at that time, what the President wanted to hear from his Ukrainian counterpart.[267] However, Ambassador Volker's assistant, Mr. Anderson, recalled "vague discussions" about addressing "Mr. Giuliani's continued calls for a corruption investigation."[268]

The quid pro quo—conditioning the Oval Office meeting that President Trump first offered the Ukrainian leader during their April 21 call on the Ukrainians' pursuit of investigations that would benefit President Trump politically—was beginning to take shape. As Ambassador Sondland testified, the conditions put on the White House meeting and on Ukraine's continued engagement with the White House would get "more insidious" with the passage of time.[269]

President Trump Invited Foreign Interference in the 2020 Election

As U.S. officials debated how to meet the President's demands as articulated by Mr. Giuliani, President Trump publicly disclosed on June 12 in an Oval Office interview with ABC News' anchor George Stephanopoulos that there was "nothing wrong with listening" to a foreign power who offered political dirt on an opponent. The President added, "I think I'd want to hear it."

Mr. Stephanopoulos then pressed the President directly, "You want that kind of interference in our elections?" to which President Trump replied, "It's not an interference, they have information. I think I'd take it."[270] President Trump also made clear that he did not think a foreign power offering damaging information on an opponent was necessarily wrong, and said only that he would "maybe" contact the FBI "*if* I thought there was something wrong."[271]

President Trump's willingness to accept foreign interference in a U.S. election during his interview with Mr. Stephanopoulos was consistent with tweets and interviews by Mr. Giuliani at this time. For example, on June 21, Mr. Giuliani tweeted:

> New Pres of Ukraine still silent on investigation of Ukrainian interference in 2016 election and alleged Biden bribery of Pres Poroshenko. Time for leadership and investigate both if you want to purge how Ukraine was abused by Hillary and Obama people.[272]

On June 18, Dr. Hill met with Ambassador Sondland at the White House. She "asked him quite bluntly" what his role was in Ukraine. Ambassador Sondland replied that "he was in charge of Ukraine."[273] Dr. Hill was taken aback and a bit irritated. She prodded Ambassador Sondland again and asked, "Who put you in charge of Ukraine?" Dr. Hill testified: "And, you know, I'll admit, I was a bit rude. And that's when he told me the President, which shut me up."[274]

Dr. Hill tried to impress upon Ambassador Sondland the "importance of coordinating" with other national security officials in the conduct of Ukraine policy, including the NSC staff and the State Department. Ambassador Sondland "retorted" that he was "coordinating with the President" and Mr. Mulvaney, "filling in" Ambassador Bolton, and talking to State Department Counselor Ulrich Brechbuhl. Ambassador Sondland asked: "Who else did he have to inform?"[275]

Dr. Hill stated that, in hindsight, with the benefit of the sworn testimony by others during the impeachment inquiry and seeing documents displayed by witnesses, she realized that she and Ambassador Sondland were working on two fundamentally different tasks. Dr. Hill testified:

> But it struck me when yesterday, when you put up on the screen Ambassador Sondland's emails and who was on these emails, and he said, These are the people who need to know, that he was absolutely right. Because he was being involved in a domestic political errand, and we were being involved in national security foreign policy, and those two things had just diverged. So he was correct. And I had not put my finger on that at the moment, but I was irritated with him and angry with him that he wasn't fully coordinating. And I did say to him, Ambassador Sondland, Gordon, I think this is all going to blow up. And here we are. [276]

Reflecting on her June 18 conversation with Ambassador Sondland, Dr. Hill concluded:

> Ambassador Sondland is not wrong that he had been given a different remit than we had been. And it was at that moment that I started to realize how those things had diverged. And I realized, in fact, that I wasn't really being fair to Ambassador Sondland, because he was carrying out what he thought he had been instructed to carry out, and we were doing something that we thought was just as—or perhaps even more important, but it wasn't in the same channel.[277]

3.　　**The President Froze Military Assistance to Ukraine**

> *The President froze military assistance to Ukraine against U.S. national security interests and over the objections of career experts.*

Overview

Since 2014, the United States has maintained a bipartisan policy of delivering hundreds of millions of dollars in security assistance to Ukraine each year. These funds benefit the security of the United States and Europe by ensuring that Ukraine is equipped to defend itself against Russian aggression. In 2019, that bipartisan policy was undermined when President Trump ordered, without justification, a freeze on military assistance to Ukraine.

For fiscal year 2019, Congress authorized and appropriated $391 million in security assistance: $250 million through the Department of Defense's (DOD) Ukraine Security Assistance Initiative and $141 million through the State Department's Foreign Military Financing program. In July 2019, however, President Trump ordered the Office of Management and Budget (OMB) to put a hold on all $391 million in security assistance to Ukraine.

The hold surprised experts from DOD and the State Department. DOD had already announced its intent to deliver security assistance to Ukraine after certifying that the country had implemented sufficient anti-corruption reforms, and the State Department was in the process of notifying Congress of its intent to deliver foreign military financing to Ukraine. In a series of interagency meetings, every represented agency other than OMB (which is headed by Mick Mulvaney, who is also the President's Acting Chief of Staff) supported the provision of assistance to Ukraine and objected to President Trump's hold. Ukraine experts at DOD, the State Department, and the National Security Council (NSC) argued that it was in the national security interest of the United States to continue to support Ukraine. Agency experts also expressed concerns about the legality of President Trump withholding assistance to Ukraine that Congress had already appropriated for this express purpose.

Despite these concerns, OMB devised a plan to implement President Trump's hold on the assistance. On July 25, 2019, OMB began using a series of footnotes in funding documents to notify DOD that the assistance funds were temporarily on hold to allow for interagency review. Throughout August and September, OMB continued to use this method and rationale to maintain the hold, long after the final interagency meeting on Ukraine assistance occurred on July 31. The hold continued despite concerns from DOD that the hold would threaten its ability to fully spend the money before the end of the fiscal year, as legally required.

On July 25—the same day as President Trump's call with President Zelensky—officials at Ukraine's embassy emailed DOD to ask about the status of the hold. By mid-August, officials at DOD, the State Department, and the NSC received numerous questions from Ukrainian officials about the hold. President Trump's hold on the Ukraine assistance was publicly reported on August 28, 2019.

Security Assistance to Ukraine is Important to U.S. National Security Interests

The United States has an interest in providing security assistance to Ukraine to support the country in its longstanding battle against Russian aggression and to shore it up as an independent and democratic country that can deter Kremlin influence in both Ukraine and other European countries. In early 2014, in what became known as the Revolution of Dignity, Ukrainian citizens demanded democratic reforms and an end to corruption, thereby forcing the ouster of pro-Kremlin Viktor Yanukovych as Ukraine's president. Shortly thereafter, Russian military forces and their proxies began an incursion into Ukraine that led to Russia's illegal annexation of the Crimean Peninsula of Ukraine, as well as the ongoing, Russian-led armed conflict in the Donbass region of eastern Ukraine. Approximately 13,000 people have been killed as a result of the conflict and over 1.4 million people have been displaced.[278]

Former U.S. Ambassador to the United Nations, Nikki Haley, noted that "militants in eastern Ukraine report directly to the Russian military, which arms them, trains them, leads them, and fights alongside them."[279] Similarly, then-Secretary of Defense James Mattis, during a visit to Ukraine in 2017, chided Russia, stating that "despite Russia's denials, we know they are seeking to redraw international borders by force, undermining the sovereign and free nations of Europe."[280]

In response to Russia's aggression, the international community imposed financial and visa sanctions on Russian individuals and entities, and committed to providing billions of dollars in economic, humanitarian, and security assistance to Ukraine to continue to support its sovereignty and democratic development.

The European Union is the single largest contributor of total foreign assistance to Ukraine, having provided €15 billion in grants and loans since 2014.[281] In addition to economic and humanitarian assistance, the United States has contributed a substantial amount of security assistance, mostly lethal and non-lethal military equipment and training, to Ukraine. In fact, the United States is the largest contributor of security assistance to Ukraine. Since 2014, the United States has delivered approximately $1.5 billion in security assistance to Ukraine.[282]

Multiple witnesses—including Ambassador William Taylor, Deputy Assistant Secretary of State George Kent, Lt. Col. Alexander Vindman, and Deputy Assistant Secretary of Defense Laura Cooper—testified that this security assistance to Ukraine is vital to the national security of the United States and Europe.[283] As Ambassador Taylor noted:

> [R]adar and weapons and sniper rifles, communication, that saves lives. It makes the Ukrainians more effective. It might even shorten the war. That's what our hope is, to show that the Ukrainians can defend themselves and the Russians, in the end, will say "Okay, we're going to stop."[284]

State Department Special Advisor for Ukraine, Catherine Croft, further emphasized that Ukrainians currently "face casualties nearly every day in defense of their own territory against Russian aggression."[285] Ambassador Taylor testified that American aid is a concrete demonstration of the United States' "commitment to resist aggression and defend freedom."[286]

Witnesses also testified that it is in the interest of the United States for Russian aggression to be halted in Ukraine. In the 20th century, the United States fought two bloody wars to resist the aggression of a hostile power that tried to change the borders of Europe by force. As Ambassador Taylor put it, Russian aggression in Ukraine "dismissed all the principles that have kept the peace and contributed to prosperity in Europe since World War II."[287]

Timothy Morrison, former Senior Director for Europe and Russia at the NSC, put the importance of U.S. assistance in stark terms:

> Russia is a failing power, but it is still a dangerous one. The United States aids Ukraine and her people so that they can fight Russia over there, and we don't have to fight Russia here.[288]

Bipartisan Support for Security Assistance to Ukraine

Congressional support for security assistance to Ukraine has been overwhelming and bipartisan. Congress provided $391 million in security assistance to Ukraine for fiscal year 2019: $250 million through the DOD-administered Ukraine Security Assistance Initiative (USAI) and $141 million through the State Department-administered Foreign Military Financing program.

On September 26, 2018, Congress appropriated $250 million for the Ukraine Security Assistance Initiative, which is funded through DOD. The funding law made clear that the funding was only "available until September 30, 2019." President Trump signed the bill into law on September 28, 2018.[289]

The Ukraine Security Assistance Initiative—a Congressionally-mandated program codifying portions of the European Reassurance Initiative, which was originally launched by the Obama Administration in 2015—authorizes DOD to provide "security assistance and intelligence support, including training, equipment, and logistics support, supplies and services, to military and other security forces of the Government of Ukraine."[290] Recognizing that strengthening Ukraine's institutions, in addition to its military, is vital to helping it break free of Russia's influence, Congress imposed conditions upon DOD before it could spend a portion of the security assistance funds. Half of the money was held in reserve until the Secretary of Defense, in coordination with the Secretary of State, certified to Congress that Ukraine had undertaken sufficient anti-corruption reforms, such as in civilian control of the military and increased transparency and accountability.[291]

On February 28, 2019, John C. Rood, Under Secretary of Defense for Policy, notified Congress that DOD intended to deliver the first half ($125 million) of assistance appropriated in September 2018 to Ukraine, including "more than $50 million of assistance to deliver counter-artillery radars and defensive lethal assistance."[292] Congress cleared the Congressional notification, which enabled DOD to begin obligating (spending) funds.[293]

For Ukraine to qualify to receive the remaining $125 million of assistance, Congress required that the Secretary of Defense, in coordination with the Secretary of State, certify that the

Government of Ukraine had taken substantial anticorruption reform actions.[294] Ms. Cooper and others at DOD conducted a review to evaluate whether Ukraine had met the required benchmarks.[295] Ms. Cooper explained that the review involved "pulling in all the views of the key experts on Ukraine defense, and coming up with a consensus view," which was then run "up the chain in the Defense Department, to ensure we have approval."[296]

On May 23, 2019, Under Secretary Rood certified to Congress that Ukraine had completed the requisite defense institutional reforms to qualify for the remaining $125 million in funds. He wrote:

> On behalf of the Secretary of Defense, and in coordination with the Secretary of State, I have certified that the Government of Ukraine has taken substantial actions to make defense institutional reforms for the purposes of decreasing corruption, increasing accountability, and sustaining improvements of combat capability enabled by U.S. assistance.[297]

Congress then cleared the related Congressional notification, which enabled DOD to begin obligating the remaining $125 million in funds.[298]

On June 18, 2019, DOD issued a press release announcing its intention to provide $250 million in security assistance funds to Ukraine "for additional training, equipment, and advisory efforts to build the capacity of Ukraine's armed forces." DOD announced that the security assistance would provide Ukraine with sniper rifles, rocket-propelled grenade launchers, and counter-artillery radars, command and control, electronic warfare detection and secure communications, military mobility, night vision, and military medical treatment.[299]

On February 15, 2019, Congress also appropriated $115 million for Ukraine through the State Department-administered Foreign Military Financing Program (FMF).[300] The Foreign Military Financing Program is administered by the State Department and provides grants or loans to foreign countries to help them purchase military services or equipment manufactured by U.S. companies in the United States. In addition to the $115 million appropriated for fiscal year 2019, approximately $26 million carried over from fiscal year 2018.[301] Thus, the total amount of foreign military financing available for Ukraine was approximately $141 million.

Before a country receives foreign military financing, the State Department must first seek Congressional approval through a notification to Congress.[302] The State Department never sent the required Congressional notification to Congress in the spring or summer of 2019. As described below, OMB blocked the notification.[303]

President Trump Had Questions About Ukraine Security Assistance

The day after DOD issued its June 18 press release announcing $250 million in security assistance funds for Ukraine, President Trump started asking OMB questions about the funding for Ukraine. On June 19, Mark Sandy, Deputy Associate Director for National Security Programs at OMB, was copied on an email from his boss, Michael Duffey, Associate Director for National Security Programs at OMB, to Elaine McCusker, Deputy Under Secretary of

Defense (Comptroller) that said that "the President had questions about the press report and that he was seeking additional information."[304] Notably, the same day, President Trump gave an interview on *Fox News* where he raised the so-called "Crowdstrike" conspiracy theory that Ukraine, rather than Russia, had interfered in the 2016 election, a line he would repeat during his July 25 call with the Ukrainian president.[305]

On June 20, in response to the President's inquiry, Ms. McCusker responded to President Trump's inquiry by providing Mr. Sandy information on the security assistance program.[306] Mr. Sandy shared the document with Mr. Duffey, who had follow-up questions about the "financial resources associated with the program, in particular," the "history of the appropriations, [and] any more details about the intent of the program."[307] Mr. Sandy said that his staff provided the relevant information to Mr. Duffey, but he did not know whether Mr. Duffey shared the information with the White House.[308]

Ms. Cooper also recalled receiving an email inquiring about DOD-administered Ukraine security assistance a "few days" after DOD's June 18, 2019 press release.[309] The email was from the Secretary of Defense's Chief of Staff, "asking for follow-up on a meeting with the President." The email contained three questions:

> And the one question was related to U.S. industry. Did U.S—is U.S. industry providing any of this equipment? The second question that I recall was related to international contributions. It asked, what are other countries doing, something to that effect. And then the third question, I don't recall—I mean, with any of these I don't recall the exact wording, but it was something to the effect of, you know, who gave this money, or who gave this funding?[310]

Like Mr. Sandy, Ms. Cooper believed that the President's inquiries were spurred by DOD's June 18 press release. She testified, "we did get that series of questions just within a few days after the press release and after that one article that had the headline."[311] Ms. Cooper noted that it was "relatively unusual" to receive questions from the President, and that she and her staff at the DOD responded "as quickly" as they could.[312] According to Ms. Cooper, DOD officials included in their answers that security assistance funding "has strong bipartisan support," but never received a response.[313]

President Trump Froze Military Assistance

Despite the fact that DOD experts demonstrated that the security assistance was crucial for both Ukraine and U.S. national security and had strong bipartisan support in Congress, President Trump ordered OMB to freeze the funds in July.

On July 3, the State Department notified DOD and NSC staff that OMB was blocking the State Department from transmitting a Congressional notification for the provision of State Department-administered security assistance to Ukraine (i.e., the $141 million in foreign military financing).[314] Because the State Department is legally required to transmit such a notification to Congress before spending funds, blocking the Congressional notification effectively barred the State Department from spending the funding.[315] Ms. Williams testified that she saw the news in a draft email that was being prepared as part of the nightly update for the National Security Advisor.[316] She agreed that the hold came "out of the blue" because it had not been discussed previously by OMB or the NSC.[317]

On or about July 12, 2019, President Trump directed that a hold be placed on security assistance funding for Ukraine. That day, Robert Blair, Assistant to the President and Senior Advisor to the Chief of Staff, sent an email to Mr. Duffey at OMB about Ukraine security assistance.[318] Mr. Sandy, who was on personal leave at the time but later received a copy of the email from Mr. Duffey, testified that in the July 12 email, Mr. Blair communicated "that the President is directing a hold on military support funding for Ukraine."[319] The email mentioned no concerns about any other country, security assistance package, or aid of any sort.[320]

On or about July 15, Mr. Morrison learned from Deputy National Security Advisor Charles Kupperman "that it was the President's direction to hold the assistance."[321] On or about July 17 or 18, 2019, Mr. Duffey and Mr. Blair again exchanged emails about Ukraine security assistance.[322] Mr. Sandy later received a copy of the emails, which showed that when Mr. Duffey asked Mr. Blair about the reason for the hold, Mr. Blair provided no explanation and instead said, "we need to let the hold take place" and then "revisit" the issue with the President.[323]

On July 18 or 19, when he returned from two weeks of personal leave, Mr. Sandy learned for the first time that the President had placed a hold on Ukraine security assistance from Mr. Duffey.[324] According to Mr. Sandy, Mr. Duffey was not aware of the reason but "there was certainly a desire to learn more about the rationale" for the hold.[325]

Agency Experts Repeatedly Objected to the Hold on Security Assistance

Between July 18 and July 31, 2019, the NSC staff convened a series of interagency meetings, at which the hold on security assistance was discussed in varying degrees of detail. Over the course of these meetings, it became evident that:

- the President directed the hold through OMB;

- no justification was provided for the hold;

- with the exception of OMB, all represented agencies supported Ukraine security assistance because it was in the national security interests of the United States; and

- there were concerns about the legality of the hold.

The first interagency meeting was held on July 18 at the Deputy Assistant Secretary level (i.e., a "sub-Policy Coordination Committee"). It was supposed to be a "routine Ukraine policy meeting."[326] Ambassador Taylor, Lt. Col. Vindman, Ms. Croft, and Mr. Kent were among the attendees. Witnesses testified that OMB announced at the meeting that President Trump had directed a hold on Ukraine security assistance. Mr. Kent testified that at the meeting, an OMB staff person announced that Acting White House Chief of Staff Mick Mulvaney "at the direction of the President had put a hold on all security assistance to the Ukraine."[327] Ambassador Taylor testified that the "directive had come from the President to the Chief of Staff to OMB" and that when he learned of the hold on military assistance, he "realized that one of the key pillars of our strong support for Ukraine was threatened."[328]

According to Ms. Croft, when Mr. Kent raised the issue of security assistance, it "blew up the meeting."[329] Ambassador Taylor testified that he and others on the call "sat in astonishment" when they learned about the hold.[330] David Holmes, Political Counselor at the U.S. Embassy in Kyiv, was also on the call. He testified he was "shocked" and thought the hold was "extremely significant."[331] He thought the hold undermined what he had understood to be longstanding U.S. policy in Ukraine.[332]

Ms. Croft testified that "the only reason given was that the order came at the direction of the President."[333] Ms. Cooper, who did not participate but received a readout of the meeting, testified that the fact that the hold was announced without explanation was "unusual."[334] Mr. Kent testified that "[t]here was great confusion among the rest of us because we didn't understand why that had happened."[335] He explained that "[s]ince there was unanimity that this [security assistance to Ukraine] was in our national interest, it just surprised all of us."[336]

With the exception of OMB, all agencies present at the July 18 meeting advocated for the lifting of the hold.[337]

There was also a lack of clarity as to whether the hold applied only to the State Department-administered Foreign Military Financing to Ukraine or whether it also applied to the DOD-administered Ukraine Security Assistance Initiative funding.[338] Ms. Cooper and her colleagues at the DOD were "concerned" about the hold.[339] After the meeting, DOD sought further clarification from the NSC and State Department about its impact on the DOD-administered funding.[340] However, there was no "specific guidance for DOD at the time."[341]

The second interagency meeting to discuss the hold on Ukraine security assistance was held at the Assistant Secretary level (i.e., a "Policy Coordination Committee") on July 23, 2019.[342] The meeting was chaired by Mr. Morrison.[343] Ms. Cooper, who participated via secure video teleconference, testified that "the White House chief of staff ha[d] conveyed that the President has concerns about Ukraine and Ukraine security assistance."[344] Jennifer Williams, Special Advisor to Vice President Pence for Europe and Eurasia, who also attended the meeting on behalf of the Vice President, testified that the "OMB representative conveyed that they had been directed by the Chief of Staff, the White House Chief of Staff, to continue holding it [the Ukraine security assistance] until further notice."[345] Similar to the July 18 meeting, the July 23 meeting did not provide clarity about whether the President's hold applied to the DOD-administered funding or only to the funds administered by the State Department.[346]

Again, no reason was provided for the hold.[347] Mr. Sandy did not attend the July 23 meeting as the representative for OMB, but he received a readout that other agencies expressed concerns about the hold. Specifically, the concerns related to the lack of rationale for the hold, the hold's implications on U.S. assistance and "overall policy toward Ukraine" and "similar legal questions."[348]

Mr. Morrison also testified that there was a discussion at the July 23 meeting about the legality of the hold, and specifically whether it is "actually legally permissible for the President to not allow for the disbursement of the funding."[349] Mr. Morrison recalled that DOD raised concerns about possible violations of the Impoundment Control Act.[350] The Impoundment Control Act gives the President the authority to delay spending, or not spend, funds *only* if Congress is notified of those intentions and approves the proposed action (see below for further discussion of the act).[351]

With the exception of OMB, all agencies present at the July 23rd meeting advocated for the lifting of the hold.[352] Ambassador Taylor explained that the State Department "made a strong statement about the importance of this assistance" and that Ms. Cooper, on behalf of DOD, "made a very strong case and continued to make a very strong case for the effectiveness" of the security assistance.[353] Lt. Col. Vindman, who also attended the meeting, testified that there was agreement that the issue should be elevated to the Agency deputies "as quickly as possible to recommend a release of security assistance."[354]

The third interagency meeting, a Deputies Small Group meeting at the Cabinet Deputies level, was held on July 26, 2019. Mr. Duffey was the OMB representative, and Mr. Sandy prepared Mr. Duffey for the meeting.[355] Mr. Sandy explained that he prepared Mr. Duffey to get policy guidance on six critical issues: (1) the reason for the hold; (2) the extent of the hold; (3) the duration of the hold; (4) the Congressional affairs approach; (5) the public affairs approach; and (6) and the diplomatic approach.[356] Mr. Sandy testified that on July 26, OMB still did not have an understanding of the reason for the hold.[357] According to Mr. Sandy, at that time, there was no discussion within OMB about the amount of money that was being contributed to Ukraine by other countries, or whether that topic was the reason for the President's hold.[358]

Mr. Morrison, Lt. Col. Vindman, Ms. Cooper, Under Secretary of State for Political Affairs David Hale, and Mr. Duffey attended the July 26 meeting. At the meeting, OMB stated that "they had guidance from the President and from Acting Chief of Staff Mulvaney to freeze the assistance."[359] It also was "stated very clearly" that the hold applied to both the State Department and Defense Department security assistance funds.[360] Ambassador Hale, as the representative for the Department of State, "advocated strongly for resuming the assistance," as did representatives from all agencies other than OMB.[361]

Mr. Morrison testified that, at the meeting, "OMB represented that—and the Chief of Staff's Office was present—that the President was concerned about corruption in Ukraine, and he wanted to make sure that Ukraine was doing enough to manage that corruption."[362] Ms. Cooper had a similar recollection but received no further understanding of what OMB meant by "corruption."[363] Ms. Cooper recalled that the deputies did not consider corruption to be a legitimate reason for the hold because they unanimously agreed that Ukraine was making sufficient progress on anti-corruption reforms, as had been certified by DOD on May 23.[364]

President Trump Continued the Hold Despite Agency Concerns About Legality

Prior to the passage of the Impoundment Control Act, presidents had frequently impounded—i.e., refused to spend—Congressionally-appropriated funds to enforce their policy priorities when they diverged from Congress'. However, most of these impoundments were small (i.e., no more than a few percent of the total program budget) or temporary (i.e., funds were released in time for them to be spent before the end of the fiscal year) and rooted in policy, rather than political interests of the President. It was not until President Nixon that presidential impoundment of funds would prompt Congress to take action citing constitutional concerns.[365]

Unlike his predecessors, Nixon undertook impoundments that were both substantial and, in some cases, permanent, which raised concerns for Congress over its Article I powers. In fact, between 1969 and 1972, Nixon impounded between 15% and 20% of Congressionally-appropriated funds in various accounts.[366]

To reassert Congressional authority over the budget, in 1973, Congress established the Joint Study Committee on Budget Control, which held a series of hearings and produced more than 4,600 pages of testimony and reports. The Joint Study Committee's findings ultimately led to the overwhelmingly bipartisan passage—over President Nixon's veto—of the Impoundment Control Act of 1974, one of a series of reform bills designed to reign in presidential power. Looking back at that moment in history, Rep. Bill Archer (R-TX), a fiscal conservative who served 30 years in the House of Representatives, including as the Chairman of the Ways and Means Committee, remarked, "the culture then was that the president had too much power…the president is abusing his power."[367]

In addition to establishing the Congressional Budget Committees and the independent Congressional Budget Office, the Impoundment Control Act also limits the circumstances under which a president can *legally* impound Congressionally-appropriated funds. According to the Act, although the President may request authority from Congress to withhold or permanently cancel the availability of budget authority, such an action is not allowed without Congressional approval. Any amount of budget authority proposed to be deferred (i.e., temporarily withheld) or rescinded (i.e., permanently withheld) must be made available for obligation unless Congress, within 45 legislative days, completes action on a bill rescinding all or part of the amount proposed for rescission.[368] The Impoundment Control Act does not permit the withholding of funds through their date of expiration, which would be a de facto rescission without Congressional approval.[369]

At the July 26 interagency meeting, senior agency officials raised serious concerns about the legality of the hold under the Impoundment Control Act. Ms. Cooper testified:

A: Well, I'm not an expert on the law, but in that meeting immediately deputies began to raise concerns about how this could be done in a legal fashion because there was broad understanding in the meeting that the funding—the State Department funding related to an earmark for Ukraine and that the DOD funding was specific to Ukraine security assistance. So the comments in the room at the deputies' level reflected a sense that there was not an understanding of how this could legally play out. And at that meeting the deputies agreed to look into the legalities and to look at what was possible.

Q: Okay. So is it fair to say the deputies thought the President was not authorized to place a hold on these funds?

A: They did not use that term, but the expression in the room that I recall was a sense that there was not an available mechanism to simply not spend money that has been in the case of USAI [DOD security assistance] already notified to Congress.[370]

Lt. Col. Vindman testified that the issue needed to be "elevated to a PC [Principals Committee] as quickly as possible to release the hold on security assistance" so that the funds could be obligated before the end of the fiscal year.[371]

A Principals Committee meeting was never convened.[372] According to Mr. Morrison, National Security Advisor John Bolton "believed that it was unnecessary, that he already had a reasonable idea of where the principals were, and he wanted to get directly to the President as early as possible in the most effective way."[373] Ambassador Bolton understood that the principals "were all supportive of the continued disbursement of the aid."[374] As had been clear since the very first interagency meeting on July 18, the lifting of the hold was "the unanimous position of the entire interagency."[375] At this point, it remained unclear to many officials why the President continued to hold the funds.

On July 31, 2019, a fourth and final interagency meeting was held at the Policy Coordination Committee level. Ms. Cooper attended the meeting on behalf of DOD. According to Ms. Cooper, the agenda "was largely focused on just routine Ukraine business, postelection follow up," and "security assistance was not actually an explicit agenda item."[376] Ms. Cooper nevertheless raised security assistance and expressed her understanding, after consulting with DOD counsel, that there were only two legally available options to implement the hold: a Presidential rescission notice to Congress (i.e., requesting that Congress "take back" funds it had already appropriated) or for the Defense Department to do a reprogramming action (i.e., use Congressionally-appropriated funds for a different purpose).[377] In either case, the law requires that the Executive Branch notify, and seek approval from, Congress before taking any action.[378]

At the July 31 meeting, Ms. Cooper emphasized to the participants that because "there are only two legally available options and we do not have direction to pursue either," DOD would have to start obligating the funds on or about August 6.[379] She explained at her deposition that DOD would have had to begin obligating the funds by that date or risk violation of the Impoundment Control Act.[380]

The Administration, however, never proposed a rescission or reprogramming of funds for Ukraine security assistance and never notified Congress of its intent to withhold funds.[381]

OMB Used Unusual Process to Implement President's Hold, Skirting Legal Concerns

OMB plays a critical role in the release of security assistance funding. The Antideficiency Act requires that, before any department or agency may spend Congressionally-appropriated funding, the Director of OMB or his delegates must "apportion" (i.e., make available to spend) the funds in writing.[382] Through this mechanism, OMB has the ability to directly impact security assistance funding or funding of any kind that is appropriated by Congress.

In parallel with the interagency meetings that occurred during the latter half of July 2019, OMB devised a way to implement the President's hold on security assistance to Ukraine, notwithstanding DOD's Congressional notifications of February 28 and May 23. Over the course of his twelve-year career at OMB, Mr. Sandy could not recall any other time when a hold had been placed on security assistance after a Congressional notification had been sent.[383]

When speaking with Mr. Duffey on or about July 18 or 19, Mr. Sandy immediately raised concerns about how to implement the hold without violating the Impoundment Control Act, which required that the funds be obligated (i.e. spent) before they expired at the end of the fiscal year, on September 30.[384] In light of that legal requirement, the hold would have to be temporary.[385] An additional hurdle was the fact that OMB had already authorized DOD to spend the security assistance funds DOD administered for fiscal year 2019.[386] Therefore, when President Trump directed the hold in July, OMB scrambled to reverse that prior authorization.

From July 19 through July 24, Mr. Sandy consulted with the OMB Office of General Counsel as well as Ms. McCusker at DOD on how to legally implement a hold on the funds.[387] Mr. Sandy's staff at OMB also conferred with OMB's Budget Review Division.[388] Based on these consultations, OMB decided to implement the hold through a series of nine funding documents, known legally as "apportionments."[389] Apportionments typically are used to convey authority to an agency to spend funds, not to withhold funds; thus, in order to bar DOD from spending money, these particular apportionments included footnotes that would impose the holds while using creative language to skirt legal concerns. Mr. Sandy testified that "the purpose of the footnote was to preclude obligation for a limited period of time but enable planning and casework to continue."[390] He also testified that this use of footnotes was unusual and that in his 12 years of OMB experience, he could "not recall another event like it."[391]

On July 25, OMB issued the first funding document implementing the hold. In this document, the relevant footnote notified DOD that the Ukraine Security Assistance Initiative funds "are not available for obligation until August 5, 2019, to allow for an interagency process to determine the best use of such funds." The footnote also stated that:

> Based on OMB's communication with DOD on July 25, 2019, OMB understands from the Department that this brief pause in obligations will not preclude DOD's timely execution of the final policy direction. DOD may continue its planning and casework for the Initiative during this period.[392]

Mr. Sandy explained that the "interagency process" referenced in the footnote referred to the NSC-led interagency meetings convened during the latter half of July, and that the August 5 date provided a "reasonable timeframe for an interagency process" to produce "clear guidance" on the hold.[393] The August 5 date was determined in consultation with Mr. Duffey at OMB and Ms. McCusker at DOD.[394]

Mr. Sandy further testified that the second sentence in the footnote—which states, in relevant part, that "OMB understands from the Department that this brief pause in obligations will not preclude DOD's timely execution of the final policy direction"—was critical to the implementation of the hold:

Well, that gets to the heart of that issue about ensuring that we don't run afoul of the Impoundment Control Act, which means that you have to allow for the timely execution. And this reflects my conversation with—conversations plural with Elaine McCusker that they can confirm that, during this brief period, they would not foresee any problem fully executing the program by the end of the fiscal year.[395]

The sentence, in effect, affirmed that if the hold remained in place only until August 5, DOD would still have sufficient time to spend all security assistance funds by September 30, 2019. President Trump, however, would continue the hold long past August 5.

Trump Appointee Took Over Signing Authority from Career Budget Expert

Since becoming Deputy Associate Director for National Security in 2013, Mr. Sandy was responsible for approving release of the funding for programs within his portfolio, including the Ukraine Security Assistance Initiative.[396] Mr. Sandy approved and signed the July 25 funding document.[397] On July 29, however, Mr. Duffey—a political appointee of President Trump whose prior position had been as Executive Director of the Republican Party of Wisconsin—told Mr. Sandy—a career civil servant with decades of experience in this area—that he would no longer be responsible for approving the release of funding for Ukraine Security Assistance Initiative.[398] Mr. Duffey also revoked the authority for approving the release of funding for Foreign Military Financing from Mr. Sandy's colleague at OMB.[399] Instead, Mr. Duffey would himself assume authority for the $250 million in DOD-administered Ukraine security assistance and authority for approving the release of funding for the $141 million in State Department-administered Foreign Military Financing to Ukraine.[400]

Mr. Duffey did not tell Mr. Sandy whether he requested this change in authority but did say that "it was in essence a joint decision reflecting both guidance from the Acting Director and also his support."[401] Over the course of several days, Mr. Duffey explained to Mr. Sandy and others in the National Security Division that "there was interest among the leadership in tracking the uses of moneys [sic] closely."[402] Mr. Duffey expressed an "interest in being more involved in daily operations" and "regarded this responsibility as a way for him to learn more about specific accounts within his area."[403]

Mr. Sandy testified that prior to July 29, he had never heard Mr. Duffey state any interest in approving the release of funding.[404] Furthermore, when they learned that Mr. Duffey was taking on this new responsibility, Mr. Sandy and other staff relayed their concerns to Mr. Duffey that it was a substantial workload.[405] Mr. Sandy also testified that "people were curious what he thought he would learn from apportionments about the accounts as opposed to the other, you know, sources of information."[406] Mr. Sandy agreed that there are more efficient ways of learning about accounts and programs, and that "I can think of other ways—other materials that I personally would find more informative."[407]

Mr. Sandy was not aware of any prior instance when a political appointee assumed this kind of funding approval authority.[408]

After the July 31 interagency meeting at which Ms. Cooper announced that DOD would have to start obligating the funds on or about August 6, Mr. Duffey sought clarification.[409] Ms. Cooper explained to Mr. Duffey that at a certain point DOD would not have sufficient time to fully obligate the funds before they expired at the end of the fiscal year. In response, Mr. Duffey "wanted more information on the precise nature of how long does it take to obligate, and how many cases, and that sort of thing."[410] Ms. Cooper referred Mr. Duffey to the DOD comptroller and to the Defense Security Cooperation Agency.[411] During the month of August, Mr. Duffey and Ms. McCusker communicated about the implementation of the hold on the Ukraine Security Assistance Initiative funds.[412]

On August 6 and August 15, Mr. Duffey approved two more funding documents that contained footnotes with language nearly identical to the footnote in the July 25 funding document that initiated the hold; the only difference was that the date funds would become available for spending was changed from August 5 to August 12.[413]

The August 6 and 15 footnotes, and all subsequent footnotes through September 10, continued to state that the hold was in place "to allow for an interagency process to determine the best use of such funds," even though the final interagency meeting regarding Ukraine security assistance occurred on July 31.[414] Not only was there no active interagency process after July, but Ms. Cooper also was not aware of any review of the funding conducted by DOD in July, August, or September.[415] In fact, Ms. Cooper noted that months before, DOD had completed its review of whether Ukraine "had made sufficient progress in meeting defense reform and anticorruption goals consistent with the NDAA," and certified to Congress in May 2019 that Ukraine had met the requirements to receive funding.[416] Similarly, Mr. Kent testified that the State Department did not conduct, and was never asked to conduct, a review of the security assistance funding administered by the State Department.[417]

At the same time that OMB was implementing the President's hold through the funding footnotes, officials inside OMB were advocating for release of the funds. On August 7, the National Security Division, International Affairs Division, and Office of Legal Counsel of OMB drafted and transmitted a memo on Ukraine security assistance to OMB Acting Director Vought "in anticipation of a principals-level discussion to address the topic."[418] The National Security Division's portion of the memorandum recommended to remove the hold because (1) the assistance was consistent with the national security strategy in terms of supporting a stable, peaceful Europe; (2) the aid countered Russian aggression; and (3) there was bipartisan support for the program.[419] Mr. Duffey approved the memorandum and agreed with the policy recommendation.[420]

Sometime in mid-August, DOD raised concerns that it might not be able to fully obligate the Defense Department administered funds before the end of the fiscal year.[421] Ms. Cooper testified that the Defense Security Cooperation Agency estimated that $100 million of aid might not be obligated in time and was at risk.[422]

Because of this, DOD concluded that it could no longer support OMB's claim in the footnote that "this brief pause in obligations will not preclude DOD's timely execution of the final policy direction."[423] As mentioned above, Mr. Sandy testified that this sentence was at "the heart of that issue about ensuring that we don't run afoul of the Impoundment Control Act." [424]

As a result of DOD's concerns, all of the subsequent footnotes issued by OMB during the pendency of the hold—approved by Mr. Duffey on August 20, 27, and 31, and September 5, 6, and 10—removed the sentence regarding DOD's ability to fully obligate by the end of the fiscal year.[425] Each footnote extended the hold for a period of two to six days.[426]

Mr. Sandy and his staff "continued to express concerns [to Mr. Duffey] about the potential implications vis-à-vis the Impoundment Control Act,"[427] and advised Mr. Duffey to consult with OMB's Office of General Counsel "on every single footnote."[428] Mr. Sandy was copied on emails with the Office of General Counsel on these topics. [429] Although Mr. Sandy understood that the Office of General Counsel supported the footnotes, he noted that there were dissenting opinions within the Office of General Counsel.[430] Concerns about whether the Administration was bending, if not breaking, the law by holding back this vital assistance contributed to at least two OMB officials resigning, including one attorney in the Office of General Counsel.[431] Mr. Sandy testified that the resignation was motivated in part by concerns about the way OMB was handling the hold on Ukraine security assistance.[432] According to Mr. Sandy, the colleague disagreed with the Office of General Counsel about the application of the Impoundment Control Act to the hold on Ukraine security assistance.[433]

Nevertheless, at the direction of the President, OMB continued to implement the hold through September 11.

Senior Officials Failed to Convince President Trump to Release the Aid in August

Sometime prior to August 16, Ambassador Bolton had a one-on-one meeting with President Trump about the aid.[434] According to Mr. Morrison, at that meeting the President "was not yet ready to approve the release of the assistance."[435] Following the meeting, Ambassador Bolton instructed Mr. Morrison to look for opportunities to get the principals together "to have the direct, in-person conversation with the President about this topic." [436]

On or about August 13 or 14, Lt. Col. Vindman was directed to draft a Presidential Decision Memorandum for Ambassador Bolton and the other principals to present to President Trump for a decision on Ukraine security assistance.[437] The memorandum, finalized on August 15, recommended that the hold should be lifted, explained why, and included the consensus views from the July 26 meeting that the funds should be released.[438] Lt. Col. Vindman received conflicting accounts about whether the memorandum was presented to the President.[439]

Mr. Morrison, who was Lt. Col. Vindman's supervisor at the NSC and agreed with the recommendation to lift the hold, testified that the memorandum was never provided to the President.[440] Mr. Morrison explained that Ambassador Bolton intended to present the memorandum to the President during an unrelated meeting in Bedminster, New Jersey, on August 15, but the "other subject matter of that meeting consumed all the time."[441] However, while at Bedminster, the principals "all represented to Ambassador Bolton that they were prepared to tell the President they endorsed the swift release and disbursement of the funding."[442]

Mr. Morrison testified that he attempted to gather the "the right group of principals" to meet with the President but was unable to do so because of scheduling issues.[443] According to Mr. Morrison, the next possible opportunity was during a trip to Warsaw, Poland at the beginning of September, but President Trump did not end up making that trip.[444]

Ms. Cooper recalled receiving an email at the end of August from Secretary of Defense Esper referencing a meeting or discussion with the President, and that there was "no decision on Ukraine."[445]

Ukrainian Officials Learned About the Hold in July 2019

Witnesses testified that officials in the Ukraine government knew of President Trump's hold on security assistance before it was publicly reported in the press on August 28, 2019. Ms. Croft testified that after July 18—when the hold was announced by OMB at the interagency meeting—it was "inevitable that it was eventually going to come out."[446]

Two individuals from the Ukrainian Embassy in Washington, D.C., approached Ms. Croft approximately a week apart "quietly and in confidence to ask me about an OMB hold on Ukraine security assistance."[447] Ms. Croft could not precisely recall the dates of these conversations, but testified that she was "very surprised at the effectiveness of my Ukrainian counterparts' diplomatic tradecraft, as in to say they found out very early on or much earlier than I expected them to."[448]

Ms. Croft explained that the Ukrainian officials came to her quietly because they would not want the hold to become public:

> I think that if this were public in Ukraine it would be seen as a reversal of our policy and would, just to say sort of candidly and colloquially, this would be a really big deal, it would be a really big deal in Ukraine, and an expression of declining U.S. support for Ukraine.[449]

DOD also received questions from the Ukraine Embassy about the status of the military assistance. Ms. Cooper testified that those occurred on July 25, 2019—the same day as President Trump's call with President Zelensky:

> On July 25th, a member of my staff got a question from a Ukraine Embassy contact asking what was going on with Ukraine security assistance, because at that time, we did not know what the guidance was on USAI [DOD-administered funds]. The OMB notice of apportionment arrived that day, but this staff member did not find out about it until later. I was informed that the staff member told the Ukrainian official that we were moving forward on USAI, but recommended that the Ukraine Embassy check in with State regarding the FMF [State Department-administered funds].[450]

On July 25, Ms. Cooper's staff received two emails from the State Department revealing that the Ukrainian Embassy was "asking about security assistance" and that "the Hill knows about the FMF situation to an extent, and so does the Ukrainian Embassy."[451]

One of Ms. Cooper's staff members reported that sometime during the week of August 6, a Ukrainian Embassy officer stated that "a Ukrainian official might raise concerns about security assistance in an upcoming meeting," but that the issue was "not, in fact, raised."[452] Ms. Cooper's staff further reported that Ukrainian officials were aware of the hold on security assistance in August.[453]

Lt. Col. Vindman testified that, by mid-August, he too was getting questions from Ukrainians about the status of the hold on security assistance:

> So to the best of my knowledge, the Ukrainians, first of all, are in general pretty sophisticated, they have their network of, you know, Ukrainian interest groups and so forth. They have bipartisan support in Congress. And certainly there are—it was no secret, at least within government and official channels, that security assistance was on hold. And to the best of my recollection, I believe there were some of these light inquires in the mid-August timeframe.[454]

While numerous individuals, including Ukrainians, were aware of the hold, it did not become publicly known until a *Politico* report on August 28, 2019.[455]

4. **The President's Meeting with the Ukrainian President Was Conditioned on An Announcement of Investigations**

> *President Trump demanded the public announcement by President Zelensky of investigations into President Trump's political rival and alleged Ukrainian interference in the 2016 U.S. election in exchange for an Oval Office meeting. The President's representatives made that quid pro quo clear to Ukrainian officials.*

Overview

After ordering the hold on security assistance to Ukraine against the unanimous advice of the relevant U.S. government agencies, President Trump used his hand-picked representatives to demand that Ukrainian leaders publicly announce investigations into his political rival, former Vice President Joe Biden, and into the debunked conspiracy theory that Ukraine, not Russia, interfered in the 2016 U.S. election. President Trump, through his agents, made clear that his demand needed to be met before a coveted White House meeting with Ukrainian President Volodymyr Zelensky would be scheduled. A face-to-face meeting with President Trump in the Oval Office would have conferred on the new Ukrainian leader much-sought prestige and would have signaled to Russia that Ukraine could continue to count on the support of the President of the United States, which was particularly important as Russia continued to wage war in eastern Ukraine.

To date, the White House meeting for President Zelensky has not occurred. Following the May 23 meeting in the Oval Office, President Trump's hand-picked representatives—the so-called "Three Amigos"—worked with the President's personal attorney, Rudy Giuliani, to pressure Ukrainian leaders to announce publicly investigations that would benefit the President's reelection campaign. Testimony of multiple witnesses and contemporaneous text messages exchanged between and among President Trump's representatives confirm that the White House meeting—and later the release of security assistance for Ukraine—was conditioned on Ukraine acquiescing to the President's demands.

In the weeks leading up to the July 25 call between President Trump and President Zelensky, President Trump's representatives repeatedly relayed the message of conditionality to Ukrainian government officials—including to President Zelensky himself—in meetings in Kyiv, Toronto, and Washington, D.C. President Zelensky and his advisors struggled to navigate these demands, recognizing that President Trump's desire that Ukraine announce these political investigations threatened to render Ukraine a "pawn" in U.S. domestic reelection politics.

An Oval Office Meeting for President Zelensky Was Important to Ukraine and U.S. National Security

A face-to-face meeting with the President of the United States in the Oval Office was critical to President Zelensky as the newly-elected Ukrainian leader sought U.S. support for his ambitious anti-corruption agenda and to repel Russian aggression. A White House meeting was also important for U.S. national security because it would have served to bolster Ukraine's negotiating position in peace talks with Russia. It also would have supported Ukraine as a bulwark against further Russian advances in Europe.

Multiple witnesses unanimously attested to the importance of a White House meeting for Ukraine and the United States. For example, David Holmes, the Political Counselor at the U.S. Embassy in Kyiv, testified that a White House meeting was "critical" to President Zelensky's ability to "encourage Russian President Putin to take seriously President Zelensky's peace efforts."[456] Likewise, Deputy Assistant Secretary George Kent explained that a White House meeting was "very important" for Ukrainians to demonstrate the strength of their relationship with "Ukraine's strongest supporter." He also said that it "makes sense" for the United States to meet with the Ukrainians as they were on "the front lines of Russian malign influence and aggression."[457]

Dr. Fiona Hill, Deputy Assistant to the President and Senior Director of European and Russian Affairs at the NSC, explained that a White House meeting would supply the new Ukrainian Government with "the legitimacy that it needed, especially vis-à-vis the Russians,"— and that the Ukrainians viewed a White House meeting as "a recognition of their legitimacy as a sovereign state."[458] Lt. Col. Alexander Vindman, the NSC Director for Ukraine, testified that a White House meeting would provide a "show of support" from "the most powerful country in the world and Ukraine's most significant benefactor," which would help the Ukrainian President "establish his bona fides" and "implement his agenda."[459]

Ambassador Kurt Volker, Special Representative for Ukraine Negotiations, also recognized that it was "a tremendous symbol of support" to have President Zelensky visit the White House.[460] He explained that a meeting "enhances [President Zelensky's] stature, that he is accepted, that he is seen at the highest level. The imagery you get from being at the White House is the best in the world, in terms of how it enhances someone's image."[461]

President Trump "Wanted to Hear from Zelensky" Before Scheduling Oval Office Meeting

Ambassador William B. Taylor, Jr. arrived in Ukraine as the new Chargé d'Affaires at the U.S. Embassy in Kyiv on June 17, 2019. After arriving, Ambassador Taylor worked to secure an Oval Office meeting between President Trump and President Zelensky. This was "an agreed-upon goal" of policymakers in both Ukraine and the United States.[462]

Ambassador Taylor worked with Ambassador Volker and Ambassador to the European Union Gordon Sondland—two of the Three Amigos—to try to schedule this meeting. Just days after beginning his new position, Ambassador Taylor learned that President Trump "wanted to hear from Zelensky" before scheduling the Oval Office meeting, but Ambassador Taylor did not understand what that meant at the time.[463] On June 27, Ambassador Sondland informed Ambassador Taylor that President Zelensky needed to "make clear" to President Trump that he, President Zelensky, was not "standing in the way of 'investigations.'"[464] Ambassador Taylor relayed this conversation to Mr. Holmes, who testified that he understood "investigations" in that context to mean the "Burisma-Biden investigations that Mr. Giuliani and his associates had been speaking about" publicly.[465]

On June 28, Secretary of Energy Rick Perry—the third of the Three Amigos—and Ambassadors Sondland, Volker, and Taylor participated in a conference call to prepare for a discussion later that day with President Zelensky. During this preparatory call, Ambassador Volker explained that he planned to be "explicit" with President Zelensky in an upcoming one-on-one meeting in Toronto, Canada. Specifically, Ambassador Volker intended to inform President Zelensky that President Trump would require Ukraine to address "rule of law, transparency, but also, specifically, cooperation on investigations to get to the bottom of things" in order to "get the meeting in the White House."[466]

For the subsequent call with President Zelensky on June 28, Ambassador Sondland sought to limit the number of U.S. government personnel listening in. According to Ambassador Taylor, Ambassador Sondland stated that he did not want to include "most of the regular interagency participants" and that "he wanted to make sure no one was transcribing or monitoring" the call when President Zelensky was patched in. Ambassador Taylor testified that he considered Ambassador Sondland's requests to be "odd."[467] During that call, President Zelensky and the U.S. officials discussed energy policy and the conflict with Russia in eastern Ukraine. The Ukrainian president also noted that he looked forward to the White House visit that President Trump had offered in a letter dated May 29.[468]

The exclusion of State Department staff and notetakers from the June 28 call was an early indication to Ambassador Taylor that separate channels of diplomacy related to Ukraine policy—an official channel and an irregular channel—were "diverging." Ambassador Taylor testified:

> This suggested to me that there were the two channels. This suggested to me that the normal channel, where you would have staff on the phone call, was being cut out, and the other channel, of people who were working, again, toward a goal which I supported, which was having a meeting to further U.S.-Ukrainian relations, I supported, but that irregular channel didn't have a respect for or an interest in having the normal staff participate in this call with the head of state.[469]

Given Ambassador Sondland's efforts to exclude staff on the June 28 call with President Zelensky, Ambassador Taylor asked Ambassadors Sondland and Volker by text message how they planned to handle informing other U.S. officials about the contents of the call. Ambassador Volker responded: "I think we just keep it among ourselves to try to build working relationship and just get the d*** date for the meeting!"[470] Ambassador Sondland then texted: "Agree with KV. Very close hold."[471] Nevertheless, Ambassador Taylor informed Mr. Kent about the call and wrote a memo for the record dated June 30 that summarized the conversation with President Zelensky.[472]

Ambassador Volker Pressed "Investigations" with President Zelensky in Toronto

On July 2, Ambassador Volker met with President Zelensky and his chief of staff on the sidelines of the Ukraine Reform Conference in Toronto. As he later texted to Ambassador Taylor, Ambassador Volker "pulled the two of them aside at the end and explained the Giuliani factor."[473] Ambassador Volker clarified that by "the Giuliani factor," he meant "a negative narrative about Ukraine" that was "being amplified by Rudy Giuliani" and was unfavorably impacting "Ukraine's image in the United States and our ability to advance the bilateral relationship."[474] Ambassador Volker later informed Ukraine's incoming Minister of Foreign Affairs, Vadym Prystaiko, about his pull-aside with President Zelensky in Toronto via text message: "I talked to him privately about Giuliani and impact on president T[rump]."[475]

On July 3, the day after his pull-aside with President Zelensky in Toronto, Ambassador Volker sent a message to Ambassador Taylor emphasizing that "The key thing is to tee up a phone call w potus and then get visit nailed down."[476] Ambassador Volker told Ambassador Taylor that during the Toronto conference, he counseled the Ukrainian president about how he could "prepare for the phone call with President Trump." Specifically, Ambassador Volker told the Ukrainian leader that President Trump "would like to hear about the investigations." [477] In his public testimony, Ambassador Volker confirmed that he mentioned "investigations" to President Zelensky in Toronto, explaining that he was "thinking of Burisma and 2016" in raising the subject, and that his "assumption" was that Ukrainian officials also understood his reference to "investigations" to be "Burisma/2016."[478]

Ambassador Volker's efforts to prepare President Zelensky for his phone call with President Trump appear to have borne fruit. As discussed further in Chapter 5, during the July 25 call, President Zelensky expressed his openness to pursuing investigations into President Trump's political rival, former Vice President Biden, and the conspiracy theory that Ukraine, rather than Russia, interfered in the 2016 U.S. election. President Zelensky also specifically referenced "Burisma" during the call.

Ambassadors Volker and Sondland Worked to Get Mr. Giuliani What He Needed

According to Ambassador Sondland, President Zelensky's commitment to make a public announcement about investigations into Burisma and the 2016 election was a "prerequisite[]" for the White House meeting.[479] In fact, Ambassador Sondland testified that the *announcement* of the investigations—and not the investigations themselves—was the price President Trump sought in exchange for a White House meeting with Ukrainian President Zelensky:

> Q: But he had to get those two investigations if that official act was going to take place, correct?
> A: He had to announce the investigations. He didn't actually have to do them, as I understood it.
> Q: Okay. President Zelensky had to announce the two investigations the President wanted, make a public announcement, correct?
> A: Correct.[480]

Ambassadors Sondland and Volker understood that they needed to work with Mr. Giuliani, who was publicly pressing for the announcement of investigations that would benefit President Trump politically. As discussed in Chapter 2, Ambassador Sondland testified that the key to overcoming President Trump's skepticism about Ukraine was satisfying the President's personal attorney. Sondland said, "Nonetheless, based on the President's direction, we were faced with a choice: We could abandon the efforts to schedule the White House phone call and a

White House visit" or "do as President Trump had directed and 'talk with Rudy'" because "it was the only constructive path open to us."[481]

Ambassador Volker discussed his intention to contact Mr. Giuliani with Mr. Kent. Ambassador Volker explained that he intended to reach out to Mr. Giuliani because it was clear that the former mayor "had influence" with President Trump "in terms of the way the President thought of Ukraine."[482] Ukrainian officials also understood the importance of working through Mr. Giuliani, something that was underscored by his successful effort to smear and remove Ambassador Marie Yovanovitch from Kyiv in late April.[483]

In response to Ambassador Volker's stated intention to reach out to Mr. Giuliani, Mr. Kent raised concerns about Mr. Giuliani's "track record," including "asking for a visa for a corrupt former prosecutor," attacking Ambassador Yovanovitch, and "tweeting that the new President needs to investigate Biden and the 2016 campaign." Mr. Kent also warned Ambassador Volker that "asking another country to investigate a prosecution for political reasons undermines our advocacy of the rule of law."[484]

On July 10, Ambassador Taylor met with Ukrainian officials in Kyiv, before their Ukrainian colleagues were scheduled to meet with National Security Advisor John Bolton at the White House later that day. At the meeting in Kyiv, the Ukrainian officials expressed that they were "very concerned" because they had heard from former Prosecutor General Yuriy Lutsenko, who had learned from Mr. Giuliani, that President Trump had decided not to meet with President Zelensky.[485]

Ambassador Taylor texted Ambassador Volker to explain the situation and advised that he had also informed T. Ulrich Brechbuhl, Counselor of the Department of State:

Volker:	Good grief. Please tell Vadym to let the official USG representatives speak for the U.S. lutsenko has his own self-Interest here…
Taylor:	Exactly what I told them.
Taylor:	And I said that RG is a private citizen.
Taylor:	I briefed Ulrich this afternoon on this.[486]

Despite his text message to Ambassador Taylor that official U.S. government representatives should be allowed to "speak for the U.S.," and notwithstanding Mr. Kent's warnings about engaging with Mr. Giuliani, Ambassador Volker almost immediately reached out to Mr. Giuliani. Four minutes after sending the text message above, Ambassador Volker texted Mr. Giuliani to request a meeting to "update you on my conversations about Ukraine." He told Mr. Giuliani that he believed he had "an opportunity to get you what you need."[487]

One hour later, around 9:00 a.m. Eastern Time, Ambassador Volker met Ukrainian presidential aide Andriy Yermak for coffee at the Trump Hotel before they traveled down Pennsylvania Avenue to their afternoon meetings at the White House.[488] Over coffee, Mr. Yermak asked Ambassador Volker to connect him to Mr. Giuliani, thus further demonstrating the Ukrainians' understanding that satisfying Mr. Giuliani's demands was a key to getting what they wanted from President Trump, namely the Oval Office meeting.[489]

July 10 White House Meetings: Ambassador Sondland
Explicitly Communicated the "Prerequisite of Investigations" to Ukrainians

On July 10, during two separate meetings at the White House, Ambassador Sondland informed senior Ukrainian officials that there was a "prerequisite of investigations" before an Oval Office meeting between President Trump and President Zelensky would be scheduled.[490]

The first meeting took place in Ambassador Bolton's office. NSC officials, including Ambassador Bolton's staff responsible for Ukraine—Dr. Hill and Lt. Col. Vindman—attended, as did the Three Amigos: Secretary Perry, Ambassador Sondland, and Ambassador Volker. The Ukrainian delegation included Mr. Yermak, a senior aide to President Zelensky, and Oleksandr "Sasha" Danyliuk, the incoming Ukrainian National Security Advisor.[491] The purpose of the meeting was twofold. The Ukrainians were seeking advice and assistance from Ambassador Bolton about how to "revamp" the Ukrainian National Security Council, and they were also "very anxious to set up a meeting, a first meeting between President Zelensky and our President."[492]

Near the end of the meeting, the Ukrainian officials raised the scheduling of the Oval Office meeting for President Zelensky. According to Dr. Hill, Ambassador Sondland, who is "a fairly big guy, kind of leaned over" and then "blurted out: Well, we have an agreement with the [White House] Chief of Staff for a meeting if these investigations in the energy sector start." Dr. Hill described that others in the room looked up from their notes, thinking the comment was "somewhat odd." Ambassador Bolton "immediately stiffened" and ended the meeting. Dr. Hill recounted that Ambassador Bolton was polite but was "very abrupt. I mean, he looked at the clock as if he had, you know, suddenly another meeting and his time was up, but it was obvious he ended the meeting," she added.[493]

Lt. Col. Vindman similarly testified that the meeting in Ambassador Bolton's office "proceeded well" until Ukrainian officials raised the meeting between President Trump and President Zelensky. The Ukrainians stated that they considered the Oval Office meeting to be "critically important in order to solidify the support for their most important international partner." When Ambassador Sondland mentioned Ukraine "delivering specific investigations in order to secure the meeting with the President," Ambassador Bolton cut the meeting short.[494]

Although Ambassador Volker did not recall any mention of "investigations" during the July 10 meeting at his deposition,[495] he later testified at his public hearing, "As I remember, the meeting [in Ambassador Bolton's office] was essentially over when Ambassador Sondland made a general comment about investigations. I think all of us thought it was inappropriate" and "not what we should be talking about."[496]

After Ambassador Bolton ended the meeting in his office, Ambassador Sondland "went out into the office in front of Ambassador Bolton" and made "unusual" arrangements for the Ukrainians, Ambassador Volker, Secretary Perry, and others to go to a second meeting in the Ward Room of the White House, located near the secure spaces of the White House Situation Room. As Dr. Hill described it, the purpose of the Ward Room meeting was "to talk to the

Ukrainians about next steps" regarding the Oval Office meeting for President Zelensky.[497] As Dr. Hill was leaving Ambassador Bolton's office, he pulled her aside and directed her to attend the Ward Room meeting to "find out what they're talking about and come back" and report to him. Dr. Hill followed his instruction.[498]

During the Ward Room meeting, which occurred after a brief photo opportunity outside the West Wing, Ambassador Sondland was more explicit in pressing the Ukrainians to undertake the investigations in order to secure an Oval Office meeting for President Zelensky. Lt. Col. Vindman testified that when the group entered the Ward Room, Ambassador Sondland began to "review what the deliverable would be in order to get the meeting," and that "to the best of my recollection, he did specifically say 'investigation of the Bidens.'" Lt. Col. Vindman said the request "was explicit. There was no ambiguity" and that Ambassador Sondland also mentioned "Burisma."[499]

Dr. Hill entered the Ward Room as the discussion was underway. She testified that "Ambassador Sondland, in front of the Ukrainians, as I came in, was talking about how he had an agreement with Chief of Staff Mulvaney for a meeting with the Ukrainians if they were going to go forward with investigations. And my director for Ukraine [Lt. Col. Vindman] was looking completely alarmed."[500] Dr. Hill recalled that Ambassador Sondland mentioned "Burisma" in the presence of the Ukrainians, in response to which Mr. Danyliuk also appeared "very alarmed" and as if he did not know what was happening.[501]

Dr. Hill confronted Ambassador Sondland, informing him that Ambassador Bolton had sent her there to ensure that the U.S. officials did not commit "at this particular juncture" to a meeting between President Trump and President Zelensky. Ambassador Sondland responded that he and the Ukrainians already had an agreement that the meeting would go forward.[502] At Dr. Hill's urging, however, Ambassador Sondland excused the Ukrainian officials, who moved into the corridor near the White House Situation Room.

Dr. Hill then told Ambassador Sondland: "Look, I don't know what's going on here, but Ambassador Bolton wants to make it very clear that we have to talk about, you know, how are we going to set up this meeting. It has to go through proper procedures." Lt. Col. Vindman relayed his own concerns to Ambassador Sondland in the Ward Room.[503] He explained that "the request to investigate the Bidens and his son had nothing to do with national security, and that such investigations were not something that the NSC was going to get involved in or push."[504]

Ambassador Sondland responded that he had had conversations with Mr. Mulvaney and he also mentioned Mr. Giuliani. Lt. Col. Vindman confirmed that Ambassador Sondland described an agreement he had with Mr. Mulvaney about the Oval Office meeting: "I heard him say that this had been coordinated with White House Chief of Staff Mr. Mick Mulvaney ... He just said that he had had a conversation with Mr. Mulvaney, and this is what was required in order to get a meeting."[505] Dr. Hill then cut the conversation short because she "didn't want to get further into this discussion at all." She testified that Ambassador Sondland "was clearly annoyed with this, but then, you know, he moved off. He said he had other meetings."[506]

Later on July 10, when Ambassador Taylor asked Ambassador Volker how the meetings went with the Ukrainian officials and whether they had resulted in a decision on a presidential call, Ambassador Volker replied: "Not good—lets talk."[507]

Following the July 10 White House meetings, Mr. Yermak followed up with Ambassador Volker by text message: "Thank you for meeting and your clear and very logical position. Will be great meet with you before my departure and discuss. I feel that the key for many things is Rudi and I ready to talk with him at any time."[508]

Concerned Officials Reported Details of This "Drug Deal" to White House Lawyers

After the Ward Room meeting, Dr. Hill returned to Ambassador Bolton's office and relayed what she had just witnessed. Ambassador Bolton was "very angry" and instructed her to report the conversation to John Eisenberg, Deputy Counsel to the President for National Security Affairs and the Legal Advisor to the National Security Council:

> And he told me, and this is a direct quote from Ambassador Bolton: You go and tell Eisenberg that I am not part of whatever drug deal Sondland and Mulvaney are cooking up on this, and you go and tell him what you've heard and what I've said.[509]

Dr. Hill explained that "drug deal" referred to Ambassador Sondland's and Mr. Mulvaney's conditioning of a White House meeting on investigations.[510] By this point, Dr. Hill explained, it was clear that investigations were "code, at least, for Burisma. Because that had been mentioned, you know, in the course of Mr. Giuliani's appearances on television."[511] Numerous U.S. officials, including Ambassadors Sondland, Volker, and Bolton, as well as Lt. Col. Vindman and others, were well aware of Mr. Giuliani's efforts to push Ukraine to pursue these political investigations.

Following the meeting with Ambassador Bolton, Dr. Hill reported what had occurred to Mr. Eisenberg. She conveyed to Mr. Eisenberg the details of the two meetings, including Ambassador Sondland's agreement with Mr. Mulvaney to provide the White House meeting if Ukraine agreed to pursue the investigations.[512] The initial conversation between Dr. Hill and Mr. Eisenberg was brief, and they scheduled a longer discussion for the next day.[513]

On July 11, Dr. Hill enlisted another NSC official who attended the July 10 meetings, Senior Director for International Energy and Environment P. Wells Griffith, to attend the longer discussion with Mr. Eisenberg.[514] Dr. Hill and Mr. Griffith went over the events of July 10 and further explained that Ambassador Sondland said that he had been communicating with Mr. Giuliani. Mr. Eisenberg was "very concerned" and stated that he would follow up. Dr. Hill understood that Mr. Eisenberg later discussed the issue with his "reporting authority," specifically, White House Counsel Pat Cipollone.[515]

Lt. Col. Vindman separately reported his concerns about the July 10 meetings to Mr. Eisenberg. He told Mr. Eisenberg that Ambassador Sondland had asked for investigations into "Bidens and Burisma," which he thought was "inappropriate."[516] Lt. Col. Vindman also reported that the investigation "Mr. Giuliani was pushing was now being pulled into a, you know, national security dialogue."[517] Mr. Eisenberg said that he would look into it and invited Lt. Col. Vindman to return if any further concerns arose. No one from the of the White House Counsel's Office, however, followed up with Lt. Col. Vindman on this issue.[518]

Dr. Hill and Lt. Col. Vindman discussed their reactions and alarm about the July 10 discussions with each other. They both believed that Ambassador Sondland's statements were inappropriate and "had nothing to do with national security," and that they would not get involved with the scheme.[519] On July 19, they also shared their concerns about Ambassador Sondland's comments during the July 10 meetings with Ambassador Taylor.[520]

Ambassador Sondland Coached President Zelensky on Investigations and Kept Senior White House and State Department Officials "In the Loop"

In mid-July, Dr. Hill was preparing to depart the NSC and transitioning her role to Timothy Morrison, who had been serving in another role at the NSC.[521] On July 13, Ambassador Sondland emailed Mr. Morrison, explaining that the "[s]ole purpose" of a presidential call was for President Zelensky to assure President Trump that, "Corruption ending, unbundling moving forward and any hampered investigations will be allowed to move forward transparently." In exchange, Ambassador Sondland wrote, the "Goal is for Potus to invite him to Oval. Volker, Perry, Bolton and I strongly recommend."[522] Later that evening, Mr. Morrison responded, "Thank you. Tracking."[523]

On July 19, a little over a week after the July 10 meetings at the White House, Ambassador Sondland spoke directly to President Zelensky about the upcoming call between the two presidents: "It was a short call. I think I said: It looks like your call is finally on, and I think it's important that you, you know, give President Trump—he wanted this—some kind of a statement about corruption."[524]

Following his call with President Zelensky, Ambassador Sondland emailed several senior Trump Administration officials, including Mr. Mulvaney, Secretary of State Michael Pompeo, Secretary Perry, and their staffs. The subject line of the July 19 email read: "I Talked to Zelensky just now." Ambassador Sondland wrote:

> He is prepared to receive Potus' call. Will assure him that he intends to run a fully transparent investigation and will "turn over every stone". He would greatly appreciate a call prior to Sunday so that he can put out some media about a "friendly and productive call" (no details) prior to Ukraine election on Sunday.[525]

Secretary Perry responded that Mr. Mulvaney had confirmed a call would be set up "for tomorrow by NSC,"[526] and Mr. Mulvaney also responded to confirm that he had asked the NSC to set up the call between the presidents for the following day, July 20.[527]

Ambassador Sondland explained that this email chain showed that "[e]veryone was in the loop" regarding his discussions with Ukrainian officials about the need for the Ukrainian leader to confirm to President Trump that he would announce the investigations. As Ambassador Sondland further testified:

It was no secret. Everyone was informed via email on July 19th, days before the Presidential call. As I communicated to the team, I told President Zelensky in advance that assurances to run a fully transparent investigation and turn over every stone were necessary in his call with President Trump.[528]

Call records reviewed by the Committees show repeated contact between Ambassador Sondland and the White House around this time. For example, on July 19, at 10:43 a.m. Eastern Time, a number associated with the White House dialed Ambassador Sondland. Four minutes later, at 10:47 a.m., Ambassador Sondland called a White House phone number and connected for approximately seven minutes.[529]

Later in the afternoon of July 19, Ambassador Sondland texted Ambassadors Volker and Taylor: "Looks like Potus call tomorrow. I spike [sic] directly to Zelensky and gave him a full briefing. He's got it."[530] Ambassador Volker replied: "Good. Had breakfast with Rudy this morning—teeing up call w Yermak Monday. Must have helped. Most impt is for Zelensky to say that he will help investigation—and address any specific personnel issues—if there are any."[531]

Mr. Giuliani Met with State Department Officials and Ukrainian Government Officials

As Ambassador Volker informed Ambassador Sondland in the above text message, on July 19, Ambassador Volker met Mr. Giuliani and his now-indicted associate Lev Parnas for breakfast at the Trump Hotel in Washington, D.C.[532] Ambassador Volker also texted Mr. Yermak to inform him that he and Mr. Giuliani were meeting that day: "Having our long anticipated breakfast today—will let you know and try to connect you directly."[533]

During the breakfast, Mr. Giuliani and Ambassador Volker discussed the discredited allegations against former Vice President Biden relating to Ukraine. Ambassador Volker testified that he pushed back against the allegations during his breakfast with Mr. Giuliani:

> One of the things that I said in that breakfast that I had with Mr. Giuliani, the only time Vice President Biden was ever discussed with me, and he was repeating—he wasn't making an accusation and he wasn't seeking an investigation—but he was repeating all of the things that were in the media that we talked about earlier about, you know, firing the prosecutor general and his son being on the company and all that.
>
> And I said to Rudy in that breakfast the first time we sat down to talk that it is simply not credible to me that Joe Biden would be influenced in his duties as Vice President by money or things for his son or anything like that. I've known him a long time, he's a person of integrity, and that's not credible.[534]

Ambassador Volker further advised Mr. Giuliani during the breakfast that the then-Ukrainian Prosecutor General, Yuriy Lutsenko, was promoting a "self-serving narrative to preserve himself in power." Mr. Giuliani agreed with Ambassador Volker and stated that he had come to that conclusion as well.[535]

Following the breakfast, Ambassador Volker connected Mr. Giuliani with Mr. Yermak by text message:

Volker: Mr Mayor — really enjoyed breakfast this morning. As discussed, connecting you here with Andrey Yermak, who is very close to President Zelensky. I suggest we schedule a call together on Monday — maybe 10am or 11am Washington time? Kurt

Giuliani: Monday 10 to 11

Yermak: Ok, thank you

Volker: I will set up call — 10 am — thanks – Kurt

Yermak: 👍[536]

On the morning of July 22, Mr. Yermak texted Ambassador Volker about the upcoming call with Mr. Giuliani, writing that it was "very good" that their discussion would take place before the call between President Trump and President Zelensky.[537] Later that day, the three men spoke by phone. Ambassador Volker described the July 22 discussion as merely an "introductory phone call,"[538] although phone records indicate that the call lasted for approximately 38 minutes.[539]

Ambassador Volker testified that during the call, Mr. Giuliani and Mr. Yermak discussed plans for an in-person meeting in Madrid in early August.[540] Afterward, Ambassador Volker texted Mr. Yermak that he thought the call had been "very useful" and recommended that Mr. Yermak send Mr. Giuliani a text message to schedule a date for the Madrid meeting.[541] Mr. Yermak texted Mr. Giuliani later that day about a plan to "take this relationship to a new level" and to meet in person as soon as possible.[542]

Later on July 22, Ambassador Volker updated Ambassador Sondland on the "great call" he "[o]rchestrated" between Mr. Giuliani and Mr. Yermak, noting that "Rudy is now advocating for phone call," an apparent reference to the call between President Trump and President Zelensky that would occur on July 25. Ambassador Volker also recommended that Ambassador Sondland inform Mr. Mulvaney that "Rudy agrees," and that he planned to convey the same information to Ambassador Bolton. Ambassador Sondland replied that Mr. Morrison of the White House NSC was also in support of the call.[543] Ambassador Volker also told Ambassador Sondland that Mr. Giuliani and Mr. Yermak would meet in person in Madrid within a couple of weeks.[544]

President Zelensky Feared Becoming "A Pawn" in U.S. Reelection Campaign

Around this time, senior Ukrainian officials informed U.S. officials that the new Ukrainian president did not want Ukraine to become enmeshed in U.S. domestic reelection politics.

On July 20, Ambassador Taylor spoke with Mr. Danyliuk, the Ukrainian national security advisor, who conveyed that President Zelensky "did not want to be used as a pawn in a U.S. reelection campaign." [545] Ambassador Taylor discussed President Zelensky's concern with Ambassador Volker and, the next day, texted Ambassador Sondland:

Taylor: Gordon, one thing Kurt and I talked about yesterday was Sasha Danyliuk's point that President Zelenskyy is sensitive about Ukraine being taken seriously, not merely as an instrument in Washington domestic, reelection politics.

Sondland: Absolutely, but we need to get the conversation started and the relationship built, irrespective of the pretext. I am worried about the alternative.[546]

Ambassador Taylor explained that his reference to "Washington domestic reelection politics" was "a reference to the investigations that Mr. Giuliani wanted to pursue."[547] According to Ambassador Taylor, President Zelensky understood what President Trump and Mr. Giuliani meant by "investigations," and "he did not want to get involved." Specifically, the Ukrainians understood that the "investigations were pursuant to Mr. Giuliani's request to develop information, to find information about Burisma and the Bidens. This was very well known in public. Mr. Giuliani had made this point clear in several instances in the beginning—in the springtime."[548] Ambassador Taylor also testified that the "whole thrust" of the activities undertaken by Mr. Giuliani and Ambassador Sondland "was to get these investigations, which Danyliuk and presumably Zelensky were resisting because they didn't want to be seen to be interfering but also to be a pawn."[549]

Despite the Ukrainian resistance, Ambassador Sondland said he believed that the public announcement of investigations would "fix" an impasse between the Ukrainian government and President Trump. When asked what he meant by "irrespective of the pretext" in his July 21 text message to Ambassador Taylor, Ambassador Sondland explained, "Well, the pretext being the agreed-upon interview or the agreed-upon press statement. We just need to get by it so that the two can meet, because, again, it was back to once they meet, all of this will be fixed."[550]

Witnesses Confirmed the President Conditioned an Oval Office Meeting on Investigations

Multiple witnesses testified that the conditioning of an Oval Office meeting on President Zelensky's announcement of investigations to benefit the President's reelection campaign came from the very top: President Trump.

Ambassador Sondland testified that he, Secretary Perry, and Ambassador Volker worked with Mr. Giuliani "at the express direction of the President of the United States."[551] Ambassador Sondland stated that "Mr. Giuliani was expressing the desires of the President of the United States, and we knew these investigations were important to the President."[552] Ambassador Sondland explained that he "followed the directions of the President" and that "we followed the President's orders."[553]

Ambassador Sondland further testified that President Trump expressed—both directly and through Mr. Giuliani—that he wanted "a public statement from President Zelensky committing to the investigations of Burisma and the 2016 election" as "prerequisites for the White House call and the White House meeting."[554] Ambassador Sondland explained:

> I know that members of this committee frequently frame these complicated issues in the form of a simple question: Was there a quid pro quo? As I testified previously with regard to the requested White House call and the White House meeting, the answer is yes.[555]

Ambassador Sondland also testified that knowledge of this quid pro quo was widespread among the President's advisers: "Everyone was in the loop" about the President's expectation that President Zelensky had to announce these specific investigations to secure an Oval Office meeting. As an example, Ambassador Sondland cited an email—copying Senior Advisor to the White House Chief of Staff Robert Blair, State Department Executive Secretary Lisa Kenna, Chief of Staff to the Secretary of Energy Brian McCormack, Mr. Mulvaney, Secretary Perry, and Secretary Pompeo—where "[e]veryone was informed."[556]

Other U.S. government officials also understood this scheme as a quid pro quo. Ambassador Taylor testified that as early as mid-July, it was "becoming clear" to him that "the meeting President Zelensky wanted was conditioned on investigations of Burisma and alleged Ukrainian influence in the 2016 elections" and that "this condition was driven by the irregular policy channel I had come to understand was guided by Mr. Giuliani."[557] Mr. Holmes similarly understood that by July, "it was made clear that some action on a Burisma/Biden investigation was a precondition for an Oval Office visit."[558] Dr. Hill testified that this quid pro quo was readily apparent after reading the July 25 call summary, explaining that it revealed that the White House meeting was used as "some kind of asset" that was "dangled out to the Ukrainian Government" to secure a political benefit.[559]

Final Preparation for Trump-Zelensky Call: Ambassador Volker Counseled Ukrainians and Ambassador Sondland Prepped President Trump

Ambassador Taylor testified that the call between President Trump and President Zelensky that ultimately occurred on July 25 was not confirmed until the last minute: "We were trying to schedule it for about a week in advance, that whole week. As I say, back and forth, yes, no, this time, that time. … it may have been about the day before that it was actually locked down, so about the 24th."[560] According to Ambassador Taylor, at least one person had prescient concerns about the call before it occurred: "Ambassador Bolton was not interested in having—did not want to have the call because he thought it was going to be a disaster. He thought that there could be some talk of investigations or worse on the call."[561]

Before the call took place on July 25, Ambassador Volker had lunch with Mr. Yermak in Kyiv. Ambassador Volker followed up with a text message to Mr. Yermak approximately 30 minutes before the call, noting that a White House visit was still on the table if, during the call, President Zelensky convinced President Trump that Ukraine would "investigate" and "get to the bottom of what happened" in 2016:

Volker: Good lunch – thanks. Heard from White House—assuming President Z convinces trump he will investigate / "get to the bottom of what happened" in 2016, we will nail down date for visit to Washington. Good luck! See you tomorrow - kurt

Ambassador Volker later informed Ambassador Sondland that he had relayed this "message" to Mr. Yermak, which Ambassador Sondland had conveyed to Ambassador Volker earlier that day:

Volker: Hi Gordon - got your message. Had a great lunch w Yermak and then passed your message to him. He will see you tomorrow. Think everything in place[562]

Ambassador Sondland testified that the "message" that Ambassador Volker conveyed to Mr. Yermak in advance of the July 25 call likely originated from an earlier conversation that Ambassador Sondland had with President Trump:

Q: So is it fair to say that this message is what you received from President Trump on that phone call that morning?
A: Again, if he testified to that, to refresh my own memory, then, yes, likely I would have received that from President Trump.
Q: But the sequence certainly makes sense, right?
A: Yeah, it does.
Q: You talked to President Trump.
A: Yeah.
Q: You told Kurt Volker to call you. You left a message for Kurt Volker. Kurt Volker sent this text message to Andriy Yermak to prepare President Zelensky and then President Trump had a phone call where President Zelensky spoke very similar to what was in this text message, right?
A: Right.
Q: And you would agree that the message in this—that is expressed here is that President Zelensky needs to convince Trump that he will do the investigations in order to nail down the date for a visit to Washington, D.C. Is that correct?
A: That's correct.[563]

Ambassador Sondland testified that he spoke with President Trump before the call with President Zelensky.[564] Mr. Morrison also confirmed that President Trump and Ambassador Sondland spoke before President Trump's call with President Zelensky.[565] Mr. Morrison stated that Ambassador Sondland emailed him on the morning of the call and listed "three topics that he was working on, the first of which was 'I spoke to the President this morning to brief him on the call.'"[566] According to Mr. Morrison, Ambassador Sondland "believed" that he helped to facilitate the July 25 call between President Trump and President Zelensky.[567]

On July 26, the day after the call between President Trump and President Zelensky, Ambassador Volker acknowledged his role in prepping President Zelensky for the call with

President Trump in a text to Mr. Giuliani: "Hi Mr Mayor – you may have heard—the President has [sic] a great phone call with the Ukrainian President yesterday. Exactly the right messages as we discussed."[568]

5.   **The President Asked the Ukrainian President to Interfere in the 2020 U.S. Election by Investigating the Bidens and 2016 Election Interference**

During a call on July 25, President Trump asked President Zelensky of Ukraine to "do us a favor though" and investigate his political opponent, former Vice President Joe Biden, and a debunked conspiracy theory that Ukraine interfered in the 2016 U.S. election. The next day, Ambassador Gordon Sondland informed President Trump that President Zelensky "was gonna do the investigation" and "anything" President Trump asked of him.

Overview

During a telephone call on July 25, 2019, President Donald J. Trump asked Ukrainian President Volodymyr Zelensky to investigate his political rival, former Vice President Joseph Biden, and a debunked conspiracy theory that Ukraine interfered in the 2016 U.S. election. President Trump also discussed the removal of Ambassador Marie Yovanovitch, former U.S. Ambassador to Ukraine, said that she was "bad news," and warned that she would "go through some things." Two witnesses who listened to the call testified that they immediately reported the details of the call to senior White House lawyers.

When asked by a reporter on October 3, 2019, what he had hoped President Zelensky would do following the call, President Trump responded: "Well, I would think that, if they were honest about it, they'd start a major investigation into the Bidens. It's a very simple answer."

Witnesses unanimously testified that President Trump's claims about former Vice President Biden and alleged Ukrainian interference in the 2016 U.S. election have been discredited. The witnesses reaffirmed that in late 2015 and early 2016, when former Vice President Biden advocated for the removal of a corrupt Ukrainian prosecutor, he acted in accordance with a "broad-based consensus" and the official policy of the United States, the European Union, and major international financial institutions. Witnesses also unanimously testified that the removal of that prosecutor made it more likely that Ukraine would investigate corruption, not less likely.

Dr. Fiona Hill, former Deputy Assistant to the President and Senior Director for European and Russian Affairs at the National Security Council, testified that the conspiracy theories about Ukrainian interference in the 2016 U.S. election touted by President Trump are a "fictional narrative that is being perpetrated and propagated by the Russian security services." She noted that President Trump's former Homeland Security Advisor Tom Bossert and former National Security Advisor H.R. McMaster repeatedly advised the President that the so-called "CrowdStrike" conspiracy theory that President Trump raised in the July 25 call is completely "debunked," and that allegations Ukraine interfered in the 2016 U.S. election are false.

Nonetheless, on July 26, 2019, U.S. Ambassador to the European Union Gordon Sondland met with senior Ukrainian officials in Kyiv and then informed President Trump that President Zelensky "was gonna do the investigation" into former Vice President Biden and alleged Ukrainian interference in the 2016 U.S. election. Ambassador Sondland added that President Zelensky would "do anything" President Trump asked of him. After the call, Ambassador Sondland told David Holmes, Counselor for Political Affairs at the U.S. Embassy in Kyiv, that President Trump "did not give a shit about Ukraine" and that he only cared about the "big stuff" that benefits his personal interests, like the "Biden investigation."

President Trump's Call with President Zelensky on July 25, 2019

On July 25, 2019, President Zelensky finally had a long-awaited phone call with Ukraine's most important international partner: The President of the United States.

It had been over three months since the two leaders first spoke. Despite a warm but largely non-substantive call on April 21, President Trump had since declined President Zelensky's invitation to attend his inauguration and directed Vice President Mike Pence not to attend either.[569] Ukrainian efforts to set a date for a promised Oval Office meeting with President Trump were stalled. As Mr. Holmes explained, following the April 21 call:

> President Zelensky's team immediately began pressing to set a date for that visit. President Zelensky and senior members of his team made clear that they wanted President Zelensky's first overseas trip to be to Washington, to send a strong signal of American support, and requested a call with President Trump as soon as possible.[570]

Before scheduling the July 25 call or a White House visit, President Trump met on June 28 with Russian President Vladimir Putin—whose armed forces were engaged in a war of attrition against U.S.-backed Ukrainian forces—on the sidelines of the G20 summit in Osaka, Japan.[571] During their meeting, President Trump and President Putin shared a joke about Russia's meddling in the 2016 U.S. election.[572]

On July 25, President Trump joined the call with President Zelensky from the Executive Residence at the White House, away from a small group of senior national security aides who would normally join him in the Oval Office for a conversation with a foreign head of state. President Trump and President Zelensky began to speak at 9:03 a.m. Washington time—4:03 p.m. in Kyiv. According to Tim Morrison, the newly-installed Senior Director for Europe and Russia on the NSC, President Zelensky spoke in Ukrainian and occasionally in "chopped English."[573] Translators interpreted the call on both sides.[574] American aides listening to the call from the White House Situation Room hoped that what was said over the next 30 minutes would provide President Zelensky with the strong U.S. endorsement he needed in order to successfully negotiate an end to the five-year-old war with Russia that had killed over 13,000 Ukrainian soldiers and to advance President Zelensky's ambitious anti-corruption initiatives in Ukraine.[575]

The Trump Administration's subject-matter experts, NSC Director for Ukraine Lt. Col. Alexander Vindman and Mr. Morrison, were both on the call.[576] They had prepared talking points for President Trump and were taking detailed notes of what both leaders said, so that they could promptly implement any agreed-upon actions.[577] They were joined by Lt. Gen. Keith Kellogg, National Security Advisor to the Vice President, and Jennifer Williams, Special Advisor to the Vice President for Europe and Russia. Assistant to the President Robert Blair, a senior aide to Acting Chief of Staff Mick Mulvaney, was also present, along with an NSC press officer.[578] Secretary of State Mike Pompeo listened from a different location, as did Dr. Charles M. Kupperman, the Deputy National Security Advisor.[579]

Notably, Secretary Pompeo did not reveal that he listened to the July 25 call when asked directly about it on *This Week* on September 22.[580] Neither Secretary Pompeo nor the State Department corrected the record until September 30, when "a senior State Department official" disclosed the Secretary of State's participation in the July 25 call.[581]

The two presidents first exchanged pleasantries. President Trump congratulated the Ukrainian leader on his party's parliamentary victory. In a nod to their shared experience as political outsiders, President Zelensky called President Trump "a great teacher" who informed his own efforts to involve "many many new people" in Ukraine's politics and "drain the swamp here in our country."[582]

The discussion turned to U.S. support for Ukraine. President Trump contrasted U.S. assistance to that of America's closest European allies, stating: "We spend a lot of effort and a lot of time. Much more than the European countries are doing and they should be helping you more than they are." The call then took a more ominous turn. President Trump stated that with respect to U.S. support for Ukraine, "I wouldn't say that it's reciprocal necessarily because things are happening that are not good but the United States has been very very good to Ukraine."[583]

President Zelensky, whose government receives billions of dollars in financial support from the European Union and its member states, responded that European nations were "not working as much as they should work for Ukraine," including in the area of enforcing sanctions against Russia.[584] He noted that "the United States is a much bigger partner than the European Union" and stated that he was "very grateful" because "the United States is doing quite a lot for Ukraine."[585]

President Zelensky then raised the issue of U.S. military assistance for Ukraine with President Trump: "I also would like to thank you for your great support in the area of defense"—an area where U.S. support is vital.[586] President Zelensky continued: "We are ready to continue to cooperate for the next steps specifically we are almost ready to buy more Javelins from the United States for defense purposes."[587] The Javelin anti-tank missiles, first transferred to Ukraine by the United States in 2018, were widely viewed by U.S. officials as a deterrent against further Russian encroachment into Ukrainian territory.[588]

Immediately after the Ukrainian leader raised the issue of U.S. military assistance to Ukraine, President Trump replied: "I would like you to do us a favor though because our country has been through a lot and Ukraine knows a lot about it."[589]

President Trump then explained the "favor" he wanted President Zelensky to do. He first requested that Ukraine investigate a discredited conspiracy theory aimed at undercutting the U.S. Intelligence Community's unanimous conclusion that the Russian government interfered in the 2016 U.S. election.[590] Specifically, President Trump stated:

> I would like you to find out what happened with this whole situation with Ukraine, they say Crowdstrike... I guess you have one of your wealthy people... The server, they say Ukraine has it. There are a lot of things that went on, the whole situation. I think you're surrounding yourself with some of the same people. I would like to have the Attorney General call you or your people and I would like you to get to the bottom of it. As you saw yesterday, that whole nonsense ended with a very poor performance by a man named Robert Mueller, an incompetent performance, but they say a lot of it started with Ukraine. Whatever you can do, it's very important that you do it if that's possible.[591]

President Trump was referencing the widely debunked conspiracy theory that the Ukrainian government—and not Russia—was behind the hack of Democratic National Committee (DNC) servers in 2016, and that the American cybersecurity firm CrowdStrike moved the DNC's servers to Ukraine to prevent U.S. law enforcement from examining them. This theory is often referred to in shorthand as "CrowdStrike" and has been promoted by the Russian government.[592]

For example, during a press conference in February 2017, just weeks after the U.S. Intelligence Community unanimously assessed in a public report that Russia interfered in the 2016 U.S. election to benefit the candidacy of Donald J. Trump, President Putin falsely asserted that "the Ukrainian government adopted a unilateral position in favour of one candidate. More than that, certain oligarchs, certainly with the approval of the political leadership, funded this candidate, or female candidate, to be more precise."[593] President Trump's reference in his July 25 telephone call to "one of your wealthy people" tracked closely with President Putin's accusations that "certain oligarchs" in Ukraine meddled in the 2016 U.S. election to support Democratic candidate Hillary Clinton.

Dr. Hill, an expert on Russia and President Putin, testified that the claim that "Russia and its security services did not conduct a campaign against our country and that perhaps, somehow for some reason, Ukraine did" is "a fictional narrative that is being perpetrated and propagated by the Russian security services themselves." Dr. Hill reaffirmed that the U.S. Intelligence Community's January 2017 conclusion that Russia interfered in the 2016 U.S. election is "beyond dispute, even if some of the underlying details must remain classified."[594]

Tom Bossert, President Trump's former Homeland Security Advisor, stated publicly that the CrowdStrike theory is "not only a conspiracy theory, it is completely debunked."[595] Dr. Hill testified that White House officials—including Mr. Bossert and former National Security Advisor H.R. McMaster—"spent a lot of time" refuting the CrowdStrike conspiracy theory to President Trump. Dr. Hill explained that Mr. Bossert and others "who were working on cybersecurity laid out to the President the facts about the interference." She affirmed that

President Trump was advised that "the alternative theory that Ukraine had interfered in the election was false."[596]

President Zelensky did not directly address President Trump's reference to CrowdStrike during the July 25 call, but he tried to assure President Trump that "it is very important for me and everything that you just mentioned earlier."[597] President Zelensky committed to proceed with an investigation, telling President Trump that he had "nobody but friends" in the new Ukrainian presidential administration, possibly attempting to rebut Rudy Giuliani's earlier claims that President Zelensky was surrounded by "enemies" of President Trump. President Zelensky then specifically noted that one of his assistants "spoke with Mr. Giuliani just recently and we are hoping very much that Mr. Giuliani will be able to travel to Ukraine and we will meet once he comes to Ukraine."[598]

Significantly, President Zelensky referenced Mr. Giuliani even before President Trump had mentioned him, demonstrating the Ukrainian leader's understanding that Mr. Giuliani represented President Trump's interests in Ukraine. The Ukrainian leader then reassured President Trump, "I also plan to surround myself with great people and in addition to that investigation" into the CrowdStrike conspiracy theory. He said, "I guarantee as the President of Ukraine that all the investigations will be done openly and candidly. That I can assure you."[599] President Trump replied, "Rudy very much knows what's happening and he is a very capable guy. If you could speak to him that would be great."[600]

Request to Investigate Bidens

President Trump then returned to his requested "favor," asking President Zelensky about the "[t]he other thing": that Ukraine investigate President Trump's U.S. political rival, former Vice President Biden, for allegedly ending an investigation into the Ukrainian energy company Burisma Holdings. Vice President Biden's son, Hunter Biden, served as a member of Burisma's board of directors. President Trump told President Zelensky:

> The other thing, There's a lot of talk about Biden's son, that Biden stopped the prosecution and a lot of people want to find out about that so whatever you can do with the Attorney General would be great. Biden went around bragging that he stopped the prosecution so if you can look into it... It sounds horrible to me.[601]

President Trump later continued, "I will have Mr. Giuliani give you a call and I am also going to have Attorney General Barr call and we will get to the bottom of it. I'm sure you will figure it out."[602]

In public remarks on October 3, 2019, a reporter asked President Trump, "what exactly did you hope Zelensky would do about the Bidens after your phone call? Exactly." President Trump responded: "Well, I would think that, if they were honest about it, they'd start a major investigation into the Bidens. It's a very simple answer."[603]

When President Trump asserted to President Zelensky during the July 25 call that former Vice President "Biden went around bragging that he stopped the prosecution," President Trump was apparently referring to Vice President Biden's involvement in the removal of the corrupt former Ukrainian prosecutor general, Viktor Shokin.

Multiple witnesses—including Dr. Hill, former U.S. Ambassador to Ukraine Marie Yovanovitch, Mr. Holmes, and Deputy Assistant Secretary of State George Kent—testified that they were not aware of any credible evidence to support the claim that former Vice President Biden acted inappropriately when he advocated for the removal of Mr. Shokin.[604] To the contrary, those witnesses confirmed that it was the official policy of the United States, the European Union, and major international financial institutions, to demand Mr. Shokin's dismissal. As Mr. Kent testified, there was "a broad-based consensus" that Mr. Shokin was "a typical Ukraine prosecutor who lived a lifestyle far in excess of his government salary, who never prosecuted anybody known for having committed a crime" and who "covered up crimes that were known to have been committed."[605] Mr. Kent further explained:

> What former Vice President Biden requested of former President of Ukraine Poroshenko was the removal of a corrupt prosecutor general, Viktor Shokin, who had undermined a program of assistance that we had spent, again, U.S. taxpayer money to try to build an independent investigator unit to go after corrupt prosecutors.[606]

As Ambassador Yovanovitch testified, the removal of a corrupt Ukrainian prosecutor general, who was not prosecuting enough corruption, increased the chance that alleged corruption in companies in Ukraine could be investigated.[607]

Mr. Shokin was a known associate of Mr. Giuliani. As described in Chapter 1, Mr. Giuliani had been communicating with Mr. Shokin since at least 2018.[608] Mr. Giuliani also lobbied the White House on behalf of Mr. Shokin to intervene earlier in 2019 when the State Department rejected a visa application for Mr. Shokin to visit the United States based upon Mr. Shokin's notorious corrupt conduct.[609] Ambassador Kurt Volker, U.S. Special Representative for Ukraine Negotiations, testified that he explicitly warned Mr. Giuliani—to no avail—against pursuing "the conspiracy theory that Vice President Biden would have been influenced in his duties as Vice President by money paid to his son."[610] Ambassador Volker affirmed that former Vice President Biden is "an honorable man, and I hold him in the highest regard."[611]

Attacks Against Ambassador Yovanovitch

During the July 25 call, President Trump also attacked Ambassador Yovanovitch, whom he had ousted as the U.S. Ambassador to Ukraine three months earlier after a concerted smear campaign perpetuated by Mr. Giuliani. As described in Chapter 1, Mr. Giuliani viewed Ambassador Yovanovitch—a decorated diplomat who had championed Ukrainian anti-corruption officials and activists—as an impediment to his activities in Ukraine.[612] President Trump told President Zelensky: "The former ambassador from the United States, the woman, was bad news and the people she was dealing with in the Ukraine were bad news so I just want to let you know that." He later added: "Well, she's going to go through some things."[613]

Ambassador Yovanovitch described her visceral reaction when she first read the call record, after the White House released it publicly on September 25, 2019. She testified, "I was shocked. I mean, I was very surprised that President Trump would—first of all, that I would feature repeatedly in a Presidential phone call, but secondly, that the President would speak about me or any ambassador in that way to a foreign counterpart."[614] When asked whether she felt "threatened" by President Trump's statement that "she's going to go through some things," Ambassador Yovanovitch answered that she did.[615]

Praise of Corrupt Former Ukrainian Prosecutor

After disparaging Ambassador Yovanovitch, who had an extensive record of combatting corruption, President Trump praised an unnamed former Ukrainian prosecutor general—referring to Yuriy Lutsenko—who was widely considered to be corrupt and had promoted false allegations against Ambassador Yovanovitch.[616] President Trump told President Zelensky: "Good because I heard you had a prosecutor who was very good and he was shut down and that's really unfair. A lot of people are talking about that, the way they shut your very good prosecutor down and you had some very bad people involved."[617] He later added, "I heard the prosecutor was treated very badly and he was a very fair prosecutor so good luck with everything."[618]

At the time of the July 25 call, Mr. Lutsenko—who was collaborating with Mr. Giuliani to smear Ambassador Yovanovitch and the Bidens—was still the Ukrainian prosecutor general. Mr. Holmes testified that Mr. Lutsenko "was not a good partner. He had failed to deliver on the promised reforms that he had committed to when he took office, and he was using his office to insulate and protect political allies while presumably enriching himself."[619] By July 2019, Mr. Holmes assessed that Mr. Lutsenko was "trying to angle to keep his job" under the new Zelensky Administration and that part of his strategy was "appealing to Rudy Giuliani and Donald Trump by pushing out these false theories about the Bidens and the 2016 election."[620]

Multiple witnesses testified that another former Ukrainian prosecutor, Mr. Shokin, was also considered to be corrupt. For example, Mr. Kent testified during his deposition that Mr. Lutsenko and Mr. Shokin were "corrupt former prosecutors" who were "peddling false information in order to extract revenge against those who had exposed their misconduct, including U.S. diplomats, Ukrainian anticorruption officials, and reform-minded civil society groups in Ukraine."[621] Ambassador Volker testified at his public hearing that Mr. Lutsenko was "not credible, and was acting in a self-serving capacity."[622] Mr. Holmes further noted that Mr. Lutsenko "resisted fully empowering truly independent anticorruption institutions that would help ensure that no Ukrainians, however powerful, were above the law."[623]

After the call, the White House press office issued a short and incomplete summary of the call, omitting major elements of the conversation. The press statement read:

> Today, President Donald J. Trump spoke by telephone with President Volodymyr Zelenskyy of Ukraine to congratulate him on his recent election. President Trump and President Zelenskyy discussed ways to strengthen the relationship between the United States and Ukraine, including energy and economic cooperation. Both leaders also expressed that they look forward to the opportunity to meet.[624]

Concerns Raised by Lieutenant Colonel Alexander Vindman

Prior to President Trump's July 25 call with President Zelensky, Lt. Col. Vindman had prepared—with Mr. Morrison's review and approval—a call briefing package, including talking points for President Trump's use. This was consistent with the NSC's regular process of preparing for the President's phone calls with foreign leaders.[625] The NSC-drafted talking points did not include any reference to Biden, Burisma, CrowdStrike, or alleged Ukrainian interference in the 2016 U.S. election.[626]

Lt. Col. Vindman testified during his deposition that, prior to the July 25 call, he was aware of concerns from former National Security Advisor John Bolton and other U.S. officials that President Trump might raise these discredited issues with President Zelensky.[627] Indeed, Ambassador Bolton had resisted scheduling the call because he believed it might be a "disaster."[628]

As he sat in the White House Situation Room listening to the leaders, Lt. Col. Vindman quickly recognized that the President's conversation was diverging from the talking points he helped prepare based on the interagency policy process, and "straying" into an "unproductive narrative" promoted by Mr. Giuliani and other "external and nongovernmental influencers"[629]—topics that Lt. Col. Vindman dubbed "stray voltage."[630]

Lt. Col. Vindman knew immediately that he had a duty to report the contents of the call to the White House lawyers. He explained, "I had concerns, and it was my duty to report my concerns to the proper—proper people in the chain of command."[631] Lt. Col. Vindman testified that President Trump's request that a foreign leader dependent on the United States open an investigation into his U.S. political opponent constituted a "demand" that President Zelensky had to meet in order to secure a White House meeting:

> So, Congressman, the power disparity between the President of the United States and the President of Ukraine is vast, and, you know, in the President asking for something, it became—there was—in return for a White House meeting, because that's what this was about. This was about getting a White House meeting. It was a demand for him to fulfill his—fulfill this particular prerequisite in order to get the meeting.[632]

Lt. Col. Vindman further testified that President Trump's demand of the Ukrainian leader was "inappropriate" and "improper," and that it would undermine U.S. national security:

> Chairman, as I said in my statement, it was inappropriate. It was improper for the President to request—to demand an investigation into a political opponent, especially a foreign power where there's, at best, dubious belief that this would be a completely impartial investigation, and that this would have significant implications if it became public knowledge, and it would be perceived as a partisan play. It would undermine our Ukraine policy, and it would undermine our national security.[633]

Within an hour of the call ending, Lt. Col. Vindman reported his concerns to John A. Eisenberg, the Deputy Counsel to the President for National Security Affairs and the Legal

Advisor to the NSC , and Michael Ellis, a Senior Associate Counsel to the President and the Deputy Legal Advisor to the NSC.[634] Lt. Col. Vindman recounted the content of the call based on his handwritten notes and told the lawyers that he believed it was "wrong" for President Trump to ask President Zelensky to investigate Vice President Biden.[635]

Concerns Raised by Timothy Morrison

After 17 years as a Republican Congressional staffer and approximately a year serving elsewhere on the NSC staff, Mr. Morrison assumed his position as the NSC's Senior Director for Europe and Russia on July 15, 2019, only 10 days before President Trump's call with President Zelensky.[636]

Before he transitioned into his new role, Mr. Morrison met with his predecessor, Dr. Hill. She advised him to stay away from efforts orchestrated by Mr. Giuliani and Ambassador Sondland to pressure Ukraine into investigating a "bucket of issues" that included "Burisma the company," and "Hunter Biden on the board."[637] Dr. Hill also warned Mr. Morrison before the July 25 call about the President's interest in alleged Ukrainian interference in the 2016 U.S. election related to the DNC server.[638]

Mr. Morrison testified that he had no knowledge of any investigations at the time, but after performing a Google search of "what is Burisma?" and seeing the name Hunter Biden, Mr. Morrison decided to "stay away."[639] Even though he was new to the portfolio, Mr. Morrison promptly concluded that because "Burisma" involved Hunter Biden, and because former Vice President Biden was running for President, such investigations could be a "problematic" area.[640] Mr. Morrison further explained that he tried to stay away from requests related to Burisma and the 2016 U.S. election because these investigations were not related to "the proper policy process that I was involved in on Ukraine," and "had nothing to do with the issues that the interagency was working on."[641]

With that background in mind, Mr. Morrison admitted he was "concerned" when, while listening to the call on July 25, he heard President Trump raise "issues related to the [DNC] server." Ultimately, Mr. Morrison said, "the call was not the full-throated endorsement of the Ukraine reform agenda that I was hoping to hear."[642]

In "fairly short order," Mr. Morrison reported the contents of the call to Mr. Eisenberg and Mr. Ellis, the NSC lawyers. He asked them to review the call, which he feared would be "damaging" if leaked.[643] Mr. Morrison stated that at the time of the call, he "did not have a view" on whether the call was "appropriate and proper."[644] He also stated that he "was not concerned that anything illegal was discussed."[645] During his deposition, however, Mr. Morrison clarified, "I did not then and I do not now opine … as to the legality" of what happened on the call.[646]

In a second meeting with Mr. Eisenberg, Mr. Morrison requested that access to the electronic files of the call record be restricted. This was an unusual request. Mr. Morrison confirmed to the Committee that he had never before asked the NSC Legal Advisor to restrict access to a presidential call record.[647] It was also unusual because Mr. Morrison raised restricting access with Mr. Eisenberg despite the fact that Mr. Morrison himself had the authority, as an NSC senior director, to recommend restrictions on the relevant files to the NSC's Executive Secretariat.

Lt. Col. Vindman also discussed restricting access to the July 25 call summary with Mr. Eisenberg and Mr. Ellis. At some point after the call, Lt. Col. Vindman discussed with the NSC lawyers the "sensitivity" of the matters raised on the call and "the fact that … there are constant leaks."[648] Lt. Col. Vindman explained that "[f]rom a foreign policy professional perspective, all of these types of calls would inherently be sensitive."[649] But the July 25 call was particularly sensitive because it could "undermine our relationship with the Ukrainians" given that it "would implicate a partisan play."[650] The NSC lawyers, therefore, believed that it was "appropriate to restrict access for the purpose of the leaks" and "to preserv[e] the integrity" of the transcript.[651] Lt. Col. Vindman recalled that Mr. Ellis raised the idea of placing the call summary on the NSC's server for highly classified information and Mr. Eisenberg "gave the go-ahead."[652]

Some weeks after his discussions with the NSC attorneys, Mr. Morrison could not locate the call record. He contacted the staff of the NSC's Executive Secretariat in search of an explanation and was informed that "John Eisenberg had directed it to be moved to a different server" utilized by the NSC staff for highly classified information.[653] This transfer occurred despite Mr. Morrison's view that the call record did not meet the requirements to be placed on the highly classified system.[654]

Mr. Eisenberg later told Mr. Morrison that the call record had been placed on the highly classified system by "mistake."[655] Even after Mr. Eisenberg stated that the call record was moved to the highly classified system by "mistake," it nevertheless remained on that system until at least the third week of September 2019, shortly before its declassification and public release by the White House.[656]

Concerns Raised by Jennifer Williams

Vice President Pence's advisor, Ms. Williams, had listened to nearly a dozen phone calls between President Trump and other heads of state prior to July 25, 2019, as well as Vice President Pence's April 23 call with President Zelensky.[657] As she sat listening to President Trump's July 25 call, she was struck by his requests relating to Vice President Biden. She stated that she believed that President Trump's comments were "unusual and inappropriate."[658]

Ms. Williams testified that she thought that "references to specific individuals and investigations, such as former Vice President Biden and his son" were "political in nature, given that the former Vice President is a political opponent of the President."[659] The comments struck her as "more specific to the President in nature, to his personal political agenda," as opposed to "a broader foreign policy objective of the United States."[660] She added, "it was the first time I had heard internally the President reference particular investigations that previously I had only heard about through Mr. Giuliani's press interviews and press reporting."[661]

Significantly, Ms. Williams, who had learned about the hold on security assistance for Ukraine on July 3, also said that the Trump-Zelensky call "shed some light on possible other motivations behind a security assistance hold."[662]

"Burisma" Omitted from Call Record

Mr. Morrison, Lt. Col. Vindman, and Ms. Williams all agreed that the publicly released record of the call was substantially accurate, but Lt. Col. Vindman and Ms. Williams both testified that President Zelensky made an explicit reference to "Burisma" that was not included in the call record. Specifically, Lt. Col. Vindman testified that his notes indicated President Zelensky used the word "Burisma"—instead of generically referring to "the company"—when discussing President Trump's request to investigate the Bidens.[663] Ms. Williams' notes also reflected that President Zelensky had said "Burisma" later in the call when referring to a "case."[664]

Lt. Col. Vindman indicated that President Zelensky's mention of "Burisma" was notable because it suggested that the Ukrainian leader was "prepped for this call." He explained that "frankly, the President of Ukraine would not necessarily know anything about this company Burisma." Lt. Col. Vindman continued, "he would certainly understand some of this—some of these elements because the story had been developing for some time, but the fact that he mentioned specifically Burisma seemed to suggest to me that he was prepped for this call."[665]

The Substance of the Call Remained Tightly Controlled

Ms. Williams testified that staff in the Office of the Vice President placed the draft call record in the Vice President's nightly briefing book on July 25.[666]

Separately, and following established protocols for coordinating U.S. government activities toward Ukraine, Lt. Col. Vindman provided Mr. Kent at the State Department with a readout. Because Mr. Kent had worked on Ukraine policy for many years, Lt. Col. Vindman sought Mr. Kent's "expert view" on the investigations requested by the President. Mr. Kent informed him that "there was no substance" behind the CrowdStrike conspiracy theory and "took note of the fact that there was a call to investigate the Bidens."[667] Recalling this conversation, Mr. Kent testified that Lt. Col. Vindman said "he could not share the majority of what was discussed [on the July 25 call] because of the very sensitive nature of what was discussed," but that Lt. Col. Vindman noted that the call "went into the direction of some of the most extreme narratives that have been discussed publicly."[668]

Ambassador Sondland Followed Up on President Trump's Request for Investigations

Soon after arriving in Kyiv from Brussels on July 25, Ambassador Sondland asked the U.S. Embassy to arrange a meeting the next day with Ukrainian presidential aide Andriy Yermak.[669]

On the morning of July 26, Ambassadors Sondland, Volker and Taylor—accompanied by Mr. Holmes, who acted as their official notetaker—went to the Presidential Administration

Building in central Kyiv for meetings with Ukrainian officials.[670] Contrary to standard procedure, Mr. Holmes and Ambassador Taylor did not receive readouts of the July 25 call, so they were unaware of what President Trump and President Zelensky had discussed.[671] Ambassador Volker also did not receive an official readout of the July 25 call from the NSC staff. He testified that Andriy Yermak, a senior aide to President Zelensky, simply characterized it as a "good call" in which "President Zelensky did reiterate his commitment to reform and fighting corruption in Ukraine."[672]

The first meeting on July 26 was with Chief of Staff to President Zelensky Andriy Bohdan.[673] Regarding the July 25 call, Mr. Holmes recalled Mr. Bohdan sharing that "President Trump had expressed interest … in President Zelensky's personnel decisions related to the Prosecutor General's office [PGO]."[674] Mr. Holmes further testified that Mr. Bohdan then "started asking … about individuals I've since come to understand they were considering appointing to different roles in the PGO."[675] Mr. Holmes explained that he "didn't understand it," and that "[i]t wasn't until I read the July 25th phone call transcript that I realized that the President [Trump] had mentioned Mr. Lutsenko in the call."[676]

Subsequently, Ambassadors Sondland, Taylor, and Volker met with President Zelensky and other senior officials. Mr. Holmes once again took notes.[677] He testified "During the meeting, President Zelensky stated that, during the July 25th call, President Trump had, quote, 'three times raised some very sensitive issues' and that he would have to follow up—he, Zelensky—would have to follow up on those issues when he and President Trump met in person."[678] After he read the transcript of the July 25 call, Mr. Holmes determined that President Zelensky's mention of "sensitive issues" was a reference to President Trump's demands for a "Burisma Biden investigation."[679]

Catherine Croft, Special Advisor to Ambassador Kurt Volker, was also in Kyiv on July 26. Although she did not attend the meeting with President Zelensky, she received a readout from Ambassadors Volker and Taylor later that day, as they were traveling in an embassy vehicle. Ms. Croft testified that her handwritten notes from that readout indicate "the President [Trump] had raised investigations multiple times" in his July 25 call with President Zelensky.[680] Ambassadors Sondland and Taylor told the Committee that they did not recall President Zelensky's comments about investigations.[681] Ambassador Volker similarly did not recall that the issue of investigations was discussed, but testified that he did not dispute the validity of "notes taken contemporaneously at the meeting."[682]

Ambassador Sondland Met One-on-One with Ukrainian Presidential Aide

The meeting with President Zelensky ended around noon.[683] After the meeting, Ambassadors Taylor and Volker departed the Presidential Administration building for a visit to the front lines of the war with Russia in eastern Ukraine.[684] Ambassador Sondland separately headed for Mr. Yermak's office. Mr. Holmes testified that, at the last minute, he received instruction from his leadership at the U.S. Embassy to join Ambassador Sondland.[685] By that point, Mr. Holmes recalled, he "was a flight of stairs behind Ambassador Sondland as he headed to meet with Mr. Yermak."[686] Mr. Holmes continued, "When I reached Mr. Yermak's office, Ambassador Sondland had already gone in to the meeting."[687] Mr. Holmes then "explained to

Mr. Yermak's assistant that I was supposed to join the meeting as the Embassy's representative and strongly urged her to let me in, but she told me that Ambassador Sondland and Mr. Yermak had insisted that the meeting be one on one with no note taker."[688] Mr. Holmes "then waited in the anteroom until the meeting ended, along with a member of Ambassador Sondland's staff and a member of the U.S. Embassy Kyiv staff."[689]

Ambassador Sondland's meeting with Mr. Yermak lasted approximately 30 minutes.[690] When it ended, Ambassador Sondland did not provide Mr. Holmes an explanation of what they discussed.[691] Ambassador Sondland later testified that he did not "recall the specifics" of his conversation with Mr. Yermak, but he believed "the issue of investigations was probably a part of that agenda or meeting."[692]

Call Between President Trump and Ambassador Sondland on July 26, 2019

After a busy morning of meetings with Ukrainian officials on July 26, Ambassador Sondland indicated that he wanted to get lunch. Mr. Holmes interjected that he would "be happy to join" Ambassador Sondland and two other State Department colleagues accompanying him "if he wanted to brief me out on his meeting with Mr. Yermak or discuss other issues."[693] Ambassador Sondland accepted the offer. The diplomats proceeded "to a nearby restaurant and sat on an outdoor terrace."[694] Mr. Holmes "sat directly across from Ambassador Sondland," close enough that they could "share an appetizer."[695]

Mr. Holmes recounted that "at first, the lunch was largely social. Ambassador Sondland selected a bottle of wine that he shared among the four of us, and we discussed topics such as marketing strategies for his hotel business."[696] Later during the meal, Ambassador Sondland "said that he was going to call President Trump to give him an update."[697] Ambassador Sondland then placed a call on his unsecure mobile phone. Mr. Holmes was taken aback. He told the Committee, "it was, like, a really extraordinary thing, it doesn't happen very often"—a U.S. Ambassador picking up his mobile phone at an outdoor cafe and dialing the President of the United States.[698]

Mr. Holmes, who was sitting directly opposite from Ambassador Sondland, said he "heard him announce himself several times, along the lines of, 'Gordon Sondland, holding for the President.' It appeared that he was being transferred through several layers of switchboards and assistants, and I then noticed Ambassador Sondland's demeanor changed and understood that he had been connected to President Trump."[699]

Mr. Holmes stated he was able to hear the first part of Ambassador Sondland's conversation with President Trump because it was "quite loud" and "quite distinctive" when the President began speaking. When President Trump started speaking, Ambassador Sondland "sort of winced and held the phone away from his ear," and "did that for the first couple exchanges."[700]

Recounting the conversation that followed, Mr. Holmes testified:

I heard Ambassador Sondland greet the President and explain he was calling from Kyiv. I heard President Trump then clarify that Ambassador Sondland was in Ukraine. Ambassador Sondland replied, yes, he was in Ukraine, and went on to state that President Zelensky, quote, "loves your ass." I then heard President Trump ask, "So he's going to do the investigation?" Ambassador Sondland replied that he is going to do it, adding that President Zelensky will do "anything you ask him to do."[701]

President Trump has denied that he spoke to Ambassador Sondland on July 26 and told reporters, "I know nothing about that."[702] But in his public testimony before the Committee, Ambassador Sondland noted that White House call records made available to his legal counsel confirmed that the July 26 call in fact occurred.[703] Ambassador Sondland further explained that Mr. Holmes's testimony—specifically, a "reference to A$AP Rocky"—refreshed his recollection about the July 26 call, which Ambassador Sondland had not originally disclosed to the Committee.[704]

Although Ambassador Sondland did not believe he mentioned the Bidens by name, he testified that with regard to the substance of his July 26 conversation with President Trump: "I have no reason to doubt that this conversation included the subject of investigations."[705] He added that he had "no reason" to doubt Mr. Holmes' testimony about the contents of the call, and that he would "have been more surprised if President Trump had not mentioned investigations, particularly given what we were hearing from Mr. Giuliani about the President's concerns."[706] Asked about his statement to President Trump that President Zelensky "loves your ass," Ambassador Sondland replied: "That sounds like something I would say. That's how President Trump and I communicate, a lot of four-letter words, in this case three letter."[707]

After the call between Ambassador Sondland and President Trump ended, Ambassador Sondland remarked to Mr. Holmes that "the President was in a bad mood," as "was often the case early in the morning."[708] Mr. Holmes, who had learned about the freeze on U.S. security assistance days earlier, was attempting to clarify the President's thinking, and said he "took the opportunity to ask Ambassador Sondland for his candid impression of the President's views on Ukraine":

> In particular, I asked Ambassador Sondland if it was true that the President did not give a shit about Ukraine. Ambassador Sondland agreed that the President did not give a shit about Ukraine. I asked, why not, and Ambassador Sondland stated, the President only cares about, quote, unquote, "big stuff." I noted there was, quote, unquote, big stuff going on in Ukraine, like a war with Russia. And Ambassador Sondland replied that he meant, quote, unquote, "big stuff" that benefits the President, like the, quote, unquote, "Biden investigation" that Mr. Giuliani was pushing. The conversation then moved on to other topics.[709]

Ambassador Sondland did not dispute the substance of Mr. Holmes' recollection of this discussion. He stated, "I don't recall my exact words, but clearly the President, beginning on May 23, when we met with him in the Oval Office, was not a big fan" of Ukraine. Asked whether President Trump "was a big fan of the investigations," Ambassador Sondland replied: "Apparently so."[710] Asked to clarify if, during his July 26 conversation with Mr. Holmes, he recalled "at least referring to an investigation that Rudy Giuliani was pushing," Ambassador Sondland replied, "I would have, yes."[711]

Mr. Holmes Informed U.S. Embassy Leadership about President Trump's Call with Ambassador Sondland

After the lunch, Mr. Holmes dropped off Ambassador Sondland at his hotel, the Hyatt Regency Kyiv. Mr. Holmes then returned to the U.S. Embassy.[712] Ambassador Taylor, the acting Ambassador in Kyiv, was still visiting the front line. So when he arrived at the Embassy, Mr. Holmes briefed his immediate supervisor, Kristina Kvien, Deputy Chief of Mission at U.S. Embassy Kyiv, about the President's call with Ambassador Sondland and Ambassador Sondland's subsequent description of President Trump's priorities for Ukraine.[713]

After taking a long-planned vacation from July 27 to August 5, Mr. Holmes told Ambassador Taylor about his lunch with Ambassador Sondland on the first day he returned to work, August 6.[714] Mr. Holmes told the Committee that he did not brief the call in detail to Ambassador Taylor because "it was obvious what the President was pressing for":

> Of course that's what's going on. Of course the President is pressing for a Biden investigation before he'll do these things the Ukrainians want. There was nodding agreement. So did I go through every single word in the call? No, because everyone by that point agreed, it was obvious what the President was pressing for.[715]

In October 2019, following the public release of testimony by several witnesses pursuant to the Committee's impeachment inquiry, Mr. Holmes reminded Ambassador Taylor about Ambassador Sondland's July 26 conversation with President Trump. Ambassador Taylor was preparing to return to Washington and testify publicly before the Committee. Mr. Holmes had been following news coverage of the inquiry and realized he had unique, firsthand evidence that "potentially bore on the question of whether the President did, in fact, have knowledge" of efforts to press the Ukrainian President to publicly announce investigations:

> I came to realize that I had firsthand knowledge regarding certain events on July 26 that had not otherwise been reported and that those events potentially bore on the question of whether the President did, in fact, have knowledge that those senior officials were using the levers of diplomatic power to influence the new Ukrainian President to announce the opening of a criminal investigation against President Trump's political opponent. It is at that point that I made the observation to Ambassador Taylor that the incident I had witnessed on July 26th had acquired greater significance, which is what he reported in his testimony last week and is what led to the subpoena for me to appear here today.[716]

Mr. Holmes testified that the July 26 call became "sort of a touchstone piece of information" for diplomats at the U.S. Embassy in Kyiv who "were trying to understand why we weren't able to get the meeting" between President Trump and President Zelensky and "what was going on with the security hold."[717] He elaborated:

I would refer back to it repeatedly in our, you know, morning staff meetings. We'd talk about what we're trying to do. We're trying to achieve this, that. Maybe it will convince the President to have the meeting. And I would say, 'Well, as we know, he doesn't really care about Ukraine. He cares about some other things. And we're trying to keep Ukraine out of our politics and so, you know, that's what we're up against.' And I would refer— use that repeatedly as a refrain.[718]

6. **The President Wanted Ukraine to Announce the Investigations Publicly**

> *In the weeks following the July 25 call, President Trump's hand-picked representatives carried out his wishes to condition a coveted White House meeting for the Ukrainian President on the public announcement of investigations beneficial to President Trump. Top U.S. officials, including the Secretary of State and Secretary of Energy, were "in the loop."*

Overview

In the weeks following the July 25 call, during which President Trump had pressed Ukrainian President Volodymyr Zelensky to "do us a favor though," the President's representatives worked to secure from the Ukrainian President a public announcement about the requested investigations as a condition for the White House meeting.

That meeting would have conferred vital support on a new president who relied on the United States to help defend his nation militarily, diplomatically, and politically against Russian aggression. U.S. Ambassador to the European Union Gordon Sondland provided testimony and quoted from documents demonstrating that he kept everyone "in the loop" about the plan, including the Secretaries of State and Energy.

Ambassadors Sondland and Volker worked closely with Mr. Giuliani, the President's personal lawyer, to help draft Ukraine's public statement. They sought to ensure that President Zelensky explicitly used the words "Burisma"—a reference to allegations about former Vice President Biden and his son—and "2016 elections."

Ukrainian officials were "very uncomfortable" with the provision of this statement, which they understood to be a requirement and a "deliverable" demanded by President Trump. The Ukrainian President was elected on a platform of rooting out public corruption, and so he resisted issuing the statement. Instead, President Zelensky's aides asked whether an official request for legal assistance with investigations had been made through appropriate channels at the U.S. Department of Justice. No such formal request was ever made. Consequently, Ukrainian officials made clear to Ambassador Volker that they did not support issuing a public statement because it could "play into" U.S. domestic politics. Nevertheless, U.S. efforts to secure a public statement continued.

Giuliani Met with Ukrainian Presidential Aide Andriy Yermak in Madrid and Discussed a White House Meeting

On July 26, the day after the call between President Trump and President Zelensky, Ambassador Volker wrote to Mr. Giuliani to confirm that he would soon be meeting with Andriy Yermak, a Ukrainian presidential aide, to "help" efforts.[719]

Ambassador Volker texted: "Please send dates when you will be in Madrid. I am seeing Yermak tomorrow morning. He will come to you in Madrid. Thanks for your help! Kurt."[720]

114

Mr. Giuliani replied that he would travel to Spain from August 1 to 5, and Ambassador Volker affirmed that he would tell the Ukrainian presidential aide to "visit with you there."[721] Ambassador Volker kept himself apprised of plans, texting Mr. Yermak on August 1 to ensure that everything was "on track" for the meeting in Spain's capital. He also asked whether Mr. Yermak planned to visit Washington.[722]

On August 2, Mr. Yermak and Mr. Giuliani met in Madrid.[723] Ambassador Volker received a meeting summary from Mr. Yermak the same day: "My meeting with Mr. Mayor was very good." Mr. Yermak added: "We asked for White House meeting during week start [sic] 16 Sept. Waiting for confirmation. Maybe you know the date?"[724]

The Madrid meeting set off a "series of discussions" among Mr. Giuliani, Ambassador Volker, and Ambassador Sondland about the need for President Zelensky to issue a public statement about the investigations into Burisma and the 2016 election conspiracy theory in order to secure a White House meeting with President Trump.[725] Ambassador Volker first spoke to Mr. Giuliani, who said that he thought Ukraine "should issue a statement."[726] Ambassador Volker then spoke to Mr. Yermak, who affirmed that the Ukrainian leader was "prepared to make a statement" that "would reference Burisma and 2016 in a wider context of bilateral relations and rooting out corruption anyway."[727]

Mr. Giuliani, acting as President Trump's personal attorney, exerted significant influence in the process. On August 4, Mr. Yermak inquired again about the presidential meeting. Ambassador Volker replied that he would speak with Mr. Giuliani later that day and would call the Ukrainian aide afterward.[728] Ambassador Volker texted the former mayor about the Madrid meeting and asked for a phone call. Mr. Giuliani replied: "It was excellent I can call a little later."[729]

Phone records obtained by the Committees show a 16 minute call on August 5 between Ambassador Volker and Mr. Giuliani.[730] Ambassador Volker texted Mr. Yermak: "Hi Andrey—had a good long talk w Rudy—call anytime—Kurt."[731] During the same period, Ambassador Volker informed Ambassador Sondland that "Giuliani was happy with that meeting," and "it looks like things are turning around."[732]

"Potus Really Wants the Deliverable" Before Scheduling a White House Visit for President Zelensky

Things had not turned around by August 7. Ambassador Volker texted Mr. Giuliani to recommend that he report to "the boss"—President Trump—about his meeting with Mr. Yermak in Madrid. He wrote:

Hi Rudy—hope you made it back safely. Let's meet if you are coming to DC. And would be good if you could convey results of your meeting in Madrid to the boss so we can get a firm date for a visit.[733]

The Committees did not find evidence that Mr. Giuliani responded to Ambassador Volker's text message.

However, call records show that the next day, on August 8, Mr. Giuliani connected with the White House Situation Room switchboard in the early afternoon, Eastern Time, for 42 seconds, and then again for one minute, 25 seconds.[734]

The same day, Mr. Giuliani texted several times with a number associated with the White House. The Committees were unable to identify the official associated with the phone number. In the mid-afternoon, someone using a telephone number associated with the Office of Management and Budget (OMB) called Mr. Giuliani, and the call lasted for nearly 13 minutes. Mr. Giuliani called the OMB number and the White House Situation Room several more times that evening, but each time connected for only a few seconds or not at all.

Rudy Giuliani Call History, August 8

Date	Connect-ing Time (EDT)	Duration of Call	Caller	Recipient
08/08/19	12:44:56	0:42	Giuliani, Rudy	White House Switchboard (Situation Room)[735]
08/08/19	12:45:38	1:25	Giuliani, Rudy	White House Switchboard (Situation Room)[736]
08/08/19	13:02:37	TEXT	Giuliani, Rudy	White House Number[737]
08/08/19	13:02:37	TEXT	Giuliani, Rudy	White House Number[738]
08/08/19	13:02:57	TEXT	Giuliani, Rudy	White House Number[739]
08/08/19	14:14:53	TEXT	White House Number	Giuliani, Rudy[740]
08/08/19	14:15:17	TEXT	Giuliani, Rudy	White House Number[741]
08/08/19	14:21:13	TEXT	Giuliani, Rudy	White House Number[742]
08/08/19	15:13:05	12:56	OMB Number	Giuliani, Rudy[743]
08/08/19	15:56:44	0:00	Giuliani, Rudy	OMB Number[744]
08/08/19	15:56:51	0:00	Giuliani, Rudy	OMB Number[745]
08/08/19	15:57:05	0:00	Giuliani, Rudy	OMB Number[746]
08/08/19	15:57:21	0:22	Giuliani, Rudy	White House Switchboard (Situation Room)[747]
08/08/19	17:20:33	0:17	Giuliani, Rudy	White House Switchboard (Situation Room)[748]
08/08/19	19:14:48	0:00	Giuliani, Rudy	White House Switchboard (Situation Room)[749]

Approximately 30 minutes after his text to Mr. Giuliani on August 7, Ambassador Volker received a text message from Mr. Yermak: "Do you have some news about White House

116

meeting date?"[750] Ambassador Volker responded that he had asked Mr. Giuliani to "weigh in," presumably with the President, "following your meeting," and that Ambassador Sondland would be speaking with President Trump on Friday, August 9. Ambassador Volker added: "We are pressing this."[751] The next day, on August 8, Mr. Yermak texted Ambassador Volker to report that he had "some news."[752] Ambassador Volker replied that he was available to speak at that time.[753]

Later on the evening of August 8, Eastern Time, Mr. Giuliani sent a text message to a phone number associated with the White House. Approximately one hour 15 minutes later, someone using an unidentified number ("-1") dialed Mr. Giuliani three times in rapid succession. Less than three minutes later, Mr. Giuliani dialed the White House switchboard for the White House Situation Room. When the call did not connect, Mr. Giuliani immediately dialed another general number for the White House switchboard and connected for 47 seconds. Approximately 16 minutes later, someone using the "-1" number called Mr. Giuliani and connected for just over four minutes.[754]

Rudy Giuliani Call History, August 8, cont.

Date	Connecting Time (EDT)	Duration of Call	Caller	Recipient
08/08/19	20:53:13	TEXT	Giuliani, Rudy	White House Number[755]
08/08/19	22:09:31	0:00	"-1"	Giuliani, Rudy[756]
08/08/19	22:09:32	0:05	"-1"	Giuliani, Rudy[757]
08/08/19	22:09:46	0:00	"-1"	Giuliani, Rudy (Cell 2)[758]
08/08/19	22:09:47	0:02	"-1"	Giuliani, Rudy (Cell 2)[759]
08/08/19	22:10:08	0:05	"-1"	Giuliani, Rudy[760]
08/08/19	22:11:52	0:00	Giuliani, Rudy	OMB Number[761]
08/08/19	22:12:16	0:00	Giuliani, Rudy	White House Switchboard (Situation Room)[762]
08/08/19	22:12:25	0:47	Giuliani, Rudy	White House Switchboard[763]
08/08/19	22:28:51	4:06	"-1"	Giuliani, Rudy[764]

Late the next morning Washington time, on August 9, Ambassador Volker texted Mr. Giuliani and Ambassador Sondland:

Hi Mr. Mayor! Had a good chat with Yermak last night. He was pleased with your phone call. Mentioned Z [President Zelensky] making a statement. Can we all get on the phone to make sure I advise Z [President

Zelensky] correctly as to what he should be saying? Want to make sure we get this done right. Thanks![765]

It is unclear which "phone call" Ambassador Volker was referencing.

Text messages and call records obtained by the Committees show that Ambassador Volker and Mr. Giuliani connected by phone twice around noon Eastern Time on August 9 for several minutes each.[766] Following the calls with Mr. Giuliani, Ambassador Volker created a three-way group chat using WhatsApp that included Ambassador Volker, Ambassador Sondland, and Mr. Yermak.[767]

At 2:24 p.m. Eastern Time on August 9, Ambassador Volker texted the group: "Hi Andrey—we have all consulted here, including with Rudy. Can you do a call later today or tomorrow your afternoon time?"[768] Ambassador Sondland texted that he had a call scheduled for 3 p.m. Eastern Time "for the three of us. [State Department] Ops will call."[769]

Call records obtained by the Committees show that on August 9, Ambassador Sondland twice called numbers associated with the White House, once in early afternoon for approximately 18 minutes, and once in late afternoon for two minutes, 25 seconds with a number associated with OMB.[770]

By early evening, minutes after his second call with OMB number, Ambassador Volker and Ambassador Sondland discussed a breakthrough they had reached in obtaining a date for a White House visit, noting that President Trump really wanted "the deliverable":

Sondland:	[Tim] Morrison ready to get dates as soon as Yermak confirms.
Volker:	Excellent!! How did you sway him? :)
Sondland:	Not sure i did. I think potus really wants the deliverable
Volker:	But does he know that?
Sondland:	Yep
Sondland:	Clearly lots of convos going on
Volker:	Ok—then that's good it's coming from two separate sources[771]

Ambassador Sondland told the Committees that the "deliverable" required by President Trump was a press statement from President Zelensky committing to "do the investigations" pushed by President Trump and Mr. Giuliani.[772]

To ensure progress, immediately after their text exchange, Ambassador Sondland recommended to Ambassador Volker that Mr. Yermak share a draft of the press statement to "avoid misunderstandings" and so they would know "exactly what they propose to cover." Ambassador Sondland explained: "Even though Ze [President Zelensky] does a live presser [press event] they can still summarize in a brief statement." Ambassador Volker agreed.[773]

As they were negotiating the language that would appear in a press statement, "there was talk about having a live interview or a live broadcast" during which President Zelensky would make the agreed-upon statement.[774] Ambassador Sondland suggested reviewing a written summary of the statement because he was "concerned" that President Zelensky would "say whatever he would say on live television and it still wouldn't be good enough for Rudy, slash, the President [Trump]."[775]

"Everyone Was in the Loop" About Plan for Ukrainians to Deliver a Public Statement about Investigations in Exchange for a White House Visit

As negotiations continued, on August 10, Mr. Yermak texted Ambassador Volker in an attempt to schedule a White House meeting *before* the Ukrainian president made a public statement in support of investigations into Burisma and the 2016 election. He wrote:

> I think it's possible to make this declaration and mention all these things. Which we discussed yesterday. But it will be logic [sic] to do after we receive a confirmation of date. We inform about date of visit about our expectations and our guarantees for future visit. Let [sic] discuss it[776]

Ambassador Volker responded that he agreed, but that first they would have to "iron out [a] statement and use that to get [a] date," after which point President Zelensky would go forward with making the statement.[777] They agreed to have a call the next day, and to include Ambassador Sondland. Mr. Yermak texted:

> Excellent. Once we have a date, will call for a press briefing, announcing upcoming visit and outlining vision for the reboot of the US-UKRAINE relationship, including, among other things, Burisma and election meddling in investigations.[778]

Ambassador Volker forwarded the message to Ambassador Sondland, and they agreed to speak with Mr. Yermak the next day.[779]

Ambassador Sondland testified that "everyone was in the loop" regarding this plan.[780] Also on August 10, Ambassador Sondland informed Ambassador Volker that he briefed T. Ulrich Brechbuhl, Counselor of the Department of State, noting: "I briefed Ulrich. All good."[781] Ambassador Sondland testified that he "may have walked [Mr. Brechbuhl] through where we were."[782] When asked if Mr. Brechbuhl briefed Secretary Pompeo, Ambassador Sondland noted that it was Mr. Brechbuhl's "habit" to "consult with Secretary Pompeo frequently."[783]

Secretary of Energy Rick Perry was also made aware of efforts to pressure Ukraine to issue a public statement about political investigations in exchange for a White House meeting. Ambassador Sondland testified:

> Mr. Giuliani conveyed to Secretary Perry, Ambassador Volker, and others that President Trump wanted a public statement from President Zelensky committing to investigations of Burisma and the 2016 election. Mr. Giuliani expressed those requests directly to the Ukrainians. Mr. Giuliani also expressed those requests directly to us. We all understood that these prerequisites for the White House call and the White House meeting reflected President Trump's desires and requirements.[784]

On August 11, Ambassador Volker requested a phone call with Ambassador Sondland and Mr. Giuliani, noting that he had heard from Mr. Yermak that the Ukrainians were "writing the statement now and will send to us."[785] According to call records obtained by the Committees, Ambassador Volker and Mr. Giuliani connected for 34 seconds.[786]

The same day, Ambassador Sondland updated Mr. Brechbuhl and Lisa Kenna, Executive Secretary of the State Department, about efforts to secure a public statement and a "big presser" from President Zelensky, which he hoped might "make the boss happy enough to authorize an invitation." He addressed the email to Secretary Pompeo:

> Mike,
> Kurt [Volker] and I negotiated a statement from Zelensky to be delivered for our review in a day or two. The contents will hopefully make the boss happy enough to authorize an invitation. Zelensky plans to have a big presser on the openness subject (including specifics) next week.[787]

Ambassador Sondland made clear in his hearing testimony that by "specifics," he meant the "2016 and the Burisma" investigations; "the boss" referred to "President Trump;" and "the invitation" referred to "the White House meeting."[788] Ms. Kenna replied to Ambassador Sondland that she would "pass to S [Secretary Pompeo]. Thank you."[789] Ambassador Sondland cited the email as evidence that "everyone was in the loop" on plans to condition a White House meeting on a public statement about political investigations.[790]

President Trump's Agents Negotiated a Draft Statement about the Investigations

In the evening of the next day, August 12, Mr. Yermak texted Ambassador Volker an initial version of the draft statement, which read:

> Special attention should be paid to the problem of interference in the political processes of the United States, especially with the alleged involvement of some Ukrainian politicians. I want to declare that this is unacceptable. We intend to initiate and complete a transparent and unbiased investigation of all available facts and episodes, which in turn will prevent the recurrence of this problem in the future.[791]

The draft statement did not explicitly mention Burisma or 2016 election interference, as expected.

On August 13, around 10 a.m. Eastern Time, Ambassador Volker texted Mr. Giuliani: "Mr mayor—trying to set up call in 5 min via state Dept. If now is not convenient, is there a time later today?"[792] Phone records show that, shortly thereafter, someone using a State Department number called Mr. Giuliani and connected for more than nine minutes.[793] Ambassador Volker told the Committees that, during the call, Mr. Giuliani stated: "If [the statement] doesn't say Burisma and 2016, it's not credible, because what are they hiding?"[794] Ambassador Volker asked whether inserting references to "Burisma and 2016" at the end of the statement would make it "more credible." Mr. Giuliani confirmed that it would.[795]

Two minutes after the call ended, Ambassador Volker sent a WhatsApp message to Ambassador Sondland and Mr. Yermak: "Hi Andrey—we spoke with Rudy. When is good to call you?"[796] Ambassador Sondland replied that it was, "Important. Do you have 5 mins."[797] They agreed to a call approximately 10 minutes later.[798] When Ambassador Sondland suggested having his "operator" in Brussels dial in the group, Ambassador Volker asked if they could "do this one on what's App?"[799] Text messages and calls in the WhatsApp cell phone application are encrypted from end-to-end, ensuring that WhatsApp employees and third parties cannot listen in or retrieve deleted communications.[800]

Shortly before the call, Ambassador Volker sent a revised draft of the proposed statement to Ambassador Sondland. It had been edited to include reference to Burisma and the 2016 elections:

> Special attention should be paid to the problem of interference in the political processes of the United States, especially with the alleged involvement of some Ukrainian politicians. I want to declare that this is unacceptable. We intend to initiate and complete a transparent and unbiased investigation of all available facts and episodes **including those involving Burisma and the 2016 US elections**, which in turn will prevent the recurrence of this problem in the future.[801]

Ambassador Sondland replied: "Perfect. Lets send to Andrey after our call."[802]

Following the call, Ambassador Volker texted Ambassador Sondland and Mr. Yermak: "Andrey—good talking—following is text with insert at the end for the 2 key items."[803] Ambassador Volker then sent to them the revised statement that included the explicit references to "Burisma and 2016 elections."[804]

Comparison of Draft Statements

Yermak Draft August 12	Giuliani-Volker-Sondland Draft August 13
Special attention should be paid to the problem of interference in the political processes of the United States, especially with the alleged involvement of some Ukrainian politicians. I want to declare that this is unacceptable. We intend to initiate and complete a transparent and unbiased investigation of all available facts and episodes, which in turn will prevent the recurrence of this problem in the future.	Special attention should be paid to the problem of interference in the political processes of the United States, especially with the alleged involvement of some Ukrainian politicians. I want to declare that this is unacceptable. We intend to initiate and complete a transparent and unbiased investigation of all available facts and episodes, **including those involving Burisma and the 2016 US elections**, which in turn will prevent the recurrence of this problem in the future.

A "Quid Pro Quo" from "the President of the United States"

Ambassador Volker testified that the language reflected what Mr. Giuliani deemed necessary for the statement to be "credible."[805] Ambassador Sondland noted the language was "proposed by Giuliani."[806] Ambassador Sondland explained that the language was a clear quid pro quo that expressed "the desire of the President of the United States":

> Mr. Giuliani's requests were a quid pro quo for arranging a White House visit for President Zelensky. Mr. Giuliani demanded that Ukraine make a public statement announcing investigations of the 2016 election/DNC server and Burisma. Mr. Giuliani was expressing the desires of the President of the United States, and we knew that these investigations were important to the President.[807]

Shortly after Ambassador Volker sent the revised statement to Mr. Yermak on August 13, Ambassador Sondland called Mr. Giuliani and connected for nearly four minutes.

Ukrainian Officials and Career State Department Became Increasingly Concerned

On August 13—while Ambassador Volker, Ambassador Sondland, and Mr. Yermak were negotiating the draft statement about investigations—Mr. Yermak asked Ambassador Volker "whether any request had ever been made by the U.S. to investigate election interference in 2016." He appeared interested in knowing whether the U.S. Department of Justice had made an official request to Ukraine's law enforcement agency for legal assistance in such a matter.[808] When Ambassador Volker sent Mr. Giuliani's approved draft statement to Mr. Yermak, he stated that he would "work on official request."[809]

Ambassador Volker testified: "When I say official request, I mean law enforcement channels, Department of Justice to law enforcement in Ukraine, please investigate was there any effort to interfere in the U.S. elections."[810] Ambassador Volker explained:

> He [Yermak] said, and I think quite appropriately, that if they [Ukraine] are responding to an official request, that's one thing. If there's no official request, that's different. And I agree with that.[811]

According to Ambassador Volker, he was merely trying to "find out" if there was ever an official request made by the Department of Justice: "As I found out the answer that we had not, I said, well, let's just not go there."[812]

On September 25, within hours of the White House's public release of the record of the July 25 call between President Trump and President Zelensky, a Justice Department spokesperson issued a statement, apparently confirming that no such formal request had been made:

> The President has not spoken with the Attorney General about having Ukraine investigate anything relating to former Vice President Biden or his son. The President has not asked

the Attorney General to contact Ukraine—on this or any other matter. The Attorney General has not communicated with Ukraine—on this or any other subject.[813]

Ukraine's current Prosecutor General Ruslan Ryaboshapka, who assumed his new position in late August 2019, confirmed the Justice Department's account. He told *The Financial Times* in late November 2019 that Attorney General Barr had made no formal request regarding a potential investigation into allegations of wrongdoing by former Vice President Biden.[814] In an apparent reference to President Trump's demand that Ukraine interfere in U.S. elections, Mr. Ryaboshapka added: "It's critically important for the west not to pull us into some conflicts between their ruling elites, but to continue to support so that we can cross the point of no return."[815]

Neither Ambassador Taylor in Ukraine nor Deputy Assistant Secretary George Kent in Washington were aware of the efforts by Ambassadors Sondland and Volker, in coordination with Mr. Giuliani, to convince Ukrainian officials to issue a statement in real time. Ambassador Taylor told the Committees that, on August 16, in a text message exchange with Ambassador Volker, he "learned that Mr. Yermak had asked that the United States submit an official request for an investigation into Burisma's alleged violations of Ukrainian law, if that is what the United States desired."[816] Ambassador Taylor noted that "a formal U.S. request to the Ukrainians to conduct an investigation based on violations of their own law" was "improper" and advised Ambassador Volker to "stay clear."[817]

Nevertheless, Ambassador Volker requested Ambassador Taylor's help with the matter.[818] "To find out the legal aspects of the question," Ambassador Taylor gave Ambassador Volker the name of an official at the Department of Justice "whom I thought would be the proper point of contact for seeking a U.S. referral for a foreign investigation."[819]

On August 15, Ambassador Volker texted Ambassador Sondland that Mr. Yermak wanted to "know our status on asking them to investigate."[820] Two days later, Ambassador Volker wrote: "Bill [Taylor] had no info on requesting an investigation—calling a friend at DOJ." Ambassador Volker testified that he was not able to connect with his contact at the Department of Justice.[821]

Mr. Kent testified that on August 15, Catherine Croft, Ambassador Volker's special assistant, approached him to ask whether there was any precedent for the United States asking Ukraine to conduct investigations on its behalf. Mr. Kent advised Ms. Croft:

> [I]f you're asking me have we ever gone to the Ukrainians and asked them to investigate or prosecute individuals for political reasons, the answer is, I hope we haven't, and we shouldn't because that goes against everything that we are trying to promote in post-Soviet states for the last 28 years, which is the promotion of the rule of law.[822]

Mr. Kent testified that the day after his conversation with Ms. Croft, he spoke with Ambassador Taylor, who "amplified the same theme" and told Mr. Kent that "Yermak was very uncomfortable" with the idea of investigations and suggested that "it should be done officially and put in writing." As a result, it became clear to Mr. Kent in mid-August that Ukraine was being pressured to conduct politically-motivated investigations. Mr. Kent told Ambassador Taylor "that's wrong, and we shouldn't be doing that as a matter of U.S. policy."[823]

After speaking to Ms. Croft and Ambassador Taylor, Mr. Kent wrote a memo to file on August 16 documenting his "concerns that there was an effort to initiate politically motivated prosecutions that were injurious to the rule of law, both in Ukraine and U.S."[824] Mr. Kent testified:

> At the time, I had no knowledge of the specifics of the [July 25] call record, but based on Bill Taylor's account of the engagements with Andriy Yermak that were engagements of Yermak with Kurt Volker, at that point it was clear that the investigations that were being suggested were the ones that Rudy Giuliani had been tweeting about, meaning Biden, Burisma, and 2016.[825]

On August 17, Mr. Yermak reached out to both Ambassador Sondland and Ambassador Volker.[826] Ambassador Sondland texted Ambassador Volker that "Yermak just tapped on me about dates. Havent responded. Any updates?"[827] Ambassador Volker responded that "I've got nothing" and stated that he was contacting the Department of Justice to find out about requesting an investigation.[828]

Ambassador Sondland then asked: "Do we still want Ze [Zelensky] to give us an unequivocal draft with 2016 and Boresma [sic]?" Ambassador Volker replied: "That's the clear message so far ..." Ambassador Sondland said that he would ask that Mr. Yermak "send us a clean draft," to which Ambassador Volker replied that he had spoken to Mr. Yermak and suggested that he and Ambassador Sondland speak the following day, August 18, to discuss "all the latest."[829]

Ambassador Volker claimed that he "stopped pursuing" the statement from the Ukrainians around this time because of concerns raised by Mr. Yermak that Yuriy Lutsenko was still the Prosecutor General. Mr. Lutsenko was likely to be replaced by President Zelensky, and because Mr. Lutsenko was alleging the same false claims that President Trump and Mr. Giuliani were demanding of President Zelensky, Ukrainian officials "did not want to mention Burisma or 2016."[830] Ambassador Volker testified that he "agreed" and advised Mr. Yermak that "making those specific refences was not a good idea" because making those statements might "look like it would play into our domestic politics."[831]

Mr. Yermak agreed and, according to Ambassador Volker, plans to put out a statement were "shelved."[832] Ambassador Volker reasoned that the plan for a public statement did not materialize partly because of "the sense that Rudy was not going to be convinced that it meant anything, and, therefore, convey a positive message to the President if it didn't say Burisma and 2016."[833] He added:

> I agreed with the Ukrainians they shouldn't do it, and in fact told them just drop it, wait till you have your own prosecutor general in place. Let's work on substantive issues like this, security assistance and all. Let's just do that. So we dropped it.[834]

Ambassador Volker testified that, "From that point on, I didn't have any further conversations about this statement."[835] Nevertheless, efforts to secure a presidential statement announcing the two investigations into the Bidens and the 2016 U.S. election interference continued well into September.

On August 19, Ambassador Sondland told Ambassador Volker that he "drove the 'larger issue' home" with Mr. Yermak: that this was bigger than just a White House meeting and was about "the relationship per se."[836] Ambassador Volker told the Committees that he understood this referred to "the level of trust that the President has with President Zelensky. He has this general negative assumption about everything Ukraine, and that's the larger issue."[837] That negative assumption would prove difficult to overcome as Ukrainian and U.S. officials sought to finally obtain a White House meeting and shake free from the White House hundreds of millions of dollars in Congressionally-approved security assistance for Ukraine.

7. **The President's Conditioning of Military Assistance and a White House Meeting on Announcement of Investigations Raised Alarm**

Following the public disclosure in late August 2019 of a hold on U.S. security assistance to Ukraine, President Trump made clear that "everything"—an Oval Office meeting and the release of taxpayer-funded U.S. security assistance—was contingent on the Ukrainian president announcing investigations into former Vice President Joe Biden and a debunked conspiracy theory about Ukrainian interference in the 2016 U.S. election. President Trump wanted the Ukrainian leader "in a public box," even as Ambassador Bill Taylor warned that it was "crazy to withhold security assistance for help with a political campaign."

Overview

On August 28, 2019, *Politico* first reported that President Trump was withholding hundreds of millions of dollars of Congressionally-appropriated U.S. security assistance from Ukraine, a fact that had been previously suspected by Ukrainian officials in July. Public revelations about the freeze raised questions about the U.S. commitment to Ukraine and harming efforts to deter Russian influence and aggression in Europe.

Around this time, American officials made clear to Ukrainians that a public announcement about investigations into Ukrainian interference in the 2016 election and former Vice President Joe Biden was a pre-condition—not only to obtain a White House meeting for President Zelensky, but also to end the freeze on military and other security assistance for Ukraine.

In early September, Ambassador Gordon Sondland conveyed President Trump's demands to both U.S. and Ukrainian officials. On September 1, he informed a senior Ukrainian official that the military aid would be released if the "prosecutor general would to go the mike [sic]" and announce the investigations. Later, on September 7, President Trump informed Ambassador Sondland that he wanted President Zelensky—not the Prosecutor General—in a "public box" and demanded that the Ukrainian president personally announce the investigations to "clear things up." Only then would Ukraine end the "stalemate" with the White House related to security assistance. President Zelensky proceeded to schedule an interview on CNN in order to announce the investigations and satisfy President Trump.

The President's efforts to withhold vital military and security assistance in exchange for political investigations troubled U.S. officials. NSC Senior Director for Europe and Russia Timothy Morrison twice reported what he understood to be the President's requirement of a quid pro quo to National Security Advisor John Bolton, who advised him to "make sure the lawyers are tracking." Ambassador Bill Taylor expressed his concerns to Ambassador Sondland, stating plainly that it was "crazy to withhold security assistance for help with a political campaign."

Secretary Pompeo and Ambassador Sondland Worked to "Break the Logjam"

President Trump's hold on security assistance persisted throughout August, without explanation to U.S. officials and contrary to the consensus recommendation of the President's national security team. At the same time, President Trump refused to schedule a coveted White House visit for President Zelensky until he announced two investigations that could benefit President Trump's reelection prospects. The confluence of those two circumstances led some American officials, including Ambassador Sondland and David Holmes, Counselor for Political Affairs at the U.S. Embassy in Kyiv, to conclude that the military assistance was conditioned on Ukraine's public announcement of the investigations.[838]

On August 20, Ambassador Kurt Volker met with Deputy Assistant Secretary of Defense Laura Cooper. Ms. Cooper and Ambassador Volker agreed that if the hold on security assistance was not lifted, "it would be very damaging to the relationship" between the U.S. and Ukraine.[839] During this meeting, Ambassador Volker mentioned that he was talking to an advisor to President Zelensky about making a statement "that would somehow disavow any interference in U.S. elections and would commit to the prosecution of any individuals involved in election interference."[840] Ambassador Volker indicated that if his efforts to get a statement were successful, the hold on security assistance might be lifted.[841]

Although he did not mention that conversation during his deposition, Ambassador Volker had a similar recollection, during his public testimony, of the meeting with Ms. Cooper. Ambassador Volker recalled discussing with Ms. Cooper the draft statement that had been coordinated with Ukrainian presidential aide Andriy Yermak—which included reference to the two investigations that President Trump demanded in the July 25 call—and that such a statement "could be helpful in getting a reset of the thinking of the President, the negative view of Ukraine that he had" which might, in turn, "unblock[] whatever hold there was on security assistance."[842]

Around this time, Ambassador Sondland sought to "break the logjam" on the security assistance and the White House meeting by coordinating a meeting between the two Presidents through Secretary of State Mike Pompeo. On August 22, Ambassador Sondland emailed Secretary Pompeo, copying the State Department's Executive Secretary, Lisa Kenna:

> Should we block time in Warsaw for a short pull-aside for POTUS to meet Zelensky? I would ask Zelensky to look him in the eye and tell him that once Ukraine's new justice folks are in place (mid-Sept) Ze should be able to move forward publicly and with confidence on those issues of importance to Potus and to the US. Hopefully, that will break the logjam.[843]

Secretary Pompeo replied, "Yes."[844]

Ambassador Sondland testified that when he referenced "issues of importance to Potus," he meant the investigation into the false allegations about Ukrainian interference in the 2016 election and the investigation into the Bidens.[845] He told the Committee that his goal was to "do what was necessary to get the aid released, to break the logjam."[846] Ambassador Sondland believed that President Trump would not release the aid until Ukraine announced the two investigations the President wanted.[847]

Ambassador Sondland testified: "Secretary Pompeo essentially gave me the green light to brief President Zelensky about making those announcements."[848] He explained:

> This was a proposed briefing that I was going to give President Zelensky, and I was going to call President Zelensky and ask him to say what is in this email. And I was asking essentially … [Secretary] Pompeo's permission to do that, which he said yes.[849]

He then forwarded the email to Ms. Kenna, seeking confirmation of "10-15 min on the Warsaw sched[ule]" for the pull-aside meeting. The Ambassador stated that he was seeking confirmation in order to brief President Zelensky. Ms. Kenna replied, "I will try for sure."[850]

On August 24, Ukraine celebrated its Independence Day. According to Mr. Holmes, Ukrainian Independence Day presented "another good opportunity to show support for Ukraine."[851] However, nobody senior to Ambassador Volker attended the festivities, even though Secretary of Defense James Mattis attended in 2017 and Ambassador Bolton attended in 2018.[852]

Two days later, on August 26, Ambassador Bolton's office requested Mr. Giuliani's contact information from Ambassador Sondland. Ambassador Sondland sent Ambassador Bolton the information directly.[853] Ambassador Sondland testified that he had "no idea" why Ambassador Bolton requested the contact information.[854]

Ambassador Bolton Visited Kyiv

On August 27, Ambassador Bolton arrived in Kyiv for an official visit. Ambassador Bolton emphasized to Andriy Bohdan, President Zelensky's chief of staff, that an upcoming meeting between Presidents Trump and Zelensky, scheduled for September 1 in Warsaw, Poland, would be "crucial to cementing their relationship."[855] Mr. Holmes, who accompanied Ambassador Bolton in Kyiv, testified that he also heard "Ambassador Bolton express to Ambassador Taylor and Mr. Morrison his frustration about Mr. Giuliani's influence with the President, making clear there was nothing he could do about it."[856]

Prior to Ambassador Bolton's departure from Kyiv, Ambassador Taylor asked to meet with him privately. Ambassador Taylor expressed his "serious concern about the withholding of military assistance to Ukraine while the Ukrainians were defending their country from Russian aggression."[857] During the conversation, Ambassador Bolton "indicated that he was very sympathetic" to Ambassador's Taylor's concerns.[858] He advised that Ambassador Taylor "send a first-person cable to Secretary Pompeo directly relaying my concerns" about the withholding of military assistance.[859]

Mr. Holmes testified that Ambassador Bolton advised during his trip that "the hold on security assistance would not be lifted prior to the upcoming meeting between President Trump and President Zelensky in Warsaw, where it would hang on whether Zelensky was able to favorably impress President Trump."[860]

Ukrainian Concern Over Military Aid Intensified After First Public Report of Hold

On August 28, 2019, *Politico* first reported that President Trump had implemented a hold on nearly $400 million of U.S. military assistance to Ukraine that had been appropriated by Congress.

Almost immediately after the news became public, Ukrainian officials expressed alarm to their American counterparts. Mr. Yermak sent Ambassador Volker a link to the *Politico* story and then texted: "Need to talk with you."[861] Other Ukrainian officials also expressed concerns to Ambassador Volker that the Ukrainian government was being "singled out and penalized for some reason."[862]

On August 29, Mr. Yermak also contacted Ambassador Taylor to express that he was "very concerned" about the hold on military assistance.[863] Mr. Yermak and other Ukrainian officials told Ambassador Taylor that they were "just desperate" and would be willing to travel to Washington to raise with U.S. officials the importance of the assistance. Ambassador Taylor described confusion among Ukrainian officials over the hold on military aid:

> I mean, the obvious question was, "Why?" So Mr. Yermak and others were trying to figure out why this was … They thought that there must be some rational reason for this being held up, and they just didn't—and maybe in Washington they didn't understand how important this assistance was to their fight and to their armed forces. And so maybe they could figure—so they were just desperate.[864]

Without any official explanation for the hold, American officials could provide little reassurance to their Ukrainian counterparts. Ambassador Taylor continued, "And I couldn't tell them. I didn't know and I didn't tell them, because we hadn't—we hadn't—there'd been no guidance that I could give them."[865]

Ambassador Taylor's First-Person Cable Described the "Folly" in Withholding Military Aid

The same day that Ambassador Taylor heard from Mr. Yermak about his concerns about the hold on military aid, Ambassador Taylor transmitted his classified, first-person cable to Washington. It was the first and only time in Ambassador Taylor's career that he sent such a cable to the Secretary of State.[866] The cable described "the folly I saw in withholding military aid to Ukraine at a time when hostilities were still active in the east and when Russia was watching closely to gauge the level of American support for the Ukrainian Government."[867]

Ambassador Taylor worried about the public message that such a hold on vital military assistance would send in the midst of Ukraine's hot war with Russia: "The Russians, as I said at my deposition, would love to see the humiliation of President Zelensky at the hands of the Americans. I told the Secretary that I could not and would not defend such a policy."[868]

The cable also sought to explain clearly "the importance of Ukraine and the security assistance to U.S. national security," according to Mr. Holmes.[869] However, Mr. Holmes worried that the national security argument might not achieve its purpose given the reasons he suspected for the hold on military aid. His "clear impression" at the time was that "the security assistance hold was likely intended by the President either as an expression of dissatisfaction with the Ukrainians, who had not yet agreed to the Burisma/Biden investigation, or as an effort to increase the pressure on them to do so."[870] Mr. Holmes viewed this as "the only logical conclusion."[871] He had "no other explanation for why there was disinterest in this [White House] meeting that the President had already offered" and there was a "hold of the security assistance with no explanation whatsoever."[872]

Ambassador Taylor never received a response to his cable, but was told that Secretary Pompeo carried it with him to a White House meeting about security assistance to Ukraine.[873]

Ambassador Sondland Told Senator Johnson
That Ukraine Aid Was Conditioned on Investigations

The next day, on August 30, Republican Senator Ron Johnson spoke with Ambassador Sondland to express his concern about President Trump's decision to withhold military assistance to Ukraine. According to Senator Johnson, Ambassador Sondland told him that if Ukraine would commit to "get to the bottom of what happened in 2016—if President Trump has that confidence, then he'll release the military spending."[874]

On August 31, Senator Johnson spoke by phone with President Trump regarding the decision to withhold aid to Ukraine.[875] President Trump denied the quid pro quo that Senator Johnson had learned of from Ambassador Sondland.[876] At the same time, however, President Trump refused to authorize Senator Johnson to tell Ukrainian officials that the aid would be forthcoming.[877]

The message that Ambassador Sondland communicated to Senator Johnson mirrored that used by President Trump during his July 25 call with President Zelensky, in which President Trump twice asked that the Ukrainian leader "get to the bottom of it," including in connection to an investigation into the debunked conspiracy theory that Ukraine interfered in the 2016 election to help Hillary Clinton.[878] To the contrary, the U.S. Intelligence Community unanimously assessed that Russia interfered in the 2016 election to help Donald Trump, as did Special Counsel Robert Mueller.[879]

In a November 18 letter to House Republicans, Senator Johnson confirmed the accuracy of the *Wall Street Journal's* account of his August 30 call with Ambassador Sondland.[880]

Ambassador Sondland testified that he had "no reason to dispute" Senator Johnson's recollection of the August 30 call and testified that by late August 2019, he had concluded that "if Ukraine did something to demonstrate a serious intention to fight corruption, and specifically addressing Burisma and the 2016, then the hold on military aid would be lifted."[881]

Ambassador Sondland Raised the Link Between Investigations and Security Assistance to Vice President Pence Before Meeting with President Zelensky

On September 1, President Trump was scheduled to meet President Zelensky in Warsaw, Poland during an event commemorating World War II. Citing the approach of Hurricane Dorian towards American soil, the President canceled his trip just days beforehand. Vice President Mike Pence traveled to Warsaw instead.[882]

Jennifer Williams, Special Advisor to the Vice President for Europe and Russia, learned of the change in the President's travel plans on August 29 and "relied heavily on the NSC briefing papers" originally prepared for President Trump. Ms. Williams recalled that "prior to leaving, [National Security Advisor to the Vice President] General Kellogg had asked, at the request of the Vice President, for an update on the status of the security assistance that was at that time still on hold." Given the public reporting about the hold on August 29, White House officials expected that President Zelensky would seek further information on the status of the funds.[883]

The delegation arrived in Warsaw and gathered in a hotel room to brief the Vice President shortly before his engagement with President Zelensky. Ambassador Bolton, who had just arrived from Kyiv, led the Ukraine briefing. He updated Vice President Pence on President Zelensky's efforts to combat corruption and explained "what the security assistance was for." Advisors in the room "agreed on the need to get a final decision on that security assistance as soon as possible so that it could be implemented before the end of the fiscal year."[884]

Before the bilateral meeting between Vice President Pence and President Zelensky, Ambassador Sondland attended a "general briefing" for the Vice President.[885] Ambassador Sondland testified that he raised concerns that the delay in security assistance had "become tied to the issue of investigations."[886] The Vice President "nodded like, you know, he heard what I said."[887]

During Ambassador Sondland's public testimony, Vice President Pence's office issued a carefully worded statement claiming that the Vice President "never had a conversation with Gordon Sondland about investigating the Bidens, Burisma, or the conditional release of financial aid to Ukraine based upon potential investigations," and that "Ambassador Gordon Sondland was never alone with the Vice President on the September 1 trip to Poland."[888] Ambassador Sondland did not testify that he specifically mentioned the Bidens, Burisma, or the conditional release of financial aid to Ukraine during his discussion with Vice President Pence, nor did he testify that he was alone with the Vice President.

Before Vice President Pence's meeting with President Zelensky, Ukrainian National Security Advisor Oleksandr "Sasha" Danyliuk wrote Ambassador Taylor, incorrectly describing the failure to provide security assistance as a "gradually increasing problem."[889] In the hours before Vice President Pence's meeting with President Zelensky, Ambassador Taylor replied, clarifying that "the delay of U.S. security assistance was an all-or-nothing proposition, in the sense that if the White House did not lift the hold prior to the end of the fiscal year, September 30th, the funds would expire and Ukraine would receive nothing."[890] Ambassador Taylor wanted to make sure Mr. Danyliuk understood that if the assistance was not provided "by the end of the fiscal year, then it goes away."[891]

President Zelensky Immediately Asked Vice President Pence About Security Assistance

As expected, at the outset of the bilateral meeting, President Zelensky immediately asked Vice President Pence about the status of U.S. security assistance. It was "the very first question" that he raised.[892] President Zelensky emphasized the multifold importance of American assistance, stating that "the symbolic value of U.S. support in terms of security assistance ... was just as valuable to the Ukrainians as the actual dollars."[893] President Zelensky also expressed concern that "any hold or appearance of reconsideration of such assistance might embolden Russia to think that the United States was no longer committed to Ukraine."[894]

According to Ms. Williams, the Vice President "assured President Zelensky that there was no change in U.S. policy in terms of our ... full-throated support for Ukraine and its sovereignty and territorial integrity."[895] Vice President Pence also assured the Ukrainian delegation that he would convey to President Trump the details of President Zelensky's "good progress on reforms, so that hopefully we could get a decision on the security assistance as soon as possible."[896]

The reassurance proved to be ineffective. *The Washington Post* later reported that one of President Zelensky's aides told Vice President Pence: "You're the only country providing us military assistance. You're punishing us."[897]

Mr. Holmes testified that President Trump's decision to cancel his Warsaw trip effectively meant that "the hold [on security assistance] remained in place, with no clear means to get it lifted."[898]

Ambassador Sondland Informed President Zelensky's Advisor that Military Aid Was Contingent on Ukraine Publicly Announcing the Investigations

After the bilateral meeting between Vice President Pence and President Zelensky, Ambassador Sondland briefly spoke to President Zelensky's aide, Mr. Yermak. Ambassador Sondland conveyed his belief that "the resumption of U.S. aid would likely not occur until Ukraine took some kind of action on the public statement that we had been discussing for many weeks" regarding the investigations that President Trump discussed during the July 25 call.[899]

Immediately following the conversation, Ambassador Sondland told Mr. Morrison what had transpired during his aside with Mr. Yermak. Mr. Morrison recounted to the Committees that Ambassador Sondland told Mr. Yermak "what could help them move the aid was if the prosecutor general would go to the mike [sic] and announce that he was opening the Burisma investigation."[900]

Mr. Morrison Reported Ambassador Sondland's Proposal to Get Ukrainians "Pulled Into Our Politics" to White House Officials and Ambassador Taylor

Mr. Morrison felt uncomfortable with "any idea that President Zelensky should allow himself to be involved in our politics."[901] He promptly reported the conversation between Ambassador Sondland and Mr. Yermak to Ambassador Bolton. Mr. Morrison had concerns with "what Gordon was proposing about getting the Ukrainians pulled into our politics."[902] Ambassador Bolton told Mr. Morrison—consistent with his own "instinct"—to "make sure the lawyers are tracking."[903] Upon his return to Washington, Mr. Morrison reported his concerns to NSC lawyers John Eisenberg and Michael Ellis.[904]

Mr. Morrison testified that, in speaking to the NSC legal advisors, he wanted to ensure "that there was a record of what Ambassador Sondland was doing, to protect the President."[905] At this point, Mr. Morrison was not certain that the President had authorized Ambassador Sondland's activities, but Mr. Morrison agreed that if the President had been aware of Ambassador Sondland's activities, the effect could be to create a paper trail that incriminated President Trump.[906]

Mr. Morrison also reported the conversation to Ambassador Taylor "because I wanted him to be in a position to advise the Ukrainians not to do it."[907] Ambassador Taylor said that he was "alarmed" to hear about the remarks to Mr. Yermak.[908] He explained that "this was the first time that I had heard that the security assistance, not just the White House meeting, was conditioned on the investigations."[909] To Ambassador Taylor, "It's one thing to try to leverage a meeting in the White House. It's another thing, I thought, to leverage security assistance … to a country at war, dependent on both the security assistance and the demonstration of support."[910]

President Trump Wanted President Zelensky in a "Public Box," and Said "Everything" Depended on Announcing the Investigations

Upon hearing from Mr. Morrison about the conditionality of the military aid on Ukraine publicly announcing the two investigations, Ambassador Taylor sent a text message to Ambassador Sondland: "Are we now saying that security assistance and WH meeting are conditioned on investigations?" Ambassador Sondland responded, "Call me."[911]

Ambassador Sondland confirmed over the phone to Ambassador Taylor that "everything"—the Oval Office meeting and the security assistance—was dependent on the Ukrainian government publicly announcing the political investigations President Trump requested on July 25. Informed by a review of contemporaneous notes that he took during his phone call, Ambassador Taylor testified:

> During that phone call, Ambassador Sondland told me that President Trump had told him that he wants President Zelensky to state publicly that Ukraine will investigate Burisma and alleged Ukrainian interference in the 2016 election. Ambassador Sondland also told me that he now recognized that he had made a mistake by earlier telling Ukrainian officials that only a White House meeting with President Zelensky was dependent on a public announcement of the investigations. In fact, Ambassador Sondland said,

133

everything was dependent on such an announcement, including security assistance. He said that President Trump wanted President Zelensky in a public box, by making a public statement about ordering such investigations.[912]

By this point, Ambassador Taylor's "clear understanding" was that President Trump would withhold security assistance until President Zelensky "committed to pursue the investigation."[913] He agreed that the U.S. position was "if they don't do this," referring to the investigations, "they are not going to get that," referring to the security assistance.[914] Ambassador Taylor also concurred with the statement that "if they don't do this, they are not going to get that" was the literal definition of a quid pro quo.[915]

Ambassador Taylor testified that his contemporaneous notes of the phone call with Ambassador Sondland reflect that Ambassador Sondland used the phrase "public box" to describe President Trump's desire to ensure that the initiation of his desired investigations was announced publicly.[916] Ambassador Sondland, who did not take contemporaneous notes of any of his conversations, did not dispute that he used those words.[917] He also testified that, when he spoke to Mr. Yermak, he believed that it would be sufficient to satisfy the requirements of President Trump and Mr. Giuliani if the new Ukrainian prosecutor general issued a statement about investigations, but his understanding soon changed.[918]

President Trump Informed Ambassador Sondland that President Zelensky Personally "Must Announce the Opening of the Investigations"

On September 7, Ambassador Sondland called Mr. Morrison to report that he had just concluded a call with President Trump. Mr. Morrison testified that Ambassador Sondland told him "that there was no quid pro quo, but President Zelensky must announce the opening of the investigations and he should want to do it."[919] This led Mr. Morrison to believe that a public announcement of investigations by the Ukrainian president—and not the prosecutor general— was a prerequisite for the release of the security assistance.[920] He reported the conversation to Ambassador Bolton, who once again instructed him to "tell the lawyers," which Mr. Morrison did.[921]

Later on September 7, Mr. Morrison relayed the substance of Ambassador Sondland's conversation with President Trump to Ambassador Taylor. Ambassador Taylor explained:

> I had a conversation with Mr. Morrison in which he described a phone conversation earlier that day between Ambassador Sondland and President Trump. Mr. Morrison said that he had a sinking feeling after learning about this conversation from Ambassador Sondland. According to Mr. Morrison, President Trump told Ambassador Sondland he was not asking for a quid pro quo, but President Trump did insist that President Zelensky go to a microphone and say he is opening investigations of Biden and 2016 election interference and that President Zelensky should want to do this himself. Mr. Morrison said that he told Ambassador Bolton and the NSC lawyers of this phone call between President Trump and Ambassador Sondland.[922]

The following day, on September 8, Ambassador Sondland texted Ambassadors Volker and Taylor: "Guys multiple convos with Ze, Potus. Lets talk." Ambassador Taylor responded one minute later, "Now is fine with me."[923] On the phone, Ambassador Sondland "confirmed that he had talked to President Trump" and that "President Trump was adamant that President Zelensky himself had to clear things up and do it in public. President Trump said it was not a quid pro quo."[924] Ambassador Sondland also shared that he told President Zelensky and Mr. Yermak that, "although this was not a quid pro quo, if President Zelensky did not clear things up in public, we would be at a stalemate."[925]

Ambassador Taylor testified that he understood "stalemate" to mean that "Ukraine would not receive the much-needed military assistance."[926] During his public testimony, Ambassador Sondland did not dispute Ambassador Taylor's recollection of events and agreed that the term "stalemate" referred to the hold on U.S. security assistance to Ukraine.[927]

Although Ambassador Sondland otherwise could not independently recall any details about his September 7 conversation with President Trump, he testified that he had no reason to dispute the testimony from Ambassador Taylor or Mr. Morrison—which was based on their contemporaneous notes—regarding this conversation.[928] Ambassador Sondland, however, did recall that President Zelensky agreed to make a public announcement about the investigations into Burisma and the Bidens and the 2016 election in an interview on CNN."[929]

According to Ambassador Taylor, Ambassador Sondland explained that President Trump was a "businessman," and that when "a businessman is about to sign a check to someone who owes him something, the businessman asks that person to pay up before signing the check."[930] Ambassador Taylor was concerned that President Trump believed Ukraine "owed him something" in exchange for the hundreds of millions of dollars in taxpayer-funded U.S. security assistance.[931] He argued to Ambassador Sondland that "the explanation made no sense. The Ukrainians did not owe President Trump anything. And holding up security assistance for domestic political gain was crazy."[932] Ambassador Sondland did not recall this exchange specifically, but did not dispute Ambassador Taylor's testimony.[933]

Ambassador Taylor Texted Ambassador Sondland that "It's Crazy to Withhold Security Assistance for Help with a Political Campaign"

Ambassador Taylor remained concerned by the President's directive that "everything" was conditioned on President Zelensky publicly announcing the investigations. He also worried that, even if the Ukrainian leader did as President Trump required, the President might continue to withhold the vital U.S. security assistance in any event. Ambassador Taylor texted his concerns to Ambassadors Volker and Sondland stating: "The nightmare is they give the interview and don't get the security assistance. The Russians love it. (And I quit.)"[934]

Ambassador Taylor testified:

"The nightmare" is the scenario where President Zelensky goes out in public, makes an announcement that he's going to investigate the Burisma and the ... interference in 2016 election, maybe among other things. He might put that in some series of investigations.

135

But ... the nightmare was he would mention those two, take all the heat from that, get himself in big trouble in this country and probably in his country as well, and the security assistance would not be released. That was the nightmare.[935]

Early in the morning in Europe on September 9, Ambassador Taylor reiterated his concerns about the President's "quid pro quo" in another series of text messages with Ambassadors Volker and Sondland:

Taylor:	The message to the Ukrainians (and Russians) we send with the decision on security assistance is key. With the hold, we have already shaken their faith in us. Thus my nightmare scenario.
Taylor:	Counting on you to be right about this interview, Gordon.
Sondland:	Bill, I never said I was "right". I said we are where we are and believe we have identified the best pathway forward. Lets hope it works.
Taylor:	As I said on the phone, I think it's crazy to withhold security assistance for help with a political campaign.[936]

By "help with a political campaign," Ambassador Taylor was referring to President Trump's 2020 reelection effort.[937] Ambassador Taylor testified: "The investigation of Burisma and the Bidens was clearly identified by Mr. Giuliani in public for months as a way to get information on the two Bidens."[938]

Ambassador Taylor framed the broader national security implications of President Trump's decision to withhold vital security assistance from Ukraine. He said:

[T]he United States was trying to support Ukraine as a frontline state against Russian attack. And, again, the whole notion of a rules-based order was being threatened by the Russians in Ukraine. So our security assistance was designed to support Ukraine. And it was not just the United States; it was all of our allies.[939]

Ambassador Taylor explained:

[S]ecurity assistance was so important for Ukraine as well as our own national interests, to withhold that assistance for no good reason other than help with a political campaign made no sense. It was counterproductive to all of what we had been trying to do. It was illogical. It could not be explained. It was crazy.[940]

Ambassador Sondland Repeated the President's Denial of a "Quid Pro Quo" to Ambassador Taylor, While He and President Trump Continued to Demand Public Investigations

In response to Ambassador Taylor's text message that it was "crazy to withhold security assistance for help with a political campaign," Ambassador Sondland denied that the President had demanded a "quid pro quo."

At approximately 5:17 a.m. Eastern Time, Ambassador Sondland responded to Ambassador Taylor:

Bill, I believe you are incorrect about President Trump's intentions. The President has been crystal clear: no quid pro quo's of any kind. The President is trying to evaluate whether Ukraine is truly going to adopt the transparency and reforms that President Zelensky promised during his campaign. I suggest we stop the back and forth by text. If you still have concerns, I recommend you give Lisa Kenna or S [Secretary Pompeo] a call to discuss them directly. Thanks.[941]

Notably, Ambassador Sondland recalled that President Trump raised the possible existence of a quid pro quo entirely on his own, without any prompting. Ambassador Sondland asked President Trump what he affirmatively wanted from Ukraine, yet President Trump reportedly responded by asserting what was not the case:

Q: Okay. During that telephone conversation with President Trump, you didn't ask the President directly if there was a quid pro quo, correct?

A: No. As I testified, I asked the question open ended, what do you want from Ukraine?

Q: President Trump was the first person to use the word "quid pro quo," correct?

A: That is correct.[942]

In contrast, Ambassador Sondland testified unequivocally there was a quid pro quo in connection to a telephone call between President Trump and President Zelensky, as well as a White House meeting for President Zelensky.[943] He acknowledged that the reference to "transparency and reforms" in his text message to Ambassador Taylor "was my clumsy way of saying he wanted these announcement to be made."[944]

Ambassador Sondland also testified that President Trump immediately followed his stated denial of a quid pro quo by demanding that President Zelensky still make a public announcement, while the military assistance remained on an unexplained hold. Ambassador Sondland agreed that President Trump said that he wanted President Zelensky to "clear things up and do it in public," as Ambassador Taylor had testified.[945] Ambassador Sondland testified that nothing on his call with President Trump changed his understanding of a quid pro quo and, at least as of September 8, he was "absolutely convinced" the White House meeting and President Trump's release of the military assistance were conditioned on the public announcement of the investigations President Trump sought.[946]

After hearing from President Trump, Ambassador Sondland promptly told the Ukrainian leader and Mr. Yermak that "if President Zelensky did not clear things up in public, we would be at a stalemate."[947] President Zelensky responded to the demand relayed by Ambassador Sondland, by agreeing to make an announcement of investigations on CNN.[948]

Regardless of when the call between President Trump and Ambassador Sondland occurred, both that phone call and Ambassador's Sondland text message denying any quid pro quo occurred *after* the White House had been informed of the whistleblower complaint discussing the hold on security assistance. The White House first received notice of the whistleblower complaint alleging wrongdoing concerning the President's July 25 call with President Zelensky on August 26—over a week before the "no quid pro quo" denial.[949] In addition, Ambassador Sondland wrote his text message on September 9, the same day that the ICIG informed the Committee of the existence of a "credible" and "urgent" whistleblower complaint that was later revealed to be related to Ukraine.[950] The Administration received prior notice of the ICIG's intent to inform the Committee.[951]

Ambassador Sondland's Testimony is the Only Evidence the Committees Received Indicating That President Trump Denied Any "Quid Pro Quo" on the Phone on September 9

Ambassador Sondland testified in his deposition that he sent a text message to Ambassador Taylor after speaking directly with President Trump on September 9. However, testimony from other witnesses and documents available to the Committees do not confirm that Ambassador Sondland and President Trump spoke on that day.

Ambassador Sondland's own testimony indicated some ambiguity in his recollection of the timing of the call. At a public hearing on November 20, Ambassador Sondland testified that he "still cannot find a record of that call [on September 9] because the State Department and the White House cannot locate it."[952] While Ambassador Sondland testified that "I'm pretty sure I had the call on that day,"[953] he acknowledged that he might have misremembered the date of the September 9 call—"I may have even spoken to him on September 6th"—and that without his call records, he could not be certain about when he spoke to President Trump.[954]

After the deposition transcripts of Ambassador Taylor and Mr. Morrison were made public, including their detailed accounts of the September 7 conversation that Ambassador Sondland had with President Trump, Ambassador Sondland submitted a written addendum to his deposition based on his "refreshed" recollection.[955] In that addendum, Ambassador Sondland amended his testimony and stated, "I cannot specifically recall if I had one or two phone calls with President Trump in the September 6-9 time frame."[956]

Furthermore, the conversation recalled by Ambassador Sondland as having taken place on September 9 is consistent with a conversation that Ambassador Sondland relayed to Mr. Morrison and Ambassador Taylor during the previous two days. Both Mr. Morrison and Ambassador Taylor, after reviewing their contemporaneous written notes, provided detailed testimony about Ambassador Sondland's description of his call with President Trump. For example, Ambassador Sondland shared with Ambassador Taylor that even though President Trump asserted that "there is no quid pro quo," President Trump "did insist that President Zelensky go to a microphone and say he is opening investigations of Biden and 2016 election interference."[957] Mr. Morrison and Ambassador Taylor both testified that this conversation occurred on September 7.[958] Ambassador Sondland acknowledged that he had no basis to dispute the recollections of Mr. Morrison and Ambassador Taylor.[959] Ambassador Sondland, who testified that he does not take notes, stated: "If they have notes and they recall that, I don't have any reason to dispute it."[960]

Text messages produced to the Committees also indicate that Ambassador Sondland spoke to President Trump prior to September 8. On September 4, Ambassador Volker texted Mr. Yermak that Ambassador Sondland planned to speak to President Trump on September 6 or 7. Ambassador Volker wrote: "Hi Andrey. Reports are that pence liked meeting and will press trump on scheduling Ze visit. Gordon will follow up with pence and, if nothing moving, will have a chance to talk with President on Saturday [September 7]."[961] Ambassador Volker then corrected himself: "Sorry—on Friday [September 6]."[962]

On Sunday, September 8, at 11:20 a.m. Eastern Time, Ambassador Sondland texted Ambassadors Taylor and Volker: "Guys multiple convos with Ze, Potus. Lets talk."[963] Shortly after this text, Ambassador Taylor testified that he spoke to Ambassador Sondland, who recounted his conversation with President Trump on September 7, as well as a separate conversation that Ambassador Sondland had with President Zelensky.

The timing of the text messages also raises questions about Ambassador Sondland's recollection. If Ambassador Sondland spoke to President Trump after receiving Ambassador Taylor's text message on September 9, and before he responded, then the timing of the text messages would mean that President Trump took Ambassador Sondland's call in the middle of the night in Washington, D.C. Ambassador Taylor sent his message on September 9 at 12:47 a.m. Eastern Time, and Ambassador Sondland responded less than five hours later at 5:19 a.m. Eastern Time.[964]

In any event, President Trump's purported denial of the "quid pro quo" was also contradicted when Acting Chief of Staff Mick Mulvaney publicly admitted that security assistance was withheld in order to pressure Ukraine to conduct an investigation into the 2016 election.

On October 17, at a press briefing in the White House, Mr. Mulvaney confirmed that President Trump withheld the essential military aid for Ukraine as leverage to pressure Ukraine to investigate the conspiracy theory that Ukraine had interfered in the 2016 U.S. election, which was also promoted by Vladimir Putin.[965] Mr. Mulvaney confirmed that President Trump "absolutely" mentioned "corruption related to the DNC server. ... No question about that."[966] When the White House press corps attempted to clarify this acknowledgement of a quid pro quo related to security assistance, Mr. Mulvaney replied: "We do that all the time with foreign policy." He continued. "I have news for everybody: get over it."[967]

8. The President's Scheme Was Exposed

President Trump lifted the hold on U.S. military assistance to Ukraine on September 11 after it became clear to the White House and President Trump that his scheme was exposed.

Overview

As news of the President's hold on military assistance to Ukraine became public on August 28, Congress, the press, and the public increased their scrutiny of President Trump's actions regarding Ukraine, which risked exposing President Trump's scheme. By this date, the White House had learned that the Inspector General of the Intelligence Community (ICIG), Michael Atkinson, had determined that a whistleblower complaint related to the same Ukraine matters was "credible" and an "urgent concern," and, pursuant to the applicable statute, recommended to the Acting Director of National Intelligence (DNI), Joseph Maguire, that the complaint should be transmitted to Congress.

In early September, bipartisan Members of both houses of Congress—publicly, and privately—expressed concerns to the White House about the hold on military assistance. On September 9, after months of internal discussion due to growing concern about the activity of President Trump's personal attorney, Rudy Giuliani, regarding Ukraine, the Chairs of the Permanent Select Committee on Intelligence, the Committee on Foreign Affairs, and the Committee on Oversight and Reform announced a joint investigation into efforts by President Trump and Mr. Giuliani, "to improperly pressure the Ukrainian government to assist the President's bid for reelection," including by withholding Congressionally-appropriated military assistance.

Later that same day, the ICIG notified Chairman Schiff and Ranking Member Nunes that, despite uniform past practice and a statutory requirement that credible, "urgent concern" complaints be provided to the intelligence committees, the Acting DNI was nevertheless withholding the whistleblower complaint from Congress. The Acting DNI later testified that his office initially withheld the complaint on the advice of the White House, with guidance from the Department of Justice.

Two days later, on September 11, the President lifted the hold on the military assistance to Ukraine. Numerous witnesses testified that they were never aware of any official reason for why the hold was either implemented or lifted.

Notwithstanding this ongoing inquiry, President Trump has continued to urge Ukraine to investigate his political rival, former Vice President Biden. For example, when asked by a journalist on October 3 what he hoped Ukraine's President would do about the Bidens in response to the July 25 call, President Trump responded: "Well, I would think that, if they were honest about it, they'd start a major investigation into the Bidens. It's a very simple answer." President Trump reiterated his affinity for the former Prosecutor General of Ukraine, Yuriy Lutsenko, whom numerous witnesses described as inept and corrupt: "And they got rid of a prosecutor who was a very tough prosecutor. They got rid of him. Now they're trying to make it the opposite way."

Public Scrutiny of President Trump's Hold on Military Assistance for Ukraine

After news of the President's freeze on U.S. military assistance to Ukraine became public on August 28, both houses of Congress increased their ongoing scrutiny of President Trump's decision.[968] On September 3, a bipartisan group of Senators, including Senator Rob Portman and Senator Ron Johnson, sent a letter to Acting White House Chief of Staff Mick Mulvaney expressing "deep concerns" that the "Administration is considering not obligating the Ukraine Security Initiative funds for 2019."[969] The Senators' letter urged that the "vital" funds be obligated "immediately."[970] On September 5, the Chairman and Ranking Member of the House Foreign Affairs Committee sent a letter to Mr. Mulvaney and Acting Director of the OMB Russell Vought expressing "deep concern" about the continuing hold on security assistance funding for Ukraine.[971]

On September 5, the *Washington Post* editorial board reported concerns that President Trump was withholding military assistance for Ukraine and a White House meeting in order to force President Zelensky to announce investigations of Mr. Biden and purported Ukrainian interference in the 2016 U.S. election. The *Post* editorial board wrote:

> [W]e're reliably told that the president has a second and more venal agenda: He is attempting to force Mr. Zelensky to intervene in the 2020 U.S. presidential election by launching an investigation of the leading Democratic candidate, Joe Biden. Mr. Trump is not just soliciting Ukraine's help with his presidential campaign; he is using U.S. military aid the country desperately needs in an attempt to extort it.

It added:

> The White House claims Mr. Trump suspended Ukraine's military aid in order for it [sic] be reviewed. But, as CNN reported, the Pentagon has already completed the study and recommended that the hold be lifted. Yet Mr. Trump has not yet acted. If his recalcitrance has a rationale, other than seeking to compel a foreign government to aid his reelection, the president has yet to reveal it.[972]

On the same day that the *Washington Post* published its editorial, Senators Christopher Murphy and Ron Johnson visited Kyiv, and met with President Zelensky. They were accompanied by Ambassador Bill Taylor and Counselor for Political Affairs David Holmes of U.S. Embassy Kyiv. President Zelensky's "first question to the Senators was about the withheld security assistance."[973] Ambassador Taylor testified that both Senators "stressed that bipartisan support for Ukraine in Washington was Ukraine's most important strategic asset and that President Zelensky should not jeopardize that bipartisan support by getting drawn into U.S. domestic politics." [974]

As Senator Johnson and Senator Murphy later recounted, the Senators sought to reassure President Zelensky that there was bipartisan support in Congress for providing Ukraine with military assistance for Ukraine and that they would continue to urge President Trump to lift the hold—as Senator Johnson had already tried, unsuccessfully, before traveling to Ukraine.[975]

Three Committees Announced Joint Investigation of President's Scheme

On September 9, the Chairs of the House Intelligence Committee, the Committee on Foreign Affairs, and the Committee on Oversight and Reform publicly announced a joint investigation of the scheme by President Trump and Mr. Giuliani "to improperly pressure the Ukrainian government to assist the President's bid for reelection."[976] The Committees had been planning and coordinating this investigation since early summer, after growing public scrutiny of Mr. Giuliani's activities in Ukraine and questions about Ambassador Yovanovitch's abrupt removal following a public smear campaign targeting her.

In a letter sent to White House Counsel Pat Cipollone the same day, the three Chairs stated that President Trump and Mr. Giuliani "appear to have acted outside legitimate law enforcement and diplomatic channels to coerce the Ukrainian government into pursuing two politically-motivated investigations under the guise of anti-corruption activity"—investigations into purported Ukrainian interference in the 2016 election and Vice President Biden and his son.[977]

With respect to the hold on Ukraine military assistance, the Chairs observed that "[i]f the President is trying to pressure Ukraine into choosing between defending itself from Russian aggression without U.S. assistance or leveraging its judicial system to serve the ends of the Trump campaign, this would represent a staggering abuse of power, a boon to Moscow, and a betrayal of the public trust."[978] The Chairs requested that the White House preserve all relevant records and produce them by September 16, including the transcript of the July 25 call between President Trump and President Zelensky.[979]

On the same day, the Chairs of the three Committees sent a similar letter to Secretary of State Mike Pompeo seeking the preservation and production of all relevant records at the Department of State by September 16.[980] To date, and as explained more fully in Section II, Secretary Pompeo has not produced a single document sought by the Committees pursuant to a lawful subpoena.

NSC Senior Director for Russia and Europe Timothy Morrison recalled seeing a copy of the letter that was sent by the three Chairs to the White House.[981] He also recalled that the three Committees' Ukraine investigation was discussed at meeting of senior-level NSC staff soon after it was publicly announced.[982] The NSC's legislative affairs staff issued a notice of the investigation to NSC staff members, although it is unclear exactly when.[983] NSC Director for Ukraine Alexander Vindman recalled discussions among NSC staff members, including Mr. Morrison's deputy, John Erath, that the investigation "might have the effect of releasing the hold" on Ukraine military assistance because it would be "potentially politically challenging" for the Administration to "justify that hold" to the Congress.[984]

Later that same day, September 9, Inspector General Atkinson sent a letter to Chairman Adam Schiff and Ranking Member Devin Nunes notifying them that an Intelligence Community whistleblower had filed a complaint with the ICIG on August 12.[985] Pursuant to a statute governing whistleblower disclosures, the Inspector General—after a condensed, preliminary review—had determined that the complaint constituted an "urgent concern" and that its allegations appeared to be "credible."[986] The Inspector General's September 9 letter did not disclose the substance or topic of the whistleblower complaint.

Contrary to uniform past practice and the clear requirements of the whistleblower statute, Acting DNI Maguire withheld the whistleblower complaint based on advice from the White House.[987] Acting DNI Maguire also relied upon an unprecedented intervention by the Department of Justice into Intelligence Community whistleblower matters to overturn the ICIG's determination based on a preliminary investigation.[988]

The White House had been aware of the whistleblower complaint weeks prior to the ICIG's letter of September 9.[989] Acting DNI Maguire testified that, after receiving the whistleblower complaint from the Inspector General on August 26, his office contacted the White House Counsel's Office for guidance.[990]

Consistent with Acting DNI Maguire's testimony, the *New York Times* reported that in late August, Mr. Cipollone and National Security Council Legal Advisor John Eisenberg personally briefed President Trump about the complaint's existence—and explained to the President that they believed the complaint could be withheld on executive privilege grounds.[991] The report alleged that Mr. Cipollone and Mr. Eisenberg "told Mr. Trump they planned to ask the Justice Department's Office of Legal Counsel to determine whether they had to disclose the complaint to lawmakers."[992]

On September 10, Chairman Schiff wrote to Acting DNI Maguire to express his concern about the Acting DNI's "unprecedented departure from past practice" in withholding the whistleblower complaint from the Congressional intelligence committees notwithstanding his "express obligations under the law" and the Inspector General's determination.[993] Chairman Schiff observed that the "failure to transmit to the Committee an urgent and credible whistleblower complaint, as required by law, raises the prospect that an urgent matter of a serious nature is being purposefully concealed from the Committee."[994]

Also on September 10, Ambassador John Bolton resigned from his position as National Security Advisor. Ambassador Bolton's deputy, Dr. Charles Kupperman, became the Acting National Security Advisor. The Committee was unable to determine if Ambassador Bolton's departure related to the matters under investigation because neither he nor Dr. Kupperman agreed to appear for testimony as part of this inquiry.

On September 13, the Office of the Director of National Intelligence (ODNI) General Counsel informed the Committee that DOJ had overruled the ICIG's determination, and that the

ODNI could not transmit the complaint to the Committee at its discretion because it involved "potentially privileged communications by persons outside the Intelligence Community"—presumably presidential communications.[995] In response, Chairman Schiff issued a subpoena to the Acting DNI on September 13 and announced to the public that ODNI was withholding a "credible" whistleblower complaint of "urgent concern."[996] Following intense pressure from the public and Congress, on September 25, the White House released the complaint to the intelligence committees and the July 25 call record to the public.[997]

President Trump Lifted the Hold on Military Assistance for Ukraine

On September 11—two days after the three Committees launched their investigation into President Trump's scheme, and one day after Chairman Schiff requested that Acting DNI Maguire produce a copy of the whistleblower complaint—President Trump lifted the hold on military assistance for Ukraine.

On the evening of September 11, prior to lifting the hold, President Trump met with Vice President Mike Pence, Mr. Mulvaney, and Senator Portman to discuss the hold.[998] Around 8:00 p.m. on September 11, the Chief of Staff's office informed Dr. Kupperman that the hold had been lifted.[999]

Just like there was no official explanation for why the hold on Ukraine security assistance was implemented, numerous witnesses testified that they were not provided with a reason for why the hold was lifted on September 11.[1000] For example, Deputy Assistant Secretary of Defense Laura Cooper testified that President Trump's lifting of the hold "really came quite out of the blue… It was quite abrupt."[1001] Jennifer Williams, Special Advisor to the Vice President for Europe and Russia, testified that from the time when she first learned about the hold on July 3 until it was lifted on September 11, she never came to understand why President Trump ordered the hold.[1002]

OMB Deputy Associate Director of National Security Programs Mark Sandy, who was the senior career official overseeing the administration of some of the Ukraine military assistance, only learned of a possible rationale for the hold in early September—after the Acting DNI had informed the White House about the whistleblower complaint.[1003] Mr. Sandy testified that he could not recall another instance "where a significant amount of assistance was being held up" and he "didn't have a rationale for as long as I didn't have a rationale in this case."[1004] However, in "early September," approximately two months after President Trump had implemented the hold, and several weeks after the White House learned of the whistleblower complaint, Mr. Sandy received an email from OMB Associate Director of National Security Programs Michael Duffey. For the first time, it "attributed the hold to the President's concern about other countries not contributing more to Ukraine" and requested "information on what additional countries were contributing to Ukraine."[1005]

Mr. Sandy testified that he was not aware of any other countries committing to provide more financial assistance to Ukraine prior to the lifting of the hold on September 11.[1006] According to Lt. Col. Vindman, none of the "facts on the ground" changed before the President lifted the hold.[1007]

After the Hold was Lifted, Congress was Forced to Pass a Law to Ensure All of the Military Aid Could Be Distributed to Ukraine

The lengthy delay created by the hold on Ukraine military assistance prevented the Department of Defense from spending all of the Congressionally-appropriated funds by the end of the fiscal year, which meant that the funds would expire on September 30 because unused funds do not roll over to the next fiscal year.[1008] This confirmed the fears expressed by Ms. Cooper, Mr. Sandy, and others related to the illegal impoundment of Congressionally-mandated funding—concerns that were discussed in some depth within the relevant agencies in late July and throughout August.[1009]

Prior to the release of the funds, DOD's internal analysis raised concerns that up to $100 million of military assistance could go unspent as a result of the hold imposed by the President.[1010] Ultimately, approximately $35 million of Ukraine military assistance—14% of the total funds—remained unspent by the end of fiscal year 2019.[1011] Typically, DOD averages between 2 and 5 percent unspent funds for similar programs, substantially less than the 14 percent left unspent in this case.[1012]

In order to ensure that Ukraine did not permanently lose $35 million of the critical military assistance frozen by the White House,[1013] Congress passed a provision on September 27—three days before funds were set to expire—to ensure that the remaining $35 million in 2019 military assistance to Ukraine could be spent.[1014] Ms. Cooper testified that such an act of Congress was unusual—indeed, she had never heard of funding being extended in this manner.[1015]

As of November 2019, Pentagon officials confirmed that the $35 million in security assistance originally held by the President and extended by Congress had still yet to be disbursed. When asked for an explanation, the Pentagon only confirmed that the funds had not yet been spent but declined to say why.[1016]

Pressure to Announce Investigations Continued After the Hold was Lifted

Before President Trump lifted the hold on security assistance, Ukrainian officials had relented to the American pressure campaign to announce the investigations and had scheduled President Zelensky to appear on CNN.[1017] Even after President Trump lifted the hold on September 11, President Zelensky did not immediately cancel his planned CNN interview.[1018]

On September 12, Ambassador Taylor personally informed President Zelensky and the Ukrainian foreign minister that President Trump's hold on military assistance had been lifted.[1019] Ambassador Taylor remained concerned, however, that "there was some indication that there might still be a plan for the CNN interview in New York" during which President Zelensky would announce the investigations that President Trump wanted Ukraine to pursue.[1020] Ambassador Taylor testified that he "wanted to be sure that that didn't happen, so I addressed it with Zelensky's staff."[1021]

On September 13, a staff member at the U.S. Embassy in Kyiv texted Mr. Holmes to relay a message that "Sondland said the Zelensky interview is supposed to be today or Monday, and they plan to announce that a certain investigation that was 'on hold' will progress."[1022] The Embassy Kyiv staffer stated that he "did not know if this was decided or if Sondland was advocating for it. Apparently he's been discussing this with Yermak."[1023]

On September 13, during a meeting in President Zelensky's office, Ukrainian presidential aide Andriy Yermak "looked uncomfortable" when Ambassador Taylor sought to confirm that there were no plans for President Zelensky to announce the investigations during a CNN interview.[1024] Although President Zelensky's National Security Advisor Oleksandr Danyliuk indicated that there were no plans for President Zelensky to do the CNN interview, Ambassador Taylor was still concerned after he and Mr. Holmes saw Mr. Yermak following the meeting.[1025] According to Ambassador Taylor, Mr. Yermak's "body language was such that it looked to me like he was still thinking they were going to make that statement."[1026] Mr. Holmes also recalled that when he and Ambassador Taylor ran ran into Mr. Yermak following the meeting, Ambassador Taylor "stressed the importance of staying out of U.S. politics and said he hoped no interview was planned," but "Mr. Yermak shrugged in resignation and did not answer, as if to indicate he had no choice."[1027]

That same day, September 13, President Zelensky reportedly met with CNN's Fareed Zakaria, who was in Kyiv to moderate the Yalta European Strategy Conference.[1028] During the meeting with Mr. Zakaria, President Zelensky did not cancel his planned CNN interview.[1029]

Conflicting advice prompted the Ukrainian foreign minister to observe in a meeting with Ambassador Volker, Ambassador Taylor, and Deputy Assistant Secretary of State George Kent, "You guys are sending us different messages in different channels."[1030]

For example, at a September 14 meeting in Kyiv attended by Ambassador Volker, Mr. Yermak, and the Ukrainian foreign minister, Ambassador Volker stated that when the two Presidents finally meet, "it's important that President Zelensky give the messages that we discussed before," apparently referring to President Zelensky's "willingness to open investigations in the two areas of interest to the President and that had been pushed previously by Rudy Giuliani."[1031] Ambassador Taylor, however, replied: "Don't do that."[1032]

On September 18 or 19, President Zelensky cancelled his scheduled interview with CNN.[1033] Although President Zelensky did not publicly announce the investigations that President Trump wanted, he remains under pressure from President Trump, particularly because he requires diplomatic, financial, and military backing from the United States, the most powerful supporter of Ukraine. That pressure continues to this day. As Mr. Holmes testified:

> [A]lthough the hold on the security assistance may have been lifted, there were still things they wanted that [the Ukrainians] weren't getting, including a meeting with the President in the Oval Office. Whether the hold—the security assistance hold continued or not, Ukrainians understood that that's something the President wanted, and they still wanted important things from the President.

And I think that continues to this day. I think they're being very careful. They still need us now going forward. In fact, right now, President Zelensky is trying to arrange a summit meeting with President Putin in the coming weeks, his first face to face meeting with him to try to advance the peace process. He needs our support. He needs President Putin to understand that America supports Zelensky at the highest levels. So this doesn't end with the lifting of the security assistance hold. Ukraine still needs us, and as I said, still fighting this war this very day.[1034]

Vice President Pence Spoke to President Zelensky

On September 18, approximately one week before President Trump was scheduled to meet with President Zelensky at the United Nations General Assembly in New York, Vice President Pence spoke with President Zelensky by telephone.[1035] According to Ms. Williams, during the call, Vice President Pence "reiterat[ed] the release of the funds" and "ask[ed] a bit more about ... how Zelensky's efforts were going."[1036]

On November 26, Ms. Williams submitted a classified addendum to her hearing testimony on November 19 related to this telephone call. According to Ms. Williams' counsel, the Office of the Vice President informed Ms. Williams' counsel that certain portions of the September 18 call, including the additional information in Ms. Williams' addendum, are classified. The Committee has requested that the Office of the Vice President conduct a declassification review so that the Committee may share this additional information regarding the substance of the September 18 call publicly. On October 9, Vice President Pence told reporters, "I'd have no objection" to the White House releasing the transcript of his calls with President Zelensky and said that "we're discussing that with White House counsel as we speak."[1037] In a November 7 interview with *Fox Business*, Vice President Pence reiterated, "I have no objection at all" to releasing records of his calls.[1038]

President Trump and Rudy Giuliani, Undeterred, Continued to Solicit Foreign Interference in Our Elections

On September 19, Rudy Giuliani was interviewed by Chris Cuomo on CNN. During the interview, Mr. Giuliani confirmed that he had urged Ukraine to investigate "the allegations that there was interference in the election of 2016, by the Ukrainians, for the benefit of Hillary Clinton[.]" When asked specifically if he had asked Ukraine to look into Vice President Biden, Mr. Giuliani replied immediately, "of course I did."

Seconds later, Mr. Giuliani attempted to clarify his admission, insisting that he had not asked Ukraine to investigate Vice President Biden but instead "to look into the allegations that related to my client [President Trump], which tangentially involved Joe Biden in a massive bribery scheme." Mr. Giuliani insisted that his conduct was appropriate, telling Mr. Cuomo later in the interview that "it is perfectly appropriate for a President to say to a leader of a foreign country, investigate this massive bribe ... that was paid by a former Vice President."[1039]

President Trump also has continued to publicly urge President Zelensky to launch an investigation of Vice President Biden and alleged 2016 election interference by Ukraine. On September 23, in a public press availability, President Trump stated:

> I put no pressure on them whatsoever. I could have. I think it would probably, possibly, have been okay if I did. But I didn't. I didn't put any pressure on them whatsoever. You know why? Because they want to do the right thing.[1040]

On September 24, in public remarks upon arriving at the opening session of the U.N. General Assembly, President Trump stated: "What Joe Biden did for his son, that's something they should be looking at."[1041]

On September 25—in a joint public press availability with President Zelensky—President Trump stated that "I want him to do whatever he can" in reference to the investigation of the Biden family. He added, "Now, when Biden's son walks away with millions of dollars from Ukraine, and he knows nothing, and they're paying him millions of dollars, that's corruption." President Trump added, "He [President Zelensky] was elected—I think, number one—on the basis of stopping corruption, which unfortunately has plagued Ukraine. And if he could do that, he's doing, really, the whole world a big favor. I know—and I think he's going to be successful."[1042]

On September 30, during his remarks at the swearing-in ceremony of Labor Secretary Eugene Scalia, President Trump stated:

> Now, the new President of Ukraine ran on the basis of no corruption. That's how he got elected. And I believe that he really means it. But there was a lot of corruption having to do with the 2016 election against us. And we want to get to the bottom of it, and it's very important that we do.[1043]

On October 2, in a public press availability, President Trump discussed the July 25 call with President Zelensky and stated that "the conversation was perfect; it couldn't have been nicer." He added:

> The only thing that matters is the transcript of the actual conversation that I had with the President of Ukraine. It was perfect. We're looking at congratulations. We're looking at doing things together. And what are we looking at? We're looking at corruption. And, in, I believe, 1999, there was a corruption act or a corruption bill passed between both—and signed—between both countries, where I have a duty to report corruption. And let me tell you something: Biden's son is corrupt, and Biden is corrupt.[1044]

On October 3, in remarks before he departed on Marine One, President Trump expressed his "hope" that Ukraine would investigate Mr. Biden and his son. Specifically, President Trump stated that he had hoped—after his July 25 conversation—that Ukraine would "start a major investigation into the Bidens." The President also stated that "by the way, likewise, China should start an investigation into the Bidens, because what happened in China is just about as bad as what happened with—with Ukraine." He addressed the corrupt prosecutor general, Yuriy

Lutsenko, who had recently been removed by Parliament: "And they got rid of a prosecutor who was a very tough prosecutor. They got rid of him. Now they're trying to make it the opposite way.[1045]

The next day, on October 4, in remarks before he departed on Marine One, the President again said:

When you look at what Biden and his son did, and when you look at other people — what they've done. And I believe there was tremendous corruption with Biden, but I think there was beyond—I mean, beyond corruption—having to do with the 2016 campaign, and what these lowlifes did to so many people, to hurt so many people in the Trump campaign—which was successful, despite all of the fighting us. I mean, despite all of the unfairness.[1046]

President Trump reiterated his willingness to solicit foreign assistance related to his personal interests: "Here's what's okay: If we feel there's corruption, like I feel there was in the 2016 campaign—there was tremendous corruption against me—if we feel there's corruption, we have a right to go to a foreign country."[1047] President Trump added that asking President Xi of China to investigate the Bidens "is certainly something we can start thinking about."[1048]

Consistent with the President's remarks after this inquiry began, Ambassador Volker understood that references to fighting "corruption" in Ukraine, when used by President Trump and Mr. Giuliani, in fact referred to the two investigations into "Burisma"—and former Vice President Biden—and the 2016 election interference that President Trump sought to benefit his reelection efforts.[1049]

The President's Scheme Undermined U.S. Anti-Corruption Efforts in Ukraine

Rather than combatting corruption in Ukraine, President Trump's ongoing efforts to urge Ukraine to pursue an investigation into former Vice President Biden undermine longstanding U.S. anti-corruption policy, which encourages countries to refrain from using the criminal justice system to investigate political opponents. When it became clear that President Trump was pressuring Ukraine to investigate his political rival, career public servants charged with implementing U.S. foreign policy in a non-partisan manner, such as Lt. Col. Vindman and Ambassador Taylor, communicated to President Zelensky and his advisors that Ukraine should avoid getting embroiled in U.S. domestic politics.[1050]

Mr. Kent, an anti-corruption and rule of law expert, explained that U.S. anti-corruption efforts prioritize "building institutional capacity so that the Ukrainian Government has the ability to go after corruption and effectively investigate, prosecute, and judge alleged criminal activities using appropriate institutional mechanisms, that is, to create and follow the rule of law. [1051]

Mr. Holmes concurred:

[O]ur longstanding policy is to encourage them [Ukraine] to establish and build rule of law institutions, that are capable and that are independent and that can actually pursue credible allegations. That's our policy. We've been doing that for quite some time with some success. So focusing on [particular] cases, including [] cases where there is an interest of the President, it's just not part of what we've done. It's hard to explain why we would do that.[1052]

Mr. Kent emphasized that when foreign government officials "hear diplomats on the ground saying one thing, and they hear other U.S. leaders saying something else," it raises concerns about the United States' credibility on anti-corruption efforts.[1053] Ambassador Taylor agreed, stating that "[o]ur credibility is based on a respect for the United States" and "if we damage that respect, then it hurts our credibility and makes it more difficult for us to do our jobs."[1054]

Mr. Kent, like many other witnesses, explained that urging Ukraine to engage in "selective politically associated investigations or prosecutions" undermined the rule of law more generally:

As a general principle, I do not believe the United States should ask other countries to engage in selective politically associated investigations or prosecutions against opponents of those in power because such selective actions undermine the rule of law, regardless of the country.[1055]

Mr. Kent agreed that pressuring Ukraine to conduct political investigations is not a part of U.S. foreign policy to promote the rule of law in Ukraine and around the world.[1056] Mr. Kent concluded that the President's request for investigations "went against U.S. policy" and "would've undermined the rule of law and our longstanding policy goals in Ukraine, as in other countries, in the post-Soviet space."[1057]

These conflicting messages came to a head at a September 14 meeting between American and Ukrainian officials in Kyiv. During that meeting, Ambassador Volker advised Mr. Yermak about the "potential problems" with investigations that the Zelensky administration was contemplating into former Ukrainian President Petro Poroshenko.[1058] Mr. Yermak retorted, "what, you mean like asking us to investigate Clinton and Biden?"[1059] Ambassador Volker did not respond.[1060]

SECTION I ENDNOTES

[1] Yovanovitch Hearing Tr. at 16-17.

[2] *Kateryna Handziuk, Ukrainian Activist, Dies From Acid Attack*, New York Times (Nov. 5, 2018) (online at www.nytimes.com/2018/11/05/world/europe/kateryna-handziuk-dies-ukraine.html).

[3] Yovanovitch Hearing Tr. at 30-31.

[4] U.S. Embassy in Ukraine, Department of State, *Ambassador Yovanovitch's Remarks at a Women of Courage Reception in Honor of Kateryna Handziuk* (Apr. 24, 2019) (online at https://ua.usembassy.gov/ambassador-yovanovitchs-remarks-at-a-women-of-courage-reception-in-honor-of-kateryna-handziuk/).

[5] U.S. Embassy in Ukraine, Department of State, *Ambassador Yovanovitch's Remarks at a Women of Courage Reception in Honor of Kateryna Handziuk* (Apr. 24, 2019) (online at https://ua.usembassy.gov/ambassador-yovanovitchs-remarks-at-a-women-of-courage-reception-in-honor-of-kateryna-handziuk/).

[6] Yovanovitch Hearing Tr. at 31.

[7] Yovanovitch Hearing Tr. at 31-32.

[8] Yovanovitch Hearing Tr. at 32.

[9] Yovanovitch Hearing Tr. at 31.

[10] Yovanovitch Hearing Tr. at 31-32.

[11] *Giuliani to Join Trump's Legal Team*, New York Times (April 19, 2018) (online at https://www.nytimes.com/2018/04/19/us/politics/giuliani-trump.html).

[12] Letter from John M. Dowd, Counsel to Igor Fruman and Lev Parnas, to Committee Staff (Oct. 3, 2019).

[13] Department of Justice, *Lev Parnas and Igor Fruman Charged with Conspiring to Violate Straw and Foreign Donor Bans* (Oct. 10, 2019) (online at www.justice.gov/usao-sdny/pr/lev-parnas-and-igor-fruman-charged-conspiring-violate-straw-and-foreign-donor-bans).

[14] Hill Dep. Tr. at 59.

[15] Yovanovitch Dep. Tr. at 28-29.

[16] *Ukraine Ousts Victor Shokin, Top Prosecutor, and Political Stability Hangs in the Balance*, New York Times (Mar. 29, 2016) (online at www.nytimes.com/2016/03/30/world/europe/political-stability-in-the-balance-as-ukraine-ousts-top-prosecutor.html).

[17] Kent Dep. Tr. at 45.

[18] Yovanovitch Dep. Tr. at 27-28.

[19] Yovanovitch Dep. Tr. at 31-32.

[20] Yovanovitch Dep. Tr. at 21.

[21] Yovanovitch Dep. Tr. at 32-33, 38 ("I think that he felt that I and the embassy were effective at helping Ukrainians who wanted reform, Ukrainians who wanted to fight against corruption, and he did not – you know, that was not in his interest.").

[22] Yovanovitch Dep. Tr. at 30.

[23] Holmes Dep. Tr. at 14.

[24] Kent-Taylor Hearing Tr. at 25.

[25] Kent-Taylor Hearing Tr. at 132.

[26] Morrison-Volker Hearing Tr. at 27.

[27] Nickolay Kapitonenko, an advisor to the Ukrainian Parliament's Foreign Policy Committee, described Giuliani as a "mythical link to the U.S." who is viewed as "an extension of Trump." *Giuliani Sits at the Center of the Ukraine Controversy*, Wall Street Journal (Sep. 26, 2019) (online at www.wsj.com/articles/giuliani-sits-at-the-center-of-the-ukraine-controversy-11569546774); David Sakvarelidze, a former Ukrainian deputy prosecutor general, stated, "Lutsenko was trying to save his political skin by pretending to be Trumpist at the end of his career." *Meet the Ukrainian Ex-Prosecutor Behind the Impeachment Furor*, New York Times (Oct. 5, 2019) (online at www.nytimes.com/2019/10/05/world/europe/ukraine-prosecutor-trump.html).

[28] Yovanovitch Dep. Tr. at 30.

[29] Donald J. Trump, Twitter (Jan. 17, 2019) (online at https://twitter.com/realdonaldtrump/status/1086096691613323265) ("Gregg Jarrett: 'Mueller's prosecutors knew the 'Dossier' was the product of bias and deception.' It was a Fake, just like so much news coverage in our Country. Nothing but a Witch Hunt, from beginning to end!").

[30] Office of the Director of National Intelligence, *Background to "Assessing Russian Activities and Intentions in Recent US Elections": The Analytic Process and Cyber Incident Attribution* (Jan. 6, 2017) (online at www.dni.gov/files/documents/ICA_2017_01.pdf); Senate Select Committee on Intelligence, *Russian Active Measures Campaigns and Interference in the 2016 U.S. Election* (May 8, 2018) (online at www.intelligence.senate.gov/publications/report-select-committee-intelligence-united-states-senate-russian-active-measures); House Permanent Select Committee on Intelligence, *Report on Russian Active Measures* (Mar. 22, 2018) (online at https://docs.house.gov/meetings/IG/IG00/20180322/108023/HRPT-115-1_1-p1-U3.pdf); House Permanent Select Committee on Intelligence, *Minority Views* (Mar. 26, 2018) (online at https://intelligence.house.gov/uploadedfiles/20180411_-_final_-_hpsci_minority_views_on_majority_report.pdf).

[31] *President Trump's Former National Security Advisor 'Deeply Disturbed' by Ukraine Scandal: 'Whole World Is Watching,'* ABC News (Sept. 29, 2019) (online at https://abcnews.go.com/Politics/president-trumps-national-security-advisor-deeply-disturbed-ukraine/story?id=65925477).

[32] *Charges of Ukrainian Meddling? A Russian Operation, U.S. Intelligence Says*, New York Times (Nov. 22, 2019) (online at https://www.nytimes.com/2019/11/22/us/politics/ukraine-russia-interference.html).

[33] Hill-Holmes Hearing Tr. at 56-57.

[34] Kent Dep. Tr. at 45.

[35] Volker Transcribed Interview Tr. at 330.

[36] Volker Transcribed Interview Tr. at 330; *Explainer: Biden, Allies, Pushed Out Ukrainian Prosecutor Because He Didn't Pursue Corruption Cases*, USA Today (Oct. 3, 2019) (online at www.usatoday.com/story/news/politics/2019/10/03/what-really-happened-when-biden-forced-out-ukraines-top-prosecutor/3785620002/).

[37] *See, e.g.*, *Ukraine Prosecutor Says No Evidence of Wrongdoing by Bidens*, Bloomberg (May 16, 2019) (online at www.bloomberg.com/news/articles/2019-05-16/ukraine-prosecutor-says-no-evidence-of-wrongdoing-by-bidens) ("Hunter Biden did not violate any Ukrainian laws -- at least as of now, we do not see any wrongdoing. A company can pay however much it wants to its board ... Biden was definitely not involved ... We do not have any grounds to think that there was any wrongdoing starting from 2014.").

[38] Notes of Call with Viktor Shokin (Jan. 23, 2019); *Ukraine Prosecutor Says No Evidence of Wrongdoing by Bidens*, Bloomberg (May 16, 2019) (online at www.bloomberg.com/news/articles/2019-05-16/ukraine-prosecutor-says-no-evidence-of-wrongdoing-by-bidens).

[39] *Giuliani Pursued Business in Ukraine While Pushing for Inquiries for Trump*, New York Times (Nov. 27, 2019) (online at www.nytimes.com/2019/11/27/nyregion/giuliani-ukraine-business-trump.html); *Ukraine Prosecutor Says No Evidence of Wrongdoing by Bidens*, Bloomberg (May 16, 2019) (online at www.bloomberg.com/news/articles/2019-05-16/ukraine-prosecutor-says-no-evidence-of-wrongdoing-by-bidens).

[40] Notes of Meeting with Yuriy Lutsenko (Jan. 25, 2019); *Ukraine Prosecutor Says No Evidence of Wrongdoing by Bidens*, Bloomberg (May 16, 2019) (online at www.bloomberg.com/news/articles/2019-05-16/ukraine-prosecutor-says-no-evidence-of-wrongdoing-by-bidens).

[41] *Giuliani Pursued Business in Ukraine While Pushing for Inquiries for Trump*, New York Times (Nov. 27, 2019) (online at www.nytimes.com/2019/11/27/nyregion/giuliani-ukraine-business-trump.html).

[42] Rudy Giuliani, Twitter (Oct. 23, 2019) (online at https://twitter.com/RudyGiuliani/status/1187168034835894272).

[43] Rudy Giuliani, Twitter (Oct. 30, 2019) (online at https://twitter.com/RudyGiuliani/status/1189667101079932928).

[44] Hill-Holmes Hearing Tr. at 19.

[45] *As Russia Collusion Fades, Ukrainian Plot to Help Clinton Emerges*, The Hill (Mar. 20, 2019) (online at https://thehill.com/opinion/campaign/435029-as-russia-collusion-fades-ukrainian-plot-to-help-clinton-emerges).

[46] *Ukraine Prosecutor General Lutsenko Admits U.S. Ambassador Didn't Give Him a Do Not Prosecute List*, The Ukrainian (Apr. 18, 2019) (online at www.unian.info/politics/10520715-ukraine-prosecutor-general-lutsenko-admits-u-s-ambassador-didn-t-give-him-a-do-not-prosecute-list.html).

[47] *As Russia Collusion Fades, Ukrainian Plot to Help Clinton Emerges*, The Hill (Mar. 20, 2019) (online at https://thehill.com/opinion/campaign/435029-as-russia-collusion-fades-ukrainian-plot-to-help-clinton-emerges).

[48] Yovanovitch Dep. Tr. at 21, 37.

[49] AT&T Document Production, Bates ATTHPSCI _20190930_00768, ATTHPSCI _20190930_00772, ATTHPSCI _20190930_00775.

[50] *As Russia Collusion Fades, Ukrainian Plot to Help Clinton Emerges*, The Hill (Mar. 20, 2019) (online at https://thehill.com/opinion/campaign/435029-as-russia-collusion-fades-ukrainian-plot-to-help-clinton emerges).

[51] Department of Justice, *Lev Parnas and Igor Fruman Charged with Conspiring to Violate Straw and Foreign Donor Bans* (Oct. 10, 2019) (online at www.justice.gov/usao-sdny/pr/lev-parnas-and-igor-fruman-charged-conspiring-violate-straw-and-foreign-donor-bans) (alleging that in May and June 2018, Mr. Parnas sought the assistance of an unnamed congressman in causing the removal or recall of the then-U.S. ambassador to Ukraine).

[52] AT&T Document Production, Bates ATTHPSCI _20190930_00775.

[53] Donald J. Trump, Twitter (Mar. 20, 2019) (online at https://twitter.com/realdonaldtrump/status/1108559080204001280).

[54] Rudy Giuliani, Twitter (Mar. 22, 2019) (online at https://twitter.com/RudyGiuliani/status/1109117167176466432); *Giuliani Slams Mueller Leak*, Fox News (April 7, 2019) (online at https://www.foxnews.com/transcript/giuliani-slams-mueller-leak).

[55] Donald Trump, Jr., Twitter (Mar. 24, 2019) (online at https://twitter.com/donaldjtrumpjr/status/1109850575926108161).

[56] Kent Dep. Tr. at 57-58.

[57] Kent Dep. Tr. at 178.

[58] Yovanovitch Dep. Tr. at 62.

[59] Hale Dep. Tr. at 37-38.

[60] Hale Dep. Tr. at 99-100.

[61] Yovanovitch Dep. Tr. at 63-64.

[62] Hale Dep. Tr. at 27.

[63] Yovanovitch Dep. Tr. at 124.

[64] Yovanovitch Dep. Tr. at 267-268.

[65] Yovanovitch Dep. Tr. at 268.

[66] Email from [Redacted] to S_All (Mar. 26, 2019) (online at www.americanoversight.org/wp-content/uploads/2019/11/AO_State_Ukraine_Docs_11-22.pdf); Email from Operations Center to [Redacted] (Mar.

29, 2019) (online at www.americanoversight.org/wp-content/uploads/2019/11/AO_State_Ukraine_Docs_11-22.pdf). (The same State Department records show that Secretary Pompeo was scheduled to have a secure call with Rep. Nunes on April 1, 2019.); Email from Operations Center to [Redacted] (Mar. 29, 2019) (online at www.americanoversight.org/wp-content/uploads/2019/11/AO_State_Ukraine_Docs_11-22.pdf).

[67] *Joe Biden's 2020 Ukrainian Nightmare: A Closed Probe is Revived*, The Hill (Apr. 1, 2019) (online at https://thehill.com/opinion/white-house/436816-joe-bidens-2020-ukrainian-nightmare-a-closed-probe-is-revived).

[68] Donald Trump, Jr., Twitter (Apr. 2, 2019) (online at https://twitter.com/donaldjtrumpjr/status/1113046659456528385).

[69] AT&T Document Production, Bates ATTHPSCI_20190930_00848-ATTHPSCI_20190930_00884. Mr. Parnas also had an aborted call that lasted 5 seconds on April 5, 2019 with an aide to Rep. Devin Nunes on the Intelligence Committee, Derek Harvey. AT&T Document Production, Bates ATTHPSCI_20190930_00876. Call records obtained by the Committees show that Mr. Parnas and Mr. Harvey had connected previously, including a four minute 42 second call on February 1, 2019, a one minute 7 second call on February 4, and a one minute 37 second call on February 7, 2019. AT&T Document Production, Bates ATTHPSCI_20190930_00617, ATTHPSCI_20190930_00630, ATTHPSCI_20190930_00641. As explained later in this Chapter, Rep. Nunes would connect separately by phone on April 10, 11, and 12 with Mr. Parnas and Mr. Giuliani. AT&T Document Production, Bates ATTHPSCI_20190930_00913- ATTHPSCI_20190930_00914; ATTHPSCI_20190930-02125.

[70] *Ukrainian to US Prosecutors: Why Don't You Want Our Evidence on Democrats?*, The Hill (Apr. 7, 2019) (online at https://thehill.com/opinion/white-house/437719-ukrainian-to-us-prosecutors-why-dont-you-want-our-evidence-on-democrats).

[71] *Ukrainian to US Prosecutors: Why Don't You Want Our Evidence on Democrats?*, The Hill (Apr. 7, 2019) (online at https://thehill.com/opinion/white-house/437719-ukrainian-to-us-prosecutors-why-dont-you-want-our-evidence-on-democrats).

[72] *Ukrainian to US Prosecutors: Why Don't You Want Our Evidence on Democrats?*, The Hill (Apr. 7, 2019) (online at https://thehill.com/opinion/white-house/437719-ukrainian-to-us-prosecutors-why-dont-you-want-our-evidence-on-democrats).

[73] *Ukrainian to US Prosecutors: Why Don't You Want Our Evidence on Democrats?*, The Hill (Apr. 7, 2019) (online at https://thehill.com/opinion/white-house/437719-ukrainian-to-us-prosecutors-why-dont-you-want-our-evidence-on-democrats).

[74] *Giuliani Slams Mueller Leak*, Fox News (Apr. 7, 2019) (online at www.foxnews.com/transcript/giuliani-slams-mueller-leak).

[75] Rudy Giuliani, Twitter (Apr. 8, 2019) (online at https://twitter.com/RudyGiuliani/status/1115171828618731520).

[76] Specifically, between April 8 and April 11, phone records show the following phone contacts:

- six calls between Mr. Giuliani and Mr. Parnas (longest duration approximately five minutes), AT&T Document Production, Bates ATTHPSCI_20190930-02115-ATTHPSCI_20190930-02131;
- four calls between Mr. Giuliani and Mr. Solomon (all on April 8, longest duration approximately one minute, 30 seconds) AT&T Document Production, Bates ATTHPSCI_20190930-02114-ATTHPSCI_20190930-02115;
- nine calls between Mr. Parnas and Mr. Solomon (longest duration four minutes, 39 seconds) AT&T Document Production, Bates ATTHPSCI_20190930-00885- ATTHPSCI_20190930-00906; and
- three calls between Mr. Parnas and Ms. Toensing (longest duration approximately six minutes), AT&T Document Production, Bates ATTHPSCI_20190930-00885- ATTHPSCI_20190930-00905.

[77] AT&T Document Production, Bates ATTHPSCI_20190930-02125, ATTHPSCI_20190930-03236.

Date	Connecting Time (ET)	Duration of Call	Caller	Recipient
04/10/19	12:00:36	0:35	Giuliani, Rudy	Nunes, Devin
04/10/19	12:10:35	0:00	Nunes, Devin	Giuliani, Rudy
04/10/19	12:10:37	0:31	Nunes, Devin	Giuliani, Rudy
04/10/19	12:11:10	SMS	UNKNOWN	Giuliani, Rudy
04/10/19	12:12:35	2:50	Giuliani, Rudy	Nunes, Devin
04/10/19	12:15:38	0:00	Giuliani, Rudy	Nunes, Devin

[78] AT&T Document Production, Bates ATTHPSCI_20190930-00902.

[79] Jay Sekulow, personal counsel to President Trump, stated that the President was disappointed that Mr. diGenova and Ms. Toensing had to withdraw due to a conflict of interest, but noted that "those conflicts do not prevent them from assisting the President in other legal matters. The President looks forward to working with them." *Trump's Legal Team Remains in Disarray as New Lawyer Will No Longer Represent Him in Russia Probe*, Washington Post (Mar. 25, 2018) (online at www.washingtonpost.com/politics/in-another-blow-to-trumps-efforts-to-combat-russia-probe-digenova-will-no-longer-join-legal-team/2018/03/25/8ac8c8d2-3038-11e8-94fa-32d48460b955_story.html).

[80] For example, between April 1 and April 7, Ms. Toensing exchanged approximately five calls with Mr. Parnas and two calls with Mr. Giuliani. In addition, on April 10, Ms. Toensing and Mr. Giuliani spoke for approximately six minutes, 19 seconds. AT&T Document Production, Bates ATTHPSCI_20190930-02126. Mr. diGenova and Ms. Toensing were also very active on social media in promoting these conspiracy theories as well as the false accusations against Ambassador Yovanovitch. *See, e.g.*, Ryan Saavedra, Twitter (Mar. 23, 2019) (online at https://twitter.com/RealSaavedra/status/1109546629672009728); Victoria Toensing, Twitter (Mar. 21, 2019) (online at https://twitter.com/VicToensing/status/1108751525239762944); Victoria Toensing, Twitter (Mar. 24, 2019) (online at https://twitter.com/VicToensing/status/1109882728101625856).

[81] Retainer Letter, diGenova & Toensing, LLP, Yuriy Lutsenko, and Kostiantyn Kulyk (Apr. 12, 2019); Retainer Letter, diGenova & Toensing, LLP, Viktor Shokin (Apr. 15, 2019).

[82] On April 12, less than a week after the latest piece in *The Hill*, Ms. Toensing signed a retainer agreement between diGenova & Toensing, LLP, Mr. Lutsenko, and his former deputy Kostiantyn Kulyk, two of the primary sources for Mr. Solomon's articles. The Committees' obtained a copy of this document which is not signed by the Ukrainians, but a spokesman for Ms. Toensing and Mr. diGenova confirmed that the firm represented Mr. Lutsenko. *See Giuliani Weighed Doing Business with Ukrainian Government*, Wall Street Journal (Nov. 27, 2019) (online at www.wsj.com/articles/giuliani-weighed-doing-business-with-ukrainian-government-11574890951).

The first paragraph of the retainer agreement sets forth the services to be provided by diGenova & Toensing, LLP to their Ukrainian clients:

> Yurii Lutsenko and Kostiantyn Kulyk ("Clients") hereby engage the firm of diGenova & Toensing, LLP ("Firm" or "Attorneys") to represent them in connection with recovery and return to the Ukraine government of funds illegally embezzled from that country and providing assistance to meet and discuss with United States government officials the evidence of illegal conduct in Ukraine regarding the United States, for example, interference in the 2016 U.S. elections.

See Retainer Letter, diGenova & Toensing, LLP, Yuriy Lutsenko, and Kostiantyn Kulyk (Apr. 12, 2019).

The scope of representation—which includes representing Mr. Lutsenko and Mr. Kulyk in meetings with U.S. officials regarding Ukrainian interference in the 2016 U.S. elections—mirrors the allegations reported in *The*

Hill, pursued by Mr. Giuliani on behalf of President Trump, and pushed by the President on his July 25 call with President Zelensky. According to the retainer agreement, Mr. Lutsenko was to pay diGenova & Toensing, LLP $25,000 per month, plus costs, for four months for this work. *See* Retainer Letter, diGenova & Toensing, LLP, Yuriy Lutsenko, and Kostiantyn Kulyk (Apr. 12, 2019).

On April 12, the same day Ms. Toensing signed the retainer agreement with Mr. Lutsenko, phone records show contacts between Ms. Toensing, Mr. Giuliani, and Mr. Parnas, as well as contacts between Mr. Parnas and Mr. Solomon, and Mr. Parnas and Rep. Nunes. In addition, among these calls are contacts between Mr. Giuliani and a phone number associated with the Office of Management and Budget (OMB), an unidentified number ("-1"), and a phone number associated with the White House:

Date	Connecting Time (ET)	Duration of Call	Caller	Recipient	Source
04/12/19	9:48:57	0:24	Toensing, Victoria	Parnas, Lev	AT&T Document Production, Bates ATTHPSCI_20190930-00908
04/12/19	10:40:19	3:25	Parnas, Lev	Toensing, Victoria	AT&T Document Production, Bates ATTHPSCI_20190930-00909
04/12/19	11:05:25	0:03	OMB Phone Number	Giuliani, Rudy	AT&T Document Production, Bates ATTHPSCI_20190930-02134
04/12/19	11:05:39	12:10	"-1"	Giuliani, Rudy	AT&T Document Production, Bates ATTHPSCI_20190930-02134
04/12/19	13:13:49	0:12	Giuliani, Rudy	White House Phone Number	AT&T Document Production, Bates ATTHPSCI_20190930-02135
04/12/19	13:18:46	0:07	Toensing, Victoria	Giuliani, Rudy	AT&T Document Production, Bates ATTHPSCI_20190930-02135
04/12/19	13:26:54	0:24	Giuliani Partners	Parnas, Lev	AT&T Document Production, Bates ATTHPSCI_20190930-00911
04/12/19	14:11:22	0:03	"-1"	Giuliani, Rudy	AT&T Document Production, Bates ATTHPSCI_20190930-02136
04/12/19	14:11:27	0:03	OMB Phone Number	Giuliani, Rudy	AT&T Document Production, Bates ATTHPSCI_20190930-02136
04/12/19	14:17:46	0:07	Toensing, Victoria	Parnas, Lev	AT&T Document Production, Bates ATTHPSCI_20190930-00912

04/12/19	15:09:22	0:02	Parnas, Lev	Giuliani, Rudy	AT&T Document Production, Bates ATTHPSCI_20190930-00912
04/12/19	15:09:32	0:01	Parnas, Lev	Giuliani, Rudy	AT&T Document Production, Bates ATTHPSCI_20190930-00912
04/12/19	15:16:09	1:38	Parnas, Lev	Solomon, John	AT&T Document Production, Bates ATTHPSCI_20190930-00912
04/12/19	15:48:09	0:03	OMB Phone Number	Giuliani, Rudy	AT&T Document Production, Bates ATTHPSCI_20190930-02137
04/12/19	16:10:49	0:00	Parnas, Lev	Giuliani, Rudy	AT&T Document Production, Bates ATTHPSCI_20190930-00913
04/12/19	16:10:51	0:02	Parnas, Lev	Giuliani, Rudy	AT&T Document Production, Bates ATTHPSCI_20190930-00913
04/12/19	16:10:51	0:02	Parnas, Lev	Giuliani, Rudy	AT&T Document Production, Bates ATTHPSCI_20190930-00913
4/12/19	16:12:53	1:00	Parnas, Lev	Nunes, Devin	AT&T Document Production, Bates ATTHPSCI_20190930-00913
04/12/19	16:54:11	0:00	Nunes, Devin	Parnas, Lev	AT&T Document Production, Bates ATTHPSCI_20190930-00913
04/12/19	16:54:13	0:02	Nunes, Devin	Parnas, Lev	AT&T Document Production, Bates ATTHPSCI_20190930-00913
04/12/19	17:07:20	1:27	Parnas, Lev	Giuliani, Rudy	AT&T Document Production, Bates ATTHPSCI_20190930-00913
04/12/19	17:17:36	7:52	Sekulow, Jay	Giuliani, Rudy	AT&T Document Production, Bates ATTHPSCI_20190930-03565
04/12/19	17:24:05	1:49	Parnas, Lev	Solomon, John	AT&T Document Production, Bates ATTHPSCI_20190930-00914

04/12/19	17:26:48	0:28	Parnas, Lev	Solomon, John	AT&T Document Production, Bates ATTHPSCI_20190930-00914
04/12/19	17:30:19	8:34	Parnas, Lev	Nunes, Devin	AT&T Document Production, Bates ATTHPSCI_20190930-00914
04/12/19	17:39:25	0:53	Parnas, Lev	Solomon, John	AT&T Document Production, Bates ATTHPSCI_20190930-00914
04/12/19	19:56:43	5:03	Giuliani, Rudy	White House Phone Number	AT&T Document Production, Bates ATTHPSCI_20190930-02139

Mr. Lutsenko and Mr. Kulyk were not the only Ukrainians who appear to have engaged with diGenova & Toensing, LLP. On April 15, Ms. Toensing signed another retainer agreement between diGenova & Toensing, LLP and former Prosecutor General Viktor Shokin. Again, the Committees' copy is not signed by Mr. Shokin. A spokesman for Ms. Toensing and Mr. diGenova acknowledged that the firm represented "Ukrainian whistleblowers," but claimed that the identities of those clients (other that Mr. Lutsenko) are protected by attorney-client privilege. *See Giuliani Weighed Doing Business with Ukrainian Government*, Wall Street Journal (Nov. 27, 2019) (online at www.wsj.com/articles/giuliani-weighed-doing-business-with-ukrainian-government-11574890951).

The first paragraph of the retainer agreement outlined the services to be rendered:

Viktor Shokin ("Client") hereby engaged the firm diGenova & Toensing, LLP ("Firm" or "Attorneys") to represent him for the purpose of collecting evidence regarding his March 2016 firing as Prosecutor General of Ukraine and the role of then-Vice President Joe Biden in such firing, and presenting such evidence to U.S. and foreign authorities.

See Retainer Letter, diGenova & Toensing, LLP, Viktor Shokin (Apr. 15, 2019).

The subject matter of the agreement—the activities of Vice President Biden—again echo Mr. Solomon's pieces in *The Hill*, conspiracy theories spread by Mr. Giuliani on behalf of President Trump, and the President's statements about Vice President Biden on his July 25 call with President Zelensky.

[83] AT&T Document Production, Bates ATTHPSCI_20190930-00947-ATTHPSCI_20190930-00950.

[84] AT&T Document Production, Bates ATTHPSCI_20190930-02222-ATTHPSCI_20190930-02223.

Date	Connecting Time (ET)	Duration of Call	Caller	Recipient
04/23/19	14:00:56	1:50	Giuliani, Rudy	Parnas, Lev
04/23/19	14:15:18	0:18	Giuliani, Rudy	White House Phone Number
04/23/19	14:15:43	0:11	Giuliani, Rudy	White House Phone Number
04/23/19	15:20:17	0:11	Giuliani, Rudy	White House Phone Number
04/23/19	15:50:23	8:28	"-1"	Giuliani, Rudy

[85] AT&T Document Production, Bates ATTHPSCI_20190930-02224.

[86] Rudy Giuliani, Twitter (Apr. 23, 2019) (online at https://twitter.com/RudyGiuliani/status/1120798794692612097).

[87] *Giuliani Fires Back at Hillary Clinton's Remarks on Mueller Probe*, Fox News (Apr. 24, 2019) (online at www.youtube.com/watch?v=FDtg8z12Q7s&feature=youtu.be).

[88] AT&T Document Production, Bates ATTHPSCI_20190930-02229- ATTHPSCI_20190930-02237.

Date	Connecting Time (ET)	Duration of Call	Caller	Recipient
04/24/19	7:17:48	0:42	OMB Phone Number	Giuliani, Rudy
04/24/19	7:47:57	0:37	Giuliani, Rudy	White House Phone Number
04/24/19	7:48:39	0:21	Giuliani, Rudy	White House Phone Number
04/24/19	7:49:00	0:31	OMB Phone Number	Giuliani, Rudy
04/24/19	7:49:00	0:20	Giuliani, Rudy	White House Phone Number
04/24/19	7:49:35	4:53	Giuliani, Rudy	White House Phone Number
04/24/19	7:54:52	0:24	Giuliani, Rudy	White House Phone Number
04/24/19	13:03:50	13:44	OMB Phone Number	Giuliani, Rudy
04/24/19	16:42:52	8:00	Parnas, Lev	Giuliani, Rudy
04/24/19	18:38:57	0:44	Giuliani, Rudy	White House Phone Number
04/24/19	18:42:43	8:42	"-1"	Giuliani, Rudy
04/24/19	20:09:14	0:06	Giuliani, Rudy	White House Phone Number
04/24/19	20:12:08	3:15	White House #	Giuliani, Rudy

[89] Yovanovitch Hearing Tr. at 31-32.

[90] Yovanovitch Dep. Tr. at 22.

[91] Yovanovitch Hearing Tr. at 21-22.

[92] Yovanovitch Dep. Tr. at 129.

[93] Yovanovitch Dep. Tr. at 139.

[94] Yovanovitch Hearing Tr. at 28.

[95] Sondland Hearing Tr. at 21.

[96] Yovanovitch Hearing Tr. at 131-132.

[97] Hale Dep. Tr. at 16-17; Hale Dep. Tr. at 112-113; Yovanovitch Hearing Tr. at 21.

[98] "I only met her when I took this job, but immediately I understood that we had an exceptional officer doing exceptional work at a very critical embassy in Kyiv. And during my visits to Kyiv, I was very impressed by

what she was doing there, to the extent that I asked her if she'd be willing to stay, if that was a possibility, because we had a gap coming up." Cooper-Hale Hearing Tr. at 63.

[99] Cooper-Hale Hearing Tr. at 64.

[100] *Biography of Marie L. Yovanovitch*, Department of State (online at https://2009-2017.state.gov/r/pa/ei/biog/261588.htm).

[101] McKinley Transcribed Interview Tr. at 37.

[102] Reeker Dep. Tr. at 26.

[103] Kent Dep. Tr. at 188-189.

[104] Yovanovitch Hearing Tr. at 18-19.

[105] Yovanovitch Hearing Tr. at 18-19.

[106] Hill-Holmes Hearing Tr. at 18-19, 45-46.

[107] Holmes Dep. Tr. at 142.

[108] *What "Corruption" Means in the Impeachment Hearings*, New Yorker (Nov. 16, 2019) (online at www.newyorker.com/news/our-columnists/the-corruption-of-the-word-corruption-and-so-much-else-amid-the-impeachment-hearings).

[109] 22 U.S.C. § 3941.

[110] Yovanovitch Hearing Tr. at 110-111.

[111] Ambassador Yovanovitch said: "Although then and now I have always understood that I served at the pleasure of the President, I still find it difficult to comprehend that foreign and private interests were able to undermine U.S. interests in this way. Individuals who apparently felt stymied by our efforts to promote stated U.S. policy against corruption, that is, to do our mission, were able to successfully conduct a campaign of disinformation against a sitting ambassador using unofficial back channels. As various witnesses have recounted, they shared baseless allegations with the President and convinced him to remove his ambassador despite the fact that the State Department fully understood that the allegations were false and the sources highly suspect." Yovanovitch Hearing Tr. at 22.

[112] Hill-Holmes Hearing Tr. at 78-79.

[113] Yovanovitch Dep. Tr. at 313-314.

[114] Yovanovitch Hearing Tr. at 22.

[115] Kent-Taylor Hearing Tr. at 25.

[116] Kent. Dep. Tr. at 131-132.

[117] Kent-Taylor Hearing Tr. at 31-32.

[118] *Comedian Volodymyr Zelensky Unseats Incumbent in Ukraine's Presidential Election, Exit Polls Show*, Washington Post (Apr. 21, 2019) (online at www.washingtonpost.com/world/as-ukraine-votes-in-presidential-runoff-a-comedian-looks-to-unseat-the-incumbent/2019/04/21/b7d69a38-603f-11e9-bf24-db4b9fb62aa2_story.html).

[119] *Comedian Volodymyr Zelensky Unseats Incumbent in Ukraine's Presidential Election, Exit Polls Show*, The Washington Post (Apr. 21, 2019) (online at www.washingtonpost.com/world/as-ukraine-votes-in-presidential-runoff-a-comedian-looks-to-unseat-the-incumbent/2019/04/21/b7d69a38-603f-11e9-bf24-db4b9fb62aa2_story.html).

[120] The White House, *Memorandum of Telephone Conversation* (Apr. 21, 2019) (online at https://assets.documentcloud.org/documents/6550349/First-Trump-Ukraine-Call.pdf).

[121] The White House, *Memorandum of Telephone Conversation* (Apr. 21, 2019) (online at https://assets.documentcloud.org/documents/6550349/First-Trump-Ukraine-Call.pdf).

[122] *Conflicting White House accounts of 1st Trump-Zelenskiy call*, The Associated Press (Nov. 15, 2019) (online at https://apnews.com/2f3c9910e0a14ec08d6d76ed93148059).

[123] The White House, *Memorandum of Telephone Conversation* (Apr. 21, 2019) (online at https://assets.documentcloud.org/documents/6550349/First-Trump-Ukraine-Call.pdf).

[124] The White House, *Memorandum of Telephone Conversation* (Apr. 21, 2019) (online at https://assets.documentcloud.org/documents/6550349/First-Trump-Ukraine-Call.pdf).

[125] The White House, *Memorandum of Telephone Conversation* (Apr. 21, 2019) (online at https://assets.documentcloud.org/documents/6550349/First-Trump-Ukraine-Call.pdf).

[126] The White House, *Memorandum of Telephone Conversation* (Apr. 21, 2019) (online at https://assets.documentcloud.org/documents/6550349/First-Trump-Ukraine-Call.pdf).

[127] The White House, *Memorandum of Telephone Conversation* (Apr. 21, 2019) (online at https://assets.documentcloud.org/documents/6550349/First-Trump-Ukraine-Call.pdf).

[128] The White House, *Memorandum of Telephone Conversation* (Apr. 21, 2019) (online at https://assets.documentcloud.org/documents/6550349/First-Trump-Ukraine-Call.pdf).

[129] The White House, *Memorandum of Telephone Conversation* (Apr. 21, 2019) (online at https://assets.documentcloud.org/documents/6550349/First-Trump-Ukraine-Call.pdf).

[130] The White House, *Memorandum of Telephone Conversation* (Apr. 21, 2019) (online at https://assets.documentcloud.org/documents/6550349/First-Trump-Ukraine-Call.pdf).

[131] Williams Dep. Tr. at 36.

[132] Williams Dep. Tr. at 37.

[133] Williams Dep. Tr. at 36.

[134] *Fox & Friends*, Fox News (Apr. 24, 2019) (online at www.youtube.com/watch?v=FDtg8z12Q7s#action=share).

[135] *Why Giuliani Singled Out 2 Ukrainian Oligarchs to Help Look for Dirt*, New York Times (Nov. 25, 2019) (online at www.nytimes.com/2019/11/25/us/giuliani-ukraine-oligarchs.html).

[136] *Ukraine's Unlikely President, Promising a New Style of Politics, Gets a Taste of Trump's Swamp,* New Yorker (Oct. 25, 2019) (online at www.newyorker.com/magazine/2019/11/04/how-trumps-emissaries-put-pressure-on-ukraines-new-president).

[137] *Why Giuliani Singled Out 2 Ukrainian Oligarchs to Help Look for Dirt*, New York Times (Nov. 25, 2019) (online at www.nytimes.com/2019/11/25/us/giuliani-ukraine-oligarchs.html).

[138] AT&T Document Production, Bates ATTHPSCI_20190930_00947; ATTHPSCI_20190930_00949; ATTHPSCI_20190930_02222; ATTHPSCI_20190930_02223.

[139] *Joe Biden Announces 2020 Run for President, After Months of Hesitation*, New York Times (Apr. 25, 2019) (online at www.nytimes.com/2019/04/25/us/politics/joe-biden-2020-announcement.html).

[140] *How the Obama White House Engaged Ukraine to Give Russia Collusion Narrative an Early Boost*, The Hill (Apr. 25, 2019) (online at https://thehill.com/opinion/white-house/440730-how-the-obama-white-house-engaged-ukraine-to-give-russia-collusion).

[141] Holmes Dep. Tr. at 17.

[142] Holmes Dep. Tr. at 116.

[143] Holmes Dep. Tr. at 116.

[144] AT&T Document Production, Bates ATTHPSCI_20190930_02245.

[145] AT&T Document Production, Bates ATTHPSCI_20190930_02245.

[146] *Sean Hannity Interviews Trump on Biden, Russia Probe, FISA Abuse, Comey*, Fox News (Apr. 26, 2019) (online at www.realclearpolitics.com/video/2019/04/26/full_video_sean_hannity_interviews_trump_on_biden_russia_probe_fisa_abuse_comey.html).

[147] Holmes Dep. Tr. at 55-56.

[148] *Sean Hannity Interviews Trump on Biden, Russia Probe, FISA Abuse, Comey*, Fox News (Apr. 26, 2019) (online at www.realclearpolitics.com/video/2019/04/26/full_video_sean_hannity_interviews_trump_on_biden_russia_probe_fisa_abuse_comey.html). As discussed later in this report, on the morning of September 25, 2019, the Department of Justice would quickly issue a statement after President Trump released the record of his July 25 call with President Zelensky. The statement asserted that that Attorney General Barr had not engaged on Ukraine matters at the President's request:

> The President has not spoken with the Attorney General about having Ukraine investigate anything relating to former Vice President Biden or his son. The President has not asked the Attorney General to contact Ukraine—on this or any other matter. The Attorney General has not communicated with Ukraine—on this or any other subject.

[149] *Cleaning Up Ukraine in the Shadow of Trump*, The Financial Times (Nov. 28, 2019) (online at www.ft.com/content/eb8e4004-1059-11ea-a7e6-62bf4f9e548a).

[150] *Cleaning Up Ukraine in the Shadow of Trump*, The Financial Times (Nov. 28, 2019) (online at www.ft.com/content/eb8e4004-1059-11ea-a7e6-62bf4f9e548a).

[151] *Biden Faces Conflict of Interest Questions That Are Being Promoted by Trump and Allies*, New York Times (May 1, 2019) (online at www.nytimes.com/2019/05/01/us/politics/biden-son-ukraine.html).

[152] *Transcript: Fox News Interview with President Trump*, Fox News (May 7, 2019) (online at www.foxnews.com/politics/transcript-fox-news-interview-with-president-trump).

[153] *Transcript: Fox News Interview with President Trump*, Fox News (May 7, 2019) (online at www.foxnews.com/politics/transcript-fox-news-interview-with-president-trump).

[154] *Foreign Affairs Issue Launch with Former Vice President Joe Biden*, Council on Foreign Relations (Jan. 23, 2018) (online at: www.cfr.org/event/foreign-affairs-issue-launch-former-vice-president-joe-biden).

[155] *Ukraine Ousts Viktor Shokin, Top Prosecutor, and Political Stability Hangs in the Balance*, New York Times (Mar. 29, 2016) (online at www.nytimes.com/2016/03/30/world/europe/political-stability-in-the-balance-as-ukraine-ousts-top-prosecutor.html).

[156] Yovanovitch Hearing Tr. at 50; Kent-Taylor Hearing Tr. at 115.

[157] *Trump Says He'd Consider Accepting Information from Foreign Governments on His Opponents*, The Washington Post (June 12, 2019) (online at www.washingtonpost.com/politics/trump-says-hed-consider-accepting-dirt-from-foreign-governments-on-his-opponents/2019/06/12/b84ba860-8d5c-11e9-8f69-a2795fca3343_story.html).

[158] AT&T Document Production, Bates ATTHPSCI_20190930_02313.

[159] AT&T Document Production, Bates ATTHPSCI_20190930_02314; ATTHPSCI_20190930_02316; ATTHPSCI_20190930_02318; ATTHPSCI 20190930 01000.

[160] Kent Dep. Tr. at 137.

[161] Kent Dep. Tr. at 137.

[162] Kent Dep. Tr. at 137.

[163] *Rudy Giuliani Plans Ukraine Trip to Push for Inquiries That Could Help Trump*, New York Times (May 9, 2019) (online at www.nytimes.com/2019/05/09/us/politics/giuliani-ukraine-trump.html).

[164] *Rudy Giuliani Plans Ukraine Trip to Push for Inquiries That Could Help Trump*, New York Times (May 9, 2019) (online at www.nytimes.com/2019/05/09/us/politics/giuliani-ukraine-trump.html).

[165] *Rudy Giuliani Plans Ukraine Trip to Push for Inquiries That Could Help Trump*, New York Times (May 9, 2019) (online at www.nytimes.com/2019/05/09/us/politics/giuliani-ukraine-trump.html).

[166] *Rudy Giuliani Plans Ukraine Trip to Push for Inquiries That Could Help Trump*, New York Times (May 9, 2019) (online at www.nytimes.com/2019/05/09/us/politics/giuliani-ukraine-trump.html).

[167] *Rudy Giuliani Plans Ukraine Trip to Push for Inquiries That Could Help Trump*, New York Times (May 9, 2019) (online at www.nytimes.com/2019/05/09/us/politics/giuliani-ukraine-trump.html).

[168] *Rudy Giuliani Plans Ukraine Trip to Push for Inquiries That Could Help Trump*, New York Times (May 9, 2019) (online at www.nytimes.com/2019/05/09/us/politics/giuliani-ukraine-trump.html).

[169] *Rudy Giuliani Plans Ukraine Trip to Push for Inquiries That Could Help Trump*, New York Times (May 9, 2019) (online at www.nytimes.com/2019/05/09/us/politics/giuliani-ukraine-trump.html).

[170] *Trump's Interest in Stirring Ukraine Investigations Sows Confusion in Kiev*, Washington Post (May 11, 2019) (online at www.washingtonpost.com/world/europe/trumps-interest-stirring-ukraine-investigations-sows-confusion-in-kiev/2019/05/11/cb94f7f4-73ea-11e9-9331-30bc5836f48e_story.html).

[171] AT&T Document Production, Bates ATTHPSCI_20190930_02321; ATTHPSCI_20190930_02322.

[172] AT&T Document Production, Bates ATTHPSCI_20190930_02320, 02321, 02322, 02323, 03612.

[173] AT&T Document Production, Bates ATTHPSCI_20190930_03614; ATTHPSCI_20190930_02326; ATTHPSCI_20190930_02327; ATTHPSCI_20190930_03614.

[174] Rudy Giuliani, Twitter (May 9, 2019) (online at https://twitter.com/RudyGiuliani/status/1126701386224156673).

[175] *Giuliani: "Massive Collusion" Between DNC, Obama Admin, Clinton People & Ukraine To Create False Info About Trump*, Real Clear Politics (May 10, 2019) (online at www.realclearpolitics.com/video/2019/05/10/giuliani_massive_collusion_between_dnc_obama_admin_clinton_peo ple__ukraine_to_create_false_info_about_trump.html).

[176] Rudy Giuliani, Twitter (May 10, 2019) (online at https://twitter.com/rudygiuliani/status/1126858889209831424?lang=en).

[177] AT&T Document Production, Bates ATTHPSCI_20190930_02334.

[178] Volker Transcribed Interview Tr. at 227; *see also* Volker Transcribed Interview Tr. at 32-33, 36 (describing the allegations).

[179] Volker Transcribed Interview Tr. at 227.

[180] AT&T Document Production, Bates ATTHPSCI_20190930_02334.

[181] AT&T Document Production, Bates ATTHPSCI_20190930_02335.

[182] AT&T Document Production, Bates ATTHPSCI_20190930_02335.

[183] AT&T Document Production, Bates ATTHPSCI_20190930_02335.

[184] *Trump: Discussing a Biden Probe with Barr Would Be 'Appropriate,'* Politico (May 10, 2019) (online at www.politico.com/story/2019/05/10/trump-biden-ukraine-barr-1317601).

[185] *Trump Denies Sending Rudy Giuliani to Ukraine to Push Biden, Election Probes*, CNBC (Nov. 27, 2019) (online at www.cnbc.com/2019/11/27/trump-denies-sending-rudy-giuliani-to-ukraine-to-push-biden-election-probes.html).

[186] *Remarks by President Trump and President Niinisto of the Republic of Finland in Joint Press Conference*, The White House (Oct. 2, 2019) (online at www.whitehouse.gov/briefings-statements/remarks-president-trump-president-niinisto-republic-finland-joint-press-conference/).

[187] *Remarks by President Trump before Marine One Departure*, The White House (Oct. 4, 2019) (online at www.whitehouse.gov/briefings-statements/remarks-president-trump-marine-one-departure-68/).

[188] *Giuliani: I didn't go to Ukraine to start an investigation, there already was one*, Fox News (May 11, 2019) (online at https://video.foxnews.com/v/6035385372001/#sp=show-clips).

[189] *Trump: Discussing a Biden probe with Barr would be 'appropriate'*, Politico (May 10, 2019) (online at www.politico.com/story/2019/05/10/trump-biden-ukraine-barr-1317601) (documenting Giuliani text message).

[190] *Trump: Discussing a Biden probe with Barr would be 'appropriate'*, Politico (May 10, 2019) (online at www.politico.com/story/2019/05/10/trump-biden-ukraine-barr-1317601) (documenting Giuliani text message).

[191] Donald J. Trump, Twitter (May 3, 2019) (online at https://twitter.com/realDonaldTrump/status/1124359594418032640)

[192] Kent Dep. Tr. at 338-339.

[193] *Remarks by President Trump and Prime Minister Orban of Hungary Before Bilateral Meeting,* The White House (May 13, 2019) (online at www.whitehouse.gov/briefings-statements/remarks-president-trump-prime-minister-orban-hungary-bilateral-meeting/).

[194] *In Hungary, a Freewheeling Trump Ambassador Undermines U.S. Diplomat's*, New York Times (Oct. 22, 2019) (online at www.nytimes.com/2019/10/22/world/europe/david-cornstein-hungary-trump-orban.html); *Hungarian prime minister earns rare rebuke from European bloc that has long backed him*, The Washington Post (Mar. 20, 2019) (online at www.washingtonpost.com/world/europe/hungarys-orban-earns-rare-rebuke-from-european-bloc-that-has-long-backed-him/2019/03/20/83be110a-4b17-11e9-8cfc-2c5d0999c21e_story.html).

[195] Kent Dep. Tr. at 339.

[196] *Remarks by President Trump and Prime Minister Orban of Hungary Before Bilateral Meeting,* The White House (May 13, 2019) (online at www.whitehouse.gov/briefings-statements/remarks-president-trump-prime-minister-orban-hungary-bilateral-meeting/).

[197] Kent Dep. Tr. at 253.

[198] Kent Dep. Tr. at 254.

[199] Williams Dep. Tr. at 37-38.

[200] Vindman-Williams Hearing Tr. at 14. Other witnesses testified that Vice President Pence may not have been able to attend on account of scheduling issues. *See* Hill Dep. Tr. at 316 ("there was a lot of scheduling issues" regarding the attempts to schedule the Vice President's participation in the delegation); Kent Dep. Tr. at 189-191 (Vice President Pence was not available); Volker Transcribed Interview Tr. at 288-290, 293 (Volker "wasn't surprised" Pence could not make it and assumed it was a matter of scheduling). However, Ms. Williams was the only staff member in the Office of the Vice President to testify before the Committees, and the only witness to testify to having heard an explanation from Vice President Pence's staff about why Vice President Pence did not attend the inauguration.

[201] Williams Dep. Tr. at 39.

[202] Holmes Dep. Tr. at 37.

[203] Holmes Dep. Tr. at 37.

[204] Rudy Giuliani, Twitter (May 18, 2019) (online at https://twitter.com/RudyGiuliani/status/1129761193755910144)

[205] *Kolomoisky: We Called Varkuch and Asked: 'Do You Support Zelensky or No?'*, Pravda (May 27, 2019) (online at www.pravda.com.ua/rus/articles/2019/05/27/7216183/).

[206] *Kolomoisky: We Called Varkuch and Asked: 'Do You Support Zelensky or No?'*, Pravda (May 27, 2019) (online at www.pravda.com.ua/rus/articles/2019/05/27/7216183/).

[207] Holmes Dep. Tr. at 16.

[208] Volker Transcribed Interview Tr. at 288-290; Vindman Dep. Tr. at 125.

[209] Holmes Dep. Tr. at 101.

[210] Holmes Dep. Tr. at 18.

[211] Holmes Dep. Tr. 17-18.

[212] Holmes Dep. Tr. at 18.

[213] Holmes Dep. Tr. at 18.

[214] Hill-Holmes Hearing Tr. at 61.

[215] Vindman-Williams Hearing Tr. at 26.

[216] Hill-Holmes Hearing Tr. at 61.

[217] Vindman-Williams Hearing Tr. at 26

[218] Vindman-Williams Hearing Tr. at 26

[219] Vindman-Williams Hearing Tr. at 26; David Holmes separately testified that Lt. Col. Vindman "made a general point about the importance of Ukraine to our national security, and he said it's very important that the Zelensky administration stay out of U.S. domestic politics." Hill-Holmes Hearing Tr. at 61.

[220] Volker Transcribed Interview Tr. at 30.

[221] Volker Transcribed Interview Tr. at 29-30.

[222] Kent Dep. Tr. at 193.

[223] Anderson Dep. Tr. at 15, 54. Ambassador Sondland testified that he did not specifically recall who arranged the May 23 meeting and conjectured that "either Rick Perry or I reached out to someone at the NSC saying: Doesn't the President want a briefing about the inauguration. And I think—I think it was Perry, if I recall correctly, that got it nailed down." Sondland Dep. Tr. at 87.

[224] Volker Transcribed Interview Tr. at 29, 303; Vindman Dep. Tr. at 168.

[225] Hill Dep. Tr. at 311.

[226] Hill Dep. Tr. at 308.

[227] Hill Dep. Tr. at 308.

[228] Hill Dep. Tr. at 309-310.

[229] Hill Dep. Tr. at 309-310.

[230] Hill Dep. Tr. at 309-310.

[231] *Nunes Ally Kash Patel Who Fought Russia Probe Gets Senior White House National Security Job*, The Daily Beast (July 31, 2019) (online at www.thedailybeast.com/kash-patel-devin-nunes-ally-who-fought-russia-probe-gets-senior-white-house-national-security-job).

[232] Volker Transcribed Interview Tr. at 304.

[233] Sondland Dep. Tr. at 25.

[234] Sondland Dep. Tr. at 25.

[235] Volker Transcribed Interview Tr. at 304.

[236] Sondland Dep. Tr. at 337; Volker Transcribed Interview Tr. at 304; Hill Dep. Tr. at 320-321 (describing Volker's readout); Croft Dep. Tr. at 90 (describing Volker's readout); Anderson Dep. Tr. at 57 (describing Volker's readout).

[237] Volker Transcribed Interview Tr. at 305.

[238] Volker Transcribed Interview Tr. at 305.

[239] Sondland Dep. Tr. at 62; Volker Transcribed Interview Tr. 305; Morrison-Volker Hearing Tr. at 40.

[240] Sondland Hearing Tr. at 71.

[241] Sondland Dep. Tr. at 26. *See also* Sondland Dep. Tr. at 87-90.

[242] Morrison-Volker Hearing Tr. at 131.

[243] Sondland Hearing Tr. at 167.

[244] In addition to the testimony cited in this paragraph, *see also* Hill Dep. Tr. at 113; Hale Dep. Tr. at 90; Taylor Dep. Tr. at 58, 285; and Reeker Dep. Tr. at 148.

[245] Kent Dep. Tr. at 195.

[246] Croft Dep. Tr. at 91.

[247] Hale Dep. Tr. at 73.

[248] Sondland Dep. Tr. at 151-152.

[249] Hill Dep. Tr. at 59-60.

[250] Sondland Hearing Tr. at 24, 27, 123-124, 125-126.

[251] Sondland Hearing Tr. at 27-30.

[252] Sondland Hearing Tr. at 22.

[253] Sondland Dep. Tr. at 77-78.

[254] Hill-Holmes Hearing Tr. at 94.

[255] Hill Dep. Tr. at 127. According to call records obtained by the Committee, Mr. Giuliani connected with Ambassador Bolton's office three times for brief calls of under a minute between April 23 and May 10, 2019—a time period that corresponds with the recall of Ambassador Yovanovitch and the acceleration of Mr. Giuliani's efforts, on behalf of President Trump, to pressure Ukraine into opening investigations that would benefit his reelection campaign. AT&T Document Production, Bates ATTHPSCI_20190930_02224, 02322, 23330.

[256] Hill Dep. Tr. at 127.

[257] Anderson Dep. Tr. at 15.

[258] Anderson Dep. Tr. at 15.

[259] Anderson Dep. Tr. at 101.

[260] Hill Dep. Tr. at 127-128.

[261] Hill Dep. Tr. at 116-117.

[262] Hill Dep. Tr. at 130.

[263] Anderson Dep. Tr. at 16.

[264] Anderson Dep. Tr. at 16; Taylor Dep. Tr. at 24-25, 167.

[265] Taylor Dep. Tr. at 25.

[266] Taylor Dep. Tr. at 25.

[267] Taylor Dep. Tr. at 25.

[268] Anderson Dep. Tr. at 16-17.

[269] Sondland Dep. Tr. at 240.

[270] *ABC News' Oval Office Interview with President Trump*, ABC News (June 13, 2019) (online at https://abcnews.go.com/Politics/abc-news-oval-office-interview-president-donald-trump/story?id=63688943).

[271] *ABC News' Oval Office Interview with President Trump*, ABC News (June 13, 2019) (online at https://abcnews.go.com/Politics/abc-news-oval-office-interview-president-donald-trump/story?id=63688943) (emphasis added).

[272] Rudy Giuliani, Twitter (June 21, 2019) (online at https://twitter.com/RudyGiuliani/status/1142085975230898176)

[273] Hill-Holmes Hearing Tr. at 77.

[274] Hill-Holmes Hearing Tr. at 91.

[275] Hill Dep. Tr. at 222-223.

[276] Hill-Holmes Hearing Tr. at 92.

[277] Hill-Holmes Hearing Tr. at 93.

[278] Office of the United Nations High Commissioner for Human Rights, *Report on the Human Rights Situation in Ukraine: 16 November 2018 to 15 February 2019* (online at https://www.ohchr.org/Documents/Countries/UA/ReportUkraine16Nov2018-15Feb2019.pdf); Office of the United Nations High Commissioner for Human Rights, *Report on the Human Rights Situation in Ukraine: 16 August to 15 November 2017* (Dec. 12, 2017) (online at https://www.ohchr.org/Documents/Countries/UA/UAReport20th_EN.pdf); Office of the United Nations High Commissioner for Human Rights, *Conflict in Ukraine Enters its Fourth Year with No End in Sight* (June 13, 2017) (online at www.ohchr.org/EN/NewsEvents/Pages/DisplayNews.aspx?NewsID=21730&LangID=E). These figures do not include the 298 civilians of 13 different nationalities killed aboard Malaysia Airlines Flight 17, which a Dutch-led joint investigation found was shot down by a Russian missile system from a Russian military unit, a conclusion supported by U.S. intelligence. *See* Dutch Safety Board, *Report on the Crash of Malaysia Airlines Flight MH17* (Oct. 13, 2015) (online at www.onderzoeksraad.nl/en/page/3546/crash-mh17-17-july-2014); *U.S. Discloses Intelligence on Downing of Malaysian Jet*, Washington Post (July 22, 2014) (online at www.washingtonpost.com/world/national-security/us-discloses-intelligence-on-downing-of-malaysian-jet/2014/07/22/b178fe58-11e1-11e4-98ee-daea85133bc9_story.html).

[279] Ambassador Nikki Haley, United States Mission to the United Nations, *Remarks at a U.N. Security Council Briefing on Ukraine* (May 29, 2018) (online at https://usun.usmission.gov/remarks-at-a-un-security-council-briefing-on-ukraine-2/).

[280] Department of Defense, *Secretary of Defense James Mattis Remarks with President Petro Poroshenko* (Aug. 24, 2017) (online at www.defense.gov/Newsroom/Speeches/Speech/Article/1291430/secretary-of-defense-james-mattis-remarks-with-president-petro-poroshenko/).

[281] European Union External Action, *EU-Ukraine Relations Factsheet* (Sept. 30, 2019) (online at https://eeas.europa.eu/headquarters/headQuarters-homepage/4081/eu-ukraine-relations-factsheet_en); NATO, *Fact Sheet: NATO's Support to Ukraine* (Nov. 2018) (www.nato.int/nato_static_fl2014/assets/pdf/pdf_2018_11/20181106_1811-factsheet-nato-ukraine-support-eng.pdf).

[282] *DOD Announces $250M to Ukraine*, U.S. Department of Defense (June 18, 2019) (online at www.defense.gov/Newsroom/Releases/Release/Article/1879340/dod-announces-250m-to-ukraine/).

[283] Kent-Taylor Hearing Tr. at 21, 28-29, 50; Vindman Dep. Tr. at 40-41, 113; Cooper Dep. Tr. at 15-16.

[284] Taylor Dep. Tr. at 153.

[285] Croft Dep. Tr. at 16.

[286] Kent-Taylor Hearing Tr. at 30.

[287] Taylor Dep. Tr. at 20.

[288] Morrison-Volker Hearing Tr. at 11.

[289] Department of Defense and Labor, Health and Human Services, and Education Appropriations Act, 2019 and Continuing Appropriations Act, 2019, Pub. L. No. 115-245, § 9013 (2018).

[290] National Defense Authorization Act for Fiscal Year 2016, Pub. L. 114-92, § 1250 (2015), amended by the National Defense Act Authorization Act for Fiscal Year 2018, Pub. L. No. 115-91, § 1234 (2017) and most recently amended by the John S. McCain National Defense Authorization Act for Fiscal Year 2019, Pub. L. No. 115-232, § 1246 (2018).

[291] National Defense Authorization Act for Fiscal Year 2017, Pub. L. No. 114-328, § 1237 (2016); National Defense Authorization Act for Fiscal Year 2018, Pub. L. No. 115-91, § 1234 (2018); John S. McCain National Defense Authorization Act for Fiscal Year 2019, Pub. L. No. 115-232, § 1246 (2018).

[292] Letter from John C. Rood, Under Secretary of Defense for Policy, Department of Defense, to Chairman Eliot L. Engel, House Committee on Foreign Affairs (sent Feb. 28, 2019, received Mar. 5, 2019).

[293] Cooper Dep. Tr. at 27-28.

[294] National Defense Authorization Act for Fiscal Year 2016, Pub. L. No. 114-92, § 1250 (2015), as amended by the National Defense Act Authorization Act for Fiscal Year 2018, Pub. L. No. 115-91, § 1234 (2017), and most recently amended by the John S. McCain National Defense Authorization Act for Fiscal Year 2019, Pub. L. No. 115-232, § 1246 (2018).

[295] Cooper Dep. Tr. at 24.

[296] Cooper Dep. Tr. at 24.

[297] Letter from John C. Rood, Under Secretary of Defense for Policy, Department of Defense, to Chairman Eliot L. Engel, House Committee on Foreign Affairs (sent May 23, 2019, received May 28, 2019).

[298] Cooper Dep. Tr. at 31-32.

[299] *DOD Announces $250M to Ukraine*, Department of Defense (June 18, 2019) (online at www.defense.gov/Newsroom/Releases/Release/Article/1879340/dod-announces-250m-to-ukraine/).

[300] Consolidated Appropriations Act, 2019, Pub. L. No. 116-6, §7046(a)(2) (2019); Conference Report to Accompany Consolidated Appropriations Act, 2019, H.R. Rep. No. 116-9, p. 869 (2019).

[301] Consolidated Appropriations Act, 2018, Pub. L. No. 115-141, Title VIII (2017).

[302] Consolidated Appropriations Act, 2019, Pub. L. No. 116-6, §7015(c) (2019); Consolidated Appropriations Act, 2018, Pub. L. No. 115-141, § 7015(c) (2017).

[303] OMB Circular No. A-11, § 22.3 (2019) (requiring that the State Department receive clearance from OMB before notifying Congress).

[304] Sandy Dep. Tr. at 25; *DOD Announces $250M to Ukraine*, Department of Defense (June 18, 2019) (online at www.defense.gov/Newsroom/Releases/Release/Article/1879340/dod-announces-250m-to-ukraine/).

[305] *Sean Hannity Interviews Donald Trump via Telephone*, Fox News (June 19, 2019) (transcript at https://factba.se/transcript/donald-trump-interview-sean-hannity-fox-telephone-june-19-2019).

[306] Sandy Dep. Tr. at 26-27.

[307] Sandy Dep. Tr. at 27-28.

[308] Sandy Dep. Tr. at 29-30.

[309] Cooper Dep. Tr. at 33-34.

[310] Cooper Dep. Tr. at 33.

[311] Cooper Dep. Tr. at 34.

[312] Cooper Dep. Tr. at 38.

[313] Cooper Dep. Tr. at 37-38.

[314] Cooper-Hale Hearing Tr. at 14; Vindman Dep. Tr. at 178-179. *See also Stalled Ukraine Military Aid Concerned Members of Congress for Months,* CNN (Sept. 30, 2019) (online at www.cnn.com/2019/09/30/politics/ukraine-military-aid-congress/index.html) (suggesting that the State Department sought OMB's approval for $141 million in FMF funds on June 21, 2019).

[315] OMB Circular No. A-11, § 22.3 (2019) (requiring that the State Department receive clearance from OMB before notifying Congress).

[316] Williams Dep. Tr. at 54-55.

[317] Williams Dep. Tr. at 55.

[318] Blair previously served as Associate Director of National Security Programs at OMB (Blair was Duffey's predecessor), and left OMB for the White House Office of Chief of Staff with Mick Mulvaney. Sandy Dep. Tr. at 36-38.

[319] Sandy Dep. Tr. at 38-39.

[320] Sandy Dep. Tr. at 39.

[321] Morrison Dep. Tr. at 161.

[322] Sandy Dep. Tr. at 141-142.

[323] Sandy Dep. Tr. at 142.

[324] Sandy Dep. Tr. at 31-32.

[325] Sandy Dep. Tr. at 41-42.

[326] Cooper Dep. Tr. at 40; *see also* Croft Dep. Tr. at 83 ("very routine low-level business").

[327] Kent Dep. Tr. at 303-305.

[328] Taylor Dep. Tr. at 27-28.

[329] Croft Dep. Tr. at 83.

[330] Taylor Dep. Tr. at 27.

[331] Holmes Dep. Tr. at 154.

[332] Holmes Dep. Tr. at 154.

[333] Croft Dep. Tr. at 15.

[334] Cooper Dep. Tr. at 45.

[335] Kent Dep. Tr. at 304.

[336] Kent Dep. Tr. at 305.

[337] Sandy Dep. Tr. at 99; Vindman Dep. Tr. at 182.

[338] Cooper Dep. Tr. at 40. Morrison, who did not attend the sub-PCC meeting but received a readout, testified that he thought OMB announced at the July 18th meeting that the hold "covered all dollars, DOD and Department of State, and it was—it was beyond funds not yet obligated to include funds that had, in fact, been obligated but not yet expended." Morrison Dep. Tr. at 161.

[339] Cooper Dep. Tr. at 40.

[340] Cooper Dep. Tr. at 44-45.

[341] Cooper Dep. Tr. at 40.

[342] Kent Dep. Tr. at 307-308.

[343] Morrison Dep. Tr. at 162.

[344] Cooper Dep. Tr. at 46.

[345] Williams Dep. Tr. at 91-92; *see also* Morrison Dep. Tr. at 162 (testifying that representatives from OMB stated that the hold "had been imposed by the chief of staff's office" and that the hold "was at the direction of the President").

[346] Cooper Dep. Tr. at 46.

[347] Morrison Dep. Tr. at 162-163; Kent Dep. Tr. at 310; Sandy Dep. Tr. at 91.

[348] Sandy Dep. Tr. at 91.

349 Morrison Dep. Tr. at 163.

350 Morrison Dep. Tr. at 163.

351 2 U.S.C. § 601 et. seq.

352 Williams Dep. Tr. at 91-92; Vindman Dep. Tr. at 182; Morrison Dep. Tr. at 162; Sandy Dep. Tr. at 99.

353 Taylor Dep. Tr. at 195.

354 Vindman Dep. Tr. at 182.

355 Sandy Dep. Tr. at 54.

356 Sandy Dep. Tr. at 54, 96-98.

357 Sandy Dep. Tr. at 97.

358 Sandy Dep. Tr. at 97.

359 Hale Dep. Tr. at 81.

360 Cooper Dep. Tr. at 47.

361 Hale Dep. Tr. at 81; *see also* Vindman Dep. Tr. at 184 ("It was unanimous consensus on the approach that we had laid out in expanding engagement, the areas of cooperation that we wanted to focus on, and that this should be elevated to a PC as quickly as possible to release the hold on security assistance because we're talking about the end of July, and time these funds were set to expire September 30th, so there was some urgency to it."); Cooper Dep. Tr. at 49 ("Although each member went around to talk about how important it [security assistance] was and how they assessed the future in Ukraine based on the recent election results.").

362 Morrison Dep. Tr. at 165.

363 Cooper Dep. Tr. at 93.

364 Cooper Dep. Tr. at 49, 93.

365 *Nixon's Presidency: Crisis for Congress*, New York Times (Mar. 5, 1973) (online at www.nytimes.com/1973/03/05/archives/nixons-presidency-crisis-for-congress-this-is-the-second-of-a.html).

366 Congressional Research Service, The Congressional Budget Act of 1974 (P.L. 93-344) Legislative History and Analysis (Feb. 26, 1975) (online at https://budgetcounsel.files.wordpress.com/2018/05/added-crs-the-congressional-budget-act-of-1974-p-l-93-344-legislative-history-and-analysis-order-code-75-94-s-february-26-1975.pdf).

367 Calvin Coolidge Presidential Foundation, *The History of the 1921 and 1974 Budget Acts* (Nov. 26, 2014); *So… this is Nixon's Fault?*, Politico (Oct. 21, 2015) (online at www.politico.com/agenda/story/2015/10/richard-nixon-congressional-budget-control-act-history-000282).

368 2 U.S.C. § 683.

369 U.S. Government Accountability Office, *Impoundment Control Act—Withholding of Funds through Their Date of Expiration* (Dec. 10, 2018) (online at www.gao.gov/assets/700/695889.pdf).

370 Cooper Dep. Tr. at 47-48. With regard to interagency discussions about the legality of the hold, Vindman testified "[s]o I'm not a legal expert, but there was a sufficient amount of—a significant amount of work done to determine whether it was legal for OMB to be able to place the hold. … I think at the—so my recollection in the [July 18th] sub-PCC was that the matter was raised; at the [July 23rd] PCC, it was tasked for further development; and I think by the time it got to our [July 26th] DSG it was determined that, you know, there was a legal basis to hold." Vindman Dep. Tr. at 185.

371 Vindman Dep. Tr. at 184.

372 Morrison Dep. Tr. at 165.

373 Morrison Dep. Tr. at 264.

374 Morrison Dep. Tr. at 264.

[375] Morrison Dep. Tr. at 264.

[376] Cooper Dep. Tr. at 51.

[377] Cooper Dep. Tr. at 51; *see also* Cooper Dep. Tr. at 113 (explaining that she relied on a conversation with DOD legal to form her understanding of the two proper legal mechanisms).

[378] 2 U.S.C. § 683.

[379] Cooper Dep. Tr. at 58-59.

[380] Cooper Dep. Tr. at 114.

[381] Cooper Dep. Tr. at 51, 57; Sandy Dep. Tr. at 147-148.

[382] 31 U.S.C. §§ 1511-1516.

[383] Sandy Dep. Tr. at 87, 163.

[384] Sandy Dep. Tr. at 34-35.

[385] Sandy Dep. Tr. at 51.

[386] Sandy Dep. Tr. at 23.

[387] Sandy Dep. Tr. at 33-35, 51-52.

[388] Sandy Dep. Tr. at 86.

[389] Sandy Dep. Tr. at 86-87.

[390] Sandy Dep. Tr. at 86.

[391] Sandy, Dep. Tr. at 87-88.

[392] SF-132 Apportionment Schedule FY 2019, OMB Footnote A4 (July 25, 2019).

[393] Sandy Dep. Tr. at 94.

[394] Sandy Dep. Tr. at 94.

[395] Sandy Dep. Tr. at 94-95; SF-132 Apportionment Schedule FY 2019, OMB Footnote A4 (July 25, 2019).

[396] Sandy Dep. Tr. at 87.

[397] SF-132 Apportionment Schedule FY 2019, OMB Footnote A4 (July 25, 2019); Sandy Dep. Tr. at 92.

[398] Sandy Dep. Tr. at 101.

[399] Sandy Dep. Tr. at 102.

[400] Sandy Dep. Tr. at 96-97, 102.

[401] Sandy Dep. Tr. at 101-102.

[402] Sandy Dep. Tr. at 63.

[403] Sandy Dep. Tr. at 63.

[404] Sandy Dep. Tr. at 102.

[405] Sandy Dep. Tr. at 64-65.

[406] Sandy Dep. Tr. at 65.

[407] Sandy Dep. Tr. at 108-109.

[408] Sandy Dep. Tr. at 104, 119-120.

[409] Cooper Dep. Tr. at 58-59.

[410] Cooper Dep. Tr. at 58-59.

[411] Cooper Dep. Tr. at 59.

[412] Sandy Dep. Tr. at 74-75, 127-128.

[413] SF-132 Apportionment Schedule FY 2019, OMB Footnote A4 (August 6, 2019); SF-132 Apportionment Schedule FY 2019, OMB Footnote A4 (August 15, 2019). Because of a drafting error in which OMB forgot to extend the date, the footnotes technically did not restrict DOD from spending funds between August 12 and August 20 (the date of the subsequent funding document reinstating the hold). However, Sandy testified that the hold was still in place and that the direction from the President remained unchanged. Sandy Dep. Tr. at 124-126.

[414] SF-132 Apportionment Schedule FY 2019, OMB Footnote A4 (August 6, 2019); SF-132 Apportionment Schedule FY 2019, OMB Footnote A4 (August 15, 2019); SF-132 Apportionment Schedule FY 2019, OMB Footnote A4 (August 20, 2019); SF-132 Apportionment Schedule FY 2019, OMB Footnote A4 (August 27, 2019); SF-132 Apportionment Schedule FY 2019, OMB Footnote A4 (August 31, 2019); SF-132 Apportionment Schedule FY 2019, OMB Footnote A4 (Sept. 5, 2019); SF-13; SF-132 Apportionment Schedule FY 2019, OMB Footnote A4 (Sept. 6, 2019); Apportionment Schedule FY 2019, OMB Footnote A4 (Sept. 10, 2019)

[415] Cooper Dep. Tr. at 91-92.

[416] Cooper Dep. Tr. at 92.

[417] Kent Dep. Tr. at 318-319.

[418] Sandy Dep. Tr. at 56-61.

[419] Sandy Dep. Tr. at 59-60.

[420] Sandy Dep. Tr. at 60-61.

[421] Sandy Dep. Tr. at 75, 127-128; Cooper Dep. Tr. at 57-58; *see also* Cooper Dep. Tr. at 59, ("And along the way, [the] Defense Security Cooperation Agency was expressing doubt that they could do it.").

[422] Cooper Dep. Tr. at 80-81. Ultimately, as described below, DOD was able to obligate all but approximately $35 million in USAI funds by September 30th. Sandy Dep. Tr. at 146-147.

[423] Sandy Dep. Tr. at 127-128.

[424] Sandy Dep. Tr. at 95.

[425] SF-132 Apportionment Schedule FY 2019 (August 20, 2019); SF-132 Apportionment Schedule FY 2019 (August 27, 2019); SF-132 Apportionment Schedule FY 2019 (August 31, 2019); SF-132 Apportionment Schedule FY 2019 (September 5, 2019); SF-132 Apportionment Schedule FY 2019 (September 6, 2019); SF-132 Apportionment Schedule FY 2019 (September 10, 2019).

[426] SF-132 Apportionment Schedule FY 2019 (August 20, 2019) (funds not available for obligation until August 26); SF-132 Apportionment Schedule FY 2019 (August 27, 2019) (funds not available for obligation until August 31); SF-132 Apportionment Schedule FY 2019 (August 31, 2019) (funds not available for obligation until September 5); SF-132 Apportionment Schedule FY 2019 (September 5, 2019) (funds not available for obligation until September 7); SF-132 Apportionment Schedule FY 2019 (September 6, 2019) (funds not available for obligation until September 11); SF-132 Apportionment Schedule FY 2019 (September 10, 2019) (funds not available for obligation until September 12).

[427] Sandy Dep. Tr. at 131.

[428] Sandy Dep. Tr. at 136-137.

[429] Sandy Dep. Tr. at 136.

[430] Sandy Dep. Tr. at 135-137, 150-155.

[431] Sandy Dep. Tr. at 149-152.

[432] Sandy Dep. Tr. at 152.

[433] Sandy Dep. Tr. at 150-156.

[434] Morrison Dep. Tr. at 266-267.

[435] Morrison Dep. Tr. at 268.

[436] Morrison Dep. Tr. at 267.

[437] Vindman Dep. Tr. at 186.

[438] Vindman Dep. Tr. at 186.

[439] Vindman Dep. Tr. at 187-188.

[440] Morrison Dep. Tr. at 167-168.

[441] Morrison Dep. Tr. at 170-171.

[442] Morrison Dep. Tr. at 265-266.

[443] Morrison Dep. Tr. at 172, 266.

[444] Morrison Dep. Tr. at 266.

[445] Cooper Dep. Tr. at 68.

[446] Croft Dep. Tr. at 86.

[447] Croft Dep. Tr. at 86-87.

[448] Croft Dep. Tr. at 86-87, 101.

[449] Croft Dep. Tr. at 97-98.

[450] Cooper-Hale Hearing Tr. at 14.

[451] Cooper-Hale Hearing Tr. at 13-14.

[452] Cooper-Hale Hearing Tr. at 14.

[453] Cooper-Hale Hearing Tr. at 15.

[454] Vindman Dep. Tr. at 221-22.

[455] *Trump Holds Up Ukraine Military Aid Meant to Confront Russia,* Politico (Aug. 28, 2019) (online at www.politico.com/story/2019/08/28/trump-ukraine-military-aid-russia-1689531).

[456] Holmes Dep. Tr. at 18. ("It is important to understand that a White House visit was critical to President Zelensky. He needed to demonstrate U.S. support at the highest levels, both to advance his ambitious anti-corruption agenda at home and to encourage Russian President Putin to take seriously President Zelensky's peace efforts.")

[457] Kent Dep. Tr. at 202. ("The President of the United States is a longtime acknowledged leader of the free world, and the U.S. is Ukraine's strongest supporter. And so in the Ukraine context, it's very important to show that they can establish a strong relationship with the leader of the United States. That's the Ukrainian argument and desire to have a meeting. The foreign policy argument is it's a very important country in the front lines of Russian malign influence and aggression. And the U.S. spends a considerable amount of our resources supporting Ukraine and therefore it makes sense.")

[458] Hill Dep. Tr. at 158. ("He was just generally concerned about actually not having a meeting because he felt that this would deprive Ukraine, the new Ukrainian Government of the legitimacy that it needed, especially vis-a-vis the Russians. So this gets to, you know, the heart of our national security dilemma. You know, the Ukrainians at this point, you know, are looking at a White House meeting or looking at a meeting with the President of the United States as a recognition of their legitimacy as a sovereign state.")

[459] Vindman Hearing Tr. at 38-39. ("The show of support for President Zelensky, still a brand-new President, frankly, a new politician on the Ukrainian political scene, looking to establish his bona fides as a regional and maybe even a world leader, would want to have a meeting with the United States, the most powerful country in the world and Ukraine's most significant benefactor, in order to be able to implement his agenda.")

[460] Volker Transcribed Interview Tr. at 59.

[461] Volker Transcribed Interview Tr. at 328.

[462] Taylor Dep. Opening Statement at 5. ("In late June, one of the goals of both channels was to facilitate a visit by President Zelensky to the White House for a meeting with President Trump, which President Trump had promised in his congratulatory letter of May 29. The Ukrainians were clearly eager for the meeting to happen. During a conference call with Ambassador Volker, Acting Assistant Secretary of State for European and Eurasian Affairs Phil Reeker, Secretary Perry, Ambassador Sondland, and Counsel of the U.S. Department of State Ulrich Brechbuhl on June 18, it was clear that a meeting between the two presidents was an agreed-upon goal.")

[463] Taylor Dep. Tr. at 25. ("[D]uring my subsequent communications with Ambassadors Volker and Sondland, they relayed to me that the President 'wanted to hear from Zelensky' before scheduling the meeting in the Oval Office. It was not clear to me what this meant.")

[464] Taylor Dep. Tr. at 25.

[465] Holmes Dep. Tr. at 20.

[466] Taylor Dep. Tr. at 25-26.

[467] Taylor Dep. Tr. at 25.

Q: But Ambassador Sondland made it clear not only that he didn't wish to include most of the regular interagency participants but also that no one was transcribing or monitoring the call as they added President Zelensky. What struck you as odd about that?

A: Same concern. That is, in the normal, regular channel, the State Department operations center that was putting the call together would stay on the line, in particular when you were having a conversation with the head of state, they would stay on the line, transcribe, take notes so that there could be a record of the discussion with this head of state. It is an official discussion. When he wanted to be sure that there was not, the State Department operations center agreed.

[468] Taylor Dep. Tr. at 26.

[469] Taylor Dep. Tr. at 127.

[470] Kurt Volker Document Production, Bates KV00000036 (Oct. 2, 2019).

[471] Kurt Volker Document Production, Bates KV00000036 (Oct. 2, 2019).

[472] Taylor Dep. Tr. at 26.

[473] Kurt Volker Document Production, Bates KV00000027 (Oct. 2, 2019).

[474] Volker Transcribed Interview Tr. at 242-243.

[475] Kurt Volker Document Production, Bates KV00000055 (Oct. 2, 2019).

[476] Kurt Volker Document Production, Bates KV00000027 (Oct. 2, 2019).

Taylor: Are you OK with me briefing Ulrich on these conversations? Maybe you

 have already?

Volker: I have not—please feel free

Volker: The key thing is to tee up a phone call w potus and then get visit nailed down

Taylor: I agree. Is Ze on board with a phone call?

Volker: Yes — bogdan was a little skeptical, but Zelensky was ok with it. Now we need to get it on potus schedule…

Taylor: The three amigos are on a roll. Let me know when I can help.

[477] Taylor Dep. Tr. at 65-66. ("Kurt told me that he had discussed how President Zelensky could prepare for the phone call with President Trump. And without going into—without providing me any details about the specific words, did talk about investigations in that conversation ... Kurt suggested that President Trump would like to hear about the investigations.")

[478] Morrison-Volker Hearing Tr. at 94.

Q: In the July 2nd or 3rd meeting in Toronto that you had with President Zelensky, you also mentioned investigations to him, right?

A: Yes

Q: And again, you were referring to the Burisma and the 2016 election.

A: I was thinking of Burisma and 2016.

Q: And you understood that that what the Ukrainians interpreted references to investigations to be, related to Burisma and the 2016 election?

A: I don't know specifically at that time if we had talked that specifically, Burisma/2016. That was my assumption, though, that they would've been thinking that too.

[479] Sondland Hearing Tr. at 27.

[480] Sondland Hearing Tr. at 43.

[481] Sondland Hearing Tr. at 21-22.

[482] Kent Dep. Tr. at 246.

[483] Hill-Holmes Hearing Tr. at 59.

[484] Kent Dep. Tr. at 246-47. ("I do not recall whether the follow-on conversation I had with Kurt about this was in Toronto, or whether it was subsequently at the State Department. But he did tell me that he planned to start reaching out to former Mayor of New York, Rudy Giuliani. And when I asked him why, he said that it was clear that the former mayor had influence on the President in terms of the way the President though of Ukraine. And I think by that moment in time, that was self-evidence to anyone who was working on the issues, and therefore, it made sense to try to engage the mayor. When I raised with Kurt, I said, about what? Because former Mayor Giuliani has a track record of, you know, asking for a visa for a corrupt former prosecutor. He attacked Masha, and he's tweeting that the new President needs to investigate Biden and the 2016 campaign. And Kurt's reaction or response to me at that was, well, if there's nothing there, what does it matter? And if there is something there, it should be investigated. My response to him was asking another country to investigate a prosecution for political reasons undermines our advocacy of the rule of law.")

[485] Kurt Volker Document Production, Bates KV00000036 (Oct. 2, 2019).

[486] Kurt Volker Document Production, Bates KV00000036 (Oct. 2, 2019).

[487] Kurt Volker Document Production, Bates KV00000006 (Oct. 2, 2019).

[488] Volker Transcribed Interview Tr. at 308; Kurt Volker Document Production, Bates KV00000018 (Oct. 2, 2019).

[489] Volker Transcribed Interview Tr. at 138.

[490] Sondland Hearing Tr. at 23.

[491] Hill Dep. Tr. at 63.

[492] Hill Dep. Tr. at 63-67, 155.

[493] Hill Dep. Tr. at 63-67, 155.

Q: Did anything happen in that meeting that was out of the ordinary?

A: Yes. At one point during that meeting, Ambassador Bolton was, you know, basically trying very hard not to commit to a meeting, because, you know – and, again, these meetings have to be well-prepared. They're not just something that you say, yes, we're going to have a meeting without there being a clear understanding of what the content of that meeting is going to be. ... And Ambassador Bolton is always – was always very cautious and always very much, you know, by the book and was not going to certainly commit to a meeting right there and then, certainly not one where it wasn't – it was unclear what the content of the meeting would be about, what kind of issues that we would discuss that would be pertaining to Ukrainian-U.S. relations. ... Then

Ambassador Sondland blurted out: Well, we have an agreement with the chief of staff for a meeting if these investigations in the energy sector start. And Ambassador Bolton immediately stiffened. He said words to the effect—I can't say word for word what he said because I was behind them sitting on the sofa with our Senior Director of Energy, and we all kind of looked up and thought that was somewhat odd. And Ambassador Bolton immediately stiffened and ended the meeting.

Q: Right then, he just ended the meeting?

A: Yeah. He said: Well, it was very nice to see you. You know, I can't discuss a meeting at this time. We'll clearly work on this. And, you know, kind of it was really nice to see you. So it was very abrupt. I mean, he looked at the clock as if he had, you know, suddenly another meeting and his time was up, but it was obvious he ended the meeting.

[494] Vindman Dep. Tr. at 17. ("The meeting proceeded well until the Ukrainians broached the subject of a meeting between the two Presidents. The Ukrainians saw this meeting as critically important in order to solidify the support for their most important international partner. Ambassador Sondland started -- when Ambassador Sondland started to speak about Ukraine delivering specific investigations in order to secure the meeting with the President, Ambassador Bolton cut the meeting short.")

[495] Volker Transcribed Interview Tr. at 310.

[496] Morrison-Volker Hearing Tr. at 23, 73, 103.

[497] Hill Dep. Tr. at 68. ("And Ambassador Sondland said to Ambassador Volker and also Secretary Perry and the other people who were with him, including the Ukrainians, to come down to—there's a room in the White House, the Ward Room, to basically talk about next steps. And that's also unusual. I mean, he meant to talk to the Ukrainians about next steps about the meeting.")

[498] Hill Dep. Tr. at 68. ("And Ambassador Bolton pulled me back as I was walking out afterwards and said: Go down to the Ward Room right now and find out what they're talking about and come back and talk to me. So I did go down.")

[499] Vindman Dep. Tr. at 64-65.

Q: And what do you recall specifically of what Sondland said to the Ukrainians—

A: Right.

Q: —in the Ward Room?

A: So that is right, the conversation unfolded with Sondland proceeding to kind of, you know, review what the deliverable would be in order to get the meeting, and he talked about the investigation into the Bidens, and, frankly, I can't 100 percent recall because I didn't take notes of it, but Burisma, that it seemed—I mean, there was no ambiguity, I guess, in my mind. He was calling for something, calling for an investigation that didn't exist into the Bidens and Burisma.

Q: Okay. Ambiguity in your mind is different from what you—

A: Sure.

Q: —actually heard?

A: Right. Correct.

Q: What did you hear Sondland say?

A: That the Ukrainians would have to deliver an investigation into the Bidens.

Q: Into the Bidens. So in the Ward Room he mentioned the word "Bidens"?

A: To the best of my recollection, yes.

Q: Okay. Did he mention 2016?

A: I don't recall.

Q: Did he mention Burisma?

A: My visceral reaction to what was being called for suggested that it was explicit. There was no ambiguity.

…

A: Again, based on my visceral reaction, it was explicit what he was calling for. And to the best of my recollection, he did specifically say "investigation of the Bidens."

…

A   So the meeting that occurred in the Ward Room referenced investigations into the Bidens, to the best of my recollection, Burisma and 2016

[500] Hill Dep. Tr. at 69.

[501] Hill Dep. Tr. at 151-52.

[502] Hill Dep. Tr. at 69-70.

[503] Vindman Dep. Tr. at 31.

Q: Did Ambassador Sondland—were the Ukrainian officials in the room when he was describing the need for these investigations in order to get the White House meeting?

A: So they were in the room initially. I think, once it became clear that there was some sort of discord amongst the government officials in the room, Ambassador Sondland asked them to step out of the room.

Q: What was the discord?

A: The fact that it was clear that I, as the representative—I, as the representative of the NSC, thought it was inappropriate and that we were not going to get involved in investigations.

Q: Did you say that to Ambassador Sondland?

A: Yes, I did.

[504] Vindman Dep. Tr. at 18.

While not specifically disagreeing with any of the content of the discussion in the Ward Room, Ambassador Sondland generally disputed Dr. Hill and Lt. Col. Vindman's accounts, saying that he did not recall "any yelling or screaming … as others have said." Sondland Hearing Tr. at 23. Neither Dr. Hill nor Lt. Col. Vindman described yelling or screaming in the meetings.

Ambassador Sondland also testified that "those recollections of protest do not square with the documentary record of our interactions with the NSC in the days and weeks that followed." Sondland Hearing Tr. at 23. As an example, Sondland provided text from a July 13 email that he sent—not to Dr. Hill, but to her successor Tim Morrison—which said that the "sole purpose" of the call between President Trump and President Zelensky was to give the former "assurances of 'new sheriff' in town." Sondland Hearing Tr. at 23. The email that Ambassador Sondland provided does not undermine Dr. Hill's or Lt. Col. Vindman's testimony that they objected to Ambassador Sondland's conduct in the Ward Room meeting. The email provided by Ambassador Sondland, however, was sent to Mr. Morrison, not Dr. Hill. Mr. Morrison had not yet started working as NSC Senior Director for Europe and was not at the July 10 meeting.

[505] Vindman Dep. Tr. at 29.

A: So I heard him say that this had been coordinated with White House Chief of Staff Mr. Mick Mulvaney.

Q: What did he say about that?

A: He just said that he had had a conversation with Mr. Mulvaney, and this is what was required in order to get a meeting.

[506] Hill Dep. Tr. at 69-70.

[507] Kurt Volker Document Production, Bates KV00000036 (Oct. 2, 2019).

[7/10/19, 2:26:06 PM] Bill Taylor: Eager to hear if your meeting with Danyliuk and Bolton resulted in a decision on a call.

[7/10/19, 10:26:13 PM] Bill Taylor: How did the meeting go?

[7/10/19, 10:29:44 PM] Kurt Volker: Not good—lets talk—kv

[508] Kurt Volker Document Production, Bates KV00000018 (Oct. 2, 2019).

[509] Hill Dep. Tr. at 70-72.

[510] Hill Dep. Tr. at 126-27.

Q: Okay. But what did you understand him to mean by that?

A: Well, based on what had happened in the July 10th meeting and Ambassador Sondland blurting out that he'd already gotten agreement to have a meeting at the White House for Zelensky if these investigations were started up again, clearly Ambassador Bolton was referring directly to those.

[511] Hill Dep. Tr. at 129.

[512] Hill Dep. Tr. at 139.   ("I told him exactly, you know, what had transpired and that Ambassador Sondland had basically indicated that there was an agreement with the Chief of Staff that they would have a White House meeting or, you know, a Presidential meeting if the Ukrainians started up these investigations again.")

[513] Hill Dep. Tr. at 139.

[514] Hill Dep. Tr. at 146-147.

[515] Hill Dep. Tr. at 158-59, 161.

Q: What was Mr. Eisenberg's reaction to what you explained to him had and Mr. Griffith had explained to him had occurred the day before?

A: Yeah. He was also concerned. I mean, he wasn't aware that Sondland, Ambassador Sondland was, you know, kind of running around doing a lot of these, you know, meetings and independently. We talked about the fact that, you know, Ambassador Sondland said he'd been meeting with Giuliani and he was very concerned about that. And he said that he would follow up on this.

[516] Vindman Dep. Tr. at 37. ("Sir, I think I—I mean, the top line I just offered, I'll restate it, which is that Mr. Sondland asked for investigations, for these investigations into Bidens and Burisma. I actually recall having that particular conversation. Mr. Eisenberg doesn't really work on this issue, so I had to go a little bit into the back story of what these investigations were, and that I expressed concerns and thought it was inappropriate.")

[517] Vindman Dep. Tr. at 36.

[518] Vindman Dep. Tr. at 38.

Q: Did he say anything to you, that, all right, I'm going to do anything with it?

A: I vaguely recall something about: I'll take a look into it. You know, there might not be anything here. We'll take a look into it, something of that nature. But—and then he offered to, you know, if I have any concerns in the future, you know, you know, that I should be open—I should be—feel free to come back and, you know, share those concerns.

Q: Did either he or anyone from the legal staff circle back to you on this issue?

A: No.

[519] Vindman Dep. Tr. at 39-40.

[520] Taylor Dep. Tr. at 29. ("In the same July 19th phone call, they gave me an account of the July 10th meeting with the Ukrainian officials at the White House. Specifically, they told me that Ambassador Sondland had connected investigations with an Oval Office meeting for President Zelensky, which so irritated Ambassador Bolton

that he abruptly ended the meeting, telling Dr. Hill and Mr. Vindman that they should have nothing to do with domestic politics.")

[521] Morrison Dep. Tr. at 12.

[522] House Permanent Select Committee on Intelligence, Written Statement of Ambassador Gordon Sondland, *Impeachment*, 116th Cong. (Nov. 20, 2019) ("2. The call between Zelensky and Potus should happen before 7/21. (Parliamentary Elections) Sole purpose is for Zelensky to give Potus assurances of 'new sheriff' in town. Corruption ending, unbundling moving forward and any hampered investigations will be allowed to move forward transparently. Goal is for Potus to invite him to Oval. Volker, Perry, Bolton and I strongly recommend.").

[523] House Permanent Select Committee on Intelligence, Written Statement of Ambassador Gordon Sondland, *Impeachment*, 116th Cong. (Nov. 20, 2019).

[524] Sondland Dep. Tr. at 227.

[525] House Permanent Select Committee on Intelligence, Opening Statement of Ambassador Gordon Sondland, Department of State, *Impeachment*, 116th Cong., at 21 (Nov. 20, 2019).

[526] House Permanent Select Committee on Intelligence, Opening Statement of Ambassador Gordon Sondland, Department of State, *Impeachment*, 116th Cong., at 21 (Nov. 20, 2019).

[527] House Permanent Select Committee on Intelligence, Opening Statement of Ambassador Gordon Sondland, Department of State, *Impeachment*, 116th Cong., at 21 (Nov. 20, 2019).

[528] Sondland Hearing Tr. at 27.

[529] Verizon Document Production. It is unclear whether this call occurred before or after Ambassador Sondland spoke with President Zelensky, and it is also unclear whether the White House caller was an Administration official or the President himself.

[530] Kurt Volker Document Production, Bates KV00000037 (Oct. 2, 2019).

[531] Kurt Volker Document Production, Bates KV00000037 (Oct. 2, 2019).

[532] Volker Transcribed Interview Tr. at 229-230.

[533] Kurt Volker Document Production, Bates KV00000018 (Oct. 2, 2019).

[534] Volker Transcribed Interview Tr. at 202-203.

[535] Volker Transcribed Interview Tr. at 232.

[536] Kurt Volker Document Production, Bates KV00000002 (Oct. 2, 2019).

[537] Kurt Volker Document Production, Bates KV00000018 (Oct. 2, 2019).

[538] Volker Transcribed Interview Tr. at 138-139.

[539] AT&T Document Production, Bates ATTHPSCI_20190930_02705.

[540] Volker Transcribed Interview Tr. at 139.

[541] Kurt Volker Document Production, Bates KV00000018 (Oct. 2, 2019).

[542] Kurt Volker Document Production, Bates KV00000002- KV00000003 (Oct. 2, 2019).

[543] Kurt Volker Document Production, Bates KV00000042 (Oct. 2, 2019).

Volker:	Orchestrated a great call w Rudy and Yermak. They are going to get together when Rudy goes to Madrid in a couple of weeks.
Volker:	In the meantime, Rudy is now advocating for phone call
Volker:	I have call into Fiona's replacement and will call Bolton if needed.
Volker:	But I can tell Bolton and you can tell Mick that Rudy agrees on a call, if that helps
Sondland:	I talked to Tim Morrison. (Fiona's replacement). He is pushing but feel free as well.

[544] Kurt Volker Document Production, Bates KV00000042 (Oct. 2, 2019).

Volker: Orchestrated a great call w Rudy and Yermak. They are going to get together when Rudy goes to Madrid in a couple of weeks.

Volker: In the meantime, Rudy is now advocating for phone call

Volker: I have call into Fiona's replacement and will call Bolton if needed.

Volker: But I can tell Bolton and you can tell Mick that Rudy agrees on a call, if that helps

Sondland: I talked to Tim Morrison. (Fiona's eplacement). He is pushing but feel free as well.

[545] Taylor Dep. Tr. at 30.

[546] Kurt Volker Document Production, Bates KV000000 37 (Oct. 2, 2019).

[547] Taylor Dep. Tr. at 74.

[548] Kent-Taylor Hearing Tr. at 68.

[549] Taylor Dep. Tr. at 177.

[550] Sondland Dep. Tr. at 183.

[551] Sondland Hearing Tr. at 17.

[552] Sondland Hearing Tr. at 18.

[553] Sondland Hearing Tr. at 19; 17.

[554] Sondland Hearing Tr. at 27.

[555] Sondland Hearing Tr. at 26.

[556] Sondland Hearing Tr. at 27.

[557] Taylor Dep. Tr. at 26.

[558] Hill-Holmes Hearing Tr. at 25.

[559] Hill Dep. Tr. at 420-421.

Q: You've mentioned repeatedly concerns that you had about, in particular, Mr. Giuliani and his efforts. When you read the call transcript of July 25th, the call record, which you must have done just a couple weeks ago, did it crystalize in your head in any way a better understanding of what was transpiring while you were there?

A: In terms of providing, you know, more information with hindsight, unfortunately, yes.

Q: And in what way?

A: The specific references, also juxtaposed with the release of the text messages by Ambassador Volker—you know, what I said before—really was kind of my worst fears and nightmares, in terms of, you know, there being some kind of effort not just to subvert the national security process but to try to subvert what really should be, you know, kind of, a diplomatic effort to, you know, kind of, set up a Presidential meeting.

Q: This may—

A: There seems to be an awful lot of people involved in, you know, basically turning a White House meeting into some kind of asset.

Q: What do you mean by "asset"?

A: Well, something that was being, you know, dangled out to the Ukrainian Government. They wanted the White House meeting very much. And this was kind of laying out that it wasn't just a question of scheduling or having, you know, the national security issues worked out, that there were all of these alternative discussions going on behind.

[560] Taylor Dep. Tr. at 174.

[561] Taylor Dep. Tr. at 174.

[562] Kurt Volker Document Production, Bates KV00000042 (Oct. 2, 2019).

[563] Sondland Hearing Tr. at 53-55.

[564] Sondland Hearing Tr. at 52-53.

[565] Morrison Dep. Tr. at 30-31, 101, 247, 256.

[566] Morrison Dep. Tr. at 31.

[567] Morrison Dep. Tr. at 111.

[568] Volker Transcribed Interview Tr. at 102-103; Kurt Volker Document Production, Bates KV00000007 (Oct. 2, 2019).

In his testimony, Ambassador Volker did not explain to the Committees what he had heard about the July 25 call put him in a position to tell Mr. Giuliani that the "right messages" were, in fact, discussed.

Ambassador Volker testified twice about the readouts that he received of the July 25 call. In his deposition, he told the Committees that he received "the same" readout from both the State Department and Mr. Yermak: that there was a message of congratulations to President Zelensky, that President Zelensky promised to fight corruption and that President Trump repeated the invitation to visit the White House. Volker Transcribed Interview Tr. at 102-103. Volker described it as a "superficial" readout. Volker Transcribed Interview Tr. at 19.

In his public testimony, Volker repeated that claim: the readouts from Mr. Yermak and Volker's U.S. sources "were largely the same, that it was a good call, that it was a congratulatory phone call for the President winning the parliamentary election." Volker-Morrison Hearing Tr. at 74. Volker did testify that he "expected" the call to cover the material in his July 25 text message – that the Ukrainians would "investigate/'get to the bottom of what happened' in 2016" – but did not receive anything more than a "barebones" description of what was said. Volker-Morrison Hearing Tr. at 87-88, 75.

If Volker is correctly describing the readouts he received, it is not clear what he heard that gave him the basis to tell Mr. Giuliani that "exactly the right messages" were discussed.

[569] Williams Dep. Tr. at 37-38.

[570] Hill-Holmes Hearing Tr. at 23.

[571] Hill-Holmes Hearing Tr. at 25.

[572] *Trump and Putin Share Joke About Election Meddling, Sparking New Furor*, New York Times (June 28, 2019) (online at www.nytimes.com/2019/06/28/us/politics/trump-putin-election.html) ("As he sat down on Friday with Mr. Putin on the sidelines of an international summit in Japan, Mr. Trump was asked by a reporter if he would tell Russia not to meddle in American elections. 'Yes, of course I will,' Mr. Trump said. Turning to Mr. Putin, he said, with a half-grin on his face and mock seriousness in his voice, 'Don't meddle in the election, President.'").

[573] Morrison Dep. Tr. at 41.

[574] Williams Dep. Tr. at 131.

[575] *See* Vindman Dep. Tr. at 42, 109; Morrison Dep. Tr. at 41.

[576] Vindman Dep. Tr. at 18; Morrison Dep. Tr. at 15.

[577] Vindman Dep. Tr. at 42-43; Morrison-Volker Hearing Tr. at 32.

[578] Morrison Dep. Tr. at 39; Vindman Dep. Tr. at 45.

[579] U.S. Embassy & Consulates in Italy, *Secretary Michael R. Pompeo and Italian Foreign Minister Luigi Di Maio at a Press Availability* (Oct. 2, 2019) (online at https://it.usembassy.gov/secretary-michael-r-pompeo-and-italian-foreign-minister-luigi-di-maio-at-a-press-availability/). Mr. Morrison testified that Dr. Kupperman was not in the Situation Room, but Mr. Morrison was informed after the fact that Dr. Kupperman was listening. Morrison

Dep. Tr. at 39-40. Ms. Williams and Lt. Col. Vindman testified that they both believed Dr. Kupperman was present, but neither had a clear recollection. Williams Dep. Tr. at 64; Vindman Dep. Tr. at 45.

[580] *See* Transcript, *This Week with George Stephanopoulos*, ABC News (Sept. 22, 2019) (online at https://abcnews.go.com/Politics/week-transcript-22-19-secretary-mike-pompeo-gen/story?id=65778332) (Q: And I want to turn to this whistleblower complaint, Mr. Secretary. The complaint involving the president and a phone call with a foreign leader to the director of national intelligence inspector general. That's where the complaint was launched by the whistle-blower. 'The Wall Street Journal' is reporting that President Trump pressed the president of Ukraine eight times to work with Rudy Giuliani to investigate Joe Biden's son. What do you know about those conversations? A: So, you just gave me a report about a I.C. whistle-blower complaint, none of which I've seen....").

[581] *Pompeo Took Part in Ukraine Call, Official Says*, Wall Street Journal (Sept. 30, 2019) (online at www.wsj.com/articles/pompeo-took-part-in-ukraine-call-official-says-11569865002).

[582] The White House, *Memorandum of Telephone Conversation* (July 25, 2019) (online at www.whitehouse.gov/wp-content/uploads/2019/09/Unclassified09.2019.pdf).

[583] The White House, *Memorandum of Telephone Conversation* (July 25, 2019) (online at www.whitehouse.gov/wp-content/uploads/2019/09/Unclassified09.2019.pdf).

[584] The White House, *Memorandum of Telephone Conversation* (July 25, 2019) (online at www.whitehouse.gov/wp-content/uploads/2019/09/Unclassified09.2019.pdf). *See* European Union External Action Service, *EU-Ukraine relations-factsheet* (Sept. 30, 2019) (online at https://eeas.europa.eu/headquarters/headquarters-Homepage/4081/eu-ukraine-relations-factsheet_en).

[585] The White House, *Memorandum of Telephone Conversation* (July 25, 2019) (online at www.whitehouse.gov/wp-content/uploads/2019/09/Unclassified09.2019.pdf).

[586] The White House, *Memorandum of Telephone Conversation* (July 25, 2019) (online at www.whitehouse.gov/wp-content/uploads/2019/09/Unclassified09.2019.pdf); Kent-Taylor Hearing Tr. at 29.

[587] The White House, *Memorandum of Telephone Conversation* (July 25, 2019) (online at www.whitehouse.gov/wp-content/uploads/2019/09/Unclassified09.2019.pdf).

[588] Vindman Dep. Tr. at 114.

[589] The White House, *Memorandum of Telephone Conversation* (July 25, 2019) (online at www.whitehouse.gov/wp-content/uploads/2019/09/Unclassified09.2019.pdf).

[590] *See* Office of the Director of National Intelligence, *Assessing Russian Activities and Intentions in Recent U.S. Elections* (Jan. 6, 2017) (online at www.dni.gov/files/documents/ICA_2017_01.pdf).

[591] The White House, *Memorandum of Telephone Conversation* (July 25, 2019) (online at www.whitehouse.gov/wp-content/uploads/2019/09/Unclassified09.2019.pdf).

[592] *Charges of Ukrainian Meddling? A Russian Operation, U.S. Intelligence Says*, New York Times (Nov. 22, 2019) (online at www.nytimes.com/2019/11/22/us/politics/ukraine-russia-interference.html).

[593] The President of Russia, *Joint News Conference with Hungarian Prime Minister Viktor Orban* (Feb. 2, 2017) (online at http://en.kremlin.ru/events/president/news/53806).

[594] Hill-Holmes Hearing Tr. at 39-40.

[595] *President Trump's Former National Security Advisor 'Deeply Disturbed' by Ukraine Scandal: 'Whole World Is Watching,'* ABC News (Sept. 29, 2019) (online at https://abcnews.go.com/Politics/president-trumps-national-security-advisor-deeply-disturbed-ukraine/story?id=65925477).

[596] Hill Dep. Tr. at 234-235.

[597] The White House, *Memorandum of Telephone Conversation* (July 25, 2019) (online at www.whitehouse.gov/wp-content/uploads/2019/09/Unclassified09.2019.pdf).

[598] The White House, *Memorandum of Telephone Conversation* (July 25, 2019) (online at www.whitehouse.gov/wp-content/uploads/2019/09/Unclassified09.2019.pdf).

[599] The White House, *Memorandum of Telephone Conversation* (July 25, 2019) (online at www.whitehouse.gov/wp-content/uploads/2019/09/Unclassified09.2019.pdf).

[600] The White House, *Memorandum of Telephone Conversation* (July 25, 2019) (online at www.whitehouse.gov/wp-content/uploads/2019/09/Unclassified09.2019.pdf).

[601] The White House, *Memorandum of Telephone Conversation* (July 25, 2019) (online at www.whitehouse.gov/wp-content/uploads/2019/09/Unclassified09.2019.pdf).

[602] The White House, *Memorandum of Telephone Conversation* (July 25, 2019) (online at www.whitehouse.gov/wp-content/uploads/2019/09/Unclassified09.2019.pdf).

[603] The White House, *Remarks by President Trump before Marine One* (Oct. 3, 2019) (online at www.whitehouse.gov/briefings-statements/remarks-president-trump-marine-one-departure-67/).

[604] Hill Dep. Tr. at 400; Kent-Taylor Hearing Tr. at 73.; Hill-Holmes Hearing Tr. at 63-64.; Yovanovitch Hearing Tr. at 49-50; Morrison-Volker Hearing Tr. at 23.

[605] Kent Dep. Tr. at 45.

[606] Kent-Taylor Hearing Tr. at 116.

[607] Yovanovitch Hearing Tr. at 50.

[608] *See* Section I, Chapter 1.

[609] Kent Dep. Tr. at 44-50.

[610] Morrison-Volker Hearing Tr. at 23.

[611] Morrison-Volker Hearing Tr. at 23.

[612] *See* Section I, Chapter 1.

[613] The White House, *Memorandum of Telephone Conversation* (July 25, 2019) (online at www.whitehouse.gov/wp-content/uploads/2019/09/Unclassified09.2019.pdf).

[614] Yovanovitch Dep. Tr. at 192-193.

[615] Yovanovitch Dep. Tr. at 192-193.

[616] Ambassador Volker was the only witness to testify that President Trump's reference to the "prosecutor" during the July 25 call was to Mr. Shokin, not Mr. Lutsenko. See Volker Dep. Tr. at 355. However, Mr. Holmes testified that, on July 26—the day after the call—he spoke with President Zelensky's Chief of Staff Andriy Bohdan who told Holmes that "President Trump had expressed interest during the previous day's phone call in President Zelensky's personnel decisions related to the Prosecutor General's office," which Mr. Holmes understood to refer to Mr. Lutsenko once he saw the July 25 call transcript. Holmes Dep. Tr. at 22, 49. In addition, in a text message to Taylor and Sondland after his July 19 breakfast with Giuliani, Volker emphasized that "Most impt [important] is for Zelensky to say" on the July 25 call "that he will help investigation—and address any specific personnel issues—if there are any." Kurt Volker Document Production, Bates KV00000037 (Oct. 2, 2019).

[617] The White House, *Memorandum of Telephone Conversation* (July 25, 2019) (online at www.whitehouse.gov/wp-content/uploads/2019/09/Unclassified09.2019.pdf).

[618] The White House, *Memorandum of Telephone Conversation* (July 25, 2019) (online at www.whitehouse.gov/wp-content/uploads/2019/09/Unclassified09.2019.pdf).

[619] Hill-Holmes Hearing Tr. at 55.

[620] Holmes Dep. Tr. at 49-50.

[621] Kent-Taylor Hearing Tr. at 25.

[622] Morrison-Volker Hearing Tr. at 19.

[623] Hill-Holmes Hearing Tr. at 18.

[624] *In-Town Pool Report #6—Ukraine Call*, White House Pool Report (July 25, 2019) (online at https://publicpool.kinja.com/subject-in-town-pool-report-6-ukraine-call-1836700221).

[625] Vindman Dep. Tr. at 42-43.

[626] Vindman-Williams Hearing Tr. at 31-33; Morrison-Volker Hearing Tr. at 34.

[627] Vindman Dep. Tr. at 46-47.

[628] Taylor Dep. Tr. at 29.

[629] Vindman Dep. Tr. at 94.

[630] Vindman Dep. Tr. at 46-47.

[631] Vindman-Williams Hearing Tr. at 28.

[632] Vindman Dep. Tr. at 147.

[633] Vindman-Williams Hearing Tr. at 28-29.

[634] Vindman Dep. Tr. at 96-97.

[635] Vindman Dep. Tr. at 97-98.

[636] Morrison-Volker Hearing Tr. at 29.

[637] Morrison Dep. Tr. at 23-24.

[638] Morrison Dep. Tr. at 41-42, 191-192.

[639] Morrison Dep. Tr. at 97.

[640] Morrison Dep. Tr. at 97.

[641] Morrison Dep. Tr. at 101.

[642] Morrison Dep. Tr. at 41.

[643] Morrison Dep. Tr. at 43.

[644] Morrison Dep. Tr. at 44.

[645] Morrison Dep. Tr. at 16.

[646] Morrison Dep. Tr. at 101.

[647] Morrison-Volker Hearing Tr. at 38.

[648] Vindman Dep. Tr. at 121.

[649] Vindman Dep. Tr. at 122.

[650] Vindman Dep. Tr. at 122-123.

[651] Vindman Dep. Tr. at 121.

[652] Vindman Dep. Tr. at 123-124.

[653] Morrison Dep. Tr. at 121.

[654] Morrison Dep. Tr. at 55-56.

[655] Morrison Dep. Tr. at 55-56, 121-123.

[656] Morrison Dep. Tr. at 270.

[657] Williams Dep. Tr. at 16, 63.

[658] Williams Dep. Tr. at 149.

[659] Vindman-Williams Hearing Tr. at 34.

[660] Williams Dep. Tr. at 148.

[661] Vindman-Williams Hearing Tr. at 29.

[662] Williams Dep. Tr. at 54, 149.

[663] Vindman Dep. Tr. at 54-55. ("There's one other substantive item in the next paragraph from Zelensky, where it says 'He or she will look into the situation specifically to the company'—it shouldn't be 'the company.' It should be 'to Burisma that you mentioned.' Because I think, you know, frankly these are not necessarily folks that are familiar with the substance. So President Zelensky specifically mentioned the company Burisma.").

[664] Vindman-Williams Hearing Tr. at 61.

[665] Vindman Dep. Tr. at 89.

[666] Williams Dep. Tr. at 68-69.
Q: Okay. When the transcript was made available to the VP's office, do you remember when that occurred?

A: My colleagues—I can't remember the precise time, but before the end of the day that day my colleagues who help prepare the Vice President's briefing book received a hard copy of the transcript from the White House Situation Room to include in that book. I didn't personally see it, but I understood that they had received it because we wanted to make sure the Vice President got it.

Q: On the 25th or 26th?

A: It was on the 25th.

[667] Vindman Dep. Tr. at 139–141.

[668] Kent Dep. Tr. at 163-165.

[669] Holmes Dep. Tr.at 107.

[670] Holmes Dep. Tr. at 21-22.

[671] Kent-Taylor Hearing Tr. at 38; Hill-Holmes Hearing Tr. at 26.

[672] Morrison-Volker Hearing Tr. at 74. ("Yes. So I was not on the phone call. I had arrived in Ukraine, and I had had that lunch with Mr. Yermak that we saw on the day of the phone call. I had been pushing for the phone call because I thought it was important to renew the personal connection between the two leaders and to congratulate President Zelensky on the parliamentary election. The readout I received from Mr. Yermak and also from the U.S. side—although I'm not exactly sure who it was on the U.S. side, but there was U.S. and a Ukrainian readout—were largely the same, that it was a good call, that it was a congratulatory phone call for the President winning the parliamentary election. President Zelensky did reiterate his commitment to reform and fighting corruption in Ukraine, and President Trump did reiterate his invitation to President Zelensky to come visit him in the White House. That's exactly what I thought the phone call would be, so I was not surprised at getting that as the readout.").

[673] Holmes Dep. Tr. at 22.

[674] Holmes Dep. Tr. at 22, 48-49.

[675] Holmes Dep. Tr. at 49.

[676] Holmes Dep. Tr. at 49.

[677] Holmes Dep. Tr. at 22.

[678] Hill-Holmes Hearing Tr. at 27.

[679] Hill-Holmes Hearing Tr. at 48-49.

[680] Croft Dep. Tr. at 118-119.

[681] Sondland Hearing Tr. at 25; Kent-Taylor Hearing Tr. at 38.

[682] Morrison-Volker Hearing Tr. at 89-90.

[683] Holmes Dep. Tr. at 64.

[684] Kent-Taylor Hearing Tr. at 38.

[685] Hill-Holmes Hearing Tr. at 27.

[686] Hill-Holmes Hearing Tr. at 27.

[687] Hill-Holmes Hearing Tr. at 27-28.

[688] Hill-Holmes Hearing Tr. at 27-28.

[689] Hill-Holmes Hearing Tr. at 27-28.

[690] Holmes Dep. Tr. at 108.

[691] Hill-Holmes Hearing Tr. at 49.

[692] Sondland Hearing Tr. at 25-26.

[693] Hill-Holmes Hearing Tr. at 28.

[694] Hill-Holmes Hearing Tr. at 28.

[695] Hill-Holmes Hearing Tr. at 49. ("The restaurant has sort of glass doors that open onto a terrace, and we were at the first tables on the terrace, so immediately outside of the interior of the restaurant. The doors were all wide open. There were—there was tables, a table for four, while I recall it being two tables for two pushed together. In any case, it was quite a wide table, and the table was set. There was sort of a table runner down the middle. I was directly across from Ambassador Sondland. We were close enough that we could, you know, share an appetizer between us, and then the two staffers were off to our right at this next table.").

[696] Hill-Holmes Hearing Tr. at 28.

[697] Hill-Holmes Hearing Tr. at 28.

[698] Holmes Dep. Tr. at 160.

[699] Hill-Holmes Hearing Tr. at 28.

[700] Hill-Holmes Hearing Tr. at 50.

Q: Now, you said that you were able to hear President Trump's voice through the receiver. How were you able to hear if it was not on speaker phone?

A: It was several things. It was quite loud when the President came on, quite distinctive. I believe Ambassador Sondland also said that he often speaks very loudly over the phone, and I certainly experienced that. When the President came on, he sort of winced and held the phone away from his ear like this, and he did that for the first couple exchanges. I don't know if he then turned the volume down, if he got used to it, if the President moderated his volume. I don't know. But that's how I was able to hear.

[701] Hill-Holmes Hearing Tr. at 28-29.

[702] *Trump Denies Discussing Ukraine Investigations with Sondland in July Phone Call*, Axios (Nov. 13, 2019) (online at: www.axios.com/trump-denies-ukraine-investigation-sondland-6063f555-2629-4f99-b2f9-fd38739c0548.html).

[703] Sondland Hearing Tr. at 26.

[704] Sondland Hearing Tr. at 46.

[705] Sondland Hearing Tr. at 26.

[706] Sondland Hearing Tr. at 26.

[707] Sondland Hearing Tr. at 48.

[708] Holmes Dep. Tr. at 25.

[709] Holmes Dep. Tr. at 25-26.

[710] Sondland Hearing Tr. at 49-50. Ambassador Sondland opined that, while he may have referred to an investigation that Mr. Giuliani was pushing as an example of an investigation that President Trump cared about, he believed that he would have said "Burisma, not Biden." He testified, however:

Q: But do you recall saying at least referring to an investigation that Rudy Giuliani was pushing? Is that something that you likely would have said?

A: I would have, yes. *Id.* at 50.

[711] Sondland Hearing Tr. at 50.

[712] Holmes Dep. Tr. at 67.

[713] Holmes Dep. Tr. at 68-69.

[714] Hill-Holmes Hearing Tr. at 30.

[715] Hill-Holmes Hearing Tr. at 107.

[716] Hill-Holmes Hearing Tr. at 34.

[717] Holmes Dep. Tr. at 80.

[718] Holmes Dep. Tr. at 80-81.

[719] Kurt Volker Document Production, Bates KV00000007 (Oct. 2, 2019).

[720] Kurt Volker Document Production, Bates KV00000007 (Oct. 2, 2019).

[721] Kurt Volker Document Production, Bates KV00000007 (Oct. 2, 2019).

[722] Kurt Volker Document Production, Bates KV00000019 (Oct. 2, 2019).

[723] Volker Transcribed Interview Tr. at 112.

[724] Kurt Volker Document Production, Bates KV00000019 (Oct. 2, 2019).

[725] Morrison-Volker Hearing Tr. at 42.

[726] Morrison-Volker Hearing Tr. at 42.

[727] Morrison-Volker Hearing Tr. at 20-21.

[728] Kurt Volker Document Production, Bates KV00000019 (Oct. 2, 2019).

[729] Kurt Volker Document Production, Bates KV00000007 (Oct. 2, 2019).

[730] AT&T Document Production, Bates ATTHPSCI_20190930_02786.

[731] Kurt Volker Document Production, Bates KV00000007 (Oct. 2, 2019).

[732] Sondland Dep. Tr. at 192-193.

[733] Kurt Volker Document Production, Bates KV00000007 (Oct. 2, 2019).

[734] AT&T Document Production, Bates ATTHPSCI_20190930_02797.

[735] AT&T Document Production, Bates ATTHPSCI_20190930_02797.

[736] *Id.*

[737] AT&T Document Production, Bates ATTHPSCI_20190930_03326.

[738] *Id.*

[739] *Id.*

[740] *Id.*

[741] *Id.*

[742] *Id.*

[743] AT&T Document Production, Bates ATTHPSCI_20190930_02798.

[744] *Id.*

[745] *Id.*

[746] *Id.*

[747] *Id.*

[748] AT&T Document Production, Bates ATTHPSCI_20190930_02799.

[749] AT&T Document Production, Bates ATTHPSCI_20190930_02801.

[750] Kurt Volker Document Production, Bates KV00000019 (Oct. 2, 2019).

[751] Kurt Volker Document Production, Bates KV00000019 (Oct. 2, 2019).

[752] Kurt Volker Document Production, Bates KV00000019 (Oct. 2, 2019).

[753] Kurt Volker Document Production, Bates KV00000019 (Oct. 2, 2019).

[754] AT&T Document Production, Bates ATTHPSCI_20190930_02802-03, 02813, 03326, 03719.

[755] AT&T Document Production, Bates ATTHPSCI_20190930_03326.

[756] AT&T Document Production, Bates ATTHPSCI_20190930_02802.

[757] AT&T Document Production, Bates ATTHPSCI_20190930_02803.

[758] AT&T Document Production, Bates ATTHPSCI_20190930_03719.

[759] *Id.*

[760] AT&T Document Production, Bates ATTHPSCI_20190930_02803.

[761] *Id.*

[762] *Id.*

[763] *Id.*

[764] *Id.*

[765] Kurt Volker Document Production, Bates KV00000004- KV00000005 (Oct. 2, 2019).

[766] Kurt Volker Document Production, Bates KV00000004- KV00000005 (Oct. 2, 2019); AT&T Document Production, Bates ATTHPSCI_20190930_02805-06.

[767] Kurt Volker Document Production, Bates KV00000023 (Oct. 2, 2019).

[768] Kurt Volker Document Production, Bates KV00000023 (Oct. 2, 2019).

[769] Kurt Volker Document Production, Bates KV00000023 (Oct. 2, 2019).

[770] Verizon Document Production.

[771] Kurt Volker Document Production, Bates KV00000042 (Oct. 2, 2019).

[772] Sondland Dep. Tr. at 290; Sondland Hearing Tr. at 100-101.

[773] Kurt Volker Document Production, Bates KV00000042 (Oct. 2, 2019).

[774] Sondland Dep. Tr. at 291.

[775] Sondland Dep. Tr. at 291.

[776] Kurt Volker Document Production, Bates KV00000019 (Oct. 2, 2019).

[777] Kurt Volker Document Production, Bates KV00000019 (Oct. 2, 2019).

[778] Kurt Volker Document Production, Bates KV00000019 (Oct. 2, 2019).

[779] Kurt Volker Document Production, Bates KV00000042 (Oct. 2, 2019).

[780] House Permanent Select Committee on Intelligence, Opening Statement of Ambassador Gordon Sondland, Department of State, *Impeachment*, 116th Cong., at 15 (Nov. 20, 2019).

[781] Kurt Volker Document Production, Bates KV00000042 (Oct. 2, 2019).

[782] Sondland Dep. Tr. at 291-292.

[783] Sondland Dep. Tr. at 291-292.

[784] House Permanent Select Committee on Intelligence, Opening Statement of Ambassador Gordon Sondland, Department of State, *Impeachment*, 116th Cong., at 14 (Nov. 20, 2019).

[785] Kurt Volker Document Production, Bates KV00000005 (Oct. 2, 2019).

[786] AT&T Document Production, Bates ATTHPSCI_20190930_02816.

[787] House Permanent Select Committee on Intelligence, Opening Statement of Ambassador Gordon Sondland, Department of State, *Impeachment*, 116th Cong., at 22 (Nov. 20, 2019).

[788] Sondland Hearing Tr. at 102.

[789] House Permanent Select Committee on Intelligence, Opening Statement of Ambassador Gordon Sondland, Department of State, *Impeachment*, 116th Cong., at 22 (Nov. 20, 2019).

[790] Sondland Hearing Tr. at 28.

[791] Kurt Volker Document Production, Bates KV00000020 (Oct. 2, 2019).

[792] Kurt Volker Document Production, Bates KV00000007 (Oct. 2, 2019).

[793] AT&T Document Production, Bates ATTHPSCI_20190930_02828.

[794] Volker Transcribed Interview Tr. at 113.

[795] Volker Transcribed Interview Tr. at 71-72.

[796] Kurt Volker Document Production, Bates KV00000023 (Oct. 2, 2019).

[797] Kurt Volker Document Production, Bates KV00000023 (Oct. 2, 2019).

[798] Kurt Volker Document Production, Bates KV00000023 (Oct. 2, 2019).

[799] Kurt Volker Document Production, Bates KV00000023 (Oct. 2, 2019).

[800] WhatsApp Security (online at www.whatsapp.com/security/) (accessed Nov. 29, 2019).

[801] Kurt Volker Document Production, Bates KV00000043 (Oct. 2, 2019).

[802] Kurt Volker Document Production, Bates KV00000043 (Oct. 2, 2019).

[803] Kurt Volker Document Production, Bates KV00000023 (Oct. 2, 2019).

[804] Kurt Volker Document Production, Bates KV00000023 (Oct. 2, 2019).

[805] Volker Transcribed Interview Tr. at 43-44, 113-114.

[806] House Permanent Select Committee on Intelligence, Opening Statement of Ambassador Gordon Sondland, Department of State, *Impeachment*, 116th Cong., at 5 (Nov. 20, 2019).

[807] Sondland Hearing Tr. at 18.

[808] Volker Transcribed Interview Tr. at 191, 197-198.

[809] Volker Transcribed Interview Tr. at 191-192.

[810] Volker Transcribed Interview Tr. at 201.

[811] Volker Transcribed Interview Tr. at 198.

[812] Volker Transcribed Interview Tr. at 197.

[813] Department of Justice, *Ukraine Statement* (Sept. 25, 2019).

[814] *Cleaning Up Ukraine in the Shadow of Trump*, The Financial Times (Nov. 28, 2019) (online at www.ft.com/content/eb8e4004-1059-11ea-a7e6-62bf4f9e548a).

[815] *Cleaning Up Ukraine in the Shadow of Trump*, The Financial Times (Nov. 28, 2019) (online at www.ft.com/content/eb8e4004-1059-11ea-a7e6-62bf4f9e548a).

[816] Taylor Dep. Opening Statement at 9.

[817] Taylor Dep. Opening Statement at 9.

[818] Volker Transcribed Interview Tr. at 196-197.

[819] Taylor Dep. Opening Statement at 9.

[820] Kurt Volker Document Production, Bates KV00000043 (Oct. 2, 2019).

[821] Volker Transcribed Interview Tr. at 196-197.

[822] Kent Dep. Tr. at 261

[823] Kent Dep. Tr. at 262-263.

[824] Kent Dep. Tr. at 264.

[825] Kent Dep. Tr. at 264-265.

[826] Kurt Volker Document Production, Bates KV00000020 (Oct. 2, 2019).

[827] Kurt Volker Document Production, Bates KV00000043 (Oct. 2, 2019).

[828] Kurt Volker Document Production, Bates KV00000043 (Oct. 2, 2019).

[829] Kurt Volker Document Production, Bates KV00000043 (Oct. 2, 2019).

[830] Volker Transcribed Interview Opening Statement at 8.

[831] Volker Transcribed Interview Tr. at 44.

[832] Morrison-Volker Hearing Tr. at 21.

[833] Volker Transcribed Interview Tr. at 259-260.

[834] Volker Transcribed Interview Tr. at 260.

[835] Morrison-Volker Hearing Tr. at 128.

[836] Kurt Volker Document Production, Bates KV00000043 (Oct. 2, 2019).

[837] Volker Transcribed Interview Tr. at 199-200.

[838] Hill-Holmes Hearing Tr. at 31-32, 68; Sondland Hearing Tr. at 55-57.

[839] Cooper Dep. Tr. at 71.

[840] Cooper Dep. Tr. at 62, 66.

[841] Cooper Dep. Tr. at 62.

[842] Morrison-Volker Hearing Tr. at 90-91.

[843] House Permanent Select Committee on Intelligence, Written Statement of Ambassador Gordon Sondland, at 23, *Impeachment,* 116th Cong. (Nov. 20, 2019).

[844] House Permanent Select Committee on Intelligence, Written Statement of Ambassador Gordon Sondland, at 23, *Impeachment,* 116th Cong. (Nov. 20, 2019).

[845] Sondland Hearing Tr. at 104.

[846] House Permanent Select Committee on Intelligence, Written Statement of Ambassador Gordon Sondland, at 18, *Impeachment,* 116th Cong. (Nov. 20, 2019).

[847] Sondland Hearing Tr. at 44.

[848] Sondland Hearing Tr. at 75.

[849] Sondland Hearing Tr. at 76.

[850] House Permanent Select Committee on Intelligence, Written Statement of Ambassador Gordon Sondland, at 23, *Impeachment,* 116th Cong. (Nov. 20, 2019).

[851] Hill-Holmes Hearing Tr. at 30.

[852] Hill-Holmes Hearing Tr. at 30.

[853] Sondland Hearing Tr. at 28.

[854] Sondland Hearing Tr. at 106.

[855] Hill-Holmes Hearing Tr. at 31-32.

[856] Hill-Holmes Hearing Tr. at 31.

[857] Kent-Taylor Hearing Tr. at 40.

[858] Taylor Dep. Tr. at 230.

[859] Kent-Taylor Hearing Tr. at 40.

[860] Hill-Holmes Hearing Tr. at 8.

[861] Kurt Volker Document Production, Bates 20 (Aug. 29, 2019).

[862] Volker Transcribed Interview Tr. at 80-81.

A: By the time it hit Politico publicly, I believe it was the end of August. And I got a text message from, it was either the Foreign Minister or—I think it was the future Foreign Minister. And, you know, basically, you're just—you're—I have to verbalize this. You're just trying to explain that we are trying this. We have a complicated system. We have a lot of players in this. We are working this. Give us time to fix it.

Q: So anybody on the Ukrainian side of things ever express like grave concern that this would not get worked out?

A: Not that it wouldn't get worked out, no, they did not. They expressed concern that, since this has now come out publicly in this Politico article, it looks like that they're being, you know, singled out and penalized for some reason. That's the image that that would create in Ukraine.

[863] Taylor Dep. Tr. at 34.

[864] Taylor Dep. Tr. at 137-138.

[865] Taylor Dep. Tr. at 137-138.

[866] Kent-Taylor Hearing Tr. at 174.

[867] Kent-Taylor Hearing Tr. at 40.

[868] Kent-Taylor Hearing Tr. at 40.

[869] Hill-Holmes Hearing Tr. at 31-32.

[870] Hill-Holmes Hearing Tr. at 31-32.

[871] Hill-Holmes Hearing Tr. at 68.

[872] Holmes Dep. Tr. at 58.

[873] Kent-Taylor Hearing Tr. at 40.

[874] *Trump, in August Call with GOP Senator, Denied Official's Claim on Ukraine Aid*, Wall Street Journal (Oct. 4, 2019) (online at www.wsj.com/articles/trump-administration-used-potential-meeting-to-pressure-ukraine-on-biden-texts-indicate-11570205661).

[875] *Trump, in August Call With GOP Senator, Denied Official's Claim on Ukraine Aid*, Wall Street Journal (Oct. 4, 2019) (online at www.wsj.com/articles/trump-administration-used-potential-meeting-to-pressure-ukraine-on-biden-texts-indicate-11570205661).

[876] Letter from Senator Ron Johnson to Ranking Member Jim Jordan, House Committee on Oversight and Reform, and Ranking Member Devin Nunes, House Permanent Select Committee on Intelligence (Nov. 18, 2019) (online at www.ronjohnson.senate.gov/public/_cache/files/e0b73c19-9370-42e6-88b1-b2458eaeeecd/johnson-to-jordan-nunes.pdf).

[877] Letter from Senator Ron Johnson to Ranking Member Jim Jordan, House Committee on Oversight and Reform, and Ranking Member Devin Nunes, House Permanent Select Committee on Intelligence (Nov. 18, 2019) (online at www.ronjohnson.senate.gov/public/_cache/files/e0b73c19-9370-42e6-88b1-b2458eaeeecd/johnson-to-jordan-nunes.pdf).

[878] The White House, *Memorandum of Telephone Conversation* (July 25, 2019) (online at www.whitehouse.gov/wp-content/uploads/2019/09/Unclassified09.2019.pdf).

[879] Office of the Director of National Intelligence, *Background to "Assessing Russian Activities and Intentions in Recent US Elections": The Analytic Process and Cyber Incident Attribution* (Jan. 6, 2017) (online at www.dni.gov/files/documents/ICA_2017_01.pdf).

[880] Letter from Senator Ron Johnson to Ranking Member Jim Jordan, Committee on Oversight and Reform, and Ranking Member Devin Nunes, Permanent Select Committee on Intelligence (Nov. 18, 2019) (online at www.ronjohnson.senate.gov/public/_cache/files/e0b73c19-9370-42e6-88b1-b2458eaeeecd/johnson-to-jordan-nunes.pdf).

[881] Sondland Hearing Tr. at 30.

[882] Volker Transcribed Interview Tr. at 251-252; Kent-Taylor Hearing Tr. at 41.

[883] Williams Dep. Tr. at 74-77.

[884] Williams Dep. Tr.at 76.

[885] Williams Dep. Tr. at 78-79.

[886] Sondland Hearing Tr. at 30.

[887] Sondland Hearing Tr. at 38. *See also* Sondland Hearing Tr. at 57:

A: I don't know exactly what I said to him. This was a briefing attended by many people, and I was invited at the very last minute. I wasn't scheduled to be there. But I think I spoke up at some point late in the meeting and said, it looks like everything is being held up until these statements get made, and that's my, you know, personal belief.

Q: And Vice President Pence just nodded his head?

A: Again, I don't recall any exchange or where he asked me any questions. I think he—it was sort of a duly noted response.

Q: Well, he didn't say, Gordon, what are you talking about?

A: No, he did not.

Q: He didn't say, what investigations?

A: He did not.

[888] *Pence Disputes that Sondland Raised Concerns to Him About Ukraine Aid-Investigations Link*, Wall Street Journal (Nov. 20, 2019) (online at www.wsj.com/livecoverage/gordon-sondland-testifies-impeachment/card/1574268547).

[889] Taylor Dep. Tr. at 190.

[890] Taylor Dep. Tr. at 35.

[891] Taylor Dep. Tr. at 190-191.

[892] Williams Dep. Tr. at 81.

[893] Williams Dep. Tr. at 82.

[894] Williams Dep. Tr. at 82-83.

[895] Williams Dep. Tr. at 83.

[896] Williams Dep. Tr. at 83.

[897] *How a CIA Analyst, Alarmed by Trump's Shadow Foreign Policy, Triggered an Impeachment Inquiry*, Washington Post (Nov. 16, 2019) (online at www.washingtonpost.com/national-security/how-a-cia-analyst-alarmed-by-trumps-shadow-foreign-policy-triggered-an-impeachment-inquiry/2019/11/15/042684a8-03c3-11ea-8292-c46ee8cb3dce_story.html).

[898] Hill-Holmes Hearing Tr. at 31.

[899] Sondland Hearing Tr. at 31.

[900] Morrison Dep. Tr. at 134.

[901] Morrison Dep. Tr. at 155.

[902] Morrison Dep. Tr. at 155.

[903] Morrison Dep. Tr. at 137.

[904] Morrison Dep. Tr. at 182.

[905] Morrison Dep. Tr. at 184.

[906] Morrison Dep. Tr. at 228.

[907] Morrison Dep. Tr. at 154.

[908] Kent-Taylor Hearing Tr. at 42.

[909] Kent-Taylor Hearing Tr. at 42.

[910] Kent-Taylor Hearing Tr. at 57.

[911] Kurt Volker Document Production, Bates 39 (Oct. 4, 2019).

[912] Kent-Taylor Hearing Tr. at 42.

[913] Taylor Dep. Tr. at 190.

[914] Taylor Dep. Tr. at 190.

[915] Taylor Dep. Tr. at 190.

[916] Kent-Taylor Hearing Tr. at 60.

[917] Sondland Hearing Tr. at 59.

[918] Sondland Hearing Tr. at 59-60.

[919] Morrison Dep. Tr. at 190-191.

[920] Morrison-Volker Hearing Tr. at 52.

[921] Morrison-Volker Hearing Tr. at 53-54; Morrison Dep. Tr. at 238.

[922] Kent-Taylor Hearing Tr. at 43-44.

[923] Kurt Volker Document Production, Bates 53 (Oct. 4, 2019).

[924] Kent-Taylor Hearing Tr. at 44.

[925] Kent-Taylor Hearing Tr. at 44.

[926] Kent-Taylor Hearing Tr. at 44.

[927] Sondland Hearing Tr. at 109-110.

[928] Sondland Hearing Tr. at 109-110.

[929] Sondland Hearing Tr. at 110-111.

[930] Kent-Taylor Hearing Tr. at 45.

[931] Kent-Taylor Hearing Tr. at 45, 63.

[932] Kent-Taylor Hearing Tr. at 45.

[933] Sondland Hearing Tr. at 110. Ambassador Volker also testified that Ambassador Sondland used the same analogy to him when discussing the release of the hold on security assistance. Morrison-Volker Hearing Tr. at 96-97.

[934] Kurt Volker Document Production, Bates 53 (Oct. 4, 2019).

[935] Taylor Dep. Tr. at 209.

[936] Kurt Volker Document Production, Bates 53 (Oct. 4, 2019).

[937] Kent-Taylor Hearing Tr. at 54.

[938] Kent-Taylor Hearing Tr. at 54.

[939] Kent-Taylor Hearing Tr. at 54.

[940] Kent-Taylor Hearing Tr. at 54.

[941] Kurt Volker Document Production, Bates 53 (Oct. 4, 2019).

[942] Sondland Dep. Tr. at 217.

[943] Sondland Hearing Tr. at 26 ("Was there a quid pro quo? As I testified previously with regard to the requested White House call and the White House meeting, the answer is yes.").

[944] Sondland Hearing Tr. at 41.

[945] Sondland Hearing Tr. at 112

[946] Sondland Hearing Tr. at 61-62.

[947] Taylor Dep. Tr. at 39.

[948] Taylor Dep. Tr. at 39.

[949] Maguire Hearing Tr. at 110; Whistleblower Compl. Appendix 2. Public reporting indicates that "[l]awyers from the White House counsel's office told Mr. Trump in late August about the complaint, explaining that they were trying to determine whether they were legally required to give it to Congress." *Trump Knew of Whistle-Blower Complaint When He Released Aid to Ukraine*, New York Times (Nov. 26, 2019) (online at www.nytimes.com/2019/11/26/us/politics/trump-whistle-blower-complaint-ukraine.html).

[950] Letter from Michael Atkinson, Inspector General of the Intelligence Community, to Chairman Adam B. Schiff and Ranking Member Devin Nunes, House Permanent Select Committee on Intelligence (Sept. 9, 2019) (online at https://intelligence.house.gov/uploadedfiles/20190909_-_ic_ig_letter_to_hpsci_on_whistleblower.pdf).

[951] Letter from Michael Atkinson, Inspector General of the Intelligence Community, to Chairman Adam B. Schiff and Ranking Member Devin Nunes, House Permanent Select Committee on Intelligence (Sept. 9, 2019) (online at https://intelligence.house.gov/uploadedfiles/20190909_-_ic_ig_letter_to_hpsci_on_whistleblower.pdf).

[952] Sondland Hearing Tr. at 118. *See also Witness Testimony and Records Raise Questions About Account of Trump's 'No Quid Pro Quo' Call*, Washington Post (Nov. 27, 2019) (online at www.washingtonpost.com/politics/witness-testimony-and-records-raise-questions-about-account-of-trumps-no-quid-pro-quo-call/2019/11/27/425545c2-0d49-11ea-8397-a955cd542d00_story.html).

[953] Sondland Hearing Tr. at 118.

[954] Sondland Hearing Tr. at 73.

[955] Statement of Ambassador Gordon Sondland at 1 (Nov. 4, 2019). This addendum did not address the July 26 telephone conversation that Sondland had with President Trump, which he only recalled following the testimony of David Holmes on November 15, 2019.

[956] Statement of Ambassador Gordon Sondland at 3 (Nov. 4, 2019).

[957] Kent-Taylor Hearing Tr. at 43-44; Morrison Dep. Tr. at 190-191.

[958] Morrison Dep. Tr. at 190-191; Kent-Taylor Hearing Tr. at 43-44.

[959] Sondland Hearing Tr. at 109.

[960] Sondland Hearing Tr. at 45, 109.

[961] Kurt Volker Document Production, Bates 20 (Oct. 4, 2019).

[962] Kurt Volker Document Production, Bates 20 (Oct. 4, 2019).

[963] Kurt Volker Document Production, Bates 53 (Oct. 4, 2019).

[964] Kurt Volker Document Production, Bates 53 (Oct. 4, 2019).

[965] The White House, *Press Briefing by Acting Chief of Staff Mick Mulvaney* (Oct. 17, 2019) (online at www.whitehouse.gov/briefings-statements/press-briefing-acting-chief-staff-mick-mulvaney/).

[966] The White House, *Press Briefing by Acting Chief of Staff Mick Mulvaney* (Oct. 17, 2019) (online at www.whitehouse.gov/briefings-statements/press-briefing-acting-chief-staff-mick-mulvaney/).

[967] The White House, *Press Briefing by Acting Chief of Staff Mick Mulvaney* (Oct. 17, 2019) (online at www.whitehouse.gov/briefings-statements/press-briefing-acting-chief-staff-mick-mulvaney/). Ambassador Taylor's testimony contradicted Mr. Mulvaney's statement about the ubiquity of such quid pro quos in American foreign policy. Ambassador Taylor testified that in his decades of military and diplomatic service, he had never seen another example of foreign aid conditioned on the personal or political interests of the President. Kent-Taylor Hearing Tr. at 55. Rather, "We condition assistance on issues that will improve our foreign policy, serve our foreign policy, ensure that taxpayers' money is well-spent." Kent-Taylor Hearing Tr. at 150.

[968] There were early concerns raised in the House and Senate about the frozen aid, even before the news became public. On August 9, the Democratic leadership of the House and Senate Appropriations Committees wrote to OMB and the White House warning that the August 3 letter apportionment might constitute an illegal impoundment of funds. They urged the Trump Administration to adhere to the law and obligate the withheld funding. Letter from Vice Chairman Patrick Leahy, Senate Committee on Appropriations, and Chairwoman Nita M. Lowey, House Committee on Appropriations, to Acting Chief of Staff Mick Mulvaney, The White House, and Acting Director Russell Vought, Office of Management and Budget (Aug. 9, 2019) (online at https://appropriations.house.gov/sites/democrats.appropriations.house.gov/files/documents/SFOPS%20Apportionment%20Letter%20Lowey-Leahy%20Signed%202019.8.9.pdf). On August 19, the Democratic leadership of the House and Senate Budget Committees wrote to OMB and the White House urging the Administration to comply with appropriations law and the Impoundment Control Act. Letter from Chairman John Yarmuth, House Committee on the Budget, and Ranking Member Bernard Sanders, Senate Committee on the Budget, to Acting Chief of Staff Mick Mulvaney, The White House (Aug. 19, 2019) (online at https://budget.house.gov/sites/democrats.budget.house.gov/files/documents/OMB%20Letter_081919.pdf).

[969] Letter from Senators Jeanne Shaheen, Rob Portman, Richard Durbin, Ron Johnson, and Richard Blumenthal to Acting White House Chief of Staff Mick Mulvaney (Sept. 3, 2019) (online at www.shaheen.senate.gov/imo/media/doc/Ukraine%20Security%20Letter%209.3.2019.pdf).

[970] Letter from Senators Jeanne Shaheen, Rob Portman, Richard Durbin, Ron Johnson, and Richard Blumenthal to Acting White House Chief of Staff Mick Mulvaney (Sept. 3, 2019) (online at www.shaheen.senate.gov/imo/media/doc/Ukraine%20Security%20Letter%209.3.2019.pdf).

[971] Letter from Chairman Eliot L. Engel and Ranking Member Michael T. McCaul, House Foreign Affairs Committee to Mick Mulvaney, Director, and Russell Vought, Acting Director, Office of Management and Budget, The White House (Sept. 5, 2019) (online at https://foreignaffairs.house.gov/_cache/files/c/4/c49328c2-941b-4c41-8c00-8c1515f0972f/D1968A9C42455BB3AFC38F97D966857B.ele-mccaul-letter-to-mulvaney-vought-on-ukraine-assistance.pdf).

[972] *Trump Tries to Force Ukraine to Meddle in the 2020 Election*, Washington Post (Sept. 5, 2019) (online at www.washingtonpost.com/opinions/global-opinions/is-trump-strong-arming-ukraines-new-president-for-political-gain/2019/09/05/4eb239b0-cffa-11e9-8c1c-7c8ee785b855_story.html).

[973] Taylor Dep. Tr. at 37-38.

[974] Taylor Dep. Tr. at 38.

[975] *See* Letter from Senator Christopher Murphy, to Chairman Adam B. Schiff, House Permanent Select Committee on Intelligence, and Acting Chairwoman Carolyn Maloney, House Committee on Oversight and Reform (Nov. 19, 2019) (online at www.murphy.senate.gov/download/111919-sen-murphy-letter-to-house-impeachment-investigators-on-ukraine) ("Senator Johnson and I assured Zelensky that Congress wanted to continue this funding, and would press Trump to release it immediately."); Letter from Senator Ron Johnson, to Ranking Member Jim Jordan, Committee on Oversight and Reform, and Ranking Member Devin Nunes, Permanent Select Committee on Intelligence (Nov. 18, 2019) (online at www.ronjohnson.senate.gov/public/_cache/files/e0b73c19-9370-42e6-88b1-b2458eaeeecd/johnson-to-jordan-nunes.pdf) ("I explained that I had tried to persuade the president to authorize me to announce the hold was released but that I was unsuccessful.").

[976] House Permanent Select Committee on Intelligence, *Three House Committees Launch Probe Into Trump and Giuliani Pressure Campaign* (Sept. 9, 2019) (online at https://intelligence.house.gov/news/documentsingle.aspx?DocumentID=685).

[977] Letter from Chairman Eliot L. Engel, House Committee on Foreign Affairs, Chairman Adam B. Schiff, House Permanent Select Committee on Intelligence, and Chairman Elijah E. Cummings, House Committee on Oversight and Reform, to Pat Cipollone, Counsel to the President, The White House (Sept. 9, 2019) (online at https://intelligence.house.gov/uploadedfiles/ele_schiff_cummings_letter_to_cipollone_on_ukraine.pdf).

[978] Letter from Chairman Eliot L. Engel, House Committee on Foreign Affairs, Chairman Adam B. Schiff, House Permanent Select Committee on Intelligence, and Chairman Elijah E. Cummings, House Committee on Oversight and Reform, to Pat Cipollone, Counsel to the President, The White House (Sept. 9, 2019) (online at https://intelligence.house.gov/uploadedfiles/ele_schiff_cummings_letter_to_cipollone_on_ukraine.pdf).

[979] Letter from Chairman Eliot L. Engel, House Committee on Foreign Affairs, Chairman Adam B. Schiff, House Permanent Select Committee on Intelligence, and Chairman Elijah E. Cummings, House Committee on Oversight and Reform, to Pat Cipollone, Counsel to the President, The White House (Sept. 9, 2019) (online at https://intelligence.house.gov/uploadedfiles/ele_schiff_cummings_letter_to_cipollone_on_ukraine.pdf).

[980] Letter from Chairman Eliot L. Engel, House Committee on Foreign Affairs, Chairman Adam B. Schiff, House Permanent Select Committee on Intelligence, and Chairman Elijah E. Cummings, House Committee on Oversight and Reform, to Michael R. Pompeo, Secretary of State (Sept. 9, 2019) (online at https://intelligence.house.gov/uploadedfiles/ele_schiff_cummings_letter_to_sec_pompeo_on_ukraine.pdf).

[981] Morrison Dep. Tr. at 245.

[982] Morrison Dep. Tr. at 245.

[983] Vindman Dep. Tr. at 303.

[984] Vindman Dep. Tr. at 304.

[985] Letter from Michael Atkinson, Inspector General of the Intelligence Community, to Chairman Adam B. Schiff and Ranking Member Devin Nunes, House Permanent Select Committee on Intelligence (Sept. 9, 2019) (online at https://intelligence.house.gov/uploadedfiles/20190909_-_ic_ig_letter_to_hpsci_on_whistleblower.pdf).

[986] Letter from Michael Atkinson, Inspector General of the Intelligence Community, to Chairman Adam B. Schiff and Ranking Member Devin Nunes, House Permanent Select Committee on Intelligence (Sept. 9, 2019) (online at https://intelligence.house.gov/uploadedfiles/20190909_-_ic_ig_letter_to_hpsci_on_whistleblower.pdf); *see also* 50 U.S.C. § 3033(k)(5) (setting forth procedures for reporting of complaints or information with respect to an "urgent concern" to Congressional intelligence committees).

[987] Maguire Hearing Tr. at 14 ("As a result, we consulted with the White House Counsel's Office, and we were advised that much of the information in the complaint was, in fact, subject to executive privilege, a privilege that I do not have the authority to waive. Because of that, we were unable to immediately share the details of the complaint with this committee but continued to consult with the White House counsels in an effort to do so.").

[988] Maguire Hearing Tr. at 15-16 ("Because the allegation on its face did not appear to fall in the statutory framework, my office consulted with the United States Department of Justice Office of Legal Counsel. … After reviewing the complaint and the Inspector General's transmission letter, the Office of Legal Counsel determined that the complaint's allegations do not meet the statutory definition concerning legal urgent concern, and found that I was not legally required to transmit the material to our oversight committee under the Whistleblower Protection Act.").

[989] Maguire Hearing Tr. at 22-23. *See also CIA's Top Lawyer Made 'Criminal Referral' on Complaint about Trump Ukraine Call*, NBC News (Oct. 4, 2019) (online at www.nbcnews.com/politics/trump-impeachment-inquiry/cia-s-top-lawyer-made-criminal-referral-whistleblower-s-complaint-n1062481) (reporting that the CIA's General Counsel, Courtney Simmons Elwood, informed NSC chief lawyer John Eisenberg about an anonymous whistleblower complaint on August 14, 2019).

[990] Maguire Hearing Tr. at 14, 21-22. On September 26, Acting DNI Maguire testified that he and the ODNI General Counsel first consulted with the White House counsel's office before discussing the whistleblower complaint with the Department of Justice's Office of Legal Counsel:

The Chairman.	I'm just trying to understand the chronology. You first went to the Office of Legal Counsel, and then you went to the White House Counsel?
Acting Director Maguire.	No, no, no, sir. No, sir. No. We went to the White House first to determine—to ask the question—
The Chairman.	That's all I want to know is the chronology. So you went to the White House first. So you went to the subject of the complaint for advice first about whether you should provide the complaint to Congress?
Acting Director Maguire.	There were issues within this, a couple of things: One, it did appear that it has executive privilege. If it does have executive privilege, it is the White House that determines that. I cannot determine that, as the Director of National Intelligence.

Id. at 21-22.

[991] *Trump Knew of Whistle-Blower Complaint When He Released Aid to Ukraine,* New York Times (Nov. 26, 2019) (online at www.nytimes.com/2019/11/26/us/politics/trump-whistle-blower-complaint-ukraine.html).

[992] *Trump Knew of Whistle-Blower Complaint When He Released Aid to Ukraine,* New York Times (Nov. 26, 2019) (online at www.nytimes.com/2019/11/26/us/politics/trump-whistle-blower-complaint-ukraine.html). The Administration repeatedly referenced privilege concerns in connection with the whistleblower complaint. *See, e.g.,* Letter from Jason Klitenic, General Counsel, Office of the Director of National Intelligence, to Chairman Adam B. Schiff, House Permanent Select Committee on Intelligence (Sept. 13, 2019) (noting that "the complaint involves confidential and *potentially privileged* communications by persons outside the Intelligence Community") (emphasis added); Letter from Jason Klitenic, General Counsel, Office of the Director of National Intelligence, to Chairman Adam B. Schiff, House Permanent Select Committee on Intelligence (Sept. 17, 2019) (characterizing subpoena to the Acting DNI for documents as demanding "sensitive and *potentially privileged*" materials and whistleblower complaint as involving "*potentially privileged* matters relating to the interests of other stakeholders within the Executive Branch") (emphasis added).

However, the White House never formally invoked executive privilege as to the whistleblower complaint. *See* Maguire Hearing Tr. at 20 ("Chairman Schiff: So they never asserted executive privilege, is that the answer?

Acting Director Maguire: Mr. Chairman, if they did, we would not have released the letters yesterday and all the information that has been forthcoming.").

[993] Letter from Chairman Adam B. Schiff, House Permanent Select Committee on Intelligence, to Joseph Maguire, Acting Director of National Intelligence (Sept. 10, 2019) (online at https://intelligence.house.gov/uploadedfiles/20190910_-_chm_schiff_letter_to_acting_dni_maguire.pdf).

[994] Letter from Chairman Adam B. Schiff, House Permanent Select Committee on Intelligence, to Joseph Maguire, Acting Director of National Intelligence (Sept. 10, 2019) (online at https://intelligence.house.gov/uploadedfiles/20190910_-_chm_schiff_letter_to_acting_dni_maguire.pdf).

[995] *See* Letter from Jason Klitenic, General Counsel, Office of the Director of National Intelligence, to Chairman Adam B. Schiff, House Permanent Select Committee on Intelligence (Sept. 13, 2019).

[996] Letter from Chairman Adam B. Schiff, House Permanent Select Committee on Intelligence, to Joseph Maguire, Acting Director of National Intelligence (Sept. 13, 2019) (online at https://intelligence.house.gov/uploadedfiles/20190913_-_chm_schiff_letter_to_acting_dni_re_whistleblower_-_subpoena.pdf).

[997] The White House, *Memorandum of Telephone Conversation* (July 25, 2019) (online at www.whitehouse.gov/wp-content/uploads/2019/09/Unclassified09.2019.pdf).

[998] Vindman Dep. Tr. at 305-06; Morrison Dep. Tr. at 242.

[999] Morrison Dep. Tr. at 242.

[1000] *See, e.g.*, Morrison Dep. Tr. at 244; Vindman Dep. Tr. at 306; Williams Dep. Tr. at 147.

[1001] Cooper Dep. Tr. at 68-69.

[1002] Williams Dep. Tr. at 147. Ms. Williams did testify that President Trump's pressure on President Zelensky to open investigations into the Bidens on the July 25 call "shed some light on possible other motivations behind a security assistance hold." Williams Dep. Tr. at 149.

[1003] Sandy Dep. Tr. at 42, 139-140. According to a press report, after Congress began investigating President Trump's scheme, the White House Counsel's Office reportedly opened an internal investigation relating to the July 25 call. As part of that internal investigation, White House lawyers gathered and reviewed "hundreds of documents" that "reveal extensive efforts to generate an after-the-fact justification" for the hold on military assistance for Ukraine ordered by President Trump. These documents reportedly include "early August email exchanges between acting chief of staff Mick Mulvaney and White House budget officials seeking to provide an explanation for withholding the funds after the president had already ordered a hold in mid-July on the nearly $400 million in security assistance." *White House Review Turns Up Emails Showing Extensive Effort to Justify Trump's Decision to Block Ukraine Military Aid*, Washington Post (Nov. 24, 2019) (online at www.washingtonpost.com/politics/white-house-review-turns-up-emails-showing-extensive-effort-to-justify-trumps-decision-to-block-ukraine-military-aid/2019/11/24/2121cf98-0d57-11ea-bd9d-c628fd48b3a0_story.html). The White House has withheld these documents from the Committee, so the Committee cannot verify the accuracy of the reporting as of the publication of this report.

[1004] Sandy Dep. Tr. at 49.

[1005] Sandy Dep. Tr. at 42, 44.

[1006] Sandy Dep. Tr. at 180.

[1007] Vindman Dep. Tr. at 306.

[1008] Cooper Dep. Tr. at 83.

[1009] Cooper Dep. Tr. at 47-48, 58, 112-114; Sandy Dep. Tr. at 34-35, 85-86, 95, 128, 139-131, 133; Morrison Dep. Tr. at 163; Kent Dep. Tr. at 308-309; Reeker Dep. Tr. at 133. News reports indicate that a confidential White House review of President Trump's hold on military assistance to Ukraine has identified hundreds of documents revealing "extensive efforts to generate an after-the-fact justification for the decision and a debate over whether the delay was legal." *White House Review Turns Up Emails Showing Extensive Effort to Justify Trump's Decision to Block Ukraine Military Aid*, Washington Post (Nov. 24, 2019) (online at www.washingtonpost.com/politics/white-house-review-turns-up-emails-showing-extensive-effort-to-justify-trumps-decision-to-block-ukraine-military-aid/2019/11/24/2121cf98-0d57-11ea-bd9d-c628fd48b3a0_story.html). According to "two people briefed on an internal White House review," in August, Acting Chief of Staff Mulvaney "asked … whether there was a legal justification for withholding hundreds of millions of dollars in military aid to Ukraine." *Mulvaney Asked About Legal Justification for Withholding Ukraine Aid*, New York Times (Nov. 24, 2019) (online at www.nytimes.com/2019/11/24/us/politics/mulvaney-ukraine-aid.html). Reports indicate that, "[e]mails show [OMB Director] Vought and OMB staffers arguing that withholding aid was legal, while officials at the National Security Council and State Department protested. OMB lawyers said that it was legal to withhold the aid, as long as they deemed it a 'temporary' hold." *White House Review Turns Up Emails Showing Extensive Effort to Justify Trump's Decision to Block Ukraine Military Aid*, Washington Post (Nov. 24, 2019) (online at www.washingtonpost.com/politics/white-house-review-turns-up-emails-showing-extensive-effort-to-justify-trumps-decision-to-block-ukraine-military-aid/2019/11/24/2121cf98-0d57-11ea-bd9d-c628fd48b3a0_story.html). The White House and State Department's obstruction of Congress has prevented the Committee from obtaining any documents on this matter and, therefore, the Committee cannot verify the accuracy of this reporting as of the publication of this report.

[1010] Cooper Dep. Tr. at 80.

[1011] Sandy Dep. Tr. at 146-147.

[1012] *See* Department of Defense, *DOD Budget Materials (FY2011-FY2018)* (online at https://comptroller.defense.gov/Budget-Materials/). In 1974, President Nixon impounded 15-20 percent of a number of specific programs, which prompted the passage of the Impoundment Control Act of 1974. Congressional Research Service, *The Congressional Budget Act of 1974 (P.L. 93-344) Legislative History and Analysis* (Feb. 26, 1975).

[1013] Department of Defense and Labor, Health and Human Services, and Education Appropriations Act, 2019 and Continuing Appropriations Act, 2019, Pub. L. No. 115-245, § 9013 (2018); Sandy Dep. Tr. at 147.

[1014] Continuing Appropriations Act 2020, and Health Extenders Act of 2019, Pub. L. No. 116-59, § 124 (2019).

[1015] Cooper Dep. Tr. at 98.

[1016] *$35 Million in Pentagon Aid Hasn't Reached Ukraine Despite White House Assurances*, L.A. Times (Nov. 19, 2019) (online at www.latimes.com/politics/story/2019-11-19/documents-show-nearly-40-million-in-ukraine-aid-delayed-despite-white-house-assurances).

[1017] *Zelensky Planned to Announce Trump's 'Quo' on My Show. Here's What Happened*, Washington Post (Nov. 14, 2019) (online at www.washingtonpost.com/opinions/zelensky-was-planning-to-announce-trumps-quid-pro-quo-on-my-show-heres-what-happened/2019/11/14/47938f32-072a-11ea-8292-c46ee8cb3dce_story.html).

[1018] *Zelensky Planned to Announce Trump's 'Quo' on My Show. Here's What Happened*, Washington Post (Nov. 4, 2019) (online at www.washingtonpost.com/opinions/zelensky-was-planning-to-announce-trumps-quid-pro-quo-on-my-show-heres-what-happened/2019/11/14/47938f32-072a-11ea-8292-c46ee8cb3dce_story.html).

[1019] Taylor Dep. Tr. at 40.

[1020] Kent-Taylor Hearing Tr. at 106.

[1021] Kent-Taylor Hearing Tr. at 106.

[1022] Hill-Holmes Hearing Tr. at 33.

[1023] Hill-Holmes Hearing Tr. at 33.

[1024] Taylor Dep. Tr. at 41.

[1025] Taylor Dep. Tr. at 217-18.

[1026] Taylor Dep. Tr. at 217-18.

[1027] Holmes Dep. Tr. at 30.

[1028] *Zelensky Planned to Announce Trump's 'Quo' on My Show. Here's What Happened*, Washington Post (Nov. 4, 2019) (online at www.washingtonpost.com/opinions/zelensky-was-planning-to-announce-trumps-quid-pro-quo-on-my-show-heres-what-happened/2019/11/14/47938f32-072a-11ea-8292-c46ee8cb3dce_story.html).

[1029] Hill-Holmes Hearing Tr. at 33; *see also Zelensky Planned to Announce Trump's 'Quo' on My Show. Here's What Happened*, Washington Post (Nov. 4, 2019) (online at www.washingtonpost.com/opinions/zelensky-was-planning-to-announce-trumps-quid-pro-quo-on-my-show-heres-what-happened/2019/11/14/47938f32-072a-11ea-8292-c46ee8cb3dce_story.html).

[1030] Kent. Dep. Tr. at 333.

[1031] Kent Dep. Tr. at 329-31.

[1032] Kent Dep. Tr. at 330.

[1033] *Zelensky Planned to Announce Trump's 'Quo' on My Show. Here's What Happened*, Washington Post (Nov. 4, 2019) (online at www.washingtonpost.com/opinions/zelensky-was-planning-to-announce-trumps-quid-pro-quo-on-my-show-heres-what-happened/2019/11/14/47938f32-072a-11ea-8292-c46ee8cb3dce_story.html).

[1034] Hill-Holmes Hearing Tr. at 46-47.

[1035] Williams Dep. Tr. at 156.

[1036] Williams Dep. Tr. at 156.

[1037] *Pence Says He's Working to Release Transcripts of His Calls with Ukraine Leader*, Politico (Oct. 9, 2019) (online at www.politico.com/news/2019/10/09/pence-ukraine-zelensky-biden-043684).

[1038] *Pence: I Don't Object To Releasing My Call Transcripts With Zelensky*, Fox Business (Nov. 7, 2019) (online at www.realclearpolitics.com/video/2019/11/07/pence_i_dont_object_to_releasing_my_call_transcripts_with_zelensky.html).

[1039] *Rudy Giuliani's Remarkable Ukraine Interview, Annotated*, Washington Post (Sept. 20, 2019) (online at www.washingtonpost.com/politics/2019/09/20/rudy-giulianis-remarkable-ukraine-interview-annotated/).

[1040] The White House, *Remarks by President Trump and President Duda of Poland Before Bilateral Meeting* (Sept. 23, 2019) (online at www.whitehouse.gov/briefings-statements/remarks-president-trump-president-duda-poland-bilateral-meeting/).

[1041] The White House, *Remarks by President Trump Upon Arriving at the U.N. General Assembly* (Sept. 24, 2019) (online at www.whitehouse.gov/briefings-statements/remarks-president-trump-upon-arriving-u-n-general-assembly-new-york-ny/).

[1042] The White House, *Remarks by President Trump and President Zelensky of Ukraine Before Bilateral Meeting* (Sept 25, 2019) (online at www.whitehouse.gov/briefings-statements/remarks-president-trump-president-zelensky-ukraine-bilateral-meeting-new-york-ny/).

[1043] The White House, *Remarks by President Trump at the Swearing-in Ceremony of Secretary of Labor Eugene Scalia* (Sept 30, 2019) (online at www.whitehouse.gov/briefings-statements/remarks-president-trump-swearing-ceremony-secretary-labor-eugene-scalia/).

[1044] The White House, *Remarks by President Trump and President Niinistö of the Republic of Finland Before Bilateral Meeting* (Oct. 2, 2019) (www.whitehouse.gov/briefings-statements/remarks-president-trump-president-niinisto-republic-finland-bilateral-meeting/).

[1045] The White House, *Remarks by President Trump Before Marine One Departure* (Oct. 3, 2019) (online at www.whitehouse.gov/briefings-statements/remarks-president-trump-marine-one-departure-67/).

[1046] The White House, *Remarks by President Trump Before Marine One Departure* (Oct. 4, 2019) (online at www.whitehouse.gov/briefings-statements/remarks-president-trump-marine-one-departure-68/).

[1047] The White House, *Remarks by President Trump Before Marine One Departure* (Oct. 4, 2019) (online at www.whitehouse.gov/briefings-statements/remarks-president-trump-marine-one-departure-68).

[1048] The White House, *Remarks by President Trump Before Marine One Departure* (Oct. 3, 2019) (online at www.whitehouse.gov/briefings-statements/remarks-president-trump-marine-one-departure-67/). These recent statements by President inviting foreign assistance for his personal political interests are consistent with his statements to George Stephanopoulos of ABC News on June 12, when President Trump indicated a desire to receive dirt on a political opponent provided by a foreign country. *ABC News' Oval Office interview with President Trump*, ABC News (Jun. 13, 2019) (online at https://abcnews.go.com/Politics/abc-news-oval-office-interview-president-donald-trump/story?id=63688943).

[1049] Morrison-Volker Hearing Tr. at 46-47, 91-92.

[1050] Vindman Dep. Tr. at 158-19; Holmes Dep. Tr. at 100; Kent-Taylor Hearing Tr. at 43.

[1051] Kent-Taylor Hearing Tr. at 24.

[1052] Hill-Holmes Hearing Tr. at 46.

[1053] Kent-Taylor Hearing Tr. at 165.

[1054] Kent-Taylor Hearing Tr. at 165.

[1055] Kent-Taylor Hearing Tr. at 24.

[1056] Kent-Taylor Hearing Tr. at 55-56.

[1057] Kent-Taylor Hearing Tr. at 164.

[1058] Kent Dep. Tr. at 329; Morrison-Volker Hearing Tr. at 138-139.

[1059] Morrison-Volker Hearing Tr. at 139.

[1060] Morrison-Volker Hearing Tr. at 139.

SECTION II.

THE PRESIDENT'S OBSTRUCTION OF THE HOUSE OF REPRESENTATIVES' IMPEACHMENT INQUIRY

1. Constitutional Authority for Congressional Oversight and Impeachment

> *Article I of the Constitution vests in the House of Representatives the "sole Power of Impeachment." Congress is authorized to conduct oversight and investigations in support of its Article I powers. The Supreme Court—and previous Presidents—have acknowledged these authorities.*

Overview

The House's Constitutional and legal authority to conduct an impeachment inquiry is clear, as is the duty of the President to cooperate with the House's exercise of this authority. The Constitution vests in the House of Representatives the "sole Power of Impeachment" as well as robust oversight powers. As the Founders intended, the courts have agreed, and prior Presidents have acknowledged, the House's sweeping powers to investigate are at their peak during an impeachment inquiry of a President. Congress has also enacted statutes to support its power to investigate and oversee the Executive Branch.

Unlike President Donald J. Trump, past Presidents who were the subject of impeachment inquiries acknowledged Congress' authority to investigate and—to varying degrees—complied with information requests and subpoenas. Even so, the House has previously determined that partial noncooperation can serve as a ground for an article of impeachment against a President as it would upend the separation of powers to allow the President to dictate the scope of an impeachment inquiry. When President Richard Nixon withheld tape recordings and produced heavily edited and inaccurate records, the House Judiciary Committee approved an article of impeachment for obstruction.

Constitutional Power of Congress to Investigate—and to Impeach

Article I of the U.S. Constitution gives the House of Representatives the "sole Power of Impeachment."[1] The Framers intended the impeachment power to be an essential check on a President who might engage in corruption or abuse power. For example, during the Constitutional Convention, George Mason stated:

> No point is of more importance than that the right of impeachment should be continued. Shall any man be above Justice? Above all shall that man be above it, who can commit the most extensive injustice? ... Shall the man who has practised corruption & by that means procured his appointment in the first instance, be suffered to escape punishment, by repeating his guilt?[2]

Congress is empowered to conduct oversight and investigations to carry out its authorities under Article I.[3] In light of the core nature of the impeachment power to the nation's Constitutional system of checks and balances, Congress' investigative authority is at its zenith during an impeachment inquiry.[4]

As the House Judiciary Committee explained during the impeachment of President Nixon:

> Whatever the limits of legislative power in other contexts—and whatever need may otherwise exist for preserving the confidentiality of Presidential conversations—in the context of an impeachment proceeding the balance was struck in favor of the power of inquiry when the impeachment provision was written into the Constitution.[5]

This conclusion echoed an early observation on the floor of the House of Representatives that the "House possessed the power of impeachment solely, and that this authority certainly implied the right to inspect every paper and transaction in any department, otherwise the power of impeachment could never be exercised with any effect."[6]

The House's "sole Power of Impeachment" is the mechanism provided by the Constitution to hold sitting Presidents accountable for serious misconduct. The Department of Justice has highlighted the importance of the impeachment power in justifying the Department's view that a sitting President cannot be indicted or face criminal prosecution while in office.[7] The Department's position that the President is immune from prosecution has not been endorsed by Congress or the courts, but as long as the Department continues to refuse to prosecute a sitting President, Congress has a heightened responsibility to exercise its impeachment power, if necessary, to ensure that no President is "above the law."[8]

The Supreme Court has recognized that Congress has broad oversight authority under the Constitution to inquire about a wide array of topics, even outside the context of impeachment:

> The power of inquiry has been employed by Congress throughout our history, over the whole range of the national interests concerning which Congress might legislate or decide upon due investigation not to legislate; it has similarly been utilized in determining what to appropriate from the national purse, or whether to appropriate. The scope of the power of inquiry, in short, is as penetrating and farreaching as the potential power to enact and appropriate under the Constitution.[9]

The Supreme Court has made clear that Congress' authority to investigate includes the authority to compel the production of information by issuing subpoenas,[10] a power the House has delegated to its committees pursuant to its Constitutional authority to "determine the Rules of its Proceedings."[11]

The Supreme Court has affirmed that compliance with Congressional subpoenas is mandatory:

> It is unquestionably the duty of all citizens to cooperate with the Congress in its efforts to obtain the facts needed for intelligent legislative action. It is their unremitting obligation to respond to subpoenas, to respect the dignity of the Congress and its committees and to testify fully with respect to matters within the province of proper investigation.[12]

Federal courts have held that the "legal duty" to respond to Congressional subpoenas extends to the President's "senior-level aides" and that the failure to comply violates the separation of powers principles in the Constitution.[13] As one court recently explained:

> [W]hen a committee of Congress seeks testimony and records by issuing a valid subpoena in the context of a duly authorized investigation, it has the Constitution's blessing, and ultimately, it is acting not in its own interest, but for the benefit of the People of the United States. If there is fraud or abuse or waste or corruption in the federal government, it is the constitutional duty of Congress to find the facts and, as necessary, take corrective action. Conducting investigations is the means that Congress uses to carry out that constitutional obligation. Thus, blatant defiance of Congress' centuries-old power to compel the performance of witnesses is not an abstract injury, nor is it a mere banal insult to our democracy. It is an affront to the mechanism for curbing abuses of power that the Framers carefully crafted for our protection, and, thereby, recalcitrant witnesses actually undermine the broader interests of the People of the United States.[14]

Laws Passed by Congress

Congress has enacted statutes to support its power to investigate and oversee the Executive Branch. These laws impose criminal and other penalties on those who fail to comply with inquiries from Congress or block others from doing so, and they reflect the broader Constitutional requirement to cooperate with Congressional investigations. For example:

- *Obstructing Congress:* Obstructing a Congressional investigation is a crime punishable by up to five years in prison. An individual is guilty of obstruction if he or she "corruptly, or by threats or force, or by any threatening letter or communication influences, obstructs, or impedes or endeavors to influence, obstruct, or impede" the "due and proper exercise of the power of inquiry under which any inquiry or investigation is being had by either House, or any committee of either House."[15]

- *Concealing Material Facts:* Concealing information from Congress is also punishable by up to five years in prison. This prohibition applies to anyone who "falsifies, conceals, or covers up" a "material fact" in connection with "any investigation or review, conducted pursuant to the authority of any committee, subcommittee, commission or office of the Congress, consistent with applicable rules of the House or Senate."[16]

- *Intimidating and Harassing Witnesses:* Intimidating witnesses in a Congressional investigation is a crime punishable by up to twenty years in prison. This statute applies to anyone who "knowingly uses intimidation, threatens, or corruptly persuades another person, or attempts to do so, or engages in misleading conduct toward another person," with the intent to "influence, delay, or prevent the testimony of any person in an official proceeding."[17] An individual who "intentionally harasses another person and thereby hinders, delays, prevents, or dissuades" a person from "attending or testifying in an official proceeding" is also guilty of a crime punishable by fines and up to three years in prison.[18]

- *Retaliating Against Employees Who Provide Information to Congress:* Employees who speak to Congress have the right not to have adverse personnel actions taken against them. Retaliatory actions taken against Executive Branch employees who cooperate with Congress may constitute violations of this law.[19] Any Executive Branch official who "prohibits or prevents" or "attempts or threatens to prohibit or prevent" any officer or employee of the federal government from speaking with Congress could have his or her salary withheld.[20]

Precedent of Previous Impeachments and Other Investigations

Unlike President Trump, past Presidents who were the subject of impeachment inquiries—including Presidents Andrew Johnson, Richard Nixon, and Bill Clinton—acknowledged Congress' authority to investigate and, to varying degrees, complied with information requests and subpoenas.

For example, President Johnson complied with the House's requests for information. According to a report subsequently adopted by the House Judiciary Committee, "There is no evidence that Johnson ever asserted any privilege to prevent disclosure of presidential conversations to the Committee, or failed to comply with any of the Committee's requests."[21]

Similarly, President Clinton provided written responses to 81 interrogatories from the House Judiciary Committee during the House's impeachment inquiry.[22]

Even President Nixon agreed to let his staff testify voluntarily in the Senate Watergate investigation, stating: "All members of the White House Staff will appear voluntarily when requested by the committee. They will testify under oath, and they will answer fully all proper questions."[23] As a result, numerous senior White House officials testified, including White House Counsel John Dean III, White House Chief of Staff H.R. Haldeman, Deputy Assistant to the President Alexander Butterfield, and Chief Advisor to the President for Domestic Affairs John D. Ehrlichman.[24] President Nixon also produced numerous documents and records in response to the House's subpoenas as part of its impeachment inquiry, including more than 30 transcripts of White House recordings and notes from meetings with the President.[25]

However, President Nixon's production of documents was incomplete. For example, he did not produce tape recordings, and transcripts he produced were heavily edited or inaccurate. President Nixon claimed that his noncompliance with House subpoenas was necessary to protect the confidentiality of Presidential conversations, but the House Judiciary Committee rejected these arguments and approved an article of impeachment for obstruction of the House's impeachment inquiry.[26]

In a letter to President Nixon, Judiciary Committee Chairman Peter Rodino explained that it would upend the separation of powers to allow the President to dictate the scope of an impeachment inquiry:

Under the Constitution it is not within the power of the President to conduct an inquiry into his own impeachment, to determine which evidence, and what version or portion of that evidence, is relevant and necessary to such an inquiry. These are matters which, under the Constitution, the House has the sole power to determine.[27]

Consistent with that long-settled understanding, other Presidents have recognized that they must comply with information requests issued in a House impeachment inquiry. In 1846, for example, President James Polk stated in a message to the House:

It may be alleged that the power of impeachment belongs to the House of Representatives, and that with a view to the exercise of this power, that House has the right to investigate the conduct of all public officers under the government. This is cheerfully admitted. In such a case, the safety of the Republic would be the supreme law; and the power of the House in the pursuit of this object would penetrate into the most secret recesses of the executive departments. It could command the attendance of any and every agent of the government, and compel them to produce all papers, public or private, official or unofficial, and to testify on oath to all facts within their knowledge.[28]

Past Presidents have also produced documents and permitted senior officials to testify in connection with other Congressional investigations, including inquiries into Presidential actions.

For example, in the Iran-Contra inquiry, President Ronald Reagan's former National Security Advisor, Oliver North, and the former Assistant to the President for National Security Affairs, John Poindexter, testified before Congress.[29] President Reagan also produced "relevant excerpts of his personal diaries to Congress."[30]

During the Clinton Administration, Congress obtained testimony from top advisors to President Bill Clinton, including Chief of Staff Mack McLarty, Chief of Staff Erskine Bowles, White House Counsel Bernard Nussbaum, and White House Counsel Jack Quinn.[31]

Similarly, in the Benghazi investigation, led by Chairman Trey Gowdy, President Barack Obama made many of his top aides available for transcribed interviews, including National Security Advisor Susan Rice and Deputy National Security Advisor for Strategic Communications Benjamin Rhodes.[32] The Obama Administration also produced more than 75,000 pages of documents in that investigation, including 1,450 pages of White House emails containing communications of senior officials on the National Security Council.[33]

2.   The President's Categorical Refusal to Comply

> *President Trump categorically directed the White House, federal departments and agencies,*
> *and federal officials not to cooperate with the House's inquiry and not to comply with duly*
> *authorized subpoenas for documents or testimony.*

Overview

Donald Trump is the first and only President in American history to openly and indiscriminately defy all aspects of the Constitutional impeachment process, ordering all federal agencies and officials categorically not to comply with voluntary requests or compulsory demands for documents or testimony.

On September 26, President Trump argued that Congress should not be "allowed" to impeach him under the Constitution and that there "should be a way of stopping it—maybe legally, through the courts." A common theme of his defiance has been his claims that Congress is acting in an unprecedented way and using unprecedented rules. However, the House has been following the same investigative rules that Republicans championed when they were in control.

On October 8, White House Counsel Pat Cipollone—acting on behalf of President Trump—sent a letter to House Speaker Nancy Pelosi and the three investigating Committees confirming that President Trump directed his entire Administration not to cooperate with the House's impeachment inquiry. Mr. Cipollone wrote: "President Trump cannot permit his Administration to participate in this partisan inquiry under these circumstances."

Mr. Cipollone's letter elicited immediate criticism from legal experts across the political spectrum. He advanced remarkably politicized arguments and legal theories unsupported by the Constitution, judicial precedent, and more than 200 years of history. If allowed to stand, the President's defiance, as justified by Mr. Cipollone, would represent an existential threat to the nation's Constitutional system of checks and balances, separation of powers, and rule of law.

The House's Impeachment Inquiry of President Trump

In January, the House of Representatives voted to adopt its rules for the 116th Congress. These rules authorized House committees to conduct investigations, hold hearings, issue subpoenas for documents and testimony, and depose witnesses.[34] Significantly, these authorities are similar to those adopted when Republicans controlled the House during previous Congresses.[35]

In April, Special Counsel Robert S. Mueller III, who was appointed by then-Deputy Attorney General Rod J. Rosenstein to investigate Russian interference in the 2016 U.S. Presidential election and potential obstruction of justice by President Trump, issued a two-volume report.[36] In connection with that report, the Committee on the Judiciary began an inquiry into "whether to approve articles of impeachment with respect to the President."[37] The Judiciary

Committee detailed its authority and intent to conduct this investigation in a series of reports, memoranda, and legal filings.[38]

On August 22, Rep. Jerrold Nadler, the Chairman of the Judiciary Committee, sent a letter requesting that the Permanent Select Committee on Intelligence, the Committee on Oversight and Reform, the Committee on Foreign Affairs, and the Committee on Financial Services provide "information, including documents and testimony, depositions, and/or interview transcripts" relevant to the "ongoing impeachment investigation relating to President Trump."[39]

In September, the Intelligence Committee, the Oversight Committee, and the Foreign Affairs Committee sent letters requesting documents and interviews from the White House and the Department of State regarding the actions of President Trump, the President's personal agent, Rudy Giuliani, and others to pressure Ukraine to launch investigations into former Vice President Joe Biden and a debunked conspiracy theory alleging Ukrainian interference in the 2016 election.[40]

On September 22, President Trump admitted to discussing former Vice President Biden and his son with the President of Ukraine during a telephone call on July 25.[41]

On September 24, Speaker Nancy Pelosi stated publicly that the House Committees were "moving forward" to "proceed with their investigations under that umbrella of impeachment inquiry." She explained that, for the past several months, the House had been "investigating in our Committees and litigating in the courts, so the House can gather 'all the relevant facts and consider whether to exercise its full Article I powers, including a constitutional power of the utmost gravity—approval of articles of impeachment.'"[42]

On September 25, the White House made public a Memorandum of Telephone Conversation of President Trump's call with President Zelensky on July 25. As discussed in detail in Section I, this call record documented how President Trump directly and explicitly asked President Zelensky to launch investigations of former Vice President Biden and the 2016 election.[43]

Following the Speaker's announcement and the release of the call record, the Intelligence Committee, the Oversight Committee, and the Foreign Affairs Committee continued their investigation, requesting documents and information, issuing subpoenas, and conducting interviews and depositions. The Committees made clear that this information would be "collected as part of the House's impeachment inquiry and shared among the Committees, as well as with the Committee on the Judiciary as appropriate."[44]

On October 31, the House voted to approve House Resolution 660, directing the Committees "to continue their ongoing investigations as part of the existing House of Representatives inquiry into whether sufficient grounds exist for the House of Representatives to exercise its Constitutional power to impeach Donald John Trump, President of the United States of America." The resolution set forth the process for holding public hearings, releasing deposition transcripts, presenting a report to the Judiciary Committee, holding proceedings within the Judiciary Committee, and submitting to the House of Representatives "such resolutions, articles of impeachment, or other recommendations as it deems proper."[45]

President Trump's Unprecedented Order Not to Comply

President Trump's categorical and indiscriminate order and efforts to block witness testimony and conceal documentary evidence from the Committees investigating his conduct as part of the House's impeachment inquiry stand in contrast to his predecessors and challenge the basic tenets of the Constitutional system of checks and balances.

Even before the House of Representatives launched its investigation regarding Ukraine, President Trump made numerous statements rejecting the fundamental authority of Congress to investigate his actions as well as those of his Administration. For example, on April 24, he stated, in response to Congressional investigations: "We're fighting all the subpoenas."[46] Similarly, during a speech on July 23, he stated: "I have an Article II, where I have to the right to do whatever I want as president."[47]

When the three investigating Committees began reviewing the President's actions as part of the House's impeachment inquiry, President Trump repeatedly challenged the investigation's legitimacy in word and deed. President Trump's rhetorical attacks appeared intended not just to dispute public reports of his misconduct, but to persuade the public that the House lacks authority to investigate the President and the inquiry is therefore invalid and fraudulent. For example, the President described the impeachment inquiry as:

- "a COUP"[48]
- "illegal, invalid, and unconstitutional"[49]
- "an unconstitutional power grab"[50]
- "Ukraine Witch Hunt"[51]
- "a continuation of the Greatest and most Destructive Witch Hunt of all time"[52]
- "a total Witch Hunt Scam by the Democrats"[53]
- "bad for the country"[54]
- "all a hoax"[55]
- "the single greatest witch hunt in American history"[56]
- "Democrat Scam"[57]
- "just another Democrat Hoax"[58]
- "a fraud against the American people"[59]
- "A Witch Hunt Scam"[60]
- "a con being perpetrated on the United States public and even the world"[61]
- "ridiculous"[62]
- "a continuation of the greatest Scam and Witch Hunt in the history of our Country"[63]
- "Ukraine Hoax"[64]
- "No Due Process Scam"[65]
- "the phony Impeachment Scam"[66]
- "the phony Impeachment Hoax"[67]

On September 26, President Trump argued that Congress should not be "allowed" to impeach him under the Constitution: "What these guys are doing—Democrats—are doing to this country is a disgrace and it shouldn't be allowed. There should be a way of stopping it—maybe legally, through the courts."[68]

A common theme of President Trump's defiance has been his claims that Congress is acting in an unprecedented way and using unprecedented rules. However, the House has been following the same investigative rules that Republicans championed when they were in control and conducted aggressive oversight of previous Administrations.[69]

White House Counsel's Letters Implementing the President's Order

On October 8, White House Counsel Pat Cipollone sent a letter to Speaker Pelosi and the three Committees explaining that President Trump had directed his entire Administration not to cooperate with the House's impeachment inquiry. He wrote:

> Consistent with the duties of the President of the United States, and in particular his obligation to preserve the rights of future occupants of his office, President Trump cannot permit his Administration to participate in this partisan inquiry under these circumstances.[70]

On October 10, President Trump confirmed that Mr. Cipollone was indeed conveying his orders, stating:

> As our brilliant White House Counsel wrote to the Democrats yesterday, he said their highly partisan and unconstitutional effort threatens grave and lasting damage to our democratic institutions, to our system of free elections, and to the American people. That's what it is. To the American people. It's so terrible. Democrats are on a crusade to destroy our democracy. That's what's happening. We will never let it happen. We will defeat them.[71]

Mr. Cipollone's letter elicited immediate criticism from legal experts from across the political spectrum.[72]

Mr. Cipollone wrote a second letter to the Committees on October 18, declaring that the White House would refuse to comply with the subpoena issued to it for documents.[73]

On November 1—after the House had already issued several subpoenas to White House and other Executive Branch officials for testimony—the Trump Administration issued a new "Letter Opinion" from Assistant Attorney General Steven A. Engel to Mr. Cipollone. The Office of Legal Counsel opinion sought to extend the reach of the President's earlier direction to defy Congressional subpoenas and to justify noncompliance by officials who could not plausibly be considered among the President's closest advisors.

Mr. Engel's opinion asserted that the House's impeachment inquiry seeks information that is "potentially protected by executive privilege" and claimed the Committees' deposition subpoenas are "invalid" and "not subject to civil or criminal enforcement" because the House's long-standing deposition rules do not allow the participation of attorneys from the White House or other government agencies.[74] These claims are without basis and unsupported by precedent.

The Letter Opinion cited statements from previous Presidents and Attorneys General that directly undercut the Administration's position. For example, President James K. Polk, stated that in an impeachment inquiry the House had power to "penetrate into the most secret recesses of the Executive Departments."[75] In addition, Attorney General Robert H. Jackson, who later served on the Supreme Court, stated that "pertinent information would be supplied in impeachment proceedings, usually instituted at the suggestion of the Department and for the good of the administration of justice."[76]

In his letters conveying the President's direction, Mr. Cipollone advanced remarkably politicized arguments and legal theories unsupported by the Constitution, judicial precedent, and more than 200 years of history. These letters effectuated the President's order and campaign to obstruct and thwart the House's exercise of its sole power of impeachment under the Constitution. They are rebutted as follows:

- **The Impeachment Inquiry is Constitutional:** According to Mr. Cipollone, "the President did nothing wrong," and "there is no basis for an impeachment inquiry."[77] President Trump has repeatedly described his call with President Zelensky as "perfect."[78] Speaking for President Trump, Mr. Cipollone also asserted that the impeachment inquiry is "partisan and unconstitutional," "a naked political strategy that began the day he was inaugurated, and perhaps even before," and that it "plainly seeks to reverse the election of 2016 and to influence the election of 2020."[79]

  However, as this report details in Section I, Congress found abundant evidence of a scheme directed by the President to solicit foreign election interference by pressing the newly-elected President of Ukraine to announce publicly politically-motivated investigations to benefit President Trump's own reelection campaign. Fundamentally, the Constitutional validity of an impeachment inquiry cannot depend on a President's view that he did nothing wrong or on the political composition of the House. Such an extreme reimagining of the Constitution would render the Article I impeachment power meaningless and provide the President with power the Constitution does not grant him to thwart, manipulate, and stonewall an impeachment inquiry conducted by the House, including by concealing information of his own misconduct.[80] Taken to its logical conclusion, the President's position would eliminate the impeachment power in every year during which a political party other than the President's is in power. Under this approach, the impeachments of President Clinton, President Nixon, and President Andrew Johnson would not have been permitted.[81]

  The purpose of an impeachment inquiry is for the House to collect evidence to determine for itself whether the President may have committed an impeachable offense warranting articles of impeachment. Because the Constitution vests the House alone with "the sole Power of Impeachment," it is not for the President to decide whether the House is exercising that power properly or prudently. The President is not free to arrogate the

212

House's power to himself—or to order across-the-board defiance of House subpoenas—based solely on his unilateral characterization of legislative motives or because he opposes the House's decision to investigate his actions.

- **The Impeachment Inquiry is Properly Authorized:** According to Mr. Cipollone, the "House has not expressly adopted any resolution authorizing an impeachment investigation" nor has it "delegated such authority to any of your Committees by rule."[82] However, nothing in either the Constitution or the House Rules requires the full House to vote to authorize an impeachment inquiry.[83] The impeachment inquiries into Presidents Andrew Johnson, Nixon, and Clinton all began prior to the House's consideration and approval of a resolution authorizing the investigations.[84] The same is true of many judicial impeachments;[85] indeed, numerous judges have been impeached without any prior vote of the full House authorizing a formal inquiry.[86] Even though Mr. Cipollone's argument is inherently invalid, the House has taken two floor votes that render it obsolete—the first on January 9 to adopt rules authorizing committees to conduct investigations, and the second on October 31 to set forth procedures for open hearings in the Intelligence Committee and for additional proceedings in the Judiciary Committee.[87] Even following passage of House Resolution 660, whereby the House confirmed the preexisting and ongoing impeachment inquiry, the President and the White House Counsel, acting on the President's behalf, have persisted in their obstructive conduct.

- **President Has No Valid Due Process Claims:** According to Mr. Cipollone, "the Committees have not established any procedures affording the President even the most basic protections demanded by due process under the Constitution and by fundamental fairness," and the Committees "have denied the President the right to cross-examine witnesses, to call witnesses, to receive transcripts of testimony, to have access to evidence," and "to have counsel present."[88] Yet, there is no requirement that the House provide these procedures during an impeachment inquiry. The Constitution vests the House with "the sole Power of Impeachment," and provides no constraints on how the House chooses to conduct its impeachment process.[89] Nevertheless, Mr. Cipollone's complaints are unfounded as the House has implemented procedural protections for the President in its exercise of its Constitutional power. House Resolution 660 authorizes procedures to "allow for the participation of the President and his counsel."[90] The Committee Report accompanying House Resolution 660 explains that these protections for the President are part of the Judiciary Committee hearing process and are "based on those provided during the Nixon and Clinton inquiries." These procedures include "that the president and his counsel are invited to attend all hearings; the ability for the president's counsel to cross-examine witnesses and object to the admissibility of testimony; and the ability of the president's counsel to make presentations of evidence before the Judiciary Committee, including the ability to call witnesses."[91]

- **Fact-Finding Was Appropriately Transparent:** According to Mr. Cipollone, the Committees conducted their proceedings "in secret."[92] This argument fundamentally misconstrues and misapprehends the fact-gathering process required at this initial stage of the House's impeachment inquiry. Unlike in the cases of Presidents Nixon and Clinton, the House conducted a significant portion of the factual investigation itself because no independent prosecutor was appointed to investigate President Trump's conduct regarding Ukraine. Attorney General William P. Barr refused to authorize a criminal investigation into the serious allegations of misconduct, and even this decision was limited to possible violations of federal campaign finance laws.[93] The investigative Committees proceeded consistent with the House's rules of procedure and in keeping with investigative best practices, including the need to reduce the risk that witnesses may try to coordinate or align testimony. As the House explained in its report accompanying House Resolution 660:

> The initial stages of an impeachment inquiry in the House are akin to those preceding a prosecutorial charging decision. Under this process, the House is responsible for collecting the evidence and, rather than weighing the question of returning an indictment, the Members of the House have the obligation to decide whether to approve articles of impeachment.[94]

The Committees have released transcripts of all interviews and depositions conducted during the investigation. As these transcripts make clear, all Members of all three Committees—including 47 Republican Members of Congress—had the opportunity to ask questions, and these transcripts are now available to the President and his counsel. These same procedures were supported by Acting White House Chief of Staff Mick Mulvaney when he served as a Member of the Oversight Committee and by Secretary of State Mike Pompeo when he served as a Member of the Benghazi Select Committee. In fact, some of the same Members and staff currently conducting depositions as part of the present impeachment inquiry participated directly in depositions during the Clinton, Bush, and Obama Administrations.[95] The Intelligence Committee also held public hearings with 12 of these witnesses.

- *Agency Attorneys Can Be (And Should Be) Excluded from Depositions:* According to Mr. Cipollone, "it is unconstitutional to exclude agency counsel from participating in congressional depositions."[96] Mr. Cipollone cites no case law to support his position— because there is none. Instead, he relies on a single opinion from the Trump Administration's Office of Legal Counsel and ignores the ample legal authority and historical precedent that clearly support the Committees' actions. For example, the Constitution expressly delegates to Congress the authority to "determine the Rules of its Proceedings,"[97] which includes the power to determine the procedures used for gathering information from witnesses whether via interview, staff deposition, or in a public hearing.[98] The basis for the rule excluding agency counsel is straightforward: it prevents agency officials who are directly implicated in the abuses Congress is investigating from trying to prevent their own employees from coming forward to tell the truth to Congress. The rule protects the rights of witnesses by allowing them to be accompanied in depositions by personal counsel. Agency attorneys have been excluded from Congressional depositions of Executive Branch officials for decades, under both Republicans and Democrats, including Chairmen Dan Burton, Henry Waxman, Darrell Issa, Jason Chaffetz, Trey Gowdy, Kevin Brady, and Jeb Hensarling, among others.[99]

- ***Congress Can Exercise Its Broad Oversight Authority:*** According to Mr. Cipollone, "you simply cannot expect to rely on oversight authority to gather information for an unauthorized impeachment inquiry that conflicts with all historical precedent and rides roughshod over due process and the separation of powers."[100] But, of course, the present impeachment inquiry does neither. Moreover, the Supreme Court has made clear that Congress' "power of inquiry" is "as penetrating and farreaching as the potential power to enact and appropriate under the Constitution."[101] The subject matter of the impeachment inquiry implicates the House's impeachment-specific as well as legislative and oversight authorities and interests. The activity under investigation, for instance, relates to a broad array of issues in which Congress has legislated and may legislate in the future, including government ethics and transparency, election integrity, appropriations, foreign affairs, abuse of power, bribery, extortion, and obstruction of justice. In fact, Members of Congress have already introduced legislation on issues related to the impeachment inquiry.[102] The House does not forfeit its Constitutional authority to investigate and legislate when it initiates an impeachment inquiry.[103] Congress passed sweeping legislative reforms following the scandal over the Watergate break-in and President Nixon's resignation.[104]

- ***"Confidentiality Interests" Do Not Eliminate Congress' Authority:*** According to Mr. Cipollone, the Administration would also not comply with the Committees' demands for documents and testimony because of unspecified Executive Branch "confidentiality interests."[105] There is no basis in the law of executive privilege for declaring a categorical refusal to respond to any House subpoena. In an impeachment inquiry, the House's need for information and its Constitutional authority are at their greatest, and the Executive's interest in confidentiality must yield. Only the President can assert executive privilege, yet he has not done so in the House's impeachment inquiry. Prior to asserting executive privilege, the Executive Branch is obligated to seek to accommodate the legitimate informational needs of Congress, which, as discussed below, it has not done.[106] In any event, much of the information sought by the Committees would not be covered by executive privilege under any theory,[107] and the privilege—where validly asserted on a particularized basis and not outweighed by the legitimate needs of the impeachment inquiry—would protect any legitimate Executive Branch interest in confidentiality.[108]

- ***President's Top Aides Are Not "Absolutely Immune":*** According to Mr. Cipollone, the President's top aides are "absolutely immune" from being compelled to testify before Congress.[109] This extreme position has been explicitly and repeatedly rejected by Congress—which has received testimony from senior aides to many previous Presidents—and by federal courts. In 2008, a federal court rejected an assertion by President George W. Bush that White House Counsel Harriet Miers was immune from being compelled to testify, noting that the President had failed to identify even a single judicial opinion to justify his claim.[110] On November 25, 2019, another federal judge rejected President Trump's claim of absolute immunity for former White House Counsel Don McGahn, concluding: "Stated simply, the primary takeaway from the past 250 years of recorded American history is that Presidents are not kings," and that "Executive branch officials are not absolutely immune from compulsory congressional process—no matter how many times the Executive branch has asserted as much over the years—even if the President expressly directs such officials' non-compliance."[111] Mr. Cipollone's position, adopted by President Trump, has thus been repudiated by Congress and the courts, and is not salvaged by Executive Branch legal opinions insisting upon a wholly fictional ground for non-compliance. In ordering categorical defiance of House subpoenas, President Trump has confirmed the unlimited breadth of his position and his unprecedented view that no branch of government—even the House—is empowered to investigate whether he may have committed constitutional offenses.

In addition to advancing specious legal arguments, President Trump has made no effort to accommodate the House's interests in conducting the impeachment inquiry. For example, the Committees first requested documents from the White House on September 9, but the White House disregarded the request.[112] The Committees made a second request on September 24, but the White House again ignored the request.[113] Finally, on October 4, the Committees transmitted a subpoena for the documents.[114] However, on October 18, the White House Counsel sent a letter stating that "the White House cannot comply with the October 4 subpoena."[115]

Since then, there has been no evidence of a willingness by the President to produce any of the documents covered by the subpoena to the White House. The State Department made passing references to potentially engaging in an "accommodations" process in response to its September 27 subpoena.[116] However, there has been no effort to do so, and departments and agencies have not produced any documents in response to subpoenas issued as part of the House impeachment inquiry. The President also made no apparent effort to accommodate the House's need for witness testimony and instead continued to flatly refuse to allow Executive Branch officials to testify.

3. **The President's Refusal to Produce Any and All Subpoenaed Documents**

> *Pursuant to the President's orders, the White House, federal departments and agencies, and key witnesses refused to produce any documents in response to duly authorized subpoenas issued pursuant to the House's impeachment inquiry.*

Overview

Following President Trump's categorical order, not a single document has been produced by the White House, the Office of the Vice President, the Office of Management and Budget, the Department of State, the Department of Defense, or the Department of Energy in response to 71 specific, individualized requests or demands for records in their possession, custody, or control. The subpoenas to federal departments and agencies remain in full force and effect. These agencies and offices also blocked many current and former officials from producing records directly to the Committees.

Certain witnesses defied the President's sweeping, categorical, and baseless order and identified the substance of key documents. Other witnesses identified numerous additional documents that the President and various agencies are withholding that are directly relevant to the impeachment inquiry.

The President's personal attorney, Mr. Giuliani, although a private citizen, also sought to rely on the President's order, as communicated in Mr. Cipollone's letter on October 8, to justify his decision to disobey a lawful subpoena for documents.

The White House

On September 9, the Committees sent a letter to White House Counsel Pat Cipollone seeking six categories of documents in response to reports indicating that, "for nearly two years, the President and his personal attorney, Rudy Giuliani, appear to have acted outside legitimate law enforcement and diplomatic channels to coerce the Ukrainian government into pursuing two politically-motivated investigations under the guise of anti-corruption activity."[117] The Committees asked the White House to voluntarily produce responsive documents by September 16.[118] The White House did not provide any response by that date.

On September 24, the Committees sent a follow-up letter requesting that the White House produce the documents by September 26.[119] Again, the White House did not provide any documents or respond by that date.

Having received no response from the White House, then-Chairman Elijah E. Cummings sent a memorandum to Members of the Committee on Oversight and Reform, which has jurisdiction over the Executive Office of the President, explaining that he was preparing to issue a subpoena in light of the White House's non-compliance and non-responsiveness. He wrote:

Over the past several weeks, the Committees tried several times to obtain voluntary compliance with our requests for documents, but the White House has refused to engage with—or even respond to—the Committees.[120]

On October 4, the Committees sent a letter to Acting White House Chief of Staff Mick Mulvaney transmitting a subpoena issued by Chairman Cummings compelling the White House to produce documents by October 18.[121]

As discussed above, on October 8, the White House Counsel sent a letter to Speaker Pelosi and the Committees stating that "President Trump cannot permit his Administration to participate in this partisan inquiry under these circumstances."[122] The White House Counsel also sent a letter on October 18, confirming that "the White House cannot comply with the October 4 subpoena to Acting Chief of Staff Mulvaney."[123]

To date, the White House has not produced a single document in response to the subpoena.[124] Instead, the White House has released to the public only two documents—call records from the President's phone calls with President Zelensky on April 21 and July 25.[125]

Witnesses who testified before the Committees have identified multiple additional documents that the President is withholding that are directly relevant to the impeachment inquiry, including but not limited to:

- briefing materials for President Trump's call with President Zelensky on July 25 prepared by Lt. Col. Alexander S. Vindman, Director for Ukraine at the National Security Council;[126]

- notes relating to the July 25 call taken by Lt. Col. Vindman and Tim Morrison, the former Senior Director for Europe and Russia on the National Security Council;[127]

- an August 15 "Presidential decision memo" prepared by Lt. Col. Vindman and approved by Mr. Morrison conveying "the consensus views from the entire deputies small group" that "the security assistance be released";[128]

- National Security Council staff summaries of conclusions from meetings at the principal, deputy, or sub-deputy level relating to Ukraine, including military assistance;[129]

- call records between President Trump and Ambassador Gordon Sondland, United States Ambassador to the European Union;[130]

- National Security Council Legal Advisor John Eisenberg's notes and correspondence relating to discussions with Lt. Col. Vindman regarding the July 10 meetings in which Ambassador Sondland requested investigations in exchange for a White House meeting;[131]

- the memorandum of conversation from President Trump's meeting in New York with President Zelensky on September 25;[132] and

- as explained below, emails and other messages between Ambassador Sondland and senior White House officials, including Acting Chief of Staff Mick Mulvaney, Senior Advisor to the Chief of Staff Rob Blair, and then-National Security Advisor John Bolton, among other high-level Trump Administration officials.[133]

The Committees also have good-faith reason to believe that the White House is in possession of and continues to withhold significantly more documents and records responsive to the subpoena and of direct relevance to the impeachment inquiry.

The Committees have closely tracked public reports that the White House is in possession of other correspondence and records of direct relevance to the impeachment inquiry. On November 24, for instance, a news report revealed that the White House had conducted a confidential, internal records review of the hold on military assistance in response to the Committees' inquiry. The review reportedly "turned up hundreds of documents that reveal extensive efforts to generate an after-the-fact justification for the decision and a debate over whether the delay was legal."[134]

Office of the Vice President

On October 4, the Committees sent a letter to Vice President Mike Pence seeking 13 categories of documents in response to reports that he and his staff were directly involved in the matters under investigation. The Committees wrote:

Recently, public reports have raised questions about any role you may have played in conveying or reinforcing the President's stark message to the Ukrainian President. The reports include specific references to a member of your staff who may have participated directly in the July 25, 2019, call, documents you may have obtained or reviewed, including the record of the call, and your September 1, 2019, meeting with the Ukrainian President in Warsaw, during which you reportedly discussed the Administration's hold on U.S. security assistance to Ukraine.[135]

The Committees asked the Vice President to produce responsive documents by October 15.[136] On that date, Matthew E. Morgan, Counsel to the Vice President, responded to the Committees by refusing to cooperate and reciting many of the same baseless arguments as the White House Counsel. He wrote:

[T]he purported "impeachment inquiry" has been designed and implemented in a manner that calls into question your commitment to fundamental fairness and due process rights. … Never before in history has the Speaker of the House attempted to launch an "impeachment inquiry" against a President without a majority of the House of Representatives voting to authorize a constitutionally acceptable process.[137]

To date, the Vice President has not produced a single document sought by the Committees and has not indicated any intent to do so going forward.

Witnesses who testified before the Committees have identified multiple additional documents that the Vice President is withholding that are directly relevant to the impeachment inquiry, including but not limited to:

- notes taken by Jennifer Williams, Special Advisor to the Vice President for Europe and Russia, during the call between President Trump and President Zelensky on July 25;[138]

- notes taken by Lt. Gen. Keith Kellogg, National Security Advisor to the Vice President, during the call between President Trump and President Zelensky on July 25;[139]

- materials regarding the July 25 call that were placed in the Vice President's briefing book that same day;[140]

- the memorandum of conversation from Vice President Pence's call with President Zelensky on September 18;[141] and

- briefing materials prepared for Vice President Pence's meeting with President Zelensky September 1 in Warsaw, Poland.[142]

The Committees also have good-faith reason to believe that the Office of the Vice President is in possession of and continues to withhold significantly more documents and records responsive to their request and of direct relevance to the impeachment inquiry.

Office of Management and Budget

On October 7, the Committees sent a letter to Russell Vought, Acting Director of the Office of Management and Budget (OMB), conveying a subpoena issued by the Intelligence Committee for nine categories of documents in response to public reports that the President directed OMB to freeze hundreds of millions of dollars in military assistance appropriated by Congress to help Ukraine counter Russian aggression. The Committees wrote:

> According to multiple press reports, at some point in July 2019, President Trump ordered Acting Chief of Staff and Office of Management and Budget (OMB) Director Mick Mulvaney to freeze the military aid to Ukraine, and Mr. Mulvaney reportedly conveyed the President's order "through the budget office to the Pentagon and the State Department, which were told only that the administration was looking at whether the spending was necessary."[143]

The subpoena compelled Acting Director Vought to produce responsive documents by October 15.[144] On that day, OMB Associate Director for Legislative Affairs Jason Yaworske responded by refusing to produce any documents and reciting many of the same baseless arguments as the White House Counsel:

> [T]he President has advised that "[g]iven that your inquiry lacks any legitimate constitutional foundation, any pretense of fairness, or even the most elementary due process protections, the Executive Branch cannot be expected to participate in

it." … President Trump cannot permit his Administration to participate in this partisan inquiry under these circumstances.[145]

To date, Acting Director Vought has not produced a single document sought by the Committees and has not indicated any intent to do so going forward.

Witnesses who testified before the Committees have identified multiple additional documents that Acting Director Vought is withholding that are directly relevant to the impeachment inquiry, including but not limited to:

- a June 19 email from OMB Associate Director of National Security Programs Michael Duffey to DOD Deputy Comptroller Elaine McCusker regarding the fact that "the President had seen a media report and he had questions about the assistance" and expressing "interest in getting more information from the Department of Defense," specifically a "description of the program";[146]

- a July 12 email from White House Assistant to the President and Senior Advisor to the Chief of Staff Robert Blair to Associate Director Duffey explaining that the "President is directing a hold on military support for Ukraine" and not mentioning any other country or security assistance package;[147] and

- an August 7 memorandum drafted in preparation for Acting Director Vought's attendance at a Principals Committee meeting on Ukrainian security assistance, which included a recommendation to lift the military assistance hold.[148]

The Committees also have good-faith reason to believe that the Office of Management and Budget is in possession of and continues to withhold significantly more documents and records responsive to the subpoena and of direct relevance to the impeachment inquiry.

Department of State

On September 9, the Committees sent a letter to Secretary of State Mike Pompeo requesting six categories of documents in response to reports that "President Trump and his personal attorney appear to have increased pressure on the Ukrainian government and its justice system in service of President Trump's reelection campaign" and "the State Department may be abetting this scheme."[149] The Committees requested that Secretary Pompeo produce responsive documents by September 16. The Secretary did not provide any documents or response by that date.

On September 23, the Committees sent a follow-up letter asking Secretary Pompeo to "inform the Committees by close of business on Thursday, September 26, 2019, whether you intend to fully comply with these requests or whether subpoenas will be necessary."[150] The Secretary did not provide any documents or respond by that date.

On September 27, the Committees sent a letter to Secretary Pompeo conveying a subpoena for documents issued by Rep. Eliot Engel, the Chairman of the Committee on Foreign Affairs, compelling the production of documents by October 4.[151]

Since Secretary Pompeo had failed to respond, the Committees also sent separate letters to six individual State Department employees seeking documents in their possession and requesting that they participate in depositions with the Committees.[152]

On October 1, Secretary Pompeo responded to the Committees for the first time. He objected to the Committees seeking documents directly from State Department employees after he failed to produce them, claiming inaccurately that such a request was "an act of intimidation and an invitation to violate federal records laws."[153] He also claimed that the Committees' inquiry was "an attempt to intimidate, bully, and treat improperly the distinguished professionals of the Department of State."[154]

To the contrary, Deputy Assistant Secretary George Kent, one of the State Department professionals from whom the Committees sought documents and testimony, testified that he "had not felt bullied, threatened, and intimidated."[155] Rather, Mr. Kent said that the language in Secretary Pompeo's letter, which had been drafted by a State Department attorney without consulting Mr. Kent, "was inaccurate."[156] Mr. Kent explained that, when he raised this concern, the State Department attorney "spent the next 5 minutes glaring at me" and then "got very angry." According to Mr. Kent, the official "started pointing at me with a clenched jaw and saying, What you did in there, if Congress knew what you were doing, they could say that you were trying to sort of control, or change the process of collecting documents."[157]

With respect to his own compliance with the subpoena for documents, Secretary Pompeo wrote that he "intends to respond to that subpoena by the noticed return date of October 4, 2019."[158]

Later on October 1, the Committees sent a letter to Deputy Secretary of State John J. Sullivan in light of new evidence that Secretary Pompeo participated on President Trump's call with President Zelensky on July 25. The Committees wrote:

> We are writing to you because Secretary Pompeo now appears to have an obvious conflict of interest. He reportedly participated personally in the July 25, 2019 call, in which President Donald Trump pressed President Volodymyr Zelensky of Ukraine to investigate the son of former Vice President Joseph Biden immediately after the Ukrainian President raised his desire for United States military assistance to counter Russian aggression.

> If true, Secretary Pompeo is now a fact witness in the impeachment inquiry. He should not be making any decisions regarding witness testimony or document production in order to protect himself or the President. Any effort by the Secretary or the Department to intimidate or prevent witnesses from testifying or withhold documents from the Committees shall constitute evidence of obstruction of the impeachment inquiry.[159]

The following day, at a press conference in Italy, Secretary Pompeo publicly acknowledged that he had been on the July 25 call between Presidents Trump and Zelensky.[160]

On October 7, Committee staff met with State Department officials who acknowledged that they had taken no steps to collect documents in response to the September 9 letter, but instead had waited for the September 27 subpoena before beginning to search for responsive records. During that conversation, the Committees made a good-faith attempt to engage the Department in the constitutionally-mandated accommodations process. The Committees requested, on a priority basis, "any and all documents that it received directly from Ambassador Sondland," as well as "documents—especially those documents identified by the witnesses as responsive—related to Ambassador Yovanovitch and DAS [Deputy Assistant Secretary] Kent." The depositions of these witnesses—Ambassador Sondland, Ambassador Yovanovitch, and Mr. Kent—were scheduled for the days shortly after that October 7 meeting. The Department's representatives stated that they would take the request back to senior State Department officials, but never provided any further response.[161]

To date, Secretary Pompeo has not produced a single document sought by the Committees and has not indicated any intent to do so going forward. In addition, the Department has ordered its employees not to produce documents in their personal possession. For example, on October 14, the Department sent a letter to Mr. Kent's personal attorney warning that "your client is not authorized to disclose to Congress any records relating to official duties."[162]

Moreover, the Department appears to have actively discouraged its employees from identifying documents responsive to the Committees' subpoena. Mr. Kent testified in his deposition that he informed a Department attorney about additional responsive records that the Department had not collected, including an email from Assistant Secretary of State for Consular Affairs David Risch, who "had spoken to Rudy Giuliani several times in January about trying to get a visa for the corrupt former prosecutor general of Ukraine, Viktor Shokin."[163] The Department attorney "objected to [Mr. Kent] raising of the additional information" and "made clear that he did not think it was appropriate for [Mr. Kent] to make the suggestion."[164] Mr. Kent responded that what he was "trying to do was make sure that the Department was being fully responsive."[165]

Certain witnesses defied the President's directive and produced the substance of key documents. For example, Ambassador Sondland attached ten exhibits to his written hearing statement.[166] These exhibits contained replicas of emails and WhatsApp messages between Ambassador Sondland and high-level Trump Administration officials, including Secretary Pompeo, Secretary Perry, Acting Chief of Staff Mick Mulvaney, and former National Security Advisor John Bolton.[167] The exhibits also contained a replica of a WhatsApp message between Ambassador Sondland and Mr. Yermak.[168]

Earlier in the investigation, Ambassador Kurt Volker had produced key text messages with Ambassador Taylor, Ambassador Sondland, President Zelensky's senior aide, Andriy Yermak, Mr. Giuliani, and others very soon after the Committees requested them and prior to Mr. Cipollone's letter on October 8 conveying the President's directive not to comply.[169]

The Department also prevented Ambassador Sondland—a current State Department employee—from accessing records to prepare for his testimony. As described above, federal law imposes fines and up to five years in prison for anyone who corruptly or by threats "impedes or endeavors to influence, obstruct, or impede" the "due and proper exercise of the power of inquiry under which any inquiry or investigation is being had by either House, or any committee of either House."[170] Ambassador Sondland explained that the Department's actions directly impeded his testimony:

> I have not had access to all of my phone records, State Department emails, and other State Department documents. And I was told I could not work with my EU Staff to pull together the relevant files. Having access to the State Department materials would have been very helpful to me in trying to reconstruct with whom I spoke and met, when, and what was said. ...

> My lawyers and I have made multiple requests to the State Department and the White House for these materials. Yet, these materials were not provided to me. They have also refused to share these materials with this Committee. These documents are not classified and, in fairness, should have been made available.[171]

He testified, "I have been hampered to provide completely accurate testimony without the benefit of those documents."[172] Ambassador Sondland also stated:

> Despite repeated requests to the White House and the State Department, I have not been granted access to all of the phone records, and I would like to review those phone records, along with any notes and other documents that may exist, to determine if I can provide more complete testimony to assist Congress.[173]

On November 22, the Department produced 99 pages of emails, letters, notes, timelines, and news articles to a non-partisan, nonprofit ethics watchdog organization pursuant to a court order in a lawsuit filed under the Freedom of Information Act (FOIA).[174] This handful of documents was limited to a narrow window of time and specific people, but it clearly indicates that the Department is withholding documents that are responsive to the Committees' requests.

For example, the Department's FOIA production contains an email from the Office Manager to the Secretary of State to "S_All" sent on March 26 which states that "S is speaking with Rudy Giuliani."[175] It also contains a March 27 email in which Madeleine Westerhout, the Personal Secretary to President Trump, facilitates another phone call between Rudy Giuliani and Secretary Pompeo.[176] These documents are directly responsive to the September 27 subpoena for "all documents and communications, from January 20, 2017 to the present, relating or referring to: Communications between any current or former State Department officials or employees and Rudolph W. Giuliani, including any text messages using personal or work-related devices."[177]

Witnesses who testified before the Committees have identified multiple additional documents that Secretary Pompeo is withholding that are directly relevant to the impeachment inquiry, including but not limited to:

- a cable on August 29 from Bill Taylor, the Chargé d'Affaires for U.S. Embassy in Kyiv, Ukraine, at the recommendation of National Security Advisor John Bolton, sent directly to Secretary Pompeo "describing the folly I saw in withholding military aid to Ukraine at a time when hostilities were still active in the east and when Russia was watching closely to gauge the level of American support for the Ukrainian Government" and telling Secretary Pompeo "that I could not and would not defend such a policy";[178]

- WhatsApp messages and emails that Ambassador Sondland replicated and provided as exhibits to the Intelligence Committee showing key communications between Ambassador Sondland and high-level Trump Administration officials, including Secretary Pompeo, Secretary Perry, Acting Chief of Staff Mick Mulvaney, and National Security Advisor John Bolton, as well as President Zelensky's senior aide, Andriy Yermak;[179]

- notes and memoranda to file from Mr. Kent, Ambassador Taylor, and others, including Ambassador Taylor's "little notebook" in which he would "take notes on conversations, in particular when I'm not in the office," such as meetings with Ukrainians or when out and receiving a phone call," as well as his "small, little spiral notebook" of calls that took place in the office;[180]

- emails among Philip Reeker, Acting Assistant Secretary of State, Bureau of European and Eurasian Affairs; David Hale, Under Secretary of State for Political Affairs; Mr. Kent; and others regarding the unsuccessful effort to issue a public statement in support of Ambassador Yovanovitch, including the "large number of emails related to the press guidance and the allegations about the Ambassador" from the "late March timeframe."[181]

The Committees also have good-faith reason to believe that the Department of State is in possession of and continues to withhold significantly more documents and records responsive to the subpoena and of direct relevance to the impeachment inquiry.

Department of Defense

On October 7, the Committees sent a letter to Secretary of Defense Mark Esper conveying a subpoena issued by the Intelligence Committee for 14 categories of documents in response to reports that the President directed a freeze of hundreds of millions of dollars in military aid appropriated by Congress to help Ukraine counter Russian aggression. The Committees wrote:

Officials at the Departments of State and Defense reportedly were "puzzled and alarmed" after learning about the White House's directive. Defense Department officials reportedly "tried to make a case to the White House that the Ukraine aid was effective and should not be looked at in the same manner as other aid," but "those arguments were ignored."[182]

The subpoena required Secretary Esper to produce responsive documents by October 15. On October 13, Secretary Esper stated in a public interview that the Department would comply with the Intelligence Committee's subpoena:

Q: Very quickly, are you going to comply with the subpoena that the House provided you and provide documents to them regarding to the halt to military aid to Ukraine?

A: Yeah we will do everything we can to cooperate with the Congress. Just in the last week or two, my general counsel sent out a note as we typically do in these situations to ensure documents are retained.

Q: Is that a yes?

A: That's a yes.

Q: You will comply with the subpoena?

A: We will do everything we can to comply.[183]

On October 15, however, Assistant Secretary of Defense for Legislative Affairs Robert R. Hood responded by refusing to produce any documents and reciting many of the same legally unsupportable arguments as the White House Counsel:

In light of these concerns, and in view of the President's position as expressed in the White House Counsel's October 8 letter, and without waiving any other objections to the subpoena that the Department may have, the Department is unable to comply with your request for documents at this time.[184]

To date, Secretary Esper has not produced a single document sought by the Committees and has not indicated any intent to do so going forward, notwithstanding his public promise to "do everything we can to comply."[185]

Witnesses who testified before the Committees have identified multiple additional documents that Secretary Esper is withholding that are directly relevant to the impeachment inquiry, including but not limited to:

- DOD staff readouts from National Security Council meetings at the principal, deputy, or sub-deputy level relating to Ukraine, including military assistance;[186]

- an email from Secretary Esper's Chief of Staff, to Laura K. Cooper, Deputy Assistant Secretary of Defense for Russia, Ukraine, and Eurasia, in late July "asking for follow-up on a meeting with the President," including information on whether "U.S. industry [is] providing any of this equipment," "international contributions" to Ukraine, and "who gave this funding";[187]

- fact sheets and other information provided by Ms. Cooper in response to the email request;[188]

- an email sent to Ms. Cooper's staff on July 25 at 2:31 p.m.—the same day as President's Trump's call with Ukrainian President Zelensky—stating that the Ukrainian Embassy was inquiring about the status of military aid, suggesting that Ukrainian officials were concerned about the status of the military aid much earlier than ever previously acknowledged by the Executive Branch;[189]

- an email sent to Ms. Cooper's staff on July 25 at 4:25 p.m. stating that the Ukrainian Embassy and The Hill newspaper had become aware of the situation with the military assistance funding;[190] and

- an email received by Ms. Cooper's staff on July 3 at 4:23 p.m. from the Department of State explaining that the Department of State "had heard the CN [Congressional Notification] is currently being blocked by OMB."[191]

The Committees also have good-faith reason to believe that the Department of Defense is in possession of and continues to withhold significantly more documents and records responsive to the subpoena and of direct relevance to the impeachment inquiry.

Department of Energy

On October 10, the Committees sent a letter to Secretary of Energy Rick Perry conveying a subpoena issued by the Intelligence Committee for ten categories of documents in response to reports about his involvement with matters under investigation. The Committees wrote:

> Recently, public reports have raised questions about any role you may have played in conveying or reinforcing the President's stark message to the Ukrainian President. These reports have also raised significant questions about your efforts to press Ukrainian officials to change the management structure at a Ukrainian state-owned energy company to benefit individuals involved with Rudy Giuliani's push to get Ukrainian officials to interfere in our 2020 election.[192]

The subpoena required Secretary Perry to produce responsive documents by October 18. On that day, Melissa F. Burnison, the Assistant Secretary of Energy for Congressional and Intergovernmental Affairs, responded by refusing to produce any documents and reciting many of the same flawed arguments as the White House Counsel:

> Pursuant to these concerns, the Department restates the President's position: "Given that your inquiry lacks any legitimate constitutional foundation, any pretense of fairness, or even the most elementary due process protections, the Executive Branch cannot be expected to participate in it."[193]

To date, Secretary Perry has not produced a single document sought by the Committees and has not indicated any intent to do so going forward.

Witnesses who testified before the Committees have identified multiple documents that Secretary Perry is withholding that are directly relevant to the impeachment inquiry, including but not limited to:

- a document passed directly from Secretary Perry to President Zelensky in a May 2019 meeting with a list of "people he trusts" that President Zelensky could seek advice from on issues of relating to "key Ukrainian energy-sector contacts," according to David Holmes, the Political Counselor at the U.S. Embassy in Kyiv;[194]

- a June 5 email from Philip Reeker, Acting Assistant Secretary of State, Bureau of European and Eurasian Affairs, to Secretary Perry and others, regarding "Zelenskyy's visit to Brussels, and the critical—perhaps historic—role of the dinner and engagement Gordon [Ambassador Sondland] coordinated";[195] and

- a July 19 email from Secretary Perry in which he states "Mick [Acting Chief of Staff Mick Mulvaney] just confirmed the call being set up for tomorrow by NSC" in reference to a call between President Trump and President Zelensky.[196]

The Committees also have good-faith reason to believe that the Department of Energy is in possession of and continues to withhold significantly more documents and records responsive to the subpoena and of direct relevance to the impeachment inquiry.

Rudy Giuliani and His Associates

On September 30, the Committees sent a letter conveying a subpoena issued by the Intelligence Committee to the President's personal attorney, Rudy Giuliani, compelling the production of 23 categories of documents relating to his actions in Ukraine.[197]

On October 15, Mr. Giuliani's counsel responded to the Committees by stating that Mr. Giuliani "will not participate because this appears to be an unconstitutional, baseless, and illegitimate 'impeachment inquiry.'"[198] He also stated: "Mr. Giuliani adopts all the positions set forth in Mr. Cipollone's October 8, 2019 letter on behalf of President Donald J. Trump."[199]

To date, Mr. Giuliani has not produced a single document sought by the Committees and has not indicated any intent to do so going forward.

On September 30, the Committees sent letters to two of Mr. Giuliani's business associates—Igor Fruman and Lev Parnas—requesting testimony and eleven categories of documents from each.[200] The Committees sought documents from Mr. Fruman and Mr. Parnas related to their efforts to influence U.S. elections.

According to press reports, Mr. Parnas and Mr. Fruman reportedly were "assisting with Giuliani's push to get Ukrainian officials to investigate former vice president Joe Biden and his son as well as Giuliani's claim that Democrats conspired with Ukrainians in the 2016 campaign." Press reports also indicate that Mr. Parnas and Mr. Fruman were involved with efforts to press Ukrainian officials to change the management structure at a Ukrainian state-owned energy company, Naftogaz, to benefit individuals involved with Mr. Giuliani's push to get Ukrainian officials to interfere in the 2020 election.[201]

On October 3, counsel to Mr. Fruman and Mr. Parnas responded to Committee staff, explaining his clients' relationship with Mr. Giuliani and President Trump:

> Be advised that Messrs. Parnas and Fruman assisted Mr. Giuliani in connection with his representation of President Trump. Mr. Parnas and Mr. Fruman have also been represented by Mr. Giuliani in connection with their personal and business affairs. They also assisted Joseph DiGenova and Victoria Toensing in their law practice.[202]

With respect to preparing Mr. Fruman and Mr. Parnas' response, their counsel wrote: "The amount of time requires is difficult to determine. [sic] but we are happy to keep you advised of our progress and engage in a rolling production of non-privileged documents."

On October 8, their counsel wrote again to Committee staff, stating:

> This is an update. We continue to meet with Mr. Parnas and Mr. Fruman to gather the facts and documents related to the many subjects and persons detailed in your September 30 letter and to evaluate all of that information in light of the privileges we raised in our last letter.[203]

On October 9, their counsel wrote to Committee staff, stating, "Please be advised that Messrs. Parnas and Fruman agree with and adopt the position of White House Counsel pertaining to Democrat inquiry."[204]

On October 10, the Committees transmitted subpoenas compelling Mr. Fruman and Mr. Parnas to produce eleven categories of documents.[205] That same day, their counsel responded:

> As I did in my recent letter of October 8, 2019, please be advised we were in the formative stages of recovering and reviewing records on October 9 when Messrs. Parnas and Fruman were arrested by the FBI and locked up in Virginia pursuant to Four Count Indictment by a Federal Grand Jury in the Southern District of New York unsealed on October 10, 2019.

> Further their records and other belongings, including materials sought by your subpoenas, were seized pursuant warrants [sic] by the FBI in several locations on the 9th or 10th of October.[206]

To date, Mr. Fruman has not produced a single document in response to his subpoena and has not indicated any intent to do so going forward.

With respect to Mr. Parnas, he obtained new counsel during the course of the impeachment inquiry. His new attorney has asserted that Mr. Parnas will cooperate with the House's inquiry, stating: "We will honor and not avoid the committee's requests to the extent they are legally proper, while scrupulously protecting Mr. Parnas' privileges including that of the Fifth Amendment."[207]

In contrast to Mr. Giuliani and Mr. Fruman, Mr. Parnas has begun rolling production of certain records in his possession, custody, or control in response to the subpoena, which the Committees are evaluating. The Committees expect Mr. Parnas' full compliance with the subpoena.

4.   **The President's Refusal to Allow Top Aides to Testify**

> *At President Trump's direction, twelve current or former Administration officials refused to testify as part of the House's impeachment inquiry, ten of whom did so in defiance of duly authorized subpoenas. The President's orders were coordinated and executed by the White House Counsel and others, and they prevented testimony from officials from the White House, National Security Council, Office of Management and Budget, Department of State, and Department of Energy.*

Overview

No other President in history has issued an order categorically directing the entire Executive Branch not to testify before Congress, including in the context of an impeachment inquiry. President Trump issued just such an order.

As reflected in White House Counsel Pat Cipollone's October 8 letter, President Trump directed all government witnesses to violate their legal obligations by defying House subpoenas—regardless of their office or position.[208] President Trump even extended his order to former officials no longer employed by the federal government. This Administration-wide effort to prevent all witnesses from providing testimony was coordinated and comprehensive.

These witnesses were warned that their refusal to testify "shall constitute evidence that may be used against you in a contempt proceeding" and "may be used as an adverse inference against you and the President."

Despite the President's unprecedented commands, the House gathered a wealth of evidence of his conduct from courageous individuals who were willing to follow the law, comply with duly authorized subpoenas, and tell the truth. Nevertheless, the President's efforts to obstruct witness testimony deprived Congress and the public of additional evidence.

In following President Trump's orders to defy duly authorized Congressional subpoenas, several Administration officials who, to date, remain under subpoena may have placed themselves at risk of being held in criminal contempt of Congress.[209] These witnesses were warned explicitly that their refusal to obey lawful orders to testify "shall constitute evidence that may be used against you in a contempt proceeding" and could also result in adverse inferences being drawn against both them and the President.[210]

Mick Mulvaney, Acting White House Chief of Staff

On November 5, the Committees sent a letter to Mick Mulvaney, the Acting White House Chief of Staff, seeking his appearance at a deposition on November 8.[211] The Committees received no response to this letter.

On November 7, the Intelligence Committee issued a subpoena compelling Mr. Mulvaney's appearance at a deposition on November 8.[212] On November 8, Mr. Mulvaney's personal attorney sent an email to Committee staff stating that "Mr. Mulvaney will not be attending the deposition today, and he is considering the full range of his legal options."[213]

Mr. Mulvaney's personal attorney provided a letter that was sent on November 8 from Mr. Cipollone, stating that "the President directs Mr. Mulvaney not to appear at the Committee's scheduled deposition on November 8, 2019."[214] Mr. Mulvaney's personal attorney also provided a letter sent on November 7 from Steven A. Engel, Assistant Attorney General at the Office of Legal Counsel of the Department of Justice, to Mr. Cipollone, stating, "Mr. Mulvaney is absolutely immune from compelled congressional testimony in his capacity as a senior advisor to the President."[215]

Mr. Mulvaney did not appear at the deposition on November 8, in defiance of the Committees' subpoena. The Committees met, and Chairman Schiff acknowledged Mr. Mulvaney's absence, stating:

> Neither Congress nor the courts recognize a blanket absolute immunity as a basis to defy a congressional subpoena. Mr. Mulvaney and the White House, therefore, have no legitimate legal basis to evade a duly authorized subpoena. The President's direction to Mr. Mulvaney to defy our subpoena can, therefore, only be construed as an effort to delay testimony and obstruct the inquiry, consistent with the White House Counsel's letter dated October 8, 2019.[216]

Chairman Schiff also explained Mr. Mulvaney's knowledge of and role in facilitating the President's conduct:

> Mr. Mulvaney's role in facilitating the White House's obstruction of the impeachment inquiry does not occur in a vacuum. Over the past several weeks, we have gathered extensive evidence of the President's abuse of power related to pressuring Ukraine to pursue investigations that would benefit the President personally and politically and jeopardize national security in doing so. Some of that evidence has revealed that Mr. Mulvaney was a percipient witness to misconduct by the President and may have had a role in certain actions under investigation. The evidence shows that Mr. Mulvaney may have coordinated with U.S. Ambassador to the European Union Gordon Sondland, Rudy Giuliani, and others to carry out President Trump's scheme to condition a White House meeting with President Zelensky on the Ukrainians' pursuit of investigations of the Bidens, Burisma holdings, and purported Ukrainian interference in the 2016 U.S. Presidential election. In addition, evidence suggests that Mr. Mulvaney may have played a central role in President Trump's attempt to coerce Ukraine into launching his desired political investigations by withholding nearly $400 million in vital security assistance from Ukraine that had been appropriated by Congress. At a White House press briefing on October 17, 2019, Mr. Mulvaney admitted publicly that President Trump ordered the hold on Ukraine security assistance to further the President's own personal political interests rather than the national interest. ...

Based on the record evidence gathered to date, we can only infer that Mr. Mulvaney's refusal to testify is intended to prevent the Committees from learning additional evidence of President Trump's misconduct and that Mr. Mulvaney's testimony would corroborate and confirm other witnesses' accounts of such misconduct. If the White House had evidence to contest those facts, they would allow Mr. Mulvaney to be deposed. Instead, the President and the White House are hiding and trying to conceal the truth from the American people. Given the extensive evidence the Committees have already uncovered, the only result of this stonewalling is to buttress the case for obstruction of this inquiry.[217]

To date, Mr. Mulvaney has not changed his position about compliance with the subpoena.[218]

Robert B. Blair, Assistant to the President and Senior Advisor to the Chief of Staff

On October 24, the Committees sent a letter to Robert B. Blair, an Assistant to the President and the Senior Advisor to Acting Chief of Staff Mulvaney, seeking Mr. Blair's appearance at a deposition on November 1.[219] On November 2, Mr. Blair's personal attorney sent a letter to the Committees stating:

Mr. Blair has been directed by the White House not to appear and testify at the Committees' proposed deposition, based on the Department of Justice's advice that the Committees may not validly require an executive branch witness to appear at such a deposition without the assistance of agency counsel. In light of the clear direction he has been given by the Executive Branch, Mr. Blair must respectfully decline to testify, as you propose, on Monday, November 4, 2019.[220]

On November 3, the Committees sent a letter to Mr. Blair's personal attorney transmitting a subpoena compelling Mr. Blair to appear at a deposition on November 4.[221]

On November 4, Mr. Blair did not appear for the scheduled deposition, in defiance of the Committees' subpoena. The Committees met and Chairman Schiff acknowledged Mr. Blair's absence, stating:

Although the committees requested a copy of the correspondence from the White House and Department of Justice, Mr. Blair's Counsel did not provide it to the Committees. This new and shifting rationale from the White House, like the others it has used to attempt to block witnesses from appearing to provide testimony about the President's misconduct, has no basis in law or the Constitution and is a serious affront to decades of precedent in which Republicans and Democrats have used exactly the same procedures to depose executive branch officials without agency counsel present, including some of the most senior aides to multiple previous Presidents.[222]

Unlike President Trump's directive to Acting Chief of Staff Mulvaney, neither Mr. Blair nor the White House have asserted that Mr. Blair is "absolutely immune" from providing testimony to Congress. To date, Mr. Blair has not changed his position or contacted the Committees about compliance with the subpoena.

Ambassador John Bolton, Former National Security Advisor

On October 30, the Committees sent a letter to the personal attorney of Ambassador John Bolton, the former National Security Advisor to President Trump, seeking his appearance at a deposition on November 7.[223] Later that day, Ambassador Bolton's personal attorney sent an email to Committee staff stating, "As you no doubt have anticipated, Ambassador Bolton is not willing to appear voluntarily."[224]

On November 7, Ambassador Bolton did not appear for the scheduled deposition. On November 8, Ambassador Bolton's personal attorney sent a letter to Douglas Letter, the General Counsel of the House of Representatives, suggesting that, if Ambassador Bolton were subpoenaed, he would file a lawsuit and would comply with the subpoena only if ordered to do so by the court. He referenced a lawsuit filed by another former official, Dr. Charles Kupperman, represented by the same attorney and stated:

> As I emphasized in my previous responses to letters from the House Chairs, Dr. Kupperman stands ready, as does Ambassador Bolton, to testify if the Judiciary resolves the conflict in favor of the Legislative Branch's position respecting such testimony.[225]

To date, Ambassador Bolton has not changed his position or come forward to testify.[226]

John A. Eisenberg, Deputy Counsel to the President for National Security Affairs and Legal Advisor, National Security Council

On October 30, the Committees sent a letter to John A. Eisenberg, the Deputy Counsel to the President for National Security Affairs and the Legal Advisor at the National Security Council, seeking his appearance at a deposition on November 4.[227] The Committees received no response to this letter.[228]

On November 1, the Committees sent a letter to Mr. Eisenberg transmitting a subpoena compelling his appearance at a deposition on November 4.[229] On November 4, Mr. Eisenberg's personal attorney sent a letter to the Committees, stating:

> Even if Mr. Eisenberg had been afforded a reasonable amount of time to prepare, the President has instructed Mr. Eisenberg not to appear at the deposition. Enclosed with this letter is the President's instruction as relayed by Pat A. Cipollone, Counsel to the President, in a letter dated November 3, 2019. We also enclose a letter, also dated November 3, 2019, from Steven A. Engel, Assistant Attorney General for the Office of Legal Counsel at the Department of Justice, to Mr. Cipollone advising that Mr. Eisenberg is "absolutely immune from compelled congressional testimony in his capacity as a senior advisor to the President." Under these circumstances, Mr. Eisenberg has no other option that is consistent with his legal and ethical obligations except to follow the direction of his client and employer, the President of the United States. Accordingly, Mr. Eisenberg will not be appearing for a deposition at this time.[230]

Enclosed was a letter sent on November 3 from Mr. Cipollone to Mr. Eisenberg's personal attorney stating that "the President directs Mr. Eisenberg not to appear at the Committee's deposition on Monday, November 4, 2019."[231] Also enclosed was a letter sent on November 3 by Assistant Attorney General Steven A. Engel to the Office of Legal Counsel of the Department of Justice to Mr. Cipollone stating:

> You have asked whether the Committee may compel Mr. Eisenberg to testify. We conclude that he is absolutely immune from compelled congressional testimony in his capacity as a senior advisor to the President.[232]

Mr. Eisenberg did not appear for the scheduled deposition, in defiance of the Committees' subpoena. The Committees met and Chairman Schiff acknowledged Mr. Eisenberg's absence, stating:

> Despite his legal obligations to comply, Mr. Eisenberg is not present here today and has therefore defied a duly authorized congressional subpoena. This morning, in an email received at 9:00 a.m., when the deposition was supposed to commence, Mr. Eisenberg's personal attorney sent a letter to the committee stating that President Trump had, quote, "instructed Mr. Eisenberg not to appear at the deposition," unquote. The attorney attached correspondence from White House counsel Pat Cipollone and a letter from the Office of Legal Counsel at Department of Justice. The OLC letter informs the White House that Mr. Eisenberg is purportedly, quote, "absolutely immune from compelled congressional testimony in his capacity as a senior advisor to the President," unquote. …
>
> Moreover, neither Congress nor the courts recognize a blanket, quote, "absolute immunity," unquote, as a basis to defy a congressional subpoena. Mr. Eisenberg and the White House, therefore, have no basis for evading a lawful subpoena. As such, the President's direction to Mr. Eisenberg to defy a lawful compulsory process can only be construed as an effort to delay testimony and obstruct the inquiry, consistent with the White House counsel's letter dated October 8, 2019. As Mr. Eisenberg was informed, the Committees may consider his noncompliance with the subpoena as evidence in a future contempt proceeding. His failure or refusal to appear, moreover, shall constitute evidence of obstruction of the House's impeachment inquiry and may be used as an adverse inference against the President. The subpoena remains in full force. The committees reserve all of their rights, including the right to raise this matter at a future Intelligence Committee proceeding, at the discretion of the chair of the committee.
>
> Mr. Eisenberg's nonappearance today adds to a growing body of evidence of the White House seeking to obstruct the White House's impeachment inquiry. To the extent the White House believes that an issue could be raised at the deposition that may implicate a valid claim of privilege, the White House may seek to assert that privilege with the Committee in advance of the deposition. To date, as has been the case in every other deposition as part of the inquiry, the White House has not done so. Mr. Eisenberg's failure to appear today also flies in the face of historical precedent. Even absent impeachment proceedings, congressional committees have deposed senior White House officials, including White House counsels and senior White House lawyers.[233]

Michael Ellis, Senior Associate Counsel to the President and Deputy Legal Advisor, National Security Council

On October 30, the Committees sent a letter to Michael Ellis, a Senior Associate Counsel to the President and the Deputy Legal Advisor at the National Security Council, seeking his appearance at a deposition on November 4.[234] On November 2, Mr. Ellis' personal attorney sent an email to Committee staff stating:

> [W]e are in receipt of an opinion from the Office of Legal Counsel providing guidance on the validity of a subpoena under the current terms and conditions and based on that guidance we are not in a position to appear for a deposition at this time.[235]

This email followed the November 1 Office of Legal Counsel opinion, discussed above, which sought to extend the reach of the President's earlier direction to defy Congressional subpoenas and provided justification for noncompliance by officials who could not plausibly be considered among the President's closest advisors.

On November 3, Mr. Ellis' personal attorney sent another email to Committee staff stating:

> [O]ur guidance is that the failure to permit agency counsel to attend a deposition of Mr. Ellis would not allow sufficient protection of relevant privileges and therefore render any subpoena constitutionally invalid. As an Executive branch employee Mr. Ellis is required to follow this guidance.[236]

On November 3, the Committees sent a letter to Mr. Ellis' personal attorney transmitting a subpoena compelling his appearance at a deposition on November 4, stating:

> Mr. Ellis' failure or refusal to comply with the subpoena, including at the direction or behest of the President or the White House, shall constitute further evidence of obstruction of the House's impeachment inquiry and may be used as an adverse inference against Mr. Ellis and the President.[237]

On November 4, Mr. Ellis did not appear for the scheduled deposition, in defiance of the Committees' subpoena. The Committees met and Chairman Schiff acknowledged Mr. Ellis' absence, stating:

> Other than the White House's objections to longstanding congressional practice, the committees are aware of no other valid constitutional privilege asserted by the White House to direct Mr. Ellis to defy this subpoena.[238]

To date, Mr. Ellis has not changed his position or contacted the Committees about compliance with the subpoena.

Preston Wells Griffith, Senior Director for International Energy and Environment, National Security Council

On October 24, the Committees sent a letter to Preston Wells Griffith, the Senior Director for International Energy and Environment at the National Security Council, seeking his appearance at a deposition on November 5.[239] On November 4, Mr. Griffith's personal attorney sent a letter to the Committees stating:

> As discussed with Committee counsel, Mr. Griffith respectfully declines to appear for a deposition before the joint Committees conducting the impeachment inquiry, based upon the direction of White House Counsel that he not appear due to agency counsel not being permitted.[240]

Later that day, the Committees sent a letter to Mr. Griffith's personal attorney transmitting a subpoena compelling his appearance at a deposition on November 5, stating:

> Mr. Griffith's failure or refusal to comply with the subpoena, including at the direction or behest of the President or the White House, shall constitute further evidence of obstruction of the House's impeachment inquiry and may be used as an adverse inference against Mr. Griffith and the President.[241]

On November 5, Mr. Griffith did not appear for the scheduled deposition, in defiance of the Committees' subpoena. The Committees met and Chairman Schiff acknowledged Mr. Griffith's absence, stating:

> Although the committees requested a copy of any written direction from the White House, Mr. Griffith's counsel has not provided any such documentation to the committees. The White House's newly invented rationale for obstructing the impeachment inquiry appears based on a legal opinion that was issued by the Department of Justice Office of Legal Counsel just last Friday, November 1. It is noteworthy and telling that OLC issued this opinion after multiple current and former White House, State Department, and Department of Defense officials testified before the committees, both voluntarily and pursuant to subpoena, all without agency counsel present. The White House's invocation of this self-serving OLC opinion should therefore be seen for what it is: a desperate attempt to staunch the flow of incriminating testimony from the executive branch officials about the President's abuse of power.[242]

To date, Mr. Griffith has not changed his position or contacted the Committees about compliance with the subpoena.

Dr. Charles M. Kupperman, Former Deputy Assistant to the President for National Security Affairs, National Security Council

On October 16, the Committees sent a letter to Dr. Charles M. Kupperman, a former Deputy Assistant to the President for National Security Affairs, seeking his appearance at a deposition on October 23.[243]

On October 25, the Intelligence Committee issued a subpoena compelling Dr. Kupperman to appear at a deposition on October 28.[244]

Later that day, Dr. Kupperman's personal attorney sent an email to Committee staff attaching a 17-page complaint in federal court seeking a declaratory judgment as to whether he should comply with the subpoena.[245] His counsel wrote:

> Pending the courts' determination as to which Branch should prevail, Dr. Kupperman will not effectively adjudicate the conflict by appearing and testifying before the Committees.[246]

Enclosed as part of the complaint was a letter sent on October 25 from Mr. Cipollone to Dr. Kupperman's personal attorney stating that "the President directs Mr. Kupperman not to appear at the Committee's scheduled hearing on Monday, October 28, 2019."[247] Also enclosed was a letter sent on October 25 from Steven A. Engel, Assistant Attorney General at the Office of Legal Counsel of the Department of Justice, to Mr. Cipollone stating that Dr. Kupperman "is absolutely immune from compelled congressional testimony in his capacity as a former senior advisor to the President."[248]

On October 26, the Committees sent a letter to Dr. Kupperman's personal attorneys, stating:

> In light of the direction from the White House, which lacks any valid legal basis, the Committees shall consider your client's defiance of a congressional subpoena as additional evidence of the President's obstruction of the House's impeachment inquiry.[249]

Later that day, Dr. Kupperman's personal attorney sent a letter to Committee staff, stating: "The proper course for Dr. Kupperman, we respectfully submit, is to lay the conflicting positions before the Court and abide by the Court's judgment as to which is correct."[250] On October 27, Dr. Kupperman's personal attorney sent a letter to Committee staff, writing: "If your clients' position on the merits of this issue is correct, it will prevail in court, and Dr. Kupperman, I assure you again, will comply with the Court's judgment."[251]

On November 5, the Committees sent a letter to Dr. Kupperman's personal attorneys withdrawing the subpoena, stating:

> The question whether the Executive Branch's "absolute immunity" theory has any basis in law is currently before the court in *Committee on the Judiciary v. McGahn*, No. 19-cv-2379 (D.D.C. filed Aug. 7, 2019). In addition to not suffering from the jurisdictional flaws in Dr. Kupperman's suit, *McGahn* is procedurally much further along.[252]

On November 8, Dr. Kupperman's personal attorney sent a letter to Douglas Letter, the General Counsel of the House of Representatives, stating that Dr. Kupperman stands ready to testify "if the Judiciary resolves the conflict in favor of the Legislative Branch's position respecting such testimony."[253]

On November 25, the district court in *McGahn* held that "with respect to senior-level presidential aides, absolute immunity from compelled congressional process simply does not exist." The court explained there is "no basis in the law" for a claim of absolute immunity regardless of the position of the aides in question or whether they "are privy to national security matters, or work solely on domestic issues."[254] To date and notwithstanding the ruling in *McGahn* as it relates to Presidential aides who "are privy to national security matters," Dr. Kupperman continues to refuse to testify, and his case remains pending in federal court.[255]

Russell T. Vought, Acting Director, Office of Management and Budget

On October 11, the Committees sent a letter to Russell T. Vought, the Acting Director of OMB, seeking his appearance at a deposition on October 25.[256] On October 21, an attorney at OMB sent an email to Committee staff stating:

> Per the White House Counsel's October 8, 2019 letter, the President has directed that "[c]onsistent with the duties of the President of the United States, and in particular his obligation to preserve the rights of future occupants of his office, [he] cannot permit his Administration to participate in this partisan inquiry under these circumstances." Therefore, Acting Director Vought will not be participating in Friday's deposition.[257]

That same day, Mr. Vought publicly stated:

> I saw some Fake News over the weekend to correct. As the WH letter made clear two weeks ago, OMB officials—myself and Mike Duffey—will not be complying with deposition requests this week. #shamprocess.[258]

On October 25, the Committees sent a letter transmitting a subpoena compelling Mr. Vought's appearance at a deposition on November 6.[259]

On November 4, Jason A. Yaworske, the Associate Director for Legislative Affairs at OMB, sent a letter to Chairman Schiff stating:

> The Office of Management and Budget (OMB) reasserts its position that, as directed by the White House Counsel's October 8, 2019, letter, OMB will not participate in this partisan and unfair impeachment inquiry. ... Therefore, Mr. Vought, Mr. Duffey, and Mr. McCormack will not appear at their respective depositions without being permitted to bring agency counsel.[260]

On November 5, Mr. Vought did not appear for the scheduled deposition, in defiance of the Committees' subpoena. The Committees met and Chairman Schiff acknowledged Mr. Vought's absence, stating:

> On Monday of this week, OMB reasserted its position that, quote, "as directed by the White House Counsel's October 8, 2019, letter, OMB will not participate in this partisan and unfair impeachment inquiry," unquote. OMB argues that the impeachment inquiry lacks basic due process protections and relies on OLC opinion that the committee cannot

lawfully bar agency counsel from depositions. This new and shifting rationale from the White House, like the others it has used to attempt to block witnesses from appearing to provide testimony about the President's misconduct, has no basis in law or the Constitution and is a serious affront to decades of precedent in which Republicans and Democrats have used exactly the same procedures to depose executive branch officials without agency counsel present, including some of the most senior aides to multiple previous Presidents.[261]

To date, Mr. Vought has not changed his position or contacted the Committees about compliance with the subpoena.

Michael Duffey, Associate Director for National Security Programs, Office of Management and Budget

On October 11, the Committees sent a letter to Michael Duffey, the Associate Director for National Security Programs at OMB, seeking his appearance at a deposition on October 23.[262]

On October 21, an attorney at OMB sent an email to Committee staff stating:

Per the White House Counsel's October 8, 2019 letter, the President has directed that "[c]onsistent with the duties of the President of the United States, and in particular his obligation to preserve the rights of future occupants of his office, [he] cannot permit his Administration to participate in this partisan inquiry under these circumstances." Therefore, Mike Duffey will not be participating in Wednesday's deposition.[263]

On October 25, the Committees sent a letter transmitting a subpoena compelling Mr. Duffey to appear at a deposition on November 5, 2019, stating:

Your failure or refusal to appear at the deposition, including at the direction or behest of the President or the White House, shall constitute evidence of obstruction of the House's impeachment inquiry and may be used as an adverse inference against the President.[264]

On November 4, Jason A. Yaworske, the Associate Director for Legislative Affairs at OMB, sent a letter to Chairman Schiff stating that, "as directed by the White House Counsel's October 8, 2019, letter," Mr. Duffey will not appear at his deposition.[265]

On November 5, Mr. Duffey did not appear for the scheduled deposition, in defiance of the Committees' subpoena. The Committees met and Chairman Schiff acknowledged Mr. Duffey's absence, stating:

This effort by the President to attempt to block Mr. Duffey from appearing can only be interpreted as a further effort by the President and the White House to obstruct the impeachment inquiry and Congress's lawful and constitutional functions.[266]

To date, Mr. Duffey has not changed his position or contacted the Committees about compliance with the subpoena.

Brian McCormack, Associate Director for Natural Resources, Energy, and Science, Office of Management and Budget

On October 24, the Committees sent a letter to Brian McCormack, the Associate Director for Natural Resources, Energy, and Science at OMB, seeking his appearance at a deposition on November 4.[267]

On November 1, the Committees sent a letter transmitting a subpoena compelling Mr. McCormack's appearance at a deposition on November 4.[268]

On November 4, Jason A. Yaworske, the Associate Director for Legislative Affairs at OMB, sent a letter to Chairman Schiff stating that, "as directed by the White House Counsel's October 8, 2019, letter," Mr. McCormack will not appear at his deposition.[269]

On November 4, Mr. McCormack did not appear for the scheduled deposition, in defiance of the Committees' subpoena. The Committees met and Chairman Schiff acknowledged Mr. McCormack's absence, stating:

> At approximately 11:30 a.m. today, committee staff received via email a letter from the Associate Director for Legislative Affairs at OMB. The letter states that, quote, "As directed by the White House counsel's October 8, 2019, letter," unquote, OMB will not participate in the House's impeachment inquiry. The letter further states that, based on the advice of the Office of Legal Counsel that, quote, "the committee cannot lawfully bar agency counsel from these depositions," unquote, Mr. McCormack will not appear at his deposition today without agency counsel present. As Mr. McCormack was informed, the committees may consider his noncompliance with a subpoena as evidence in a future contempt proceeding. His failure or refusal to appear, moreover, shall constitute evidence of obstruction of the House's impeachment inquiry and may be used as an adverse inference against the President.[270]

To date, Mr. McCormack has not changed his position or contacted the Committees about compliance with the subpoena.

T. Ulrich Brechbuhl, Counselor, Department of State

On September 13, the Committees sent a letter to Secretary of State Mike Pompeo seeking transcribed interviews with Counselor T. Ulrich Brechbuhl and other officials.[271] The Committees received no direct, substantive response to this letter.

On September 27, the Committees sent a letter informing Secretary Pompeo that Mr. Brechbuhl's deposition was being scheduled on October 8, stating:

On September 13, the Committees wrote to request that you make State Department employees available for transcribed interviews. We asked you to provide, by September 20, dates by which the employees would be made available for transcribed interviews. You failed to comply with the Committees' request.[272]

That same day, the Committees sent a letter directly to Mr. Brechbuhl seeking his appearance at a deposition on October 8.[273]

On October 1, Secretary Pompeo sent a letter to the Committees stating, "Based on the profound procedural and legal deficiencies noted above, the Committee's requested dates for depositions are not feasible."[274]

Later that day, the Committees sent a letter to Deputy Secretary of State John J. Sullivan stating that the State Department "must immediately halt all efforts to interfere with the testimony of State Department witnesses before Congress."[275]

On October 2, Mr. Brechbuhl's personal attorney sent an email to Committee staff stating:

> My law firm is in the process of being formally retained to assist Mr. Brechbuhl in connection with this matter. It will take us some time to complete those logistics, review the request and associated request for documents, and to meet with our client to insure he is appropriately prepared for any deposition. It will not be possible to accomplish those tasks before October 8, 2019. Thus, as I am sure that you can understand, Mr. Brechbuhl will not be able to appear on that date as he requires a sufficient opportunity to consult with counsel. Moreover, given the concerns expressed in Secretary Pompeo's letter of October 1, 2019, to Chairman Engel, any participation in a deposition would need to be coordinated with our stakeholders.[276]

On October 8, Committee staff sent an email to Mr. Brechbuhl's personal attorney stating: "The Committees have agreed to reschedule Mr. Brechbuhl's deposition to Thursday, October 17. Please confirm that Mr. Brechbuhl intends to appear voluntarily."[277] On October 9, Committee staff sent an email to Mr. Brechbuhl's personal attorney asking him to "confirm by COB today whether Mr. Brechbuhl intends to appear voluntarily."[278] Later that day, Mr. Brechbuhl's personal attorney sent an email to Committee staff stating, "I am still seeking clarification from the State Department regarding this deposition."[279]

On October 25, the Committees sent a letter to Mr. Brechbuhl's personal attorney transmitting a subpoena compelling Mr. Brechbuhl's appearance at a deposition on November 6.[280]

On November 5, Mr. Brechbuhl's personal attorney sent a letter to the Committees stating:

> Mr. Brechbuhl respects the important Constitutional powers vested in the United States Congress. And, indeed, he would welcome the opportunity to address through testimony

242

an existing inaccuracy in the public record—the false claim that Mr. Brechbuhl in any way personally participated in the telephone call between President Trump and President Zelensky that occurred on July 25, 2019. However, Mr. Brechbuhl has received a letter of instruction from the State Department, directing that he not appear. The State Department letter of instruction asserts significant Executive Branch interests as the basis for direction not to appear and also asserts that the subpoena Mr. Brechbuhl received is invalid. The letter is supported by analysis from the United States Department of Justice. We are also aware that litigation has recently been initiated in the United States District Court for the District of Columbia that may bear on resolving the significant issues now arising between the Committees and the President. Given these circumstances, Mr. Brechbuhl is not able to appear on November 6, 2019.[281]

On November 6, Mr. Brechbuhl did not appear for the scheduled deposition, in defiance of the Committees' subpoena. The Committees met and Chairman Schiff acknowledged Mr. Brechbuhl's absence, stating:

The committees requested a copy of the State Department's letter and the Department of Justice analysis, but Mr. Brechbuhl's attorney has not responded. While the letter from Mr. Brechbuhl's attorney provides only vague references to unidentified executive branch interests and a DOJ analysis as the basis for the State Department's blocking of Mr. Brechbuhl's testimony, the Department's latest obstruction of this inquiry appears to be predicated on the opinion issued by the Department of Justice Office of Legal Counsel just last Friday, November 1, well after the subpoena was issued to Mr. Brechbuhl. It is noteworthy and telling that the OLC issued this opinion only after multiple State Department officials testified in this inquiry, both voluntarily and pursuant to subpoena, all without agency counsel present. Indeed, this morning, the third-highest-ranking official at the State Department, Under Secretary David Hale, appeared and has begun testifying in accordance with his legal obligations pursuant to a subpoena.[282]

The Committees sent Mr. Brechbuhl's personal attorney two separate inquiries asking him to provide a copy of the "letter of instruction" that Mr. Brechbuhl claimed to have received from the State Department directing him to defy a congressional subpoena.[283] Mr. Brechbuhl's personal attorney furnished the Committees with a copy of the letter on December 2. The State Department's letter to Mr. Brechbuhl is dated November 4, 2019.[284]

To date, Mr. Brechbuhl has not changed his position or contacted the Committees about compliance with the subpoena.

Secretary Rick Perry, Department of Energy

On November 1, the Committees sent a letter to Secretary of Energy Rick Perry seeking his appearance at a deposition on November 6, stating:

Your failure or refusal to appear at the deposition, including at the direction or behest of the President or the White House, shall constitute evidence of obstruction of the House's impeachment inquiry and may be used as an adverse inference against the President.[285]

On November 5, an attorney at the Department of Energy sent a letter to the Committees stating:

> Please be advised that the Secretary will not appear on Wednesday, November 6, 2019, at 2:00 pm for a deposition to be conducted jointly by the Permanent Select Committee on Intelligence, the Committee on Foreign Affairs, and the Committee on Oversight and Reform.[286]

To date, Secretary Perry has not changed his position or come forward to testify.

5.   The President's Unsuccessful Attempts to Block Key Witnesses

Despite President Trump's explicit orders that no Executive Branch employees should cooperate with the House's impeachment inquiry and efforts by federal agencies to limit the testimony of those who did, multiple key officials complied with duly authorized subpoenas and provided critical testimony at depositions and public hearings. These officials adhered to the rule of law and obeyed lawful subpoenas.

Overview

Despite President Trump's orders that no Executive Branch employees should cooperate with the House's impeachment inquiry, multiple key officials complied with duly authorized subpoenas and provided critical testimony at depositions and public hearings. These officials not only served their nation honorably, but they fulfilled their oath to support and defend the Constitution of the United States.

In addition to the President's broad orders seeking to prohibit all Executive Branch employees from testifying, many of these witnesses were personally directed by senior political appointees not to cooperate with the House's impeachment inquiry. These directives frequently cited or enclosed copies of Mr. Cipollone's October 8 letter conveying the President's order not to comply.

For example, the State Department, relying on President Trump's order, attempted to block Ambassador Marie Yovanovitch from testifying, but she fulfilled her legal obligations by appearing at a deposition on October 11 and a hearing on November 15. More than a dozen current and former officials followed her courageous example by testifying at depositions and public hearings over the course of the last two months. The testimony from these witnesses produced overwhelming and clear evidence of President Trump's misconduct, which is described in detail in Section I of this report.

Ambassador Marie Yovanovitch, Former
U.S. Ambassador to Ukraine, Department of State

On September 13, the Committees sent a letter to Secretary of State Mike Pompeo seeking a transcribed interview with Ambassador Marie Yovanovitch and other State Department officials.[287] The Committees received no direct, substantive response to this letter.

On September 27, the Committees sent a letter informing Secretary Pompeo that Ambassador Yovanovitch's deposition was being scheduled on October 2, stating:

On September 13, the Committees wrote to request that you make State Department employees available for transcribed interviews. We asked you to provide, by September 20, dates by which the employees would be made available for transcribed interviews. You failed to comply with the Committees' request.[288]

Also on September 27, the Committees sent a letter directly to Ambassador Yovanovitch seeking her appearance at a deposition on October 2.[289]

On October 1, Secretary Pompeo sent a letter to the Committees stating:

Therefore, the five officials subject to your letter may not attend any interview or deposition without counsel from the Executive Branch present to ensure that the Executive Branch's constitutional authority to control the disclosure of confidential information, including deliberative matters and diplomatic communications, is not impaired.[290]

After further discussions with Ambassador Yovanovitch's counsel, her deposition was rescheduled for October 11. On October 10, Brian Bulatao, the Under Secretary of State for Management, sent a letter to Ambassador Yovanovitch's personal attorney directing Ambassador Yovanovitch not to appear for her deposition and enclosing Mr. Cipollone's October 8 letter stating that President Trump and his Administration would not participate in the House's impeachment inquiry. Mr. Bulatao's letter stated:

Accordingly, in accordance with applicable law, I write on behalf of the Department of State, pursuant to the President's instruction reflected in Mr. Cipollone's letter, to instruct your client (as a current employee of the Department of State), consistent with Mr. Cipollone's letter, not to appear before the Committees under the present circumstances.[291]

That same day, October 10, when asked whether he intended to block Ambassador Yovanovitch from testifying the next day, President Trump stated: "You know, I don't think people should be allowed. You have to run a country, I don't think you should be allowed to do that."[292]

On the morning of Ambassador Yovanovitch's deposition on October 11, the Committees sent a letter to her personal attorney transmitting a subpoena compelling her appearance, stating:

In light of recent attempts by the Administration to direct your client not to appear voluntarily for the deposition, the enclosed subpoena now compels your client's mandatory appearance at today's deposition on October 11, 2019.[293]

Later on October 11, Ambassador Yovanovitch's personal attorney sent a letter to Mr. Bulatao, stating:

In my capacity as counsel for Ambassador Marie Yovanovitch, I have received your letter of October 10, 2019, directing the Ambassador not to appear voluntarily for her scheduled deposition testimony on October 11, 2019 before the Committee on Foreign Affairs, the Permanent Select Committee on Intelligence, and the Committee on Oversight and Reform in connection with the House of Representatives's impeachment inquiry. Just this morning, the Ambassador received a subpoena issued by the House Permanent Select Committee on Intelligence, requiring her to appear for the deposition as scheduled. Although the Ambassador has faithfully and consistently honored her professional duties as a State Department employee—including at all times following her abrupt termination as U.S. Ambassador to Ukraine—she is unable to obey your most recent directive. As the recipient of a duly issued congressional subpoena, Ambassador Yovanovitch is, in my judgment, legally obligated to attend the depositions as scheduled.[294]

Ambassador Yovanovitch participated in the deposition on October 11, in compliance with the Committees' subpoena.[295] During her deposition, Ambassador Yovanovitch's personal attorney confirmed that "she received a direction by the Under Secretary to decline to appear voluntarily."[296]

On November 15, the Committees transmitted a subpoena to Ambassador Yovanovitch compelling her to testify at a public hearing of the Intelligence Committee that same day.[297] Ambassador Yovanovitch complied with the Committees' subpoena and testified at the public hearing. During the hearing, Chairman Schiff acknowledged Ambassador Yovanovitch's compliance, stating:

> Ambassador, I want to thank you for your decades of service. I want to thank you, as Mr. Maloney said, for being the first one through the gap. What you did in coming forward and answering a lawful subpoena was to give courage to others that also witnessed wrongdoing, that they, too, could show the same courage that you have, that they could stand up, speak out, answer questions, they could endure whatever threats, insults may come their way. And so in your long and distinguished career you have done another great public service in answering the call of our subpoena and testifying before us today.[298]

Ambassador Gordon Sondland, U.S. Ambassador to the European Union, Department of State

On September 27, 2019, the Committees sent a letter informing Secretary Pompeo that Ambassador Gordon Sondland's deposition was being scheduled on October 10.[299] That same day, the Committees sent a letter directly to Ambassador Sondland seeking his appearance at the deposition.[300] On October 1, Secretary Pompeo sent a letter to the Committees stating that Ambassador Sondland "may not attend" the deposition.[301]

After further discussions with Ambassador Sondland's personal attorney, his deposition was rescheduled for October 8. On October 7, Mr. Bulatao sent a letter to Ambassador Sondland's personal attorney, stating:

> Based on consultations with the White House, the State Department hereby instructs your client, Ambassador Gordon Sondland, not to appear tomorrow for his voluntary deposition based on the Executive Branch confidentiality interests remaining to be addressed, including, in particular, the Committee's refusal to permit agency counsel to appear.[302]

On October 8, Ambassador Sondland's personal attorney sent an email to the Committees stating:

> I am incredibly disappointed to report that, overnight, the State Department advised that it will direct Ambassador Sondland not to appear before the Committee this morning. While we have not yet gotten written confirmation of that direction, we wanted to advise you of this development at the earliest opportunity. As the sitting US Ambassador to the EU and employee of the State Department, Ambassador Sondland is required to follow this direction. I hope that whatever concerns the Department has can be resolved promptly and that Ambassador Sondland's testimony can be scheduled at the earliest opportunity. I am very sorry for the inexcusably late notice, but we are sharing this with you as soon as it was confirmed to us. Ambassador Sondland is personally disappointed that he will not be able to answer the Committee's questions this morning.[303]

On October 8, the Committees sent a letter to Ambassador Sondland transmitting a subpoena compelling his appearance at a deposition on October 16, stating:

> The Committees have not received any communication directly from the White House or the State Department about this matter. In light of Secretary Pompeo's direct intervention to block your appearance before our Committees, we are left with no choice but to compel your appearance at a deposition pursuant to the enclosed subpoena.[304]

On October 14, the Committees sent a letter to Ambassador Sondland stating:

> We hereby write to memorialize our agreement with your counsel, Mr. Robert Luskin, Esq., to adjourn the date and time of your document production and deposition to October 17, 2019, at 9:30 a.m. at the Capitol, HVC-304.[305]

Ambassador Sondland participated in the deposition on October 17, in compliance with the Committees' subpoena.[306] During the deposition, Ambassador Sondland's personal attorney stated:

> But we also wish to emphasize that it's his belief, and ours, that the Committee should have access to all relevant documents, and he regrets that they have not been provided in advance of his testimony. Having those documents would lead to a more fulsome and accurate inquiry into the matters at hand. Indeed, Ambassador Sondland has not had access to all of the State Department records that would help him refresh his recollection in anticipation of this testimony.[307]

During the deposition, Ambassador Sondland stated:

> I was truly disappointed that the State Department prevented me at the last minute from testifying earlier on October 8, 2019. But your issuance of a subpoena has supported my appearance here today, and I'm pleased to provide the following testimony.[308]

On November 4, Ambassador Sondland's personal attorney transmitted to the Committees a sworn declaration from Ambassador Sondland, which supplemented his deposition testimony and noted that despite "repeated requests to the White House and the State Department," he still had not been granted access to records he sought to review to determine if he could "provide more complete testimony to assist Congress."[309]

On November 20, the Committees transmitted a subpoena to Ambassador Sondland compelling him to testify at a public hearing of the Intelligence Committee that same day.[310] Ambassador Sondland complied with the Committees' subpoena and testified at the public hearing. During the hearing, Ambassador Sondland described the direction he received from the White House:

> Q: Ambassador Sondland, in your deposition, you lamented, quote: I was truly disappointed that the State Department prevented me at the last minute from testifying earlier on October 8, 2019, but your issuance of a subpoena has supported my appearance here today, and I am pleased to provide the following testimony. So it is clear that the White House, the State Department did not want you to testify at that deposition. Is that correct?
>
> A: That is correct.
>
> Q: And since then, you have on numerous occasions during your opening statement today indicated that you have not been able to access documents in the State Department. Is that correct?
>
> A: Correct.
>
> Q: So you have been hampered in your ability to provide testimony to this committee. Is that correct?
>
> A: I have been hampered to provide completely accurate testimony without the benefit of those documents.[311]

George P. Kent, Deputy Assistant Secretary of State, Bureau of European and Eurasian Affairs, Department of State

On September 13, 2019, the Committees sent a letter to Secretary of State Pompeo seeking a transcribed interview with Deputy Assistant Secretary of State George Kent and other State Department officials.[312] The Committees received no direct, substantive response to this letter.

On September 27, the Committees sent a letter informing Secretary Pompeo that Mr. Kent's deposition was being scheduled on October 7.[313] That same day, the Committees sent a letter directly to Mr. Kent seeking his appearance at the deposition on that date.[314] Later that day, Mr. Kent sent an email to Committee staff acknowledging receipt of the Committees' request and copying an official from the Office of Legislative Affairs at the Department of State.[315] On October 1, Secretary Pompeo sent a letter to the Committees stating that Mr. Kent "may not attend" the deposition.[316]

After consulting with Mr. Kent's personal attorney, the Committees rescheduled his deposition for October 15.[317] On October 10, Under Secretary Bulatao sent a letter to Mr. Kent's personal attorney enclosing the White House Counsel's letter of October 8, and stating:

> I write on behalf of the Department of State, pursuant to the President's instruction reflected in Mr. Cipollone's letter, to instruct your client (as a current employee of the Department of State), consistent with Mr. Cipollone's letter, not to appear before the Committees under the present circumstances.[318]

On October 15, the Committees sent a letter to Mr. Kent's personal attorney transmitting a subpoena compelling him to appear at a deposition on that date.[319]

Mr. Kent participated in the deposition on October 15, in compliance with the Committees' subpoena.[320] During the deposition, he stated:

> As you all know, I am appearing here in response to your congressional subpoena. If I did not appear I would have been exposed to being held in contempt. At the same time, I have been instructed by my employer, the U.S. Department of State, not to appear. I do not know the Department of State's views on disregarding that order.[321]

On November 13, the Committees transmitted a subpoena to Mr. Kent compelling him to testify at a public hearing before the Intelligence Committee on that day.[322] Mr. Kent complied with the Committees' subpoena and testified at the public hearing. During the hearing, Mr. Kent described the direction he received from the White House, stating that he "received, initially, a letter directing me not to appear. And once the committees issued a subpoena, I was under legal obligation to appear, and I am here today under subpoena."[323]

Ambassador William B. Taylor, Jr., Chargé d'Affaires for U.S. Embassy in Kyiv, Department of State

On October 4, 2019, the Committees sent a letter to Deputy Secretary of State John Sullivan seeking a deposition with Ambassador William B. Taylor, Jr. on October 15.[324] That same day, the Committees sent a letter directly to Ambassador Taylor seeking his appearance at the deposition.[325]

On October 14, after consulting with Ambassador Taylor's counsel, the Committees sent a letter to Ambassador Taylor stating: "We hereby write to adjourn the date and time of your deposition to Tuesday, October 22, 2019, at 9:30 a.m. at the Capitol, HVC-304."[326]

On October 22, the Committees transmitted a subpoena to Ambassador Taylor's personal attorneys compelling Ambassador Taylor to appear at a deposition on that date, stating:

> In light of recent attempts by the Administration to direct witnesses not to appear voluntarily for depositions, the enclosed subpoena compels your client's mandatory appearance at today's deposition.[327]

Ambassador Taylor participated in the deposition on October 22, in compliance with the Committees' subpoena. During the deposition, Ambassador Taylor's personal attorney stated, in regard to communications with the Department of State:

> They sent us the directive that said he should not appear under I think the quote is under the present circumstances. We told the majority that we could not appear; he'd been instructed not to. We saw the pattern.[328]

On November 13, the Committees transmitted a subpoena to Ambassador Taylor compelling him to testify at a public hearing of the Intelligence Committee that same day.[329] Ambassador Taylor complied with the Committees' subpoena and testified at the public hearing. During the hearing, Ambassador Taylor described the direction he received from the State Department:

> Q: Ambassador, were you also asked not to be part of the deposition?
> A: Mr. Quigley, I was told by the State Department: Don't appear under these circumstances. That was in the letter to me. And when I got the subpoena, exactly as Mr. Kent said, that was different circumstances and obeyed a legal subpoena. So, yes, sir, I'm here for that reason.[330]

Catherine Croft and Christopher Anderson, Department of State

On October 24, 2019, the Committees sent letters to the personal attorney representing two State Department officials, Catherine Croft and Christopher Anderson, seeking their attendance at depositions on October 30 and November 1, respectively.[331]

On October 25, their attorney sent a letter to the Committees acknowledging receipt of the Committees' requests and stating that "we are in the process of contacting the Office of the Legal Advisor of the Department of State in an effort to learn the disposition of that Office with regard to the Committee's request."[332]

On October 28, Under Secretary Bulatao sent letters to the personal attorney for Ms. Croft and Mr. Anderson. Both letters enclosed the White House Counsel's October 8 letter and stated:

> Pursuant to Mr. Cipollone's letter and in light of these defects, we are writing to inform you and Ms. Croft of the Administration-wide direction that Executive Branch personnel "cannot participate in [the impeachment] inquiry under these circumstances."[333]

On October 30, the Committees transmitted subpoenas to the personal attorney for Ms. Croft and Mr. Anderson compelling their appearance at depositions on October 30, stating:

> In light of recent attempts by the Administration to direct witnesses not to appear voluntarily for depositions, the enclosed subpoenas compel your clients' mandatory appearance.[334]

Ms. Croft and Mr. Anderson participated in their depositions on October 30, in compliance with the Committees' subpoenas.[335] During Ms. Croft's deposition, her personal attorney stated:

> On October 28th, 2019, Ms. Croft received a letter through her lawyers from Under Secretary of State Brian Bulatao, in which we were instructed that Ms. Croft cannot participate in the impeachment inquiry being conducted by the House of Representatives and these committees. Under Secretary Bulatao's letter stated that these instructions were issued pursuant to a directive from the Office of White House Counsel. Nonetheless, Ms. Croft has been served with a valid subpoena, and so she is obliged to be here today.[336]

During Mr. Anderson's deposition, his personal attorney stated:

> On October 28th, 2019, Mr. Anderson received a letter, through his lawyers, from Under Secretary of State Brian Bulatao in which we were instructed that Mr. Anderson cannot participate in the impeachment inquiry being conducted by the House of Representatives and these committees. Under Secretary Bulatao's letter stated that these instructions were issued pursuant to a directive from the Office of White House Counsel. Nonetheless, Mr. Anderson has been served with a valid subpoena, and so he is obliged to be here today.[337]

Laura K. Cooper, Deputy Assistant Secretary of Defense for Russia, Ukraine, and Eurasia, Department of Defense

On October 11, the Committees sent a letter to Deputy Assistant Secretary of Defense Laura K. Cooper seeking her attendance at a deposition on October 18.[338]

After consulting with Ms. Cooper's personal attorney, the Committees rescheduled her deposition for October 23.

On October 22, Deputy Secretary of Defense David L. Norquist sent a letter to Ms. Cooper's personal attorney, stating:

> This letter informs you and Ms. Cooper of the Administration-wide direction that Executive Branch personnel "cannot participate in [the impeachment] inquiry under these circumstances" [Tab C]. In the event that the Committees issue a subpoena to compel Ms. Cooper's appearance, you should be aware that the Supreme Court has held, in *United States v. Rumely*, 345 U.S. 41 (1953), that a person cannot be sanctioned for refusing to comply with a congressional subpoena unauthorized by House Rule or Resolution.[339]

On October 23, the Committees sent an email transmitting a subpoena compelling Ms. Cooper to appear at a deposition on that date, stating:

In light of recent attempts by the Administration to direct witnesses not to appear voluntarily for depositions, the enclosed subpoena compels your client's mandatory appearance at today's deposition.[340]

Ms. Cooper participated in the deposition on October 23, in compliance with the Committees' subpoena.[341]

During her deposition, Ms. Cooper stated with regard to the Department of Defense, "They instructed me yesterday not to participate."[342]

On November 20, the Committees transmitted a subpoena to Ms. Cooper compelling her to testify at a public hearing before the Intelligence Committee on that day.[343] Ms. Cooper complied with the Committees' subpoena and testified at the public hearing.[344]

Mark Sandy, Deputy Associate Director of National Security Programs, Office of Management and Budget

On November 5, the Committees sent a letter to Mark Sandy, the Deputy Associate Director of National Security Programs at OMB, seeking his appearance at a deposition on November 8.[345] On November 6, Mr. Sandy responded to confirm receipt of the Committees' letter.[346]

On November 7, an attorney at OMB sent an email to Committee staff stating:

In light of the Committee's rules that prohibit agency counsel from being present in a deposition of an executive branch witness and consistent with the November 1, 2019 OLC letter opinion addressing this issue, OMB has directed Mr. Sandy not to appear at tomorrow's deposition.[347]

After consulting with Mr. Sandy's personal attorney, the Committees rescheduled his deposition for November 16.

On November 16, the Committees sent an email transmitting a subpoena compelling Mr. Sandy to appear at a deposition on that date, stating:

In light of recent attempts by the Administration to direct witnesses not to appear voluntarily for depositions, the enclosed subpoena compels your client's mandatory appearance.[348]

Mr. Sandy participated in the deposition on November 16, in compliance with the Committees' subpoena.[349] During his deposition, Mr. Sandy also testified that the Administration sent his personal attorney an official communication with further direction, stating: "It did direct me to have my personal counsel ask for a postponement until agency counsel could accompany me."[350]

Dr. Fiona Hill, Former Deputy Assistant to the President and
Senior Director for Europe and Russian Affairs, National Security Council

On October 9, 2019, the Committees sent a letter seeking Dr. Hill's testimony at a deposition on October 14.[351] On October 13, Dr. Hill's personal attorney informed the White House that she intended to appear at the scheduled deposition.[352] On October 14, the White House sent a letter to Dr. Hill's personal attorney stating that "Dr. Hill is not authorized to reveal or release any classified information or any information subject to executive privilege."[353] Also on October 14, the Committees sent Dr. Hill a subpoena seeking her testimony the same day.[354] Dr. Hill complied and participated in the deposition.[355]

On November 18, Dr. Hill's personal attorney sent a letter to the White House stating that Dr. Hill had been invited to provide testimony at a public hearing on November 21, and stating: "We continue to disagree with regard to the parameters of executive privilege as you articulated it on October 14 and our prior telephone calls."[356] On November 20, the White House sent a letter to Dr. Hill's personal attorney stating that Dr. Hill "continues to be bound by important obligations to refrain from disclosing classified information or information subject to executive privilege in her upcoming testimony before the House Permanent Select Committee on Intelligence."[357] On November 21, the Committees sent Dr. Hill a subpoena seeking her testimony the same day.[358] Dr. Hill also complied with this subpoena and testified at the public hearing.[359]

Lieutenant Colonel Alexander S. Vindman,
Director for Ukraine, National Security Council

On October 16, 2019, the Committees sent a letter seeking Lt. Col. Alexander Vindman's testimony at a deposition on October 24.[360] After discussions with Lt. Col. Vindman's personal attorneys, the deposition was rescheduled to October 29. On October 29, the Committees sent Lt. Col. Vindman a subpoena seeking his testimony the same day.[361] Lt. Col. Vindman complied.[362] In addition, on November 19, the Committees conveyed a subpoena seeking Lt. Col. Vindman's testimony at a public hearing that same day.[363] Lt. Col. Vindman also complied with this subpoena and testified at the public hearing.[364]

Timothy Morrison, Former Deputy Assistant to the President
and Senior Director for Europe and Russia, National Security Council

On October 16, 2019, the Committees sent a letter to Timothy Morrison seeking his testimony at a deposition on October 25.[365] After discussions with Mr. Morrison's personal attorney, the deposition was rescheduled to October 31. On October 31, the Committees sent Mr. Morrison a subpoena seeking his testimony the same day.[366] Mr. Morrison complied.[367] In addition, on November 19, the Committees conveyed a subpoena seeking Mr. Morrison's testimony at a public hearing that same day.[368] Mr. Morrison also complied with this subpoena and testified at the public hearing.[369]

David Hale, Under Secretary for Political Affairs, Department of State

On November 1, 2019, the Committees sent a letter seeking Under Secretary David Hale's testimony at a deposition on November 6.[370] On November 5, Mr. Hale's counsel wrote to the Committees, stating that Mr. Hale would be willing to testify pursuant to a subpoena.[371]

On November 6, the Committees sent Mr. Hale a subpoena seeking his testimony the same day.[372] Mr. Hale complied.[373] In addition, on November 20, the Committees conveyed a subpoena seeking Mr. Hale's testimony at a public hearing that same day.[374] Mr. Hale also complied with this subpoena and testified at the public hearing.[375]

David Holmes, Counselor for Political Affairs at the
U.S. Embassy in Kyiv, Ukraine, Department of State

On November 12, 2019, the Committees sent a letter to Political Counselor David Holmes' personal attorney seeking his testimony at a deposition on November 15.[376] On November 15, the Committees conveyed a subpoena to Mr. Holmes' personal attorney seeking his testimony the same day.[377] Mr. Holmes complied.[378] In addition, on November 21, the Committees conveyed a subpoena seeking Mr. Holmes' testimony at a public hearing that same day.[379] Mr. Holmes also complied with this subpoena and testified at the public hearing.[380]

Ambassador P. Michael McKinley, Former Senior Advisor
to the Secretary of State, Department of State

On October 12, 2019, Committee staff emailed Ambassador P. Michael McKinley requesting his voluntary participation in a transcribed interview on October 16.[381] On October 14, the Committees sent a letter formalizing this request.[382] On October 16, Ambassador McKinley participated in the scheduled transcribed interview.[383]

Ambassador Philip T. Reeker, Acting Assistant Secretary,
Bureau of European and Eurasian Affairs, Department of State

On October 16, 2019, the Committees sent a letter seeking Ambassador Philip T. Reeker's testimony at a deposition on October 23.[384] On October 25, the Committees sent Ambassador Reeker a subpoena seeking his testimony on October 26.[385] Ambassador Reeker complied and testified at the scheduled deposition.[386]

Ambassador Kurt Volker, Former U.S. Special Representative
for Ukraine Negotiations, Department of State

On September 13, 2019, the Committees wrote a letter to Secretary Pompeo requesting the testimony of four witnesses, including Ambassador Kurt Volker.[387] On September 27, the Committees sent a follow up letter to Secretary Pompeo, noting that Ambassador Volker's deposition had been scheduled for October 3.[388] On that same day, the Committees sent a letter directly to Ambassador Volker, seeking his testimony at the deposition scheduled for October 3.[389]

On October 1, Secretary Pompeo responded to the Committees, refusing to make Ambassador Volker available on the requested date.[390] On October 2, the Department of State wrote a letter to Ambassador Volker's counsel instructing Ambassador Volker not to reveal classified or privileged information and prohibiting Ambassador Volker from producing any government documents.[391]

On October 2, Ambassador Volker produced copies of text messages in response to the Committees' request.[392] On October 3, Ambassador Volker voluntarily participated in a transcribed interview.[393] In addition, on November 19, Ambassador Volker testified voluntarily at a public hearing.[394]

Jennifer Williams, Special Advisor for Europe and Russia, Office of the Vice President

On November 4, 2019, the Committees sent a letter to Jennifer Williams seeking her testimony at a deposition on November 7.[395] On November 7, the Committees sent Ms. Williams a subpoena seeking her testimony the same day.[396] Ms. Williams complied.[397] On November 11, Ms. Williams sent a letter to Chairman Schiff to make one amendment to her deposition testimony.[398] In addition, on November 19, the Committees conveyed a subpoena seeking Ms. William's testimony at a public hearing on November 19.[399] Ms. Williams also complied with this subpoena and testified at the public hearing.[400]

6. The President's Intimidation of Witnesses

> *President Trump publicly attacked and intimidated witnesses who came forward to comply with duly authorized subpoenas and testify about his conduct. The President also threatened and attacked an Intelligence Community whistleblower.*

Overview

President Trump engaged in a brazen effort to publicly attack and intimidate witnesses who came forward to comply with duly authorized subpoenas and testify about his conduct, raising grave concerns about potential violations of the federal obstruction statute and other criminal laws intended to protect witnesses appearing before Congressional proceedings. President Trump issued threats, openly discussed possible retaliation, made insinuations about witnesses' character and patriotism, and subjected them to mockery and derision. The President's attacks were broadcast to millions of Americans—including witnesses' families, friends, and coworkers—and his actions drew criticism from across the political spectrum, including from his own Republican supporters.

It is a federal crime to intimidate or seek to intimidate any witness appearing before Congress. This statute applies to all citizens, including federal officials. Violations of this law can carry a criminal sentence of up to 20 years in prison.

This campaign of intimidation risks discouraging witnesses from coming forward voluntarily, complying with mandatory subpoenas for documents and testimony, and disclosing evidence that may support consideration of articles of impeachment.

Ambassador Marie Yovanovitch, Former
U.S. Ambassador to Ukraine, Department of State

As discussed above, President Trump removed Marie Yovanovitch as the U.S. Ambassador to Ukraine in May 2019 following a concerted effort by Rudy Giuliani, his associates Lev Parnas and Igor Fruman, and others to spread false conspiracy theories about her. The smearing of the Ambassador was part of the larger campaign undertaken by Mr. Giuliani at President Trump's direction and in his capacity as President Trump's representative. During her deposition on October 11, Ambassador Yovanovitch explained that she felt threatened and "very concerned" after she read President Trump's statements about her during his July 25 call with President Zelensky, including President Trump's claim that "she's going to go through some things."[401]

On November 15, Ambassador Yovanovitch testified at a public hearing that she was "shocked" and "devastated" by the President's statements about her:

> I was shocked and devastated that I would feature in a phone call between two heads of state in such a manner, where President Trump said that I was bad news to another world

leader and that I would be "going through some things." So I was—it was—it was a terrible moment. A person who saw me actually reading the transcript said that the color drained from my face. I think I even had a physical reaction. I think, you know, even now, words kind of fail me.[402]

Ambassador Yovanovitch was also asked about her reaction to the President's comment that she would "go through some things." She acknowledged feeling threatened, stating: "It didn't sound good. It sounded like a threat."[403]

As Ambassador Yovanovitch was in the process of testifying before the Committee, President Trump tweeted an attack against her. He wrote:

> Everywhere Marie Yovanovitch went turned bad. She started off in Somalia, how did that go? Then fast forward to Ukraine, where the new Ukrainian President spoke unfavorably about her in my second phone call with him. It is a U.S. President's absolute right to appoint ambassadors.[404]

During the hearing, Chairman Schiff asked Ambassador Yovanovitch for her reaction to the President's attacks:

> Q: Ambassador, you've shown the courage to come forward today and testify, notwithstanding the fact you were urged by the White House or State Department not to; notwithstanding the fact that, as you testified earlier, the President implicitly threatened you in that call record. And now, the President in real-time is attacking you. What effect do you think that has on other witnesses' willingness to come forward and expose wrongdoing?
> A: Well, it's very intimidating.
> Q: It's designed to intimidate, is it not?
> A: I—I—I mean, I can't speak to what the President is trying to do, but I think the effect is to be intimidating.
> Q: Well, I want to let you know, Ambassador, that some of us here take witness intimidation very, very seriously.[405]

In response to the President's attacks, Rep. Liz Cheney, Chair of the House Republican Caucus, stated that the President "was wrong" and that Ambassador Yovanovitch "clearly is somebody who's been a public servant to the United States for decades and I don't think the President should have done that."[406] Rep. Francis Rooney, also a Republican, stated: "I don't necessarily think it's right to be harassing or beating up on our professional diplomatic service."[407]

Even after these rebukes, the President continued to attack and threaten Ambassador Yovanovitch. For example, in an interview on November 22, President Trump stated: "This was not an angel, this woman, okay? And there are a lot of things that she did that I didn't like. And we will talk about that at some time."[408]

Lieutenant Colonel Alexander S. Vindman,
Director for Ukraine, National Security Council

On October 29, President Trump tweeted that Lt. Col. Alexander Vindman is a "Never Trumper."[409] When asked by a reporter what evidence he had for his claim, the President responded: "We'll be showing that to you real soon. Okay?"[410] President Trump continued attacking Lt. Col. Vindman during his testimony on November 19, seeking to question his loyalty to the United States. The President retweeted: "Lt. Col. Vindman was offered the position of Defense Minister for the Ukrainian Government THREE times!"[411] Allies of the President also questioned Lt. Col. Vindman's loyalty to the country and amplified the smear.[412]

For his part, Lt. Col. Vindman stated during his testimony:

I want to take a moment to recognize the courage of my colleagues who have appeared and are scheduled to appear before this Committee. I want to state that the vile character attacks on these distinguished and honorable public servants is reprehensible.[413]

Ambassador William B. Taylor, Jr., Chargé d'Affaires for
U.S. Embassy in Kyiv, Department of State

On October 23, one day after Ambassador William Taylor's deposition, the President sent a tweet comparing "Never Trumper Republicans" to "human scum."[414] An hour later, he described Ambassador Taylor in a tweet as a "Never Trumper."[415]

On October 25, the President discussed Ambassador Taylor's testimony with reporters, and again dismissed the Ambassador as a "Never Trumper." After a reporter noted that Secretary of State Mike Pompeo had hired Ambassador Taylor, the President responded: "Hey, everybody makes mistakes." He then had the following exchange about Ambassador Taylor:

Q: Do you want him out now as the top diplomat?
A: He's a Never Trumper. His lawyer is the head of the Never Trumpers. They're a dying breed, but they're still there.[416]

On the morning of November 13, just before Ambassador Taylor and George Kent testified at a public hearing, the President tweeted: "NEVER TRUMPERS!"[417]

Jennifer Williams, Special Advisor for
Europe and Russia, Office of the Vice President

On November 17, two days before Jennifer Williams testified at a public hearing, President Trump sent a tweet attacking her and stating that "she should meet with the other Never Trumpers, who I don't know & mostly never even heard of, & work out a better presidential attack!"[418] During the hearing, Rep. Jim Himes asked Ms. Williams what impression the President's tweet had made on her. She responded: "It certainly surprised me. I was not expecting to be called out by name." Rep. Himes noted that the tweet "surprised me, too, and it looks an awful lot like witness intimidation and tampering, and an effort to try to get you to perhaps shape your testimony today."[419]

Threats of Retaliation

The President suggested that witnesses who testified as part of the impeachment inquiry could face retaliation. For example, on November 16, the President sent a pair of tweets indicating that three witnesses appearing before the impeachment inquiry could face dismissals as a result of their testimony. The President tweeted language he attributed to radio host Rush Limbaugh:

"My support for Donald Trump has never been greater than it is right now. It is paramountly obvious watching this, these people have to go. You elected Donald Trump to drain the Swamp, well, dismissing people like Yovanovitch is what that looks like. Dismissing people like Kent ... and Taylor, dismissing everybody involved from the Obama holdover days trying to undermine Trump, getting rid of those people, dismissing them, this is what it looks like. It was never going to be clean, they were never going to sit by idly and just let Trump do this!" Rush L[420]

Intelligence Community Whistleblower

In addition to his relentless attacks on witnesses who testified in connection with the House's impeachment inquiry, the President also repeatedly threatened and attacked a member of the Intelligence Community who filed an anonymous whistleblower complaint raising an "urgent concern" regarding the President's conduct. The whistleblower filed the complaint confidentially with the Inspector General of the Intelligence Community, as authorized by the relevant whistleblower law. Federal law prohibits the Inspector General from revealing the whistleblower's identity.[421] Federal law also protects the whistleblower from retaliation.[422]

On September 9, the Inspector General notified Congress that this individual had filed a credible complaint regarding an "urgent concern," but that the Acting Director of National Intelligence was withholding the complaint from Congress—contrary to his statutory obligation to have submitted the complaint to the congressional intelligence committees by no later than September 2.[423] On September 13, 2019, the Intelligence Committee issued a subpoena to the Acting Director of National Intelligence for the whistleblower's complaint and other records.[424]

On September 26, the Intelligence Committee received the declassified whistleblower complaint and made it available to the public.[425]

That day, the President issued a chilling threat against the whistleblower and those who provided information to the whistleblower regarding the President's misconduct, suggesting that they could face the death penalty for treason. President Trump stated:

I want to know who's the person who gave the whistle-blower the information because that's close to a spy. You know what we used to do in the old days when we were smart with spies and treason, right? We used to handle it a little differently than we do now.[426]

In response, the Committees warned President Trump to stop attacking the whistleblower, stating:

> The President's comments today constitute reprehensible witness intimidation and an attempt to obstruct Congress' impeachment inquiry. We condemn the President's attacks, and we invite our Republican counterparts to do the same because Congress must do all it can to protect this whistleblower, and all whistleblowers. Threats of violence from the leader of our country have a chilling effect on the entire whistleblower process, with grave consequences for our democracy and national security.[427]

Yet the President's attacks did not stop. Instead, he continued to threaten the whistleblower, publicly questioned the whistleblower's motives, disputed the accuracy of the whistleblower's account, and encouraged others to reveal the whistleblower's identity. The President's focus on the whistleblower has been obsessive, with the President making more than 100 public statements about the whistleblower over a period of just two months. For example, the President stated:

- "I want to meet not only my accuser, who presented SECOND & THIRD HAND INFORMATION, but also the person who illegally gave this information, which was largely incorrect, to the 'Whistleblower.' Was this person SPYING on the U.S. President? Big Consequences!"[428]
- "I think it's outrageous that a Whistleblower is a CIA agent."[429]
- "But what they said is he's an Obama person. It was involved with Brennan; Susan Rice, which means Obama. But he was like a big—a big anti-Trump person. Hated Trump."[430]
- "The Whistleblower got it sooo wrong that HE must come forward. The Fake News Media knows who he is but, being an arm of the Democrat Party, don't want to reveal him because there would be hell to pay. Reveal the Whistleblower and end the Impeachment Hoax!"[431]
- "But the whistleblower should be revealed because the whistleblower gave false stories. Some people would call it a fraud; I won't go that far. But when I read it closely, I probably would. But the whistleblower should be revealed."[432]
- "I think that the whistleblower gave a lot of false information."[433]
- "The whistleblower is not a whistleblower. He's a fake. ... Everybody knows who the whistleblower is. And the whistleblower is a political operative."[434]

In response to a request from Intelligence Committee Ranking Member Devin Nunes to call the whistleblower to testify at an open hearing, Chairman Schiff underscored the danger posed by the President's threats against the whistleblower and why the whistleblower's testimony was now unnecessary:

> The Committee also will not facilitate efforts by President Trump and his allies in Congress to threaten, intimidate, and retaliate against the whistleblower who courageously raised the initial alarm. It remains the duty of the Intelligence Committee to protect whistleblowers, and until recently, this was a bipartisan priority. The

whistleblower has a right under laws championed by this Committee to remain anonymous and to be protected from harm.

The impeachment inquiry, moreover, has gathered an ever-growing body of evidence—from witnesses and documents, including the President's own words in his July 25 call record—that not only confirms, but far exceeds, the initial information in the whistleblower's complaint. The whistleblower's testimony is therefore redundant and unnecessary. In light of the President's threats, the individual's appearance before us would only place their personal safety at grave risk.[435]

Until President Trump's attacks on the whistleblower, Republicans and Democrats were united in protecting whistleblowers' right to report abuses of power and be free from retaliation.[436] For example, Rep. Nunes, serving in 2017 as Chairman of the Intelligence Committee, spoke in defense of whistleblowers, stating: "We want people to come forward and we will protect the identity of those people at all cost."[437] He also stated:

As you know, and I've said this several times, we don't talk about sources at this committee. ... The good thing is, is that we have continued to have people come forward, voluntarily, to this committee and we want to continue that and I will tell you that that will not happen if we tell you who our sources are and people that come—come to the committee. [438]

Other Republican Members of Congress have opposed efforts to expose the whistleblower. For example, Senator Charles Grassley stated:

This person appears to have followed the whistleblower protection laws and ought to be heard out and protected. We should always work to respect whistleblowers' requests for confidentiality. Any further media reports on the whistleblower's identity don't serve the public interest—even if the conflict sells more papers or attracts clicks.[439]

Senator Richard Burr, the Chair of the Senate Select Committee on Intelligence, affirmed that he would "never" want the identity of the whistleblower revealed and stated, "We protect whistleblowers. We protect witnesses in our committee."[440]

Senator Mitt Romney also called for support of the whistleblower's rights, stating: "[W]histleblowers should be entitled to confidentiality and privacy, because they play a vital function in our democracy."[441]

SECTION II ENDNOTES

[1] U.S. Const. Art. I, § 2, cl. 5.

[2] Statement of George Mason, Madison Debates (July 20, 1787).

[3] *McGrain v. Daugherty*, 273 U.S. 135 (1927) ("We are of [the] opinion that the power of inquiry—with process to enforce it—is an essential and appropriate auxiliary to the legislative function."); *Eastland v. United States Servicemen's Fund*, 421 U.S. 491 (1975) ("the power to investigate is inherent in the power to make laws"); *Committee on the Judiciary v. McGahn*, Case No. 1:19-cv-02379, Memorandum Opinion, Doc. No. 46 (D.D.C. Nov. 25, 2019) ("[T]he House of Representatives has the constitutionally vested responsibility to conduct investigations of suspected abuses of power within the government, and to act to curb those improprieties, if required."). As of this report, an appeal is pending in the D.C. Circuit. No. 19-5331 (D.C. Cir.).

[4] *Cf. Nixon v. Fitzgerald*, 457 U.S. 731 (1982) ("Vigilant oversight by Congress also may serve to deter Presidential abuses of office, as well as to make credible the threat of impeachment."); *Senate Select Committee on Presidential Campaign Activities v. Nixon*, 498 F.2d 725 (D.C. Cir. 1974) (discussing in dicta the "inquiry into presidential impeachment" opened by the House Judiciary Committee regarding President Nixon and explaining, "The investigative authority of the Judiciary Committee with respect to presidential conduct has an express constitutional source."); *In re Report & Recommendation of June 5, 1972 Grand Jury Concerning Transmission of Evidence to House of Representatives*, 370 F. Supp. 1219 (D.D.C. 1974) ("[I]t should not be forgotten that we deal in a matter of the most critical moment to the Nation, an impeachment investigation involving the President of the United States. It would be difficult to conceive of a more compelling need than that of this country for an unswervingly fair inquiry based on all the pertinent information."). In 1833, Justice Joseph Story reasoned—while explaining why pardons cannot confer immunity from impeachment—that, "The power of impeachment will generally be applied to persons holding high office under the government; and it is of great consequence that the President should not have the power of preventing a thorough investigation of their conduct, or of securing them against the disgrace of a public conviction by impeachment, should they deserve it. The constitution has, therefore, wisely interposed this check upon his power." Joseph L. Story, 3 *Commentaries on the Constitution of the United States* § 1501 (1873 ed., T.M. Cooley (ed.)).

[5] House Committee on the Judiciary, *Impeachment of Richard M. Nixon, President of the United States,* 93rd Cong. (1974) (H. Rep. 93-1305).

[6] Statement of Rep. William Lyman, Annals of Congress, 4th Cong. 601 (1796).

[7] Department of Justice, Office of Legal Counsel, *A Sitting President's Amenability to Indictment and Criminal Prosecution* (Oct. 16, 2000) (explaining that a President "who engages in criminal behavior falling into the category of 'high Crimes and Misdemeanors'" is "always subject to removal from office upon impeachment by the House and conviction by the Senate") (online at www.justice.gov/sites/default/files/olc/opinions/2000/10/31/op-olc-v024-p0222_0.pdf).

[88] *Id.* ("Moreover, the constitutionally specified impeachment process ensures that the immunity [of a sitting President from prosecution] would not place the President 'above the law.'"). President Trump's personal lawyers have staked out the more extreme position that the President may not be <u>investigated</u> by law enforcement agencies while in office. For example, President Trump's personal attorney asserted in court that the President could not be investigated by local authorities if he committed murder while in office. *If Trump Shoots Someone on 5th Ave., Does He Have Immunity? His Lawyer Says Yes,* New York Times (Oct. 23, 2019) (online at www.nytimes.com/2019/10/23/nyregion/trump-taxes-vance.html). A federal district court and appeals court rejected this argument. *Trump v. Vance*, 941 F.3d 631 (2nd Cir. 2019) ("presidential immunity does not bar the enforcement of a state grand jury subpoena directing a third party to produce non-privileged material, even when the subject matter under investigation pertains to the President"); *Trump v. Vance,* 395 F. Supp. 3d 283 (S.D.N.Y. 2019) (calling the President's claims of "unqualified and boundless" immunity from judicial process "repugnant to the nation's governmental structure and constitutional values"). The case is currently being appealed.

[9] *Barenblatt v. U.S*, 360 U.S. 109 (1959).

[10] *McGrain v. Daugherty*, 273 U.S. 135 (1927) ("A legislative body cannot legislate wisely or effectively in the absence of information respecting the conditions which the legislation is intended to affect or change; and where the legislative body does not itself possess the requisite information—which not infrequently is true—recourse must

be had to others who do possess it. Experience has taught that mere requests for such information often are unavailing, and also that information which is volunteered is not always accurate or complete; so some means of compulsion are essential to obtain what is needed."); *Eastland v. United States Servicemen's Fund*, 421 U.S. 491 (1975) ("the subpoena power may be exercised by a committee acting, as here, on behalf of one of the Houses"); *Committee on the Judiciary v. Miers*, 558 F. Supp. 2d 84 (D.D.C. 2008) ("In short, there can be no question that Congress has a right—derived from its Article I legislative function—to issue and enforce subpoenas, and a corresponding right to the information that is the subject of such subpoenas. ... Congress's power of inquiry is as broad as its power to legislate and lies at the very heart of Congress's constitutional role. Indeed, the former is necessary to the proper exercise of the latter: according to the Supreme Court, the ability to compel testimony is 'necessary to the effective functioning of courts and legislatures.'") (citation omitted).

[11] U.S. Const. Art. I, § 5, cl. 2.

[12] *Watkins v. United States*, 354 U.S. 178 (1957).

[13] *See Committee on the Judiciary v. Miers*, 558 F. Supp. 2d 84 (D.D.C. 2008) ("Thus, federal precedent dating back as far as 1807 contemplates that even the Executive is bound to comply with duly issued subpoenas.").

[14] *Committee on the Judiciary v. McGahn*, Case No. 1:19-cv-02379, Memorandum Opinion, Doc. No. 46 (D.D.C. Nov. 25, 2019). As of this report, an appeal is pending in the D.C. Circuit. No. 19-5331 (D.C. Cir.).

[15] 18 U.S.C. § 1505.

[16] 18 U.S.C. § 1001 (also prohibiting making "any materially false, fictitious, or fraudulent statement or representation" or making or using "any false writing or document knowing the same to contain any materially false, fictitious, or fraudulent statement or entry" in connection with a Congressional investigation).

[17] 18 U.S.C. § 1512(b); *See also* 18 U.S.C. § 1515(a) (defining "official proceeding" to include "a proceeding before the Congress").

[18] 18 U.S.C. § 1512(d).

[19] *See, e.g.*, 5 U.S.C. § 2302; 10 U.S.C. § 1034; P.L. 113-126.

[20] P.L. 116-6, § 713 ("No part of any appropriation contained in this or any other Act shall be available for the payment of the salary of any officer or employee of the Federal Government, who ... prohibits or prevents, or attempts or threatens to prohibit or prevent, any other officer or employee of the Federal Government from having any direct oral or written communication or contact with any Member, committee, or subcommittee of the Congress in connection with any matter pertaining to the employment of such other officer or employee or pertaining to the department or agency of such other officer or employee in any way, irrespective of whether such communication or contact is at the initiative of such other officer or employee or in response to the request or inquiry of such Member, committee, or subcommittee.").

[21] House Committee on the Judiciary, *Impeachment of Richard M. Nixon, President of the United States*, 93rd Cong. (1974) (H. Rep. 93-1305).

[22] House Committee on the Judiciary, *Impeachment of William Jefferson Clinton, President of the United States*, 105th Cong. (1998) (H. Rep. 105-830).

[23] The White House, *The President's Remarks Announcing Developments and Procedures to be Followed in Connection with the Investigation* (Apr. 17, 1973). President Nixon initially stated that members of his "personal staff" would "decline a request for a formal appearance before a committee of the Congress," but reversed course approximately one month later. The White House, *Statement by the President, Executive Privilege* (Mar. 12, 1973).

[24] *See, e.g.*, Senate Select Committee on Presidential Campaign Activities, Testimony of John Dean, *Watergate and Related Activities, Phase I: Watergate Investigation*, 93rd Cong. (June 25, 1973); Senate Select Committee on Presidential Campaign Activities, Testimony of H.R. Haldeman, *Watergate and Related Activities, Phase I: Watergate Investigation*, 93rd Cong. (July 30, 1973); Senate Select Committee on Presidential Campaign Activities, Testimony of Alexander Butterfield, *Watergate and Related Activities, Phase I: Watergate Investigation*, 93rd Cong. (July 16, 1973); Senate Select Committee on Presidential Campaign Activities, Testimony of John Ehrlichman, *Watergate and Related Activities, Phase I: Watergate Investigation*, 93rd Cong. (July 24, 1973).

[25] *See* House Committee on the Judiciary, *Impeachment of Richard M. Nixon, President of the United States*, 93rd Cong. (1974) (H. Rep. 93-1305).

[26] *Id.*

[27] *Id.* (quoting letter from Chairman Peter W. Rodino, Jr., House Committee on the Judiciary, to President Richard M. Nixon (May 30, 1974)).

[28] H.R. Jour., 29th Cong., 1st Sess., 693 (Apr. 20, 1846).

[29] Senate Select Committee on Secret Military Assistance to Iran and the Nicaraguan Opposition and House Select Committee to Investigate Covert Arms Transactions with Iran, Testimony of Oliver North, *Iran-Contra Investigation: Joint Hearings Before the House Select Committee to Investigate Covert Arms Transactions with Iran and the Senate Select Committee on Secret Military Assistance to Iran and the Nicaraguan Oppositions*, 100th Cong. (July 7, 1987); Senate Select Committee on Secret Military Assistance to Iran and the Nicaraguan Opposition and House Select Committee to Investigate Covert Arms Transactions with Iran, Testimony of John Poindexter, *Iran-Contra Investigation: Joint Hearings Before the House Select Committee to Investigate Covert Arms Transactions with Iran and the Senate Select Committee on Secret Military Assistance to Iran and the Nicaraguan Oppositions*, 100th Cong. (July 15, 1987).

[30] *Committee on the Judiciary v. McGahn*, Civ. No. 1:19-cv-02379, Memorandum Opinion, Doc. No. 46 (D.D.C. Nov. 25, 2019). As of this report, an appeal is pending in the D.C. Circuit. No. 19-5331 (D.C. Cir.).

[31] Committee on Government Reform, Democratic Staff, *Congressional Oversight of the Clinton Administration* (Jan. 17, 2006) (online at https://wayback.archive-it.org/4949/20141031200116/http://oversight-archive.waxman.house.gov/documents/20060117103516-91336.pdf) (noting that Republican Dan Burton, Chairman of the Committee on Government Reform, deposed 141 Clinton Administration officials during his tenure).

[32] Select Committee on the Events Surrounding the 2012 Terrorist Attack in Benghazi, *Final Report of the Select Committee on the Events Surrounding the 2012 Terrorist Attack in Benghazi*, 114th Cong. (2016) (H. Rep. 114-848) (noting that the Select Committee interviewed or received testimony from 107 people—none of whom was instructed not to appear—including 57 current and former State Department officials such as Secretary of State Hillary Clinton, Chief of Staff and Counselor to the Secretary Cheryl Mills, Deputy Chief of Staff and Director of Policy Planning, Jacob Sullivan, and Deputy Chief of Staff for Operations Huma Abedin; 24 Defense Department officials such as Secretary Leon Panetta and General Carter Ham; and 19 Central Intelligence Agency officials such as Director David Petraeus and former Deputy Director Michael Morell).

[33] *Id.* (including productions of 71,640 pages of State Department documents, 300 pages of CIA intelligence analyses, 200 pages of FBI documents, 900 pages of Defense Department documents, and 750 pages of National Security Agency documents).

[34] *See, e.g.*, House rule X, clause 2(a) (assigning "general oversight responsibilities" to committees); House Rule XI, clause 2(m) (authorizing Committees to "hold such hearings as it considers necessary" and to "require, by subpoena or otherwise, the attendance and testimony of such witnesses and the production of such books, records, correspondence, memoranda, papers, and documents as it considers necessary"); H.Res. 6 (2019) (granting deposition authority to committees); 116th Congress Regulations for Use of Deposition Authority, Congressional Record (Jan. 25, 2019) (establishing procedures for committee depositions).

[35] *See, e.g.*, House Rules (2017); H.Res. 5 (2017); 115th Congress Staff Deposition Authority Procedures, Congressional Record (Jan. 13, 2017).

[36] Special Counsel Robert S. Mueller III, Department of Justice, *Report on The Investigation Into Russian Interference In The 2016 Presidential Election*, Vol. I (March 2019) (online at www.justice.gov/storage/report.pdf); Special Counsel Robert S. Mueller, III, Department of Justice, *Report on The Investigation Into Russian Interference In The 2016 Presidential Election*, Vol. II (March 2019) (online at www.justice.gov/storage/report_volume2.pdf).

[37] *See* H. Res. 430; *see also* H. Rep. 116-105 (2019) (the purposes of the Judiciary Committee's investigation include "considering whether any of the conduct described in the Special Counsel's Report warrants the Committee in taking any further steps under Congress' Article I powers," including "whether to approve articles of impeachment with respect to the President or any other Administration official").

[38] *See* Letter from Chairman Jerrold Nadler, House Committee on the Judiciary, to Chairman Adam B. Schiff, House Permanent Select Committee on Intelligence, Chairman Maxine Waters, House Committee on Financial Services, Chairman Elijah E. Cummings, House Committee on Oversight and Reform, and Chairman Eliot L. Engel, House Committee on Foreign Affairs (Aug. 22, 2019) (online at https://judiciary.house.gov/sites/democrats.judiciary.house.gov/files/documents/FiveChairsLetter8.22.pdf).

[39] *Id.*

[40] Letter from Chairman Eliot L. Engel, House Committee on Foreign Affairs, Chairman Adam B. Schiff, House Permanent Select Committee on Intelligence, and Chairman Elijah E. Cummings, House Committee on Oversight and Reform, to Pat A. Cipollone, Counsel to the President, The White House (Sept. 9, 2019) (online at https://intelligence.house.gov/uploadedfiles/ele_schiff_cummings_letter_to_cipollone_on_ukraine.pdf); Letter from Chairman Eliot L. Engel, House Committee on Foreign Affairs, Chairman Adam B. Schiff, House Permanent Select Committee on Intelligence, and Chairman Elijah E. Cummings, House Committee on Oversight and Reform, to Secretary Michael R. Pompeo, Department of State (Sept. 9, 2019) (online at https://intelligence.house.gov/uploadedfiles/ele_schiff_cummings_letter_to_sec_pompeo_on_ukraine.pdf); Letter from Chairman Eliot L. Engel, Committee on Foreign Affairs, Chairman Adam B. Schiff, Permanent Select Committee on Intelligence, and Chairman Elijah E. Cummings, Committee on Oversight and Reform, to Secretary Michael R. Pompeo, Department of State (Sept. 13, 2019) (online at https://oversight.house.gov/sites/democrats.oversight.house.gov/files/2019-09-13.EEC%20ELE%20Schiff%20re%20Ukraine.pdf).

[41] The White House, *Remarks by President Trump Before Marine One Departure* (Sept. 22, 2019) (online at www.whitehouse.gov/briefings-statements/remarks-president-trump-marine-one-departure-66/) ("We had a great conversation. The conversation I had was largely congratulatory. It was largely corruption—all of the corruption taking place. It was largely the fact that we don't want our people, like Vice President Biden and his son, creating to the corruption already in the Ukraine.").

[42] Speaker of the House Nancy Pelosi, *Pelosi Remarks Announcing Impeachment Inquiry* (Sept. 24, 2019) (online at www.speaker.gov/newsroom/92419-0).

[43] The White House, *Memorandum of Telephone Conversation* (July 25, 2019) (online at www.whitehouse.gov/wp-content/uploads/2019/09/Unclassified09.2019.pdf).

[44] *See, e.g.*, Letter from Chairman Elijah E. Cummings, House Committee on Oversight and Reform, Chairman Adam B. Schiff, House Permanent Select Committee on Intelligence, and Chairman Eliot L. Engel, House Committee on Foreign Affairs, to Mick Mulvaney, Acting Chief of Staff, The White House (Oct. 4, 2019) (online at https://oversight.house.gov/sites/democrats.oversight.house.gov/files/documents/2019-10-04.EEC%20Engel%20Schiff%20to%20Mulvaney-WH%20re%20Subpoena.pdf).

[45] H. Res. 660 (2019).

[46] *Trump Vows Stonewall of 'All' House Subpoenas, Setting Up Fight Over Powers*, New York Times (Apr. 24, 2019) (online at www.nytimes.com/2019/04/24/us/politics/donald-trump-subpoenas.html).

[47] *While Bemoaning Mueller Probe, Trump Falsely Says the Constitution Gives Him 'The Right to do Whatever I Want'*, Washington Post (July 23, 2019) (online at www.washingtonpost.com/politics/2019/07/23/trump-falsely-tells-auditorium-full-teens-constitution-gives-him-right-do-whatever-i-want/).

[48] Donald J. Trump, Twitter (Oct. 1, 2019) (online at https://twitter.com/realDonaldTrump/status/1179179573541511176).

[49] *At Louisiana Rally, Trump Lashes Out at Impeachment Inquiry and Pelosi,* New York Times (Oct. 11, 2019) (online at www.nytimes.com/2019/10/11/us/trump-rally-louisiana-lake-charles.html).

[50] Donald J. Trump, Twitter (Oct. 18, 2019) (online at https://twitter.com/realDonaldTrump/status/1185374394350215169) (purporting to quote former Rep. Jason Chaffetz).

[51] Donald J. Trump, Twitter (Sept. 21, 2019) (online at https://twitter.com/realDonaldTrump/status/1175409914384125952).

[52] Donald J. Trump, Twitter (Sept. 24, 2019) (online at https://twitter.com/realDonaldTrump/status/1176559970390806530).

[53] Donald J. Trump, Twitter (Sept. 24, 2019) (online at https://twitter.com/realDonaldTrump/status/1176623010230525953).

[54] The White House, *Remarks by President Trump and President Salih of Iraq Before Bilateral Meeting* (Sept. 24, 2019) (online at www.whitehouse.gov/briefings-statements/remarks-president-trump-president-salih-iraq-bilateral-meeting-new-york-ny-2/).

[55] The White House, *Remarks by President Trump and President Bukele of El Salvador Before Bilateral Meeting* (Sept. 25, 2019) (online at www.whitehouse.gov/briefings-statements/remarks-president-trump-president-bukele-el-salvador-bilateral-meeting-new-york-ny/).

[56] The White House, *Remarks by President Trump in a Multilateral Meeting on the Bolivarian Republic of Venezuela* (Sept. 25, 2019) (online at www.whitehouse.gov/briefings-statements/remarks-president-trump-multilateral-meeting-bolivarian-republic-venezuela-new-york-ny/).

[57] Donald J. Trump, Twitter (Sept. 26, 2019) (online at https://twitter.com/realDonaldTrump/status/1177285017636093953).

[58] Donald J. Trump, Twitter (Oct. 1, 2019) (online at https://twitter.com/realDonaldTrump/status/1179023004241727489).

[59] Donald J. Trump, Twitter (Oct. 5, 2019) (online at https://twitter.com/realDonaldTrump/status/1180482408522629120).

[60] Donald J. Trump, Twitter (Oct. 8, 2019) (online at https://twitter.com/realDonaldTrump/status/1181761045486080002).

[61] The White House, *Remarks by President Trump at Signing of Executive Orders on Transparency in Federal Guidance and Enforcement* (Oct. 9, 2019) (online at www.whitehouse.gov/briefings-statements/remarks-president-trump-signing-executive-orders-transparency-federal-guidance-enforcement/).

[62] Donald J. Trump, Twitter (Oct. 9, 2019) (online at https://twitter.com/realDonaldTrump/status/1181913137483829250).

[63] Donald J. Trump, Twitter (Oct. 9, 2019) (online at https://twitter.com/realdonaldtrump/status/1181969511697788928).

[64] Donald J. Trump, Twitter (Oct. 20, 2019) (online at https://twitter.com/realDonaldTrump/status/1186035686396321793).

[65] Donald J. Trump, Twitter (Nov. 12, 2019) (online at https://twitter.com/realDonaldTrump/status/1194214569591394304).

[66] Donald J. Trump, Twitter (Nov. 24, 2019) (online at https://twitter.com/realDonaldTrump/status/1198733640722718725).

[67] Donald J. Trump, Twitter (Nov. 26, 2019) (online at https://twitter.com/realDonaldTrump/status/1199352977934487553).

[68] The White House, *Remarks by President Trump Upon Air Force One Arrival* (Sept. 26, 2019) (online at www.whitehouse.gov/briefings-statements/remarks-president-trump-upon-air-force-one-arrival-prince-georges-county-md/).

[69] *See, e.g.,* Co-Equal, *Investigative Rules and Practices Followed by House Republicans* (online at www.co-equal.org/guide-to-congressional-oversight/investigative-rules-and-practices-followed-by-house-republicans). *See also* Committee on Government Reform, Democratic Staff, *Congressional Oversight of the Clinton Administration* (Jan. 17, 2006) (online at https://wayback.archive-it.org/4949/20141031200116/http://oversight-archive.waxman.house.gov/documents/20060117103516-91336.pdf) (noting that House Republicans conducted hundreds of confidential depositions of both political appointees and career officials without agency counsel present, with one Committee alone conducting over 140 depositions of Clinton Administration officials).

[70] Letter from Pat A. Cipollone, Counsel to the President, The White House, to House Speaker Nancy Pelosi, Chairman Adam B. Schiff, House Permanent Select Committee on Intelligence, Chairman Eliot L. Engel, House Committee on Foreign Affairs Committee, and Chairman Elijah E. Cummings, House Committee on Oversight and Reform (Oct. 8, 2019) (online at www.whitehouse.gov/wp-content/uploads/2019/10/PAC-Letter-10.08.2019.pdf).

[71] *Speech: Donald Trump Holds a Political Rally in Minneapolis, Minnesota*, Factbase Videos (Oct. 10, 2019) (online at www.youtube.com/watch?time_continue=742&v=_y8Al_mGwmc&feature=emb_logo).

[72] Gregg Nunziata, a former legal counsel and senior policy advisor to Senator Marco Rubio, stated: "This letter is bananas. A barely-lawyered temper tantrum." Gregg Nunziata, Twitter (Oct. 8, 2019) (online at https://twitter.com/greggnunziata/status/1181685021926662144). Jonathan Turley, a law professor who has represented House Republicans, stated: "A President cannot simply pick up his marbles and leave the game because he does not like the other players. A refusal to cooperate with a constitutionally mandated process can itself be an abuse of power." *White House Issues Defiant Letter Refusing to Cooperate in Impeachment Proceedings*, Res Ipsa Loquitur (Oct. 9, 2019) (online at https://jonathanturley.org/2019/10/09/white-house-issues-defiant-letter-refusing-to-cooperate-in-impeachment-proceedings/). Preet Bharara, the former U.S. Attorney for the Southern District of New York, stated, "It's one of the worst letters I've seen from the White House counsel's office." George Conway, a prominent conservative attorney, called Mr. Cipollone's letter "a disgrace to the country, a disgrace to the presidency, and a disgrace to the legal profession." He accused the White House of "clearly engaging in obstructionist tactics." *Diagnosing Trump (with George Conway)*, Stay Tuned with Preet Bharara (Oct. 9, 2019) (online at https://cafe.com/stay-tuned-transcript-diagnosing-trump-with-george-conway/). Mr. Conway also stated: "I cannot fathom how any self respecting member of the bar could affix his name to this letter. It's pure hackery, and it disgraces the profession." George T. Conway, III, Twitter (Oct. 8, 2019) (online at https://twitter.com/gtconway3d/status/1181685229687394307).

[73] Letter from Pat A. Cipollone, Counsel to the President, The White House, to Acting Chairwoman Carolyn Maloney, House Committee on Oversight and Reform, Chairman Adam B. Schiff, House Permanent Select Committee on Intelligence Chairman Eliot L. Engel, Chairman, House Committee on Foreign Affairs (Oct. 18, 2019).

[74] Department of Justice, Office of Legal Counsel, *Exclusion of Agency Counsel from Congressional Depositions in the Impeachment Context* (Nov. 1, 2019) (online at www.justice.gov/olc/file/1214996/download).

[75] Department of Justice, Office of Legal Counsel, *Legal Aspects of Impeachment: An Overview* (1974) (quoting President James K. Polk) (online at www.justice.gov/olc/page/file/980036/download).

[76] *Position of the Executive Department Regarding Investigative Reports*, 40 Op. Atty Gen. 45 (1941).

[77] Letter from Pat A. Cipollone, Counsel to the President, The White House, to House Speaker Nancy Pelosi, Chairman Adam B. Schiff, House Permanent Select Committee on Intelligence, Chairman Eliot L. Engel, House Committee on Foreign Affairs Committee, and Chairman Elijah E. Cummings, House Committee on Oversight and Reform (Oct. 8, 2019) (online at www.whitehouse.gov/wp-content/uploads/2019/10/PAC-Letter-10.08.2019.pdf).

[78] *See, e.g.*, The White House, *Remarks by President Trump and President Salih of Iraq Before Bilateral Meeting* (Sept. 24, 2019) (online at www.whitehouse.gov/briefings-statements/remarks-president-trump-president-salih-iraq-bilateral-meeting-new-york-ny/) ("The phone call was perfect."); The White House, *Remarks by President Trump Upon Arriving at the U.N. General Assembly* (Sept. 24, 2019) (online at www.whitehouse.gov/briefings-statements/remarks-president-trump-upon-arriving-u-n-general-assembly-new-york-ny/) ("That call was perfect."); Donald J. Trump, Twitter (Nov. 11, 2019) (online at https://twitter.com/realDonaldTrump/status/1193615188311912449) ("The call to the Ukrainian President was PERFECT.").

[79] Letter from Pat A. Cipollone, Counsel to the President, The White House, to House Speaker Nancy Pelosi, Chairman Adam B. Schiff, House Permanent Select Committee on Intelligence, Chairman Eliot L. Engel, House Committee on Foreign Affairs Committee, and Chairman Elijah E. Cummings, House Committee on Oversight and Reform (Oct. 8, 2019) (online at www.whitehouse.gov/wp-content/uploads/2019/10/PAC-Letter-10.08.2019.pdf).

[80] *See* House Committee on the Judiciary, *Impeachment of Richard M. Nixon, President of the United States*, 93rd Cong. (1974) (H. Rep. 93-1305) (Impeachment Article III: "In refusing to produce these papers and things, Richard M. Nixon, substituting his judgment as to what materials were necessary for the inquiry, interposed the powers of the presidency against the lawful subpoenas of the House of Representatives, thereby assuming to himself functions and judgments necessary to the exercise of the sole power of impeachment vested by the Constitution in the House of Representatives.").

[81] In this case, one Republican Member of the House of Representatives supported impeaching President Trump—Rep. Justin Amash from Michigan. In explaining his support, Rep. Amash noted the importance of upholding Congress' "duties under our Constitution" rather than "loyalty to a political party." After Rep. Amash announced his support for impeachment, President Trump denounced him as a "total lightweight" and a "loser." Rep. Amash subsequently declared that he was leaving the Republican party. *See* Justin Amash, Twitter (May 18, 2019) (online at https://twitter.com/justinamash/status/1129831626844921862); *Trump Calls Representative Justin Amash a 'Loser' Over Impeachment Talk,* New York Times (May 19, 2019) (online at www.nytimes.com/2019/05/19/us/politics/trump-justin-amash-impeachment.html); *Justin Amash: Our politics is in a partisan death spiral. That's why I'm leaving the GOP*, Washington Post (July 4, 2019) (online at www.washingtonpost.com/opinions/justin-amash-our-politics-is-in-a-partisan-death-spiral-thats-why-im-leaving-the-gop/2019/07/04/afbe0480-9e3d-11e9-b27f-ed2942f73d70_story.html).

[82] Letter from Pat A. Cipollone, Counsel to the President, The White House, to Acting Chairwoman Carolyn Maloney, House Committee on Oversight and Reform, Chairman Adam B. Schiff, House Permanent Select Committee on Intelligence, Chairman Eliot L. Engel, Chairman, House Committee on Foreign Affairs (Oct. 18, 2019).

[83] Jefferson's Manual of Parliamentary Practice § 603 (stating that "various events have been credited with setting an impeachment in motion," including "facts developed and reported by an investigating committee of the House"). On October 25, 2019, a federal district court affirmed that "no governing law requires" the House to hold a such a vote. *In re Application of the Committee on the Judiciary, United States House of Representatives*, 2019 U.S. Dist. LEXIS 184857 (D.D.C. 2019). More than 300 legal scholars agreed, concluding that "the Constitution does not mandate the process for impeachment and there is no constitutional requirement that the House of Representatives authorize an impeachment inquiry before one begins." *An Open Letter from Legal Scholars on Trump Impeachment Inquiry* (Oct. 17, 2019) (online at www.law.berkeley.edu/wp-content/uploads/2019/10/Open-Letter-from-Legal-Scholars-re-Impeachment.pdf).

[84] *In re Application of the Committee on the Judiciary, United States House of Representatives,* 2019 U.S. Dist. LEXIS 184857 (D.D.C. 2019).

[85] *See, e.g.,* 3 Deschler Ch. 14 § 5 (discussing impeachment of Justice William O. Douglas).

[86] *See, e.g.*, H. Res. 87, 101st Cong. (1989) (impeachment of Judge Walter L. Nixon, Jr.); H. Res. 461, 99th Cong. (1986) (impeachment of Judge Harry E. Claiborne).

[87] H. Res. 6 (2019); H. Res. 660 (2019). In addition, on June 11, 2019, the House approved House Resolution 430, which, in part, authorized the House Committee on the Judiciary to seek judicial enforcement of subpoenas in the ongoing investigation related to Special Counsel Mueller's report. The resolution granted the Committee "any and all necessary authority under Article I of the Constitution" to seek judicial enforcement. The accompanying report by the House Committee on Rules explained that this authority is intended to further the Judiciary Committee's ongoing investigation, the purpose of which includes assessing whether to recommend "articles of impeachment with respect to the President." H. Rep. 116-108, quoting H. Rep. 116-105.

[88] Letter from Pat A. Cipollone, Counsel to the President, The White House, to House Speaker Nancy Pelosi, Chairman Adam B. Schiff, House Permanent Select Committee on Intelligence, Chairman Eliot L. Engel, House Committee on Foreign Affairs Committee, and Chairman Elijah E. Cummings, House Committee on Oversight and Reform (Oct. 8, 2019) (online at www.whitehouse.gov/wp-content/uploads/2019/10/PAC-Letter-10.08.2019.pdf). President Trump has also made these claims directly, stating: "we had a great two weeks watching these crooked politicians, not giving us due process, not giving us lawyers, not giving us the right to speak, and destroying their witnesses," and "we weren't allowed any rights." *Speech: Donald Trump Holds a Political Rally in Sunrise, Florida*, Factbase Videos (Nov. 26, 2019) (online atwww.youtube.com/watch?v=zoRcCRULQl8&feature=youtu.be).

[89] Indeed, Mr. Cipollone articulated no basis under the Constitution for his various "due process" demands—and there is no such basis, especially when the House is engaged in a fact-finding investigation as part of its efforts to ascertain whether to consider articles of impeachment. *See* H. Rept. 116-266 (2019).

[90] H. Res. 660 (2019).

[91] H. Rept. 116-266 (2019) ("The purpose of providing these protections is to ensure that the president has a fair opportunity to present evidence to the Judiciary Committee if it must weigh whether to recommend articles of impeachment against him to the full House.").

[92] Letter from Pat A. Cipollone, Counsel to the President, to House Speaker Nancy Pelosi, Chairman Adam B. Schiff, House Permanent Select Committee on Intelligence, Chairman Eliot L. Engel, House Committee on Foreign Affairs, and Chairman Elijah E. Cummings, Committee on Oversight and Reform (Oct. 8, 2019) (online at www.whitehouse.gov/wp-content/uploads/2019/10/PAC-Letter-10.08.2019.pdf).

[93] In a September 25, 2019, statement, a Department of Justice spokesperson stated: "The Attorney General was first notified of the President's conversation with Ukrainian President Zelensky several weeks after the call took place, when the Department of Justice learned of a potential referral. The President has not spoken with the Attorney General about having Ukraine investigate anything relating to former Vice President Biden or his son. The President has not asked the Attorney General to contact Ukraine—on this or any other matter. The Attorney General has not communicated with Ukraine—on this or any other subject. Nor has the Attorney General discussed this matter, or anything relating to Ukraine, with Rudy Giuliani." As to the President's conduct with regard to Ukraine, the Department stated: "In August, the Department of Justice was referred a matter relating to a letter the Director of National Intelligence had received from the Inspector General for the Intelligence Community regarding a purported whistleblower complaint. The Inspector General's letter cited a conversation between the President and Ukrainian President Zelensky as a potential violation of federal campaign finance law, while acknowledging that neither the Inspector General nor the complainant had firsthand knowledge of the conversation. Relying on established procedures set forth in the Justice Manual, the Department's Criminal Division reviewed the official record of the call and determined, based on the facts and applicable law, that there was no campaign finance violation and that no further action was warranted. All relevant components of the Department agreed with this legal conclusion, and the Department has concluded the matter." Statement of Kerri Kupec, Spokesperson, Department of Justice (Sept. 25, 2019) (as emailed by the Department of Justice to the House Permanent Select Committee on Intelligence).

[94] H. Rept. 116-266 (2019) (The report continued: "As previously described, an impeachment inquiry is not a criminal trial and should not be confused with one. The president's liberty is not at stake and the constitutional protections afforded a criminal defendant do not as a matter of course apply. The constitutionally permitted consequences of impeachment are limited to immediate removal from office and potentially being barred from holding future federal office. Moreover, it is the Senate that conducts the trial to determine whether the conduct outlined in the articles warrant the president's removal from office, which requires a 2/3 majority vote. Indeed, given the nature of the ongoing investigation into the Ukraine matter, President Trump has received additional procedural protections. During closed door depositions held by HPSCI and others related to the Ukraine matter, minority members have been present and granted equal time to question witnesses brought before the committees. This is unlike the process in the preceding two presidential impeachment inquiries, which relied significantly upon information gathered by third-party investigators.").

[95] *See* Committee on Government Reform, Democratic Staff, *Congressional Oversight of the Clinton Administration* (Jan. 17, 2006) (online at https://wayback.archive-it.org/4949/20141031200116/http://oversight-archive.waxman.house.gov/documents/20060117103516-91336.pdf) (explaining that when Rep. Dan Burton served as Chairman of the Committee on Government Reform, the Committee deposed 141 Clinton Administration officials without agency counsel present—including White House Chief of Staff Mack McLarty; White House Chief of Staff Erskine Bowles; White House Counsel Bernard Nussbaum; White House Counsel Jack Quinn; Deputy White House Counsel Bruce Lindsey; Deputy White House Counsel Cheryl Mills; Deputy White House Chief of Staff Harold Ickes; Chief of Staff to the Vice President Roy Neel; and Chief of Staff to the First Lady Margaret Williams).

[96] Letter from Pat A. Cipollone, Counsel to the President, The White House, to House Speaker Nancy Pelosi, Chairman Adam B. Schiff, House Permanent Select Committee on Intelligence, Chairman Eliot L. Engel, House Committee on Foreign Affairs, and Chairman Elijah E. Cummings, Committee on Oversight and Reform

(Oct. 8, 2019) (online at www.whitehouse.gov/wp-content/uploads/2019/10/PAC-Letter-10.08.2019.pdf). On November 1, 2019, after the House approved H. Res. 660, the Administration continued to press this spurious claim, with the Office of Legal Counsel issuing an opinion asserting that "Congressional committees participating in an impeachment inquiry may not validly compel executive branch witnesses to testify about matters that potentially involve information protected by executive privilege without the assistance of agency counsel." Department of Justice, Office of Legal Counsel, *Exclusion of Agency Counsel from Congressional Depositions in the Impeachment Context* (Nov. 1, 2019) (online at www.justice.gov/olc/file/1214996/download). As discussed in this section, this position is entirely unsupported by judicial precedent and erroneous.

[97] U.S. Const., Art. I, sec. 5, cl. 2.

[98] The regulations that govern House depositions state: "Only members, Committee staff designated by the chair or ranking minority member, an official reporter, the witness, and the witness's counsel are permitted to attend. Observers or counsel for other persons, including counsel for government agencies, may not attend." 116th Congress Regulations for Use of Deposition Authority, Congressional Record, H1216 (Jan. 25, 2019) (online at www.congress.gov/116/crec/2019/01/25/CREC-2019-01-25-pt1-PgH1216-2.pdf).

[99] Committee on Oversight and Reform, *Committee Depositions in the House of Representatives: Longstanding Republican and Democratic Practice of Excluding Agency Counsel* (Nov. 5, 2019) (online at https://oversight.house.gov/sites/democrats.oversight.house.gov/files/Committee%20Depositions%20in%20the%20House%20of%20Representatives_Longstanding%20Republican%20and%20Democratic%20Practice%20of%20Excluding%20Agency%20Counsel.pdf).

[100] Letter from Pat A. Cipollone, Counsel to the President, The White House, to House Speaker Nancy Pelosi, Chairman Adam B. Schiff, House Permanent Select Committee on Intelligence, Chairman Eliot L. Engel, House Committee on Foreign Affairs Committee, and Chairman Elijah E. Cummings, House Committee on Oversight and Reform (Oct. 8, 2019).

[101] *Barenblatt v. United States*, 360 U.S. 109 (1959).

[102] *See, e.g.*, S. 2537 (requiring an investigation by the State Department Inspector General into the withholding of aid to Ukraine, directing the President to immediately obligate previously appropriated funds, and authorizing funds to counter Russian influence); H.R. 3047 (providing support to Ukraine to defend its independence, sovereignty, and territorial integrity).

[103] *In re Application of the Committee on the Judiciary, United States House of Representatives*, 2019 U.S. Dist. LEXIS 184857 (D.D.C. 2019), quoting *Trump v. Mazars United States*, 2019 U.S. App. LEXIS 30475 (D.D.C. 2019) ("Nothing 'in the Constitution or case law ... compels Congress to abandon its legislative role at the first scent of potential illegality and confine itself exclusively to the impeachment process.'").

[104] *See, e.g.*, the 1974 Amendments to the Freedom of Information Act, P.L. 93-502; Ethics in Government Act of 1978, P.L. 95-52; Presidential Records Act of 1978, P.L. 95-591; Federal Election Campaign Act Amendments of 1974, P.L. 93-443.

[105] Letter from Pat A. Cipollone, Counsel to the President, The White House, to House Speaker Nancy Pelosi, Chairman Adam B. Schiff, House Permanent Select Committee on Intelligence, Chairman Eliot L. Engel, House Committee on Foreign Affairs Committee, and Chairman Elijah E. Cummings, House Committee on Oversight and Reform (Oct. 8, 2019) (online at www.whitehouse.gov/wp-content/uploads/2019/10/PAC-Letter-10.08.2019.pdf); Letter from Pat A. Cipollone, Counsel to the President, The White House, to Acting Chairwoman Carolyn Maloney, House Committee on Oversight and Reform, Chairman Adam B. Schiff, House Permanent Select Committee on Intelligence Chairman Eliot L. Engel, Chairman, House Committee on Foreign Affairs (Oct. 18, 2019).

[106] *United States v. American Tel. & Tel. Co.*, 567 F.2d 121 (D.C. Cir. 1977) ("Rather, each branch should take cognizance of an implicit constitutional mandate to seek optimal accommodation through a realistic evaluation of the needs of the conflicting branches in the particular fact situation.").

[107] For example, on November 22, 2019, the Department of State produced to a private party 99 pages of emails, letters, notes, timelines, and news articles under a court order pursuant to the Freedom of Information Act. *State Department Releases Ukraine Documents to American Oversight*, American Oversight (Nov. 22, 2019) (online at www.americanoversight.org/state-department-releases-ukraine-documents-to-american-oversight).

[108] Even if the President were to make a colorable assertion of executive privilege, which he has not, the Supreme Court has held that the privilege is not absolute. In the context of a grand jury subpoena, the Supreme Court found that the President's "generalized assertion of privilege must yield to the demonstrated, specific need for evidence in a pending criminal trial." *United States v. Nixon*, 418 U.S. 683 (1974). Similarly, the D.C. Circuit has held that executive privilege is a "qualified" privilege and that "courts must balance the public interests at stake in determining whether the privilege should yield in a particular case, and must specifically consider the need of the party seeking privileged evidence." *In re Sealed Case*, 121 F.3d 729 (D.C. Cir. 1997). As described above, Congress' need for information during an impeachment inquiry is particularly "compelling." *In re Report & Recommendation of June 5, 1972 Grand Jury Concerning Transmission of Evidence to House of Representatives*, 370 F. Supp. 1219 (D.D.C. 1974) ("[I]t should not be forgotten that we deal in a matter of the most critical moment to the Nation, an impeachment investigation involving the President of the United States. It would be difficult to conceive of a more compelling need than that of this country for an unswervingly fair inquiry based on all the pertinent information.").

[109] *See, e.g.,* Letter from Pat A. Cipollone, Counsel to the President, The White House, to William Pittard, Counsel to Mick Mulvaney, Acting Chief of Staff, The White House (Nov. 8, 2019) (asserting that Acting Chief of Staff Mick Mulvaney "is absolutely immune from compelled congressional testimony with respect to matters related to his service as a senior advisor to the President" and that "[s]ubjecting a senior presidential advisor to the congressional subpoena power would be akin to requiring the President himself to appear before Congress on matters relating to the performance of his constitutionally assigned executive functions").

[110] *Committee on the Judiciary v. Miers*, 558 F. Supp. 2d 53 (D.D.C. 2008) ("The Executive cannot identify a single judicial opinion that recognizes absolute immunity for senior presidential advisors in this or any other context. That simple yet critical fact bears repeating: the asserted absolute immunity claim here is entirely unsupported by existing case law. In fact, there is Supreme Court authority that is all but conclusive on this question and that powerfully suggests that such advisors do not enjoy absolute immunity. The Court therefore rejects the Executive's claim of absolute immunity for senior presidential aides.").

[111] *Committee on the Judiciary v. McGahn,* Case No. 1:19-cv-02379, Memorandum Opinion, Doc. No. 46 (D.D.C. Nov. 25, 2019). As of this report, an appeal is pending in the U.S. Court of Appeals for the D.C. Circuit. No. 19-5331 (D.C. Cir.).

[112] Letter from Chairman Eliot L. Engel, House Committee on Foreign Affairs, Chairman Adam B. Schiff, House Permanent Select Committee on Intelligence, and Chairman Elijah E. Cummings, House Committee on Oversight and Reform, to Pat A. Cipollone, Counsel to the President, The White House (Sept. 9, 2019) (online at https://intelligence.house.gov/uploadedfiles/ele_schiff_cummings_letter_to_cipollone_on_ukraine.pdf).

[113] Letter from Chairman Eliot L. Engel, House Committee on Foreign Affairs, Chairman Adam B. Schiff, House Permanent Select Committee on Intelligence, and Chairman Elijah E. Cummings, House Committee on Oversight and Reform, to Pat A. Cipollone, Counsel to the President, The White House (Sept. 24, 2019) (online at https://intelligence.house.gov/uploadedfiles/2019-09-24.eec_engel_schiff_to_cipollone-wh_re_potus_ukraine.pdf).

[114] Letter from Chairman Elijah E. Cummings, House Committee on Oversight and Reform, Chairman Adam B. Schiff, House Permanent Select Committee on Intelligence, and Chairman Eliot L. Engel, House Committee on Foreign Affairs, to Pat A. Cipollone, Counsel to the President, The White House (Oct. 4, 2019) (online at https://oversight.house.gov/sites/democrats.oversight.house.gov/files/documents/2019-10-04.EEC%20Engel%20Schiff%20to%20Mulvaney-WH%20re%20Subpoena.pdf).

[115] Letter from Pat A. Cipollone, Counsel to the President, The White House, to Acting Chairwoman Carolyn Maloney, House Committee on Oversight and Reform, Chairman Adam B. Schiff, House Permanent Select Committee on Intelligence, and Chairman Eliot L. Engel, House Committee on Foreign Affairs, (Oct. 18, 2019).

[116] Email from Bureau of Legislative Affairs, Department of State, to Committee Staff (Oct. 2, 2019).

[117] Letter from Chairman Eliot L. Engel, House Committee on Foreign Affairs, Chairman Adam B. Schiff, House Permanent Select Committee on Intelligence, and Chairman Elijah E. Cummings, House Committee on Oversight and Reform, to Pat A. Cipollone, Counsel to the President, The White House (Sept. 9, 2019) (online at https://intelligence.house.gov/uploadedfiles/ele_schiff_cummings_letter_to_cipollone_on_ukraine.pdf).

[118] *Id.*

[119] Letter from Chairman Eliot L. Engel, House Committee on Foreign Affairs, Chairman Adam B. Schiff, House Permanent Select Committee on Intelligence, and Chairman Elijah E. Cummings, House Committee on Oversight and Reform, to Pat A. Cipollone, Counsel to the President, The White House (Sept. 24, 2019).

[120] Memorandum from Chairman Elijah E. Cummings to Members of the House Committee on Oversight and Reform, Notice of Intent to Issue Subpoenas (Oct. 2, 2019) (online at https://oversight.house.gov/sites/democrats.oversight.house.gov/files/documents/2019-10-02.COR%20WH%20Subpoena%20Memo%20and%20Schedule.pdf).

[121] Letter from Chairman Elijah E. Cummings, House Committee on Oversight and Reform, Chairman Adam B. Schiff, House Permanent Select Committee on Intelligence, and Chairman Eliot L. Engel, House Committee on Foreign Affairs, to Pat A. Cipollone, Counsel to the President, The White House (Oct. 4, 2019) (online at https://oversight.house.gov/sites/democrats.oversight.house.gov/files/documents/2019-10-04.EEC%20Engel%20Schiff%20to%20Mulvaney-WH%20re%20Subpoena.pdf).

[122] Letter from Pat A. Cipollone, Counsel to the President, The White House, to Speaker Nancy Pelosi, Chairman Adam B. Schiff, House Permanent Select Committee on Intelligence, Chairman Eliot L. Engel, House Committee on Foreign Affairs, and Chairman Elijah E. Cummings, House Committee on Oversight and Reform (Oct. 8, 2019) (online at www.whitehouse.gov/wp-content/uploads/2019/10/PAC-Letter-10.08.2019.pdf).

[123] Letter from Pat A. Cipollone, Counsel to the President, The White House, to Acting Chairwoman Carolyn Maloney, House Committee on Oversight and Reform, Chairman Adam B. Schiff, House Permanent Select Committee on Intelligence, and Chairman Eliot L. Engel, House Committee on Foreign Affairs, (Oct. 18, 2019).

[124] On September 13, the Intelligence Committee issued a subpoena pursuant to its oversight authority to the Acting Director of National Intelligence to compel the production of a complaint submitted by an Intelligence Community whistleblower, as well as other records. The Intelligence Committee issued this subpoena before Speaker Pelosi announced on September 24 that the Intelligence Committee and other committees would be continuing their work under the umbrella of the impeachment inquiry being conducted by the Judiciary Committee. As a result, this subpoena should not be conflated with subpoenas issued as part of the impeachment inquiry. *See* Letter from Chairman Adam B. Schiff, House Permanent Select Committee on Intelligence, to Joseph Maguire, Acting Director of National Intelligence, Office of the Director of National Intelligence (Sept. 13, 2019).

[125] The White House, *Memorandum of Telephone Conversation* (Apr. 21, 2019) (online at http://cdn.cnn.com/cnn/2019/images/11/15/4-21-19.trump-zelensky.call.pdf); The White House, *Memorandum of Telephone Conversation* (July 25, 2019) (online at www.whitehouse.gov/wp-content/uploads/2019/09/Unclassified09.2019.pdf).

[126] Vindman-Williams Hearing Tr. at 31-32.

[127] Vindman Dep. Tr. at 53; Morrison Dep. Tr. at 19-20.

[128] Vindman Dep. Tr. at 186-187; Morrison Dep. Tr. at 166-167.

[129] *See, e.g.*, Cooper Dep. Tr. at 42-43.

[130] Sondland Hearing Tr. at 78-79.

[131] Vindman Dep. Tr. at 36-37.

[132] Holmes Dep. Tr. at 31.

[133] House Permanent Select Committee on Intelligence, Opening Statement of Ambassador Gordon Sondland, Department of State, *Impeachment*, 116th Cong. (Nov. 20, 2019).

[134] The review reportedly uncovered "early August email exchanges between acting chief of staff Mick Mulvaney and White House budget officials seeking to provide an explanation for withholding the funds after the president had already ordered a hold in mid-July on the nearly $400 million in security assistance." The review also reportedly included interviews with "some key White House officials involved in handling Ukraine aid and dealing with complaints and concerns in the aftermath of the call between Trump and Zelensky." *White House Review Turns Up Emails Showing Extensive Effort to Justify Trump's Decision to Block Ukraine Military Aid,* Washington Post (Nov. 24, 2019) (online at www.washingtonpost.com/politics/white-house-review-turns-up-emails-showing-

extensive-effort-to-justify-trumps-decision-to-block-ukraine-military-aid/2019/11/24/2121cf98-0d57-11ea-bd9d-c628fd48b3a0_story.html).

[135] Letter from Chairman Eliot L. Engel, House Committee on Foreign Affairs, Chairman Adam B. Schiff, House Permanent Select Committee on Intelligence, and Chairman Elijah E. Cummings, House Committee on Oversight and Reform, to Vice President Michael Pence, Office of the Vice President (Oct. 4, 2019) (online at https://oversight.house.gov/sites/democrats.oversight.house.gov/files/documents/2019-10-04.EEC%20Engel%20Schiff%20%20re%20Request%20to%20VP%2010-04-19%20Letter%20and%20Schedule.pdf).

[136] *Id.*

[137] Letter from Matthew E. Morgan, Counsel to the Vice President, Office of the Vice President, to Chairman Elijah E. Cummings, House Committee on Oversight and Reform, Chairman Eliot L. Engel, House Committee on Foreign Affairs, and Chairman Adam B. Schiff, House Permanent Select Committee on Intelligence (Oct. 15, 2019).

[138] Vindman-Williams Hearing Tr. at 61.

[139] Williams Dep. Tr. at 129.

[140] Vindman-Williams Hearing Tr. at 15.

[141] Vindman-Williams Hearing Tr. at 23-24.

[142] Williams Dep. Tr. at 74-75.

[143] Letter from Chairman Adam B. Schiff, House Permanent Select Committee on Intelligence, Chairman Eliot L. Engel, House Committee on Foreign Affairs, and Chairman Elijah E. Cummings, House Committee on Oversight and Reform, to Acting Director Russell T. Vought, Office of Management and Budget (Oct. 7, 2019) (online at https://intelligence.house.gov/uploadedfiles/2019-10-07.eec_engel_schiff_to_vought-_omb_re_subpoena.pdf).

[144] *Id.*

[145] Letter from Jason Yaworske, Associate Director for Legislative Affairs, Office of Management and Budget, to Chairman Adam B. Schiff, House Permanent Select Committee on Intelligence (Oct. 15, 2019).

[146] Sandy Dep. Tr. at 23-26.

[147] Sandy Dep. Tr. at 36-41.

[148] Sandy Dep. Tr. at 57-60, 62-63.

[149] Letter from Chairman Eliot L. Engel, House Committee on Foreign Affairs, Chairman Adam B. Schiff, House Permanent Select Committee on Intelligence, and Chairman Elijah E. Cummings, House Committee on Oversight and Reform, to Secretary Michael R. Pompeo, Department of State (Sept. 9, 2019) (online at https://intelligence.house.gov/uploadedfiles/ele_schiff_cummings_letter_to_sec_pompeo_on_ukraine.pdf).

[150] Letter from Chairman Eliot L. Engel, House Committee on Foreign Affairs, Chairman Adam B. Schiff, House Permanent Select Committee on Intelligence, and Chairman Elijah E. Cummings, House Committee on Oversight and Reform, to Secretary Michael R. Pompeo, Department of State (Sept. 23, 2019).

[151] Letter from Chairman Eliot L. Engel, House Committee on Foreign Affairs, Chairman Adam B. Schiff, House Permanent Select Committee on Intelligence, and Chairman Elijah E. Cummings, House Committee on Oversight and Reform, to Secretary Michael R. Pompeo, Department of State (Sept. 27, 2019) (online at https://oversight.house.gov/sites/democrats.oversight.house.gov/files/documents/2019-09-27.EEC%20Engel%20Schiff%20%20to%20Pompeo-%20State%20re%20Document%20Subpoena.pdf).

[152] Letter from Chairman Adam B. Schiff, House Permanent Select Committee on Intelligence, Chairman Elijah E. Cummings, House Committee on Oversight and Reform, and Chairman Eliot L. Engel, House Committee on Foreign Affairs, to Ambassador Gordon Sondland, Department of State (Oct. 8, 2019) (online at https://oversight.house.gov/sites/democrats.oversight.house.gov/files/documents/2019-10-08.EEC%20Engel%20Schiff%20to%20Sondland%20re%20Subpoena.pdf); Letter from Chairman Eliot L. Engel,

House Committee on Foreign Affairs, Chairman Adam B. Schiff, House Permanent Select Committee on Intelligence, and Chairman Elijah E. Cummings, House Committee on Oversight and Reform, to Ambassador William Taylor, Department of State (Oct. 4, 2019); Letter from Chairman Eliot L. Engel, House Committee on Foreign Affairs, Chairman Adam B. Schiff, House Permanent Select Committee on Intelligence, and Chairman Elijah E. Cummings, House Committee on Oversight and Reform, to Counselor T. Ulrich Brechbuhl, Department of State (Sept. 27, 2019) (online at https://intelligence.house.gov/uploadedfiles/20190927_-_eec_engel_schiff_to_brechbuhl_re_individual_deposition_request.pdf); Letter from Chairman Eliot L. Engel, House Committee on Foreign Affairs, Chairman Adam B. Schiff, House Permanent Select Committee on Intelligence, and Chairman Elijah E. Cummings, House Committee on Oversight and Reform, to Deputy Assistant Secretary George P. Kent, Department of State (Sept. 27, 2019); Letter from Chairman Eliot L. Engel, House Committee on Foreign Affairs, Chairman Adam B. Schiff, House Permanent Select Committee on Intelligence, and Chairman Elijah E. Cummings, House Committee on Oversight and Reform, to Ambassador Kurt Volker, Department of State (Sept. 27, 2019); Letter from Chairman Eliot L. Engel, House Committee on Foreign Affairs, Chairman Adam B. Schiff, House Permanent Select Committee on Intelligence, and Chairman Elijah E. Cummings, House Committee on Oversight and Reform, to Ambassador Marie Yovanovitch, Department of State (Sept. 27, 2019).

[153] Letter from Secretary Michael R. Pompeo, Department of State, to Chairman Eliot L. Engel, House Committee on Foreign Affairs (Oct. 1, 2019) (Secretary Pompeo sent identical letters to Chairman Elijah. E. Cummings, House Committee on Oversight and Reform, and Chairman Adam B. Schiff, House Permanent Select Committee on Intelligence, the same day).

[154] *Id.*

[155] Kent Dep. Tr. at 27.

[156] Kent Dep. Tr. at 33-34.

[157] Kent Dep. Tr. at 34-35.

[158] Letter from Secretary Michael R. Pompeo, Department of State, to Chairman Eliot L. Engel, House Committee on Foreign Affairs (Oct. 1, 2019) (Secretary Pompeo sent identical letters to Chairman Elijah. E. Cummings, House Committee on Oversight and Reform, and Chairman Adam B. Schiff, House Permanent Select Committee on Intelligence, the same day).

[159] Letter from Chairman Eliot L. Engel, House Committee on Foreign Affairs, Chairman Adam B. Schiff, House Permanent Select Committee on Intelligence, and Chairman Elijah E. Cummings, House Committee on Oversight and Reform, to Deputy Secretary John J. Sullivan, Department of State (Oct. 1, 2019) (online at https://foreignaffairs.house.gov/_cache/files/4/6/4683bc86-be2a-49fc-9e76-7cdbf669592f/98BEBD8006DE62BA36BEBD175775F744.2019-10-1-ele-abs-eec-to-depsec-sullivan.pdf).

[160] *Pompeo: 'I Was on the Phone Call' with Trump and Ukrainian President*, CNN (Oct. 2, 2019) (online at www.cnn.com/2019/10/02/politics/mike-pompeo-ukraine-call/index.html).

[161] Email from Committee Staff to Bureau of Legislative Affairs, Department of State (Oct. 7, 2019).

[162] Letter from Brian Bulatao, Under Secretary of State for Management, Department of State, to Andrew Wright, Counsel to Deputy Assistant Secretary George P. Kent, Department of State (Oct. 14, 2019).

[163] Kent Dep. Tr. at 30-31, 46.

[164] Kent Dep. Tr. at 32.

[165] Kent Dep. Tr. at 35.

[166] House Permanent Select Committee on Intelligence, Opening Statement of Ambassador Gordon Sondland, Department of State, *Impeachment*, 116th Cong. (Nov. 20, 2019).

[167] *Id.*

[168] *Id.* In addition, Dr. Fiona Hill, the former Senior Director for European and Russian Affairs at the National Security Council, produced calendar entries relating to relevant meetings. Fiona Hill Document Production, Bates Hill0001 through Hill0049 (Oct. 13, 2019).

[169] Kurt Volker Document Production, Bates KV00000001-KV00000065 (Oct. 3, 2019).

[170] 18 U.S.C. § 1505.

[171] House Permanent Select Committee on Intelligence, Opening Statement of Ambassador Gordon Sondland, Department of State, *Impeachment*, 116th Cong., at 3-4 (Nov. 20, 2019).

[172] Sondland Hearing Tr. at 160.

[173] Declaration of Ambassador Gordon Sondland, Department of State, at 3 (Nov. 4, 2019).

[174] *State Department Releases Ukraine Documents to American Oversight*, American Oversight (Nov. 22, 2019) (online at www.americanoversight.org/state-department-releases-ukraine-documents-to-american-oversight); *American Oversight v. Dep't of State*, Case No. 19-cv-2934, Doc. No. 15 (D.D.C. November 25, 2019).

[175] Email from Office Manager to the Secretary of State to S_All (Mar. 26, 2019) (online at www.americanoversight.org/wp-content/uploads/2019/11/AO_State_Ukraine_Docs_11-22.pdf).

[176] Email from Madeleine Westerhout to State Department Official, (Mar. 27, 2019) (online at www.americanoversight.org/wp-content/uploads/2019/11/AO_State_Ukraine_Docs_11-22.pdf).

[177] Letter from Chairman Eliot L. Engel, House Committee on Foreign Affairs, Chairman Adam B. Schiff, House Permanent Select Committee on Intelligence, and Chairman Elijah E. Cummings, House Committee on Oversight and Reform, to Secretary Michael R. Pompeo, Department of State (Sept. 27, 2019) (online at https://oversight.house.gov/sites/democrats.oversight.house.gov/files/documents/2019-09-27.EEC%20Engel%20Schiff%20%20to%20Pompeo-%20State%20re%20Document%20Subpoena.pdf).

[178] Taylor Dep. Tr. at 33-34.

[179] House Permanent Select Committee on Intelligence, Opening Statement of Ambassador Gordon Sondland, Department of State, *Impeachment*, 116th Cong., at 20-23 (Nov. 20, 2019).

[180] Taylor Dep. Tr. at 45-46.

[181] Hale Dep. Tr. at 147-148.

[182] Letter from Chairman Adam B. Schiff, House Permanent Select Committee on Intelligence, Chairman Eliot L. Engel, House Committee on Foreign Affairs, and Chairman Elijah E. Cummings, House Committee on Oversight and Reform, to Secretary Mark Esper, Department of Defense (Oct. 7, 2019) (online at https://intelligence.house.gov/uploadedfiles/2019-10-07.eec_engel_schiff_to_esper-dod_re_subpoena.pdf).

[183] *Transcript: Secretary of Defense Mark Esper on "Face the Nation," October 13, 2019*, CBS News (Oct. 13, 2019) (online at www.cbsnews.com/news/transcript-secretary-of-defense-mark-esper-on-face-the-nation-october-13-2019/).

[184] Letter from Robert R. Hood, Assistant Secretary of Defense for Legislative Affairs, Department of Defense, to Chairman Adam B. Schiff, House Permanent Select Committee on Intelligence, Chairman Eliot L. Engel, House Committee on Foreign Affairs, and Chairman Elijah E. Cummings, House Committee on Oversight and Reform (Oct. 15, 2019).

[185] *Transcript: Secretary of Defense Mark Esper on "Face the Nation," October 13, 2019*, CBS News (Oct. 13, 2019) (online at www.cbsnews.com/news/transcript-secretary-of-defense-mark-esper-on-face-the-nation-october-13-2019/).

[186] *See, e.g.*, Cooper Dep. Tr. at 42-43.

[187] Cooper Dep. Tr. at 33.

[188] Cooper Dep. Tr. at 33-38.

[189] Cooper Hearing Tr. at 13-14.

[190] Cooper Hearing Tr. at 14.

[191] Cooper Hearing Tr. at 14.

[192] Letter from Chairman Eliot L. Engel, House Committee on Foreign Affairs, Chairman Adam B. Schiff, House Permanent Select Committee on Intelligence, and Chairman Elijah E. Cummings, House Committee on Oversight and Reform, to Secretary Rick Perry, Department of Energy (Oct. 10, 2019) (online at https://oversight.house.gov/sites/democrats.oversight.house.gov/files/documents/2019-10-10.EEC%20Engel%20Schiff%20to%20Perry-DOE%20Joint%20Cover%20Letter%20re%20Subpoena.pdf).

[193] Letter from Melissa F. Burnison, Assistant Secretary for Congressional and Intergovernmental Affairs, Department of Energy, to Chairman Eliot L. Engel, House Committee on Foreign Affairs, Chairman Adam B. Schiff, House Permanent Select Committee on Intelligence, and Chairman Elijah E. Cummings, House Committee on Oversight and Reform (Oct. 18, 2019).

[194] Hill-Holmes Hearing Tr. at 160.

[195] House Permanent Select Committee on Intelligence, Opening Statement of Ambassador Gordon Sondland, Department of State, *Impeachment*, 116th Cong. (Nov. 20, 2019).

[196] House Permanent Select Committee on Intelligence, Opening Statement of Ambassador Gordon Sondland, Department of State, *Impeachment*, 116th Cong. (Nov. 20, 2019).

[197] Letter from Chairman Chairman Adam B. Schiff, House Permanent Select Committee on Intelligence, Eliot L. Engel, House Committee on Foreign Affairs, and Chairman Elijah E. Cummings, House Committee on Oversight and Reform, to Rudy Giuliani (Sept. 30, 2019) (online at https://oversight.house.gov/sites/democrats.oversight.house.gov/files/documents/20190930%20-%20Giuliani%20HPSCI%20Subpoena%20Letter.pdf).

[198] Letter from Jon A. Sale, Counsel to Rudy Giuliani, to Committee Staff (Oct. 15, 2019).

[199] *Id.*

[200] Letter from Chairman Adam B. Schiff, House Permanent Select Committee on Intelligence, Chairman Eliot L. Engel, House Committee on Foreign Affairs, and Chairman Elijah E. Cummings, House Committee on Oversight and Reform, to Igor Fruman (Sept. 30, 2019) (online at https://oversight.house.gov/sites/democrats.oversight.house.gov/files/documents/20190930%20-%20Fruman%20Letter%20and%20Doc%20Request%20Schedule.pdf); Letter from Chairman Adam B. Schiff, House Permanent Select Committee on Intelligence, Chairman Eliot L. Engel, House Committee on Foreign Affairs, and Chairman Elijah E. Cummings, House Committee on Oversight and Reform, to Lev Parnas (Sept. 30, 2019) (online at https://oversight.house.gov/sites/democrats.oversight.house.gov/files/documents/20190930%20-%20Parnas%20Letter%20and%20Doc%20Request%20Schedule.pdf).

[201] Letter from Chairman Adam B. Schiff, House Permanent Select Committee on Intelligence, Chairman Eliot L. Engel, House Committee on Foreign Affairs, and Chairman Elijah E. Cummings, House Committee on Oversight and Reform, to John M. Dowd, Counsel to Igor Fruman and Lev Parnas (Oct. 10, 2019) (online at https://intelligence.house.gov/uploadedfiles/2019-10-09.eec_engel_schiff_to_parnas_fruman_re_subpoena.pdf).

[202] Letter from John M. Dowd, Counsel to Igor Fruman and Lev Parnas, to Committee Staff (Oct. 3, 2019).

[203] Letter from John M. Dowd, Counsel to Igor Fruman and Lev Parnas, to Committee Staff (Oct. 8, 2019).

[204] Email from John M. Dowd, Counsel to Igor Fruman and Lev Parnas, to Committee Staff (Oct. 9, 2019).

[205] Email from Committee Staff to John M. Dowd, Counsel to Igor Fruman and Lev Parnas (Oct. 10, 2019).

[206] Email from John M. Dowd, Counsel to Igor Fruman and Lev Parnas, to Committee Staff (Oct. 10, 2019).

[207] *Exclusive: Giuliani Associate Parnas Will Comply with Trump Impeachment Inquiry—Lawyer*, Reuters (Nov. 4, 2019) (online at www.reuters.com/article/us-usa-trump-impeachment-parnas-exclusiv/exclusive-giuliani-associate-now-willing-to-comply-with-trump-impeachment-inquiry-lawyer-idUSKBN1XE297). On November 23, 2019, Mr. Parnas' attorney informed the press that "Mr. Parnas learned from former Ukrainian Prosecutor General Victor Shokin that [Ranking Member Devin] Nunes had met with Shokin in Vienna last December." According to the report, "Parnas says he worked to put Nunes in touch with Ukrainians who could help Nunes dig up dirt on Biden and Democrats in Ukraine, according to Bondy." *Exclusive: Giuliani Associate Willing to Tell Congress Nunes Met with Ex-Ukrainian Official to Get Dirt on Biden,* CNN (Nov. 23, 2019) (online at

www.cnn.com/2019/11/22/politics/nunes-vienna-trip-ukrainian-prosecutor-biden/index.html). On November 24, 2019, Mr. Parnas' attorney told press that his client had arranged skype and phone calls earlier this year between Ranking Member Nunes' staff and Ukraine's chief anti-corruption prosecutor, Nazar Kholodnytsky, as well as a deputy in Ukraine's Prosecutor General's office, Konstantin Kulik. According to Mr. Parnas' attorney, Ranking Member Nunes had actually planned a trip to Ukraine instead of the calls, but cancelled the trip when his staff realized it would require alerting Chairman Schiff about the travel. *Giuliani Associate Parnas Wants to Testify that Nunes Aides Hid Ukraine Meetings on Biden Dirt from Schiff*, CNBC (Nov. 24, 2019) (online at www.cnbc.com/2019/11/24/giuliani-ally-would-testify-that-nunes-staffers-hid-ukraine-meetings-from-schiff.html).

[208] Letter from Pat A. Cipollone, Counsel to the President, The White House, to House Speaker Nancy Pelosi, Chairman Adam B. Schiff, House Permanent Select Committee on Intelligence, Chairman Eliot L. Engel, House Committee on Foreign Affairs Committee, and Chairman Elijah E. Cummings, House Committee on Oversight and Reform (Oct. 8, 2019) (online at www.whitehouse.gov/wp-content/uploads/2019/10/PAC-Letter-10.08.2019.pdf).

[209] *See* 2 U.S.C. §§ 192, 194. Witnesses who received subpoenas that were subsequently withdrawn would not face a similar risk of being held in contempt of Congress.

[210] *See, e.g.*, Email from Committee Staff to Mick Mulvaney, Acting Chief of Staff, The White House (Nov. 7, 2019) ("Your failure or refusal to comply with the subpoena, including at the direction or behest of the President, shall constitute further evidence of obstruction of the House's impeachment inquiry and may be used as an adverse inference against you and the President. Moreover, your failure to appear shall constitute evidence that may be used against you in a contempt proceeding.").

[211] Letter from Chairman Eliot L. Engel, House Committee on Foreign Affairs, Chairman Adam B. Schiff, House Permanent Select Committee on Intelligence, and Acting Chairwoman Carolyn B. Maloney, House Committee on Oversight and Reform, Mick Mulvaney, Acting Chief of Staff, The White House (Nov. 5, 2019) (online at https://oversight.house.gov/sites/democrats.oversight.house.gov/files/2019-11-05.CBM%20Engel%20Schiff%20to%20Mulvaney-WH%20re%20Depo%20Notice.pdf).

[212] House Permanent Select Committee on Intelligence, Subpoena to Mick Mulvaney, Acting Chief of Staff, The White House (Nov. 7, 2019).

[213] Email from William Pittard, Counsel to Mick Mulvaney, Acting Chief of Staff, The White House, to Committee Staff (Nov. 8, 2019).

[214] Letter from Pat A. Cipollone, Counsel to the President, The White House, to William Pittard, Counsel to Mick Mulvaney, Acting Chief of Staff, The White House (Nov. 8, 2019) (online at www.whitehouse.gov/wp-content/uploads/2019/10/PAC-Letter-10.08.2019.pdf).

[215] Letter from Steven A. Engel, Assistant Attorney General, Office of Legal Counsel, Department of Justice, to Pat A. Cipollone, Counsel to the President, The White House (Nov. 7, 2019).

[216] Mulvaney Dep. Tr. at 5.

[217] Mulvaney Dep. Tr. at 7-9.

[218] On November 8, 2019, Mr. Mulvaney filed a motion in federal court seeking to join a lawsuit, discussed below, filed by Dr. Charles Kupperman seeking a declaratory judgment as to whether he should comply with the Committees' subpoena. On November 11, 2019, Mr. Mulvaney withdrew his request to join the case. *White House Chief of Staff Mulvaney Drops Bid to Join Kupperman Impeachment Lawsuit,* Washington Post (Nov. 11, 2019) (online at www.washingtonpost.com/local/legal-issues/bolton-and-kupperman-reject-white-house-chief-of-staff-mulvaneys-bid-to-join-impeachment-lawsuit/2019/11/11/cdf40226-04ac-11ea-8292-c46ee8cb3dce_story.html).

[219] Letter from Chairman Eliot L. Engel, House Committee on Foreign Affairs, Chairman Adam B. Schiff, House Permanent Select Committee on Intelligence, and Acting Chairwoman Carolyn B. Maloney, House Committee on Oversight and Reform, to Robert B. Blair, Assistant to the President and Senior Advisor to the Chief of Staff, The White House (Oct. 24, 2019).

[220] Letter from Whitney C. Ellerman, Counsel to Robert B. Blair, Assistant to the President and Senior Advisor to the Chief of Staff, The White House, to Chairman Eliot L. Engel, House Committee on Foreign Affairs,

Chairman Adam B. Schiff, House Permanent Select Committee on Intelligence, and Acting Chairwoman Carolyn B. Maloney, House Committee on Oversight and Reform (Nov. 2, 2019).

[221] Letter from Chairman Adam B. Schiff, House Permanent Select Committee on Intelligence, Acting Chairwoman Carolyn B. Maloney, House Committee on Oversight and Reform, and Chairman Eliot L. Engel, House Committee on Foreign Affairs, to Whitney C. Ellerman, Counsel to Robert B. Blair, Assistant to the President and Senior Advisor to the Chief of Staff, The White House (Nov. 3, 2019); House Permanent Select Committee on Intelligence, Subpoena to Robert B. Blair, Assistant to the President and Senior Advisor to the Chief of Staff, The White House (Nov. 3, 2019).

[222] Blair Dep. Tr. at 6-7.

[223] Letter from Chairman Eliot L. Engel, House Committee on Foreign Affairs, Chairman Adam B. Schiff, House Permanent Select Committee on Intelligence, and Acting Chairwoman Carolyn B. Maloney, House Committee on Oversight and Reform, to Charles J. Cooper and Michael W. Kirk, Counsel to Ambassador John Bolton, Former National Security Advisor, The White House (Oct. 30, 2019).

[224] Email from Charles J. Cooper, Counsel to Ambassador John Bolton, Former National Security Advisor, The White House, to Committee Staff (Oct. 30, 2019).

[225] Letter from Charles J. Cooper, Counsel to Ambassador John Bolton, Former National Security Advisor, The White House, to Douglas N. Letter, General Counsel, House of Representatives (Nov. 8, 2019).

[226] In early November 2019, Ambassador Bolton's personal attorney also informed Committee staff that if the Committees were to issue a subpoena to compel his testimony, he would seek to join the lawsuit filed by Dr. Kupperman. On November 24, 2019, Chairman Schiff stated, "We've certainly been in touch with his lawyer and what we've been informed by his lawyer—because we invited him and he did not choose to come in and testify, notwithstanding the fact that his deputy Fiona Hill and his other deputy Colonel Vindman and Tim Morrison and others on the National Security Council have shown the courage to come in—is if we subpoena him, they will sue us in court." *Schiff Pushes Bolton to Testify But Will Not Go to Court to Force Him*, CNN (Nov. 24, 2019) (online at www.cnn.com/2019/11/24/politics/adam-schiff-house-democrats-impeachment-state-of-the-union-cnntv/index.html).

[227] Letter from Chairman Eliot L. Engel, House Committee on Foreign Affairs, Chairman Adam B. Schiff, House Permanent Select Committee on Intelligence, and Acting Chairwoman Carolyn B. Maloney, House Committee on Oversight and Reform, to John A. Eisenberg, Deputy Counsel to the President for National Security Affairs and Legal Advisor to the National Security Council, National Security Council, The White House (Oct. 30, 2019).

[228] Eisenberg Dep. Tr. at 6 ("Mr. Eisenberg never acknowledged receipt or otherwise responded to the committees' deposition request, nor did any official at the White House.").

[229] Letter from Chairman Eliot L. Engel, House Committee on Foreign Affairs, Chairman Adam B. Schiff, House Permanent Select Committee on Intelligence, and Acting Chairwoman Carolyn B. Maloney, House Committee on Oversight and Reform, to John A. Eisenberg, Deputy Counsel to the President for National Security Affairs and Legal Advisor to the National Security Council, National Security Council, The White House (Nov. 1, 2019); House Permanent Select Committee on Intelligence, Subpoena to John A. Eisenberg, Deputy Counsel to the President for National Security Affairs and Legal Advisor to the National Security Council, The White House (Nov. 1, 2019).

[230] Letter from William A. Burck, Counsel to John A. Eisenberg, Deputy Counsel to the President for National Security Affairs and Legal Advisor to the National Security Council, National Security Council, The White House, to Chairman Eliot L. Engel, House Committee on Foreign Affairs, Chairman Adam B. Schiff, House Permanent Select Committee on Intelligence, and Acting Chairwoman Carolyn B. Maloney, House Committee on Oversight and Reform (Nov. 4, 2019).

[231] Letter from Pat A. Cipollone, Counsel to the President, The White House, to William A. Burck, Counsel to John A. Eisenberg, Deputy Counsel to the President for National Security Affairs and Legal Advisor to the National Security Council, National Security Council, The White House (Nov. 3, 2019).

[232] Letter from Steven A. Engel, Assistant Attorney General, Office of Legal Counsel, Department of Justice, to Pat A. Cipollone, Counsel to the President, the White House (Nov. 3, 2019).

[233] Eisenberg Dep. Tr. at 6-8.

[234] Letter from Chairman Eliot L. Engel, House Committee on Foreign Affairs, Chairman Adam B. Schiff, House Permanent Select Committee on Intelligence, and Acting Chairwoman Carolyn B. Maloney, House Committee on Oversight and Reform, to Michael Ellis, Senior Associate Counsel to the President and Deputy Legal Advisor to the National Security Council, National Security Council, The White House (Oct. 30, 2019).

[235] Email from Paul Butler, Counsel to Michael Ellis, Senior Associate Counsel to the President and Deputy Legal Advisor to the National Security Council, National Security Council, The White House, to Committee Staff (Nov. 2, 2019).

[236] Email from Paul Butler, Counsel to Michael Ellis, Senior Associate Counsel to the President and Deputy Legal Advisor to the National Security Council, National Security Council, The White House, to Committee Staff (Nov. 3, 2019).

[237] Letter from Chairman Adam B. Schiff, House Permanent Select Committee on Intelligence, Acting Chairwoman Carolyn B. Maloney, House Committee on Oversight and Reform, Chairman Eliot L. Engel, House Committee on Foreign Affairs, to Paul W. Butler, Counsel to Michael Ellis, Senior Associate Counsel to the President and Deputy Legal Advisor to the National Security Council, National Security Council, The White House (Nov. 3, 2019); House Permanent Select Committee on Intelligence, Subpoena to Michael Ellis, Senior Associate Counsel to the President and Deputy Legal Advisor to the National Security Council, National Security Council, The White House (Nov. 3, 2019).

[238] Ellis Dep. Tr. at 7.

[239] Letter from Chairman Eliot L. Engel, House Committee on Foreign Affairs, Chairman Adam B. Schiff, House Permanent Select Committee on Intelligence, and Acting Chairwoman Carolyn B. Maloney, House Committee on Oversight and Reform, to Preston Wells Griffith, Senior Director for International Energy and Environment, National Security Council (Oct. 24, 2019).

[240] Letter from Karen D. Williams, Counsel to Preston Wells Griffith, Senior Director for International Energy and Environment, National Security Council, to Chairman Eliot L. Engel, House Committee on Foreign Affairs, Chairman Adam B. Schiff, House Permanent Select Committee on Intelligence, and Acting Chairwoman Carolyn B. Maloney, House Committee on Oversight and Reform (Nov. 4, 2019).

[241] Letter from Chairman Adam B. Schiff, House Permanent Select Committee on Intelligence, Acting Chairwoman Carolyn B. Maloney, House Committee on Oversight and Reform, and Chairman Eliot L. Engel, House Committee on Foreign Affairs, to Karen D. Williams, Counsel to Preston Wells Griffith, Senior Director for International Energy and Environment, National Security Council (Nov. 4, 2019); House Permanent Select Committee on Intelligence, Subpoena to Preston Wells Griffith, Senior Director for International Energy and Environment, National Security Council (Nov. 4, 2019).

[242] Griffith Dep. Tr. at 5-6.

[243] Letter from Chairman Eliot L. Engel, House Committee on Foreign Affairs, Chairman Adam B. Schiff, House Permanent Select Committee on Intelligence, and Chairman Elijah E. Cummings, House Committee on Oversight and Reform, to Dr. Charles M. Kupperman, Former Deputy Assistant to the President for National Security Affairs, National Security Council (Oct. 16, 2019).

[244] Email from Committee Staff to Charles J. Cooper and Michael W. Kirk, Counsel to Dr. Charles M. Kupperman, Former Deputy Assistant to the President for National Security Affairs, National Security Council (Oct. 25, 2019); House Permanent Select Committee on Intelligence, Subpoena to Dr. Charles M. Kupperman, Former Deputy Assistant to the President for National Security Affairs, National Security Council (Oct. 25, 2019).

[245] Compl., *Kupperman v. U.S. House of Representatives et al.*, No. 19 Civ. 3224 (D.D.C. filed Oct. 25, 2019).

[246] Email from Michael W. Kirk, Counsel to Dr. Charles M. Kupperman, Former Deputy Assistant to the President for National Security Affairs, National Security Council, to Committee Staff (Oct. 25, 2019).

[247] Letter from Pat A. Cipollone, Counsel to the President, The White House, to Charles J. Cooper, Counsel to Dr. Charles M. Kupperman, Former Deputy Assistant to the President for National Security Affairs, National Security Council (Oct. 25, 2019).

[248] Letter from Steven A. Engel, Assistant Attorney General, Office of Legal Counsel, Department of Justice, to Pat A. Cipollone, Counsel to the President, The White House (Oct. 25, 2019).

[249] Letter from Chairman Adam B. Schiff, House Permanent Select Committee on Intelligence, Chairman Eliot L. Engel, House Committee on Foreign Affairs, and Acting Chairwoman Carolyn B. Maloney, House Committee on Oversight and Reform, to Charles J. Cooper and Michael W. Kirk, Counsel to Dr. Charles M. Kupperman, Former Deputy Assistant to the President for National Security Affairs, National Security Council (Oct. 26, 2019).

[250] Letter from Charles J. Cooper, Counsel to Dr. Charles M. Kupperman, Former Deputy Assistant to the President for National Security Affairs, National Security Council, to Committee Staff (Oct. 26, 2019).

[251] Letter from Charles J. Cooper, Counsel to Dr. Charles M. Kupperman, Former Deputy Assistant to the President for National Security Affairs, National Security Council, to Committee Staff (Oct. 27, 2019).

[252] Letter from Chairman Eliot L. Engel, House Committee on Foreign Affairs, Chairman Adam B. Schiff, House Permanent Select Committee on Intelligence, and Acting Chairwoman Carolyn B. Maloney, House Committee on Oversight and Reform to Charles J. Cooper and Michael W. Kirk, Counsel to Dr. Charles M. Kupperman, Former Deputy Assistant to the President for National Security Affairs, National Security Council, (Nov. 5, 2019).

[253] Letter from Charles J. Cooper, Counsel to Dr. Charles M. Kupperman, Former Deputy Assistant to the President for National Security Affairs, National Security Council, to Douglas N. Letter, General Counsel, House of Representatives (Nov. 8, 2019).

[254] *Committee on the Judiciary v. McGahn*, Memorandum Opinion (D.D.C. Nov. 25, 2019) ("To make the point as plain as possible, it is clear to this Court for the reasons explained above that, with respect to senior-level presidential aides, absolute immunity from compelled congressional process simply does not exist. Indeed, absolute testimonial immunity for senior-level White House aides appears to be a fiction that has been fastidiously maintained over time through the force of sheer repetition in OLC opinions, and through accommodations that have permitted its proponents to avoid having the proposition tested in the crucible of litigation. And because the contention that a President's top advisors cannot be subjected to compulsory congressional process simply has no basis in the law, it does not matter whether such immunity would theoretically be available to only a handful of presidential aides due to the sensitivity of their positions, or to the entire Executive branch. Nor does it make any difference whether the aides in question are privy to national security matters, or work solely on domestic issues."). As of this report, an appeal is pending in the D.C. Circuit. No. 19-5331 (D.C. Cir.).

[255] *See, Kupperman v. U.S. House of Representatives, et al.*, No. 19 Civ. 3224 (D.D.C.). As of this report, the House Defendants' Motion to Dismiss (Nov. 14, 2019), ECF No. 41, remains pending. Although the Committee will not reissue the subpoena to Dr. Kupperman and the court case is moot, he could choose to appear on a voluntary basis to assist Congress in the discharge of its Constitutional responsibilities.

[256] Letter from Chairman Eliot L. Engel, House Committee on Foreign Affairs, Chairman Adam B. Schiff, House Permanent Select Committee on Intelligence, and Chairman Elijah E. Cummings, House Committee on Oversight and Reform, to Acting Director Russell T. Vought, Office of Management and Budget (Oct. 11, 2019).

[257] Email from Jessica L. Donlon, Deputy General Counsel for Oversight, Office of Management and Budget, to Committee Staff (Oct. 21, 2019).

[258] Russell T. Vought, Twitter (Oct. 21, 2019) (online at https://twitter.com/RussVought45/status/1186276793172578306?s=20).

[259] Letter from Chairman Eliot L. Engel, House Committee on Foreign Affairs, Chairman Adam B. Schiff, House Permanent Select Committee on Intelligence, and Acting Chairwoman Carolyn B. Maloney, House Committee on Oversight and Reform, to Acting Director Russell T. Vought, Office of Management and Budget (Oct. 25, 2019).

[260] Letter from Jason A. Yaworske, Associate Director for Legislative Affairs, Office of Management and Budget, to Chairman Adam B. Schiff, House Permanent Select Committee on Intelligence (Nov. 4, 2019).

[261] Vought Dep. Tr. at 10-11.

[262] Letter from Chairman Eliot L. Engel, House Committee on Foreign Affairs, Chairman Adam B. Schiff, House Permanent Select Committee on Intelligence, and Chairman Elijah E. Cummings, House Committee on Oversight and Reform, to Associate Director Michael Duffey, Office of Management and Budget (Oct. 11, 2019).

[263] Email from Jessica L. Donlon, Deputy General Counsel for Oversight, Office of Management and Budget, to Committee Staff (Oct. 21, 2019).

[264] Letter from Chairman Eliot L. Engel, House Committee on Foreign Affairs, Chairman Adam B. Schiff, House Permanent Select Committee on Intelligence, and Acting Chairwoman Carolyn B. Maloney, House Committee on Oversight and Reform, to Michael Duffey, Associate Director of National Security Programs, Office of Management and Budget (Oct. 25, 2019) (online at https://intelligence.house.gov/uploadedfiles/20191025_-_letter_duffey_re_subpoena.pdf); House Permanent Select Committee on Intelligence, Subpoena to Michael Duffey, Associate Director of National Security Programs, Office of Management and Budget (Oct. 25, 2019).

[265] Letter from Jason A. Yaworske, Associate Director for Legislative Affairs, Office of Management and Budget, to Chairman Adam B. Schiff, House Permanent Select Committee on Intelligence (Nov. 4, 2019).

[266] Duffey Dep. Tr. at 7.

[267] Letter from Chairman Eliot L. Engel, House Committee on Foreign Affairs, Chairman Adam B. Schiff, House Permanent Select Committee on Intelligence, and Acting Chairwoman Carolyn B. Maloney, House Committee on Oversight and Reform, to Brian McCormack, Associate Director for Natural Resources, Energy, and Science, Office of Management and Budget (Oct. 24, 2019).

[268] Letter from Chairman Eliot L. Engel, House Committee on Foreign Affairs, Chairman Adam B. Schiff, House Permanent Select Committee on Intelligence, and Acting Chairwoman Carolyn B. Maloney, House Committee on Oversight and Reform, to Brian McCormack, Associate Director for Natural Resources, Energy, and Science, Office of Management and Budget (Nov. 1, 2019); House Permanent Select Committee on Intelligence, Subpoena to Brian McCormack, Associate Director for Natural Resources, Energy, and Science, Office of Management and Budget (Nov. 1, 2019).

[269] Letter from Jason A. Yaworske, Associate Director for Legislative Affairs, Office of Management and Budget, to Chairman Adam B. Schiff, House Permanent Select Committee on Intelligence (Nov. 4, 2019).

[270] McCormack Dep. Tr. at 6.

[271] Letter from Chairman Eliot L. Engel, House Committee on Foreign Affairs, Chairman Adam B. Schiff, House Permanent Select Committee on Intelligence, and Chairman Elijah E. Cummings, House Committee on Oversight and Reform, to Secretary Michael R. Pompeo, Department of State (Sept. 13, 2019).

[272] Letter from Chairman Eliot L. Engel, House Committee on Foreign Affairs, Chairman Adam B. Schiff, House Permanent Select Committee on Intelligence, and Chairman Elijah E. Cummings, House Committee on Oversight and Reform, to Secretary Michael R. Pompeo, Department of State (Sept. 27, 2019) (internal citations omitted) (online at https://oversight.house.gov/sites/democrats.oversight.house.gov/files/documents/2019-09-27.EEC%20Engel%20Schiff%20%20to%20Pompeo-%20State%20re%20Depositions.pdf).

[273] Letter from Chairman Eliot L. Engel, House Committee on Foreign Affairs, Chairman Adam B. Schiff, House Permanent Select Committee on Intelligence, and Chairman Elijah E. Cummings, House Committee on Oversight and Reform, to T. Ulrich Brechbuhl, Counselor, Department of State (Sept. 27, 2019).

[274] Letter from Secretary Michael R. Pompeo, Department of State, to Chairman Eliot L. Engel, House Committee on Foreign Affairs (Oct. 1, 2019) (Secretary Pompeo sent identical letters to Chairman Elijah. E. Cummings, House Committee on Oversight and Reform, and Chairman Adam B. Schiff, House Permanent Select Committee on Intelligence, the same day).

[275] Letter from Chairman Eliot L. Engel, House Committee on Foreign Affairs, Chairman Adam B. Schiff, House Permanent Select Committee on Intelligence, and Chairman Elijah E. Cummings, House Committee on Oversight and Reform, to Deputy Secretary of State John J. Sullivan, Department of State (Oct. 1, 2019) (online at https://oversight.house.gov/sites/democrats.oversight.house.gov/files/documents/2019-10-01%20ELE%20ABS%20EEC%20TO%20DEPSEC%20SULLIVAN.pdf).

[276] Email from Ronald J. Tenpas, Counsel to T. Ulrich Brechbuhl, Counselor, Department of State, to Committee Staff (Oct. 2, 2019).

[277] Email from Committee Staff, to Ronald J. Tenpas, Counsel to T. Ulrich Brechbuhl, Counselor, Department of State (Oct. 8, 2019).

[278] Email from Committee Staff, to Ronald J. Tenpas, Counsel to T. Ulrich Brechbuhl, Counselor, Department of State (Oct. 9, 2019).

[279] Email from Ronald J. Tenpas, Counsel to T. Ulrich Brechbuhl, Counselor, Department of State, to Committee Staff (Oct. 9, 2019).

[280] Letter from Chairman Eliot L. Engel, House Committee on Foreign Affairs, Chairman Adam B. Schiff, House Permanent Select Committee on Intelligence, and Acting Chairwoman Carolyn B. Maloney, House Committee on Oversight and Reform, to T. Ulrich Brechbuhl, Counselor, Department of State (Oct. 25, 2019); House Permanent Select Committee on Intelligence, Subpoena to T. Ulrich Brechbuhl, Counselor, Department of State (Oct. 25, 2019).

[281] Letter from Ronald J. Tenpas, Counsel to T. Ulrich Brechbuhl, Counselor, Department of State to Chairman Adam B. Schiff, House Permanent Select Committee on Intelligence, Chairman Eliot L. Engel, House Committee on Foreign Affairs, and Acting Chairwoman Carolyn B. Maloney, House Committee on Oversight and Reform (Nov. 5, 2019).

[282] Brechbuhl Dep. Tr. at 4-5.

[283] Email from Committee staff to Ronald J. Tenpas, Counsel to T. Ulrich Brechbuhl, Counselor, Department of State (Nov. 5, 2019); Email from Committee Staff to Ronald J. Tenpas, Counsel to T. Ulrich Brechbuhl, Counselor (Nov. 22, 2019).

[284] Letter from Brian Bulatao, Under Secretary of State for Management, to Ronald J. Tenpas, Counsel to T. Ulrich Brechbuhl, Counselor, Department of State (Nov. 4, 2019.)

[285] Letter from Chairman Eliot L. Engel, House Committee on Foreign Affairs, Chairman Adam B. Schiff, House Permanent Select Committee on Intelligence, and Acting Chairwoman Carolyn B. Maloney, House Committee on Oversight and Reform, to Secretary Rick Perry, Department of Energy (Nov. 1, 2019).

[286] Letter from General Counsel Bill Cooper, Department of Energy, to Chairman Adam B. Schiff, House Permanent Select Committee on Intelligence, Chairman Eliot L. Engel, House Committee on Foreign Affairs, and Acting Chairwoman Carolyn B. Maloney, House Committee on Oversight and Reform (Nov. 5, 2019).

[287] Letter from Chairman Eliot L. Engel, House Committee on Foreign Affairs, Chairman Adam B. Schiff, House Permanent Select Committee on Intelligence, and Chairman Elijah E. Cummings, House Committee on Oversight and Reform, to Secretary Michael R. Pompeo, Department of State (Sept. 13, 2019).

[288] Letter from Chairman Eliot L. Engel, House Committee on Foreign Affairs, Chairman Adam B. Schiff, House Permanent Select Committee on Intelligence, and Chairman Elijah E. Cummings, House Committee on Oversight and Reform, to Secretary Michael R. Pompeo, Department of State (Sept. 27, 2019) (internal citations omitted).

[289] Letter from Chairman Eliot L. Engel, House Committee on Foreign Affairs, Chairman Adam B. Schiff, House Permanent Select Committee on Intelligence, and Chairman Elijah E. Cummings, House Committee on Oversight and Reform, to Ambassador Marie Yovanovitch, Former U.S. Ambassador to Ukraine, Department of State (Sept. 27, 2019).

[290] Letter from Secretary Michael R. Pompeo, Department of State, to Chairman Eliot L. Engel, House Committee on Foreign Affairs (Oct. 1, 2019) (Secretary Pompeo sent identical letters to Chairman Elijah. E. Cummings, House Committee on Oversight and Reform, and Chairman Adam B. Schiff, House Permanent Select Committee on Intelligence, the same day).

[291] Letter from Brian Bulatao, Under Secretary of State for Management, Department of State, to Lawrence S. Robbins, Counsel to Ambassador Marie Yovanovitch, Former U.S. Ambassador to Ukraine, Department of State (Oct. 10, 2019).

[292] The White House, *Remarks by President Trump Before Marine One Departure* (Oct. 10, 2019) (online at www.whitehouse.gov/briefings-statements/remarks-president-trump-marine-one-departure-69/).

[293] Letter from Chairman Adam B. Schiff, House Permanent Select Committee on Intelligence, Chairman Eliot L. Engel, House Committee on Foreign Affairs, and Chairman Elijah E. Cummings, House Committee on Oversight and Reform, to Lawrence S. Robbins, Counsel to Ambassador Marie Yovanovitch, Former U.S. Ambassador to Ukraine, Department of State (Oct. 11, 2019); House Permanent Select Committee on Intelligence, Subpoena to Ambassador Marie Yovanovitch, Former U.S. Ambassador to Ukraine, Department of State (Oct. 11, 2019).

[294] Letter from Lawrence S. Robbins, Counsel to Ambassador Marie Yovanovitch, Former U.S. Ambassador to Ukraine, Department of State, to Brian Bulatao, Under Secretary of State for Management, Department of State (Oct. 11, 2019) (citations omitted).

[295] Yovanovitch Dep. Tr.

[296] *Id.* at 70.

[297] Email from Committee Staff to Lawrence S. Robbins, Counsel to Ambassador Marie Yovanovitch, Former U.S. Ambassador to Ukraine, Department of State (Nov. 15, 2019); House Permanent Select Committee on Intelligence, Subpoena to Ambassador Marie Yovanovitch, Former U.S. Ambassador to Ukraine, Department of State (Nov. 15, 2019).

[298] Yovanovitch Hearing Tr. at 157-158.

[299] Letter from Chairman Elijah E. Cummings, House Committee on Oversight and Reform, Chairman Eliot L. Engel, House Committee on Foreign Affairs, and Chairman Adam B. Schiff, House Permanent Select Committee on Intelligence, to Secretary Michael R. Pompeo, Department of State (Sept. 27, 2019) (internal citations omitted) (online at https://oversight.house.gov/sites/democrats.oversight.house.gov/files/documents/2019-09-27.EEC%20Engel%20Schiff%20%20to%20Pompeo-%20State%20re%20Depositions.pdf).

[300] Letter from Chairman Elijah E. Cummings, House Committee on Oversight and Reform, Chairman Eliot L. Engel, House Committee on Foreign Affairs, and Chairman Adam B. Schiff, House Permanent Select Committee on Intelligence, to Ambassador Gordon Sondland, U.S. Ambassador to the European Union, Department of State (Sept. 27, 2019).

[301] Letter from Secretary Michael R. Pompeo, Department of State, to Chairman Eliot L. Engel, House Committee on Foreign Affairs (Oct. 1, 2019) (Secretary Pompeo sent identical letters to Chairman Elijah. E. Cummings, House Committee on Oversight and Reform, and Chairman Adam B. Schiff, House Permanent Select Committee on Intelligence, the same day).

[302] Letter from Brian Bulatao, Under Secretary of State for Management, Department of State, to Robert Luskin, Counsel to Ambassador Gordon Sondland, U.S. Ambassador to the European Union, Department of State (Oct.7, 2019).

[303] Email from Robert Luskin, Counsel to Ambassador Gordon Sondland, U.S. Ambassador to the European Union, Department of State, to Committee Staff (Oct. 8, 2019).

[304] Letter from Chairman Adam B. Schiff, House Permanent Select Committee on Intelligence, Chairman Elijah E. Cummings, House Committee on Oversight and Reform, and Chairman Eliot L. Engel, House Committee on Foreign Affairs, to Ambassador Gordon Sondland, U.S. Ambassador to the European Union, Department of State (Oct. 8, 2019); House Permanent Select Committee on Intelligence, Subpoena to Ambassador Gordon Sondland, U.S. Ambassador to the European Union, Department of State (Oct. 11, 2019).

[305] Letter from Chairman Adam B. Schiff, House Permanent Select Committee on Intelligence, Chairman Elijah E. Cummings, House Committee on Oversight and Reform, and Chairman Eliot L. Engel, House Committee on Foreign Affairs, to Ambassador Gordon Sondland, U.S. Ambassador to the European Union, Department of State (Oct. 14, 2019).

[306] Sondland Dep. Tr.

[307] *Id.* at 16.

[308] *Id.* at 17.

[309] Letter from Robert Luskin, Counsel to Ambassador Gordon Sondland, U.S. Ambassador to the European Union, Department of State, to Chairman Adam B. Schiff, House Permanent Select Committee on

Intelligence (Nov. 4, 2019); Declaration of Ambassador Gordon Sondland, U.S. Ambassador to the European Union, Department of State (Nov. 4, 2019).

[310] House Permanent Select Committee on Intelligence, Subpoena to Ambassador Gordon Sondland, U.S. Ambassador to the European Union, Department of State (Nov. 20, 2019).

[311] Sondland Hearing Tr. at 160.

[312] Letter from Chairman Eliot L. Engel, House Committee on Foreign Affairs, Chairman Adam B. Schiff, House Permanent Select Committee on Intelligence, and Chairman Elijah E. Cummings, House Committee on Oversight and Reform, to Secretary Michael R. Pompeo, Department of State (Sept. 13, 2019).

[313] Letter from Chairman Eliot L. Engel, House Committee on Foreign Affairs, Chairman Adam B. Schiff, House Permanent Select Committee on Intelligence, and Chairman Elijah E. Cummings, House Committee on Oversight and Reform, to Secretary Michael R. Pompeo, Department of State (Sept. 27, 2019) (online at https://oversight.house.gov/sites/democrats.oversight.house.gov/files/documents/2019-09-27.EEC%20Engel%20Schiff%20%20to%20Pompeo-%20State%20re%20Depositions.pdf) (internal citations omitted).

[314] Letter from Chairman Eliot L. Engel, House Committee on Foreign Affairs, Chairman Adam B. Schiff, House Permanent Select Committee on Intelligence, and Chairman Elijah E. Cummings, House Committee on Oversight and Reform, to George P. Kent, Deputy Assistant Secretary of State, Bureau of European and Eurasian Affairs, Department of State (Sept. 27, 2019).

[315] Email from George P. Kent, Deputy Assistant Secretary of State, Bureau of European and Eurasian Affairs, Department of State, to Committee Staff (Sept. 27, 2019).

[316] Letter from Secretary Michael R. Pompeo, Department of State, to Chairman Eliot L. Engel, House Committee on Foreign Affairs (Oct. 1, 2019) (Secretary Pompeo sent identical letters to Chairman Elijah. E. Cummings, House Committee on Oversight and Reform, and Chairman Adam B. Schiff, House Permanent Select Committee on Intelligence, the same day).

[317] Email from Committee Staff to Andrew M. Wright, Counsel to George P. Kent, Deputy Assistant Secretary of State, Bureau of European and Eurasian Affairs, Department of State (Oct. 8, 2019).

[318] Letter from Brian Bulatao, Under Secretary of State for Management, Department of State, to Andrew M. Wright, Counsel to George P. Kent, Deputy Assistant Secretary of State, Bureau of European and Eurasian Affairs, Department of State (Oct. 10, 2019).

[319] Letter from Chairman Adam B. Schiff, House Permanent Select Committee on Intelligence, Chairman Eliot L. Engel, House Committee on Foreign Affairs, and Chairman Elijah E. Cummings, House Committee on Oversight and Reform, to Andrew M. Wright, Counsel to George P. Kent, Deputy Assistant Secretary of State, Bureau of European and Eurasian Affairs, Department of State (Oct. 15, 2019); House Permanent Select Committee on Intelligence, Subpoena to George P. Kent, Deputy Assistant Secretary of State, Bureau of European and Eurasian Affairs, Department of State (Oct. 15, 2019).

[320] Kent Dep. Tr.

[321] *Id.* at 17.

[322] House Permanent Select Committee on Intelligence, Subpoena to George P. Kent, Deputy Assistant Secretary of State, Bureau of European and Eurasian Affairs, Department of State (Nov. 20, 2019).

[323] Kent-Taylor Hearing Tr. at 142-143.

[324] Letter from Chairman Eliot L. Engel, House Committee on Foreign Affairs, Chairman Adam B. Schiff, House Permanent Select Committee on Intelligence, and Chairman Elijah E. Cummings, House Committee on Oversight and Reform, to John J. Sullivan, Deputy Secretary of State, Department of State (Oct. 4, 2019).

[325] Letter from Chairman Eliot L. Engel, House Committee on Foreign Affairs, Chairman Adam B. Schiff, House Permanent Select Committee on Intelligence, and Chairman Elijah E. Cummings, House Committee on Oversight and Reform, to Ambassador William B. Taylor, Jr., Chargé d'Affaires, U.S. Embassy, Kyiv, Department of State (Oct. 4, 2019).

326 Letter from Chairman Adam B. Schiff, House Permanent Select Committee on Intelligence, Chairman Elijah E. Cummings, House Committee on Oversight and Reform, and Chairman Eliot L. Engel, House Committee on Foreign Affairs, to Ambassador William B. Taylor, Jr., Ambassador William B. Taylor, Jr., Chargé d'Affaires, U.S. Embassy, Kyiv, Department of State (Oct. 14, 2019).

327 Email from Committee Staff to John B. Bellinger, III, and Jeffrey H. Smith, Counsel to Ambassador William B. Taylor, Jr., Chargé d'Affaires, U.S. Embassy, Kyiv, Department of State (Oct. 22, 2019); House Permanent Select Committee on Intelligence, Subpoena to Ambassador William B. Taylor, Jr., Chargé d'Affaires, U.S. Embassy, Kyiv, Department of State (Oct. 22, 2019).

328 Taylor Dep. Tr. at 83.

329 House Permanent Select Committee on Intelligence, Subpoena to Ambassador William B. Taylor, Jr., Chargé d'Affaires, U.S. Embassy, Kyiv, Department of State (Nov. 13, 2019).

330 Kent-Taylor Hearing Tr. at 143.

331 Letter from Chairman Eliot L. Engel, House Committee on Foreign Affairs, Chairman Adam B. Schiff, House Permanent Select Committee on Intelligence, and Acting Chairwoman Carolyn B. Maloney, House Committee on Oversight and Reform, to Mark J. MacDougall, Counsel to Catherine Croft, Foreign Service Officer, Department of State (Oct. 24, 2019); Letter from Chairman Eliot L. Engel, House Committee on Foreign Affairs, Chairman Adam B. Schiff, House Permanent Select Committee on Intelligence, and Acting Chairwoman Carolyn B. Maloney, House Committee on Oversight and Reform, to Mark J. MacDougall, Counsel to Christopher Anderson, Foreign Service Officer, Department of State (Oct. 24, 2019).

332 Letter from Mark J. MacDougall, Counsel to Catherine Croft, Foreign Service Officer, Department of State, and Christopher Anderson, Foreign Service Officer, Department of State, to Committee Staff (Oct. 25, 2019).

333 Letter from Brian Bulatao, Under Secretary of State for Management, Department of State, to Mark J. MacDougall, Counsel to Catherine Croft, Foreign Service Officer, Department of State (Oct. 28, 2019) (bracketed text in original); Letter from Brian Bulatao, Under Secretary of State for Management, Department of State, to Mark J. MacDougall, Counsel to Christopher Anderson, Foreign Service Officer, Department of State (Oct. 28, 2019) (bracketed text in original); see Letter from Pat A. Cipollone, Counsel to the President, The White House, to Speaker Nancy Pelosi, Chairman Elijah E. Cummings, House Committee on Oversight and Reform, Chairman Eliot L. Engel, House Committee on Foreign Affairs, and Chairman Adam B. Schiff, House Permanent Select Committee on Intelligence (Oct. 8, 2019).

334 Email from Committee Staff to Mark J. MacDougall and Abbey McNaughton, Counsel to Catherine Croft, Foreign Service Officer, Department of State and Christopher Anderson, Foreign Service Officer, Department of State (Oct. 30, 2019); House Permanent Select Committee on Intelligence, Subpoena to Catherine Croft, Foreign Service Officer, Department of State (Oct. 30, 2019); House Permanent Select Committee on Intelligence, Subpoena to Christopher Anderson, Foreign Service Officer, Department of State (Oct. 30, 2019).

335 Croft Dep. Tr.; Anderson Dep. Tr.

336 Croft Dep. Tr. at 12.

337 Anderson Dep. Tr. at 11-12.

338 Letter from Chairman Eliot L. Engel, House Committee on Foreign Affairs, Chairman Adam B. Schiff, House Permanent Select Committee on Intelligence, and Chairman Elijah E. Cummings, House Committee on Oversight and Reform, to Laura K. Cooper, Deputy Assistant Secretary of Defense for Russia, Ukraine, Eurasia, Department of Defense (Oct. 11, 2019).

339 Letter from Deputy Secretary of Defense David L. Norquist to Daniel Levin, Counsel to Laura K. Cooper, Deputy Assistant Secretary of Defense for Russia, Ukraine, Eurasia, Department of Defense (Oct. 22, 2019).

340 Email from Committee Staff to Dan Levin, Counsel to Laura K. Cooper, Deputy Assistant Secretary of Defense for Russia, Ukraine, Eurasia, Department of Defense (Oct. 23, 2019); House Permanent Select Committee on Intelligence, Subpoena to Laura K. Cooper, Deputy Assistant Secretary of Defense for Russia, Ukraine, Eurasia, Department of Defense (Oct. 23, 2019).

[341] Cooper Dep. Tr.

[342] *Id.* at 108.

[343] Email from Committee Staff to Dan Levin, Counsel to Laura K. Cooper, Deputy Assistant Secretary of Defense for Russia, Ukraine, Eurasia, Department of Defense (Nov. 20, 2019); House Permanent Select Committee on Intelligence, Subpoena to Laura K. Cooper, Deputy Assistant Secretary of Defense for Russia, Ukraine, Eurasia, Department of Defense (Nov. 20, 2019).

[344] Cooper-Hale Hearing Tr.

[345] Letter from Chairman Adam B. Schiff, House Permanent Select Committee on Intelligence, Acting Chairwoman Carolyn B. Maloney, House Committee on Oversight and Reform, and Chairman Eliot L. Engel, House Committee on Foreign Affairs, to Mark Sandy, Deputy Associate Director of National Security Programs, Office of Management and Budget (Nov. 5, 2019).

[346] Email from Mark Sandy, Deputy Associate Director of National Security Programs, Office of Management and Budget, to Committee Staff (Nov. 6, 2019).

[347] Email from Jessica L. Donlon, Deputy General Counsel for Oversight, Office of Management and Budget, to Committee Staff (Nov. 7, 2019).

[348] Email from Committee Staff to Barbara Van Gelder, Counsel to Mark Sandy, Deputy Associate Director of National Security Programs, Office of Management and Budget (Nov. 16, 2019); House Permanent Select Committee on Intelligence, Subpoena to Mark Sandy, Deputy Associate Director of National Security Programs, Office of Management and Budget (Nov. 16, 2019).

[349] Sandy Dep. Tr.

[350] Sandy Dep. Tr. at 161.

[351] Letter from Chairman Eliot L. Engel, House Committee on Foreign Affairs, Chairman Adam B. Schiff, House Permanent Select Committee on Intelligence, and Chairman Elijah E. Cummings, House Committee on Oversight and Reform, to Dr. Fiona Hill, Former Deputy Assistant to the President and Senior Director for Europe and Russian Affairs, National Security Council (Oct. 9, 2019).

[352] Letter from Lee S. Wolosky, Counsel to Dr. Fiona Hill, Former Deputy Assistant to the President and Senior Director for Europe and Russian Affairs, National Security Council, to Michael M. Purpura, Deputy Counsel and Deputy Assistant to the President, The White House, and Patrick F. Philbin, Deputy Counsel and Deputy Assistant to the President, The White House (Oct. 13, 2019).

[353] Letter from Michael M. Purpura, Deputy Counsel and Deputy Assistant to the President, The White House, to Lee S. Wolosky, Counsel to Dr. Fiona Hill, Former Deputy Assistant to the President and Senior Director for Europe and Russian Affairs, National Security Council (Oct. 14, 2019).

[354] Email from Committee Staff to Lee S. Wolosky and Samuel S. Ungar, Counsel to Dr. Fiona Hill, Former Deputy Assistant to the President and Senior Director for Europe and Russian Affairs, National Security Council (Oct. 14, 2019); House Permanent Select Committee on Intelligence, Subpoena to Dr. Fiona Hill, Former Deputy Assistant to the President and Senior Director for Europe and Russian Affairs, National Security Council (Oct. 14, 2019).

[355] Hill Dep. Tr.

[356] Letter from Lee S. Wolosky, Counsel to Dr. Fiona Hill, Former Deputy Assistant to the President and Senior Director for Europe and Russian Affairs, National Security Council, to Michael M. Purpura, Deputy Counsel and Deputy Assistant to the President, The White House (Nov. 18, 2019).

[357] Letter from Michael M. Purpura, Deputy Counsel and Deputy Assistant to the President, The White House, to Lee S. Wolosky, Counsel to Dr. Fiona Hill, Former Deputy Assistant to the President and Senior Director for Europe and Russian Affairs, National Security Council (Nov. 20, 2019).

[358] Email from Committee Staff to Lee S. Wolosky and Samuel S. Ungar, Counsel to Dr. Fiona Hill, Former Deputy Assistant to the President and Senior Director for Europe and Russian Affairs, National Security Council (Nov. 21, 2019); House Permanent Select Committee on Intelligence, Subpoena to Dr. Fiona Hill, Former

Deputy Assistant to the President and Senior Director for Europe and Russian Affairs, National Security Council (Nov. 21, 2019).

[359] Hill-Holmes Hearing Tr.

[360] Letter from Chairman Eliot L. Engel, House Committee on Foreign Affairs, Chairman Adam B. Schiff, House Permanent Select Committee on Intelligence, and Chairman Elijah E. Cummings, House Committee on Oversight and Reform, to Lieutenant Colonel Alexander S. Vindman, Director for Ukraine, National Security Council (Oct. 16, 2019).

[361] Email from Committee Staff, to Michael Volkov and Matt Stankiewicz, Counsel to Lieutenant Colonel Alexander S. Vindman, Director for Ukraine, National Security Council (Oct. 29, 2019); House Permanent Select Committee on Intelligence, Subpoena to Lieutenant Colonel Alexander S. Vindman, Director for Ukraine, National Security Council (Oct. 29, 2019).

[362] Vindman Dep. Tr. (During the deposition, Lieutenant Colonel Vindman stated: "I was subpoenaed to appear here. You know, absent a subpoena, I would believe I was operating under the President's guidance to not appear, but I was subpoenaed and I presented myself." Vindman Dep. Tr. at 232).

[363] Email from Committee Staff, to Michael Volkov and Matt Stankiewicz, Counsel to Lieutenant Colonel Alexander S. Vindman, Director for Ukraine, National Security Council (Nov. 19, 2019); House Permanent Select Committee on Intelligence, Subpoena to Lieutenant Colonel Alexander S. Vindman, Director for Ukraine, National Security Council (Nov. 19, 2019).

[364] Vindman-Williams Hearing Tr.

[365] Letter from Chairman Eliot L. Engel, House Committee on Foreign Affairs, Chairman Adam B. Schiff, House Permanent Select Committee on Intelligence, and Chairman Elijah E. Cummings, House Committee on Oversight and Reform, to Timothy Morrison, Former Deputy Assistant to the President and Senior Director for Europe and Russia, National Security Council (Oct. 16, 2019).

[366] Email from Committee Staff to Barbara Van Gelder, Counsel to Timothy Morrison, Former Deputy Assistant to the President and Senior Director for Europe and Russia, National Security Council (Oct. 31, 2019); House Permanent Select Committee on Intelligence, Subpoena to Timothy Morrison, Former Deputy Assistant to the President and Senior Director for Europe and Russia, National Security Council (Oct. 31, 2019).

[367] Morrison Dep. Tr.

[368] Email from Committee Staff to Barbara Van Gelder, Counsel to Timothy Morrison, Former Deputy Assistant to the President and Senior Director for Europe and Russia, National Security Council (Nov. 19, 2019); House Permanent Select Committee on Intelligence, Subpoena to Timothy Morrison, Former Deputy Assistant to the President and Senior Director for Europe and Russia, National Security Council (Nov. 19, 2019).

[369] Morrison-Volker Hearing Tr.

[370] Letter from Chairman Eliot L. Engel, House Committee on Foreign Affairs, Chairman Adam B. Schiff, House Permanent Select Committee on Intelligence, and Acting Chairwoman Carolyn B. Maloney, House Committee on Oversight and Reform, to David Hale, Under Secretary of State for Political Affairs, Department of State (Nov. 1, 2019).

[371] Letter from Brian A. Glasser, Counsel to David Hale, Under Secretary of State for Political Affairs, Department of State, to Chairman Adam B. Schiff, House Permanent Select Committee on Intelligence, Chairman Eliot L. Engel, House Committee on Foreign Affairs, and Acting Chairwoman Carolyn B. Maloney, House Committee on Oversight and Reform (Nov. 5, 2019).

[372] Email from Committee Staff to Brian Glasser and Cary Joshi, Counsel for David Hale, Under Secretary of State for Political Affairs, Department of State (Nov. 6, 2019); House Permanent Select Committee on Intelligence, Subpoena to David Hale, Under Secretary of State for Political Affairs, Department of State (Nov. 6, 2019).

[373] Hale Dep. Tr.

[374] Email from Committee Staff to Brian A. Glasser, Counsel to David Hale, Under Secretary of State for Political Affairs, Department of State (Nov. 20, 2019); House Permanent Select Committee on Intelligence, Subpoena to David Hale, Under Secretary of State for Political Affairs, Department of State (Nov. 20, 2019).

[375] Cooper-Hale Hearing Tr.

[376] Letter from Chairman Adam B. Schiff, House Permanent Select Committee on Intelligence, Acting Chairwoman Carolyn B. Maloney, House Committee on Oversight and Reform, and from Chairman Eliot L. Engel, House Committee on Foreign Affairs, to Kenneth L. Wainstein, Counsel to David Holmes, Political Counselor at the U.S. Embassy in Kyiv, Ukraine, Department of State (Nov. 12, 2019).

[377] Email from Committee Staff to Kenneth L. Wainstein, Paul J. Nathanson, and Katherine Swan, Counsel to David Holmes, Political Counselor at the U.S. Embassy in Kyiv, Ukraine, Department of State (Nov. 15, 2019); House Permanent Select Committee on Intelligence, Subpoena to David Holmes, Political Counselor at the U.S. Embassy in Kyiv, Ukraine, Department of State (Nov. 15, 2019).

[378] Holmes Dep. Tr.

[379] Email from Committee Staff to Kenneth L. Wainstein, Paul J. Nathanson, and Katherine Swan, Counsel to David Holmes, Political Counselor at the U.S. Embassy in Kyiv, Ukraine, Department of State (Nov. 21, 2019); House Permanent Select Committee on Intelligence, Subpoena to David Holmes, Political Counselor at the U.S. Embassy in Kyiv, Ukraine, Department of State (Nov. 21, 2019).

[380] Hill-Holmes Hearing Tr.

[381] Email from Committee Staff to Ambassador P. Michael McKinley, Former Senior Advisor to the Secretary of State, Department of State (Oct. 12, 2019).

[382] Letter from Chairman Eliot L. Engel, House Committee on Foreign Affairs, Chairman Adam B. Schiff, House Permanent Select Committee on Intelligence, and Chairman Elijah E. Cummings, House Committee on Oversight and Reform, to John B. Bellinger, III, Counsel to Ambassador P. Michael McKinley, Former Senior Advisor to the Secretary of State, Department of State (Oct. 14, 2019).

[383] McKinley Transcribed Interview Tr.

[384] Letter from Chairman Eliot L. Engel, House Committee on Foreign Affairs, Chairman Adam B. Schiff, House Permanent Select Committee on Intelligence, and Chairman Elijah E. Cummings, House Committee on Oversight and Reform, to Ambassador Philip T. Reeker, Acting Assistant Secretary, Bureau of European and Eurasian Affairs, Department of State (Oct. 16, 2019).

[385] Letter from Chairman Adam B. Schiff, House Permanent Select Committee on Intelligence, Chairman Eliot L. Engel, House Committee on Foreign Affairs, and Acting Chairwoman Carolyn B. Maloney, House Committee on Oversight and Reform, to Margaret E. Daum, Counsel to Ambassador Philip T. Reeker, Acting Assistant Secretary, Bureau of European and Eurasian Affairs, Department of State (Oct. 25, 2019); House Permanent Select Committee on Intelligence, Subpoena to Ambassador Philip T. Reeker, Acting Assistant Secretary, Bureau of European and Eurasian Affairs, Department of State (Oct. 25, 2019).

[386] Reeker Dep. Tr.

[387] Letter from Chairman Eliot L. Engel, House Committee on Foreign Affairs, Chairman Adam B. Schiff, House Permanent Select Committee on Intelligence, and Chairman Elijah E. Cummings, House Committee on Oversight and Reform, to Secretary Michael R. Pompeo, Department of State (Sept. 13, 2019).

[388] Letter from Chairman Eliot L. Engel, House Committee on Foreign Affairs, Chairman Adam B. Schiff, House Permanent Select Committee on Intelligence, and Chairman Elijah E. Cummings, House Committee on Oversight and Reform, to Secretary Michael R. Pompeo, Department of State (Sept. 27, 2019).

[389] Letter from Chairman Eliot L. Engel, House Committee on Foreign Affairs, Chairman Adam B. Schiff, House Permanent Select Committee on Intelligence, and Chairman Elijah E. Cummings, House Committee on Oversight and Reform, to Ambassador Kurt Volker, U.S. Special Representative for Ukraine Negotiations, Department of State (Sept. 27, 2019).

[390] Letter from Secretary Michael F. Pompeo, Department of State, to Chairman Eliot L. Engel, House Committee on Foreign Affairs (Oct. 1, 2019) (Identical letters transmitted to Chairman Schiff and Chairman Cummings).

[391] Letter from Marik A. String, Acting Legal Advisor, Department of State, to Margaret E. Daum, Counsel to Ambassador Kurt Volker, U.S. Special Representative for Ukraine Negotiations, Department of State (Oct. 2, 2019).

[392] Letter from Margaret E. Daum, Counsel to Ambassador Kurt Volker, U.S. Special Representative for Ukraine Negotiations, Department of State, to Chairman Eliot L. Engel, House Committee on Foreign Affairs, Chairman Adam B. Schiff, House Permanent Select Committee on Intelligence, and Chairman Elijah E. Cummings, House Committee on Oversight and Reform (Oct. 2, 2019); Kurt Volker Document Production, Bates KV00000001 – KV00000065 (Oct. 2, 2019).

[393] Volker Transcribed Interview Tr.

[394] Morrison-Volker Hearing Tr.

[395] Letter from Chairman Adam B. Schiff, House Permanent Select Committee on Intelligence, and Acting Chairwoman Carolyn B. Maloney, House Committee on Oversight and Reform, and Chairman Eliot L. Engel, House Committee on Foreign Affairs, to Justin Shur, Counsel to Jennifer Williams, Special Advisor for Europe and Russia, Office of the Vice President (Nov. 4, 2019).

[396] Email from Committee Staff to Justin Shur, Counsel to Jennifer Williams, Special Advisor for Europe and Russia, Office of the Vice President (Nov. 7, 2019); House Permanent Select Committee on Intelligence, Subpoena to Jennifer Williams, Special Advisor for Europe and Russia, Office of the Vice President (Nov. 7, 2019).

[397] Williams Dep. Tr.

[398] Letter from Jennifer Williams, Special Advisor for Europe and Russia, Office of the Vice President, Justin Shur, Emily K. Damrau, and Caleb Hayes-Deats, Counsel to Jennifer Williams, Special Advisor for Europe and Russia, Office of the Vice President, to Chairman Adam B. Schiff, House Permanent Select Committee on Intelligence (Nov. 11, 2019).

[399] Email from Committee Staff to Justin Shur and Caleb Hayes-Deats, Counsel to Jennifer Williams, Special Advisor for Europe and Russia, Office of the Vice President (Nov. 19, 2019); House Permanent Select Committee on Intelligence, Subpoena to Jennifer Williams, Special Advisor for Europe and Russia, Office of the Vice President (Nov. 19, 2019).

[400] Vindman-Williams Hearing Tr.

[401] Yovanovitch Dep. Tr. at 193.

[402] Yovanovitch Hearing Tr. at 37-38.

[403] Yovanovitch Hearing Tr. at 38.

[404] Donald J. Trump, Twitter (Nov. 15, 2019) (online at https://twitter.com/realDonaldTrump/status/1195356198347956224).

[405] Yovanovitch Hearing Tr. at 46.

[406] *The Latest: Ousted Ukraine Ambassador Has Her Say in Hearing,* Associated Press (Nov. 16, 2019) (online at https://apnews.com/2f420045618b4106b6fa7419a3d75b8e).

[407] *Impeachment Inquiry Hearing with Former US Ambassador to Ukraine*, CNN (Nov. 15, 2019) (online at www.cnn.com/politics/live-news/impeachment-hearing-11-15-19/h_fb32b149181437e02e5d937c6fc64f35). During a recess in the hearing at which Ambassador Yovanovitch was testifying, a federal jury returned a verdict of guilty against President Trump's longest-serving political advisor, Roger Stone, on seven criminal counts, including witness tampering and obstruction of Congress' investigation into Russian interference in the 2016 election and possible links to President Trump's campaign. Mr. Stone used threats and intimidation to attempt to persuade a witness to withhold information and lie to Congress. He has yet to be sentenced. *See Roger Stone Guilty on All Counts of Lying to Congress, Witness Tampering*, Washington Post (Nov. 15, 2019) (online at www.washingtonpost.com/local/public-safety/roger-stone-jury-weighs-evidence-and-a-defense-move-to-make-case-

about-mueller/2019/11/15/554fff5a-06ff-11ea-8292-c46ee8cb3dce_story.html). Mr. Stone was convicted of giving false and misleading statements to the Intelligence Committee, failing to produce and lying about the existence of records responsive to Committee requests, and attempting to persuade a witness to give false testimony to the Committee. Among other acts of witness tampering, Mr. Stone told the witness to "Stonewall it. Plead the Fifth" and to "be honest w fbi" that "there was no back channel." He also called the witness a "rat" and "stoolie" and threatened retaliation. *United States v. Roger Stone*, Indictment, No. 1:19-cr-00018-ABJ (Jan. 24, 2019). Mr. Stone was convicted of violating 18 U.S.C. § 1505 (obstruction), 18 U.S.C. § 1001 (false statements), and 18 U.S.C. § 1512(b) (witness tampering).

[408] *Fox and Friends*, Fox News (Nov. 22, 2019) (online at www.youtube.com/watch?v=WNqKhRcpktU).

[409] Donald J. Trump, Twitter (Oct. 23, 2019) (online at https://twitter.com/realDonaldTrump/status/1189167309455331328).

[410] The White House, *Remarks by President Trump Before Marine One Departure* (Nov. 3, 2019) (online at www.whitehouse.gov/briefings-statements/remarks-president-trump-marine-one-departure-74/).

[411] Donald J. Trump, Twitter (Nov. 19, 2019) (retweeting Dan Scavino Jr., Twitter (Nov. 19, 2019) (online at https://twitter.com/Scavino45/status/1196860213233684480)).

[412] *See, e.g, Berman Shocked by Republican's Attacks on US War Vet*, CNN (Oct. 29, 2019) (online at www.cnn.com/videos/politics/2019/10/29/duffy-berman-spar-over-vindman-loyalty newday-vpx.cnn) (former Rep. Sean Duffy claiming that Lt. Col Vindman "has an affinity, I think for the Ukraine," that "it seems very clear that he is incredibly concerned about Ukrainian defense," and that "I don't know that he's concerned about American policy"); *see also* Rudy Giuliani, Twitter (Oct. 30, 2019) (online at https://twitter.com/RudyGiuliani/status/1189732605383630850) (claiming that Lt. Col. Vindman was "giving advice to two countries" and stating that "I thought he worked for US").

[413] House Permanent Select Committee on Intelligence, Written Statement of Lieutenant Colonel Alexander S. Vindman, Impeachment, 116th Cong. (Nov. 19, 2019).

[414] Donald J. Trump, Twitter (Oct. 23, 2019) (online at https://twitter.com/realDonaldTrump/status/1187063301731209220).

[415] Donald J. Trump, Twitter (Oct. 23, 2019) (online at https://twitter.com/realDonaldTrump/status/1187080923961012228).

[416] The White House, *Remarks by President Trump Before Marine One Departure* (Oct. 25, 2019) (online at www.whitehouse.gov/briefings-statements/remarks-president-trump-marine-one-departure-72/).

[417] Donald J. Trump, Twitter (Nov. 13, 2019) (online at https://twitter.com/realdonaldtrump/status/1194608482793795584).

[418] Donald J. Trump, Twitter (Nov. 17, 2019) (online at https://twitter.com/realDonaldTrump/status/1196155347117002752).

[419] Vindman-Williams Hearing Tr. at 97.

[420] Donald J. Trump, Twitter (Nov. 16, 2019) (online at https://twitter.com/realDonaldTrump/status/1195727871765073921); Donald J. Trump, Twitter (Nov. 16, 2019) (online at https://twitter.com/realDonaldTrump/status/1195727879780360193).

[421] 50 U.S.C. § 3033(g)(3) (when a complaint is received from a member of the Intelligence Community, "the Inspector General shall not disclose the identity of the employee without the consent of the employee, unless the Inspector General determines that such disclosure is unavoidable during the course of the investigation or the disclosure is made to an official of the Department of Justice responsible for determining whether a prosecution should be undertaken").

[422] 50 U.S.C. § 3234(b).

[423] Letter from Michael K. Atkinson, Inspector General of the Intelligence Community, to Chairman Adam B. Schiff, House Permanent Select Committee on Intelligence, and Ranking Member Devin Nunes, House Permanent Select Committee on Intelligence (Sept. 9, 2019); *see also* 50 U.S.C. § 3033(k)(5)(C) ("Upon receipt of

the transmittal from the ICIG, the Director *shall* within 7 calendar days of such receipt, forward such transmittal to the congressional intelligence committees, together with any comments the Director considers appropriate.")

[424] Letter from Chairman, Adam B. Schiff, House Permanent Select Committee on Intelligence, to Joseph Maguire, Acting Director of National Intelligence, Office of the Director of National Intelligence (Sept. 13, 2019).

[425] House Permanent Select Committee on Intelligence, *House Intelligence Committee Releases Whistleblower Complaint* (Sept. 26, 2019) (online at https://intelligence.house.gov/news/documentsingle.aspx?DocumentID=708).

[426] *Listen: Audio of Trump Discussing Whistleblower at Private Event: 'That's Close to a Spy,'* Los Angeles Times (Sept. 26, 2019) (online at www.latimes.com/politics/story/2019-09-26/trump-at-private-breakfast-who-gave-the-whistle-blower-the-information-because-thats-almost-a-spy).

[427] House Permanent Select Committee on Intelligence, *Chairmen Warn President to Stop Attacking Whistleblower and Witnesses to His Misconduct and to Halt Efforts to Obstruct Impeachment Inquiry* (Sept. 26, 2019) (online at https://intelligence.house.gov/news/documentsingle.aspx?DocumentID=709).

[428] Donald J. Trump, Twitter (Sept. 29, 2019) (online at https://twitter.com/realDonaldTrump/status/1178442765736333313?s=20).

[429] Donald J. Trump, Twitter (Oct. 4, 2019) (online at https://twitter.com/realDonaldTrump/status/1180123504924151809).

[430] The White House, *Remarks by President Trump Before Marine One Departure* (Nov. 3, 2019) (online at www.whitehouse.gov/briefings-statements/remarks-president-trump-marine-one-departure-74/).

[431] Donald J. Trump, Twitter (Nov. 3, 2019) (online at https://twitter.com/realdonaldtrump/status/1191000516580519937).

[432] The White House, *Remarks by President Trump Before Marine One Departure* (Nov. 3, 2019) (online at www.whitehouse.gov/briefings-statements/remarks-president-trump-marine-one-departure-74/).

[433] The White House, *Remarks by President Trump Before Marine One Departure* (Nov. 4, 2019) (online at www.whitehouse.gov/briefings-statements/remarks-president-trump-marine-one-departure-75/).

[434] The White House, *Remarks by President Trump After Tour of Apple Manufacturing Plant* (Nov. 20, 2019) (online www.whitehouse.gov/briefings-statements/remarks-president-trump-tour-apple-manufacturing-plant-austin-tx/).

[435] Letter from Chairman Adam B. Schiff to Ranking Member Devin Nunes, House Permanent Select Committee on Intelligence (Nov. 9, 2019).

[436] In 2017, every Republican Member of Congress joined a unanimous vote in the House of Representatives to increase penalties for retaliation against whistleblowers. U.S. House of Representatives, Roll Call Vote Approving S. 585, The Dr. Chris Kirkpatrick Whistleblower Protection Act of 2017 (Oct. 12, 2017) (420 yeas, 0 nays) (online at www.govtrack.us/congress/votes/115-2017/h568).

[437] *House Intelligence Chair News Conference*, C-SPAN (Mar. 24, 2017) (online at www.c-span.org/video/?425953-1/paul-manafort-volunteered-intelligence-committee-chairman-nunes).

[438] *Id.*

[439] Office of Senator Chuck Grassley, *Grassley Statement Regarding Intel Community Whistleblower* (Oct. 1, 2019) (online at www.grassley.senate.gov/news/news-releases/grassley-statement-regarding-intel-community-whistleblower).

[440] *Senate Intel Chair Doesn't Want Whistleblower's Identity Disclosed*, The Hill (Nov. 7, 2019) (online at https://thehill.com/homenews/senate/469455-senate-intel-chair-doesnt-want-whistleblowers-identity-disclosed).

[441] *Republicans Break with Trump and Rand Paul on Whistleblower Unmasking*, Politico (Nov. 5, 2019) (online at www.politico.com/news/2019/11/05/rand-paul-trump-whistleblower-065917).

APPENDIX A: KEY PEOPLE AND ENTITIES

Anderson, Christopher J.	Special Advisor for Ukraine Negotiations, Department of State, August 2017-July 2019
Atkinson, Michael K.	Inspector General of the Intelligence Community, May 2018-present
Avakov, Arsen	Ukrainian Minister of Internal Affairs, February 2014-present
Bakanov, Ivan	Head of Security Service of Ukraine, August 2019-present; First Deputy Chief of the Security Service of Ukraine, May 2019-August 2019
Barr, William P.	Attorney General, Department of Justice, February 2019-present
Biden, Hunter	Son of former Vice President Joe Biden
Biden, Joseph R., Jr.	U.S. Vice President, January 2009-January 2017
Blair, Robert B.	Assistant to the President and Senior Advisor to the Chief of Staff, February 2019-present
Bohdan (Bogdan), Andriy	Head of Ukrainian Presidential Administration, May 2019-present
Bolton, John	National Security Advisor, March 2018-September 2019
Brechbuhl, T. Ulrich	Counselor, Department of State, May 2018-present
Bulatao, Brian	Under Secretary of State for Management, Department of State, May 2019-present
Burisma Holdings	Ukrainian energy company
Cipollone, Pat	White House Counsel, December 2018-present
Clinton, Hillary Rodham	Democratic Presidential candidate, November 2016
Cooper, Laura K.	Deputy Assistant Secretary of Defense for Russia, Ukraine, Eurasia, Department of Defense, 2016-present
Croft, Catherine M.	Special Advisor for Ukraine Negotiations, Department of State, July 2019-present; Ukraine director, National Security Council, July 2017-July 2018

CrowdStrike	Cybersecurity company; object of conspiracy theories claiming that CrowdStrike framed Russia in hack of the DNC server in the 2016 U.S. election
Danyliuk (Danylyuk), Oleksandr "Sasha"	Secretary, Ukrainian National Security and Defense Council, May 2019-September 2019
diGenova, Joseph	Attorney allegedly working for President Trump to obtain information from Ukrainian officials on the Bidens
Duffey, Michael	Associate Director, National Security Programs, Office of Management and Budget, May 2019-present
Eisenberg, John	Legal Advisor to the National Security Council and Deputy Counsel to the President for National Security Affairs, February 2017-present
Ellis, Michael	Senior Associate Counsel to the President and Deputy Legal Advisor to the National Security Council, March 2017-present
Elwood, Courtney Simmons	General Counsel, Central Intelligence Agency, June 2017-present
Engel, Steven A.	Assistant Attorney General, Office of Legal Counsel, Department of Justice, November 2017-present
Esper, Mark	Secretary of Defense, Department of Defense, July 2019-present; Acting Secretary of Defense, June 2019-July 2019
Fruman, Igor	Giuliani associate named in indictment unsealed on October 10, 2019
Giuliani, Rudolph "Rudy"	President Trump's agent and personal attorney
Griffith, P. Wells	Senior Director for International Energy and Environment, National Security Council, April 2018-present
Hale, David M.	Under Secretary of State for Political Affairs, Department of State, August 2018-present
Hannity, Sean	Host of *Hannity*, Fox News, January 2009-present
Hill, Fiona	Deputy Assistant to the President and Senior Director for European and Russian Affairs, National Security Council, April 2017-July 2019
Hochstein, Amos J.	Supervisory Board Member, Naftogaz, November 2017-present

Holmes, David A.	Political Counselor, U.S. Embassy in Kyiv, Ukraine, August 2017-present
Johnson, Ron	Senator from Wisconsin, Chairman, Senate Homeland Security and Governmental Affairs Committee, January 2015-present
Kellogg, Keith	National Security Advisor to the Vice President, April 2018-present
Kenna, Lisa D.	Executive Secretary in the Office of the Secretary, Department of State, June 2017-present
Kent, George P.	Deputy Assistant Secretary of State, Bureau of European and Eurasian Affairs, September 2018-present; Deputy Chief of Mission in Kyiv, Ukraine, 2015-2018
Kholodnitsky, Nazar	Head, Ukrainian Specialized Anti-Corruption Prosecutor's Office, November 2015-present
Klitenic, Jason	General Counsel, Office of the Director of National Intelligence
Kulyk, Konstiantyn	Deputy Head of the Ukrainian Department of International Legal Cooperation of the Prosecutor General's Office, November 2018-November 2019
Kupperman, Charles M.	Deputy National Security Advisor, January 2019-September 2019
Kushner, Jared	Assistant to the President and Senior Advisor, 2017-present
Kvien, Kristina	Deputy Chief of Mission, U.S. Embassy in Kyiv, May 2019-present
Lutsenko, Yuriy	Ukrainian Prosecutor General, May 2016-August 2019
McCormack, Brian	Associate Director for Natural Resources, Office of Management and Budget, September 2019-present; Chief of Staff, Department of Energy, March 2017-September 2019
McKinley, P. Michael	Senior Advisor to the Secretary, Department of State, May 2018-October 2019
McKusker, Elaine A.	Deputy Under Secretary of Defense (Comptroller), Department of Defense, August 2017-present
Maguire, Joseph	Acting Director of National Intelligence, August 2019-present

Manafort, Paul	Chairman, Donald J. Trump presidential campaign, May 2016-August 2016; convicted in August 2018 on two counts of bank fraud, five counts of tax fraud, and one count of failure to disclose a foreign bank account
Morrison, Tim	Deputy Assistant to the President for National Security, National Security Council, July 2019-October 2019
Mueller, Robert S., III	Special Counsel, Department of Justice, May 2017-May 2019
Mulvaney, John Michael "Mick"	Acting Chief of Staff, White House, January 2019-present
Murphy, Chris	Senator from Connecticut, Ranking Member, Subcommittee on Near East, South Asia, Central Asia, and Counterterrorism, Senate Committee on Foreign Relations, formerly Ranking Member, Subcommittee on Europe and Regional Security Cooperation, Senate Committee on Foreign Relations, January 2017-January 2019
Naftogaz	Ukrainian state-owned national gas company
Parnas, Lev	Giuliani associate named in indictment unsealed on October 10, 2019
Patel, Kashyap "Kash"	Senior Director for Counterterrorism, National Security Council, July 2019-present; former Staff, Directorate of International Organizations and Alliances, National Security Council, February 2019-July 2019; former National Security Advisor, House Permanent Select Committee on Intelligence, March 2018-January 2019; former Senior Counsel for Counterterrorism, House Permanent Select Committee on Intelligence, April 2017-March 2018
Pence, Michael R.	Vice President, January 2017-present
Pennington, Joseph	Chargé d'Affaires, of the U.S. Embassy in Ukraine, May 2019
Perez, Carol Z.	Director General of the Foreign Service and Director of Human Services, January 2019-present
Perry, James Richard "Rick"	Secretary of Energy, March 2017-December 2019
Pompeo, Michael	Secretary of State, April 2018-present
Poroshenko, Petro	President of Ukraine, June 2014-May 2019

Portman, Robert	U.S. Senator from Ohio, January 2011-present; Chairman, Permanent Subcommittee on Investigations, Senate Homeland Security and Governmental Affairs Committee, January 2015-present
Purpura, Michael	Deputy Counsel to the President, December 2018-present
Putin, Vladimir	Russian President, May 2012-present
Reeker, Philip T.	Acting Assistant Secretary, Bureau of European and Eurasian Affairs, Department of State, March 2019-present
Rood, John C.	Under Secretary of Defense for Policy, Department of Defense, January 2018-present
Sandy, Mark	Deputy Associate Director for National Security at the Office of Management and Budget, December 2013-present; Acting Director of the Office of Management and Budget, January 2017-February 2017
Sekulow, Jay	Personal attorney for President Trump
Shokin, Viktor	Ukrainian Prosecutor General of Ukraine, February 2015-March 2016
Short, Marc	Chief of Staff to Vice President Mike Pence, February 2019-present
Solomon, John	Author of articles promoting debunked conspiracy theories about the Bidens, Crowdstrike, and the 2016 U.S. election
Sondland, Gordon	U.S. Ambassador to the European Union, July 2018-present
String, Marik	Acting Legal Advisor, Office of the Legal Advisor, Department of State, June 2019-present
Sullivan, John J.	Deputy Secretary of State, Department of State, June 2017-present
Taylor, William B., Jr.	Chargé d'Affaires for the U.S. Embassy in Kyiv, Ukraine, June 2019-present
"Three Amigos"	Secretary of Energy Rick Perry, Ambassador Gordon Sondland, and Ambassador Kurt Volker
Toensing, Victoria	Attorney allegedly working "off the books" for President Trump to obtain information from Ukrainian officials on the Bidens

Trump, Donald J.   U.S. President, January 2017-present

Trump, Donald J., Jr.   Son of President Trump

Vindman, Alexander S.   Director for Ukraine, National Security Council, July 2018-present; Lieutenant Colonel, U.S. Army

Volker, Kurt   U.S. Special Representative for Ukraine Negotiations, Department of State, July 2017-September 2019

Vought, Russell T.   Acting Director, Office of Management and Budget, January 2019-present

Whistleblower   Author of complaint declassified by the Office of the Director of National Intelligence on September 25, 2019

Williams, Jennifer   Special Advisor for Europe and Russia, Office of the Vice President, April 2019-present

Yermak, Andriy   Assistant to the President of Ukraine, May 2019-present

Yovanovitch, Marie L.   U.S. Ambassador to Ukraine, August 2016-May 2019

Zakaria, Fareed   Host, *Fareed Zakaria GPS*, June 2008-present

Zelensky, Volodymyr   President of Ukraine, May 2019-present

APPENDIX B: ABBREVIATIONS AND COMMON TERMS

AntAC	Anti-Corruption Action Center
CDA	Chargé d'Affaires / Acting Ambassador
CIA	Central Intelligence Agency
Chargé d'Affaires	Acting Ambassador
CN	Congressional Notification
COM	Chief of Mission
DAS	Deputy Assistant Secretary
DC	Deputies Committee
DCM	Deputy Chief of Mission
DNI	Director of National Intelligence
DNC	Democratic National Committee
DOD	Department of Defense
DOE	Department of Energy
DOJ	Department of Justice
DOS	Department of State
DSCA	Defense Security Cooperation Agency
EDI	European Deterrence Initiative
ERI	European Reassurance Initiative
FBI	Federal Bureau of Investigation
FMF	Foreign Military Financing
FMS	Foreign Military Sales
FSB	Russian Federal Security Service
IC	Intelligence Community
ICIG	Inspector General for the Intelligence Community
IO	Bureau of International Organizations
IG	Inspector General
Legatt	Legal Attaché
LNG	Liquefied Natural Gas
MEMCON	Memorandum of Conversation
MLAT	Mutual Legal Assistance Treaty
NABU	National Anti-Corruption Bureau of Ukraine
NBU	National Bank of Ukraine
NDAA	National Defense Authorization Act
NSC	National Security Council
ODNI	Office of the Director of National Intelligence
OFAC	Office of Foreign Assets Control
OMB	Office of Management and Budget
OSCE	Organization for Security and Co-operation in Europe
OVP	Office of the Vice President
PAC	Political Action Committee
PC	Principals Committee
PCC	Policy Coordination Committee
PDB	President's Daily Briefing
PDM	Presidential Decision Memorandum

PGO	Prosecutor General's Office
SAPO	Specialized Anti-Corruption Prosecutor's Office
SBU	Security Service of Ukraine
SDN	Specially Designated Nationals and Blocked Persons
SMM	Special Monitoring Mission
SOC	Summary of Conclusions
SVTC	Secure Video Teleconference
TCG	Trilateral Contact Group
UNSCR	United Nations Security Council Resolution
USAI	Ukraine Security Assistance Initiative
USAID	United States Agency for International Development
WHSR	White House Situation Room
YES	Yalta European Strategy

What follows is the full text of the response
by Republican Representatives Devin Nunes, Jim Jordan, and
Michael McCaul to the Trump-Ukraine Impeachment
Inquiry Report issued by the House Permanent Select Committee on
Intelligence. Turn the book over to read the House report.

REPORT OF EVIDENCE
IN THE DEMOCRATS' IMPEACHMENT
INQUIRY IN THE
HOUSE OF REPRESENTATIVES

REPORT of EVIDENCE in the DEMOCRATS' IMPEACHMENT INQUIRY in the HOUSE of REPRESENTATIVES

Republican
Staff Report Prepared for
Representatives
Devin Nunes,
Jim Jordan, and
Michael T. McCaul

REPORT of EVIDENCE in the DEMOCRATS' IMPEACHMENT INQUIRY in the HOUSE of REPRESENTATIVES

Republican
Staff Report Prepared for
Representatives
Devin Nunes,
Jim Jordan, and
Michael T. McCaul

MELVILLE HOUSE
BROOKLYN · LONDON

Report of Evidence in the Democrats'
Impeachment Inquiry in the House of Representatives

Republican Staff Report Prepared For Devin Nunes, Ranking
Member Permanent Select Committee on Intelligence,
Jim Jordan, Ranking Member Committee on Oversight and
Reform, and Michael T. McCaul, Ranking Member Committee
on Foreign Affairs

First Melville House printing December 2019

Melville House Publishing

46 John Street

Brooklyn NY 11201

mhpbooks.com

ISBN: 978-1-61219-870-5

Cover design by Marina Drukman

Prepress production by Beste M. Doğan

Printed in the United States of America

10 9 8 7 6 5 4 3 2 1

REPORT OF EVIDENCE IN THE DEMOCRATS' IMPEACHMENT INQUIRY IN THE HOUSE OF REPRESENTATIVES

Republican Staff Report Prepared For

Devin Nunes
Ranking Member
Permanent Select Committee on Intelligence

Jim Jordan
Ranking Member
Committee on Oversight and Reform

Michael T. McCaul
Ranking Member
Committee on Foreign Affairs

December 2, 2019

EXECUTIVE SUMMARY

On November 8, 2016, nearly 63 million Americans from around the country chose Donald J. Trump to be the 45th President of the United States. Now, less than a year before the next presidential election, 231 House Democrats in Washington, D.C., are trying to undo the will of the American people.[*] As one Democrat admitted, the pursuit of this extreme course of action is because they want to stop President Trump's re-election.[†]

Democrats in the House of Representatives have been working to impeach President Trump since his election. Democrats introduced four separate resolutions in 2017 and 2018 seeking to impeach President Trump.[‡] In January 2019, on their first day in power, House Democrats again introduced articles of impeachment.[§] That same day, a newly elected Congresswoman promised to an audience of her supporters, "we're going to go in there and we're going to impeach the [expletive deleted]."[**] Her comments are not isolated. Speaker Nancy Pelosi called President Trump "an impostor" and said it is "dangerous" to allow American voters to evaluate his performance in 2020.[††]

The Democrats' impeachment inquiry is not the organic outgrowth of serious misconduct; it is an orchestrated campaign to upend our political system. The Democrats are trying to impeach a duly elected President based on the accusations and assumptions of unelected bureaucrats who disagreed with President Trump's policy initiatives and processes. They are trying to impeach President Trump because some unelected bureaucrats were discomforted by an elected President's telephone call with Ukrainian President Volodymyr Zelensky. They are trying to impeach President Trump because some unelected bureaucrats chafed at an elected President's "outside the beltway" approach to diplomacy.

The sum and substance of the Democrats' case for impeachment is that President Trump abused his authority to pressure Ukraine to investigate former Vice President Joe Biden, President Trump's potential political rival, for President Trump's benefit in the 2020 election. Democrats say this pressure campaign encompassed leveraging a White House meeting and the release of U.S. security assistance to force the Ukrainian President to succumb to President Trump's political wishes. Democrats say that Mayor Rudy Giuliani, the President's personal attorney, and a "shadow" group of U.S. officials conspired to benefit the President politically.

The evidence presented does not prove any of these Democrat allegations, and none of the Democrats' witnesses testified to having evidence of bribery, extortion, or any high crime or misdemeanor.

---

[*] H. Res. 660, 116th Cong. (2019) (Roll call vote 604).
[†] *Weekends with Alex Witt* (MSNBC television broadcast May 5 2019) (interview with Rep. Al Green).
[‡] H., Res. 705, 115th Cong. (2018); H. Res. 646, 115th Cong. (2017); H. Res. 621, 115th Cong. (2017); H. Res. 438, 115th Cong. (2017).
[§] H. Res. 13, 116th Cong. (2019).
[**] Amy B. Wong, *Rep. Rashida Tlaib profanely promised to impeach Trump. She's not sorry.*, Wash. Post, Jan. 4, 2019.
[††] Emily Tillett, *Nancy Pelosi says Trump's attacks on witnesses "very significant" to impeachment probe*, CBS News, Nov. 15, 2019; Dear Colleague Letter from Speaker Nancy Pelosi (Nov. 18, 2019).

The evidence does not support the accusation that President Trump pressured President Zelensky to initiate investigations for the purpose of benefiting the President in the 2020 election. The evidence does not support the accusation that President Trump covered up the summary of his phone conversation with President Zelensky. The evidence does not support the accusation that President Trump obstructed the Democrats' impeachment inquiry.

At the heart of the matter, the impeachment inquiry involves the actions of only two people: President Trump and President Zelensky. The summary of their July 25, 2019, telephone conversation shows no *quid pro quo* or indication of conditionality, threats, or pressure—much less evidence of bribery or extortion. The summary reflects laughter, pleasantries, and cordiality. President Zelensky has said publicly and repeatedly that he felt no pressure. President Trump has said publicly and repeatedly that he exerted no pressure.

Even examining evidence beyond the presidential phone call shows no *quid pro quo*, bribery, extortion, or abuse of power. The evidence shows that President Trump holds a deep-seated, genuine, and reasonable skepticism of Ukraine due to its history of pervasive corruption. The President has also been vocal about his skepticism of U.S. foreign aid and the need for European allies to shoulder more of the financial burden for regional defense. Senior Ukrainian officials under former President Petro Poroshenko publicly attacked then-candidate Trump during the 2016 campaign—including some senior Ukrainian officials who remained in their positions after President Zelensky's term began. All of these factors bear on the President's state of mind and help to explain the President's actions toward Ukraine and President Zelensky.

Understood in this proper context, the President's initial hesitation to meet with President Zelensky or to provide U.S. taxpayer-funded security assistance to Ukraine without thoughtful review is entirely prudent. Ultimately, President Zelensky took decisive action demonstrating his commitment to promoting reform, combatting corruption, and replacing Poroshenko-era holdovers with new leadership in his Administration. President Trump then released security assistance to Ukraine and met with President Zelensky in September 2019—all without Ukraine taking any action to investigate President Trump's political rival.

House Democrats allege that Ukraine felt pressure to bend to the President's political will, but the evidence shows a different reality. Ukraine felt good about its relationship with the United States in the early months of the Zelensky Administration, having had several high-level meetings with senior U.S. officials between July and September. Although U.S. security assistance was temporarily paused, the U.S. government did not convey the pause to the Ukrainians because U.S. officials believed the pause would get worked out and, if publicized, may be mischaracterized as a shift in U.S. policy towards Ukraine. U.S. officials said that the Ukrainian government in Kyiv never knew the aid was delayed until reading about it in the U.S. media. Ambassador Kurt Volker, the key American interlocutor trusted by the Ukrainian government, said the Ukrainians never raised concerns to him until after the pause became public in late August.

The Democrats' impeachment narrative ignores Ukraine's dramatic transformation in its fight against endemic corruption. President Trump was skeptical of Ukrainian corruption and his Administration sought proof that newly-elected President Zelensky was a true reformer. And

after winning a parliamentary majority, the new Zelensky administration took rapid strides to crack down on corruption. Several high-level U.S. officials observed firsthand these anti-corruption achievements in Kyiv, and the security assistance was released soon afterward.

The Democrats' impeachment narrative also ignores President Trump's steadfast support for Ukraine in its war against Russian occupation. Several of the Democrats' witnesses described how President Trump's policies toward Ukraine to combat Russian aggression have been substantially stronger than those of President Obama—then under the stewardship of Vice President Biden. Where President Obama and Vice President Biden gave the Ukrainians night-vision goggles and blankets, the Trump Administration provided the Ukrainians with lethal defensive assistance, including Javelin anti-tank missiles.

The Democrats nonetheless tell a story of an illicit pressure campaign run by President Trump through his personal attorney, Mayor Giuliani, to coerce Ukraine to investigate the President's political rival by withholding a meeting and security assistance. There is, however, no direct, firsthand evidence of any such scheme. The Democrats are alleging guilt on the basis of hearsay, presumptions, and speculation—all of which are reflected in the anonymous whistleblower complaint that sparked this inquiry. The Democrats' narrative is so dependent on speculation that one Democrat publicly justified hearsay as "better" than direct evidence.[‡‡] Where there are ambiguous facts, the Democrats interpret them in a light most unfavorable to the President. In the absence of real evidence, the Democrats appeal to emotion—evaluating how unelected bureaucrats *felt* about the events in question.

The fundamental disagreement apparent in the Democrats' impeachment inquiry is a difference of world views and a discomfort with President Trump's policy decisions. To the extent that some unelected bureaucrats believed President Trump had established an "irregular" foreign policy apparatus, it was because they were not a part of that apparatus. There is nothing illicit about three senior U.S. officials—each with official interests relating to Ukraine—shepherding the U.S.-Ukraine relationship and reporting their actions to State Department and NSC leadership. There is nothing inherently improper with Mayor Giuliani's involvement as well because the Ukrainians knew that he was a conduit to convince President Trump that President Zelensky was serious about reform.

There is also nothing wrong with asking serious questions about the presence of Vice President Biden's son, Hunter Biden, on the board of directors of Burisma, a corrupt Ukrainian company, or about Ukraine's attempts to influence the 2016 presidential election. Biden's Burisma has an international reputation as a corrupt company. As far back as 2015, the Obama State Department had concerns about Hunter Biden's role on Burisma's board. Ukrainian anti-corruption activists noted concerns as well. Publicly available—and irrefutable—evidence shows how senior Ukrainian government officials sought to influence the 2016 U.S. presidential election in opposition to President Trump's candidacy, and that some in the Ukrainian embassy in Washington worked with a Democrat operative to achieve that goal. While Democrats reflexively dismiss these truths as conspiracy theories, the facts are indisputable and bear heavily on the Democrats' impeachment inquiry.

[‡‡] *"Impeachment Inquiry: Ambassador William B. Taylor and Mr. George Kent": Hearing before the H. Perm. Sel. Comm. on Intelligence, 116th Cong. (2019) (statement of Rep. Mike Quigley).*

* * *

In our system of government, power resides with the American people, who delegate executive power to the President through an election once every four years. Unelected officials and career bureaucrats assist in the execution of the laws. The unelected bureaucracy exists to serve the elected representatives of the American people. The Democrats' impeachment narrative flips our system on its head in service of their political ambitions.

The Democrats' impeachment inquiry, led by House Intelligence Committee Chairman Adam Schiff, is merely the outgrowth of their obsession with re-litigating the results of the 2016 presidential election. Despite their best efforts, the evidence gathered during the Democrats' partisan and one-sided impeachment inquiry does not support that President Trump pressured Ukraine to investigate his political rival to benefit the President in the 2020 presidential election. The evidence does not establish any impeachable offense.

But that is not for Democrats' want of trying.

For the first phase of the Democrats' impeachment inquiry, Chairman Schiff led the inquiry from his Capitol basement bunker, preventing transparency on the process and accountability for his actions. Because the fact-finding was unclassified, the closed-door process was purely for information control. This arrangement allowed Chairman Schiff—who had already publicly fabricated evidence and misled Americans about his interaction with the anonymous whistleblower—to selectively leak information to paint misleading public narratives, while simultaneously imposing a gag rule on Republican members. From his basement bunker, Chairman Schiff provided no due process protections for the President and he directed witnesses called by the Democrats not to answer Republican questions. Chairman Schiff also ignored Republican requests to secure the testimony of the anonymous whistleblower, despite promising earlier that the whistleblower would provide "unfiltered testimony."

When the Democrats emerged from the bunker for the public phase of their impeachment inquiry, Chairman Schiff continued to deny fundamental fairness and minority rights. Chairman Schiff interrupted Republican Members and directed witnesses not to answer Republican questions. Chairman Schiff refused to allow Republicans to exercise the limited procedural rights afforded to them. Chairman Schiff rejected witnesses identified by Republicans who would inject some semblance of fairness and objectivity. Chairman Schiff denied Republican subpoenas for testimony and documents, violating the Democrats' own rules to vote down these subpoenas with no notice to Republicans.

Speaker Pelosi, Chairman Schiff, and House Democrats seek to impeach President Trump—not because they have proof of a high crime or misdemeanor, but because they disagreed with the President's actions and his policies. But in our system of government, the President is accountable to the American people. The accountability to the American people comes at the ballot box, not in House Democrats' star chamber.

FINDINGS

Democrats allege that President Trump pressured Ukraine to initiate investigations into his political rival, former Vice President Biden, for the purpose of benefiting the President in the 2020 U.S. presidential election. The evidence does not support the Democrats' allegations. Instead, the findings outlined below are based on the evidence presented and information available in the public realm.

- President Trump has a deep-seated, genuine, and reasonable skepticism of Ukraine due to its history of pervasive corruption.

- President Trump has a long-held skepticism of U.S. foreign assistance and believes that Europe should pay its fair share for mutual defense.

- President Trump's concerns about Hunter Biden's role on Burisma's board are valid. The Obama State Department noted concerns about Hunter Biden's relationship with Burisma in 2015 and 2016.

- There is indisputable evidence that senior Ukrainian government officials opposed President Trump's candidacy in the 2016 election and did so publicly. It has been publicly reported that a Democratic National Committee operative worked with Ukrainian officials, including the Ukrainian Embassy, to dig up dirt on then-candidate Trump.

- The evidence does not establish that President Trump pressured Ukraine to investigate Burisma Holdings, Vice President Joe Biden, Hunter Biden, or Ukrainian influence in the 2016 election for the purpose of benefiting him in the 2020 election.

- The evidence does not establish that President Trump withheld a meeting with President Zelensky for the purpose of pressuring Ukraine to investigate Burisma Holdings, Vice President Joe Biden, Hunter Biden, or Ukrainian influence in the 2016 election.

- The evidence does not support that President Trump withheld U.S. security assistance to Ukraine for the purpose of pressuring Ukraine to investigate Burisma Holdings, Vice President Joe Biden, Hunter Biden, or Ukrainian influence in the 2016 election.

- The evidence does not support that President Trump orchestrated a shadow foreign policy apparatus for the purpose of pressuring Ukraine to investigate Burisma Holdings, Vice President Joe Biden, Hunter Biden, or Ukrainian influence in the 2016 election.

- The evidence does not support that President Trump covered up the substance of his telephone conversation with President Zelensky by restricting access to the call summary.

- President Trump's assertion of longstanding claims of executive privilege is a legitimate response to an unfair, abusive, and partisan process, and does not constitute obstruction of a legitimate impeachment inquiry.

TABLE OF CONTENTS

TABLE OF NAMES

Christopher Anderson	Foreign Service Officer, U.S. Department of State
Michael Atkinson	Inspector General of the Intelligence Community (May 2018–present)
Arsen Avakov	Ukrainian Minister of Internal Affairs (February 2014–present)
Hunter Biden	Board Member, Burisma Holdings (April 2014–October 2019)
Joseph R. Biden	Vice President of the United States (January 2009–January 2017)
Robert Blair	Senior Advisor to the White House Chief of Staff (January 2019–present)
Andriy Bohdan	Head of Ukrainian Office of Presidential Administration (May 2019–present)
John Bolton	U.S. National Security Advisor (April 2018–September 2019)
T. Ulrich Brechbuhl	Counselor to the U.S. Secretary of State, U.S. Department of State (May 2018–present)
Alexandra Chalupa	Former contractor, Democratic National Committee
Valeriy Chaly	Ukrainian Ambassador to the United States (July 2015–July 2019)
Laura Cooper	Deputy Assistant Secretary of Defense for Russia, Ukraine, and Eurasia, U.S. Department of Defense
Catherine Croft	Foreign Service Officer, U.S. Department of State Director for European Affairs, National Security Council (July 2017–July 2018)
Oleksandr Danylyuk	Secretary of the Ukrainian National Security and Defense Council (May 2019–September 2019)
Michael Duffey	Associate Director for National Security Programs, U.S. Office of Management and Budget (May 2019–present)
John Eisenberg	Legal Advisor, National Security Council (2017–present)
Michael Ellis	Deputy Legal Advisor, National Security Council (March 2017–present)
Rudy Giuliani	Mayor of New York City (1994–2001) Personal Attorney to President Trump (April 2018–present)
Preston Wells Griffith	Associate Director for Natural Resources, Energy & Science, U.S. Office of Management and Budget (April 2018–present)
David Hale	Under Secretary of State for Political Affairs, U.S. Department of State (August 2018–present)
Fiona Hill	Senior Director for European and Russian Affairs, National Security Council (April 2017–July 2019)
David Holmes	Political Counselor, U.S. Embassy Kyiv[§§] (August 2017–present)

[§§] Consistent with the U.S. Board on Geographic Names, this report spells the Ukrainian capital as "Kyiv" throughout.

Keith Kellogg	National Security Advisor to the Vice President (April 2018–present)
George Kent	Deputy Assistant Secretary of State, Bureau of European and Eurasian Affairs, U.S. Department of State (September 2018–present)
Igor Kolomoisky	Co-owner, PrivatBank Co-owner, 1+1 Media Group
Charles Kupperman	U.S. Deputy National Security Advisor (January 2019–September 2019)
Serhiy Leshchenko	Ukrainian Member of Parliament (November 2014–July 2019)
Yuriy Lutsenko	Prosecutor General of Ukraine (May 2016–August 2019)
Joseph Maguire	Acting U.S. Director of National Intelligence (August 2019–present)
Brian McCormack	Associate Director for Natural Resources, Energy & Science, U.S. Office of Management and Budget (September 2018–present)
Michael McKinley	Senior Advisor to the U.S. Secretary of State, U.S. Department of State (November 2018–October 2019)
Tim Morrison	Senior Director for European and Russian Affairs, National Security Council (July 2019–November 2019)
Mick Mulvaney	Director of the U.S. Office of Management and Budget (February 2017–present) Acting Chief of Staff to the President (January 2019–present)
Nellie Ohr	Contractor, Fusion GPS
Mike Pence	Vice President of the United States (January 2017–present)
Rick Perry	U.S. Secretary of Energy (March 2017–present)
Mike Pompeo	U.S. Secretary of State (April 2018–present)
Petro Poroshenko	President of Ukraine (June 2014–May 2019)
Vadym Prystaiko	Minister of Foreign Affairs of Ukraine (August 2019–present)
Philip Reeker	Acting Assistant Secretary of State, Bureau of European and Eurasian Affairs, U.S. Department of State (March 2019–present)
Mark Sandy	Deputy Associate Director for National Security, U.S. Office of Management and Budget (December 2013–present)
Viktor Shokin	Prosecutor General of Ukraine (February 2015–March 2016)
Oksana Shulyar	Deputy Chief of Mission, Embassy of Ukraine to the U.S.
Gordon Sondland	U.S. Ambassador to the European Union (July 2018–present)
William Taylor	U.S. Ambassador to Ukraine (June 2006–May 2009) U.S. Chargé d'Affaires, *a.i.*, U.S. Embassy Kyiv (June 2019–present)
Andrii Telizhenko	Political officer, Embassy of Ukraine to the U.S.
Donald J. Trump	President of the United States (January 2017–present)

Alexander Vindman	Director for European Affairs, National Security Council (July 2018–present)
Kurt Volker	U.S. Special Representative for Ukraine Negotiations, U.S. Department of State (July 2017–September 2019)
Russell Vought	Acting Director, U.S. Office of Management and Budget
Kathryn Wheelbarger	Acting Assistant Secretary of Defense for International Affairs, U.S. Department of Defense (November 2018–present)
Jennifer Williams	Special Adviser for Europe and Russia, Office of the Vice President
Viktor Yanukovych	President of Ukraine (February 2010–February 2014)
Arseniy Yatsenyuk	Prime Minister of Ukraine (February 2014–April 2016)
Andrey Yermak	Adviser to President of Ukraine Volodymyr Zelensky
Marie Yovanovitch	U.S. Ambassador to Ukraine (August 2016–May 2019)
Volodymyr Zelensky***	President of Ukraine (May 2019–present)
Mykola Zlochevsky	Co-founder, Burisma Holdings (2002–present) Ukrainian Minister of Ecology and Natural Resources (July 2010–April 2012)

*** Although some sources use alternate spellings of the Ukrainian President's surname, this report uses the spelling "Zelensky" for consistency throughout.

I.   **The evidence does not establish that President Trump pressured the Ukrainian government to investigate his political rival for the purpose of benefiting him in the 2020 U.S. presidential election.**

Democrats have alleged that President Trump exerted pressure on Ukrainian President Zelensky to force the Ukrainian government to manufacture "dirt" or otherwise investigate a potential Democrat candidate in the 2020 U.S. presidential election for President Trump's political benefit.[1] Democrats allege that President Trump sought to use the possibility of a White House meeting with President Zelensky and release of U.S. security assistance to Ukraine as leverage to force Ukraine to help the President politically. Democrats allege that President Trump orchestrated a "shadow" foreign policy apparatus that worked to accomplish the President's political goals.

The evidence obtained in the Democrats' impeachment inquiry, however, does not support these Democrat allegations. In fact, witnesses called by the Democrats denied having any awareness of criminal activity or an impeachable offense. Rep. John Ratcliffe asked Ambassador Bill Taylor and Deputy Assistant Secretary George Kent whether they were "assert[ing] there was an impeachable offense in [the July 25] call."[2] Neither said there was.[3] Rep. Chris Stewart asked Ambassador Marie Yovanovitch if she had any information about President Trump's involvement in criminal activity.[4] Ambassador Yovanovitch said no.[5] Rep. Ratcliffe asked National Security Council (NSC) staff member LTC Alexander Vindman and Office of the Vice President special adviser Jennifer Williams if they have labeled the President's conduct as "bribery."[6] Both said no.[7] Rep. Elise Stefanik asked Ambassador Kurt Volker, the U.S. special envoy for Ukraine negotiations, and Tim Morrison, the NSC senior director for Europe, whether they saw any bribery, extortion, or *quid pro quo*.[8] Both said no.[9]

Contrary to Democrat assertions, the evidence does not show that President Trump pressured President Zelensky to investigate his political rival during the July 25 phone call. The best evidence of the conversation—the call summary—shows no evidence of conditionality, threats, or pressure. President Zelensky and President Trump have both said there was no

---

[1] *"Whistleblower Disclosure": Hearing of the H. Perm. Sel. Comm. on Intelligence*, 116th Cong. (2019) (statement of Rep. Adam Schiff, Chairman); Rep. Adam Schiff (@RepAdamSchiff), Twitter (Oct. 12, 2019, 2:53 p.m.), https://twitter.com/repadamschiff/status/1183138629130035200; *Lieu accuses Trump of asking Ukraine to "manufacture dirt" on Biden*, The Hill, Sept. 25, 2019.

[2] *"Impeachment Inquiry: Ambassador William B. Taylor and Mr. George Kent": Hearing before the H. Perm. Sel. Comm. on Intelligence*, 116th Cong. (2019).

[3] *Id.*

[4] *"Impeachment Inquiry: Ambassador Marie Yovanovitch": Hearing before the H. Perm. Sel. Comm. on Intelligence*, 116th Cong. (2019).

[5] *Id.*

[6] *"Impeachment Inquiry: LTC Alexander Vindman and Ms. Jennifer Williams": Hearing before the H. Perm. Sel. Comm. on Intelligence*, 116th Cong. (2019). This report abbreviates military titles consistent with the U.S. Government Printing Office style manual. *See* U.S. Gov't Printing Off., Style Manual 227 (2016).

[7] *Id.*

[8] *"Impeachment Inquiry: Ambassador Kurt Volker and Mr. Timothy Morrison": Hearing before the H. Perm. Sel. Comm. on Intelligence*, 116th Cong. (2019).

[9] *Id.*

1

pressure, the initial read-out from the State Department and the Ukrainian government reflected no concerns, and the NSC leadership saw no illegality or impropriety with the call.

The evidence does not show that President Trump withheld a meeting with President Zelensky to pressure Ukraine to investigate his political rival. The evidence shows that President Trump has a long-standing, deep-seated skepticism of Ukraine due to its history of pervasive corruption. President Zelensky was a political newcomer with untested views on anti-corruption and a close association with a Ukrainian oligarch. Even so, President Trump agreed to invite President Zelensky to the White House, and in the interim, Ukrainian officials had several high-level meetings with U.S. officials. President Trump and President Zelensky met in September 2019 without Ukraine ever taking any action on investigating President Trump's political rival.

In addition, the evidence does not show that President Trump withheld U.S. security assistance to Ukraine to pressure Ukraine to investigate his political rival. The evidence shows that President Trump has a skepticism of U.S. taxpayer-funded foreign aid and believes Europe should carry more financial burden for its regional defense. Although U.S. security assistance was paused temporarily, Democrats' witnesses denied there being any direct link to investigations of the President's political rival. Both the Ukrainian government and President Trump separately denied any linkage. U.S. officials did not tell the Ukrainian officials about the delay because they thought it would get worked out. Ambassador Volker, a senior U.S. diplomat and primary interlocutor with senior Ukrainian government officials, testified that the Ukrainians did not raise concerns to him about a delay in aid until after the pause was made public in late August 2019. The U.S. security assistance to Ukraine was ultimately disbursed without Ukraine taking any action to investigate President Trump's political rival.

The evidence does not show that President Trump established a "shadow" foreign policy apparatus to pressure Ukraine to investigate his political rival. The President has broad Constitutional authority over U.S. foreign policy, and President Trump is likely suspicious of the national security apparatus due to continual leaks of sensitive information and the resistance within the federal bureaucracy. The three U.S. officials who Democrats accuse of conducting an "irregular" foreign policy channel had legitimate responsibilities for Ukraine policy. They kept the State Department and NSC aware of their actions. To the extent Mayor Giuliani was involved, he was in communication with these officials and the Ukrainians did not see him as speaking on behalf of the President.

Although Democrats reflexively criticize President Trump for promoting "conspiracy theories" about Hunter Biden's role on Burisma's board or Ukrainian attempts to influence the 2016 election, evidence suggests there are legitimate questions about both issues. The Democrats' witnesses testified that it would be appropriate for Ukraine to investigate allegations of corruption in Ukraine.

Finally, there are fundamental flaws with the anonymous whistleblower complaint that initiated the Democrats' impeachment inquiry. The complaint contained inaccurate and misleading information that prejudiced the public understanding of President Trump's conversation with President Zelensky. The whistleblower had no firsthand knowledge of the events in question and a bias against President Trump. The whistleblower communicated with

Chairman Schiff or his staff prior to submitting the whistleblower complaint to the Inspector General of the Intelligence Community. Several witnesses contradicted assertions made by the anonymous whistleblower. The whistleblower's complaint did not accurately reflect the tone and substance of the phone call, which is unsurprising given the whistleblower's reliance on secondhand information that had likely already been colored by biases of the original sources.

A. The evidence does not establish that President Trump pressured President Zelensky during the July 25 phone call to investigate the President's political rival for the purpose of benefiting him in the 2020 election.

On July 25, 2019, President Trump and President Zelensky spoke by telephone.[10] This conversation would later serve as the basis for the anonymous whistleblower complaint and the spark for the Democrats' impeachment inquiry. Contrary to allegations that President Trump pressured Ukraine to investigate a domestic political rival during this call,[11] the evidence shows that President Trump did not pressure President Zelensky to investigate his political rival.

The call summary and initial read-outs of the conversation reflect no indication of conditionality, coercion, or intimidation—elements that would have been present if President Trump had used his authority to pressure President Zelensky to investigate his political rival. Importantly, both President Zelensky and President Trump have said publicly there was no pressure or anything inappropriate about their conversation. The anonymous whistleblower complaint—which sparked the impeachment inquiry—contains sensational rhetoric about the July 25 phone conservation that has prejudged subsequent views of the call.

1. The call summary does not reflect any improper pressure or conditionality to pressure Ukraine to investigate President Trump's political rival.

The best evidence of the telephone conversation between President Trump and President Zelensky is the contemporaneous summary prepared by the White House Situation Room. The Democrats' witnesses described how National Security Council (NSC) policy staffers and White House Situation Room duty officers typically listen in on presidential conversations with foreign leaders to transcribe the contents of the conversation.[12] This process occurred for President Trump's July 25 phone call with President Zelensky.

---

[10] President Trump had spoken with then-President-elect Zelensky on April 21, 2019, to congratulate him on his election. *See* The White House, *Memorandum of Telephone Conversation* (Apr. 21, 2019). This conversation too contained no indication of pressure, intimidation or threats. *See id.*

[11] *See, e.g.*, Josh Dawsey et al., *How Trump and Giuliani pressured Ukraine to investigate the President's rivals*, Wash. Post, (Sept. 20, 2019).

[12] *See, e.g.*, Deposition of Dr. Fiona Hill, in Wash., D.C., at 297-300 (Oct. 14, 2019) [hereinafter "Hill deposition"]. Although some have alleged that the presence of ellipses in the call summary connotes missing text, witnesses testified that call summaries often use ellipses to denote unfinished thoughts and not to "read too much" into the use of ellipses. *See, e.g., id.* at 307. LTC Vindman testified in his closed-door deposition that any editing decisions or missing words were not done maliciously. *See* Deposition of LTC Alexander Vindman, in Wash., D.C., at 253 (Oct. 29, 2019) [hereinafter "Vindman deposition"]. In his public testimony, LTC Vindman explained that although the summary did not mention the word "Burisma," it was "not a significant omission." *Impeachment Inquiry: LTC Alexander Vindman and Ms. Jennifer Williams*, *supra* note 6. Morrison testified in his deposition that he believed

As transcribed, the call summary denotes laughter, pleasantries, and compliments exchanged between President Trump and President Zelensky. The summary does not evince any threats, coercion, intimidation, or indication of conditionality. Democrats even acknowledged that the call summary reflected no *quid pro quo*.[13] The summary bears absolutely no resemblance to House Intelligence Committee Chairman Adam Schiff's self-described "parody" interpretation of the call, which the Chairman performed at a public hearing on September 26.[14]

The summary of the July 25 phone call begins by President Trump congratulating President Zelensky on a "great victory," a "terrific job," and a "fantastic achievement."[15] President Zelensky reciprocated by complimenting President Trump, saying:

> Well, yes, to tell you the truth, we are trying to work hard because we wanted to drain the swamp here in our country. We brought in many, many new people. Not the old politicians, not the typical politicians, because we want to have a new format and a new type of government. You are a great teacher for us and in that.[16]

President Trump expressed his concern that European countries were not providing their fair share in terms of assistance to Ukraine[17]—a topic about which President Trump has been vocal.[18] President Zelensky responded that President Trump was "absolutely right" and that he had expressed concerns to German Chancellor Angela Merkel and French President Emmanuel Macron.[19] President Zelensky thanked President Trump for U.S. military support and said Ukraine was "almost ready to buy more Javelins from the United States for defense purposes."[20]

President Trump then transitioned to discuss the allegation that some Ukrainian officials sought to influence the 2016 U.S. presidential election. Although Democrats have seized on the President's phrasing—"I would like you to do us a favor though"[21]—to accuse the President of pressuring President Zelensky to target his 2020 political rival for his political benefit,[22] they omit the remainder of his sentence. The full sentence shows that President Trump was not asking President Zelensky to investigate his political rival, but rather asking him to assist in "get[ting] to

---

the call memorandum was an "accurate and complete" reflection of the substance of the call. Deposition of Timothy Morrison, in Wash., D.C., at 60 (Oct. 31, 2019) [hereinafter "Morrison deposition"].

[13] *See, e.g.*, *MSNBC Live with Craig Melvin* (MSNBC television broadcast Sept. 25, 2019) (interview with Rep. Ro Khanna) (saying evidence of a *quid pro quo* on the call summary is "irrelevant").

[14] *Whistleblower Disclosure*, *supra* note 1.

[15] The White House, *Memorandum of Telephone Conversation* 1 (July 25, 2019).

[16] *Id.* at 2.

[17] *Id.*

[18] *See infra* section I.C.2.

[19] *Memorandum of Telephone Conversation*, *supra* note 15, at 2.

[20] *Id.*

[21] *Id.* at 3.

[22] *See, e.g.*, *Whistleblower Disclosure*, *supra* note 1 (statement of Rep. Adam Schiff, Chairman).

the bottom" of potential Ukrainian involvement in the 2016 election.[23] This reading is supported by President Trump's subsequent reference to Special Counsel Robert Mueller, who had testified the day before about his findings,[24] and to Attorney General William Barr, who had initiated an official inquiry into the origins of the U.S. government's 2016 Russia investigation.[25]

President Zelensky did not express any concern that President Trump had raised the allegations about Ukrainian influence in the 2016 election. In fact, President Zelensky responded by reiterating his commitment to cooperation between Ukraine and the United States and mentioning that he had recalled the Ukrainian Ambassador to the United States, Valeriy Chaly.[26] Ambassador Chaly had authored an op-ed in *The Hill* during the height of the presidential campaign in 2016 criticizing a statement that President Trump had made by Crimea.[27] President Zelensky said he planned to surround himself with "the best and most experienced people" and pledged that "as the President of Ukraine that all the investigations will be done openly and candidly."[28] President Zelensky also raised former New York Mayor Rudy Giuliani, saying "we are hoping very much that Mr. Giuliani will be able to travel to Ukraine and we will meet once he comes to Ukraine."[29]

The call summary shows that the discussion then intertwined several different topics. In response to President Zelensky's statement about new personnel, President Trump and President Zelensky discussed the position of prosecutor general.[30] President Zelensky did not express any discomfort discussing the prosecutor general position. He said the new prosecutor general would be "100% my person, my candidate" and said the prosecutor would look into the matters raised by President Trump to "mak[e] sure to restore the honesty" of the investigation.[31] President Zelensky later said "we will be very serious about the case and will work on the investigation."[32]

In response to President Zelensky's reference to Mayor Giuliani, President Trump said Mayor Giuliani is "a highly respected man" who "very much knows what's happening and he is a very capable guy."[33] President Trump said that he would ask Mayor Giuliani to call President Zelensky, along with Attorney General Barr, to "get to the bottom of it."[34] President Zelensky did not express any concern about Mayor Giuliani's engagement—in fact, President Zelensky, not President Trump, first referenced Mayor Giuliani in the conversation.

---

[23] *Memorandum of Telephone Conversation*, *supra* note 15, at 3. The President's reference to "Crowdstrike" during the conversation refers to a cybersecurity firm that examined the Democratic National Committee server following intrusion by the Russian government in 2016.

[24] *"Oversight of the Report on the Investigation into Russian Interference in the 2016 Presidential Election: Former Special Counsel Robert S. Mueller, III": Hearing before the H. Comm. on the Judiciary*, 116th Cong. (2019).

[25] *See, e.g.*, Adam Goldman et al., *Barr assigns U.S. Attorney in Connecticut to review origins of Russia inquiry*, N.Y. Times, May 13, 2019.

[26] *Memorandum of Telephone Conversation*, *supra* note 15, at 3.

[27] Valeriy Chaly, *Ukraine's ambassador: Trump's comments send wrong message to world*, The Hill, Aug. 4, 2016.

[28] *Memorandum of Telephone Conversation*, *supra* note 15, at 3.

[29] *Id.*

[30] *Id.* at 3-4.

[31] *Id.* at 4.

[32] *Id.* at 5.

[33] *Id.* at 3-4.

[34] *Id.* at 4.

President Trump then raised former U.S. Ambassador to Ukraine, Marie Yovanovitch, saying that she was "bad news" and "the people she was dealing with in the Ukraine were bad news."[35] President Zelensky did not express any hesitancy in discussing the ambassador. Contrary to Democrats' assertion that he felt obligated to agree with President Trump's assessment, President Zelensky stated his independent negative assessment of Ambassador Yovanovitch:

> Her attitude toward me was far from the best as she admired the previous President and she was on his side. She would not accept me as a new President well enough.[36]

President Trump also raised in passing—using the transition phrase "the other thing"—the topic of Vice President Joe Biden's son, Hunter Biden, referring to his position on the board of a Ukrainian energy company, Burisma, known for its corruption.[37] President Trump said "a lot of people want to find out about that so whatever you can do with the Attorney General would be great."[38] President Zelensky did not reply to President Trump's reference to the Bidens, and the two did not discuss the topic substantively.

The call concluded with President Zelensky raising energy cooperation between Ukraine and the United States and with President Trump reiterating his invitation for President Zelensky to visit the White House.[39]

Although some later expressed concern about the call, the call summary—the best evidence of the conversation—shows no indication of conflict, intimidation, or pressure. President Trump never conditioned a White House meeting on any action by President Zelensky. President Trump never mentioned U.S. security assistance to Ukraine. President Zelensky never verbalized any disagreement, hostility, or concern about any facet of the U.S.-Ukrainian relationship.

2. President Zelensky has publicly and repeatedly said he felt no pressure to investigate President Trump's political rival.

Since President Trump declassified and publicly released the content of his July 25 phone conversation with President Zelensky, President Zelensky and other senior Ukrainian officials have publicly and repeatedly asserted that President Zelensky felt no pressure to investigate President Trump's political rival. President Zelensky has variously asserted, "nobody pushed . . . me," "I was never pressured," and there was no "blackmail."

---

[35] *Id.*
[36] *Id.*
[37] *Id.*
[38] *Id.*
[39] *Id.* at 5.

On September 25, President Zelensky and President Trump met face-to-face for a bilateral meeting on the margins of the 74th United Nations (U.N.) General Assembly in New York. The presidents jointly participated in a media availability, during which President Zelensky asserted that he felt no pressure.[40] President Zelensky said then:

> Q. President Zelensky, have you felt any pressure from President Trump to investigate Joe Biden and Hunter Biden?
>
> A. I think you read everything. So I think you read text. I'm sorry, but I don't want to be involved to democratic, open elections — elections of USA. *No, you heard that we had, I think, good phone call. It was normal. We spoke about many things. And I — so I think, and you read it, that nobody pushed — pushed me*.[41]

President Zelensky again reiterated that he was not pressured to investigate President Trump's political rival during an interview with a Kyodo News, a Japanese media outlet, published on October 6. Kyodo News quoted President Zelensky as saying, "I was never pressured and there were no conditions being imposed" on a White House meeting or U.S. security assistance to Ukraine.[42] President Zelensky denied "reports by U.S. media that [President] Trump's requests were conditions" for a White House meeting or U.S. security assistance.[43]

On October 10, during an all-day media availability in Kyiv, President Zelensky again emphasized that he felt no pressure to investigate President Trump's political rival. President Zelensky said there was "no blackmail" during the conversation, explaining: "This is not corruption. It was just a call."[44]

In addition, on September 21—before President Trump had even declassified and released the call summary—Ukrainian Foreign Minister Vadym Prystaiko denied that President Trump had pressured President Zelensky to investigate President Trump's political rival.[45] Foreign Minister Prystaiko said:

> *I know what the conversation was about and I think there was no pressure*. There was talk, conversations are different, leaders have the right to discuss any problems that exist. This conversation was

[40] Press Release, The White House, Remarks by President Trump and President Zelensky of Ukraine Before Bilateral Meeting (Sept. 25, 2019), *available at* https://www.whitehouse.gov/briefings-statements/remarks-president-trump-president-zelensky-ukraine-bilateral-meeting-new-york-ny/.
[41] *Id.* (emphasis added).
[42] *Ukraine president denies being pushed by Trump to investigate Biden*, Kyodo News, Oct. 6, 2019.
[43] *Id.*
[44] *Ukraine's president says 'no blackmail' in Trump call*, BBC, Oct. 10, 2019.
[45] *"Trump did not pressure Zelenskyy, Ukraine is independent state" – Foreign Minister Prystaiko*, Hromadske, Sept. 21, 2019.

long, friendly, and it touched on a lot of questions, including those requiring serious answers.[46]

Similarly, Ambassador Bill Taylor explained that he had dinner with Oleksandr Danylyuk, then-Secretary of the National Security and Defense Council, the night of the phone conversation between President Trump and President Zelensky.[47] He explained that Danylyuk said that the Ukrainian government "seemed to think that the call went fine, the call went well. He wasn't disturbed by anything. He wasn't disturbed that he told us about the phone call."[48]

President Zelensky's repeated denials that President Trump pressured him to investigate domestic political rival—corroborated by Foreign Minister Prystaiko's similar denial—carry significant weight.

3. President Trump has publicly and repeatedly said he did not pressure President Zelensky to investigate his political rival.

Like President Zelensky, President Trump has repeatedly and publicly stated that he did not pressure President Zelensky to investigate his political rival. During the September 25 bilateral meeting with President Zelensky, President Trump said to the assembled members of the media: "There was no pressure. And you know there was—and, by the way, you know there was no pressure. All you have to do it see it, what went on the call."[49] When asked whether he wanted President Zelensky to "do more" to investigate Vice President Biden, President Trump responded: "No. I want him to do whatever he can. This was not his fault; he wasn't there. He's just been here recently. But whatever he can do in terms of corruption, because the corruption is massive."[50]

Despite the President's statements, some allege that an overheard conversation the day after President Trump's conversation with President Zelensky shows that the President sought to pressure President Zelensky. On July 26, following a meeting with President Zelensky, Ambassador Gordon Sondland, the U.S. Ambassador to the European Union, telephoned President Trump from Kyiv.[51] According to a subsequent account of David Holmes, a Political Counselor at U.S. Embassy Kyiv, Ambassador Sondland told the President that he was in Ukraine and stated President Zelensky "loves your ass."[52] Holmes recounted that President Trump asked Ambassador Sondland, "So he's going to do the investigation?"[53] Ambassador Sondland allegedly replied, "He's going to do it."[54]

---

[46] *Id.* (emphasis added).
[47] Deposition of Ambassador William B. Taylor, in Wash., D.C., at 80 (Oct. 22, 2019).
[48] *Id.*
[49] Remarks by President Trump and President Zelensky of Ukraine Before Bilateral Meeting, *supra* note 40.
[50] *Id.*
[51] Deposition of David Holmes, in Wash., D.C., at 23-25 (Nov. 15, 2019) [hereinafter "Holmes deposition"]. Ambassador Sondland did not mention this phone call in his deposition. *See generally* Deposition of Ambassador Gordon D. Sondland, in Wash., D.C. (Oct. 17, 2019) [hereinafter "Sondland deposition"].
[52] Holmes deposition, *supra* note 51, at 24
[53] *Id.*
[54] *Id.*

8

This conversation is not definitive evidence that President Trump pressured President Zelensky to investigate his political rival. First, according to Ambassador Sondland, it was not clear that President Trump meant an investigation into the Bidens. In his closed-door deposition, Ambassador Sondland testified that he only had "five or six" conversations with the President and did not mention this particular conversation.[55] In his public testimony, however, Ambassador Sondland suddenly recalled the conversation, saying that it "did not strike me as significant at the time" and that the primary purpose of the call was to discuss rapper A$AP Rocky, who was imprisoned in Sweden.[56] Ambassador Sondland testified that he has no recollection of discussing Vice President Biden or his son, Hunter Biden, with President Trump.[57]

Second, Holmes testified that although he disclosed Ambassador Sondland's conversation with the President to multiple friends on multiple occasions, he did not feel compelled to disclose it to the State Department or Congress until weeks into the impeachment inquiry.[58] Although Holmes testified that he told his boss, Ambassador Taylor, about the call on August 6 and received a "knowing" response, and that he referred to the call often in staff meetings, Ambassador Taylor testified publicly that he was "not aware of this information" at the time of his October 22 deposition, and that he only became aware of the Holmes account on November 8, 2019, two days after his hearing was publicly announced, at which point he referred it (for the first time) to the Legal Adviser for the Department of State.[59]

4. **Read-outs of the phone call from both the State Department and the Ukrainian government did not reflect that President Trump pressured President Zelensky to investigate his political rival.**

Immediately following the telephone conversation between President Trump and President Zelensky, senior U.S. and Ukrainian government officials provided read-outs of the conversation. According to witness testimony, none of these read-outs indicated that the conversation between the presidents was substantively concerning.

Ambassador Volker testified that he received informal read-outs of the call from both his State Department assistant and his high-level Ukrainian contacts.[60] These read-outs did not indicate any concern with the phone call. Ambassador Volker explained:

[55] Sondland deposition, *supra* note 51, at 56.

[56] *"Impeachment Inquiry: Ambassador Gordon Sondland": Hearing before the H. Perm. Sel. Comm. on Intelligence*, 116th Cong. (2019).

[57] *Id.*

[58] Holmes deposition, *supra* note 51, at 31, 158-62.

[59] *Id.* at 81-82, 121-22, 167; *see generally* Taylor deposition, *supra* note 47; *Impeachment Inquiry: Ambassador William B. Taylor and Mr. George Kent, supra* note 2.

[60] Transcribed interview of Ambassador Kurt Volker, in Wash., D.C., at 102-03 (Oct. 3, 2019) [hereinafter "Volker transcribed interview"]. Ambassador Volker's assistant at the time, Catherine Croft, testified that she only received a read-out of the phone call was based on what President Zelensky told Ambassador Volker, Ambassador Taylor, and Ambassador Sondland on July 26. Deposition of Catherine Croft, in Wash., D.C., at 16 (Oct. 30, 2019) [hereinafter "Croft deposition"].

A. I got an oral readout from the staffer who works for me in the State Department and our chargé, as well as from Andrey Yermak, who had been on the call in Ukraine himself.

Q. So you got two readouts?

A. Yeah.

Q. One from each side?

A. Correct.

Q. What was the top line message you got from the State Department?

A. Well, they were the same, actually, which is interesting. But the message was congratulations from the President to President Zelensky; President Zelensky reiterating that he is committed to fighting corruption and reform in the Ukraine; and President Trump reiterating an invitation for President Zelensky to visit him at the White House. That was it.[61]

In fact, in his public testimony, Ambassador Volker testified that President Zelensky was "very upbeat about the fact of the call."[62]

Ambassador Sondland received a summary of the phone call from his staff.[63] Ambassador Sondland testified that he was pleased to learn that it was a "good call."[64] George Kent, the Deputy Assistant Secretary of State covering Ukraine, testified that he received a read-out of the call from NSC staffer LTC Alexander Vindman.[65] According to Kent, although LTC Vindman said the "atmospherics" of the conversation was cooler and reserved, LTC Vindman did not mention Vice President Biden's name or anything relating to 2016.[66]

In addition, the Office of the President of Ukraine issued an official statement following the phone call.[67] The official statement also signaled no concern about the call or any indication of coercion, intimidation, or pressure from President Trump. The statement read in full:

President of Ukraine Volodymyr Zelensky had a phone conversation with President of the United States Donald Trump. President of the United States congratulated Ukraine on successful holding free and

---

[61] Volker transcribed interview, *supra* note 60, at 102-03.
[62] *Impeachment Inquiry: Ambassador Kurt Volker and Timothy Morrison*, *supra* note 8.
[63] Sondland deposition, *supra* note 51, at 116.
[64] *Id.*
[65] Deposition of George Kent, in Wash., D.C., at 163 (Oct. 15, 2019) [hereinafter "Kent deposition"].
[66] *Id.* at 163-65
[67] Press Release, Office of the President of Ukraine, Volodymyr Zelenskyy had a phone conversation with President of the United States (July 25, 2019), *available at* https://www.president.gov.ua/en/news/volodimir-zelenskij-proviv-telefonnu-rozmovu-z-prezidentom-s-56617.

democratic parliamentary elections as well as Volodymyr Zelensky with victory the Servant of the People Party.

Donald Trump is convinced that the new Ukrainian government will be able to quickly improve image of Ukraine, complete investigation of corruption cases, which inhibited the interaction between Ukraine and the USA.

He also confirmed continued support of the sovereignty and territorial integrity of Ukraine by the United States and the readiness of the American side to fully contribute to the implementation of a Large-Scale Reform Program in our country.

Volodymyr Zelensky thanked Donald Trump for US leadership in preserving and strengthening the sanctions pressure on Russia.

The Presidents agreed to discuss practical issues of Ukrainian-American cooperation during the visit of Volodymyr Zelensky to the United States.[68]

The initial read-outs of the July 25 telephone conversation between President Trump and President Zelensky provide compelling evidence that the key message conveyed during the conversation was about fighting corruption in Ukraine—and not about digging up dirt on President Trump's political rival for the President's political benefit.

5. The National Security Council leadership did not see the call as illegal or improper.

The evidence shows that the NSC leadership did not see the telephone conversation between President Trump and President Zelensky as improper. Timothy Morrison, who served as the Deputy Assistant to the President for National Security, listened in on the conversation.[69] He testified that he was concerned information from the call could leak, but he was not concerned that anything discussed on the call was illegal or improper.[70]

LTG Keith Kellogg, Vice President Pence's National Security Advisor, also listened in on the July 25 telephone conversation.[71] LTG Kellogg stated that like Morrison: "I heard nothing wrong or improper on the call. I had and have no concerns."[72] LTG Kellogg's subordinate, Jennifer Williams, testified that although she found the call to be "unusual," she did not raise

---

[68] *Id.*

[69] Morrison deposition, *supra* note 12, at 15.

[70] *Id.* at 16, 60-61.

[71] The White House, Statement from Lieutenant General Keith Kellogg, National Security Advisor to Vice President Mike Pence (Nov. 19, 2019) [hereinafter "Statement from Lieutenant General Kellogg"].

[72] *Id.*

concerns to LTG Kellogg.[73] LTG Kellogg similarly noted that Williams never raised concerns to him.[74]

Morrison's subordinate, LTC Vindman, listened in on the conversation.[75] At the time of the call, LTC Vindman handled Ukraine policy for the NSC.[76] He testified that he was concerned by the conversation and raised his concerns to the NSC's Legal Advisor, John Eisenberg.[77] Eisenberg, according to LTC Vindman, did not share the concern.[78] LTC Vindman did not raise any concerns to Morrison, his immediate supervisor.[79] In his public testimony, Morrison explained that he had concerns with LTC Vindman's judgment and deviation from the chain of command.[80]

The evidence suggests that any wider concerns about the July 25 phone call originated from LTC Vindman. Williams testified that she discussed the call with no one outside the NSC.[81] LTC Vindman, on the other hand, testified that he discussed the phone call with two people outside of the NSC, Deputy Assistant Secretary Kent and an unidentified intelligence community employee.[82] Deputy Assistant Secretary Kent explained that LTC Vindman felt "uncomfortable" and would not share the majority of the substance of the conversation.[83] According to Kent's recollection, LTC Vindman did not mention that the conversation included any reference to Vice President Biden.[84]

6. The anonymous, secondhand whistleblower complaint misstated details about the July 25 call, which has falsely colored the call's public characterization.

The anonymous whistleblower did not listen in on the July 25 call between President Trump and President Zelensky. The whistleblower's subsequent complaint about the conversation, compiled with secondhand information, misstated key details about the conversation.

The whistleblower sensationally alleged that President Trump "sought to pressure the Ukrainian leader to take actions to help the President's 2020 reelection bid."[85] The call summary, however, contains no reference to 2020 or President Trump's reelection bid.[86]

---

[73] Deposition of Jennifer Williams, in Wash., D.C., at 129 (Nov. 7, 2019) [hereinafter "Williams deposition"]; *Impeachment Inquiry: LTC Alexander Vindman and Ms. Jennifer Williams, supra* note 6.
[74] Statement from Lieutenant General Kellogg, *supra* note 71.
[75] Vindman deposition, *supra* note 12, at 18.
[76] *Id.* at 16.
[77] *Id.* at 96.
[78] *Id.* at 97, 258.
[79] Morrison deposition, *supra* note 12, at 59.
[80] *Impeachment Inquiry: Ambassador Kurt Volker and Mr. Timothy Morrison, supra* note 8.
[81] *Impeachment Inquiry: LTC Alexander Vindman and Ms. Jennifer Williams, supra* note 6.
[82] *Id.*
[83] Kent deposition, *supra* note 65, at 163-64.
[84] *Id.* at 165-66.
[85] Letter to Richard Burr, Chairman, S. Sel. Comm. on Intelligence, & Adam Schiff, Chairman, H. Perm. Sel. Comm. on Intelligence 2 (Aug. 12, 2019) [hereinafter "Whistleblower letter"].
[86] *Memorandum of Telephone Conversation, supra* note 15.

The whistleblower alleged that President Trump "pressured" President Zelensky to "initiate or continue an investigation into the activities of former Vice President Joseph Biden and his son, Hunter Biden."[87] The call summary, however, shows that President Trump referenced the Bidens only in passing and that the presidents did not discuss the topic substantively.[88]

The whistleblower alleged that President Trump "pressured" President Zelensky to "locate and turn over servers used by the Democratic National Committee (DNC) and examined by the U.S. cyber security firm Crowdstrike."[89] The call summary, however, demonstrates that while President Trump mentioned Crowdstrike and "the server," President Trump never made any request that President Zelensky locate or turn over any material.[90]

The whistleblower alleged that President Trump "praised Ukraine's Prosecutor General, Mr. Yuriy Lutsenko, and suggested that Mr. Zelensky might want to keep him in his position."[91] The call summary is not clear about which prosecutor general President Trump is referring to—Ambassador Volker testified he believed President Trump was referring to Lutsenko's predecessor, Viktor Shokin[92]—and President Trump never specifically referenced Lutsenko.[93] President Trump also never suggested or intimated that President Zelensky should "keep [Lutsenko] in his position."[94]

The whistleblower also alleged that T. Ulrich Brechbuhl, Counselor to Secretary of State Mike Pompeo, listened in on the July 25 phone call.[95] Subsequent reporting, confirmed by a letter sent by Brechbuhl's attorney, indicated that Brechbuhl was not on the call.[96]

* * *

Setting aside the whistleblower's mischaracterization of President Trump's phone call with President Zelensky, the best available evidence shows no coercion, threats, or pressure for Ukraine to investigate the President's political rival for the President's political benefit. The call summary shows no *quid pro quo*, the initial read-outs relayed no substantive concerns, and both President Zelensky and President Trump have repeatedly said publicly there was no pressure. These facts refute the Democrats' allegations.

---

[87] Whistleblower letter, *supra* note 85, at 2.
[88] *Memorandum of Telephone Conversation*, *supra* note 15.
[89] Whistleblower letter, *supra* note 85, at 2.
[90] *Memorandum of Telephone Conversation*, *supra* note 15, at 3.
[91] Whistleblower letter, *supra* note 85, at 3.
[92] Volker transcribed interview, *supra* note 60, at 355.
[93] *Memorandum of Telephone Conversation*, *supra* note 15.
[94] *Id.*
[95] Whistleblower letter, *supra* note 85, at 3.
[96] Christina Ruffini (@EenaRuffini), Twitter (Sept. 26, 2019, 12:41 p.m.), https://twitter.com/EenaRuffini/status/1177307225024544768; Letter from Ronald Tenpas to Adam Schiff, Chairman, H. Perm. Sel. Comm. on Intelligence (Nov. 5, 2019).

B. **The evidence does not establish that President Trump withheld a meeting with President Zelensky to pressure Ukraine to investigate the President's political rival for the purpose of benefiting him in the 2020 election.**

Democrats allege that President Trump withheld a meeting with President Zelensky as a way of pressuring Ukraine to investigate President Trump's political rival.[97] Here, too, the evidence obtained during the impeachment inquiry does not support this allegation. President Trump and President Zelensky met *without* Ukraine ever investigating Vice Present Biden or his son, Hunter Biden.

The evidence strongly suggests, instead, that President Trump was reluctant to meet with President Zelensky for a different reason—Ukraine's long history of pervasive corruption and uncertainty about whether President Zelensky would break from this history and live up to his anti-corruption campaign platform. The Democrats' witnesses described how President Trump has a deep-seated and genuine skepticism of Ukraine due to its corruption and that the President's view was reasonable. Because of President Trump's skepticism and because President Zelensky was a first-time candidate with relatively untested views, Ukraine and U.S. officials sought to convince President Trump that President Zelensky was the "real deal" on reform. President Trump ultimately signed a letter to President Zelensky on May 29 inviting him to the White House.

Although there were several months between President Trump's invitation on May 29 and the bilateral meeting on September 25, the evidence does not show the delay was intentional or aimed at pressuring President Zelensky. The Democrats' witnesses described the difficulty in scheduling high-level meetings and how an anticipated presidential meeting in Poland in early September was cancelled due to Hurricane Dorian. Nonetheless, U.S. foreign policy officials believed that the Ukrainian government felt good about its relationship with the Trump Administration because of several high-level bilateral meetings held between May and September 2019, including President Zelensky's meeting with Vice President Pence on September 1. Ultimately, of course, President Trump and President Zelensky met during the U.N. General Assembly in New York on September 25, without Ukraine taking steps to investigate President Trump's political rival.

1. **Ukraine has a long history of pervasive corruption.**

Since it became an independent nation following the collapse of the Soviet Union, Ukraine has been plagued by systemic corruption. *The Guardian* has called Ukraine "the most corrupt nation in Europe"[98] and Ernst & Young cites Ukraine among the three most-corrupt nations of the world.[99]

---

[97] *See, e.g.*, Karoun Demirjian et al., *Officials' texts reveals belief that Trump wanted probes as condition of Ukraine meeting*, Wash. Post, Oct. 4, 2019.
[98] Oliver Bullough, *Welcome to Ukraine, the Most Corrupt Nation in Europe*, Guardian, (Feb. 6, 2015).
[99] *See, e.g.*, *14th Global Fraud Survey*, Ernst & Young, (2016), https://www.ey.com/Publication/vwLUAssets/EY-corporate-misconduct-individual-consequences/$FILE/EY-corporate-misconduct-individual-consequences.pdf (noting that 88% of Ukrainian's agree that "bribery/corrupt practices happen widely in business in [Ukraine]"). *See also* Viktor Tkachuk, *People First: The Latest in the Watch on Ukrainian Democracy*, Kyiv Post, (Sept. 11, 2012),

The United States Agency for International Development (USAID) explained Ukraine's history of corruption in a 2006 report:

> From the early 1990s, powerful officials in [the Ukrainian] government and politics acquired and privatized key economic resources of the state. As well, shadowy businesses, allegedly close to organized crime, became powerful economic forces in several regions of the country. Over the course of the past decade, these business groupings—or clans—as they became called, grew into major financial-industrial structures that used their very close links with and influence over government, political parties, the mass media and the state bureaucracy to enlarge and fortify their control over the economy and sources of wealth. They used ownership ties, special privileges, relations with government and direct influence over the courts and law enforcement and regulatory organizations to circumvent weaknesses in governmental institutions.[100]

Corruption is so pervasive in Ukraine that in 2011, 68.8% of Ukrainian citizens reported that they had bribed a public official within the preceding twelve months.[101] Bribery and facilitation payments[102] are common schemes by which Ukrainian officials demand payment in exchange for ensuring public services are delivered either on time or at all.[103] Corruption also presents an obstacle to private and public business in Ukraine.[104] In 2011, then-President Petro Poroshenko estimated that 15%, or $7.4 billion, of the state budget "ends up in the pockets of officials" through corrupt public procurement practices.[105]

Pervasive corruption in Ukraine has been one of the primary impediments to Ukraine joining the European Union.[106] Corruption-related concerns also figure prominently in the E.U.-Ukrainian Association Agreement, the document establishing a political and economic

---

https://www.kyivpost.com/article/opinion/op-ed/people-first-the-latest-in-the-watch-on-ukrainian-democracy-5-312797.html.

[100] U.S. Agency for International Development, Final Report, Corruption Assessment: Ukraine (2006), https://pdf.usaid.gov/pdf_docs/PNADK247.pdf.

[101] *Fighting Corruption in Ukraine: Ukrainian Style*, Gorshenin Inst., (Mar. 7, 2011), http://gpf-europe.com/upload/iblock/333/round_table_eng.pdf.

[102] *See* Facilitation Payments, *Corruption Dictionary*, Ganintegrity.com, (last visited Oct. 23, 2019), https://www.ganintegrity.com/portal/corruption-dictionary/. Facilitation payments, also known as "grease payments," are a form of bribery made with the purpose of expediting or securing the performance of a routine action to which the payer is legally entitled. *Id.*

[103] *People & Corruption: Citizens' Voices from Around the World*, Transparency Int'l, (2017), https://www.transparency.org/whatwedo/publication/people_and_corruption_citizens_voices_from_around_the_world.

[104] *Id.*

[105] Mark Rachkevych, *Under Yanukovych, Ukraine Slides Deeper in Ranks of Corrupt Nations*, Kyiv Post, (Dec. 1, 2011).

[106] *See, e.g.*, Vladimir Isachenkov, *Ukraine's integration into West dashed by war and corruption*, Assoc. Press, Mar. 26, 2019.

association between the E.U. and Ukraine.[107] The Agreement was entered into with the intent of Ukraine committing to gradually conform to E.U. technical and consumer standards.

State Department witnesses called by the Democrats during the impeachment inquiry confirmed Ukraine's reputation for corruption. Deputy Assistant Secretary of State George Kent described Ukraine's corruption problem as "serious" and said corruption has long been "part of the high-level dialogue" between the United States and Ukraine.[108] Ambassador Bill Taylor said corruption in Ukraine is a "big issue."[109] Ambassador Kurt Volker testified that "Ukraine has a long history of pervasive corruption throughout the economy[,] throughout the country, and it has been incredibly difficult for Ukraine as a country to deal with this, to investigate it, to prosecute it."[110] He later elaborated:

> Ukraine had for decades a reputation of being just a corrupt place. There are a handful of people who own a disproportionate amount of the economy. Oligarchs, they use corruption as kind of the coin of the realm to get what they want, including influencing the Parliament, the judiciary, the government, state-owned industries. And so businessmen generally don't want to invest in Ukraine, even to this day, because they just fear that it's a horrible environment to be working in, and they don't want to put – expose themselves to that risk. I would have to believe that President Trump would be aware of that general climate.[111]

2. President Trump has a deep-seated, genuine, and reasonable skepticism of Ukraine due to its history of pervasive corruption.

Multiple Democrat witnesses offered firsthand testimony of President Trump's skeptical view of Ukraine, as far back as September 2017. Ambassador Volker explained: "President Trump demonstrated that he had a very deeply rooted negative view of Ukraine based on past corruption. And that's a reasonable position. Most people who would know anything about Ukraine would think that."[112] He elaborated that the President's concern about Ukraine was genuine,[113] and that this concern contributed to a delay in the meeting with President Zelensky. He explained:

---

[107] E.U.-Ukraine Ass'n Agreement, art. 14, Mar. 21, 2014, 57 Off. J. of the E.U. L161/3 ("In their cooperation on justice, freedom and security, the Parties shall attach particular importance to the consolidation of the rule of law and the reinforcement of institutions at all levels in the areas of administration in general and law enforcement and the administration of justice in particular. Cooperation will, in particular, aim at strengthening the judiciary, improving its efficiency, safeguarding its independence and impartiality, and combating corruption. Respect for human rights and fundamental freedoms will guide all cooperation on justice, freedom and security.").
[108] Kent deposition, *supra* note 65 at 105, 151.
[109] Taylor deposition, *supra* note 47, at 86.
[110] Volker transcribed interview, *supra* note 60, at 76.
[111] *Id.* at 148-49.
[112] *Id.* at 30.
[113] *Id.* at 295.

16

So the issue as I understood it was this deep-rooted, skeptical view of Ukraine, a negative view of Ukraine, preexisting 2019, you know, going back. When I started this, I had one other meeting with President Trump and [then-Ukrainian] President Poroshenko. It was in September of 2017. And at that time he had a very skeptical view of Ukraine. So I know he had a very deep-rooted skeptical view. And my understanding at the time was that even though he agreed in the [May23] meeting that we had with him, say, okay, I'll invite him, he didn't really want to do it. And that's why the meeting kept being delayed and delayed. [114]

Other testimony confirms Ambassador Volker's statements. Former U.S. Ambassador to Ukraine Marie Yovanovitch confirmed the President's skepticism, saying that she observed it during President Trump's meeting with President Poroshenko in September 2017.[115] She testified:

Q. Were you aware of the President's deep-rooted skepticism about Ukraine's business environment?

A. Yes.

Q. And what did you know about that?

A. That he—I mean, he shared that concern directly with President Poroshenko in their first meeting in the Oval Office.[116]

Dr. Fiona Hill, NSC Senior Director for Europe, also testified that President Trump was "quite publicly" skeptical of Ukraine and that "everyone has expressed great concerns about corruption in Ukraine."[117] Catherine Croft, a former NSC director, similarly attested to President's Trump skepticism when she staffed President Trump for two Ukraine matters in 2017, explaining: "Throughout both, I heard, directly and indirectly, President Trump described Ukraine as a corrupt country."[118]

3. Senior Ukrainian government officials publicly attacked President Trump during the 2016 campaign.

President Trump's skepticism about Ukraine was compounded by statements made by senior Ukrainian government officials in 2016 that were critical of then-candidate Trump and supportive of his opponent, former Secretary of State Hillary Clinton. Although Democrats have attempted to discredit these assertions as "debunked," the statements by Ukrainian leaders speak

---

[114] *Id.* at 41.
[115] Deposition of Ambassador Marie Yovanovitch, in Wash., D.C., at 142 (Oct. 11, 2019).
[116] *Id.*
[117] Hill deposition, *supra* note 12, at 118.
[118] Croft deposition, *supra* note 60, at 14.

17

for themselves and shed light on President Trump's mindset when interacting with President Zelensky in 2019.

In August 2016, less than three months before the election, Valeriy Chaly, then-Ukrainian Ambassador to the United States, authored an op-ed in the Washington-based publication *The Hill* criticizing candidate Trump for comments he made about Russia's occupation of Crimea.[119] Ambassador Chaly wrote that candidate Trump's comments "have raised serious concerns in [Kyiv] and beyond Ukraine."[120] Although President Zelensky dismissed Ambassador Chaly on July 19, 2019,[121] the ambassador's op-ed remains on the website of the Ukrainian Embassy in the U.S. as of the date of this report.[122]

Later that month, the *Financial Times* published an article asserting that Trump's candidacy led "Kyiv's wider political leadership to do something they would never have attempted before: intervene, however indirectly, in a US election."[123] The article quoted Serhiy Leshchenko, a Ukrainian Member of Parliament, to detail how the Ukrainian government was supporting Secretary Clinton's candidacy.[124] The article explained:

> Though most Ukrainians are disillusioned with the country's current leadership for stalled reforms and lackluster anti-corruption efforts, Mr. Leshchenko said events of the past two years had locked Ukraine on to a pro-western course. ***The majority of Ukraine's politicians, he added, are "on Hillary Clinton's side."***[125]

The *Financial Times* reported that during the U.S. presidential campaign, former Ukrainian Prime Minister Arseniy Yatsenyuk had warned on Facebook that candidate Trump "challenged the very values of the free world."[126] On Twitter, Ukrainian Internal Affairs Minister Arsen Avakov called Trump a "clown" who is "an even bigger danger to the US than terrorism."[127] In a Facebook post, Avakov called Trump "dangerous for Ukraine and the US" and said that Trump's Crimea comments were the "diagnosis of a dangerous misfit."[128] Avakov continues to serve in President Zelensky's government.

Multiple Democrat witnesses testified that these Ukrainian actions during the 2016 election campaign likely also colored President Trump's views of President Zelensky. Ambassador Volker said:

---

[119] *See* Chaly, *supra* note 27.
[120] *Id.*
[121] *Zelensky dismisses Valeriy Chaly from post of Ukraine's envoy to US*, Kyiv Post (July 19, 2019).
[122] Embassy of Ukraine in the United States of America, *Op-ed by Ambassador of Ukraine to the USA Valeriy Chaly for the Hill: "Trump's comments send wrong message to world,"* https://usa.mfa.gov.ua/en/press-center/publications/4744-posol-ukrajini-vislovlyuvannya-trampa-nadsilajuty-nevirnij-signal-svitu.
[123] Roman Olearchyk, *Ukraine's leaders campaign against 'pro-Putin' Trump*, Financial Times, Aug. 28, 2016.
[124] *Id.*
[125] *Id.* (emphasis added).
[126] *Id.*
[127] Kenneth P. Vogel & David Stern, *Ukrainian efforts to sabotage Trump backfire*, Politico, Jan. 11, 2017.
[128] *Id.*

Q. And you mentioned that the President was skeptical, had a deep-rooted view of the Ukraine. Is that correct?

A. That is correct.

Q. And that, whether fair or unfair, he believed there were officials in Ukraine that were out to get him in the run-up to his election?

A. That is correct.

Q. So, to the extent there are allegations lodged, credible or uncredible, if the president was made aware of those allegations, whether it was via The Hill or, you know, via Mr. Giuliani or via cable news, if the President was made aware of these allegations, isn't it fair to say that he may, in fact, have believed they were credible?

A. Yes, I believe so.[129]

Ambassador Sondland similarly testified:

Q. Did [President Trump] mention anything about Ukraine's involvement in the 2016 election?

A. I think he said: They tried to take me down. He kept saying that over and over.

Q. In connection with the 2016 election?

A. Probably, yeah.

Q. That was what your understanding was?

A. That was my understanding, yeah.[130]

4. **U.S. foreign policy officials were split on President Zelensky, a political novice with untested views on anti-corruption and a close relationship with a controversial oligarch.**

Evidence obtained during the Democrats' impeachment inquiry shows that the U.S. foreign policy apparatus was divided on the question of whether President Trump should meet with President Zelensky. President Zelensky was a first-time candidate and a newcomer to the Ukrainian political scene. Although President Zelensky ran on an anti-corruption and reform platform, the Democrats' witnesses explained that the State Department was unsure how he

---

[129] Volker transcribed interview, *supra* note 60, at 70-71.
[130] Sondland deposition, *supra* note 51, at 75.

would govern as president. In addition, others in the U.S. government worried about President Zelensky's association with Ukrainian oligarch Igor Kolomoisky.

President Zelensky won a landslide victory on April 21, 2019, defeating incumbent President Petro Poroshenko by a 73-24 percent margin.[131] The win came as a surprise to many.[132] At the time of his election, Mr. Zelensky was a comedic television personality. Ambassador Volker testified that "Zelensky kind of came up out of nowhere. . . . When he arose kind of meteorically, as an outside figure and a popular candidate, I think it did take everybody by surprise."[133]

Ambassador Yovanovitch also testified that Zelensky's election came as a surprise. She explained:

> And I think that there was, you know, as is true, I think, probably in any country during Presidential elections, a lot of – a lot of concerns among people. This was I think a big surprise for the political elite of Ukraine, which is relatively small. And so, I don't think they saw it coming really until the very end. And, so, there was surprise and, you know, all the stages of grief, anger, disbelief, how is this happening?[134]

Ambassador Yovanovitch agreed that President Zelensky was an "untried" politician:

> Q. And how did you feel about [Zelensky winning the election]? What were your views of Zelensky? Did you think he was going to be a good advocate for the anticorruption initiatives, as he was campaigning on?
>
> A. We didn't know. I mean, he was an untried politician. Obviously, he has a background as a comedian, as an actor, as a businessperson, but we didn't know what he would be like as a President.[135]

Ambassador Sondland testified that there was a difference in opinion regarding whether to schedule a call between Presidents Trump and Zelensky. Ambassador Sondland recalled that he, Ambassador Volker, and Secretary Perry advocated for a call between the presidents, while NSC officials disagreed.[136]

Evidence suggests that U.S. officials had concerns about some people surrounding President Zelensky. Ambassador Volker testified that President Zelensky's chief of presidential administration, Andriy Bohdan, had earlier been an attorney for "a very famous oligarch in

---

[131] *Ukraine election: Comedian Zelensky wins presidency by landside*, BBC News (Apr. 22, 2019*)*.
[132] *Id.*
[133] Volker transcribed interview, *supra* note 60 at 152-53.
[134] Yovanovitch deposition, *supra* note 115, at 73-74.
[135] *Id.* at 74.
[136] Sondland note 51, at 27-28.

Ukraine."[137] Senator Ron Johnson, who attended President Zelensky's inauguration in May 2019, recalled "concern over rumors that [President] Zelensky was going to appoint Andriy Bohdan, the lawyer for oligarch Igor Kolomoisky, as his chief of staff. The delegation [to the inauguration] viewed Bohdan's rumored appointment to be contrary to the goal of fighting corruption and maintaining U.S. support."[138] President Zelensky appointed Bohdan to be head of presidential administration in May 2019.[139]

In addition, Dr. Hill explained that the NSC had a concern about President Zelensky's relationship with Kolomoisky, an oligarch who had owned the television station on which Zelensky's comedy show aired.[140] Under the Poroshenko regime, the Ukrainian government had accused Kolomoisky of embezzling from PrivatBank, which he co-owned, causing Kolomoisky to flee Ukraine.[141] According to Ambassador Volker, "the Ukrainian taxpayer officially is bailing out the bank for the money that Kolomoisky stole. Because the IMF provides budgetary support to Ukraine, we [the U.S. taxpayers] actually ended up bailing out this bank."[142]

Ambassador Taylor testified that he discussed these concerns about Kolomoisky directly with President Zelensky:

> [T]he influence of one particular oligarch over Mr. Zelensky is of particular concern, and that's this fellow Kolomoisky, so – and Kolomoisky has growing influence. And this is one of the concerns that I have expressed to President Zelensky and his team on several occasions very explicitly, saying that, you know, Mr. President, Kolomoisky was not elected. You were elected and he, Mr. Kolomoisky, is increasing his influence in your government, which could cause you to fail. So I've had that conversation with him a couple of times.[143]

Kolomoisky returned to Ukraine following President Zelensky's victory.[144]

5. **President Trump extended an invitation to the White House to President Zelensky on three occasions without conditions.**

The evidence demonstrates that President Trump had a deep skepticism of Ukraine based on its history of pervasive corruption. This inherent skepticism, coupled with certain Ukrainian government officials' criticism of candidate Trump during the 2016 campaign and President Zelensky's untested views, contributed to President Trump's reticence to meet with President

---

[137] Volker transcribed interview, *supra* note 60, at 137.
[138] Letter from Sen. Ron Johnson to Jim Jordan, Ranking Member, H. Comm. on Oversight & Reform, & Devin Nunes, Ranking Member, H. Perm. Sel. Comm. on Intelligence 3 (Nov. 18, 2019).
[139] Roman Olearchyk, *Volodymyr Zelensky hires oligarch's lawyer as chief of staff*, Financial Times, May 22, 2019.
[140] Hill deposition, *supra* note 12, at 76-77.
[141] Andrew E. Kramer, *Oligarch's return raises alarm in Ukraine*, N.Y. Times, May 16, 2019.
[142] Volker transcribed interview, *supra* note 60, at 246.
[143] Taylor deposition, *supra* note 47, at 86.
[144] Kramer, *supra* note 141.

Zelensky. In spring and summer 2019, however, the President extended an invitation to the White House to President Zelensky on three occasions—without any conditions.

On April 21, 2019, President Trump placed a brief congratulatory call to President-elect Zelensky.[145] President Trump said: "When you're settled in and ready, I'd like to invite you to the White House."[146] The presidents did not discuss any investigations, and President Trump placed no conditions on his invitation.

On May 23, President Trump met with Ambassador Volker, Ambassador Sondland, Secretary Perry, and Senator Johnson—the senior U.S. officials who had comprised the official U.S. delegation to President Zelensky's inauguration days before. The delegation sought to convey to President Trump a positive impression of President Zelensky.[147] According to Ambassador Volker:

> President Trump demonstrated that he had a very deeply rooted negative view of Ukraine based on past corruption. And that's a reasonable position. Most people who would know anything about Ukraine would think that. That's why it was important that we wanted to brief him, because we were saying, it's different, this guy is different. But the President had a very deeply rooted negative view. We urged that he invite President Zelensky to meet with him at the White House. He was skeptical of that. We persisted. And he finally agreed, okay, I'll do it.[148]

Later in his transcribed interview, Ambassador Volker provided more context for the May 23 discussion:

> What I heard from President Trump in the meeting in the oval office was blanket, like, "this—these are terrible people, this is a corrupt country," you know, "I don't believe it." I made the argument that President Zelensky is the real deal, he is going to try to fix things, and, you know, he just did not believe it. He waved it off. So there's a general issue there.
>
> He did not mention investigations to me in that meeting, or call for investigations. I was not aware that he did so in the July 25th call later. His attitude towards Ukraine was just general and negative.[149]

Ambassador Sondland similarly testified that President Trump expressed negative views about Ukraine in this meeting and mentioned how "they tried to take me down" in 2016.[150]

---

[145] *Memorandum of Telephone Conversation, supra* note 10.
[146] *Id.*
[147] Hill deposition, *supra* note 12, at 320.
[148] Volker transcribed interview, *supra* note 60, at 30-31.
[149] *Id.* at 280.
[150] Sondland deposition, *supra* note 51, at 74-75.

Although Ambassador Sondland said he was discouraged by the President's viewpoint, he was pleased and surprised that the President later agreed to invite President Zelensky to the White House.[151]

Senator Johnson recalled that in this meeting, President Trump "expressed strong reservations about support for Ukraine. He made it crystal clear that he viewed Ukraine as a thoroughly corrupt country both generally and, specifically, regarding rumored meddling in the 2016 election."[152] Senator Johnson further explained:

> It was obvious that [the President's] viewpoint and reservations were strongly held, and that we would have a significant sales job ahead of us in getting him to change his mind. I specifically asked him to keep his viewpoint and reservations private and not to express them publicly until he had a chance to meet [President] Zelensky. He agreed to do so, but he added that he wanted [President] Zelensky to know exactly how he felt about the corruption in Ukraine prior to any future meeting.[153]

Senator Johnson recounted that he did not recall President Trump mentioning Burisma or the Bidens, but it was "obvious" that President Trump was aware of "rumors that corrupt actors in Ukraine might have played a part in helping create the false Russia collusion narrative."[154]

On May 29, President Trump wrote to President Zelensky to invite him to Washington, D.C. "as soon as we can find a mutually convenient time."[155] President Trump's letter did not mention any investigations and placed no conditions on President Zelensky's invitation to the White House. On July 25, during their phone conversation, President Trump reiterated his invitation to President Zelensky, again without conditions.[156]

6. Despite difficulty scheduling a face-to-face presidential meeting, senior Ukrainian officials interacted often with senior American officials between May and September 2019.

By late May 2019, President Trump had formally extended an invitation for President Zelensky to visit the White House. Although the two presidents did not meet face-to-face until September 25, the Democrats' witnesses testified that presidential meetings can often take time to schedule and that senior Ukrainian officials met frequently with American counterparts in the

---

[151] *Id.* at 74, 81, 85-87.
[152] Letter from Sen. Ron Johnson, *supra* note 138, at 4.
[153] *Id.*
[154] *Id.*
[155] Letter from President Donald J. Trump to His Excellency Volodymyr Zelenskyy, President of Ukraine (May 29, 2019). Dr. Hill testified that Ambassador Sondland claimed he had dictated the paragraph inviting President Zelensky to the White House, *see* Hill deposition, *supra* note 12, at 74; however, Ambassador Sondland testified that he had no role in drafting the letter. Sondland deposition, *supra* note 51, at 81.
[156] *Memorandum of Telephone Conversation, supra* note 15.

interim.[157] Ambassador Volker explained that the new Zelensky regime was "actually feeling pretty good by then" about its relationship with the Trump Administration.[158]

On June 4, President Zelensky attended an Independence Day dinner at the U.S. mission to the E.U. hosted by Ambassador Sondland and also attended by White House Senior Advisor Jared Kushner.[159]

On July 3, while in Toronto, Canada, for the Ukraine Reform Conference, President Zelensky met with Ambassador Volker and Deputy Assistant Secretary of State George Kent.[160]

On July 9, Oleksandr Danylyuk, then-Secretary of the National Security and Defense Council of Ukraine, and Andrey Yermak, a senior adviser to President Zelensky, met with LTG Keith Kellogg, Vice President Pence's National Security Advisor; Jennifer Williams, a special advisor covering European issues for Vice President Pence; and NSC staff member LTC Alexander Vindman.[161]

On July 10, Danylyuk and Yermak met at the White House with National Security Advisor John Bolton, Secretary Perry, Ambassador Volker, Ambassador Sondland, Dr. Hill, and LTC Vindman.[162]

On July 25, President Trump and President Zelensky spoke by telephone.[163]

On July 26, President Zelensky met with Ambassador Volker, Ambassador Sondland, and Ambassador Taylor in Kyiv.[164] Ambassador Volker testified that the meeting was scheduled before the presidents' phone call.[165] He said President Zelensky was "pleased that the call had taken place . . . . They thought it went well. And they were encouraged again because the President had asked them to pick dates for coming to the White House."[166]

On August 27, President Zelensky met with National Security Advisor Bolton in Kyiv.[167]

On September 1, President Zelensky met with Vice President Pence in Warsaw, Poland, after an event commemorating the 80th anniversary of the beginning of World War II.[168] President Trump had been scheduled to attend but was forced to cancel due to Hurricane

---

[157] Kent deposition, *supra* note 65, at 231; Volker transcribed interview, *supra* note 60, at 127.
[158] Volker transcribed interview, *supra* note 60, at 127.
[159] Sondland deposition, *supra* note 51, at 26-27, 148-49.
[160] Kent deposition, *supra* note 65, at 241; Volker transcribed interview, *supra* note 60, at 137.
[161] Williams deposition, *supra* note 73, at 51-53.
[162] Volker transcribed interview, *supra* note 60, at 66-67; Hill deposition, *supra* note 12, at 62-63.
[163] *Memorandum of Telephone Conversation*, *supra* note 15.
[164] Volker transcribed interview, *supra* note 60, at 312-33; Sondland deposition, *supra* note 51, at 29.
[165] Volker transcribed interview, *supra* note 60, at 102.
[166] *Id.* at 313.
[167] Taylor deposition, *supra* note 47, at 229-30.
[168] The White House, Readout of Vice President Mike Pence's Meeting with Ukrainian President Volodymyr Zelenskyy (Sept. 1, 2019); Taylor deposition, *supra* note 47, at 34-35.

Dorian.[169] According to Ambassador Taylor's testimony, Vice President Pence reiterated President Trump's views for "Europeans to do more to support Ukraine and that he wanted the Ukrainians to do more to fight corruption."[170]

On September 17, Secretary of State Pompeo had a telephone conversation with Ukrainian Foreign Minister Vadym Prystaiko.[171] According to a readout from the U.S. Embassy in Kyiv, Secretary Pompeo "affirmed U.S. support for Ukraine as it advances critical reforms to tackle corruption, strengthen the rule of law, and foster an economic environment that promotes competition and investment. The Secretary expressed unwavering U.S. support for Ukraine's sovereignty and territorial integrity."[172]

On September 18, President Zelensky and Vice President Pence spoke by telephone.[173] The two discussed President Zelensky's upcoming meeting with President Trump on the margins of the U.N. General Assembly and Ukraine's effort to address its corruption challenges.[174]

7. The evidence does not establish a linkage between a White House meeting and Ukrainian investigations into President Trump's political rival.

The evidence in the Democrats' impeachment inquiry does not show that a White House meeting was conditioned on Ukraine's willingness to investigate President Trump's political rival. Although the anonymous whistleblower, citing "multiple" secondhand sources, alleged that President Trump sought to withhold a meeting to pressure President Zelensky to "play ball,"[175] publicly available information contradicts the whistleblower's claim. For example, Andrey Yermak, a senior adviser to President Zelensky, admitted in an August 2019 *New York Times* article that he discussed with Mayor Giuliani both meeting between President Trump and President Zelensky and investigations.[176] The *Times* reported, however, that Yermak and Mayor Giuliani "did not discuss a link between the two."[177]

Other firsthand testimony obtained during the impeachment inquiry supports this finding. For example, Ambassador Volker, the key interlocutor with the Ukrainian government, clearly testified that there was no "linkage" between a White House meeting and Ukrainian actions to investigate President Trump's political rival. He explained:

> Q. Did the President ever withhold a meeting with President Zelensky
> until the Ukrainians committed to investigating those allegations?

---

[169] Volker transcribed interview, *supra* note 60, at 130; Taylor deposition, *supra* note 47, at 35.
[170] Taylor deposition, *supra* note 47, at 35.
[171] U.S. Embassy in Ukraine, Secretary Michael R. Pompeo's Call with Ukrainian Foreign Minister Vadym Prystayko (Sept. 17, 2019), https://ua.usembassy.gov/secretary-michael-r-pompeos-call-with-ukrainian-foreign-minister-vadym-prystayko/.
[172] *Id.*
[173] The White House, Readout of Vice President Mike Pence's Phone Call with President of Ukraine (Sept. 18, 2019).
[174] *Id.*; *see also* Volker transcribed interview, *supra* note 60, at 317-18.
[175] Whistleblower letter, *supra* note 85, at 7.
[176] Kenneth P. Vogel & Andrew E. Kramer, *Giuliani renews push for Ukraine to investigate Trump's political opponents*, N.Y. Times, Aug. 21, 2019.
[177] *Id.*

A. We had a difficult time scheduling a bilateral meeting between President Zelensky and President Trump.

Q. Ambassador Volker, that was a yes-or-no question.

A. Well, if I – can you repeat the question then?

Q. Sure. Did President Trump ever withhold a meeting with President Zelensky or delay a meeting with President Zelensky until the Ukrainians committed to investigate the allegations that you just described concerning the 2016 Presidential election?

A. The answer to the question is no, if you want a yes-or-no answer. But the reason the answer is no is we did have difficulty scheduling a meeting, but there was no linkage like that.[178]

***

Q. So before we move to the text messages, I want to ask you a clarifying question. You said that you were not aware of any linkage between the delay in the Oval Office meeting between President Trump and President Zelensky and the Ukrainian commitment to investigate the two allegations as you described them, correct?

A. Correct.[179]

Ambassador Sondland was the only witness to allege a *quid pro quo* with respect to a White House meeting. However, to the extent that Ambassador Sondland testified that he believed a White House meeting was conditioned on Ukrainian actions, his belief was that a meeting was conditioned on a public statement about anti-corruption—not on investigations into President Trump's political rival.[180] Ambassador Sondland testified in his closed-door deposition that "nothing about the request raised any red flags for me, Ambassador Volker, or Ambassador Taylor."[181] In his public testimony, Ambassador Sondland clarified that he *believed* there was linkage, but that President Trump had never discussed with him any preconditions for a White House visit by President Zelensky.[182]

In addition, there is conflicting testimony about what occurred during a July 10 meeting between two senior Ukrainian officials and senior U.S. officials in National Security Advisor John Bolton's office. Ambassador Volker, Ambassador Sondland, Secretary Perry joined

---

[178] Volker transcribed interview, *supra* note 60, at 35-36.
[179] *Id.* at 40.
[180] Sondland deposition, *supra* note 51, at 30, 331.
[181] *Id.* at 30.
[182] *Impeachment Inquiry: Ambassador Gordon Sondland, supra* note 56.

Ambassador Bolton to meet with Oleksandr Danylyuk, then-Secretary of Ukraine's National Security and Defense Council, and Andrey Yermak, an adviser to President Zelensky.[183] Dr. Hill and LTC Vindman from the NSC staff attended as well.[184]

Dr. Hill and LTC Vindman alleged that during the meeting, Ambassador Sondland raised potential Ukrainian actions on investigations, leading Ambassador Bolton to abruptly end the meeting.[185] Dr. Hill recounted that Ambassador Bolton told her to brief the NSC Legal Advisor, John Eisenberg, and said he would not be a part of what he termed a "drug deal."[186]

Although Dr. Hill testified that she confronted Ambassador Sondland over his discussion of investigations,[187] Ambassador Sondland testified in his closed-door deposition that "neither Ambassador Bolton, Dr. Hill, or anyone else on the NSC staff ever expressed any concerns to me about our efforts . . . or, most importantly, any concerns that we were acting improperly."[188] Ambassador Sondland testified in his deposition that he recalled no "unpleasant conversation" with Dr. Hill.[189] Likewise, although Ambassador Volker assessed that the meeting was "not good," he said it was because Danylyuk poorly conveyed the appropriate top-level message to Ambassador Bolton during the meeting.[190]

In his public testimony, Ambassador Volker acknowledged that Ambassador Sondland made a "general comment about investigations," but he disputed that the July 10 meeting ended abruptly.[191] He also testified that preconditions were not discussed during the meeting.[192] Although Ambassador Sondland denied in his closed-door depositions that he raised investigations during July 10 meeting,[193] he acknowledged that he did in his public testimony.[194] Even still, Ambassador Sondland denied that the July 10 meeting ended abruptly: "I don't recall any abrupt ending of the meeting or people storming out or anything like that. That would have been very memorable if someone had stormed out of a meeting, based on something I said."[195] He explained that Dr. Hill never raised concerns to him, and that any discussion of investigations did not mention specific investigations.[196] He testified:

> Q. And, in fact, after the meeting, you went out and you took a picture, right?

---

[183] Sondland deposition, *supra* note 51, at 27; Volker transcribed interview, *supra* note 60, at 50-51.
[184] Hill deposition, *supra* note 12, at 63; Vindman deposition, *supra* note 12, at 17-18.
[185] Hill deposition, *supra* note 12, at 67; Vindman deposition, *supra* note 12, at 17.
[186] Hill deposition, *supra* note 12, at 70-71.
[187] *Id.* at 68-71. Dr. Hill testified that she also had a "blow up" with Ambassador Sondland in June about Ukraine, saying that Ambassador Sondland got "testy." *Id.* at 113.
[188] Sondland deposition, *supra* note 51, at 28.
[189] *Id.* at 114.
[190] Volker transcribed interview, *supra* note 60, at 66.
[191] *Impeachment Inquiry: Ambassador Kurt Volker and Mr. Timothy Morrison, supra* note 8.
[192] *Id.*
[193] *Id.* at 109-10.
[194] *Impeachment Inquiry: Ambassador Gordon Sondland, supra* note 56.
[195] *Id.*
[196] *Id.*

27

A. Yeah. We – Ambassador Bolton – or his assistant indicated that he was out of time, that he needed – he had another meeting to attend. And we all walked out of the White House. Everyone was smiling, everyone was happy, and we took a picture on the lawn on a nice sunny day.

Q. Okay. Then did you retire to the Ward Room?

A. I think Secretary Perry asked to use the Ward Room to continue the conversation. And the real subject that was under debate – and it wasn't an angry debate, it was a debate – should the call from President Trump to President Zelensky be made prior to the parliamentary elections in Ukraine or after the parliamentary elections? And there was good reason for both. We felt – Ambassador Perry, Ambassador Volker, and I thought it would help President Zelensky to have President Trump speak to him prior to the parliamentary elections, because it would give President Zelensky more credibility, and ultimately he would do better with his people in the parliamentary elections. Others, I believe, pushed back and said, no, it's not appropriate to do it before. It should be done after. And ultimately, it was done after.

Q. Okay. There was no mention of Vice President Biden in the Ward Room?

A. Not that I remember, no.

Q. Or any specific investigation?

A. Just the generic investigations.[197]

Contemporaneous evidence contradicts the idea that there was serious discord during the meeting. Following the meeting, Ambassador Bolton retweeted a statement from Secretary Perry about the July 10 meeting, writing it was a "great discussion . . . on U.S. support for Ukrainian reforms and the peaceful restoration of Ukrainian territory."[198] The picture in the tweet of the U.S. and Ukrainian officials—taken immediately after the meeting in Ambassador Bolton's office[199]—shows smiling faces and no indication of hostility or discord between Ambassador Bolton and Ambassador Sondland.

---

[197] *Id.*
[198] John Bolton (@AmbJohnBolton), Twitter (July 10, 2019, 4:39 p.m.), https://twitter.com/AmbJohnBolton/status/1149100798632026112.
[199] Sondland deposition, *supra* note 51, at 110.

Figure 1: Ambassador Bolton tweet following July 10 meeting

Figure 2: Picture of smiling U.S. and Ukrainian officials following July 10 meeting

8. The evidence does not establish that President Trump directed Vice President Pence not to attend President Zelensky's inauguration to pressure Ukraine to investigate the President's political rival.

The evidence also does not establish that President Trump directed Vice President Pence not to attend President Zelensky's inauguration as a means of pressuring Ukraine to investigate the President's political rival. During their initial April 21 phone call, President Trump told President Zelensky that a "great" representative of the U.S. would attend the Zelensky inauguration.[200] The anonymous whistleblower alleged that President Trump later "instructed Vice President Pence to cancel his planned travel to Ukraine to attend President Zelensky's

---

[200] Memorandum of Telephone Conversation, *supra* note 10.

inauguration . . . . [I]t was also 'made clear' to them that the President did not want to meet with Mr. Zelensky until he saw how Zelensky 'chose to act' in office."[201] The evidence in the Democrats' impeachment inquiry does not support this assertion.

Although Jennifer Williams, a special adviser in the Office of the Vice President, testified in her closed-door deposition that a colleague told her that President Trump directed Vice President Pence not to attend the inauguration,[202] she had no firsthand knowledge of any such direction or the reasons given for any such direction.[203] Williams explained that the Office of the Vice President provided three dates—May 30, May 31 and June 1—during which Vice President Pence would be available to attend the inauguration.[204] Williams explained that "if it wasn't one of those dates it would be very difficult or impossible" for Vice President Pence to attend.[205] Neither the Secret Service nor advance teams deployed to Ukraine to prepare for Vice President Pence's travel.[206]

During this same period, Vice Present Pence was planning travel to Ottawa, Canada, on May 30 to promote the U.S.-Mexico-Canada Agreement (USMCA).[207] Williams acknowledged in her public testimony that the Office of the Vice President had "competing trips . . . for the same window."[208] Williams elaborated that due to international travel by President Trump and Vice President Pence, there was a "narrow window" within which Vice President Pence was able to attend President Zelensky's inauguration.[209] Dr. Hill explained that the President and Vice President cannot travel internationally at the same time, testifying that Vice President Pence's attendance at President Zelensky's inauguration was just dependent on scheduling and she had no knowledge that the Vice President was directed not to attend the inauguration.[210]

Ultimately, on May 16, the Ukrainian Parliament scheduled President Zelensky's inauguration for only four days later, May 20, which was a date not offered by the Vice President's Office.[211] Williams testified that this scheduling posed a problem: "To be honest, we hadn't looked that closely at the Vice President's schedule before the President's trip [to Japan]

---

[201] Whistleblower letter, *supra* note 85, at app. 1-2.
[202] Williams deposition, *supra* note 73, at 37.
[203] *Impeachment Inquiry: LTC Alexander Vindman and Ms. Jennifer Williams*, *supra* note 6.
[204] Williams deposition, *supra* note 73, at 58; *Impeachment Inquiry: LTC Alexander Vindman and Ms. Jennifer Williams*, *supra* note 6.
[205] Williams deposition, *supra* note 73, at 58.
[206] *Id.* at 59.
[207] *See* The White House, Joint Statement by Vice President Mike Pence and Canadian Prime Minister Justin Trudeau (May 30, 2019).
[208] *Impeachment Inquiry: LTC Alexander Vindman and Ms. Jennifer Williams*, *supra* note 6.
[209] *Id.*
[210] *"Impeachment Inquiry: Dr. Fiona Hill and Mr. David Holmes": Hearing before the H. Perm. Sel. Comm. on Intelligence*, 116th Cong. (2019); Hill deposition, *supra* note 12, at 185 ("It depended on the date. I mean, we were hoping, you know, if others couldn't attend that [Vice President Pence] could. I mean, I myself couldn't attend because of the date, that the way that it – again, there were several different dates, and then the date that was announced in May was very quickly announced."); *id.* at 316 ("And it was going to be very tight for the Vice President to make it for the inauguration. So I, you know, have no knowledge that he was actually ordered not to go, but it was going to be very difficult for him to go.").
[211] Kent deposition, *supra* note 65, at 189.

at the end of May just because we weren't expecting the Ukrainians to look at that timeframe."[212] Kent explained that this short notice sent the State Department "scrambl[ing]" to find a U.S. official to lead the delegation.[213] Secretary Pompeo was traveling, so the decision was made to ask Secretary Perry to lead the delegation.[214] On May 20, the day of President Zelensky's inauguration, Vice President Pence attended an event in Jacksonville, Florida, to promote the USMCA.[215]

9. President Trump and President Zelensky met during the United Nations General Assembly in September 2019 without any Ukrainian action to investigate President Trump's political rival.

On September 25, President Trump and President Zelensky met during the U.N. General Assembly in New York.[216] Ambassador Volker said that President Trump and President Zelensky had a "positive" meeting. He testified:

> Q. Turning back to President Trump's skepticism of Ukraine and the corruption there, do you think you made any inroads in convincing him that Zelensky was a good partner?
>
> A. I do. I do. I attended the President's meeting with President Zelensky in New York on, I guess it was the 25th of September. And I could see the body language and the chemistry between them was positive, and I felt that this is what we needed all along.[217]

Ambassador Taylor testified that the meeting was "good" and President Trump "left pleased that they had finally met face to face."[218] Ambassador Taylor said there was no discussion about investigations during the September 25 meeting.[219]

Notably, President Trump and President Zelensky met in New York without Ukraine ever investigating President Trump's political rival.

* * *

The evidence presented in the impeachment inquiry does not support the Democrats' assertion that President Trump sought to withhold a White House meeting to pressure the Ukrainian government to investigate the President's political rival. President Trump and President Zelensky met in September 2019 *without* Ukraine ever investigating Vice President Biden or Hunter Biden.

---

[212] Williams deposition, *supra* note 73, at 60.

[213] Kent deposition, *supra* note 65, at 190.

[214] *Id.* at 190-91.

[215] The White House, Remarks by Vice President Pence at America First Policies Event USMCA: A Better Deal for American Worker (May 20, 2019).

[216] Remarks by President Trump and President Zelensky of Ukraine Before Bilateral Meeting, *supra* note 40.

[217] Volker transcribed interview, *supra* note 60, at 87-88.

[218] Taylor deposition, *supra* note 47, at 288.

[219] *Id.*

Contrary to the assertions in the anonymous whistleblower complaint, the evidence shows that President Trump has a genuine, deep-seated, and reasonable skepticism of Ukraine given its history of pervasive corruption. In addition, U.S. foreign policy officials were divided on whether President Trump should meet with President Zelensky, in part due to President Zelensky's close association with an oligarch accused of embezzlement. In May 2019, President Trump formally invited President Zelensky to the White House. For several months, there were attempts to arrange a meeting between President Trump and President Zelensky. Although President Trump indicated during their July 25 call that they may meet in Warsaw in September, Hurricane Dorian forced President Trump to cancel. Vice President Pence met with President Zelensky instead. President Trump and President Zelensky ultimately met without Ukraine ever investigating any of President Trump's political rival.

C. The evidence does not establish that President Trump withheld U.S. security assistance to Ukraine to pressure Ukraine to investigate the President's political rival for the purpose of benefiting him in the 2020 election.

Democrats allege that President Trump conspired to withhold U.S. security assistance to Ukraine as a way of pressuring Ukraine to investigate President Trump's political rival.[220] Here, too, the evidence obtained during the impeachment inquiry does not support this allegation.

The evidence suggests a far less nefarious reality. Just as President Trump holds a deep-seated skepticism about Ukraine, the President is highly skeptical of foreign assistance. Any examination of the President's actions must consider this factor. President Trump has been vocal about his view that U.S. allies in Europe should contribute a fair share for regional security. As Ukrainian government officials worked with U.S. officials to convince President Trump that President Zelensky was serious about reform and worthy of U.S. assistance, they discussed a public statement conveying that commitment. Although the security assistance was paused in July, it is not unusual for U.S. foreign assistance to become delayed. Assistance to Ukraine has been delayed before. Most telling, the Trump Administration has been stronger than the Obama Administration in providing Ukraine with lethal defensive arms to deter Russian aggression.

The Democrats' witnesses testified that U.S. security assistance to Ukraine was not conditioned on Ukrainian action on investigations. U.S. officials did not raise the issue of the delay in security assistance with Ukrainian officials because they viewed it as a bureaucratic issue that would be resolved. The Ukrainian government in Kyiv was not even aware that the aid was paused until it was reported publicly, only two weeks before the aid was released, as senior U.S. officials confidently predicted it would be. Ultimately, the U.S. disbursed security assistance to Ukraine *without* Ukraine ever investigating Vice Present Biden or his son, Hunter Biden.

---

[220] *See, e.g.*, Rishika Dugyala, *Democratic Senator: 'No doubt' Ukraine 'felt pressure'*, Politico (Oct. 27, 2019).

1. President Trump has been skeptical about U.S. taxpayer-funded foreign assistance.

Evidence suggests that President Trump is generally skeptical of U.S. taxpayer-funded foreign assistance. President Trump's skepticism of U.S. taxpayer-funded foreign assistance is long-standing. On June 16, 2015, when President Trump announced his candidacy for president, he said:

> It is time to stop sending jobs overseas through bad foreign trade deals. We will renegotiate our trade deals with the toughest negotiators our country has… the ones who have actually read "The Art of the Deal" and know how to make great deals for our country.
>
> It is time to close loopholes for Wall Street and create far more opportunities for small businesses.
>
> It is necessary that we invest in our infrastructure, *stop sending foreign aid to countries that hate us and use that money to rebuild our tunnels, roads, bridges and schools—and nobody can do that better than me.*[221]

During the 2016 presidential campaign, then-candidate Trump continued to express his skepticism of U.S. taxpayer-funded foreign aid. In March 2016, he told the *Washington Post*, "I do think it's a different world today and I don't think we should be nation building anymore. I think it's proven not to work. And we have a different country than we did then. You know we have 19 trillion dollars in debt. . . . And I just think we have to rebuild our country."[222] That same month, then-candidate Trump told the *New York Times*, "We're going to be friendly with everybody, but we're not going to be taken advantage of by anybody. . . . I think we'll be very worldview [*sic*], but we're not going to be ripped off anymore by all of these countries."[223]

As president, President Trump has sought to reduce U.S. taxpayer-funded foreign assistance. In his fiscal year 2018 budget proposal, the President proposed "to reduce or end direct funding for international programs and organizations whose missions do not substantially advance U.S. foreign policy interests. The Budget also renews attention on the appropriate U.S. share of international spending . . . for many other global issues where the United States currently pays more than its fair share."[224] The President's 2020 budget proposal—submitted in March 2019—likewise "supports America's reliable allies, but reflects a new approach toward countries that have taken unfair advantage of the United States' generosity."[225] The President's

---

[221] Donald Trump, Announcement of Candidacy for President of the United States, in New York, N.Y. (June 16, 2015) (emphasis added).

[222] *A transcript of Donald Trump's meeting with the Washington Post editorial board*, Wash. Post, Mar. 21, 2016.

[223] Maggie Haberman & David Sanger, *Transcript: Donald Trump Expounds on His Foreign Policy Views*, N.Y. Times, Mar. 26, 2016.

[224] Budget of the U.S. Government Fiscal Year 2018 at 13 (May 23, 2017).

[225] Budget of the U.S. Government Fiscal Year 2020 at 71 (Mar. 11, 2019).

Budget specifically sought "greater accountability by international partners along with donor burden sharing that is more balanced."[226]

Testimony from the Democrats' witnesses reinforces the President's skepticism of foreign assistance. Ambassador Taylor, U.S. chargé *a.i.* in Kyiv, testified that on August 22, 2019, he had a phone conversation with NSC Senior Director for Europe Tim Morrison in which Morrison said that the "President doesn't want to provide any assistance at all."[227] Morrison testified that President Trump generally does not like giving foreign aid to other countries and believes U.S. "ought not" to be the only country providing security assistance.[228] LTC Vindman, the NSC director handling Ukraine policy, similarly testified that President Trump is skeptical of foreign aid.[229]

In fact, evidence suggests that President Trump sought to review U.S. taxpayer-funded foreign assistance across the board. Ambassador David Hale, the Under Secretary of State for Political Affairs, testified that the Trump Administration was undertaking a "review" of foreign assistance globally.[230] He testified:

> Q. You mentioned that there was a foreign assistance review undergoing –
>
> A. Yes.
>
> Q. – at that time. What can you tell us about that?
>
> A. Well, it had been going on for quite a while, and the concept, you know, the administration did not want to take a, sort of, business-as-usual approach to foreign assistance, a feeling that once a country has received a certain assistance package, it's a – it's something that continues forever. It's very difficult to end those programs and to make sure that we have a very rigorous measure of why we are providing the assistance.
>
> We didn't go to zero base, but almost a zero-based concept that each assistance program and each country that receives the program had to be evaluated that they were actually worthy beneficiaries of our assistance; that the program made sense; that we have embarked on, you know, calling everything that we do around the world countering violent extremism, but, rather, that's actually focused on tangible and proven means to deal with extremist problems; that we avoid nation-building strategies; and that we not provide assistance to countries that are lost to us in terms of policy, to our adversaries.

---

[226] *Id.* at 73.

[227] Taylor deposition, *supra* note 47, at 33.

[228] Morrison deposition, *supra* note 12, at 78-79, 132.

[229] *Impeachment Inquiry: LTC Alexander Vindman and Ms. Jennifer Williams*, *supra* note 6.

[230] Deposition of Ambassador David Hale, in Wash., D.C., at 80 (Nov. 6, 2019) [hereinafter "Hale deposition"].

Q. And do you know if the President also had concerns about whether the allies of Ukraine, in this example, were contributing their fair share?

A. That's another factor in the foreign affairs review is appropriate burden sharing. But it was not, in the deputies committee meeting, OMB [the U.S. Office of Management and Budget] did not really explain why they were taking the position other than they had been directed to do so.

Q. Okay. You are aware of the President's skeptical views on foreign assistance? Right?

A. Absolutely.

Q. And that's a genuinely held belief, correct?

A. It is what guided the foreign affairs review.

Q. Okay. It's not just related to Ukraine?

A. Absolutely not. It's global in nature.[231]

2. President Trump has been clear and consistent in his view that Europe should pay its fair share for regional defense.

Since his 2016 presidential campaign, President Trump has emphasized his view that U.S. foreign assistance should be spent wisely and cautiously. As President, he has continued to be critical of sending U.S. taxpayer dollars to foreign countries and asked our allies to share the financial burden for international stewardship.

In a March 2016 interview with the *New York Times*, then-candidate Trump said: "Now, I'm a person that—you notice I talk about economics quite a bit [in foreign policy] because it is about economics, because we don't have money anymore because we've been taking care of so many people in so many different forms that we don't have money."[232] Then-candidate Trump elaborated about the North Atlantic Treaty Organization (NATO), a collective defense alliance between the U.S., Canada, and European countries:

> I mean, we defend everybody. (Laughs.) We defend everybody. No matter who it is, we defend everybody. We're defending the world. But we owe, soon, it's soon to be $21 trillion. You know, it's 19 now but it's soon to be $21 trillion. But we defend everybody. When in doubt, come to the United States. We'll defend you. In some cases

---

[231] *Id.* at 81-83.
[232] Haberman & Sanger, *supra* note 223.

free of charge. And in all cases for a substantially, you know, greater amount. We spend a substantially greater amount than what the people are paying.[233]

That same month, candidate Trump spoke to CBS News about U.S. spending to NATO. He said then:

> NATO was set up when we were a richer country. We're not a rich country anymore. We're borrowing, we're borrowing all of this money . . . NATO is costing us a fortune and yes, we're protecting Europe with NATO but we're spending a lot of money. Number one, I think the distribution of costs has to be changed.[234]

As president, President Trump has continued to press European allies to contribute more NATO defense. For example, in a tweet on July 9, 2018, President Trump wrote:

> The United States is spending far more on NATO than any other Country. This is not fair, nor is it acceptable. While these countries have been increasing their contributions since I took office, they must do much more. Germany is at 1%, the U.S. is at 4%, and NATO benefits.......[235]

Jens Stoltenberg, the NATO Secretary-General, acknowledged in an interview that President Trump's message has "helped" NATO member countries to increase defense spending, commending the President on "his strong message on burden sharing."[236]

NSC Senior Director Tim Morrison explained the President's specific views about burden sharing regarding Ukraine during his public testimony. He testified:

> Q. And the President was also interested, was he not, in better understanding opportunities for increased burden sharing among the Europeans?
>
> A. Yes.
>
> Q. And what can you tell us about that?
>
> A. The President was concerned that the United States seemed to – to bear the exclusive brunt of security assistance to Ukraine. He wanted to see the Europeans step up and contribute more security assistance.

---

[233] *Id.*

[234] Shayna Freisleben, *A Guide to Trump's Past Comments about NATO*, CBS News, (Apr. 12, 2017).

[235] Donald J. Trump (@realDonaldTrump), Twitter (Jul. 9, 2018, 7:55 a m.), https://twitter.com/realDonaldTrump/status/1016289620596789248.

[236] David Greene, *After Trump's NATO Criticism, Countries Spend More on Defense*, NPR.org, (May 18, 2018).

Q. And was there any interagency activity, whether it be with the State Department for or the Defense Department, in coordination by the National Security Council, to look into that a little bit for the President?

A. We were surveying the data to understand who was contributing what and sort of in what categories.

Q. And so the President's evinced concerns, the interagency tried to address them?

A. Yes.[237]

In his public testimony, LTC Vindman confirmed the President's concerns about U.S. allies sharing the burden for mutual defense.[238]

3. U.S. foreign aid is often conditioned or paused, and U.S. security assistance to Ukraine has been paused before.

U.S. taxpayer-funded assistance to foreign governments is not an entitlement. The United States often conditions foreign aid on actions by recipient nations. In addition, foreign aid can, and often does, get delayed for various reasons. The pause of U.S. security assistance to Ukraine in this case is therefore not presumptive evidence of misconduct.

The United States conditions foreign assistance to a number of nations as a result of concerns about corruption, human rights abuses, or other issues. On October 31, 2019, the Trump Administration announced that it would withhold $105 million in security assistance for Lebanon shortly after the resignation of Lebanese Prime Minister Saad al-Hariri.[239] In September 2019, the State Department announced that it was withholding $160 million in aid from Afghanistan, citing corruption.[240] In June 2019, the Administration told Congress that it would reallocate $370 million in aid to Central American nations and suspend an additional $180 million in an effort to incentivize those countries to reduce the number of migrants reaching the U.S. border.[241] In 2017, President Trump froze $195 million in security assistance to Egypt—one of the largest recipients of U.S. aid—due to frustration with the country's poor track record on human rights and a recently enacted law regarding nongovernmental organizations.[242]

---

[237] *Impeachment Inquiry: Ambassador Kurt Volker and Mr. Timothy Morrison, supra* note 8.

[238] *Impeachment Inquiry: LTC Alexander Vindman and Ms. Jennifer Williams, supra* note 6.

[239] Patricia Zengerle & Mike Stone, *Exclusive: U.S. withholding $105 million in security aid for Lebanon- sources*, Reuters, Oct. 31, 2019.

[240] Tal Axelrod, *US withholds $160M in Afghan aid citing corruption*, The Hill, Sept. 9, 2019.

[241] Lesley Wroughton & Patricia Zengerle, *As promised, Trump slashes aid to Central America over migrants*, Reuters, Jun. 17, 2019.

[242] Gardiner Harris & Declan Walsh, *U.S. Slaps Egypt on Human Rights Record and Ties to North Korea*, N.Y. Times, Aug. 22, 2017.

The Democrats' witnesses explained that it is not unusual for foreign aid to be paused or even withheld. Ambassador Taylor testified that U.S. aid to foreign countries can be paused in various instances, such as a Congressional hold.[243] Ambassador Volker testified that foreign assistance can be delayed for a multitude of reasons and that "this hold on security assistance [to Ukraine] was not significant."[244] Ambassador Volker elaborated during his public testimony:

> Q. Ambassador Volker, you testified during your deposition that aid, in fact, does get held up from time-to-time for a whole assortment of reasons. Is that your understanding?
>
> A. That is true.
>
> Q. And sometimes the holdups are rooted in something at OMB, sometimes it's at the Defense Department, sometimes it's at the State Department, sometimes it's on the Hill. Is that correct?
>
> A. That is correct.
>
> Q. And so, when the aid was held up for 55 days for Ukraine, that didn't in and of itself strike you as uncommon?
>
> A. No. It's something that had happened in my career in the past. I had seen holdups of assistance. I just assumed it was part of the decision-making process. Somebody had an objection, and we had to overcome it.[245]

Ambassador David Hale, the Under Secretary of State for Political Affairs, agreed that U.S. taxpayer-funded aid has been paused from several countries around the world for various reasons and, in some cases, for unknown reasons.[246] Ambassador Hale elaborated:

> We've often heard at the State Department that the President of the United States wants to make sure that foreign assistance is reviewed scrupulously to make sure that it's truly in U.S. national interests, and that we evaluate it continuously, so that it meets certain criteria that the President has established.[247]

Ambassador Hale explained that the NSC launched a review of U.S. foreign assistance to ensure U.S. taxpayer money was spent efficiently and to advance "[t]he principle of burden sharing by allies and other like-minded states."[248] Dr. Hill, the NSC's Senior Director for Europe, testified that as she was leaving NSC in July 2019, "there had been more scrutiny" to assistance:

---

[243] Taylor deposition, *supra* note 47, at 170-71.
[244] Volker transcribed interview, *supra* note 60, at 78-80.
[245] *Impeachment Inquiry: Ambassador Kurt Volker and Mr. Timothy Morrison*, *supra* note 8.
[246] *"Impeachment Inquiry: Ms. Laura Cooper and Mr. David Hale": Hearing before the H. Perm. Sel. Comm. on Intelligence*, 116th Cong. (2019).
[247] *Id.*
[248] *Id.*

As I understood them, there had been a directive for whole-scale review of our foreign policy, foreign policy assistance, and the ties between our foreign policy objectives and the assistance. This had been going on actually for many months. And in the period when I was wrapping up my time there, there had been more scrutiny than specific assistance to specific sets of countries as a result of that overall view – review.[249]

The Democrats' witnesses also described how U.S. foreign assistance to Ukraine has been delayed in the past. Dr. Hill testified that security assistance to Ukraine has been paused before "at multiple junctures" during her time at NSC, even with bipartisan support for the assistance.[250] Dr. Hill testified:

Q. On the issue of the security assistance freeze, had assistance for Ukraine ever been held up before during your time at NSC?

A. Yes.

Q. For what – and when was that?

A. At multiple junctures. You know, it gets back to the question that [Republican staff] asked before. There's often a question raised about assistance, you know, a range of assistance –

Q. But for Ukraine specifically?

A. Yeah, that's correct.

Q. Okay. Even though there's been bipartisan support for the assistance?

A. Correct.[251]

Catherine Croft, a former NSC director, offered an example in her deposition, explaining that OMB paused the sale of Javelin missiles to Ukraine in November or December 2017.[252] This pause, too, was eventually lifted and Ukraine received the missiles.[253]

---

[249] *Impeachment Inquiry: Dr. Fiona Hill and Mr. David Holmes, supra* note 210.
[250] Hill deposition, *supra* note 12, at 304.
[251] *Id.* at 303-04.
[252] Croft deposition, *supra* note 60, at 67.
[253] *Id.* at 68.

4. Despite President Trump's skepticism, the Trump Administration's policies have shown greater commitment and support to Ukraine than those of the Obama Administration.

Several of the Democrats' witnesses testified that President Trump has taken a stronger stance in supporting Ukraine. Dr. Hill testified that President Trump's decision to support Ukraine with lethal defensive weapons was a more robust policy than under the Obama Administration.[254] Ambassador Taylor characterized President Trump's policy as a "substantial improvement."[255] Ambassador Yovanovitch agreed, testifying:

> And I actually felt that in the 3 years that I was there, partly because of my efforts, but also the interagency team, and President Trump's decision to provide lethal weapons to Ukraine, that our policy actually got stronger over the three last 3 years [*sic*].[256]

She added:

> Q. Can you testify to the difference [to] the changes in aid to Ukraine with the new administration starting in 2017? The different initiatives, you know, as far as providing lethal weapons and –
>
> A. Yeah. Well, I think that most of the assistance programs that we had, you know, continued, and due to the generosity of the Congress actually were increased. And so that was a really positive thing, I think, for Ukraine and for us. In terms of lethal assistance, we all felt *it was very significant that this administration made the decision to provide lethal weapons to Ukraine*.[257]

Ambassador Volker also explained how President Trump's policies of providing lethal defensive assistance to Ukraine have been "extremely helpful" in deterring Russian aggression in Ukraine.[258] He explained:

> So there has been U.S. assistance provided to Ukraine for some time, under the Bush administration, Obama administration, and now under the Trump administration. I was particularly interested in the security assistance and lethal defensive weapons. The reason for this is this was something that the Obama administration did not approve. They did not want to send lethal defensive arms to Ukraine.
>
> I fundamentally disagreed with that decision. It is not my – you know, I was just a private citizen, but that's my opinion. I thought

---

[254] Hill deposition, *supra* note 12, at 196.
[255] Taylor deposition, *supra* note 47, at 155.
[256] Yovanovitch deposition, *supra* note 115, at 140-41 (emphasis added).
[257] *Id.* at 144.
[258] Volker transcribed interview, *supra* note 60, at 87.

that this is a country that is defending itself against Russian aggression. They had their military largely destroyed by Russia in 2014 and '15 and needed the help. And humanitarian assistance is great, and nonlethal assistance, you know, MREs and blankets and all, that's fine, but if you're being attacked with mortars and artilleries and tanks, you need to be able to fight back.

The argument against this assistance being provided, the lethal defensive assistance, was that it would be provocative and could escalate the fighting with Russia. I had a fundamentally different view that if we did not provide it, it's an inducement to Russia to keep up the aggression, and there's no deterrence of Russia from trying to go further into Ukraine. So I believed it was important to help them rebuild their defensive capabilities and to deter Russia. It's also a symbol of U.S. support.

So I argued very strongly from the time I was appointed by Secretary Tillerson that the rationale for why we were not providing lethal defensive assistance to me doesn't hold water and that is a much stronger rationale that we should be doing it.

That eventually became administration policy. It took a while, but Secretary Tillerson, you know, he wanted to think it through, see how that would play out. How would the allies react to this? How would Russia react to this? How would the Ukrainians handle it? And we managed those issues. Secretary Mattis was very much in favor. And they met. I did not meet with the President about this, but they met with the President and the President approved it.[259]

5. Although security assistance to Ukraine was paused in July 2019, several witnesses testified that U.S. security assistance was not linked to any Ukrainian action on investigations.

Several witnesses testified that U.S. security assistance was not linked to or conditioned on any Ukrainian action to investigate President Trump's political rival. Even after U.S. officials learned in early- to mid-July that the security assistance had been paused for unknown reasons, evidence suggests that there was not a link between U.S. security assistance and Ukrainian action to investigate President Trump's political rival.

LTC Vindman testified that he learned about a pause on security assistance on July 3.[260] Morrison said he learned of the pause around July 15.[261] According to Ambassador Taylor, he learned via conference call on July 18 that OMB had paused the security assistance to

---

[259] *Id.* at 84-86.
[260] Vindman deposition, *supra* note 12, at 178.
[261] Morrison deposition, *supra* note 12, at 16.

Ukraine.[262] Ambassador Taylor relayed that according to the OMB representative on the call, the pause was done at the direction of the President and the chief of staff.[263] Although a reason was not provided for the pause at the time, OMB official Mark Sandy testified that he learned in early September 2019 that the pause was related "to the President's concern about other countries contributing more to Ukraine."[264]

Despite the pause, testimony from the Democrats' witnesses suggests the assistance was not linked to Ukraine investigating President Trump's political rival. Ambassador Volker, the key intermediary between the Ukrainian government and U.S. officials, testified that he was aware of no *quid pro quo* and that the Ukrainian government never raised concerns to him about a *quid pro quo*.[265] He said that when Ambassador Taylor raised questions about the appearance of a *quid pro quo*, "I discussed with him that there is no linkage here. I view this as an internal thing, and we are going to get it fixed."[266] Ambassador Volker further explained that even if Ukrainians perceived the aid was linked to investigations, they "never raised" that possibility with him.[267] Ambassador Volker believed that given the trust he had developed with the Ukrainian government, the Ukrainians would have come to him with concerns about the security assistance.[268]

House Intelligence Committee Chairman Adam Schiff attempted to get Ambassador Volker to testify in his closed-door deposition that the Ukrainian government would have felt pressure to investigate President Trump's political rival once they learned that the security assistance was delayed.[269] Ambassador Volker refused to accept Chairman Schiff's conclusion. He testified:

> Q. The request is made. And even though the suspension may have occurred earlier, the request is made to investigate the Bidens, and then Ukraine learns, for mysterious reasons, hundreds of millions in military support is being withheld. Do I have the chronology correct?
>
> A. Yes.
>
> Q. At the point they learned that, wouldn't that give them added urgency to meet the President's request on the Bidens?
>
> A. I don't know the answer to that. The –

---

[262] Taylor deposition, *supra* note 47, at 27.

[263] *Id.* at 28.

[264] Deposition of Mark Sandy, in Wash., D.C., at 42 (Nov. 16, 2019). Sandy testified that in early September, OMB received "requests for information on what additional countries were contributing to Ukraine." *Id.* at 44. OMB provided that information sometime in the first week of September. *Id.* at 82.

[265] Volker transcribed interview, *supra* note 60, at 170, 300-01.

[266] *Id.* at 130.

[267] *Id.* at 284.

[268] *Id.* at 300-01.

[269] *Id.* at 124-28.

Q. Ambassador –

A. When that – no –

Q. – as a career diplomat, you can't venture –

A. But, Congressman, this is why I'm trying to the say the context is different, because at the time they learned that, if we assume it's August 29th, they had just had a visit from the National Security Advisor, John Bolton. That's a high level meeting already. He was recommending and working on scheduling the visit of President Zelensky to Washington. We were also working on a bilateral meeting to take place in Warsaw on the margins of a commemoration on the beginning of World War II. And in that context, I think the Ukrainians felt like things are going the right direction, and they had not done anything on – they had not done anything on an investigation, they had not done anything on a statement, and things were ramping up in terms of their engagement with the administration. So I think they were actually feeling pretty good by then.

Q. Ambassador, I find it remarkable as a career diplomat that you have difficulty acknowledging that when Ukraine learned that their aid had been suspended for unknown reasons, that this wouldn't add additional urgency to a request by the President of the United States. I find that remarkable.[270]

During his public testimony, in an exchange with Rep. Mike Turner, Ambassador Volker reiterated that there was no linkage between U.S. security assistance and investigations. He testified:

Q. Did the President of the United States ever say to you that he was not going to allow aid from the United States to go to the Ukraine unless there were investigations into Burisma, the Bidens, or the 2016 elections?

A. No, he did not.

Q. Did the Ukrainians ever tell you that they understood that they would not get a meeting with the President of the United States, a phone call with the President of the United States, military aid or foreign aid from the United States unless they undertook investigations of Burisma, the Bidens, or the 2016 elections?

A. No, they did not.

---

[270] *Id.* at 126-28 (question and answer with Chairman Adam Schiff).

Q. So I would assume, then, that the Ukrainians never told you that [Mayor] Giuliani had told them that, in order to get a meeting with the President, a phone call with the President, military aid or foreign aid from the United States, that they would have to do these investigations.

A. No.[271]

Similarly, Deputy Assistant Secretary Kent testified in his closed-door deposition that he also did not "associate" the security assistance to investigations."[272] Kent relayed how Ambassador Taylor had told him that Ambassador Sondland was "pushing" President Zelensky to give an interview during the Yalta European Strategy (YES) conference in Kyiv in mid-September.[273] Ambassador Taylor told Kent that the "hope" was if President Zelensky gave a public signal on investigations, the security assistance pause would lift; however, Ambassador Taylor asserted that "both Tim Morrison and Gordon Sondland said that they did not believe the two issues were linked."[274]

During his sworn deposition, Ambassador Sondland testified that he could not recall "any discussions with the White House about withholding U.S. security assistance from Ukraine in exchange for assistance with President Trump's 2020 election campaign."[275] Ambassador Sondland testified that he was "never" aware of any preconditions on the delay of security assistance to Ukraine, or that the aid was tied to Ukraine undertaking any investigations.[276]

Although media reports allege that Ambassador Sondland later recanted this testimony to "confirm" a *quid pro quo*,[277] those reports exaggerate the supplemental information that Ambassador Sondland later provided. In a written supplement to his deposition testimony, Ambassador Sondland asserted that by the beginning of September 2019, "in the absence of any credible explanation for the suspension of aid, [he] ***presumed*** that the aid suspension had become linked to the proposed anti-corruption statement."[278] Ambassador Sondland asserted that he spoke to Yermak in Warsaw on September 1 and conveyed that U.S. aid would not "likely" flow until Ukraine provided an anti-corruption statement.[279] Yermak, however, in an interview with *Bloomberg*, disputed Ambassador Sondland's account, saying that he "bumped into" Ambassador Sondland and "doesn't remember any reference to military aid."[280]

---

[271] *Impeachment Inquiry: Ambassador Kurt Volker and Mr. Timothy Morrison, supra* note 8.

[272] Kent deposition, *supra* note 65, at 323.

[273] *Id.* at 269.

[274] *Id.; see also id.* at 323.

[275] Sondland deposition, *supra* note 51, at 35.

[276] *Id.* at 197.

[277] *See, e.g.*, Andrew Desiderio & Kyle Cheney, *Sondland reverses himself on Ukraine, confirming quid pro quo*, Politico, Nov. 5, 2019.

[278] Declaration of Ambassador Gordon D. Sondland at ¶ 4 (Nov. 4, 2019) (emphasis added) [hereinafter "Sondland declaration"].

[279] *Id.* at ¶ 5.

[280] Stephanie Baker & Daryna Krasnolutska, *Ukraine's fraught summer included a rogue embassy in Washington*, Bloomberg, Nov. 22, 2019.

44

Ambassador Sondland's addendum does not prove a nefarious *quid pro quo*. At most, and even discounting Yermak's subsequent denial, the addendum shows that as of September 1, Ambassador Sondland assumed there was a connection and relayed this assumption to Yermak— an assumption that the President would later tell Ambassador Sondland was inaccurate.[281]

During his deposition, Ambassador Taylor testified that he spoke by phone with Ambassador Sondland on September 8.[282] Ambassador Taylor recounted how Ambassador Sondland told him that President Trump wanted President Zelensky to "clear things up and do it in public" but there was no "*quid pro quo*."[283]

On September 9, Ambassador Sondland texted Ambassador Volker and Ambassador Taylor: "The President has been crystal clear: no *quid pro quo*'s [*sic*] of any kind. The President is trying to evaluate whether Ukraine is truly going to adopt the transparency and reforms that President Zelensky promised during his campaign."[284] When asked about this text message during his transcribed interview, Ambassador Volker testified that "Gordon was repeating here what we all understood."[285]

In his public testimony, Ambassador Taylor clarified his statement from his closed-door deposition that he had "clear understanding" that Ukraine would not receive security assistance until President Zelensky committed to investigations.[286] He explained his "clear understanding" came from Ambassador Sondland, who acknowledged that he had *presumed* there to be a linkage. In an exchange with Rep. Jim Jordan, Ambassador Taylor testified:

> Q. So what I'm wondering is, where did you get this clear understanding?
>
> A. As I testified, Mr. Jordan, this came from Ambassador Sondland.
>
>   ***
>
> Q. You said you got this from Ambassador Sondland.
>
> A. That is correct. Ambassador Sondland also said he had talked to President Zelensky and Mr. Yermak and had told them that, although this was not a *quid pro quo*, if President Zelensky did not clear things up in public, we would be at a stalemate. That was the – that was one point.
>
>   ***

---

[281] *See infra* note 297 and accompanying text.
[282] Taylor deposition, *supra* note 47, at 39.
[283] *Id.*
[284] Text message from Gordon Sondland to William Taylor and Kurt Volker (Sept. 9, 2019, 5:19 a.m.) [KV00000053].
[285] Volker transcribed interview, *supra* note 60, at 170.
[286] *Impeachment Inquiry: Ambassador William B. Taylor and Mr. George Kent, supra* note 2.

Q. All right. So, again, just to recap, you had three meetings with President Zelensky; no linkage in those three meetings came up. Ambassador Zelensky didn't announce that he was going [to] do any investigation of the Bidens or Burisma before the aid was released. He didn't –

A. That was President –

Q. – do a tweet, didn't do anything on CNN, didn't do any of that. President Zelensky. Excuse me.

A. Yeah. Right.

Q. And then what you have in front of you is an addendum that Mr. Sondland made to his testimony that we got a couple weeks ago. It says, "Declaration of Ambassador Gordon Sondland. I, Gordon Sondland, do hereby swear and affirm as follows." I want to you look at point number two, bullet point number two, second sentence. "Ambassador Taylor recalls that Mr. Morrison told Ambassador Taylor that I told Mr. Morrison that I conveyed this message to Mr. Yermak on September 1st, 2019, in connection with Vice President Pence's visit to Warsaw and a meeting with President Zelensky." Now, this is his clarification. Let me read it one more time. "Ambassador Taylor recalls that Mr. Morrison told Ambassador Taylor that I told Mr. Morrison that I had conveyed this message to Mr. Yermak on September 1st, 2019, in connection with Vice President Pence's visit to Warsaw and a meeting with President Zelensky." We've got six people having four conversations in one sentence, and you just told me this is where you got your clear understanding, which – I mean, even though you had three opportunities with President Zelensky for him to tell you, "You know what? We're going to do these investigations to get the aid," he didn't tell you, three different times. Never makes an announcement, never tweets about it, never does the CNN interview. Ambassador, you weren't on the call, were you? The President – you didn't listen in on President Trump's call and President Zelensky's call?

A. I did not.

Q. You never talked with Chief of Staff Mulvaney.

A. I never did.

Q. You never met the President.

46

A. That's correct.

Q. You had three meetings again with Zelensky and it didn't come up.

A. And two of those, they had never heard about it, as far as I know, so there was no reason for it to come up.

Q. And President Zelensky never made an announcement. This is what I can't believe. And you're their star witness. You're their first witness.

A. Mr. Jordan –

Q. You're the guy. You're the guy based on this, based on – I mean, I've seen church prayer chains that are easier to understand than this.[287]

During his public testimony, Ambassador Sondland made clear that no one had ever told him that the security assistance was tied to Ukraine investigating the President's political rival. In particular, Ambassador Sondland explained that "President Trump never told me directly that the aid was conditioned on the meetings."[288] In an exchange with Rep. Turner, Ambassador Sondland elaborated:

Q. What about the aid? [Ambassador Volker] says that they weren't tied, that the aid was not tied—

A. And I didn't say they were conclusively tied either. I said I was presuming it.

Q. Okay. And so the President never told you they were tied.

A. That is correct.

Q. So your testimony and [Ambassador Volker's] testimony is consistent, and the President did not tie aid to investigations.

A. That is correct.

***

Q. So no one told you, not just the President. [Mayor] Giuliani didn't tell you. [Acting Chief of Staff] Mulvaney didn't tell you. Nobody— [Secretary] Pompeo didn't tell you. Nobody else on this planet told

---

[287] *Impeachment Inquiry: Ambassador William B. Taylor and Mr. George Kent, supra* note 2.
[288] *Impeachment inquiry: Ambassador Gordon Sondland, supra* note 56.

you that Donald Trump was tying aid to these investigations. Is that correct?

A. I think I already testified to that.

Q. No. Answer the question. Is it correct? No one on this planet told you that Donald Trump was tying aid to the investigations? Because if your answer is yes, then the chairman is wrong and the headline on CNN is wrong. No one on this planet told you that President Trump was tying aid to investigations, yes or no?

A. Yes.[289]

6. President Trump rejected any linkage between U.S. security assistance and Ukrainian action on investigations.

The evidence also shows that when President Trump was asked about a potential linkage between U.S. security assistance and Ukrainian investigations into the President's political rival, the President vehemently denied any connection. This evidence is persuasive because the President made the same denial twice to two separate senior U.S. officials in private, where there is no reason for the President to be anything less than completely candid.

In an interview with the *Wall Street Journal* and a detailed written submission to the impeachment inquiry, Senator Ron Johnson, the Chairman of the Senate Foreign Relations Subcommittee on Europe, disclosed that he spoke to President Trump on August 31, after learning from Ambassador Sondland that U.S. security assistance may be linked to Ukraine's willingness to demonstrate its commitment to fight corruption.[290] Senator Johnson explained that his purpose for calling President Trump was "to inform President Trump of my upcoming trip to Ukraine and to try to persuade him to authorize me to tell [President] Zelensky that the hold would be lifted on military aid."[291]

Senator Johnson recounted that President Trump was "not prepared" to lift the pause on security assistance to Ukraine, citing Ukrainian corruption and frustration that Europe did not share more of the burden.[292] Echoing his continual statements about U.S. allies sharing the financial burden for mutual defense, President Trump told Senator Johnson: "Ron, I talk to Angela [Merkel, German chancellor] and ask her, 'why don't you fund these things,' and she tells me, 'because we know you will.' We're schmucks, Ron. We're schmucks."[293]

When Senator Johnson raised the potential of a linkage between U.S. security assistance and investigations, President Trump vehemently denied it.[294] According to Senator Johnson,

---

[289] *Id.*

[290] Letter from Sen. Johnson, *supra* note 138, at 5; Siobhan Hughes & Rebecca Ballhaus, *Trump, in August call with GOP Senator, denied official's claim on Ukraine aid*, Wall St. J., Oct. 4, 2019.

[291] Letter from Sen. Johnson, *supra* note 138, at 5.

[292] *Id.*

[293] *Id.*

[294] *Id.*

Without hesitation, President Trump immediately denied such an arrangement existed. As reported in the *Wall Street Journal*, I quoted the President as saying, "[Expletive deleted]—No way. I would never do that. Who told you that?" *I have accurately characterized his reaction as adamant, vehement and angry* – there was more than one expletive that I have deleted.[295]

At the end of the phone call, President Trump circled back to Senator Johnson's request to release the pause on security assistance. President Trump said: "Ron, I understand your position. We're reviewing it now, and you'll probably like my final decision."[296] This conversation occurred on August 31, well before the Democrats initiated their impeachment inquiry, and undermines the assertion that the President fabricated legitimate reasons for the pause in security assistance in response to the Democrats' impeachment inquiry.

During his deposition, Ambassador Sondland testified that he called President Trump on September 9 and asked him "What do you want from Ukraine?" The President's response was "Nothing. There is no *quid pro quo*."[297] During his deposition, Ambassador Sondland testified:

> Q. So when you telephoned the President, tell us what happened.

> A. Well, from the time that the aid was help up until I telephoned the President there were a lot of rumors swirling around as to why the aid had been help up, including they wanted a review, they wanted Europe to do more. There were all kinds of rumors. And I know in my few previous conversations with the President he's not big on small talk to I would have one shot to ask him. And rather than asking him, "Are you doing X because of X or because of Y or because of Z?" *I asked him one open-ended question: What do you want from Ukraine? And as I recall, he was in a very bad mood. It was a very quick conversation. He said: I wanted nothing. I want no* quid pro quo. *I want Zelensky to do the right thing. And I said: What does that mean? And he said: I want him to do what he ran on.*[298]

When asked about his conversation with Senator Johnson—which prompted Senator Johnson to call President Trump—Ambassador Sondland testified that he was "speculating" about the linkage between security assistance and investigations.[299] He explained:

> I noticed in the media [Senator Johnson] had come out and said that he and I had a conversation on the phone about it. And he had said

---

[295] *Id.* (emphasis added).
[296] *Id.*
[297] Sondland deposition, *supra* note 51, at 106.
[298] *Id.* at 105-06 (emphasis added).
[299] *Id.* at 196.

that I told him – this is in the media report, and I haven't discussed this with him since that media report – that I had said there was a *quid pro quo*. And I don't remember telling him that because I'm not sure I knew that at that point. I think what I might have done is I might have been speculating – I hope there's no, I hope this isn't being held up for nefarious reasons.[300]

Although Democrats and some in the media believe that Acting Chief of Staff Mick Mulvaney confirmed the existence of a *quid pro quo* during an October 2019 press briefing,[301] a careful reading of his statements shows otherwise. Chief of Staff Mulvaney cited President Trump's concerns about Ukrainian corruption and foreign aid in general as the "driving factors" in the temporary pause on security assistance.[302] He explained that Ukraine's actions in the 2016 election "was part of the thing that [the President] was worried about in corruption with that nation."[303] Chief of Staff Mulvaney specified, however, that "the money held up had absolutely nothing to do with [Vice President] Biden."[304]

7. Senior U.S. officials never substantively discussed the delay in security assistance with Ukrainian officials before the July 25 call.

Evidence also suggests that the senior levels of the Ukrainian government did not know that U.S. security assistance was delayed until some point after the July 25 phone call between President Trump and President Zelensky. Although the assistance was delayed at the time of the July 25 call, President Trump never raised the assistance with President Zelensky or implied that the aid was in danger. As Ambassador Volker testified, because Ukrainian officials were unaware of the pause on security assistance, "there was no leverage implied."[305] This evidence undercuts the allegation that the President withheld U.S. security assistance to pressure President Zelensky to investigate his political rival.

Most of the Democrats' witnesses, including Ambassador Taylor, traced their knowledge of the pause to a July 18 interagency conference call, during which OMB announced a pause on security assistance to Ukraine.[306] However, the two U.S. diplomats closest the Ukrainian government—Ambassador Volker and Ambassador Taylor—testified that Ukraine did not know about the delay "until the end of August," six weeks later, after it was reported publicly by *Politico* on August 28.[307]

---

[300] *Id.*

[301] *Impeachment Inquiry: Dr. Fiona Hill and Mr. David Holmes, supra* note 210 (statement of Rep. Adam Schiff, Chairman); Aaron Blake, *Trump's acting chief of staff admits it: There was a Ukraine quid pro quo*, Wash. Post, Oct. 17, 2019.

[302] The White House, Press Briefing by Acting Chief of Staff Mick Mulvaney (Oct. 17, 2019).

[303] *Id.*

[304] *Id.*

[305] Volker transcribed interview, *supra* note 60, at 124-25.

[306] *See, e.g.*, Taylor deposition, *supra* note 47, at 27.

[307] Volker transcribed interview, *supra* note 60, at 125, 266-67; Taylor deposition, *supra* note 47, at 119-20.

Ambassador Volker, the chief interlocutor with the Ukrainian government, testified that he never informed the Ukrainians about the delay.[308] The Ukrainian government only raised the issue with Ambassador Volker after reading about the delay in *Politico* in late August.[309] Explaining why the delay was not "significant, Ambassador Volker testified:

> Q. Looking back on it now, is [the delayed security assistance] something, in the grand scheme of things, that's very significant? I mean, is this worthy of investigating, or is this just another chapter in the rough and tumble world of diplomacy and foreign assistance?
>
> A. In my view, this hold on security assistance was not significant. I don't believe – in fact, I am quite sure that at least I, Secretary Pompeo, the official representatives of the U.S., never communicated to Ukrainians that it is being held for a reason. We never had a reason. And I tried to avoid talking to Ukrainians about it for as long as I could until it came out in *Politico* a month later because I was confident we were going to get it fixed internally.[310]

During his public testimony, Ambassador Volker confirmed that he did not have any communication with the Ukrainian government about the pause on U.S. security assistance until they raised the topic with him.[311] Morrison likewise testified that he avoided discussing the pause on security assistance with the Ukrainian government.[312]

Ambassador Taylor similarly testified that the Ukrainian government was not aware of the pause on U.S. security assistance until late August 2019. In an exchange with Rep. Ratcliffe, he explained:

> Q. So, based on your knowledge, nobody in the Ukrainian government became aware of a hold on military aid until 2 days later, on August 29th.
>
> A. That's my understanding.
>
> Q. That's your understanding. And that would have been well over a month after the July 25th call between President Trump and President Zelensky.
>
> A. Correct.
>
> Q. So you're not a lawyer, are you, Ambassador Taylor?

---

[308] Volker transcribed interview, *supra* note 60, at 80.
[309] *Id.* at 80-81; Text message from Andrey Yermak to Kurt Volker, (Aug. 29, 2019, 03:06:14 AM), [KV00000020]; *see* Caitlin Emma & Connor O'Brien, *Trump holds up Ukraine military aid meant to confront Russia*, Politico, Aug. 28, 2019.
[310] Volker transcribed interview, *supra* note 60, at 80.
[311] *Impeachment Inquiry: Ambassador Kurt Volker and Mr. Timothy Morrison, supra* note 8.
[312] *Id.*

A. I am not.

Q. Okay. So the idea of a *quid pro quo* is it's a concept where there is a demand for an action or an attempt to influence action in exchange for something else. And in this case, when people are talking about a *quid pro quo*, that something else is military aid. So, if nobody in the Ukrainian government is aware of a military hold at the time of the Trump-Zelensky call, then, as a matter of law and as a matter of fact, there can be no *quid pro quo* based on military aid. I just want to be real clear that, again, as of July 25th, you have no knowledge of a *quid pro quo* involving military aid.

A. July 25th is a week after the hold was put on the security assistance. And July 25th, they had a conversation between the two presidents where it was not discussed.

Q. And to your knowledge, nobody in the Ukrainian government was aware of the hold?

A. That is correct.[313]

Likewise, Philip Reeker, the Acting Assistant Secretary of State for Europeans Affairs, testified that he was unaware of any U.S. official conveying to a Ukrainian official that President Trump sought political investigations.[314] Acting Assistant Secretary Reeker testified that he was not aware of whether Ambassador Volker or Ambassador Sondland had such conversations with the Ukrainians.[315]

Some witnesses testified that the Ukrainian embassy made informal inquiries about the status of the security assistance. LTC Vindman recalled receiving "light queries" from his Ukrainian embassy counterparts about the aid in either early- or mid-August, but he was unable to pinpoint specific dates, or even the week, that he had such conversations.[316] LTC Vindman testified that Ukrainian questions about the delay were not "substantive" or "definitive" until around the time of the Warsaw summit, on September 1.[317] State Department official Catherine Croft testified that two individuals from the Ukrainian embassy approached her about a pause on security assistance at some point before August 28, but Croft told them she "was confident that any issues in process would get resolved."[318] Deputy Assistant Secretary of Defense Laura Cooper testified publicly that her staff received inquiries from the Ukrainian embassy in July that "there was some kind of issue" with the security assistance; however, she did not know what the Ukrainian government knew at the time.[319]

---

[313] Taylor deposition, *supra* note 47, at 119-20.
[314] Deposition of Philip Reeker in Wash., D.C., at 149 (Oct. 26, 2019).
[315] *Id.* at 150.
[316] Vindman deposition, *supra* note 12, at 135-37, 189-90.
[317] *Id.* at 189-90.
[318] Croft deposition, *supra* note 60, at 86-87.
[319] *Impeachment Inquiry: Ms. Laura Cooper and Mr. David Hale, supra* note 246.

Although this evidence suggests that Ukrainian officials in Washington were vaguely aware of an issue with the security assistance before August 28, the evidence does not show that the senior leadership of Ukrainian government in Kyiv was aware of the pause until late August. A *New York Times* story claimed that unidentified Ukrainian officials were aware of a delay in "early August" 2019 but said there was no stated link between that delay and any investigative demands.[320] However, a subsequent *Bloomberg* story reported that President Zelensky "and his key advisers learned of [the pause on U.S. security assistance] only in a *Politico* report in late August."[321]

The *Bloomberg* story detailed how Ukraine's embassy in Washington—led by then-Ambassador Chaly, who had been appointed by President Zelensky's predecessor—went "rogue" in the early months of the Zelensky administration.[322] According to Andrey Yermak, a close adviser to President Zelensky, the Ukrainian embassy officials, who were loyal to former President Poroshenko, did not inform President Zelensky that there was any issue with the U.S. security assistance.[323] This information explains the conflicting testimony between witnesses like LTC Vindman and Deputy Assistant Secretary Cooper, who testified that the Ukrainian embassy raised questions about the security assistance, and Ambassador Volker and Ambassador Taylor, who testified that the Zelensky government did not know about any pause in security assistance.

According to the Ukrainian government, President Zelensky and his senior advisers only learned of the pause on security assistance from *Politico*—severely undercutting the idea that President Trump was seeking to pressure Ukraine to investigate his political rival.

8. The Ukrainian government denied any awareness of a linkage between U.S. security assistance and investigations.

Publicly available information also shows clearly that the Ukrainian government leadership denied any awareness of a linkage between U.S. security assistance and investigations into the President's political rival. The Ukrainian government leaders made this assertion following public reports that Ambassador Sondland had raised the potential connection in early September. This understanding is supported by information provided by Senator Johnson.

In Ambassador Sondland's addendum to his closed-door testimony, dated November 5, 2019, he wrote how he came to perceive a connection between security assistance and the investigations. He wrote:

> [B]y the beginning of September 2019, and in the absence of any credible explanation for the suspension of aid, I presumed that the aid suspension had become linked to the proposed anti-corruption

---

[320] Andrew E. Kramer & Kenneth P. Vogel, *Ukraine knew of aid freeze by early August, undermining Trump defense*, N.Y. Times, Oct. 23, 2019.
[321] Baker & Krasnolutska, *supra* note 280.
[322] *Id.*
[323] *Id.*

statement. . . . And it would have been natural for me to have voiced what I had presumed to Ambassador Taylor, Senator Johnson, the Ukrainians, and Mr. Morrison.[324]

Following media reports of Ambassador Sondland's addendum, Ukrainian Foreign Minister Prystaiko told the media that Ambassador Sondland had not linked the security assistance to Ukrainian action on investigations.[325] He said: "Ambassador Sondland did not tell us, and certainly did not tell me, about a connection between the assistance and the investigations."[326] Minister Prystaiko went further to say that he was never aware of any connection between security assistance and investigations: "*I have never seen a direct relationship between investigations and security assistance*. Yes, the investigations were mentioned, you know, in the conversation of the presidents. But there was no clear connection between these events."[327]

Senator Johnson explained that he had three meetings with senior Ukrainian government officials in June and July 2019.[328] Two of meetings were with Oleksandr Danylyuk, then-secretary of Ukraine's National Security and Defense Council, and Valeriy Chaly, then-Ukrainian Ambassador to the U.S.[329] Senator Johnson said that none of the these Ukrainian officials raised any concerns with him about security assistance or investigations: "At no time during those meetings did anyone from Ukraine raise the issue of the withholding of military aid or express concerns regarding pressure being applied by the president or his administration."[330]

9. The Ukrainian government considered issuing a public anti-corruption statement to convey that President Zelensky was "serious and different" from previous Ukrainian regimes.

Evidence shows that in light of President Trump's deep-rooted skepticism about Ukraine, and working in tandem with senior U.S. officials, the Ukrainian government sought to convince President Trump that the new regime took corruption seriously. This commitment took two potential forms: a public statement that Ukraine would investigate corruption or a media interview about investigations. Although the parties later discussed the inclusion of specific investigations proposed by Mayor Giuliani, U.S. officials explained that the intent of the statement was to convey a public commitment to anti-corruption reform and that they did not associate the statement with an investigation of the President's political rival.

Ambassador Volker explained the goal of having Ukraine convey President Zelensky's commitment to reform and fighting corruption in a public message. He testified:

A. So the issue as I understood it was this deep-rooted, skeptical view of Ukraine, a negative view of Ukraine, preexisting 2019, you know,

---

[324] Sondland declaration, *supra* note 278, at ¶4.
[325] *U.S. envoy Sondland did not link Biden probe to aid: Ukraine minister*, Reuters, Nov. 14, 2019.
[326] *Id.*
[327] *Id.* (emphasis added).
[328] Letter from Sen. Ron Johnson, *supra* note 138, at 4.
[329] *Id.*
[330] *Id.* at 4-5.

going back. When I started this I had one other meeting with President Trump and President Poroshenko. It was in September of 2017. And at that time he had a very skeptical view of Ukraine. So I know he had a very deep-rooted skeptical view. And my understanding at the time was that even though he agreed in the [May 23] meeting that we had with him, say, okay, I'll invite him, he didn't really want to do it. And that's why the meeting kept being delayed and delayed. And we ended up at a point in talking with the Ukrainians – who we'll come to this, but, you know, who had asked to communicate with Giuliani – that they wanted to convey that they really are different. And we ended up talking about, well, then, make a statement about investigating corruption and your commitment to reform and so forth.

Q. Is that the statement that you discussed in your text messages –

A. Yes.

Q. – around August of 2019?

A. Yes.

Q. Okay.

A. Yeah. To say make a statement along those lines. And *the thought behind that was just trying to be convincing that they are serious and different from the Ukraine of the past.*[331]

Ambassador Volker elaborated during his public testimony that a public statement is not unusual. He explained:

I didn't find it that unusual. I think when you're dealing with a situation where I believe the President was highly skeptical about President Zelensky being committed to really changing Ukraine after his entirely negative view of the country, that he would want to hear something more from President Zelensky to be convinced that, "Okay, I'll give this guy a chance."[332]

The Democrats' witnesses explained how the idea of a public statement arose. Ambassador Volker testified that Andrey Yermak, a senior adviser to President Zelensky, sent him a draft statement following Yermak's meeting with Mayor Giuliani on August 2.[333] Ambassador Volker said that he believed the statement was "valuable for getting the Ukrainian

---

[331] Volker transcribed interview, *supra* note 60, at 41-42 (emphasis added).
[332] *Impeachment Inquiry: Ambassador Kurt Volker and Mr. Timothy Morrison, supra* note 8.
[333] Volker transcribed interview, *supra* note 60, at 71.

Government on the record about their commitment to reform and change and fighting corruption because I believed that would be helpful in overcoming this deep skepticism that the President had about Ukraine."[334] Ambassador Volker, however, did not see the statement as a "necessary condition" for President Zelensky securing a White House meeting.[335]

Ambassador Volker explained that although the statement evolved to include specific references to "Burisma" and "2016," the goal was still to show that President Zelensky was "different." He testified:

> Q. And the draft statement went through some iterations. Is that correct?
>
> A Yeah. It was pretty quick, though. I don't know the timeline exactly. We have it. But, basically, Andrey [Yermak] sends me a text. I share it with Gordon Sondland. We have a conversation with Rudy to say: The Ukrainians are looking at this text. Rudy says: Well, if it doesn't say Burisma and if it doesn't say 2016, what does it mean? You know, it's not credible. You know, they're hiding something. And so we talked and I said: So what you're saying is just at the end of the – same statement, just insert Burisma and 2016, you think that would be more credible? And he said: Yes. So I sent that back to Andrey, conveyed the conversation with him – because he had spoken with Rudy prior to that, not me – conveyed the conversation, and Andrey said that he was not – he did not think this was a good idea, and I shared his view.
>
> Q. You had testified from the beginning you didn't think it was a good idea to mention Burisma or 2016.
>
> A. Correct.
>
> Q. But then, as I understand it, you came to believe that if we're going to do the statement, maybe it's necessary to have that reference in there, correct?
>
> A. I'd say I was in the middle. I wouldn't say I thought it was necessary to have it in there because I thought the target here is not the specific investigations. The target is getting Ukraine to be seen as credible in changing the country, fighting corruption, introducing reform, that Zelensky is the real deal. You may remember that there was a statement that Rudy Giuliani made when he canceled his visit to Ukraine in May of 2019 that President Zelensky is surrounded by enemies of the United States. And I just knew that to be

---

[334] *Id.*

[335] *Impeachment Inquiry: Ambassador Kurt Volker and Mr. Timothy Morrison, supra* note 8

fundamentally not true. And so I think, when you talk about overcoming skepticism, that's kind of what I'm talking about, getting these guys out there publicly saying: We are different.[336]

Although subsequent reporting has connoted a connection between "Burisma" and the Bidens,[337] the Democrats' witnesses testified that they did not have that understanding while working with the Ukrainian government about a potential statement. Ambassador Volker explained that "there is an important distinction about Burisma" and that Vice President Biden or Hunter Biden were "never part of the conversation" with the Ukrainians.[338] He also testified that the Ukrainians did not link Burisma to the Bidens: "They never mentioned Biden to me."[339] Ambassador Volker also made clear that following his initial conversation with Mayor Giuliani in May 2019, Mayor Giuliani "never brought up Biden or Bidens with me again. And so when we talked or heard Burisma, I literally meant Burisma and that, not the conflation of that with the Bidens."[340]

Ambassador Sondland testified that he was unaware that "Burisma" may have meant "Biden" until the White House released the July 25th call transcript on September 25.[341] In fact, Ambassador Sondland testified that he recalled no discussions with any State Department or White House official about former Vice President Joe Biden or Hunter Biden.[342] Ambassador Sondland testified that he did not recall Mayor Giuliani ever discussing the Bidens with him.[343]

Testimony and text messages reflect that Ambassador Volker, Ambassador Sondland, and Ambassador Taylor communicated about Ukraine's commitment to fight corruption throughout the summer. Ambassador Taylor testified that in a phone conversation on June 27, Ambassador Sondland told him that President Zelensky "needed to make clear to President Trump that he, President Zelensky, was not standing in the way of 'investigations.'"[344] Ambassador Taylor said he did not know to what "investigations" Ambassador Sondland was referring, but that Ambassador Volker "intended to pass that message [to President Zelensky] in Toronto several days later."[345]

In early July, Ambassador Volker explained the dynamic directly to President Zelensky in Toronto, emphasizing the need to demonstrate a commitment to reform. Ambassador Volker testified:

---

[336] Volker transcribed interview, *supra* note 60, at 71-73.
[337] *See, e.g.*, Paul Sonne, Michael Kranish, & Matt Viser, *The gas tycoon and the vice president's son: The story of Hunter Biden's foray into Ukraine,* Wash. Post, Sept. 28, 2019.
[338] Volker transcribed interview, *supra* note 60, at 73.
[339] *Id.* at 193.
[340] *Id.* at 213.
[341] Sondland deposition, *supra* note 51, at 70.
[342] *Id.* at 33. Ambassador Sondland testified that Burisma was "one of many examples" of Ukrainian corruption. *Id.* Ambassador Sondland mentioned Naftogaz as another example of Ukrainian corruption and lack of transparency that "[came] up at every conversation." *Id.* at 71, 99.
[343] *Id.* at 33.
[344] Taylor deposition, *supra* note 47, at 25.
[345] *Id.* at 62-65.

I believe [Mayor Giuliani] was getting bad information, and I believe that his negative messaging about Ukraine would be reinforcing the President's already negative position about Ukraine. So I discussed this with President Zelensky when I saw him in Toronto on July 3rd, and I said I think this is a problem that we have Mayor Giuliani – so I didn't discuss his meeting with Lutsenko then. That came later. I only learned about that later. But I discussed even on July 3rd with President Zelensky that you have a problem with your message of being, you know, clean, reform, that we need to support you, is not getting – or is getting countermanded or contradicted by a negative narrative about Ukraine, that it is still corrupt, there's still terrible people around you. At this time, there was concern about his chief of presidential administration, Andriy Bohdan, who had been a lawyer for a very famous oligarch in Ukraine. And so I discussed this negative narrative about Ukraine that Mr. Giuliani seemed to be furthering with the President.[346]

On July 21, Ambassador Sondland sent a text message to Ambassador Taylor that read: "[W]e need to get the conversation started and the relationship built, irrespective of the pretext. I am worried about the alternative."[347] Ambassador Sondland testified that the word "pretext" concerned agreement on an interview or press statement and that the "alternative" was no engagement at all between President Trump and President Zelensky.[348] Ambassador Sondland testified that he viewed giving a press interview or making a press statement as different from pressuring Ukraine to investigate political rival.[349]

On August 9, Ambassador Sondland sent a text message to Ambassador Volker, writing in part: "I think potus [*sic*] really wants the deliverable."[350] Ambassador Sondland testified that "deliverable" referred to the Ukrainian press statement.[351] Ambassador Volker testified that President Trump wanted a public commitment to reform as a "deliverable":

> Q. And what – yeah, what did you understand what the President wanted by deliverable?
>
> A. That statement that had been under conversation.
>
> Q. That was the deliverable from Zelensky that the President wanted before he would commit to –

---

[346] Volker transcribed interview, *supra* note 60, at 137.

[347] Text message from Gordon Sondland to Kurt Volker & William Taylor (July 21, 2019, 4:45 a m.) [KV00000037].

[348] Sondland deposition, *supra* note 51, at 183-84.

[349] *Id.* at 170-71.

[350] Text message from Gordon Sondland to Kurt Volker (Aug. 9, 2019, 5:47 p m.) [KV00000042].

[351] Sondland deposition, *supra* note 51, at 290.

A. *He wanted to see that they're going to come out publicly and commit to reform, investigate the past*, et cetera.[352]

According to Ambassador Taylor, on September 8, Ambassador Sondland relayed to Ambassador Taylor that he had told President Zelensky and Yermak that if President Zelensky "did not clear things up in public, we would be at a stalemate."[353] Ambassador Taylor interpreted Ambassador Sondland's use of "stalemate" to mean that there would be no security assistance to Ukraine.[354] Ambassador Taylor recounted that Ambassador Sondland said that President Trump is a businessman and businessmen ask for something before "signing a check."[355] Ambassador Taylor testified that he understood that "signing a check" related to security assistance.[356] Ambassador Sondland did not recall the conversation with Ambassador Taylor and denied making a statement about President Trump seeking something for signing a check to Ukraine.[357] He testified:

> Q. So you hadn't – did you ever, in the course of this, ever make a statement to the effect of, you know, we're cutting a big check to the Ukraine, you know, what should we get for his?
>
> A. That's not something I would have said. I don't remember that at all.
>
> Q. Okay. So you've never made a statement relating the aid to conditions that the Ukrainians ought to comply with?
>
> A. I don't remember that, no.
>
> Q. But if someone suggested that you made that statement, that would be out of your own character, you're saying?
>
> A. Yes.[358]

Although Ambassador Sondland's statements imply that the President personally sought a conditionality on the security assistance, other witnesses testified that Ambassador Sondland had a habit of exaggerating his interactions with President Trump.[359] Ambassador Sondland himself acknowledged that he only spoke with the President five or six times, one of which was a Christmas greeting.[360] It is not readily apparent that Ambassador Sondland was speaking on behalf of President Trump in this context.

---

[352] Volker transcribed interview, *supra* note 60, at 184 (emphasis added).
[353] Taylor deposition, *supra* note 47, at 39.
[354] *Id.*
[355] *Id.* at 40
[356] *Id.*
[357] Sondland deposition, *supra* note 51, at 198-99, 351.
[358] *Id.* at 198-99.
[359] Hill deposition, *supra* note 12, at 240-41; Kent deposition, *supra* note 65, at 257.
[360] Sondland deposition, *supra* note 51, at 56.

10. President Zelensky never raised a linkage between security assistance and investigations in his meetings with senior U.S. government officials.

Between July 18—the date on which OMB announced the pause on security assistance to Ukraine during an interagency conference call—and September 11—when the pause was lifted—President Zelensky had five separate meetings with high-ranking U.S. government officials. The evidence shows that President Zelensky never raised any concerns in those meeting that he felt pressure to investigate President Trump's political rival or that U.S. security assistance to Ukraine was conditioned on any such investigations.

On July 25, President Zelensky spoke by telephone with President Trump. Although President Zelensky noted a desire to purchase additional Javelin missiles from the United States—an expenditure separate from security assistance—the call summary otherwise does not show that the President discussed a pause on U.S. security assistance to Ukraine.[361]

On July 26, President Zelensky met in Kyiv with Ambassador Volker, Ambassador Taylor, and Ambassador Sondland.[362] According to Ambassador Sondland's closed-door deposition, President Zelensky did not raise any concern about a pause on security assistance or a linkage between the aid and investigations into President Trump's political rival.[363]

On August 27, President Zelensky met in Kyiv with President Trump's then-National Security Advisor John Bolton.[364] According to Ambassador Taylor, President Zelensky and Ambassador Bolton did not discuss U.S. security assistance.[365]

On September 1, President Zelensky met in Warsaw with Vice President Pence, after the existence of the security assistance pause became public. Tim Morrison, Senior Director at the NSC, testified that President Zelensky raised the security assistance directly with Vice President Pence during their meeting.[366] According to Morrison, Vice President Pence relayed President Trump's concern about corruption, the need for reform in Ukraine, and his desire for other countries to contribute more to Ukrainian defense.[367] As Jennifer Williams, senior adviser for Europe in the Office of the Vice President, testified:

> Once the cameras left the room, the very first question that President Zelensky had was about the status of security assistance. And the VP responded by really expressing our ongoing support for Ukraine, but wanting to hear from President Zelensky, you know, what the status of his reform efforts were that he could then convey back to

---

[361] *Memorandum of Telephone Conversation, supra* note 15.
[362] Taylor deposition, *supra* note 47, at 31; Sondland deposition, *supra* note 51, at 29.
[363] Sondland deposition, *supra* note 51, at 252.
[364] Taylor deposition, *supra* note 47, at 33.
[365] *Id.*
[366] Morrison deposition, *supra* note 12, at 131-34.
[367] *Id.*

the President, and also wanting to hear if there was more that European countries could do to support Ukraine.[368]

Vice President Pence did not discuss any investigations with President Zelensky.[369] Morrison said that Vice President Pence spoke to President Trump that evening, who was "still skeptical" due to the fact that U.S. allies were not adequately contributing to Ukraine.[370] Although Ambassador Sondland claimed in his public hearing that he informed Vice President Pence of his assumption of a link between security assistance and investigations in advance of the Vice President's meeting with President Zelensky,[371] the Vice President's office said Ambassador Sondland never raised investigations or conditionality on the security assistance.[372]

On September 5, President Zelensky met in Kyiv with Senator Ron Johnson, Senator Chris Murphy, and Ambassador Taylor.[373] President Zelensky raised the issue of the security assistance, and Senator Johnson relayed to him what President Trump had told Senator Johnson during their August 31 conversation.[374] Senator Murphy then warned President Zelensky "not to respond to requests from American political actors or he would risk losing Ukraine's bipartisan support."[375] Senator Johnson recalled that he did not comment on Senator Murphy's statement but began discussing a potential presidential meeting.[376] To help President Zelensky understand President Trump's mindset, Senator Johnson "tried to portray [President Trump's] strongly held attitude and reiterated the reasons President Trump consistently gave [Senator Johnson] for his reservations regarding Ukraine: endemic corruption and inadequate European support."[377] Senator Johnson recounted how President Zelensky raised no concerns about pressure:

> This was a very open, frank, and supportive discussion. There was no reason for anyone on either side not to be completely honest or to withhold any concerns. *At no time during this meeting—or any other meeting on this trip—was there any mention by [President] Zelensky or any Ukrainian that they were feeling pressure to do anything in return for military aid*, not even after [Senator] Murphy warned them about getting involved in the 2020 election—which would have been the perfect time to discuss any pressure.[378]

---

[368] Williams deposition, *supra* note 73, at 81.

[369] *Impeachment Inquiry: Ambassador Kurt Volker and Mr. Timothy Morrison, supra* note 8; *Impeachment Inquiry: LTC Alexander Vindman and Ms. Jennifer Williams, supra* note 6. In fact, Williams testified that Vice President Pence has "never brought up" these investigations. *Impeachment Inquiry: LTC Alexander Vindman and Ms. Jennifer Williams, supra* note 6.

[370] Morrison deposition, *supra* note 12, at 133-34.

[371] *Impeachment Inquiry: Ambassador Gordon Sondland, supra* note 56.

[372] Office of the Vice President, Statement from VP Chief of Staff Marc Short (Nov. 20, 2019). In addition, the summary of President Trump's July 25 call with President Zelensky was not included in Vice President Pence's briefing book for his meeting with President Zelensky. Williams deposition, *supra* note 73, at 108.

[373] Sen. Johnson letter, *supra* note 138, at 6.

[374] *Id.*

[375] *Id.* at 7.

[376] *Id.*

[377] *Id.*

[378] *Id.* at 8 (emphasis added).

After Senator Johnson offered his perspective, Senator Murphy similarly provided an account of the September 5 meeting.[379] Senator Murphy did not dispute the facts as recounted by Senator Johnson, including that President Zelensky raised no concerns about feeling pressure to investigate the President's political rival.[380] Senator Murphy, however, interpreted President Zelensky's silence to mean that he felt pressure.[381] This "interpretation"—based on what President Zelensky did not say—is unpersuasive in light of President Zelensky's repeated and consistent statements that he felt no pressure.[382]

11. In early September 2019, President Zelensky's government implemented several anti-corruption reform measures.

Publicly available information shows that following the seating of Ukraine's new parliament, the Verkhovna Rada (Rada), on August 29, 2019, the Zelensky government initiated aggressive anti-corruption reforms. Almost immediately, President Zelensky appointed a new prosecutor general and opened Ukraine's Supreme Anti-Corruption Court.[383] On September 3, the Rada passed a bill that removed parliamentary immunity.[384] President Zelensky signed the bill on September 11.[385] On September 18, the Rada approved a bill streamlining corruption prosecutions and allowing the Supreme Anti-Corruption Court to focus on high-level corruption cases.[386]

Witnesses described how these legislative initiatives instilled confidence that Ukraine was delivering on anti-corruption reform. NSC staffer LTC Vindman testified that the Rada's efforts were significant.[387] In his deposition, Ambassador Taylor lauded President Zelensky for this demonstrable commitment to reform. He testified:

> President Zelensky was taking over Ukraine in a hurry. He had appointed reformist ministers and supported long-stalled anticorruption legislation. He took quick executive action, including opening Ukraine's High Anti-Corruption Court, which was established under previous Presidential administration but was never allowed to operate. . . . With his new parliamentary majority, President Zelensky changed the Ukrainian constitution to remove absolute immunity from Rada deputies, which had been the source of raw corruption for decades.[388]

---

[379] Letter from Sen. Chris Murphy to Adam Schiff, Chairman, H. Perm. Sel. Comm. on Intelligence, & Carolyn Maloney, Acting Chairwoman, H. Comm. on Oversight & Reform (Nov. 19, 2019).

[380] *Id.* at 5.

[381] *Id.*

[382] *See supra* Section I.A.2.

[383] Stefan Wolff & Tatyana Malyarenko, *In Ukraine, Volodymyr Zelenskiy must tread carefully or may end up facing another Maidan uprising*, The Conversation, Nov. 11, 2019.

[384] *Bill on lifting parliamentary immunity submitted to Zelensky for signature*, Unian, Sept. 4, 2019.

[385] *Zelensky signs law on stripping parliamentary immunity*, Interfax-Ukraine, Sept. 11, 2019.

[386] *Anti-corruption Court to receive cases from NABU, SAPO*, 112 UA, Sept. 18, 2019.

[387] *Impeachment Inquiry: LTC Alexander Vindman and Ms. Jennifer Williams*, *supra* note 6.

[388] Taylor deposition, *supra* note 47, at 22-23.

Likewise, NSC Senior Director Tim Morrison recalled that President Zelensky's team had literally been working through the night on anti-corruption reforms. He testified:

> Q: And after the Rada was seated, do you know if President Zelensky made an effort to implement those [anti-corruption] reforms?
>
> A: I do.
>
> Q: And what reforms generally can you speak to?
>
> A: Well, he named a new prosecutor general. That was something that we were specifically interested in. He had his party introduce a spate of legislative reforms, one of which was particularly significant was stripping Rada members of their parliamentary immunity. That passed fairly quickly, as I recall. Those kinds of things.
>
> Q: And within what time period were some of those initial reforms passed?
>
> A: Very, very quickly.
>
> Q: Okay. So in the month of August?
>
> A: When we were – when Ambassador Bolton was in Ukraine and he met with President Zelensky, we observed that everybody on the Ukrainian side of the table was exhausted, because they had been up for days working on, you know, reform legislation, working on the new Cabinet, to get through as much as possible on the first day.
>
> Q: Remind me again of Ambassador Bolton's visit. Was that August, at the end of August?
>
> A: It was at the end of August. It was between the G7 and the Warsaw commemoration
>
> Q: So by Labor Day, for example?
>
> A: I seem to recall we were – we – we were there on the opening day of the Rada. President – President Zelensky met with Ambassador Bolton on the opening day of the Rada, and they were in an all-night session. Yeah. So, I mean, things were happening that day.[389]

These actions by the Ukrainian government in early September 2019 are significant in demonstrating President Zelensky's commitment to fighting corruption. Although the

---

[389] Morrison deposition, *supra* note 12, at 128-29.

Department of Defense had certified Ukraine met its anti-corruption benchmarks in Spring 2019, that certification occurred before President Zelensky's inauguration.[390] Deputy Assistant Secretary of Defense Laura Cooper testified during her public hearing that the anti-corruption review examined the efforts of the Poroshenko administration and that President Zelensky had appointed a new Minister of Defense.[391]

As President Trump told Ambassador Sondland on September 9, he sought "nothing" from the Ukrainian government; he only wanted President Zelensky to "do what he ran on."[392] President Zelensky had run on an anti-corruption platform, and these early aggressive actions provided confirmation that he was the "real deal," as U.S. officials advised President Trump.

12. The security assistance was ultimately disbursed to Ukraine in September 2019 without any Ukrainian action to investigate President Trump's political rival.

On September 11, President Trump met with Vice President Pence, Senator Rob Portman, and Acting Chief of Staff Mick Mulvaney to discuss U.S. security assistance to Ukraine.[393] As recounted by NSC Senior Director Tim Morrison, the group discussed whether President Zelensky's progress on anti-corruption reform—which Vice President Pence discussed during his bilateral meeting with President Zelensky on September 1—was significant enough to justify releasing the aid.[394] He testified:

> I believe Senator Portman was relating, and I believe the Vice President as well, related their view of the importance of the assistance. The Vice President was obviously armed with his conversation with President Zelensky, and they were – they convinced the President that the aid should be disbursed immediately.[395]

Following this meeting, the President decided to lift the pause on U.S. security assistance to Ukraine.[396] The release was conveyed to the interagency the following morning.[397] The U.S. disbursed this assistance without Ukraine ever acting to investigate President Trump's political rival.

Democrats cannot show conclusively that the Trump Administration lifted the pause on security assistance only as a result of their impeachment inquiry. In a private conversation with Senator Johnson on August 31, President Trump signaled that the aid would be released, saying then: "We're reviewing it now, and you'll probably like my final decision."[398] A number of other

---

[390] Deposition of Laura Cooper, in Wash., D.C., at 19, 99 (Oct. 23, 2019).
[391] *Impeachment Inquiry: Ms. Laura Cooper and Mr. David Hale*, *supra* note 246.
[392] Sondland deposition, *supra* note 51, at 106.
[393] Morrison deposition, *supra* note 12, at 242-43.
[394] *Id.* at 243.
[395] *Id.*.
[396] *Id.* at 211.
[397] *Id.*
[398] Letter from Sen. Johnson, *supra* note 138, at 5.

events occurred within the same period. President Zelensky implemented serious anti-corruption reforms in Ukraine and OMB conducted a review of foreign assistance globally and provided data on what other countries contribute to Ukraine. Bipartisan senators contacted the White House, telling the Administration that the Senate would act legislatively to undo the pause on security assistance.[399] In fact, Senator Dick Durbin credited the release of the security assistance to the Senate's potential action.[400] Senator Durbin said, "It's beyond a coincidence that they released it the night before our vote in the committee."[401]

* * *

The evidence does not support the Democrats' allegation that President Trump sought to withhold U.S. security assistance to Ukraine to pressure President Zelensky to investigate his political rival for the President's political benefit. The Democrats' witnesses denied the two were linked. The U.S. officials never informed the Ukrainian government that the security assistance was delayed, and senior Ukrainian officials did not raise concerns to U.S. officials until after the delay was publicly reported. President Trump never raised the security assistance during his phone call with President Zelensky. President Zelensky never voiced concerns about pressure or conditionality on security assistance in any meetings he had with senior U.S. government officials. U.S. security assistance ultimately flowed to Ukraine without the Ukrainian government taking any action to investigate President Trump's political rival.

D. **The evidence does not establish that President Trump set up a shadow foreign policy apparatus to pressure Ukraine to investigate the President's political rival for the purpose of benefiting him in the 2020 election.**

Democrats allege that President Trump established an unauthorized, so-called "shadow" foreign policy apparatus to pressure Ukraine to investigate his political rival to benefit the President in the 2020 election.[402] Democrats also alleged that President Trump's recall of Ambassador Yovanovitch was a "politically motivated" decision to appease "allies of President Trump."[403] Although the Constitution gives the President broad authority to conduct the foreign policy of the United States, the Democrats say that President Trump abused his power by disregarding the traditional State Department bureaucratic channels for his personal political benefit. These allegations fall flat.

It is impossible to fairly assess the facts without appreciating the circumstances in which they occurred. From the very first days of the Trump Administration—indeed even before it began—the unelected bureaucracy rejected President Trump and his policies. The self-proclaimed "resistance" organized protests and parody social media accounts, while high-level

---

[399] *See* Byron York, *Why did Trump release Ukraine aid? The answer is simple*, Wash. Exam., Nov. 24, 2019.
[400] Caitlin Emma et al., *Trump administration backs off hold on Ukraine military aid*, Politico, Sept. 12, 2019.
[401] *Id.*
[402] Press Release, H. Comm. On Foreign Affairs, Engel Floor Remarks on Resolution for Open Hearings on Trump's Abuse of Power (Oct. 31, 2019); Adam Schiff (@RepAdamSchiff) (Nov. 6, 2019, 10:58 AM), https://twitter.com/RepAdamSchiff/status/1192154367199260672.
[403] Press Release, H. Comm. on Foreign Affairs, Engel & Hoyer Statement on U.S. Ambassador to Ukraine Masha Yovanovitch (May 7, 2019).

bureaucrats received praise from colleagues for openly defying the Administration's policies. Leaks of secret information became almost daily occurrence, including details about the President's sensitive conversations with foreign leaders. Meanwhile, the Department of Justice and FBI spent 22 months thoroughly investigating false allegations that the Trump campaign had colluded with the Russian government in the 2016 election.

The evidence shows that following President Zelensky's inauguration, the three senior U.S. officials who attended his inauguration—Ambassador Kurt Volker, Ambassador Gordon Sondland, and Secretary Rick Perry—assumed responsibility for shepherding the U.S.-Ukrainian relationship. Contrary to assertions of an "irregular" foreign policy channel, all three men were senior U.S. leaders who had important official interests in Ukraine. The three men maintained regular communication with the NSC and the State Department about their work in Ukraine.

Following President Zelensky's inauguration, Ambassador Volker, Ambassador Sondland, and Secretary Perry sought to convince President Trump of Ukraine's commitment to reform. In that meeting, President Trump referenced Mayor Rudy Giuliani, who had experience in Ukraine. When President Zelensky's adviser Andrey Yermak asked Ambassador Volker to connect him with Mayor Giuliani, Ambassador Volker did so because he believed it would advance U.S.-Ukrainian interests. Mayor Giuliani informed Ambassador Volker about his communications with Yermak. Volker and Yermak both have said that Mayor Giuliani did not speak on behalf of the President in these discussions.

Some pockets of the State Department and NSC grumbled that Ambassador Volker, Ambassador Sondland, and Secretary Perry had become so active in U.S-Ukraine policy. Others criticized Ambassador Marie Yovanovitch's recall or fretted about Mayor Giuliani's involvement. Yet, despite these bureaucratic misgivings, there is no evidence that the involvement of Ambassador Volker, Ambassador Sondland, Secretary Perry, or Mayor Giuliani was illegal or hurt U.S. strategic interests. There is also no evidence that President Trump made this arrangement or recalled Ambassador Yovanovitch for the purpose of pressuring Ukraine to investigate the President's political rival for his benefit in the 2020 presidential election.

1. **The President has broad Constitutional authority to conduct the foreign policy of the United States.**

The Constitution vests the President of the United States with considerable authority over foreign policy.[404] The President is the Commander-in-Chief of U.S. Armed Forces. The President has the power to make treaties with foreign nations, and he appoints and receives "Ambassadors and other public ministers."[405] The Supreme Court has explained that the Constitution gives the President "plenary and exclusive authority" over the conduct of foreign affairs.[406] The President is the "sole organ of the federal government" with respect to foreign affairs.[407]

---

[404] U.S. Const. Art. II.
[405] *Id.*
[406] United States v. Curtiss-Wright Export Corp., 299 U.S. 304, 320 (1936).
[407] *Id.* Although the President makes treaties with the advice and consent of the Senate; the President alone negotiates. *Cf.* H. Jefferson Powell, *The President's Authority Over Foreign Affairs: An Executive Branch Perspective*, 67 Geo. Wash. L. Rev. 527, 546-47 (1999). Dealings with foreign nations require "caution and unity of design," which depend on the President's authority to speak with "one voice" on behalf of U.S. interests. *Id.* at 546.

2. **President Trump was likely skeptical of the established national security apparatus as a result of continual leaks and resistance from the federal bureaucracy.**

In the wake of President Trump's electoral victory in 2016, he faced almost immediate intransigence from unelected—and often anonymous—federal employees. Since then, the "Resistance" has protested President Trump and leaked sensitive national security information about the Trump Administration's policies and objectives. In this context, one can see how President Trump would be justifiably skeptical of the national security apparatus.

Since the beginning of the Trump Administration, leaks of sensitive national security information have occurred at unprecedented rate. As the *Washington Post* noted, "[e]very presidential administration leaks. So far, the Trump White House has gushed."[408] According to an analysis from the Senate Homeland Security and Governmental Affairs Committee in May 2017, the Trump Administration faced about one national security leak per day—flowing seven times faster in the Trump Administration than during the Obama or Bush Administrations.[409] Unelected bureaucrats leaked details about President Trump's private conversations with world leaders and the investigation into Russian interference in the 2016 election.[410]

In Kimberley Strassel's book *Resistance (At All Costs)*, she described the Resistance as "the legions of Americans who were resolutely opposed to the election of Trump, and who remain angrily determined to remove him from office."[411] This resistance included anonymous federal employees who criticized President Trump and his policies on parody U.S. government social media accounts.[412] This resistance included high-level bureaucrats—including then-Acting Attorney General Sally Yates—who openly defied implementing Administration policies.[413] The resistance included an anonymous employee who published an op-ed in the *New York Times* in September 2018 titled, "I Am Part of the Resistance Inside the Trump Administration," detailing how he or she and other unelected bureaucrats were actively working at odds with the President.[414] The op-ed earned the anonymous employee a book deal.[415]

The "Resistance" extended to the U.S. national security apparatus as well, including FBI agents investigating unproven allegations of collusion between the Trump campaign and the Russian government.[416] An FBI lawyer working the investigation, and later assigned to Special Counsel Robert Mueller's office, texted another FBI employee, "Vive le resistance," in the

---

[408] Paul Farhi, *The Trump administration has sprung a leak. Many of them, in fact*, Wash. Post, Feb. 5, 2017.
[409] Maj. Staff on S. Comm. on Homeland Sec. & Gov't Affairs, 115th Cong., State Secrets: How An Avalanche Of Media Leaks Is Harming National Security (2017) [hereinafter "HSGAC report"].
[410] *Id.*
[411] Kimberley Strassel, Resistance (At All Costs): How Trump Haters Are Breaking America (2019).
[412] Kimberley A. Strassel, *Whistleblowers and the Real Deep State*, Wall St. J., Oct. 11, 2019.
[413] *Id.*
[414] *I Am Part of the Resistance Inside the Trump Administration*, N.Y. Times, Sep. 5, 2018.
[415] Alexa Diaz, *Anonymous Trump official who wrote 'resistance' op-ed to publish tell-all book*, L.A. Times, Oct. 22, 2019.
[416] Special Counsel Robert S. Mueller, III, *Report On The Investigation Into Russian Interference In The 2016 Presidential Election*, 1-2. Vol. 1 (2019) [hereinafter "Mueller report"].

month that President Trump was elected.[417] In the week after election night, FBI Agent Peter Strzok and FBI lawyer Lisa Page—who were both involved in the Russia collusion investigation—wrote to each other: "OMG THIS IS F*CKING TERRIFYING" and "I bought all the president's men. Figure I needed to brush up on watergate [*sic*]."[418]

The FBI surveilled Trump campaign associates using evidence delivered by Christopher Steele—a confidential human source funded by then-candidate Trump's political opponents and who admitted he was "desperate" that Donald Trump lose the election.[419] During her deposition, Dr. Hill testified that Steele's reporting was likely a bogus Russia misinformation campaign against Steele.[420] Yet, the FBI accepted Steele's information and used it to obtain surveillance warrants on Trump campaign associate Carter Page.[421] Ultimately, Special Counsel Mueller's report concluded that the Trump campaign did not conspire or coordinate with Russian election interference actions.[422] In considering the President's mindset, this context cannot be ignored.

3. The President has the constitutional authority to remove Ambassador Yovanovitch.

U.S. ambassadors are the President's representatives abroad, serving at the pleasure of the President. Every ambassador interviewed during this impeachment inquiry recognized and appreciated this fact.[423] Even Ambassador Yovanovitch understood that the President could remove any ambassador at any time for any reason, although she unsurprisingly disagreed with the reason for her removal.[424] The removal of Ambassador Yovanovitch, therefore, is not *per se* evidence of wrongdoing for the President's political benefit.

Evidence suggests that President Trump likely had concerns about Ambassador Yovanovitch's ability to represent him in Ukraine,[425] and that then-Ukrainian President

---

[417] Inspector Gen., Dep't of Justice, *A Review of Various Actions by the Federal Bureau of Investigation and Department of Justice in Advance of the 2016 Election*, 396, 419 (2018).

[418] *Id.* at 397, 400.

[419] F.B.I., Dep't of Just., 302 Interview with Bruce Ohr on Dec. 19, 2016 at 3.

[420] *See* Hill deposition, *supra* note 12, at 177-180 ("I think it was a rabbit hole . . . . The way that the Russians operate is that they will use whatever conduit they can to put out information that is both real and credible but that also masks a great deal of disinformation . . . .").

[421] Transcribed Interview of Sally Moyer, in Wash., D.C., at 162 (Oct. 23, 2018).

[422] Mueller report, *supra* note 416.

[423] Sondland deposition, *supra* note 51, at 19; Volker transcribed interview, *supra* note 60, at 88-89; Transcribed interview of Ambassador Michael McKinley, in Wash., D.C., at 37 (Oct. 16, 2019) [hereinafter "McKinley transcribed interview"]; Yovanovitch deposition, *supra* note 115, at 23; Taylor deposition, *supra* note 47, at 297; Hale deposition, *supra* note 230, at 38.

[424] Yovanovitch deposition, *supra* note 115, at 23. Evidence suggests that Ambassador Yovanovitch took steps to gain the President's trust. Deputy Assistant Secretary of State George Kent testified that Ambassador Yovanovitch taped videos in which she proclaimed support for the Trump Administration's foreign policies. Kent deposition, *supra* note 65, at 118-19. Ambassador Yovanovitch testified that she sought Ambassador Sondland's guidance on how to address negative news reports critical of her work as Ambassador to Ukraine. She said that Ambassador Sondland told her to "go big or go home" in publicly supporting the President. Yovanovitch deposition, *supra* note 115, at 267-28, 306-07. Ambassador Sondland, however, testified that he did not recall advising Ambassador Yovanovitch to make a public statement. Sondland deposition, *supra* note 51, at 58-59.

[425] Memorandum of Telephone Conversation, *supra* note 15.

Poroshenko had authorized an effort to criticize Ambassador Yovanovitch.[426] Ambassador Volker testified that he had no firsthand knowledge of Ambassador Yovanovitch criticizing the President; however, he said that "President Trump would understandably be concerned if that was true because you want to have trust and confidence in your Ambassadors."[427]

Despite recognizing the President's prerogative to dismiss ambassadors, some in the U.S. foreign policy apparatus voiced concerns about Ambassador Yovanovitch's removal. Ambassador McKinley testified that he resigned from the State Department because he believed that it failed to protect its diplomats.[428] However, Ambassador McKinley did not resign when he first learned that Ambassador Yovanovitch had been called home, despite knowing that she had been recalled.[429] He only resigned months later, after the whistleblower's account and the President's comments to President Zelensky about Ambassador Yovanovitch during the July 25 call transcript became public.[430]

Ambassador Yovanovitch testified that her removal from Kyiv had little effect on her career with the State Department. Her post was scheduled to end only a matter of weeks after her recall.[431] Although she had considered extending her tour, a decision had not been officially made.[432] Ambassador Yovanovitch explained that she had been planning to retire following her tour in Ukraine and "[s]o I don't think from a State Department point of view [the recall] has had any effect."[433] The recall also did not affect her compensation.[434] Ambassador Yovanovitch explained that the State Department was helpful in securing her a position with Georgetown University.[435]

4. Ambassador Volker, Ambassador Sondland, and Secretary Perry were all senior U.S. government officers with official interests in Ukraine policy.

Contrary to allegations that President Trump orchestrated a "shadow" foreign policy channel to pressure Ukraine to investigate his political rival, evidence shows that the U.S. interactions with Ukraine were led by senior U.S. officials. These officials, Ambassador Volker, Ambassador Sondland, and Secretary Perry, had attended President Zelensky's inauguration in May 2019 and all had official interests in U.S. policy toward Ukraine.

Ambassador Volker explained that "we viewed ourselves as having been empowered as a Presidential delegation to go there, meet, make an assessment [of whether President Zelensky was a legitimate anti-corruption reformer], and report" to President Trump.[436] He said that they

---

[426] Kent deposition, *supra* note 65, at 232.
[427] Volker transcribed interview, *supra* note 60, at 90.
[428] McKinley transcribed interview, *supra* note 423, at 20, 24-25.
[429] *Id.* at 33-34.
[430] *Id.* at 35-36. *See also* Karen DeYoung, *Senior adviser to Pompeo resigns*, Wash. Post, Oct. 10, 2019.
[431] Yovanovitch deposition, *supra* note 115, at 114-16, 140.
[432] *Id.* at 22, 114-16, 122.
[433] *Id.* at 139-40.
[434] *Impeachment Inquiry: Ambassador Marie Yovanovitch, supra* note 4.
[435] Yovanovitch deposition, *supra* note 115, at 139.
[436] Volker transcribed interview, *supra* note 60, at 206.

assumed responsibility to "shepherd this [U.S.-Ukrainian] relationship together as best we could."[437] The delegation assumed this responsibility at a time when the U.S. government lacked an experienced chief of mission in Kyiv.

Importantly, cutting against the idea of a "shadow" channel, each of these three men had an official role with respect to U.S. policy toward Ukraine.[438] Ambassador Volker described his role as the Special Representative for Ukraine Negotiations as "supporting democracy and reform in Ukraine, helping Ukraine better defend itself and deter Russian aggression, and leading U.S. negotiating efforts to end the war and restore Ukraine's territorial integrity."[439] As Ambassador to the European Union, Ambassador Sondland said that Ukraine issues were "central" to his responsibilities.[440] In addition, the Department of Energy, led by Secretary Perry, has significant equities in energy policies in Ukraine.[441]

In the absence of a seasoned chief of mission in Kyiv—before Ambassador Taylor's arrival—these three individuals assumed responsibility following President Zelensky's inauguration for shepherding U.S. engagement with President Zelensky's government. That each individual had an official interest in U.S. policy toward Ukraine undercuts the notion that they engaged in "shadow" diplomacy for illegitimate purposes.

5. Referencing Ukrainian corruption, President Trump told Ambassador Volker, Ambassador Sondland, and Secretary Perry to talk to Mayor Giuliani.

Evidence suggests that Mayor Giuliani's negative assessment of President Zelensky may have reinforced President Trump's existing skepticism about Ukraine and its history of corruption. In May 2019, Mayor Giuliani said that President-elect Zelensky was "surrounded by enemies" of President Trump.[442] When the U.S. delegation to President Zelensky's inauguration later tried to assure President Trump that President Zelensky was different, the President referenced Mayor Giuliani as someone knowledgeable about Ukrainian corruption and told the men to talk to Mayor Giuliani.[443] Testimony differs, however, on whether the President's reference to Mayor Giuliani was a direction or an aside. Either way, because President Trump—constitutionally, the nation's "sole organ of foreign affairs"[444]—raised Mayor Giuliani as

---

[437] *Id.* at 67.

[438] *See Impeachment Inquiry: Dr. Fiona Hill and Mr. David Holmes, supra* note 210.

[439] Volker transcribed interview, *supra* note 60, at 13.

[440] Sondland deposition, *supra* note 51, at 20. During her deposition, Dr. Hill testified that Ambassador Sondland told her that President Trump had "given him broad authority on all things related to Europe, that he was the President's point man on Europe." Hill deposition, *supra* note 12, at 60. Dr. Hill later acknowledged it that Ambassador Sondland could have been exaggerating, explaining that she often saw Ambassador Sondland coming out of West Wing saying he was seeing the President but she learned later that he was really seeing other staff. *Id.* at 204.

[441] James Osborne, *What Rick Perry was doing in Ukraine*, Houston Chronicle, Oct. 16, 2019.

[442] *See* Charles Creitz, *Giuliani cancels Ukraine trip, says he'd be 'walking into a group of people that are enemies of the US,'* Fox News, May 11, 2019.

[443] Sondland deposition, *supra* note 51, at 25. According to public reports, Mayor Giuliani has over a decade of experience working in Ukraine. *See, e.g.,* Rosalind S. Helderman et al., *Impeachment Inquiry Puts New Focus on Giuliani's Work for Prominent Figures in Ukraine,* Wash. Post, Oct. 2, 2019.

[444] *Curtiss-Wright Export Corp.*, 299 U.S. at 320.

someone knowledgeable about Ukraine, this arrangement is not evidence of an unsanctioned and nefarious "shadow" foreign policy apparatus.

On May 23, the U.S. delegation to President Zelensky's inauguration briefed President Trump about their impressions of President Zelensky. Ambassador Sondland testified that the President relayed concerns about Ukrainian corruption, saying "Ukraine is a problem," "tried to take me down," and "talk to Rudy."[445] During his transcribed interview, Ambassador Volker elaborated:

Q. And can you describe the discussion –

A. Yes.

Q. – that occurred?

A Yes. The President started the meeting and started with kind of a negative assessment of the Ukraine. As I've said earlier –

Q. Yep.

A. – it's a terrible place, all corrupt, terrible people, just dumping on Ukraine.

Q. And they were out to get me in 2016.

A. And they were out to get – and they tried to take me down.

Q. In 2016?

A. Yes. And each of us took turns from this delegation giving our point of view, which was that this is a new crowd, it's a new President, he is committed to doing the right things. I believe I said, he agrees with you. That's why he got elected. It is a terrible place, and he campaigned on cleaning it up, and that's why the Ukrainian people supported him.

So, you know, we strongly encouraged him to engage with this new President because he's committed to fighting all of those things that President Trump was complaining about.

Q. And how did the President react?

A. He just didn't believe it. He was skeptical. And he also said, that's not what I hear. I hear, you know, he's got some terrible people

---

[445] Sondland deposition, *supra* note 51, at 61-62, 75.

around him. And he referenced that he hears from Mr. Giuliani as part of that.

Q. Can you explain a little bit more about what the President said about Rudy Giuliani in that meeting?

A. He said that's not what I hear. I hear a whole bunch of other things. And I don't know how he phrased it with Rudy, but it was – I think he said, not as an instruction but just as a comment, talk to Rudy, you know. He knows all of these things, and they've got some bad people around him. And that was the nature of it. It was clear that he also had other sources. It wasn't only Rudy Giuliani. I don't know who those might be, but he – or at least he said, I hear from people.[446]

In his public testimony, Ambassador Volker reiterated that he did not understand the President's comment, "talk to Rudy," to be a direction.[447] He explained:

I didn't take it as an instruction. I want to be clear about that. He said: That's not what I hear. You know, when we were giving him our assessment about President Zelensky and where Ukraine is headed: That's not what I hear. I hear terrible things. He's got terrible people around him. Talk to Rudy. And I understood, in that context, him just saying that's where he hears it from. I didn't take it as an instruction."[448]

Ambassador Sondland, however, in both his closed-door deposition and his public testimony, characterized the President's comment as a "direction."[449] In an interview with the *Wall Street Journal*, Energy Secretary Rick Perry stated that he called Mayor Giuliani following the May 23 meeting, and that Mayor Giuliani told him "to be careful with regards" to President Zelensky.[450] Secretary Perry said "he never heard the president, any of his appointees, Mr. Giuliani, or the Ukrainian regime discuss the possibility of specifically investigating former Vice President Joe Biden, a Democratic presidential contender, and his son Hunter Biden."[451]

[446] Volker transcribed interview, *supra* note 60, at 304-05. Deputy Assistant Secretary Kent testified that Dr. Hill relayed to him that President Trump had conversations with Viktor Orban, the Prime Minister of Hungary, and Vladimir Putin, the President of Russia, which he said may have also colored President Trump's view of Ukraine. Kent deposition, *supra* note 65, at 253-54.
[447] *Impeachment Inquiry: Ambassador Kurt Volker and Mr. Timothy Morrison*, *supra* note 8.
[448] *Id.*
[449] *Impeachment Inquiry: Ambassador Gordon Sondland*, *supra* note 56; Sondland deposition, *supra* note 51, at 25-26.
[450] Timothy Puko & Rebecca Ballhaus, *Rick Perry called Rudy Giuliani at Trump's direction on Ukraine concerns*, Wall St. J., Oct. 16, 2019.
[451] *Id.*

6. At the Ukrainian government's request, Ambassador Volker connected them with Mayor Giuliani to change his impression about the Zelensky regime.

Evidence shows that the Ukrainian government, and specifically Zelensky adviser Andrey Yermak, initiated contact with Mayor Giuliani—and not the other way around—to attempt to refute Mayor Giuliani's views about President Zelensky. Yermak later told *Bloomberg* that he had informed both Republicans and Democrats in Congress in July 2019 that he planned to engage with Mayor Giuliani and heard no objections.[452]

According to Ambassador Volker, in May 2019, he "became concerned that a negative narrative about Ukraine fueled by assertions made by Ukraine's departing prosecutor general" was reaching President Trump via Mayor Giuliani.[453] In July, Ambassador Volker shared his concerns with Yermak, who asked Ambassador Volker to connect him with Mayor Giuliani directly.[454] Ambassador Volker explained:

> After sharing my concerns with the Ukrainian leadership, an adviser to President Zelensky asked me to connect him to the President's personal lawyer, Mayor Rudy Giuliani. I did so. I did so solely because I understood that the new Ukrainian leadership wanted to convince those, like Mayor Giuliani, who believed such a negative narrative about Ukraine, that times have changed and that, under President Zelensky, Ukraine is worthy of U.S. support. I also made clear to the Ukrainians on a number of occasions that Mayor Giuliani is a private citizen and the President's personal lawyer and that he does not represent the United States Government.[455]

Ambassador Volker was clear during his transcribed interview that his action connecting Yermak with Mayor Giuliani was in the best interests of the United States. He testified:

> Q. And so any of the facts here, you connecting Mr. Giuliani with Mr. Yermak and to the extent you were facilitating Mr. Giuliani's communication with anybody in the Ukraine, you were operating under the best interests of the United States?
>
> A. Absolutely.
>
> Q. And to the extent Mr. Giuliani is tight with the President, has a good relationship with him, has the ability to influence him, is it fair to say that, at times, it was in the U.S.'s interest to have Mr. Giuliani connecting with these Ukrainian officials?

---

[452] Baker & Krasnolutska, *supra* note 280.
[453] Volker transcribed interview, *supra* note 60, at 18.
[454] *Id.; see also id.* at 137-38.
[455] *Id.* at 18.

A. Yes. I would say it this way: It was I think in the U.S. interest for the information that was reaching the President to be accurate and fresh and coming from the right people. And if some of what Mr. Giuliani believed or heard from, for instance, the former [Ukrainian] Prosecutor General Lutsenko was self-serving, inaccurate, wrong, et cetera, I think correcting that perception that he has is important, because to the extent that the President does hear from him, as he would, you don't want this dissonant information reaching the President.[456]

In an interview with *Bloomberg*, Yermak explained that he sought to engage with Mayor Giuliani to "dispel the notion that the new Ukraine government was corrupt."[457] Yermak said the Zelensky regime was "surprised" that Mayor Giuliani believed them to be "enemies of the U.S." and they sought to ask Mayor Giuliani directly why he believed that.[458] Yermak recounted how, before his engaged with Mayor Giuliani, he sought bipartisan feedback from Congress about this approach.[459] He said that he spoke with "the top national security advisers to the minority and majority leaders in both the U.S. House and Senate" and told them that "he planned to talk to [Mayor] Giuliani to explain the nation's reform agenda and to urge him not to communicate with Ukraine through the media."[460] Yermak recalled, "Everyone said: 'good idea.'"[461]

7. The Ukrainian government understood that Mayor Giuliani was not speaking on behalf of President Trump.

Ambassador Volker was the chief interlocutor with the Ukrainian government. He described himself as someone who had the Ukrainian government's trust and who offered them counsel on how to address the negative narrative about Ukrainian corruption.[462] Ambassador Volker testified that the Ukrainian government did not view Mayor Giuliani as President Trump's "agent" on whose behalf he spoke.[463] Instead, the Ukrainians saw Mayor Giuliani as a one-way method for conveying information to President Trump about President Zelensky's commitment to reform.

Under examination by House Intelligence Committee Chairman Adam Schiff in his closed-door deposition, Ambassador Volker was resolute that the Ukrainian government saw Mayor Giuliani as someone who "had the President's ear," not someone who spoke for the President. He explained:

Q. You understood that the Ukrainians recognized that Rudy Giuliani represented the President, that he was an agent of the President, that

---

[456] *Id.* at 69-70.
[457] Baker & Krasnolutska, *supra* note 280.
[458] *Id.*
[459] *Id.*
[460] *Id.*
[461] *Id.*
[462] Volker transcribed interview, *supra* note 60, at 168-69.
[463] *Id.* at 116.

he was a direct channel to the President. Ukrainian officials you were dealing with would have understood that, would they not?

A. *I would not say that they thought of him as an agent*, but that he was a way of communicating, that you could get something to Giuliani and he would be someone who would be talking to the President anyway, so it would flow information that way.

Q. So this was someone who had the President's ear?

A. Yes. That's fair.[464]

In his public testimony, Ambassador Volker reiterated that Mayor Giuliani was not speaking on the President's behalf. He explained:

> I made clear to the Ukrainians that Mayor Giuliani was a private citizen, the President's personal lawyer, and not representing the U.S. Government. Likewise, in my conversations with Mayor Giuliani, I never considered him to be speaking on the President's behalf, or giving instructions. Rather, the information flow was the other way, from Ukraine to Mayor Giuliani, in the hopes that this would clear up the information reaching President Trump.[465]

During her closed-door deposition, Dr. Hill confirmed this assessment, explaining that she could not say that Mayor Giuliani was acting on President Trump's behalf.[466]

Andrey Yermak, in an August 2019 *New York Times* article, said it was also not clear to him whether Mayor Giuliani was speaking on behalf of President Trump.[467] According to the *Times*, Mayor Giuliani "explicitly stated that he was not" speaking on behalf of the President.[468] President Trump confirmed this fact in a November 2019 interview, explaining that he did not direct Mayor Giuliani's Ukraine activities.[469]

8. Ambassador Volker, Ambassador Sondland, and Secretary Perry kept the National Security Council and the State Department informed about their actions.

As Ambassador Volker, Ambassador Sondland, and Secretary Perry engaged with Ukrainian government officials, they maintained communications with the State Department and NSC. This coordination undercuts any notion that President Trump orchestrated a "shadow" foreign policy apparatus to work outside of the State Department or NSC.

---

[464] *Id.* (emphasis added).

[465] *Impeachment Inquiry: Ambassador Kurt Volker and Mr. Timothy Morrison, supra* note 8.

[466] Hill deposition, *supra* note 12, at 424-25.

[467] Kramer & Vogel, *supra* note 176.

[468] *Id.*

[469] Daniel Chaitin, *'I didn't direct him': Trump denies sending Giuliani to Ukraine*, Wash. Exam., Nov. 26, 2019.

Ambassador Volker testified that "while executing my duties, I kept my colleagues at the State Department and National Security Council informed and also briefed Congress about my actions."[470] Ambassador Volker and Ambassador Sondland also communicated regularly with Ambassador Bill Taylor once he became the chargé d'affaires, *a.i.*, in Kyiv.[471] These briefings went as high as the Counselor to the Secretary of State, Ulrich Brechbuhl.[472]

In his public testimony, Ambassador Sondland explained that it was "no secret" what he, Ambassador Volker, and Secretary Perry were doing. As he stated, "[w]e kept the NSC apprised of our efforts, including specifically our efforts to secure a public statement from the Ukrainians that would satisfy President Trump's concerns."[473] Ambassador Sondland testified that "everyone was in the loop," although he conceded that he "presumed" a connection between investigations and security assistance without speaking to President Trump, Acting Chief of Staff Mulvaney, or Mayor Giuliani.[474]

9. **Although some in the U.S. foreign policy establishment bristled, the roles of Ambassador Volker, Ambassador Sondland, and Secretary Perry and their interactions with Mayor Giuliani did not violate the law or harm national security.**

Evidence suggests that some in the U.S. foreign policy establishment disliked the involvement of Ambassador Volker, Ambassador Sondland, and Secretary Perry in the U.S.-Ukrainian relationship. Some also expressed discomfort with Mayor Giuliani's interactions with Ukrainian officials. However, the use of private citizens, such as Mayor Giuliani, to assist effectuating U.S. foreign policy goals on specific issues is not *per se* inappropriate and the Democrats' witnesses testified that the use of private citizens can sometimes beneficial. There is no evidence that the arrangement here violated any laws or harmed national security.

Some of the Democrats' witnesses criticized the non-traditional diplomacy. Ambassador Taylor testified about his concern for what he characterized as "two channels" of U.S. policy-making in Ukraine: a regular, State Department channel and an "irregular, informal" channel featuring Ambassador Volker, Ambassador Sondland, Secretary Perry, and Mayor Giuliani.[475] Deputy Assistant Secretary Kent testified that he was concerned that discussions were occurring outside the "formal policy process."[476]

Dr. Hill, too, disapproved of a non-traditional channel of communication, testifying that she disagreed with Ambassador Volker's decision to engage with Mayor Giuliani.[477] Dr. Hill

[470] Volker transcribed interview, *supra* note 60, at 19.
[471] *See* generally text messages exchanged between Kurt Volker and Gordon Sondland [KV00000036-39].
[472] Volker transcribed interview, *supra* note 60, at 59.
[473] *Impeachment Inquiry: Ambassador Gordon Sondland*, *supra* note 56.
[474] *Id.*
[475] Taylor deposition, *supra* note 47, at 23-24.
[476] Kent deposition, *supra* note 65, at 266-67.
[477] Hill deposition, *supra* note 12, at 113-14. Ambassador Sondland recounted that when he met with Dr. Hill prior to her departure from the White House in mid-July, she was "pretty upset about her role" in the Administration and

characterized Ambassador Sondland's conduct as a "domestic political errand."[478] However, by the time that Dr. Hill left the NSC on July 19, Ambassador Volker had only met with Mayor Giuliani once and Ambassador Sondland had never communicated with him.[479] Mayor Giuliani did not meet with the Ukrainian government until early August.[480]

Despite this criticism, Ambassador Volker said that Ambassador Taylor never raised concerns to him about an "irregular" foreign policy channel.[481] The Democrats' witnesses also explained that unorthodox foreign policy channels are not unusual and can actually be helpful to advance U.S. interests. Ambassador Taylor testified that non-traditional channels of diplomacy "can be helpful."[482] Ambassador Volker testified that he always operated with the best interests of the U.S. in mind and to advance "U.S. foreign policy goals with respect to Ukraine."[483]

The impeachment inquiry has uncovered no clear evidence that President Trump directed Ambassador Volker, Ambassador Sondland, and Secretary Perry to work with Mayor Giuliani for the purpose of pressuring Ukraine to investigate his political rival. In fact, the evidence suggests that the White House actively worked to stop potential impropriety. When Mayor Giuliani attempted to obtain a visa for former Ukrainian Prosecutor General Viktor Shokin to travel to the U.S. in January 2019, the White House shut down the effort.[484] The State Department had denied Shokin's visa and Mayor Giuliani apparently appealed to the White House.[485] According to Deputy Assistant Secretary Kent, in settling the matter, White House senior advisor Rob Blair said: "I heard what I need to know to protect the interest of the President."[486] Shokin did not receive a visa.

* * *

The evidence does not support the Democrats' allegation that President Trump set up a shadow foreign policy apparatus to pressure Ukraine to investigate the President's political rival for his political benefit in the 2020 election. The Constitution vests the President with broad authority over U.S. foreign relations. The U.S. officials accused of conducting "shadow" foreign policy—Ambassador Volker, Ambassador Sondland, and Secretary Perry—were all senior leaders with official interests in Ukraine who informed the State Department and NSC of their actions. Mayor Giuliani, whom President Trump referenced in the May 23 meeting with these three U.S. officials, also had experience in Ukraine.

---

so mad that Ambassador Sondland said he had "never seen anyone so upset." Sondland deposition, *supra* note 51, at 266-67, 307. In her public testimony, Dr. Hill explained that she was angry with Ambassador Sondland for not coordinating with her sufficiently. *Impeachment Inquiry: Dr. Fiona Hill and Mr. David Holmes*, *supra* note 210.

[478] *Impeachment Inquiry: Dr. Fiona Hill and Mr. David Holmes*, *supra* note 210.

[479] *Impeachment Inquiry: Ambassador Kurt Volker and Mr. Timothy Morrison*, *supra* note 8; *Impeachment Inquiry: Ambassador Gordon Sondland*, *supra* note 56.

[480] *Impeachment Inquiry: Ambassador Kurt Volker and Mr. Timothy Morrison*, *supra* note 8.

[481] *Impeachment Inquiry: Ambassador Kurt Volker and Mr. Timothy Morrison*, *supra* note 8.

[482] Taylor deposition, *supra* note 47, at 177.

[483] Volker transcribed interview, *supra* note 60, at 15, 69.

[484] Kent deposition, *supra* note 65, at 48-49.

[485] *Id*. at 48-49.

[486] *Id*. at 143.

The Ukrainian government asked Ambassador Volker to connect them with Mayor Giuliani to help change Mayor Giuliani's skeptical view of President Zelensky and "clear up" information flowing to the President. The Ukrainian government saw Mayor Giuliani as someone who had the President's ear but they did not see him as speaking on behalf of the President. While some in the U.S. foreign policy establishment disagreed with these actions, there is no indication it harmed national security or violated any laws. Notably, Ambassador Volker said he operated at all times with the U.S. national interest in mind. Ultimately, Ukraine took no actions to investigate President Trump's political rival.

E. President Trump is not wrong to raise questions about Hunter Biden's role with Burisma or Ukrainian government officials' efforts to influence the 2016 campaign.

Democrats allege that President Trump and Mayor Giuliani are spreading "conspiracy theories" by raising questions about Hunter Biden's role on the board of Burisma and certain Ukrainian government officials' efforts to influence the 2016 election.[487] The evidence available, however, shows that there are legitimate, unanswered questions about both issues. As Ukraine implements anti-corruption reforms, it is appropriate for the country to examine these allegations.

The Democrats' witnesses described how Burisma has long been a subject of controversy in Ukraine. The company's founder, Mykola Zlochevsky, was Ukraine's Minister of Ecology and Natural Resources from 2010 to 2012. In that role, he allegedly granted Burisma licenses for certain mineral deposits. Hunter Biden and other well-connected Democrats joined Burisma's board at a time when the company faced criticism. Hunter Biden's role on Burisma was concerning enough to the Obama State Department that it raised the issue with Vice President Biden's office and even prepared Ambassador Yovanovitch for a potential question on the topic at her confirmation hearing in 2016.

The extent of Ukraine's involvement in the 2016 election draws a much more visceral denial from Democrats, despite harsh rhetoric from prominent Democrats condemning foreign interference in U.S. election. It is undisputed that the then-Ukraine Ambassador to the U.S. authored an op-ed criticizing candidate Trump in U.S. media at the height of the presidential campaign. It is undisputed that senior Ukrainian officials made negative and critical comments about candidate Trump. In addition, a well-researched January 2017 article in *Politico* chronicles attempts by some Ukrainian government officials to harm candidate Trump. The article quotes a former DNC contractor and Ukrainian embassy staffer to show how the Ukrainian embassy worked with Democrat operatives and the media to hurt President Trump's candidacy.

1. It is appropriate for Ukraine to investigate allegations of corruption in its country.

As Ukraine adopts anti-corruption reforms, the United States has encouraged the country's leaders to investigate and prosecute corruption. Deputy Assistant Secretary of State for

---

[487] *See, e.g., Impeachment Inquiry: Ambassador Gordon Sondland, supra* note 56; *Impeachment Inquiry: Ambassador William B. Taylor and Mr. George Kent, supra* note 2;

European and Eurasian Affairs George Kent described Ukraine's corruption problem as "serious" and said corruption has long been "part of the high-level dialogue" between the United States and Ukraine.[488] Ambassador Marie Yovanovitch, the former U.S. Ambassador to Ukraine, testified that in Ukraine "corruption is not just prevalent, but frankly is the system."[489] Although Ukraine has established various anti-corruption prosecutors, courts, and investigative agencies to address the pervasive problem, corruption remains a problem.[490]

The Democrats' witnesses testified that it is appropriate for Ukraine to investigate allegations of corruption, including allegations about Burisma and 2016 election influence. Dr. Fiona Hill, Senior Director for Europe at the NSC, explained that it is "not actually . . . completely ridiculous" for President Zelensky's administration to investigate allegations of corruption arising from prior Ukrainian administrations.[491] Ambassador Volker testified that he "always thought [it] was fine" for Ukraine to investigate allegations about 2016 election influence.[492] Ambassador Yovanovitch testified:

> Q. Ambassador Volker mentioned the fact that to the extent there are corrupt Ukrainians and the United States is advocating for the Ukraine to investigate themselves, that certainly would be an appropriate initiative for U.S. officials to advocate for. Is that right?
>
> A. If that's what took place.[493]

With President Trump's deep-seated and genuine concern about corruption in Ukraine, it is not unreasonable that he would raise two examples of concern in a conversation with President Zelensky. Democrats are fundamentally wrong to argue that President Trump urged President Zelensky to "manufacture" or "dig up" "dirt" by raising these issues. As Ambassador Volker testified:

> Q. Would you say that President Trump in the phone call – and you've read the transcript and you're familiar with all the parties – was asking President Zelensky to manufacture dirt on the Bidens?
>
> A. No. And I've seen that phrase thrown around a lot. And I think there's a difference between the manufacture or dig up dirt versus finding out did anything happen in the 2016 campaign or did anything happen with Burisma. I think – or even if he's asking them to investigate the Bidens, it is to find out what facts there may be rather than to manufacture something.

---

[488] Kent deposition, *supra* note 65, at 105, 151.
[489] Yovanovitch deposition, *supra* note 115, at 18.
[490] *Id.* at 79-80.
[491] Hill deposition, *supra* note 12, at 394.
[492] Volker transcribed interview, *supra* note 60, at 146.
[493] Yovanovitch deposition, *supra* note 115, at 294.

Q. It is not an accurate statement of what the President was asking Ukraine to sum it up as saying that President Trump was asking Ukraine to manufacture dirt?

A. Yeah, I agree with that.[494]

2. There are legitimate concerns surrounding Hunter Biden's position on the board of Ukrainian energy company Burisma during his father's term as Vice President of the United States.

Burisma Holdings had a reputation in Ukraine as a corrupt company.[495] The company was founded by Mykola Zlochevsky, who served as Ukraine's Minister of Ecology and Natural Resources from 2010 to 2012.[496] During Zlochevsky's tenure in the Ukrainian government, Burisma received oil exploration licenses without public auctions.[497]

According to the *New York Times*, Hunter Biden and two other well-connected Democrats—Christopher Heinz, then-Secretary of State John Kerry's stepson, and Devon Archer—"were part of a broad effort by Burisma to bring in well-connected Democrats during a period when the company was facing investigations backed not just by domestic Ukrainian forces but by officials in the Obama administration."[498] Hunter Biden joined Burisma's board when his father, Vice President Joe Biden, acted as the Obama Administration's point person on Ukraine.[499]

The appearance of a conflict of interest raised concerns during the Obama Administration. In May 2014, the *Washington Post* reported "[t]he appointment of the vice president's son to a Ukrainian oil board looks nepotistic at best, nefarious at worst. No matter how qualified Biden is, it ties into the idea that U.S. foreign policy is self-interested, and that's a narrative Vladimir Putin has pushed during Ukraine's crisis."[500] The *Post* likened Hunter Biden's position with Burisma to "children of Russian politicians" who take "executive positions in companies at the top of the Forbes 500 list, and China's 'princelings' [who] have a similar habit."[501]

Deputy Assistant Secretary of State George Kent testified that while he served as acting Deputy Chief of Mission in Kyiv in early 2015, he raised concerns directly to Vice President Biden's office about Hunter Biden's service on Burisma's board.[502] Kent said that the "message"

---

[494] Volker transcribed interview, *supra* note 60, at 212-213.

[495] Kent deposition, *supra* note 65, at 83.

[496] Paul Sonne & Laura Mills, *Ukrainians see conflict in Biden's anticorruption message*, Wall St. J., Dec. 7, 2015.

[497] *Id.*

[498] Kenneth P. Vogel & Iuliia Mendel, *Biden faces conflicts of interest questions that are being promoted by Trump and allies*, N.Y. Times, May 1, 2019.

[499] Adam Taylor, *Hunter Biden's new job at a Ukrainian gas company is a problem for U.S. soft power*, Wash. Post, May 14, 2014.

[500] *Id.*

[501] *Id.*

[502] Kent deposition, *supra* note 65, at 226-27.

he received back was that because Vice President Biden's elder son, Beau, was dying of brain cancer at the time, there was no "bandwidth" to deal with any other family issues.[503]

In December 2015, the *Wall Street Journal* reported that Ukrainian anti-corruption activists complained that Vice President Biden's anti-corruption message "is being undermined as his son receives money" from Zlochevsky.[504] According to the *Journal*, "some anticorruption campaigners here [in Kyiv] worry the link with Mr. Biden may protect Mr. Zlochevsky from being prosecuted in Ukraine."[505]

Ambassador Yovanovitch testified that the Obama State Department actually prepared her to address Hunter Biden's role on Burisma if she received a question about it during her Senate confirmation hearing to be ambassador to Ukraine in June 2016. She explained:

Q. And you may have mentioned this when we were speaking before lunch, but when did the issues related to Burisma first get to your attention? Was that as soon as you arrived in country?

A. Not really. I first became aware of it when I was being prepared for my Senate confirmation hearing. So I'm sure you're familiar with the concept of questions and answer and various other things. And so there was one there about Burisma, and so, you know, that's when I first heard that word.

Q. Were there any other companies that were mentioned in connection with Burisma?

A. I don't recall.

Q. And was it in the general sense of corruption, there was a company bereft with corruption?

A. The way the question was phrased in this model Q&A was, what can you tell us about Hunter Biden's, you know, being named to the board of Burisma?

***

Q. Did anyone at the State Department – when you were coming on board as the new ambassador, did anyone at the State Department brief you about this tricky issue, that Hunter Biden was on the board of this company and the company suffered from allegations of corruption, and provide you guidance?

---

[503] *Id.*
[504] Sonne & Mills, *supra*, note 496.
[505] *Id.*

A. Well, there was that Q&A that I mentioned.[506]

According to testimony, the Obama State Department actually took steps to prevent the U.S. government from associating with Burisma. In his closed-door deposition, Deputy Assistant Secretary Kent recounted a story about how he stopped a taxpayer-funded partnership with Burisma in mid-2016.[507] He said he learned that Burisma sought to cosponsor a U.S. Agency for International Development (USAID) program to encourage Ukrainian school children to develop ideas for clean energy.[508] Kent said he advised USAID not to work with Burisma due to its reputation for corruption.[509]

U.S. law enforcement in the past has examined employment arrangements in which a company hires a seemingly unqualified individual to influence government action. In 2016, the Obama Justice Department fined a Hong Kong subsidiary of a multinational bank for a scheme similar to Burisma's use of Hunter Biden and other well-connected Democrats.[510] There, the company hired otherwise unqualified candidates to "influence" officials toward favorable business outcomes.[511] At the time, then-Assistant Attorney General Leslie Caldwell explained that "[a]warding prestigious employment opportunities to unqualified individuals in order to influence government officials is corruption, plain and simple."[512]

During their public testimony, Democrat witnesses testified that Hunter Biden's role on Burisma's board of directors created the potential for the appearance of a conflict of interest. LTC Vindman testified that Hunter Biden did not appear qualified to serve on Burisma's board.[513] Deputy Assistant Secretary Kent explained that the issues surrounding Burisma were worthy of investigation by Ukrainian authorities.[514] Kent testified:

Q. But given Hunter Biden's role on Burisma's board of directors, at some point, you testified in your deposition that you expressed some concern to the Vice President's office. Is that correct?

A. That is correct.

Q. And what did they do about that concern that you expressed?

A. I have no idea. I reported my concern to the Office of the Vice President.

---

[506] Yovanovitch deposition, *supra* note 115, at 150-53.

[507] Kent deposition, *supra* note 65, at 88, 102-03.

[508] *Id.* at 103

[509] *Id.* at 102.

[510] Press Release, U.S. Dep't of Justice, JPMorgan's Investment Bank in Hong Kong Agrees to Pay $72 Million Penalty for Corrupt Hiring Scheme in China (Nov. 17, 2016), https://www.justice.gov/opa/pr/jpmorgan-s-investment-bank-hong-kong-agrees-pay-72-million-penalty-corrupt-hiring-scheme.

[511] *Id.*

[512] *Id.*

[513] *Impeachment Inquiry: LTC Alexander Vindman and Ms. Jennifer Williams, supra* note 6.

[514] *Impeachment Inquiry: Ambassador William B. Taylor and Mr. George Kent, supra* note 2.

Q. Okay. That was the end of it? Nobody –

A. Sir, you would have to ask people who worked in the Office of the Vice President during 2015.

Q. But after you expressed a concern of a perceived conflict of interest, at the least, the Vice President's engagement in the Ukraine didn't decrease, did it?

A. Correct, because the Vice President was promoting U.S. policy objectives in Ukraine.

Q. And Hunter Biden's role on the board of Burisma didn't cease, did it?

A. To the best of my knowledge, it didn't. And my concern was that there was the possibility of a perception of a conflict of interest.[515]

Similarly, in her public testimony, Ambassador Yovanovitch agreed that concerns about Hunter Biden's presence on Burisma's board were legitimate. In an exchange with Rep. Ratcliffe, she testified:

Q. You understood from Deputy Assistant Secretary George Kent's testimony, as it's been related to you that he testified a few days ago, do you understand that that arrangement, Hunter Biden's role on the Burisma board, caused him enough concern that, as he testified in his statement, that "in February of 2015, I raised my concern that Hunter Biden's status as a board member could create the perception of a conflict of interest." Then he went on to talk about the Vice President's responsibilities over the Ukraine – or over Ukraine – Ukrainian policy as one of those factors. Do you recall that?

A. Yes.

Q. Did you ever – do you agree with that?

A. Yes.

Q. That it was a legitimate concern to raise?

A. I think that it could raise the appearance of a conflict of interest.

***

---

[515] *Id.*

83

> Q. But the legitimate concern about Hunter Biden's role was legitimate, correct?

> A. I think it creates a concern that there could be an appearance of conflict of interest.[516]

During her public testimony, Dr. Hill testified:

> Q. Dr. Hill, you told us during your deposition that, indeed, that there are perceived conflict of interest troubles when the child of a government official is involved with something that government official has an official policy role in, correct?

> A. I think any family member of any member of the U.S. Government, Congress or the Senate, is open to all kinds of questions about optics and of perhaps undue outside influence, if they take part in any kind of activity that could be misconstrued as being related to their parent or the family member's work. So as a matter of course, yes, I do think that's the case.[517]

Despite this evidence, House Intelligence Committee Chairman Adam Schiff has prevented Republican Members from fully assessing the role of Hunter Biden on Burisma's board of directors. Chairman Schiff refused to invite Hunter Biden and Devon Archer to testify during public hearings.[518] Chairman Schiff declined to concur with a Republican subpoena for Hunter Biden to testify in a closed-door deposition.[519] Chairman Schiff declined to concur with a Republican subpoena for documents relating to Hunter Biden's role on Burisma.[520]

In addition to Burisma, there are questions about why the Ukrainian government fired then-Prosecutor General Shokin—according to Vice President Biden, at his insistence[521]—when it did not fire his successor, Prosecutor General Yuriy Lutsenko. Although Shokin and Lutsenko were both seen by State Department officials as corrupt and ineffective prosecutors, there was no effort to remove Lutsenko to the same degree or in the same way as there was with Shokin.[522] Ambassador Yovanovitch testified:

> Q. And was he, in your experience – because you're very knowledgeable about the region, so when I ask you in your opinion, you have a very informed opinion – was Lutsenko better or worse than Shokin?

---

[516] *Impeachment Inquiry: Ambassador Marie Yovanovitch, supra* note 4.

[517] *Impeachment Inquiry: Dr. Fiona Hill and Mr. David Holmes, supra* note 210.

[518] *See, e.g.,* Allan Smith, *Democrats push back on GOP effort to have whistleblower, Hunter Biden testify,* NBC News, Nov. 10, 2019.

[519] *Impeachment Inquiry: Ms. Laura Cooper and Mr. David Hale, supra* note 246.

[520] *Id.*

[521] Council on Foreign Relations, Foreign Affairs Issue Launch with Former Vice President Joe Biden (Jan. 23, 2018).

[522] Kent deposition, *supra* note 65, at 90-98, 144-49.

A. I mean, honestly, I don't know. I mean, I think they're cut from the same cloth.

***

Q. There was never as much of a clamor to remove Lutsenko as there was Shokin. Is that fair to say?

A. Yeah, I think that's fair.

Q. And what do you account for that?

A. I would say that there was, I think, still a hope that one could work with Mr. Lutsenko. There was also that prospect of Presidential elections coming up, and as seemed likely by, you know, December, January, February, whatever the time was, that there would be a change of government. And I think we certainly hoped that Mr. Lutsenko would be replaced in the natural order of things, which is, in fact, what happened. We also had more leverage before. I mean, this was not easy. President Poroshenko and Mr. Shokin go way back. In fact, I think that they are godfathers to each other's children. So this was, you know, this was a big deal. But we had assistance, as did the IMF, that we could condition.[523]

Evidence suggests that Lutsenko's misconduct was not trivial. Deputy Assistant Secretary Kent explained that the U.S. government became disillusioned with Lutsenko in 2017 when he exposed an undercover investigator working to catch Ukrainian government officials selling fraudulent biometric passports.[524] Kent said that Lutsenko's actions could have resulted in terrorists obtaining fraudulent biometric passports.[525] Whereas Shokin only served for little over a year, Lutsenko served for years until President Zelensky removed him.[526] Although both prosecutors were regarded as ineffective and corrupt, the U.S. government only took an official position with respect to Shokin's removal and never as to Lutsenko's.[527]

3. There are legitimate questions about the extent to which Ukrainian government officials worked to oppose President Trump's candidacy in the 2016 election.

Democrats reflexively oppose any discussion about whether senior Ukrainian government officials worked to oppose President Trump's candidacy and support former Secretary Clinton during the 2016 election. Calling these allegations "debunked" and "conspiracy theories," Democrats ignore irrefutable evidence that is inconvenient for their

---

[523] Yovanovitch deposition, *supra* note 115, at 102-03.
[524] Kent deposition, *supra* note 65, at 145-47.
[525] *Id.* at 147-48.
[526] *Id.* at 95-103.
[527] *Id.* at 95.

political narrative. The facts, however, show outstanding questions about Ukrainian influence in the 2016 presidential election—questions that the Democrats' witnesses said would be appropriate for Ukraine to examine.

Prominent Democrats expressed concern about foreign interference in U.S. elections when they believed that the Russian government colluded with the Trump campaign in 2016. For example, in a 2017 hearing about Russian election interference, then-Ranking Member Schiff said that the "stakes are nothing less than the future of liberal democracy."[528] But where evidence suggests that Ukraine also sought to influence the election to the benefit of the Clinton campaign, now-Chairman Schiff and fellow Democrats have held their outrage.

Democrats have posited a false choice: that influence in the 2016 election is binary—it could have been conducted by Russia or by Ukraine, but not both. This is nonsense. Under then-Chairman Devin Nunes, Republicans on the House Intelligence Committee issued a report in March 2018 detailing Russia's active measures campaign against the United States.[529] But Russian interference in U.S. elections does not preclude Ukrainian officials from also attempting to influence the election. As Ambassador Volker testified during his public hearing, it is possible for more than one country to influence U.S. elections.[530]

Indisputable evidence shows that senior Ukrainian government officials sought to influence the 2016 election in favor of Secretary Clinton and against then-candidate Trump. In August 2016, then-Ukrainian Ambassador to the United States, Valeriy Chaly, wrote an op-ed in *The Hill* criticizing Trump's policies toward Ukraine.[531] The same month, the *Financial Times* reported that Trump's candidacy led "Kyiv's wider political leadership to do something they would never have attempted before: intervene, however indirectly, in a US election."[532] Ukrainian parliamentarian Serhiy Leshchenko explained that Ukraine was "on Hillary Clinton's side.[533] Other senior Ukrainian officials called candidate Trump a "clown," a "dangerous misfit," and "dangerous," and alleged that candidate Trump "challenged the very values of the free world."[534]

Other publicly available information reinforces the conclusion that senior Ukrainian government officials worked in 2016 to support Secretary Clinton. A January 2017 *Politico* article by current-*New York Times* reporter Ken Vogel detailed the Ukrainian effort to "sabotage" the Trump campaign.[535] Although Democrats reflexively dismiss the information presented in this article, neither *Politico* nor Vogel have retracted the story.

---

[528] *Open hearing on Russian Active Measures Campaign: Hearing before the H. Perm. Sel. Comm. on Intelligence*, 115th Cong. (2017)

[529] H. Perm. Sel. Comm. on Intelligence, Report on Russian Active Measures (Mar. 2018).

[530] *Impeachment Inquiry: Ambassador Kurt Volker and Mr. Timothy Morrison, supra* note 8

[531] *See* Chaly, *supra* note 27.

[532] Olearchyk, *supra* note 123.

[533] *Id.*

[534] *Id.*; Vogel & Stern, *supra* note 127.

[535] Vogel & Stern, *supra* note 127.

According to Vogel's reporting, the Ukrainian government worked with a Democrat operative and the media in 2016 to boost Secretary Clinton's candidacy and hurt President Trump's. Vogel wrote:

> Ukrainian government officials tried to help Hillary Clinton and undermine Trump by publicly questioning his fitness for office. They also disseminated documents implicating a top Trump aide in corruption and suggested they were investigating the matter, only to back away after the election. And they helped Clinton's allies research damaging information on Trump and his advisers, a *Politico* investigation found.[536]

Vogel reported how Alexandra Chalupa, a Ukrainian-American contractor paid by the DNC and working with the DNC and the Clinton campaign, "traded information and leads" about Paul Manafort, Trump's campaign manager, with staff at the Ukrainian embassy.[537] Chalupa also told Vogel that the Ukrainian embassy "worked directly with reporters researching Trump, Manafort, and Russia to point them in the right directions."[538] With the DNC's encouragement, Chalupa asked Ukrainian embassy staff "to try to arrange an interview in which [Ukrainian President] Poroshenko might discuss Manafort's ties to [Russia-aligned former Ukrainian President Viktor] Yanukovych."[539]

Vogel also spoke on the record to Andrii Telizhenko, a political officer in the Ukrainian Embassy under Ambassador Chaly, who corroborated Chalupa's account.[540] Telizhenko said that he was instructed by Ambassador Chaly's top aide, Oksana Shulyar, to "help Chalupa research connections between Trump, Manafort, and Russia" with the goal of generating a hearing in Congress.[541] Telizhenko also told Vogel that he was instructed not to speak to the Trump campaign:

> We had an order not to talk to the Trump team, because he was critical of Ukraine and the government and his critical position on Crimea and the conflict. I was yelled at when I proposed to talk to Trump. The ambassador said not to get involved – Hillary is going to win.[542]

---

[536] *Id.*

[537] *Id.* In April 2019, then-Ambassador Chaly issued a statement to *The Hill* denying that the Ukrainian embassy sought to influence the election. *See Official April 25, 2019 statement of the Ukrainian embassy in Washington to The Hill concerning the activities of Democratic National Committee Alexandra Chalupa during the 2016 U.S. election*, https://www.scribd.com/document/432699412/Ukraine-Chaly-Statement-on-Chalupa-042519.

[538] Vogel & Stern, *supra* note 127.

[539] *Id.* Interestingly, in August 2019, when Chairman Schiff tweeted an allegation that U.S. security assistance to Ukraine was tied up with Ukrainian investigations, Alexandra Chalupa replied that she had "a lot of information on this topic." *See* Adam Schiff (@RepAdamSchiff), Twitter (Aug. 28, 2019, 5:17 p.m.), https://twitter.com/RepAdamSchiff/status/1166867471862829056. It is unknown whether Chalupa ever provided information to Chairman Schiff or his staff.

[540] Vogel & Stern, *supra* note 127.

[541] *Id.*

[542] *Id.*

Vogel also reported on the actions of Ukrainian parliamentarian Leshchenko, who spoke out against Manafort, in part, to show that candidate Trump was a "pro-Russia candidate."[543] A separate congressional investigation in 2018 learned that Leshchenko was a source for Fusion GPS, the opposition research firm hired by the DNC's law firm, Perkins Coie, to gather information about candidate Trump.[544] Fusion GPS received information about Manafort that may have originated from Leshchenko.[545]

The Democrats' witnesses in the impeachment inquiry testified that the allegations of Ukrainian influence in the 2016 election were appropriate to examine.[546] Asked about the *Politico* reporting, Ambassador Taylor said that, if true, it is "disappointing" that some Ukrainian officials worked against President Trump. He testified:

> Q. So isn't it possible that Trump administration officials might have a good-founded belief, whether true or untrue, that there were forces in the Ukraine that were operating against them?
>
> A. [B]ased on this [January 2017] *Politico* article, which, again, surprises me, disappoints me because I think it's a mistake for any diplomat or any government official in one country to interfere in the political life of another country. That's disappointing.[547]

Ambassador Taylor testified that he was "surprise[ed] [and] disappoint[ed]" that Avakov, an influential member of the Ukrainian government—who still serves in President Zelensky's government—had criticized President Trump during the 2016 campaign.[548] He testified:

> Q. What do you know about Avakov?
>
> A. So he is the Minister of Internal Affairs and was the Minister of Internal Affairs under President Poroshenko as one of only two carryovers from the Poroshenko Cabinet to the Zelensky Cabinet. He, as I think I mentioned earlier when we were talking about Lutsenko, the Minister of Interior, which Avakov is now, controls the police, which gives him significant influence in the government.
>
> Q. Avakov, he's a relatively influential Minister. Is that right?
>
> A. That is correct.

---

[543] *Id.*; Olearchyk, *supra* note 123.
[544] Transcribed Interview of Nellie Ohr, in Wash., D.C., at 113-15 (Oct. 19, 2018).
[545] *Id.*
[546] *See, e.g.*, Volker transcribed interview, *supra* note 60, at 146.
[547] Taylor deposition, *supra* note 47, at 101.
[548] *Id.* at 98-99.

Q. Does it concern you that at one time he was being highly critical of candidate Trump?

A. It does.

Q. And did you ever have any awareness of that before I called your attention to this?

A. I haven't. This is surprising. Disappointing, but—[549]

Despite this testimony, Chairman Schiff has prevented Republican Members from fully assessing the nature and extent of Ukraine's influence in the 2016 election. Chairman Schiff refused to invite Alexandra Chalupa or Fusion GPS contractor Nellie Ohr to testify during public hearings.[550] Chairman Schiff declined to concur with a Republican subpoena for documents relating to the DNC's communications with the Ukrainian government.[551] Chairman Schiff declined to concur with a Republican subpoena for documents relating to the DNC's work with Alexandra Chalupa.[552]

* * *

There are legitimate concerns about Burisma's corruption and Hunter Biden's role on the company's board, and Ukrainian government officials' actions to support Secretary Clinton over President Trump in the 2016 election. Democrats reflexively dismiss these concerns because acknowledging them would require an admission that past U.S. assistance to Ukraine may have been misspent. As Ambassador Yovanovitch testified:

> I think most Americans believe that there shouldn't be meddling in our elections. And if Ukraine is the one that had been meddling in our elections, I think the support that all of you [in Congress] have provided to Ukraine over the last almost 30 years, I don't know that – I think people would ask themselves questions about that.[553]

Similarly, other career foreign service employees spoke about their emotional investment in U.S. foreign assistance to Ukraine. Speaking about his reaction to the recent events in Ukraine, Ambassador Taylor testified that he feels a strong "emotional attachment, bond, connection to this country and these people."[554] Deputy Assistant Secretary Kent, according to current State Department employee and former NSC staffer Catherine Croft, likewise "has a lot of emotion tied into" U.S. policy toward Ukraine, saying he "feels very strongly in all aspects of our policy

---

[549] *Id.*
[550] *See, e.g.*, Riley Beggin, *House Democrats deny Republicans' request for whistleblower testimony*. Vox, Nov. 10, 2019.
[551] *Impeachment Inquiry: Ms. Laura Cooper and Mr. David Hale, supra* note 246.
[552] *Id.*
[553] Yovanovitch deposition, *supra* note 115, at 137.
[554] Taylor deposition, *supra* note 47, at 273.

with regard to Ukraine."[555] President Trump's world view threatens these personal, subjective interests, which may explain why some are so eager to discount these allegations.

F. The anonymous whistleblower who served as the basis for the impeachment inquiry has no firsthand knowledge of events and a bias against President Trump.

Democrats built their impeachment inquiry on the foundation of the anonymous whistleblower complaint submitted to the Inspector General of the Intelligence Community on August 12. This foundation is fundamentally flawed.

The anonymous whistleblower acknowledged having no firsthand knowledge about the events he or she described. As a result, his or her complaint mischaracterized important facts and portrayed events in an inaccurate light. The anonymous whistleblower reportedly had a professional relationship with Vice President Joe Biden, which, if true, biases the whistleblower's impressions of the events as they relate to Vice President Biden. The anonymous whistleblower also reportedly communicated initially with House Intelligence Committee Chairman Adam Schiff, who has been an ardent and outspoken critic of President Trump, or his staff. Chairman Schiff's early secret awareness of the issue tainted the objectivity of the Democrats' impeachment inquiry.

To this day, only one Member of Congress—Chairman Schiff—knows the identity of the individual whose words sparked the impeachment of the President. Chairman Schiff has prevented any objective assessment of the whistleblower's credibility or knowledge. Chairman Schiff declined to invite the whistleblower to testify as part of the Democrats' impeachment inquiry, but only after Chairman Schiff's or his staff's communications with the whistleblower came to light.[556] Chairman Schiff rejected a Republican subpoena for documents relating to the drafting of the whistleblower complaint and the whistleblower's personal memorandum written shortly after the July 25 telephone conversation.[557]

The public reporting about the existence of a whistleblower and his or her sensational allegations about President Trump generated tremendous public interest. But Americans cannot assess the credibility, motivations, or biases of the whistleblower. This analysis is necessary because the whistleblower's inaccurate assertions, coupled with Chairman Schiff's selective leaks of cherry-picked information, have prejudiced the public narrative surrounding President Trump's telephone call with President Zelensky.

1. The anonymous whistleblower acknowledged having no firsthand knowledge of the events in question.

The anonymous whistleblower has no direct, firsthand knowledge of the events described in his or her complaint. In the complaint, the whistleblower acknowledged, "I was not a direct

---

[555] Croft deposition, *supra* note 60, at 105-06.
[556] *See, e.g.*, Beggin, *supra* note 550.
[557] *Impeachment Inquiry: Ms. Laura Cooper and Mr. David Hale*, *supra* note 246.

witness to most of the events described," and admitted that he or she was not on the July 25 call between President Trump and President Zelensky.[558] Instead, the anonymous whistleblower relied upon indirect, secondhand information provided by others—individuals who are also still unidentified. The whistleblower's lack of firsthand knowledge undermines the credibility of his or her accusations.

Testimony provided by officials with firsthand knowledge of the events rebuts the whistleblower's allegations. Ambassador Sondland testified that some of the concerns in the August 12 whistleblower complaint may be inaccurate or hyperbole.[559] For example, both Ambassador Volker and Ambassador Sondland testified that the whistleblower incorrectly alleged "that State Department officials, including Ambassadors Volker and Sondland, had spoken with Mr. Giuliani to 'contain the damage' to U.S. national security."[560] The ambassadors also disagreed with the whistleblower's statement that they helped Ukrainian leadership "'navigate' the demands" from President Trump.[561]

In addition, Ambassador Sondland took issue with the whistleblower's characterization of efforts to arrange a meeting between President Trump and President Zelensky. The whistleblower complaint stated:

> During this same timeframe, multiple U.S. officials told me [the anonymous whistleblower] that the Ukrainian leadership was led to believe that a meeting or phone call between the President and President Zelensky would depend on whether Zelensky showed willingness to "play ball" on the issues that had been publicly aired by Mr. Lutsenko and Mr. Giuliani.[562]

Ambassador Sondland testified that he never heard U.S. officials use the expression "play ball" in this context.[563]

2. Press reports suggest that the anonymous whistleblower acknowledged having a professional relationship with former Vice President Biden.

The anonymous whistleblower reportedly acknowledged having a professional relationship with Vice President Biden. This admission is important because Vice President Biden was referenced in passing on the July 25 call and is a potential opponent of President Trump in the 2020 presidential election. It stands to reason that a mention of Vice President Biden—no matter how brief or innocuous—could stir the passion of someone who had a professional relationship with him.

---

[558] Whistleblower letter, *supra* note 85, at 1; *see also* Letter from Hon. Michael Atkinson, Inspector Gen. of the Intelligence Cmty., to Hon. Joseph Maguire, Acting Dir. Of Nat'l Intelligence (Aug. 26, 2019).
[559] Sondland deposition, *supra* note 51, at 259-64, 311-14.
[560] Volker transcribed interview, *supra* note 60, at 100-01; Sondland deposition, *supra* note 51, at 261-62, 313.
[561] Volker transcribed interview, *supra* note 60, at 101; Sondland deposition, *supra* note 51, at 259-61, 311-12.
[562] Whistleblower letter, *supra* note 85, at 7.
[563] Sondland deposition, *supra* note 51, at 264.

On August 26, 2019, Inspector General Atkinson wrote to Acting Director of National Intelligence (DNI) Joseph Maguire stating that he found "some indicia of an arguable political bias on the part of the [anonymous whistleblower] in favor of a rival political candidate . . . ."[564] News reports later reported that the "rival political candidate" referenced in Atkinson's letter was a 2020 Democrat presidential candidate with whom that the whistleblower acknowledged having a "professional relationship."[565]

Subsequent news reports explained that the whistleblower is a CIA analyst who had been detailed to the NSC and would have worked closely with Vice President Biden's office.[566] This relationship is significant because President Obama relied upon Vice President Biden to be the Obama Administration's point person for Ukrainian policy.[567] This relationship suggests that aside from any partisan bias in support of Vice President Biden's 2020 presidential campaign, the whistleblower may also have had a bias in favor of Vice President Biden's Ukrainian policies instead of those of President Trump.

3. The anonymous whistleblower secretly communicated with Chairman Schiff or his staff.

According to an admission from Chairman Schiff, the anonymous whistleblower communicated with Chairman Schiff's staff prior to submitting his or her complaint. This early, secret involvement of Chairman Schiff severely prejudices the objectivity of the whistleblower's allegations, given Chairman Schiff's obsession with attacking President Trump for partisan gain.

Since 2016, Chairman Schiff has been a chief ringleader in Congress for asserting that President Trump colluded with Russia, going so far as to allege that he had secret evidence of collusion.[568] Now Chairman Schiff is the investigator-in-chief of President Trump's July 25 phone call with Ukrainian President Zelensky. Chairman Schiff led the investigation's first phase from behind the closed doors of his Capitol basement bunker, even though the depositions were all unclassified. Chairman Schiff did so purely for information control—allowing him to leak selected pieces of information to paint a misleading public narrative.

Chairman Schiff has publicly fabricated evidence about President Trump's July 25 phone call and misled the American public about his awareness of the whistleblower allegations. On September 26, at a public hearing of the House Intelligence Committee, Chairman Schiff opened the proceedings by fabricating the contents of President Trump's call with President Zelensky to

---

[564] Letter from Hon. Michael Atkinson, Inspector General of the Intelligence Community, to Hon. Joseph Maguire, Dir. Of Nat'l Intelligence, Office of the Dir. of Nat'l Intelligence (Aug. 26, 2019).

[565] Byron York, *Whistleblower Had 'Professional' Tie to 2020 Democratic Candidate,* Wash. Exam., Oct. 8, 2019.

[566] *See generally* Rob Crilly, Steven Nelson, & David Drucker, *Joe Biden Worked with Whistleblower When he was Vice President, Officials Reveal,* Wash. Exam., Oct. 10, 2019; Ben Feuerherd, *Whistleblower May Have Worked with Joe Biden in White House: Report,* N.Y. Post, Oct. 10, 2019; Julian Barnes, Michael Schmidt, Adam Goldman, & Katie Benner, *White House Knew of Whistleblower's Allegations Soon After Trump's Call with Ukraine Leader,* N.Y. Times, Sept. 26, 2019.

[567] Greg Myre, *What Were the Bidens Doing in Ukraine? 5 Questions Answered,* Nat'l Pub. Radio, Sept. 24, 2019.

[568] *See, e.g.,* Kelsey Tamborrino, *Warner: 'Enormous amounts of evidence' of possible Russia collusion,* Politico, Mar. 3, 2019.

make the conversation seem sinister.[569] Pretending to be President Trump, Chairman Schiff said in part:

> I hear what you want. I have a favor I want from you though. And I'm going to say this only seven times so you better listen good. I want you to make up dirt on my political opponent, understand. Lots of it.[570]

These words were never uttered by President Trump. When Chairman Schiff rightly faced criticism for his actions, he blamed others for not understanding that he was joking.[571] Republicans sought to hold Chairman Schiff accountable for his fabrication of evidence; however, Democrats prevented the House from voting on a censure resolution.[572]

In October 2019, the *New York Times* reported that the whistleblower contacted a staff member on the House Intelligence Committee—chaired by Chairman Schiff—after asking a colleague to convey his or her concerns about the July 25 call to the CIA's top lawyer.[573] Chairman Schiff, however, had denied ever communicating directly with the whistleblower,[574] and the whistleblower failed to disclose that he or she had contacted Chairman Schiff's staff when asked by the Intelligence Community Inspector General.[575] Chairman Schiff acknowledged his early awareness of the whistleblower's allegations only after he was caught.[576] The *Washington Post* gave Chairman Schiff "Four Pinocchios"—its worst rating—for "clearly ma[king] a statement that was false."[577]

Chairman Schiff's early awareness of the whistleblower complaint explains why he publicly posited a connection between paused U.S. security assistance and Ukrainian investigations well before the whistleblower complaint became public. On August 28, 2019, before the public became aware of the whistleblower complaint or any allegations that U.S. security assistance to Ukraine was linked to Ukraine investigating President Trump's political rival, Chairman Schiff made such a connection in a tweet.[578] According to the *New York Times*, Chairman Schiff knew "the outlines" of the anonymous whistleblower complaint at the time that he issued this tweet.[579]

---

[569] *Whistleblower disclosure, supra* note 1.
[570] *Id.*
[571] *Id.*
[572] Katherine Tully-McManus, *Republican effort to censure Adam Schiff halted*, Roll Call, Oct. 21, 2019.
[573] Julian Barnes, Michael Schmidt, & Matthew Rosenberg, *Schiff Got Early Account of Accusations as Whistleblower's Concerns Grew*, N.Y. Times, Oct. 2, 2019.
[574] *See, e.g.*, Glenn Kessler, *Schiff's false claim his committee had not spoken to the whistleblower*, Wash. Post, Oct. 4, 2019.
[575] Andrew O'Reilly, *Schiff Admits He Should Have Been 'Much More Clear' About Contact with Whistleblower*, Fox News, Oct. 13, 2019.
[576] *Schiff Got Early Account of Accusations as Whistleblower's Concerns Grew, supra* note 573.
[577] *Schiff's false claim his committee had not spoken to the whistleblower, supra* note 574.
[578] Adam Schiff (@RepAdamSchiff), Twitter, (Aug. 28, 2019, 8:17 PM), https://twitter.com/RepAdamSchiff/status/1166867471862829056.
[579] Barnes, Schmidt, & Rosenberg, *supra* note 573.

Figure 3: Chairman Schiff's August 28 tweet linking aid to investigations

Chairman Schiff's early awareness also explains why he pressured Inspector General Atkinson to produce the whistleblower's complaint to Congress, despite Acting DNI Maguire's determination that transmittal was not required because the complaint did not meet the legal definition of "urgent concern."[580]

* * *

The allegations of the anonymous whistleblower—the foundation for the Democrats' impeachment inquiry—are fundamentally flawed. The whistleblower acknowledged having no direct, firsthand knowledge of the events he or she described. The whistleblower reportedly acknowledged a professional relationship with Vice President Joe Biden, which, if true, suggests a bias toward Vice President Biden and against President Trump. Finally, the whistleblower secretly communicated with staff of Chairman Schiff, who subsequently misled the public about this communication.

If Democrats are serious about impeaching the President—about undoing the will of the American people—they cannot limit the evidence and information available to the House of Representatives. The motivations, biases, and credibility of the anonymous whistleblower are necessary aspects of any serious examination of the facts in question.

---

[580] U.S. Dep't of Justice, Office of Legal Counsel, "Urgent Concern" Determination by the Inspector General of the Intelligence Community 2 (2019).

II. The evidence does not establish that President Trump engaged in a cover-up of his interactions with Ukrainian President Zelensky.

Democrats also argue that President Trump is engaged in a cover-up of his July 25 telephone conversation by hiding evidence of his alleged wrongdoing.[581] There is no basis for this allegation. The President has been transparent about the issues surrounding the anonymous whistleblower complaint and the telephone call with President Zelensky.

On September 24, Speaker Pelosi launched the impeachment inquiry based solely on reports of the telephone call between President Trump and President Zelensky. She had not listened to the conversation; she had not read the call summary or the whistleblower complaint. The following day, to offer unprecedented transparency and prove there was no *quid pro quo*, President Trump declassified the July 25 call summary for the American people to read for themselves. President Trump also released a redacted version of the anonymous whistleblower complaint and he released the summary of his April 21 telephone conversation with President Zelensky. Even the Democrats' best evidence of a "cover-up"—the restricted access to the call summary—is unpersuasive. Evidence suggests that the call summary was restricted not for a malicious intention but as a result of the proliferation of leaks by unelected bureaucrats, including leaks of President Trump's conversations with foreign leaders.

A. President Trump declassified and released publicly the summary of his July 25 phone call with President Zelensky.

On July 25, President Trump and President Zelensky spoke by telephone.[582] Normally, presidential conversations with foreign leaders are presumptively classified because "[t]he unauthorized disclosure of foreign government information is presumed to cause damage to the national security."[583] In fact, the call summary of President Trump's call with President Zelensky was initially marked as classified.[584]

On September 25, after questions arose about the contents of the phone call, President Trump chose to declassify and release the transcript in the interest of full transparency. He wrote on Twitter: "I am currently at the United Nations representing our Country, but have authorized the release tomorrow of the complete, fully declassified and unredacted transcript of my phone conversation with President Zelensky of Ukraine."[585] The President stressed his goal that Americans could read for themselves the contents of the call: "You will see it was a very friendly and totally appropriate call. No pressure unlike Joe Biden and his son, NO quid pro quo! This is

---

[581] *See, e.g.*, Speaker Nancy Pelosi, Transcript of Pelosi Weekly Press Conference (Sept. 26, 2019) ("The [whistleblower] complaint reports 'repeated abuse of an electronics record system designed to store classified, sensitive national security information, which the White House used to hide information of a political nature.' This is a cover-up. This is a cover-up.").

[582] Memorandum of Telephone Conversation, *supra* note 15.

[583] Exec. Order 13,526 (2009).

[584] *See* Memorandum of Telephone Conversation, *supra* note 15.

[585] Donald J. Trump (@realDonaldTrump), Twitter (Sept. 24, 2019, 11:12 a m.), https://twitter.com/realdonaldtrump/status/1176559966024556544.

nothing more than a continuation of the Greatest and most Destructive Witch Hunt of all time."[586]

B. President Trump released a redacted version of the classified anonymous whistleblower complaint.

Like the call summary, the anonymous whistleblower complaint was initially classified. The complaint was reportedly "hand delivered . . . to Capitol Hill" hours after President Trump released the call summary.[587] Although a limited number of Members of Congress—like Chairman Schiff—could access the classified complaint, the American public could not. The President released a redacted version of the anonymous whistleblower complaint so that every American could read it for themselves.[588]

C. President Trump released publicly the summary of his April 21 phone call with President Zelensky.

President Trump first spoke by telephone with President Zelensky on April 21, 2019, the date on which President Zelensky won the Ukrainian presidential election.[589] On November 15, the President publicly released the summary of this April conversation.[590] President Trump explained that he chose to release the summary of this call to "continue being the most transparent President in history."[591]

D. The Trump Administration has experienced a surge in sensitive leaks, including details of the President's communications with foreign leaders.

The Trump Administration has experienced an unprecedented number of potentially damaging leaks from the U.S. national security apparatus.[592] According to a report from the Senate Homeland Security and Governmental Affairs Committee in May 2017, these leaks have flowed seven times faster under President Trump than during former Presidents Obama and Bush's administrations—averaging almost one per day.[593] The report explained:

---

[586] Donald J. Trump (@realDonaldTrump), Twitter (Sept. 24, 2019, 11:12 a m.), https://twitter.com/realdonaldtrump/status/1176559970390806530.

[587] Dana Bash, et al, *Whistleblower complaint about Trump declassified and may be released Thursday*, CNN, Sept. 26, 2019.

[588] *Whistleblower complaint says White House tried to "lock down" Ukraine call records*, CBS News, Sept. 26, 2019.

[589] *Memorandum of Telephone Conversation*, *supra* note 10.

[590] Mark Mazzetti & Eileen Sullivan, *Rough transcript of Trump's first phone call with Ukrainian leader released*, N.Y. Times, Nov. 15, 2019.

[591] Donald J. Trump (@realDonaldTrump), Twitter (Nov. 11, 2019, 3:35 p.m.), https://twitter.com/realDonaldTrump/status/1194035922066714625.

[592] HSGAC report, *supra* note 409.

[593] *Id.*

From the morning of President Trump's inauguration, when major newspapers published information about highly sensitive intelligence intercepts, news organizations have reported on an avalanche of leaks from officials across the U.S. government. Many disclosures have concerned the investigations of alleged Russian interference in the 2016 election, with the world learning details of whose communications U.S. intelligence agencies are monitoring, what channels are being monitored, and the results of those intercepts. All such revelations are potential violations of federal law, punishable by jail time.

But the leak frenzy has gone far beyond the Kremlin and has extended to other sensitive information that could harm national security. President Trump's private conversations with other foreign leaders have shown up in the press, while secret operations targeting America's most deadly adversaries were exposed in detail.

As *The New York Times* wrote in a candid self-assessment: "Journalism in the Trump era has featured a staggering number of leaks from sources across the federal government." No less an authority than President Obama's CIA director called the deluge of state secrets "appalling." These leaks do not occur in a vacuum. They can, and do, have real world consequences for national security.[594]

As the *Washington Post* explained, "Every presidential administration leaks. So far, the Trump White House has gushed."[595] Sensitive national security information—for which public disclosure could harm U.S. interests—found its way into mainstream news outlets such as the *New York Times*, the *Washington Post*, NBC, and *Associated Press*.[596] This unfortunate reality helps to explain the circumstances by which the NSC handled the summary of President Trump's July 25 telephone conversation with President Zelensky.

E. The evidence does not establish that access to the July 25 call summary was restricted for inappropriate reasons.

The anonymous whistleblower complaint alleged that NSC staffers deliberately placed the call summary of the July 25 call on a highly secure server to hide its contents.[597] This allegation has not been proven. In fact, the Democrats' witnesses testified that it was mistakenly place on a highly classified server. Evidence suggests that call summaries of the President's conversations with other foreign leaders have been subject to restricted access due to a pattern of leaks.

---

[594] *Id.*
[595] Paul Farhi, *The Trump administration has sprung a leak. Many of them, in fact*, Wash. Post, Feb. 5, 2017.
[596] HSGAC report, *supra* note 409.
[597] Whistleblower letter, *supra* note 85.

As the Trump Administration dealt with an unprecedented number of national security leaks, it sought to take appropriate precautions. Public reporting indicates that the NSC began restricting access to summaries of the President's communications with foreign leaders following the leak of President Trump's conversation in May 2017 with senior Russian officials.[598] Dr. Fiona Hill, the former NSC Senior Director for Europe, testified that a summary of this meeting was not initially restricted and that details of the conversation "seemed to immediately end up in the press."[599] Following this leak, the White House began a practice of restricting access to summaries of calls and meetings with foreign leaders.[600] Current and former White House officials said that it made sense to restrict access to calls given the number of leaks.[601]

With respect to the summary of President Trump's conversation with President Zelensky on July 25, NSC Senior Director Tim Morrison testified in his closed-door deposition that although he "was not concerned that anything illegal was discussed," he was concerned about a leak of the summary of President Trump's call with President Zelensky.[602] He explained that he was "concerned about how the contents [of the call summary] would be used in Washington's political process."[603] In his public testimony, Morrison elaborated:

> Q. And you were concerned about it leaking because you were worried about how it would play out in Washington's polarized political environment, correct?
>
> A. Yes.
>
> Q. And you were also worried how that would lead to the bipartisan support here in Congress towards Ukraine, right?
>
> A. Yes.
>
> Q. And you were also concerned that it might affect the Ukrainians' perception negatively.
>
> A. Yes.
>
> Q. And, in fact, all three of those things have played out, haven't they?
>
> A. Yes.[604]

---

[598] *See, e.g.*, Julian E. Barnes et al., *White House Classified Computer System is Used to Hold Transcripts of Sensitive Calls*, N.Y. Times, Sept. 29, 2019.
[599] Hill deposition, *supra* note 12, at 294.
[600] Barnes, et al., *supra* note 598.
[601] *Id.*
[602] Morrison deposition, *supra* note 12, at 16.
[603] *Id.* at 44.
[604] *Impeachment Inquiry: Ambassador Kurt Volker and Timothy Morrison*, *supra* note 8.

LTC Vindman—the NSC staffer who raised concerns about the contents of call—testified there was no "malicious intent" in restricting access to the summary.[605] Morrison also testified that call summary was mistakenly placed on a secure server with restricted access.[606] He explained:

> Q. And were you ever provided with an explanation for why [the call summary] was placed in the highly classified system?
>
> A. Yes.
>
> Q. What was the explanation you were given?
>
> A. It was a mistake.
>
> Q. It was a mistake?
>
> A. Yes.[607]

In his public testimony, Morrison reiterated that the placement of the call summary on a secure server was an administrative error.[608] He explained that NSC Legal Advisor John Eisenberg sought to restrict access to the summary, but that his direction was mistakenly interpreted to mean placing the summary on a secure server.[609] He testified:

> I spoke with the NSC Executive Secretariat staff, asked them why [the summary had been removed from the normal server]. And they did their research, and they informed me it had been moved to the higher classification system at the direction of John Eisenberg, whom I then asked why. I mean, that's – if that was the judgment he made, that's not necessarily mine to question, but I didn't understand it. And he essentially told me, "I gave no such direction." He did his own inquiry, and he represented back to me that it was – his understanding was that it was a kind of administrative error, that when he also gave direction to restrict access, the Executive Secretariat staff understood that as an apprehension that there was something in the content of the [call summary] that could not exist on the lower classification system.[610]

Morrison also explained that there was no malicious intent in moving the transcript to the secure server.[611]

---

[605] Vindman deposition, *supra* note 12, at 124.
[606] Morrison deposition, *supra* note 12, at 54-57.
[607] *Id.* at 54.
[608] *Impeachment Inquiry: Ambassador Kurt Volker and Timothy Morrison, supra* note 8.
[609] *Id.*
[610] *Id.*
[611] *Id.*

To the extent Democrats allege that President Trump sought to cover up his July 25 telephone conversation with President Zelensky, the facts do not support such a charge. Indeed, President Trump has declassified and publicly released the July 25 call summary. He has also released a redacted version of the classified anonymous whistleblower complaint and released the call summary of his first phone call with President Zelensky, on April 21. Although the July 25 call summary was located on a secure White House server prior to its public release, testimony shows that its placement on the server was an "administrative error." In light of substantial leaks of sensitive national security information—including the President's conversations with foreign leaders—testimony shows that the NSC Legal Advisor sought to restrict access to the summary. In attempting to carry out this direction, the NSC executive secretariat staff incorrectly placed the summary on a secure server. Taken, together, these facts do not establish that President Trump sought to cover up his interactions with President Zelensky.

III. The evidence does not establish that President Trump obstructed Congress in the Democrats' impeachment inquiry.

Democrats allege that President Trump has obstructed Congress by declining to participate in Speaker Pelosi's impeachment inquiry.[612] Under any fair assessment of the facts, however, President Trump has not obstructed Congress. In fact, the President personally urged at least one witness to cooperate with the Democrats' impeachment inquiry and to testify truthfully.[613] But Democrats cannot and should not impeach President Trump for declining to submit himself to an abusive and unfair process.

In the Democrats' impeachment inquiry, fairness is not an asset guaranteed or even recognized. Democrats have told witnesses in the inquiry that a failure to adhere strictly to their demands "shall constitute evidence of obstruction of the House's impeachment inquiry and may be used as an adverse inference against the President."[614] Democrats have threatened to withhold the salaries for agency employees as punishment for not meeting Democrat demands.[615] As Chairman Schiff explained the Democrat logic, any disagreement with Democrats amounts to obstruction: "The failure to produce this witness, the failure to produce these documents, we consider yet additionally strong evidence of obstruction of the constitutional functions of Congress, a coequal branch of government."[616]

The Democrats' actions are fundamentally abusive. In any just proceeding, the President ought to be afforded an opportunity to raise defenses without Democrats considering it to be *de facto* evidence of obstruction. In any just proceeding, investigators would not impute the conduct of a witness to the President or use a witness's refusal to cooperate with an unfair process as an "adverse inference" against the President.

The Democrats' obstruction arguments are also divorced from historical precedent for House impeachment proceedings and basic legal concepts of due process and the presumption of innocence. Past bipartisan precedent for presidential impeachment inquiries guaranteed fundamental fairness by authorizing bipartisan subpoena authority; providing the President unrestricted access to information presented; and allowing the President's counsel to identify relevant witnesses and evidence, cross examine witnesses, and respond to evidence collected. These guarantees of due process and fundamental fairness are not present in the Democrats' impeachment resolution against President Trump.

Congressional oversight of the Executive Branch is an important and serious undertaking designed to improve the efficiency and accountability of the federal government. The White House has said that it is willing to work with Democrats on legitimate congressional oversight

---

[612] *See, e.g.*, Amber Phillips, *How the House Could Impeach Trump for Obstructing its Probe*, Wash. Post, Oct. 8, 2019.
[613] Sondland deposition, *supra* note 51, at 38.
[614] *See, e.g.*, letter from Eliot L. Engel, Chairman, H. Comm. on Foreign Affairs, et al. to John Eisenberg, Nat'l Sec. Council (Oct. 30, 2019).
[615] *See* letter from Eliot L. Engel, Chairman, H. Comm. on Foreign Affairs, et al. to John J. Sullivan, Dep. Sec'y, Dep't of State (Oct. 1, 2019).
[616] Phillips, *supra* note 612.

requests.[617] However, public statements from prominent Democrats suggest they are pursuing impeachment purely for partisan reasons—that they seeking to prevent President Trump's reelection in 2020.[618] The Democrats' unfair and abusive impeachment process confirms that they are not interested in pursuing a full understanding of the facts.

Even despite the Democrats' partisan rhetoric and unfair process, President Trump has been transparent about his interactions with Ukrainian President Zelensky. President Trump has released to the public documents directly relevant the subject matter and he has spoken publicly about the issues. Democrats cannot justly condemn President Trump for declining to submit to their abusive and fundamentally unfair process.

A. Democrats have abandoned long-standing precedent by failing to guarantee due process and fundamental fairness in their impeachment inquiry.

The two recent impeachment investigations into presidents by the House of Representatives were largely identical to each other despite the passage of two decades. In 1974, the House authorized an impeachment inquiry into President Nixon by debating and passing House Resolution 803.[619] This resolution authorized the Committee on the Judiciary to issue subpoenas, including those offered by the minority; to sit and act without regard to whether the House stood in recess; and to expend funds in the pursuit of the investigation.[620] In 1998, the House passed House Resolution 581, a nearly identical resolution authorizing an impeachment inquiry into President Clinton.[621]

In 1974, the House undertook this action because "the rule of the House defining the jurisdiction of committees does not place jurisdiction over impeachment matters in the Judiciary Committee. In fact, it does not place such jurisdiction anywhere."[622] Passing a resolution authorizing the inquiry was "a necessary step if we are to meet our obligations [under the Constitution]."[623] By passing the resolution, the House sought to make "[t]he committee's investigative authority . . . fully coextensive with the power of the House in an impeachment investigation . . . ."[624]

Notably, in empowering the Judiciary Committee to conduct the Nixon impeachment inquiry, the House granted subpoena power to the minority, an action that was "against all precedents" at the time.[625] During debate, Members made it "crystal clear that the authority given to the minority [ranking] member and to the chairman, the right to exercise authority [to issue a

---

[617] See letter from Pat A. Cipollone, Counsel to the President to Speaker Nancy Pelosi et al. 8 (Oct. 8, 2019).
[618] See, e.g., Weekends with Alex Witt (MSNBC television broadcast May 5 2019) (interview with Rep. Al Green).
[619] H. Res. 803, 93rd Cong. (1974).
[620] See Id.
[621] H. Res. 581, 105th Cong. (1998).
[622] 130 Cong. Rec. 2351 (Feb. 6, 1974) (statement of Rep. Hutchinson).
[623] Id. at 2350 (statement of Rep. Rodino).
[624] H.R. Rep. No. 93-774, at 3 (1974).
[625] 130 Cong. Rec. at 2352 (statement of Rep. Brooks).

subpoena], is essentially the same. It is the same. Both are subject to a veto by a majority of the membership of that committee."[626]

In 1998, the House similarly passed a resolution authorizing an impeachment inquiry because the "[Judiciary] Committee decided that it must receive authorization from the full House before proceeding . . . ."[627] The Judiciary Committee reached this conclusion "[b]ecause impeachment is delegated solely to the House of Representatives by the Constitution, [and therefore] the full House of Representatives should be involved in critical decision making regarding various stages of impeachment."[628]

In putting forth this resolution for consideration by the House, the Judiciary Committee made several commitments with respect to ensuring "procedural fairness" of the impeachment inquiry. For instance, the Judiciary Committee voted to allow the President or his counsel to be present at all executive sessions and open hearings and to allow the President's counsel to cross examine witnesses, make objections regarding relevancy, suggest additional evidence or witnesses that the committee should receive, and to respond to the evidence collected.[629]

The fundamental fairness and due process protections guaranteed in the Nixon and Clinton impeachment proceedings are missing from Speaker Pelosi's impeachment inquiry. The Democrats' impeachment inquiry offers a veneer of legitimacy that hides a deeply partisan and one-sided process. The impeachment resolution passed by Democrats in the House—against bipartisan opposition—allows Democrats to maintain complete control of the proceedings.[630] The resolution denies Republicans co-equal subpoena authority and requires the Democrat chairmen to concur with Republican subpoenas—unlike Democrat subpoenas, which the chairmen may issue with no Republican input.[631] The Democrat impeachment resolution requires Republicans to specifically identify and explain the need for witnesses 72 hours before the first impeachment hearing—without a similar requirement for Democrats.[632] Most importantly, the Democrats' resolution excludes the President's counsel from House Intelligence Committee Chairman Adam Schiff's proceedings and provides House Judiciary Committee Chairman Jerry Nadler with discretion to do the same.[633] In short, these partisan procedures dramatically contradict the bipartisan Nixon and Clinton precedents.

B. Democrats have engaged in an abusive process toward a pre-determined outcome.

Since the beginning of the 116 Congress, Democrats have sought to impeach President Trump. Just hours after her swearing in, Rep. Rashida Tlaib told a crowd at a public event that

---

[626] *Id.*
[627] H.R. Rep. No. 105-795, at 24 (1998).
[628] *Id.*
[629] *Id.* at 25-26.
[630] H. Res. 660, 116th Cong. (2019).
[631] *Id.*
[632] *Id.*
[633] *Id.*

"[Democrats are] going to go in there, and we're going to impeach the [expletive deleted]."[634] Rep. Brad Sherman introduced articles of impeachment against President Trump on the very first day of the Democrat majority.[635] Rep. Al Green separately introduced articles of impeachment in July 2019, and even forced the House to consider the measure.[636] The House tabled Rep. Green's impeachment resolution by an overwhelming bipartisan majority—332 ayes to 95 nays.[637]

Such a fervor to impeach a political opponent for purely partisan reasons was what Alexander Hamilton warned of as the "greatest danger" in Federalist No. 65: that "the decision [to impeach] will be regulated more by the comparative strength of parties, than by the real demonstrations of innocence or guilt."[638] Indicative of this partisan fervor, Democrats have already forced the House to consider three resolutions of impeachment—offered by Democrats after no investigation, report, or process of any kind—since President Trump took office.[639]

During the consideration of articles of impeachment against President Clinton, Democrats argued that "[i]f we are to impeach the President, it should be at the end of a fair process. . . . [and not through decisions] made on a strictly partisan basis."[640] Rep. Zoe Lofgren, now a senior member of the Judiciary Committee, testified then before the Rules Committee on the resolution authorizing the Clinton impeachment inquiry. She said:

> Under our Constitution, the House of Representatives has the sole power of impeachment. This is perhaps our single most serious responsibility short of a declaration of war. Given the gravity and magnitude of this undertaking, only a fair and bipartisan approach to this question will ensure that truth is discovered, honest judgments rendered, and the constitutional requirement observed. Our best yardstick is our historical experience. We must compare the procedures used today with what Congress did a generation ago when a Republican President was investigated by a Democratic House.[641]

However, Speaker Pelosi's impeachment inquiry has been divorced from historical experience and has borne no markings of a fair process. During the first several weeks, the Speaker asserted that a vote authorizing the inquiry was unnecessary.[642] This process allowed Chairman Schiff to conduct his partisan inquiry behind closed doors with only a limited group of Members present. It also allowed Chairman Schiff to selectively leak cherry-picked information

---

[634] Nicholas Fandos, *Rashida Tlaib's Expletive-Laden Cry to Impeach Trump Upends Democrats' Talking Points*, N.Y. Times, Jan. 4, 2019.
[635] H. Res. 13, 116th Cong. (2019).
[636] H. Res. 498, 116th Cong. (2019).
[637] *Id.* (Roll call vote 483).
[638] Federalist No. 65 (Alexander Hamilton).
[639] *See* H. Res. 646, 115th Cong. (2018); H. Res. 705, 115th Cong. (2018); H. Res. 498, 116th Cong. (2019).
[640] Impeachment Inquiry: William Jefferson Clinton, President of the United States, 105th Cong., Consideration of Articles of Impeachment 82 (Comm. Print 1998) (statement of Rep. Bobby Scott).
[641] *Hearing before the Committee on Rules on H. Res. 525*, 105th Cong., 2d Sess. 108 (1998).
[642] *See, e.g.*, Haley Byrd, *Kevin McCarthy Calls on Nancy Pelosi to Suspend Impeachment Inquiry*, CNN, Oct. 3, 2019.

to paint a misleading public narrative. Chairman Schiff failed to respond to Republican requests for witnesses,[643] and directed witnesses not to answer questions from Republicans.[644] Chairman Schiff even declined to share closed-door deposition transcripts with Republican Members.[645]

During the public hearings, despite the modicum of minority rights outlined in the Democrats' impeachment resolution, Chairman Schiff has continued to trample long-held minority rights. Chairman Schiff interrupted Republican Members during questioning and directed witnesses not to answer Republican questions.[646] Chairman Schiff declined to invite all the witnesses identified by Republicans as relevant to the inquiry.[647] Chairman Schiff declined to honor Republican subpoenas for documents and witnesses, and then violated House rules and the Democrats' impeachment resolution to vote down the subpoenas without sufficient notice or even any debate.[648]

This is the very sort of process that Democrats had previously decried as "what happens when a legislative chamber is obsessively preoccupied with investigating the opposition rather than legislating for the people who elected them to office."[649] Rep. Jerrold Nadler, now chairman of the Judiciary Committee, once argued that:

> The effect of impeachment is to overturn the popular will of voters as expressed in a national election. . . . *There must never be a narrowly voted impeachment or an impeachment substantially supported by one of our major political parties and largely opposed by the other*. Such an impeachment would lack legitimacy and produce the divisiveness and bitterness in our politics for years to come and will call into question the very legitimacy of our political institutions.[650]

During the impeachment proceedings for President Clinton, Democrats warned against "dump[ing] mountains of salacious, uncross-examined and otherwise untested materials onto the Internet, and then . . . sorting through boxes of documents to selectively find support for a foregone conclusion."[651] But now, in Speaker Pelosi's impeachment inquiry, as conducted by Chairman Schiff, the Democrats' old warnings have become the very process by which their current impeachment inquiry has proceeded.

---

[643] Letter from Jim Jordan, Ranking Member, H. Comm. on Oversight & Reform, et al., to Adam Schiff, Chairman, H. Perm. Sel. Comm. on Intelligence (Oct. 23, 2019).

[644] *See, e.g.*, Vindman deposition, *supra* note 12, at 78-80, 103-05.

[645] *See, e.g.*, Deirdre Shesgreen & Bart Jansen, *House Republicans complain about limited access to closed-door House impeachment investigation sessions*, USA Today, Oct. 16, 2019.

[646] *See, e.g., Impeachment Inquiry: Ambassador William B. Taylor and Mr. George Kent, supra* note 2; *Impeachment Inquiry: Ambassador Marie Yovanovitch, supra* note 4.

[647] *See, e.g.*, Beggin, *supra* note 550.

[648] *Impeachment Inquiry: Ms. Laura Cooper and Mr. David Hale, supra* note 246.

[649] Impeachment Inquiry: William Jefferson Clinton, President of the United States, *supra* note 640, at 94 (statement of Rep. Zoe Lofgren).

[650] *Id.* at 77 (statement of Rep. Jerrold Nadler) (emphasis added).

[651] *Id.* at 82 (statement of Rep. Bobby Scott).

C. President Trump may raise privileges and defenses in response to unfair, abusive proceedings.

Speaker Pelosi's impeachment inquiry, as conducted by Chairman Schiff, has abandoned due process and the presumption of innocence that lies at the heart of western legal systems.[652] Due to this abusive conduct and the Democrats' relentless attacks on the Trump Administration, President Trump may be rightly concerned about receiving fair treatment from House Democrats during this impeachment inquiry.

During the Clinton impeachment proceedings, Rep. Bobby Scott, now a senior member of the Democrat caucus, argued that the impeachment process should "determine[], with a presumption of innocence, whether those allegations [against President Clinton] were true by using cross-examination of witnesses and other traditionally reliable evidentiary procedures."[653] Similarly, Rep. Jerrold Nadler argued then that "[w]e have been entrusted with the grave and awesome duty by the American people, by the Constitution and by history. We must exercise that duty responsibly. At a bare minimum, that means *the President's accusers must go beyond hearsay and innuendo and beyond demands that the President prove his innocence of vague and changing charges*."[654]

Furthermore, Democrats had previously argued that the assertion of privileges by a president does not constitute an impeachable offense. During the Clinton impeachment proceedings, Rep. Scott stated:

> At the hearing when I posed the question of whether any of the witnesses on the hearing's second panel believed that the count involving invoking executive privilege should be considered an impeachable offense, the clear consensus on the panel was that the charge was not an impeachable offense. In fact, one Republican witness said, I do not think invoking executive privilege even if frivolously, and I believe it was frivolous in these circumstances, that that does not constitute an impeachable offense.[655]

Despite this prior commitment to due process and a presumption of innocence, the Democrats now favor a presumption of guilt. Chairman Schiff has said publicly that the Trump Administration and witnesses asserting their constitutional rights and seeking to test the soundness of subpoenas have formed "a very powerful case against the president for obstruction, an article of impeachment based on obstruction."[656] Similarly, Chairman Schiff has made clear

---

[652] *See, e.g., Id.* at 102 (statement of Rep. Maxine Waters) ("As Members of Congress have sworn to uphold the Constitution, we must always insist on equal and just treatment under the law. The presumption of innocence until proven guilty is central and basic to our system of justice.").

[653] *Id.* at 82 (statement of Rep. Bobby Scott).

[654] *Id.* at 78 (statement of Rep. Jerrold Nadler) (emphasis added).

[655] *Id.* at 83 (statement of Rep. Bobby Scott).

[656] Kyle Cheney, *Trump Makes 'Very Powerful Case' for Impeachment Based on Obstruction, Schiff Warns*, Politico, Oct. 28, 2019.

that he will simply assume that a witness's testimony is adverse to the President when that witness or the President asserts a right or privilege.[657] These are not the hallmarks of a fair and transparent process; these are the tell-tale signs of a star chamber.

D. Although declining to submit to the Democrats' abusive and unfair process, President Trump has released information to help the American public understand the issues.

Just twenty-seven minutes after President Trump's inauguration on January 20, 2017, the *Washington Post* reported that the "campaign to impeach President Trump has begun."[658] As the *Post* reported:

> The effort to impeach President Donald John Trump is already underway. At the moment the new commander in chief was sworn in, a campaign to build public support for his impeachment went live at ImpeachDonaldTrumpNow.org, spearheaded by two liberal advocacy groups aiming to lay the groundwork for his eventual ejection from the White House. . . . The impeachment drive comes as Democrats and liberal activists are mounting broad opposition to stymie Trump's agenda.[659]

In 2017 and 2018, Democrats introduced four separation resolution in the House with the goal of impeaching President Trump.[660] On January 3, 2019, on the Democrats' first day in power, Rep. Al Green again introduced articles of impeachment.[661] That same day, Rep. Rashida Tlaib promised, "we're going to go in there and we're going to impeach the [expletive deleted]."[662]

In this context, it is difficult to see the Democrats' impeachment inquiry as anything other than a partisan effort to undo the results of the 2016 election. Rep. Green said on MSNBC in May 2019, "If we don't impeach this President, he will get re-elected."[663] Even as Democrats have conducted their impeachment inquiry, Speaker Pelosi has called President Trump "an impostor" and said it is "dangerous" to allow American voters to evaluate his performance in

---

[657] *See Id.* ("Schiff also argued that the president is seeking to block Kupperman because he is concerned about a high-level source corroborating damning testimony that Trump pressured Ukraine to open investigations of his political rivals—and condition military aid and a White House visit on bending the European ally to his will.").
[658] Matea Gold, *The campaign to impeach President Trump has begun*, Wash. Post, Jan. 20, 2017.
[659] *Id.*
[660] H., Res. 705, 115th Cong. (2018); H. Res. 646, 115th Cong. (2017); H. Res. 621, 115th Cong. (2017); H. Res. 438, 115th Cong. (2017).
[661] H. Res. 13, 116th Cong. (2019).
[662] Amy B. Wong, *Rep. Rashida Tlaib profanely promised to impeach Trump. She's not sorry.*, Wash. Post, Jan. 4, 2019.
[663] *Weekends with Alex Witt, supra* note 618.

2020.[664] The Democrats' impeachment process has mirrored this rhetoric, stacking the deck against the President.[665]

Even so, the President is not entirely unwilling to cooperate with the Democrats' demands. In October 2019, Pat A. Cipollone, the Counsel to the President, wrote to Speaker Pelosi and the chairmen of the three "impeachment" committees:

> If the Committees wish to return to the regular order of oversight requests, we stand ready to engage in that process as we have in the past, in a manner consistent with well-established bipartisan constitutional protections and a respect for the separation of powers enshrined in our Constitution.[666]

Speaker Pelosi did not respond to Mr. Cipollone's letter. President Trump explained that he would "like people to testify" but he is resisting the Democrats' unfair and abusive process "for future Presidents and the Office of the President."[667]

Although the Democrats' abusive and unfair process has prevented his cooperation with the Democrats' impeachment inquiry, President Trump has nonetheless been transparent about his conduct. On September 25, President Trump declassified and released to the public the summary of his July 25 phone conversation with President Zelensky, stressing his goal that Americans could read for themselves the contents of the call: "You will see it was a very friendly and totally appropriate call."[668] On November 15, President Trump released to the public the summary of this April 21 phone conversation with President Zelensky in the interest of transparency.[669] In addition, President Trump has spoken publicly about his actions, as has Acting Chief of Staff Mick Mulvaney.[670]

Congress has a serious and important role to play in overseeing the Executive Branch. When the House of Representatives considers impeachment of a president, bipartisan precedent dictates fundamental fairness and due process. In pursuing impeachment of President Trump, however, Democrats have abandoned those principles, choosing instead to use impeachment as a tool to pursue their partisan objectives. While the President has declined to submit himself to the Democrats' unfair and abusive process, he has still made an effort to be transparent with the Americans to whom he is accountable. Under these abusive and unfair circumstances, the Democrats cannot establish a charge of obstruction.

---

[664] Emily Tillett, *Nancy Pelosi says Trump's attacks on witnesses "very significant" to impeachment probe*, CBS News, Nov. 15, 2019; Dear Colleague Letter from Speaker Nancy Pelosi (Nov. 18, 2019).

[665] *See* H. Res. 660, 116th Cong. (2019).

[666] Letter from Pat A. Cipollone, *supra* note 617.

[667] Donald J. Trump (@realDonaldTrump), Twitter (Nov. 26, 2019, 7:43 a m.), https://twitter.com/realDonaldTrump/status/1199352946187800578.

[668] Donald J. Trump (@realDonaldTrump), Twitter (Sept. 24, 2019, 11:12 a m.), https://twitter.com/realdonaldtrump/status/1176599970390806530.

[669] Donald J. Trump (@realDonaldTrump), Twitter (Nov. 11, 2019, 3:35 p.m.), https://twitter.com/realDonaldTrump/status/1194035922066714625.

[670] *See, e.g.*, The White House, Remarks by President Trump before Marine One Departure (Nov. 20, 2019); Press Briefing by Acting Chief of Staff Mick Mulvaney, *supra* note 302.

IV. Conclusion

The impeachment of a president is one of the gravest and most solemn duties of the House of Representatives. For Democrats, impeachment is a tool for settling political scores and re-litigating election results with which they disagreed. This impeachment inquiry and the manner in which the Democrats are pursuing it sets a dangerous precedent.

The Democrats have not established an impeachable offense. The evidence presented in this report does not support a finding that President Trump pressured President Zelensky to investigate his political rival for the President's benefit in the 2020 election. The evidence does not establish that President Trump withheld a White House meeting to pressure President Zelensky to investigate his political rival to benefit him in the 2020 election. The evidence does not support that President Trump withheld U.S. security assistance to pressure President Zelensky to investigate his political rival for the President's benefit in the 2020 election. The evidence does not establish that President Trump orchestrated a shadow foreign policy apparatus to pressure President Zelensky to investigate his political rival to benefit him in the 2020 election.

The best evidence of President Trump's interaction with President Zelensky is the "complete and accurate" call summary prepared by the White House Situation Room staff. The summary shows no indication of conditionality, pressure, or coercion. Both President Trump and President Zelensky have denied the existence of any pressure. President Zelensky and his senior advisers in Kyiv did not even know that U.S. security assistance to Ukraine was paused until it was publicly reported in U.S. media. Ultimately, Ukraine received the security assistance and President Zelensky met with President Trump, all without Ukraine ever investigating President Trump's political rival. These facts alone severely undercut the Democrat allegations.

The evidence in the Democrats' impeachment inquiry shows that President Trump is skeptical about U.S. taxpayer-funded foreign assistance and strongly believes that European allies should shoulder more of the financial burden for regional defense. The President also has deeply-rooted, reasonable, and genuine concerns about corruption in Ukraine, including the placement of Vice President Biden's son on the board of a Ukrainian energy company notorious for corruption at a time when Vice President Biden was the Obama Administration's point person for Ukraine policy. There is also compelling and indisputable evidence that Ukrainian government officials—some working with a Democrat operative—sought to influence the U.S. presidential election in 2016 in favor of Secretary Clinton and in opposition to President Trump.

The Democrats' impeachment narrative ignores the President's state of mind and it ignores the specific and concrete actions that the new Zelensky government took to address pervasive Ukrainian corruption. The Democrats' case rests almost entirely on hearsay, presumption, and emotion. Where there are ambiguous facts, the Democrats interpret them in a light most unfavorable to the President. The Democrats also flatly disregard any perception of potential wrongdoing with respect to Hunter Biden's presence on the board of Burisma Holdings or Ukrainian influence in the 2016 election.

The evidence presented also does not support allegations that President Trump covered-up his conversation with President Zelensky by restricting access to it. In light of leaks of other presidential conversations with world leaders, the White House took reasonably steps to restrict access to the July 25 call summary. The summary was mistakenly placed on a secure server; however, the Democrats' witnesses explained that there was no nefarious conduct or malicious intent associated with this action.

Likewise, the evidence presented does not support allegations that President Trump obstructed the Democrats' impeachment inquiry by raising concerns about an unfair and abusive process. The Democrats deviated from prior bipartisan precedent for presidential impeachment and denied Republican attempts to inject basic fairness and objectivity into their partisan and one-sided inquiry. The White House has signaled that it is willing to work with Democrats but President Trump cannot be faulted for declining to submit himself to the Democrats' star chamber. Even so, President Trump has been transparent with the American people about his actions, releasing documents and speaking publicly about the subject matter.

The Democrats' impeachment inquiry paints a picture of unelected bureaucrats within the foreign policy and national security apparatus who fundamentally disagreed with President Trump's style, world view, and decisions. Their disagreements with President Trump's policies and their discomfort with President Trump's actions set in motion the anonymous, secondhand whistleblower complaint. Democrats seized on the whistleblower complaint to fulfill their years-old obsession with removing President Trump from office.

The unfortunate collateral damage of the Democrats' impeachment inquiry is the harm done to bilateral U.S.-Ukraine relations, the fulfillment of Russian President Vladimir Putin's desire to sow discord within the United States, and the opportunity costs to the American people. In the time that Democrats spent investigating the President, Democrats could have passed legislation to implement the U.S.-Mexico-Canada Agreement, lower the costs of prescription drugs, or secure our southern border. Instead, the Democrats' obsession with impeaching President Trump has paralyzed their already-thin legislative agenda. Less than a year before the 2020 election and Democrats in the House still cannot move on from the results of the last election.